Quarters for entering port.

The
Naval
Officer's
Guide

EIGHTH EDITION

by
ARTHUR A. AGETON
Rear Admiral, U. S. Navy (Retired)

with
WILLIAM P. MACK
Vice Admiral, U. S. Navy

NAVAL INSTITUTE PRESS

LIBRARY OF CONGRESS CATALOGUE CARD No. 43–4401

ISBN 0-87021-432-2

For J.L.G.A.
who, better than anyone,
knows the travail of
the course we follow

Preface to the Eighth Edition

This book is intended as a compendium of useful information for the guidance of newly commissioned officers in the United States Navy. It will provide abundant instruction and counsel for their consideration, both during the period of adjustment following first commission and in the formative years that follow. The material should prove useful not only on sea duty, but during service in the naval shore establishment as well. Women officers also should find this volume instructive and helpful.

Although the opinions or assertions contained in this guide are not to be considered as official or as reflecting the views of the Department of the Navy, no effort has been spared to make this work authoritative and interesting. Pertinent extracts have been made from various official publications by permission of the Department of the Navy. These extracts, together with a detailed index, make this guide a ready source of reference for many naval occasions.

This has been in no sense a "one man" book. The author has sought the benefit of the experience and guidance of many officers in preparing the text, which was checked in manuscript for accuracy and completeness by officers well versed in the subject matter under discussion.

Grateful acknowledgement is made to the following, who furnished source material or checked the text in manuscript: Admiral Arleigh A. Burke, USN (Ret.); Admiral H. P. Smith, USN; Vice Admiral B. J. Semmes, USN; Rear Admiral S. Sherwood, SC, USN; Rear Admiral E. J. Peltier, CEC, USN (Ret.); Rear Admiral W. C. Mott, USN (Ret.); Vice Admiral Frank Virden, USN (Ret.); Rear Admiral R. O. Canada, MC, USN; Captain T. M. D. Davis, SC, USN (Ret.), Secretary-Treasurer, Navy Mutual Aid; Commander F. C. Huntley, USN; Commander L. W. Roberts, SC, USN; Commander Roy de S. Horn, USN (Ret.); Chief Supply Clerk R. S. Boreen, USN; Mr. F. C. Dyer, of the Bureau of Naval Personnel; Miss Ruth Tarrant of the Office of Naval Intelligence; to Mr. D. Dejanikus and Mr. David R. Raynolds of the Department of State; and to Captain J. R. Thompson, USN, and Lieutenant Commander O. A. Meining, USN, of the Promotion and Retirement and Retired Activities Sections and the many other officers and personnel of BUPERS, who thoroughly checked this edition for accuracy and completeness. Special acknowledgement is due Mr. C. Gibson Schaeffer, of the McGraw-Hill Book Company, who edited the guide through two formidable earlier editions, and the late Rear Admiral Bruce McCandless, USN (Ret.), who guided the fifth edition from manuscript to published book. For the Appendix on Military Law, the author owes special thanks to Lieutenant Commander Edward M. Byrne, JAGC, USN, the author of *Military Law: A Handbook for the Navy and Marine Corps,* also published by the Naval Institute. For the Appendix on Roads to a Naval Commission, the author is grateful for the assistance of Lieutenant Anthony F. Walsh, USNR, in Officer Programs, Recruiting Division, Bureau of Naval Personnel.

For my collaborator, Vice Admiral William P. Mack, USN, who brought to the preparation of this edition his extensive naval experience and vast knowledge of the Armed Forces, and his writing skill to well over half of the manuscript, my deep appreciation for the added scope and authenticity which his participation has contributed to the finished book.

ARTHUR A. AGETON

Washington, D.C.
April 1970

Foreword

The young American seeking a career of challenge, promise, achievement, and responsibility will find all of these in full measure as an officer in the United States Navy. Few professions offer such rich opportunities for the early development of leadership capability or require so early an exercise of the full spectrum of individual talents.

The Navy is a highly technical service whose people are constantly called upon to fulfill the demands of a rapidly improving technological environment. The quest for excellence and the mastery of new developments in technical fields are essential to our continued effectiveness in defense of our country.

The naval officer is simultaneously a leader, an operator, a manager, and, oftentimes, a diplomat. Awareness of those events and factors which shape our nation and the world is vital. Thorough knowledge and professional performance in seamanship, in airmanship, or in his technical specialty are indispensable. The effective leadership of men and the prudent management of funds and resources are essential to the achievement of the naval officer's commission.

In addition to the traditional requirements for integrity and honor, the young officer of today's Navy must have the ability to master the complex, evaluate a changing environment, and use the full range of his personal capabilities to move the Navy forward into the exciting challenges of the future. Never has more been required of the men who would join the leadership of this honored profession. Never have the satisfactions of meaningful service been greater.

T. H. MOORER
Admiral, U. S. Navy
Chief of Naval Operations

Contents

CHAPTER 1

Our Navy and the Challenge of Seapower

> *The most effective victory is one which is attained with the least possible damage to nonmilitary targets and a minimum of casualties among the civil population, with the objective of bringing war to a successful conclusion with a minimum of wartime cost and postwar chaos.*
>
> —ADMIRAL THOMAS C. KINKAID,
> WASHINGTON, OCTOBER 12, 1949

The Role of Today's Navy

101. THE MISSION OF THE NAVY. Military policy derives its strength and direction from foreign policy. It therefore follows that our military strategy must be consonant with our foreign policy. Inseparable from the political objectives of our government, the military capabilities of our armed services must include a proper balance of military forces to provide the exact degree of force at the proper time and place to support those objectives.

The mission and the functions of our Navy are fully stated in Section 1001. Of briefer scope and of vital importance to the naval officer is the following statement of the Credo of the United States Navy:

GUARDIAN OF OUR COUNTRY

The United States Navy is responsible for maintaining control of the sea and is a ready force on watch at home and overseas capable of strong action to preserve the peace or of instant offensive action to win in war. It is upon the maintenance of this control that our country's glorious future depends; the United States Navy exists to make it so.

WE SERVE WITH HONOR

Tradition, valor, and victory are the Navy's heritage from the past. To these may be added dedication, discipline, and vigilance as the watchwords of the present and the future. At home or on distant stations we serve with pride, confident in the respect of our country, our shipmates, and our families. Our responsibilities sober us; our adversities strengthen us. Service to God and Country is our special privilege. We serve with honor.

THE FUTURE OF THE NAVY

The Navy will always employ new weapons, new techniques, and greater power to protect and defend the United States on the sea, under the sea, and in the air. Now and in the future, control of the sea gives the United States her greatest advantage for the maintenance of peace and for victory in war. Mobility, surprise, dispersal, and offensive power are the keynotes of the new Navy. The roots of the Navy lie in a strong belief in the future, in continued dedication to our tasks, and in reflection on our heritage from the past. Never have our opportunities and our responsibilities been greater.

102. THE PRINCIPLES OF WAR. War is—or should be—directed along rational lines of thought. These lines of thought, called the principles of war, are discovered just as are the principles of physics, or morality, or flight—through both experience and theory.

The Principles of War are seven in number, and the first of these is the *Principle of the Objective*. A nation's objectives must be sound and must be based upon valid national capabilities and priorities. Only then can the objectives of its armed forces also be sound.

In general, the great objective of navies is to command, or to dispute someone else's command of, the sea including the sea's surface, the airspace above it, and the depths beneath its surface.

On the tactical level, for example, a destroyer division commodore's objective may be either to protect a convoy or to sink a hostile submarine lurking nearby. It is important for him to be clear as to what his true objective is. If his true objective is the protection of the convoy, he should concentrate his destroyers on that even if it means that after a time he must drop his effort to sink the submarine. To do otherwise would leave the convoy open to the danger of destruction by other submarines.

Whatever the objective, the *Principle of Concentration* helps one achieve it, for by concentrating his destroyers on the protection of the convoy, the commodore has a better chance of achieving his objective than if he scatters their efforts about in a number of other tasks. He is also working in accordance with the *Principle of Econ-*

omy of Force, which calls for the use of all the force necessary to accomplish one's objective, and to do that as rapidly as possible. (This is perhaps the most easily misunderstood of the principles. It does *not* mean that one should use the *least possible* force which might eventually accomplish the mission.)

Should a threat to the convoy develop on the starboard bow, the commodore might well concentrate his forces, bringing destroyers in from the port quarter. This is simply the use of the *Principle of Mobility*, which is perhaps the most distinctive characteristic of naval power.

Should the convoy encounter a threat from the air, a carrier, which had been employing her attack planes to support Marines on the ground a few hundred miles distant, might be called upon to protect the convoy with her fighter aircraft. Obviously, mobility is involved here, as the carrier moves from supporting the Marines to protecting the convoy, but so is the *Principle of Flexibility:* not only is the carrier able to carry out different tasks, using different types of weapons, launched by different types of aircraft against difftrent types of targets, but also she can carry out these tasks in different areas.

In any event, if they are to succeed in their joint objective of protecting the convoy, the destroyer division commander and the carrier captain must work together, either under the direction of one or the other of them, or under the orders and leadership of some other officer superior to both of them. This is the *Principle of Command Authority*. Assuming that they have succeeded in their joint objective, the protection of the convoy, one can say that they acted in accordance with the *Principle of Security*, so far as the convoy was concerned. They may then wish to go to a base for repair and resupply. For that to be done well, the base must be protected from the enemy, either by distance or by force. Protected in either fashion, this, too, would be an example of the Principle of Security.

103. UNITED STATES SEAPOWER. Themistocles (514-449 B.C.) said "He who commands the sea has command of everything." Khair-Ed-Din (Barbarossa), who died in 1546, said "He who rules on the sea will very shortly rule on the land also." Sir Walter Raleigh, in his *Historie of the World, 1616,* wrote "Whosoever commands the sea commands the trade; whosoever commands the trade of the world commands the riches of the world, and consequently the world itself." George Washington in a letter to the Marquis de la Fayette on 15

November 1781 wrote "Without a decisive naval force we can do nothing definitive, and with it everything honorable and glorious." The naval historian-philosopher Alfred T. Mahan wrote in his *The Influence of Sea Power Upon History, 1890*, "It is not the taking of individual ships or convoys, be they few or many, that strikes down the money power of a nation; it is the possession of that overbearing power on the sea which drives the enemy flag from it, or allows it to appear only as the fugitive; and by controlling the great common, closes the highways by which commerce moves to and from the enemy's shores. This overbearing power can only be exercised by great navies." In an address to the House of Commons on 11 October 1940, Winston Churchill said, "When we speak of command of the seas, it does not mean command of every part of the sea at the same moment, or at every moment. It only means that we can make our will prevail ultimately in any part of the seas which may be selected for operations, and thus indirectly make our will prevail in every part of the seas." Admiral Arleigh A. Burke wrote in the United States Naval Institute *Proceedings* in 1962, "To control the sea, the Navy must be capable of destroying the source of weapons which threaten ships and operations at sea—submarine bases, air bases, missile bases, and any other base from which control of the sea can be challenged."

There are many aspects of sea power: military and naval, maritime, economic, political, legal, etc., but the naval officer has chosen as his prime concern the military and naval aspects of seapower, although he may deal with one or more of the other aspects in an indirect or direct manner from time to time during his naval career.

The seapower of the United States Navy is made up of ships. Their number varies continually. At the time of this writing the Navy has 20 aircraft carriers, 12 cruisers, 25 frigates, 177 destroyers, 45 ocean escorts, 135 submarines, 121 amphibious warfare ships, 90 mine warfare ships, and 169 auxiliary ships.

The seapower of the United States Navy is made up of aircraft, missiles, and guns. Naval aviation has attack (e.g. A-4 Skyhawk, A-5 Vigilante, A-6 Intruder, and A-7 Corsair II) aircraft; fighter (F-4 Phantom II and F-8 Crusader) aircraft; patrol and antisubmarine (P-2 Neptune, P-3 Orion, and S-2 Tracker) aircraft; utility aircraft; observation aircraft; cargo, transport, airborne early warning, and VSTOL aircraft, as well as helicopters (H-3 Sea King and H-46 Sea Knight). Guided missiles and rockets are Navy weapons. The Polaris and Poseidon are ballistic missiles launched from submarines to destroy land or sea targets. Sea Sparrow, Terrier, Talos, Tartar, and Standard Missile are guided missiles launched from surface vessels to intercept aerial targets in defensive or offensive roles. Sparrow III, Phoenix, and Sidewinder are guided missiles launched from the air to intercept aerial targets. Bullpup, Shrike, Standard ARM, Walleye, and Condor are guided missiles launched from the air to destroy land or sea targets. ASROC is a rocket-propelled depth charge or torpedo launched from a ship to destroy submarines. SUBROC is a rocket launched from a submarine to destroy enemy submarines. Torpedoes, mines, big guns, and small arms comprise the balance of the naval arsenal.

The seapower of the United States Navy is made up of men; the Navy has over 85,000 officers and 680,000 enlisted men stationed in all parts of the world, land-based and sea-based.

The Navy believes in seapower, but the Navy does not believe in a single ship, a single aircraft, a single missile, a single weapons system, a single officer, or a single enlisted man as the answer to attaining seapower. All ships, aircraft, weapons, and people in the United States Navy constitute seapower. And seapower can be used quickly, flexibly, discriminately, and selectively to the degree any particular situation dictates.

The roles of all the armed forces are played best if they are coordinated, for the combined strength of the Army, Navy, Marine Corps, Air Force, and Coast Guard employed in concert is far greater than the sum of these separate strengths. The Navy must project and protect the combat power of the other services overseas. In war or peace 98 percent of all goods go by ship.

But, no matter how awesome the structure of seapower, man is still the vital element of the defense team. Men make decisions; men fight battles; and men win or lose wars.

104. THE FUTURE OF THE OFFICER IN OUR MODERN NAVY. Our Navy is a unique military force. The ports and cities of nearly all the countries of the world know its ships and officers and men. Its capability ranges all the way from a show of force through limited warfare with conventional weapons to general warfare with nuclear weapons. Carriers and submarines, Marine expeditionary troops and supporting naval amphibious forces, cruisers, destroyers and destroyer escorts— all the wide spectrum of naval power—will long be with us. The young officer may look forward to an active, interesting, challenging, and useful career in the Navy. Keeping always in mind his primary mission—to prepare for, and to conduct, naval operations in wartime—he will find that the Navy of the present and the future will need all of his intelligence, initiative, leadership, and skill, and also the historic requirement that he know the ways of the sea.

In the semi-peace of the cold war, he has important responsibilities in psychological warfare. Whether conscious of it or not, he provides good—or bad—propaganda for our American way of life. We have had to learn again the old lesson—we cannot buy friendship or respect. The issue of friendship and respect for Americans and American ideals versus anti-Americanism can depend upon such small things as a loud-mouthed, boastful tourist; a drunken sailor; a supercilious, ill-mannered officer—or upon an understanding and courteous respect for the traditions, attitudes, and strange customs of another people among whom we live. In his duty abroad, living in a country or passing through as a tourist on sea duty, the naval officer must realize that, although he helps to carry the Big Stick, he must also tread softly. He must recognize early that, in taking leave ashore in foreign countries, he and his shipmates are the foreigners. To many a local citizen, the naval officer or enlisted man will provide his only acquaintance with ideas and impressions of America. The navyman must learn to accommodate himself readily to the ways of the people of another land.

Our purpose must be not just to combat communism and other enemies throughout the world, but also to testify to the efficacy of democratic processes and the virtues of the freedom and dignity of the individual. This competition is for much more than military superiority at the point of conflict—it is a struggle for the hearts and minds of men. We possess a dynamic program to which we can point with pride before the world as a means to a better life for all depressed peoples. Our country's long continuing success in practical democracy and widely shared industrial progress has been an explosive force in the world for almost two centuries. We are not defenders of a *status quo*—our philosophy and our people are an active, positive force for change in the world. We must demonstrate abroad that we and our way of life are aligned with the economic, political, and cultural aspirations of all those peoples who are desperately striving for improvement through change.

C H A P T E R 2

First Station

We are ready now.
—COMMANDER J. K. TAUSSIG, USN, FIRST
UNITED STATES DESTROYERS TO EUROPE, 1917

201. INTRODUCTION. You are now a naval officer. You may have acquired this status by any of the roads to a naval commission outlined in Appendix 3. A letter has come advising you that your appointment as an officer in the Navy or Naval Reserve has been approved. Your commission awaits your oath of office for delivery. There are a number of forms which you must fill out and return promptly to the Chief of Naval Personnel via your commanding officer or Naval District Headquarters.

First Papers

202. FIRST PAPER WORK. You will want to accept your commission immediately. To do so, you must complete your acceptance and oath of office form (NavPers 287, 339, 962 or 2688) and send it to the Bureau of Naval Personnel. With this form, you must enclose a number of other forms that have been forwarded to you. If possible, fill in the forms on a typewriter.

The following are usually submitted:

- Acceptance and oath of office.
- Officers Report of Home of Record.
- Officers Photograph Submission Sheet.

These forms contain adequate, detailed instructions for their completion. Your ship, station or unit Personnel Officer will be glad to assist you with this paper work.

7

203. ACTIVE DUTY. If you are being commissioned in the Regular Navy or the Naval Reserve in time of war or national emergency, shortly after you receive your commission you may expect orders to active duty. This is a thrilling but perplexing experience. What should you do first? When should you report? How do you get transportation? To whom should you report on arrival? What will be your duties? How will you like your new station in life? What will your new associates be like?

FIGURE 201. A "Little Ship" takes it over the bow in heavy weather. The new officer must early learn to accustom himself to the ways of the sea.

These are only a few of the questions which will arise in your mind. Your first step should be to make a careful study of your orders. A sample set of first orders follows:

703750/1100
Pers-B124-mat-3
12 May 19—

BUPERS ORDER
183589

ENS Jacob N. Jones, USN
Yale University, New Haven, Connecticut

Via CO, NROTC UNIT

Upon acceptance appointment and when directed proceed Naval Amphibious Base, Little Creek, Va., report CO, Naval Amphibious School, Little Creek, temporary duty under instruction about three weeks Course G-00-6518, class convening 19 Jun and about one week Course G-3B-6585, class convening 10 Jul.

COMPTEMDIRDET proceed port in which USS GUADALCANAL (LPH-7) may be, arrival report CO duty numerical relief ENS James H. Smith, USNR.

Accounting data 1761453.2250 R 22 N2F6 2G CIC 1/N2F6/1/C/5/3750

In complying with these orders refer to reverse side for explanation of items listed below.
Item 23; 40; 91- fifteen POE(c)(a)(2) (b)- NLT 0800 19 Jun and NET 17 Jun LCREEK; 94; 100- 12 Jun

While traveling via government air outside CONUS class III priority certified.

CO comply current BUPERSINST 4650.14.

C. K. DUNCAN

Copy to:
COMFIVE
CO USS GUADALCANAL (LPH-7)
CO NAVPHIBSCOL LITTLE CREEK NAVPHIBASE NORVA*
JACKET

916-4/00
Ser: 1234
14 May 19—

FIRST ENDORSEMENT on BUPERS ltr 703750/1100 Pers-B124-mat-3 of 12 May 19—

From: Commanding Officer, NROTC Unit, Yale University, New Haven, Connecticut
To: ENS Jacob N. JONES, USN

Subj: Orders

1. Delivered for compliance.

S. D. JOHNSON

To provide information which will later be required as endorsements by the Disbursing Officer in taking up your pay accounts or paying mileage and other transportation claims, record the place, date, and hour of receipt of orders, when you left home (if applicable), when you arrived at naval station or recruiting station for physical examination and departed therefrom, and when you proceeded from the first station to which you reported and any subsequent station to which ordered. Other endorsements will be made on your original orders by various authorities as required in carrying out these orders. Be sure that sufficient copies are similarly endorsed.

In this sample case, the Guadalcanal will probably be in Norfolk, Virginia on the day you are to report. However, ship movements are uncertain, and you will save yourself time and money if you confirm the ship's location. This information, and other facts and advice can be best obtained by writing a formal (but unofficial) letter to the Executive Officer of your new ship. A good example of a form to use follows:

925 Elm Avenue
New Haven, Conn.
1 June 19—

Executive Officer
USS GUADALCANAL (LPH-7)
c/o Fleet Post Office
New York, New York

Dear Sir:

I have just received orders to report to the GUADALCANAL at Norfolk, Virginia about 20 June 19—. My present intention is to arrive one day early and to report for duty about 0800, 19 June 19—. If the GUADALCANAL is scheduled to be absent from Norfolk on this date, I would appreciate advice as to whether I should report at some other time.

I am married, but have no children, and my wife will remain in New Haven temporarily.

I have no particular naval qualifications as yet, but majored in Electrical Engineering at Yale and feel that I could do well in the Engineering Department.

I am looking forward to service in the GUADALCANAL with great pleasure.

Very respectfully,

Jacob N. Jones
Ensign, USN

The Executive Officer will probably answer promptly, giving you all the information you need.

Orders to active duty, prepared by the Bureau of Naval Personnel, customarily provide sufficient time for a new officer to settle his personal affairs. If you have a wife and other dependents, you should, at this time, consider and make your plans for their welfare. If sea duty is in prospect after your initial indoctrination, you should check life-insurance policies, your will, and final arrangements for the support of your family (see Chapter 17).

If ordered to sea duty, you will wish to see your family comfortably settled before your departure. As ship movements are often confidential and unpredictable, the experienced officer usually settles his family in the ship's home port, so that he will be able to be with his wife and children more.

If you are first ordered to a school for a period of indoctrination, as is often the case with officers newly commissioned, it is not advisable to take your family with you. Duty at indoctrination schools is of a temporary nature. You will probably be required to live in student quarters, and your time will be very fully occupied from reveille to taps.

It may be unwise to ship your household effects to your first station. Before trying to settle your family permanently, see how your initial duty goes and what your prospects are.

Travel

204. EXECUTION OF ORDERS. Some additional forms of duty and travel may be included in your orders. If a BuPers Manual is available you should check closely the applicable provisions of that manual. If none be available, the following general information will help.

Form of Orders. The most common order that a naval officer receives is referred to as a "proceed" order. This wording indicates that the officer has 4 days plus "travel time" in which to report. However, there are cases of "proceed" orders that are not so readily interpreted. In the case of orders to proceed on "temporary additional duty," orders should be interpreted as allowing 4 days in which to proceed, plus travel time to arrive at your temporary-duty station. However, no "proceed" time is allowed for returning or continuing to your permanent-duty station. In complying with "temporary additional duty orders," and particularly when the duty involves training, it is wise not to take the 4 days' "proceed" time unless your particular needs urgently require that they be taken. In most cases, discretion is given to the Commanding Officer as to when he may direct an officer to proceed to a temporary-duty station. Your special needs will be taken into consideration by your Commanding Officer.

A per diem allowance is made to an officer whenever the Bureau of Naval Personnel considers that the temporary additional duty would cause the officer monetary loss or hardship were such an allowance not granted.

"Temporary duty under instruction" orders to one station and "upon completion" to another station for active duty or for further temporary duty under instruction, such orders being embraced in one set of orders, do not allow the 4 days' "proceed" time to the second station, even though the orders might read "to proceed." If, however, there is a separate set of orders to proceed to each station, the 4 days are allowed for each change of duty.

As indicated in BuPers Manual, when an officer is granted delay, to count as leave, in obeying proceed orders, the date of reporting is computed in the following sequence: Take the date of detachment and add to it the number of whole days' proceed and travel time. This will give the date on which the officer would report without any authorized delay. To this add the authorized delay which will give the latest day on which to report.

Remember, you are not reporting from leave but for duty after being granted a delay in reporting. You must, therefore, report *before midnight on the reporting date*.

See also BuPers Manual, or an information form attached to your orders, for such phraseology of orders and their interpretation as "Hereby detached," "Detached on or about," "Detached when relieved," "Proceed immediately," "Proceed without delay," etc.

Travel Time. Travel time is based on mileage tables contained in Joint Travel Instructions. For ordinary commercial means of transportation other than those described below in this section, the following table gives the number of days' travel time for distances between points of departure and destination over any usually traveled route by through service:

DISTANCE, MILES	TRAVEL TIME, DAYS
0 to 720	1
721 to 1,440	2
1,441 to 2,160	3
2,161 to 2,880	4
2,881 or over	5

By Privately Owned Vehicle. In the absence of instructions to the contrary on permanent change of station, officers may elect to travel via privately owned vehicle without specific authority. When so traveling, one day per 300 miles is the rate used to compute the amount of travel time allowed. The distance via the shortest usually traveled route given in the official mileage tables divided by 300 is the period of travel time allowed. Any distance of 150 miles or more in excess of 300-mile multiples is credited as an additional day. When travel was performed by privately owned vehicle, you so endorse your orders. Unless permission is obtained from the Bureau of Naval Personnel to travel by private vehicle under temporary additional duty orders or blanket or repeated travel orders, the allowance for travel time is as given in the table above.

By Air. For complete travel by air, travel time is allowed for travel by direct through routes, with use of first available connection at points of change, on the basis of 1 day's travel time for each 24 hours or fraction thereof actually in a travel status. For travel within the continental United States, only 1 day's travel time is allowed. Endorse your orders with time of departure from city at old station and time of arrival in city of new station.

Overseas and to Foreign Station. Orders to foreign station or to stations beyond the continental limits of the United States usually specify the method of transportation and the carrier from the port or airport of embarkation. The travel time while en route at sea in a liner or government transport is the actual time required for the passage. If by air, the principles given above apply (see also Chapter 16).

Combinations of the Methods of Travel. When travel is performed partly by one method and partly by another—as, for example, driving from your present duty station to a port or airport of embarkation— travel time is computed by a combination of the above described methods as may be applicable for the various portions of the travel. You should consult the nearest naval activity prior to commencing travel if you are in doubt as to computation.

205. TRANSPORTATION. You are now ready to arrange your transportation. Study your orders carefully to determine what kinds of transportation are authorized. Refer to Appendix 4, Section 20 for detailed information on transportation allowances, types of travel and travel advice for yourself and dependents.

Luggage. Your personal luggage deserves your careful attention, as does that of your wife if you are married. Pieces should be selected from the standpoints of serviceability, ruggedness—for they will certainly be called upon to "take it"—appearance and, of course, cost. Large, heavy and bulky pieces are a curse; you may have to do a lot of the carrying yourself and two small or medium-sized pieces are far easier to handle than one large one. You would be wise and humane to impress this upon your wife, if you have or acquire one, as she probably will have to struggle with them herself on numerous occasions. Avoid anything larger than a foot locker.

A Navy Exchange or a Post Exchange is an excellent place to purchase such items; their prices are usually rock-bottom and through experience will be carrying the most popular pieces and usually only those that you will need.

You will require at least one suitcase and at least one foot locker. A canvas zipper handbag will be very useful on many occasions: short trips, overnight visits, many forms of athletics, etc. A small leather zipper bag or case that will hold your shaving gear, soap, etc., will be particularly useful in traveling.

All your foot lockers should be stenciled with your name on all sides, top and bottom. Suitcases should be monogrammed with your initials. (Rank is best left off any marking as it probably will change.) Extra keys, properly tagged, are advisable. The matter of insurance on your baggage while traveling also should be considered—losses do occur.

You can save yourself a lot of unnecessary trouble by packing the things you will need on a trip in one suitcase; then only that one has to go into the passenger accommodation with you on a train, or into a hotel or motel—the others can be checked through or left in the car. Foot lockers will be seen only at the beginning and end of a trip.

When you report aboard a ship you will be expected to unpack your gear promptly and send the empty lockers and suitcases (except, perhaps, one bag) to a designated stowage where they will not be immediately accessible. Shore stations generally are more liberal but also have rules concerning stowage of luggage.

As soon as you have ascertained the probable location of your ship (Section 203) you should express the foot locker to your ship or station. In your hand luggage pack the uniform in which you expect to report (with its accessories, of course) and sufficient additional clothing and personal equipment to last through your trip and for the first day aboard. Upon arrival in the area in which you are to report, shift into the proper uniform prior to reporting. The uniform of the day will be either service dress blue or khaki or in some locations, tropical white long. If in doubt as to the proper uniform of the day, call the Officer of the Day of the local Naval Base or other activity, or the Officer of the Day of the station to which you are ordered. As a general guide, khaki is worn in most areas from April to October and blue service the remainder of the year. If you are able to do so, include one each of service dress blue, khaki, and white in your hand luggage.

Uniforms

206. UNIFORMS. The U. S. Navy Uniform Regulations give complete and detailed information as to the regulation uniforms required of a naval officer. You are urged to study this publication carefully. If you are of the Regular Navy, you must purchase all your own uniforms. If you are of the Naval Reserve, you are required to purchase with your own funds certain prescribed articles of uniform, but you will apply to the first Disbursing Officer who takes up your pay accounts for your uniform gratuity on first appointment.

Source. The Naval Uniform Shop, 3rd Avenue and 29th Street, Brooklyn, N. Y. 10032, and its many branches in Washington, Philadelphia, Annapolis, Norfolk, Pensacola, Great Lakes (Illinois), Seattle, San Francisco, Pearl Harbor, San Diego, and other naval bases, and most Navy Exchanges, are excellent sources for uniforms and accoutrements for both men and women officers. Articles purchased have the advantages that they are regulation in all respects, that any branch Shop will make necessary alterations, and that your measurements are kept on file to facilitate reorders. Should you wish to patronize other naval tailors, be sure to select a reliable firm and to ensure that the uniforms and equipment you purchase are regulation and of good quality.

Quality. To buy an article of uniform of inferior quality is the poorest kind of economy, for shoddy material will not justify its cost and certainly will not stand up under the rigorous requirements of sea duty. Know something about materials so that you will have personal knowledge that you are getting value for your money.

Check your uniforms against the specifications given in the U. S. Navy Uniform Regulations. Purchase of nonstandard articles made of unauthorized materials is troublesome, not only to the individual but also to the Navy Department. Avoid the salesman whose sales talk in offering you a nonstandard garment includes some such statement as, "All the officers at Pensacola buy these trousers." The better merchants will try to sell you regulation uniforms; but, if you insist, they will sell you nonregulation garments. Individuality is a characteristic of great value, but officers should try to express their individuality in excellent care of their uniforms rather than by wearing eccentric-looking uniforms.

The incidental articles of uniform such as shirts, collars, ties, underwear, socks, and shoes can be purchased almost anywhere. Ship's Stores and Navy Exchanges frequently carry these items and will usually give you a better price than you can get anywhere else in the locality. Buy conventional articles that are plain rather than fancy. Most officers wear low white collars, good-quality black silk ties, underwear of any type that pleases them, nylon, silk, cotton or wool

FIGURE 202. Uniforms, Male Officers. *Top row, left to right,* Full Dress, Blue; Service Dress, Blue (gray gloves optional); Dinner Dress, Blue (with miniature ribbons); Service Dress, Blue with White Trousers; Blue Working (with white cap cover). *Middle row,* Dinner Dress, White Jacket (with gold cummerbund); Full Dress, White; Service Dress, White; Tropical White Long; Tropical White. *Bottom row,* Service Dress, Khaki; Khaki Working; Tropical Khaki, Long; Tropical Khaki; Dungaree Working.

socks, and conservative shoes without excessive decoration in the leather. White shirts either may be of the neckband variety or may have the collar attached, with or without attached cuffs. It is advisable to buy at least some neckband shirts and stiff collars, for these present a much neater appearance for official and semiformal occasions.

For khaki shirts buy a good grade of military cotton drill, for this is the only material that will withstand the rough treatment of sea duty. A number of officers have been buying a very heavy shirt, similar to that worn by enlisted men in the U. S. Army. This is satisfactory in a moderate summer climate; but in the tropics or at any station where the humidity is high, these shirts are unnecessarily uncomfortable. Brown shoes are prescribed for wear with khaki and aviation green uniforms.

White uniforms are a special problem. The best answer is to select your tailor rather than your uniform. One uniform tailor has been making white uniforms for naval officers for many years and has the biggest clientele in the service. Although his prices are high, the quality of his material and tailoring has brought him excellent business through the years. Poorly tailored whites of inferior material can look worse on an officer than any other uniform.

In purchasing the small items of uniform, do not forget the Ships' Stores and Navy Exchanges run as government activities by the supply officers. Here you can get such items as underwear, both summer and winter, handkerchiefs, bath towels, and socks. The enlisted man's shoe is satisfactory for shipboard wear and is excellent for service in the field. The heavy blue shirt carried for chief petty officers is useful for officers, especially on night watches. From the Marine Quartermaster on large ships, you can purchase some items of khaki uniform.

Advice about purchasing uniforms and uniform equipment all boils down to this: Get good material, have it made up by a good tailor, keep it in good condition, and wear it smartly. In the long run, the buyer gets what he pays for.

U. S. Navy Uniform Regulations contain a list of uniform articles titled "Minimum outfit" for officers. After arrival at your ship or station, check your uniforms against this list. However, it is recommended that you delay buying optional items until you arrive at your ship or station. You will need additional items for sports, civilian wear and for general living. The following list is a general guide for equipment and clothing to be taken to sea on your first ship.

WHAT TO TAKE TO SEA

AMOUNT	ARTICLE
2	Service dress, blue
2	Service dress, khaki
2	Service dress, white
1	Dark civilian suit
1	Lightweight civilian suit
1	Overcoat
2	Working uniform, green (for aviators)
4	Khaki trousers, working
1	Muffler
1	Sweater
1 pair	Shoes, white
2 pair	Shoes, black
2 pair	Shoes, brown
2	Caps, combination with 2 white, 1 khaki, 1 khaki working, and 1 rain cover (1 green for aviators)
2	Caps, garrison, khaki
1 pair	Overshoes
1 pair	Slippers
1 pair	Sneakers
12 suits	Underwear (light)
4	White shirts, with collars attached
2	White Shirts, without collar
6	White shirts, tropical
6	Khaki shirts, long
6	Khaki shirts, tropical
4	Collars, or 1 package paper collars
2	Black ties and 1 tie clip
1	Black bow tie
12 pairs	Black socks (to include some wool)
6 pairs	White socks
6 pairs	Khaki socks
1	Bathrobe
12	Handkerchiefs
2 pairs	White gloves
1 pair	Gray gloves, dress
1 pair	Heavy gloves (wool or fleece-lined)
1 each	Belts, white, black, khaki
1 pair	Suspenders (optional)
1 pair	Garters
3 pairs	Pajamas
2	Polo shirts (athletics)
2	Shorts, or 1 shorts and 1 slacks (athletics)
1 pair	Swimming trunks
2 sets	Buttons and ribbons if rated
2 pairs	Shoulder marks
2 sets	Collar devices
2 sets	Garrison cap insignia

AMOUNT	ARTICLE
1	Sewing kit
1	Whisk broom
1 set	Collar buttons and cuff links
1	Fountain pen
1	Tennis racket, set of golf clubs,* or other desired athletic gear (optional)
1	Sword, with sword belt

Toilet articles as selected, to include razors and blades, 2 toothbrushes, shaving soap and brush, toothpaste, toilet soap, nail file, comb, and hairbrush

* May not be desirable on small ships because of space limitations. Permission of C.O. of a minewarfare vessel must be obtained.

The items above, excluding athletic gear and overcoat, should pack into one foot locker or sea bag and one handbag. At least one white shirt, one khaki shirt and two sets of underwear and socks should be of the drip dry variety for use in traveling.

If your first station is ashore or at an indoctrination school, you will not necessarily need all of the above uniforms at once. Some indoctrination schools will send you a letter when your orders are issued giving information on uniforms immediately required. If you do not receive such a list, you should have the following uniform equipment upon reporting:

AMOUNT	ARTICLE
1	Service dress, blue
2	Service dress, white (if summer)
1	Service dress, khaki
2	Working uniform (green for aviators)
1	Cap, combination with 1 white, 1 khaki and 1 rain cover (1 green for aviators)
2	Ties, black
1	Shoulder marks
1	Collar marks
1	Overcoat
1	Shoes, black
1	Shoes, white (if summer)
1	Shoes, khaki
6	Shirts, white, attached collars
6	Shirts, khaki
4	Shirts, khaki, tropical

Women officers should arrive at a shore station with the minimum outfit prescribed by U. S. Navy Regulations.

ITEM	QUANTITY	ITEM	QUANTITY
Coats:		Jacket, light blue[1]	2
Blue[1]	2	Lingerie ....as required	
White	1	Necktie, black	2
Dress, gray	1	Overcoat, blue	1
Gloves:		Overshoes	1 pr.
Black	1 pr.	Scarf, white	1
White	2 pr.	Shirts, white[2]	6
Handbags:		Shoes:	
Black	1	Black dress	1 pr.
White	1	Black service	1 pr.
Hat, combination, complete ..	1	White dress	1 pr.
Hat Covers:		Skirts:	
Light Blue	1	Blue[1]	2
White	2	Light blue[1]	2
Havelock, blue	1	White	1
Insignia ....as required		Stockings, beige[2]	6 pr.

[1] Nurse Corps officers and officers of the Women's Specialists Section, Medical Service Corps, required to have but 1 each of these items.

[2] Nurse Corps officers and officers of the Women's Specialists Section, Medical Service Corps, are required to have but four each of these items.

Nurse Corps Uniforms. Officers of the Nurse Corps are required to possess the following items of uniform in addition to those prescribed above. Optional for officers of the Women's Specialist Section, Medical Service Corps.

ITEM	QUANTITY	ITEM	QUANTITY
Caps:		Dress, white indoor duty	8
White indoor duty	2	Stockings, white	3 pr.
Cuff buttons, white or gold ...	1 pr.	Shoes, white indoor duty	1 pr.

Aviation Uniforms. Officers of the Nurse Corps designated as Flight Nurses and serving as such are required to possess the following uniforms in addition to those previously prescribed.

ITEM	QUANTITY	ITEM	QUANTITY
Caps, garrison:		Skirts:	
Green	2	Green	2
Khaki	2	Khaki	2
Jacket, green	1	Slacks:	
Shirt, khaki	4	Green	2
		Khaki	2

FIGURE 203. Uniform, Women Officers. *Top row, left to right,* Service Dress, Blue; Service Dress, White; Service Dress, Light Blue; Full Dress, Blue. *Middle row,* Full Dress, White; Formal Dress, Blue; Formal Dress, White; Service Dress, Blue (modified). *Bottom row,* Blue Working; Nurse's Indoor Duty, White.

Optional Articles of Uniform. The following articles are optional:

ITEM	ITEM
Anklets:	Rain, lightweight
Beige[1]	Raincoats:
Blue	Blue
White	Blue, lightweight
Cape[2]	Shirts:
Caps, garrison:	Blue chambray
Blue	Shoes:
Light blue	Gymnasium
Caps, visor:	Shorts, blue denim
Green[1]	Skirt, blue evening dress
Khaki[1]	Slacks:
Havelock, blue, lightweight	Blue denim
Hood:	Blue serge
Rain	Sweater, blue

[1] Flight Nurses only
[2] Nurse Corps officers and officers of the Women's Specialist Section, Medical Service Corps, only.

207. WEARING OF UNIFORMS. Figure 202 illustrates the proper wearing of service dress blue and service dress khaki, the two uniforms most likely to be worn when reporting. After reporting, refer to a copy of Uniform Regulations for additional uniform questions. If you are not already in the uniform of the day you should, of course, shift into it immediately. Figure 204 shows the proper installation of the sword knot, which is attached to the sword of a Navy commissioned officer. Attaching the knot for the first time is a little tricky and you may require some guidance.

208. DESIGNATIONS OF UNIFORM. The Senior Officer Present Afloat (SOPA) or Naval District Commandant prescribes the uniform of the day. For special occasions such as official calls and visits the uniform is prescribed by Navy Regulation and is set forth in the Table of Honors, Chapter 5. For dinners and other special occasions the uniform is usually prescribed by the host, and for other occasions you are expected to wear the appropriate uniform or civilian attire. The following will serve as a general guide:

(a) *Service Dress.* Service Dress, Blue and White, are the basic naval uniforms and are generally worn on all occasions except when Evening, Dinner, Full, or Working Dress is prescribed. Service Dress, Khaki, is an additional uniform for use in warm weather. It is generally substituted for Service Dress, White, during working hours on board ship and on shore where white is not practical. Service Dress, Khaki, may be designated as the uniform of the day in lieu of Service Dress, White. It is normally worn in lieu of white by officers serving on shore with troops under arms and by officers on shore patrol duty.

FIGURE 204. The proper installation
of the sword knot.

(b) *Full Dress.* Full Dress, Blue or White, is worn when changing command, on official visits with honors as prescribed in Chapter 21 of Navy Regulations, on visits of ceremony, occasions of state, and on formal occasions on board ship. For drill with troops, Service Dress, Blue or White, with sword may be prescribed. Gray gloves in lieu of white shall be worn with Service Dress, Blue, with sword and when the overcoat is worn with either Full Dress, Blue, or Service Dress, Blue, with sword.

(c) *Evening Dress.* Evening Dress is worn at official formal functions at which civilians would normally wear evening clothes with white tie.

(d) *Dinner Dress.* Dinner Dress is worn at ordinary official social functions at which civilians would normally wear dinner dress with black tie.

(e) *Working Dress.* Aviation Green Working is worn when engaged in work at aviation activities, flying, or on board vessels serv-

SERVICE

ARMY	NAVY	AIR FORCE	MARINES	
STAFF SGT. MAJOR / COMMAND SGT. MAJOR / SPEC. 9	MASTER CHIEF P.O.	CHIEF MASTER SGT. / CHIEF MASTER SGT. OF THE AF	SGT. MAJOR / MASTER GUNNERY SGT.	E-9
1ST SGT. / MASTER SGT. / SPEC. 8	SENIOR CHIEF P.O.	SENIOR MASTER SGT.	1ST SGT. / MASTER SGT.	E-8
SGT. 1ST CLASS / SPEC. 7	CHIEF P.O.	MASTER SGT.	GUNNERY SGT.	E-7
STAFF SGT. / SPEC. 6	P.O. 1ST CLASS	TECHNICAL SGT.	STAFF SGT.	E-6
SGT. / SPEC. 5	P.O. 2ND CLASS	STAFF SGT.	SGT.	E-5
CORPORAL / SPEC. 4	P.O. 3RD CLASS	SGT.	CORPORAL	E-4
PRIVATE 1ST CLASS	SEAMAN	AIRMAN 1ST CLASS	LANCE CORPORAL	E-3
PRIVATE	SEAMAN APPRENTICE	AIRMAN	PRIVATE 1ST CLASS	E-2
PRIVATE	SEAMAN RECRUIT	BASIC AIRMAN	PRIVATE	E-1

FIGURE 205. Comparative enlisted insignia of the United States Armed Forces by pay grades.

icing aircraft, or at advanced bases. Dungarees are worn when engaged in work which might soil other uniforms.

(f) *Tropical.* Tropical is worn in hot weather when prescribed.

The individual items which should be worn as part of designated uniforms are shown in Figures 202 and 203. For more detailed information consult U. S. Navy Uniform Regulations.

209. CARE OF UNIFORMS. Uniform regulations, Chapter 11, gives excellent advice concerning care of uniforms. Proper wearing, care, and use of your uniforms will pay good dividends in improved personal appearance and in savings. Change your uniforms carefully to avoid ripping linings or weakening seams. Always hang unused uniforms on good hangers.

Keep shoe trees in your shoes. Do not leave the care of your shoes completely to your stewardsman. Well-kept shoes will save your feet and add to your appearance.

Learn to fold uniforms, shirts, and other equipment stored in drawers so that wrinkling does not result. Store uniforms in plastic bags or other coverings and hang so that motion of ship or closing of steel doors does not rub or cut them. Articles such as shoes or shirts can wear through in a few days of heavy weather if not stored in drawers so that they cannot slide.

Purchase and use of a cap stretcher will assure that your cap covers are well pressed and fitted. The cap is a very obvious part of your uniform. Much of your appearance depends on the attention you pay to your cap, shoes, shirt collar, and tie.

Gold buttons may be cleaned with soap, water and an old toothbrush. The cleaning of gold lace should be left to an experienced tailor.

The cleaning and laundering of uniforms, even in small ships, is becoming increasingly efficient. Leave the removal of stains to expert cleaners. If you need to remove a stain in an emergency, consult Uniform Regulations for the proper solvent and procedure to use.

210. AWARDS. Awards are decorations, medals, badges, ribbons, or other appurtenances awarded to an individual or to the unit of which he is a part. Naval officers may wear those United States awards to which they are entitled as listed in the Navy and Marine Corps Awards Manual (NavPers 15790). Foreign awards may be worn when authorized by the Chief of Naval Personnel.

Large medals are the decorations originally presented to the individual. Miniature medals are half-scale replicas of the large ones. Badges are awards without suspension ribbons. Service ribbons are

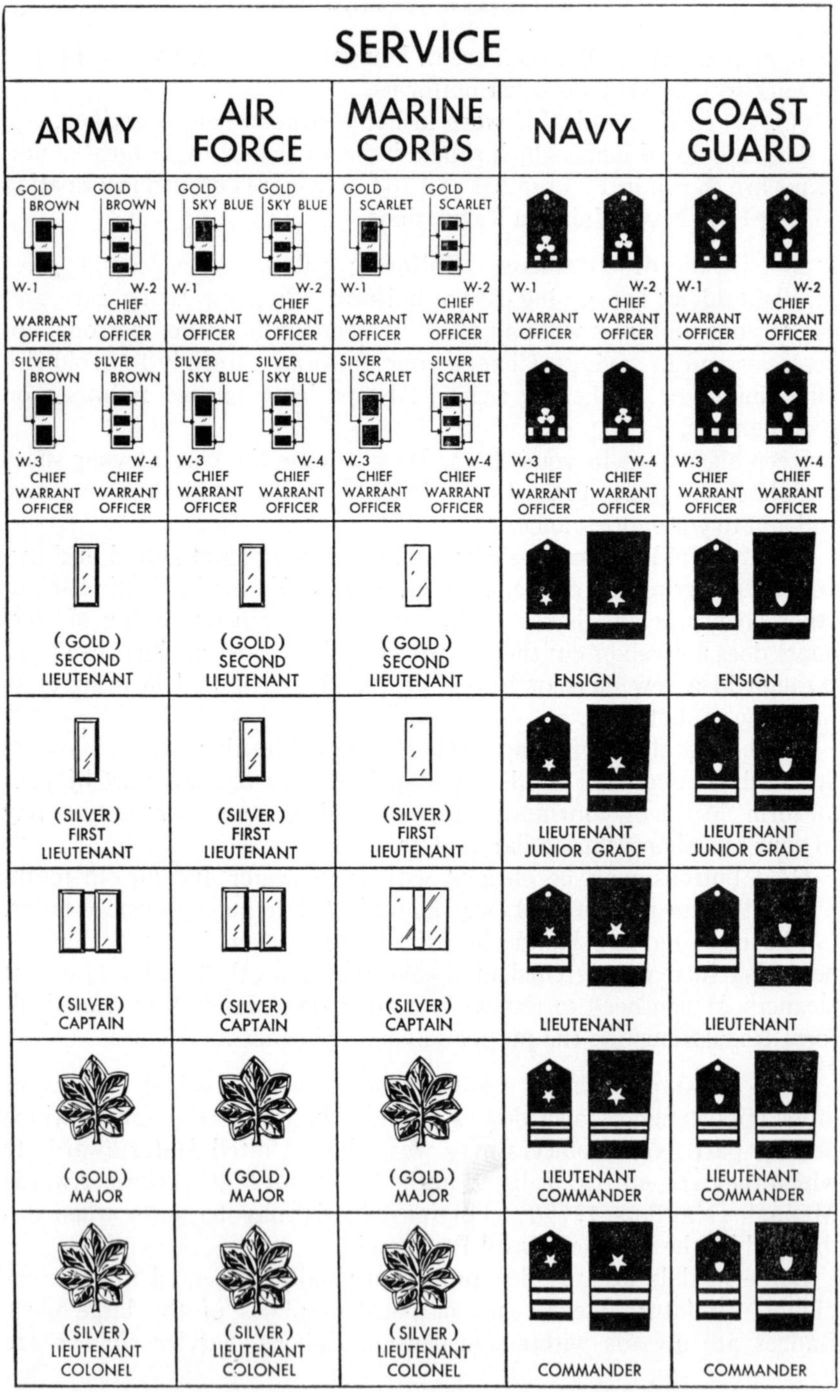

SERVICE				
ARMY	**AIR FORCE**	**MARINE CORPS**	**NAVY**	**COAST GUARD**
GOLD BROWN / GOLD BROWN W-1 / W-2 CHIEF WARRANT OFFICER / WARRANT OFFICER	GOLD SKY BLUE / GOLD SKY BLUE W-1 / W-2 CHIEF WARRANT OFFICER / WARRANT OFFICER	GOLD SCARLET / GOLD SCARLET W-1 / W-2 CHIEF WARRANT OFFICER / WARRANT OFFICER	W-1 / W-2 CHIEF WARRANT OFFICER / WARRANT OFFICER	W-1 / W-2 CHIEF WARRANT OFFICER / WARRANT OFFICER
SILVER BROWN / SILVER BROWN W-3 CHIEF / W-4 CHIEF WARRANT OFFICER / WARRANT OFFICER	SILVER SKY BLUE / SILVER SKY BLUE W-3 CHIEF / W-4 CHIEF WARRANT OFFICER / WARRANT OFFICER	SILVER SCARLET / SILVER SCARLET W-3 CHIEF / W-4 CHIEF WARRANT OFFICER / WARRANT OFFICER	W-3 CHIEF / W-4 CHIEF WARRANT OFFICER / WARRANT OFFICER	W-3 CHIEF / W-4 CHIEF WARRANT OFFICER / WARRANT OFFICER
(GOLD) SECOND LIEUTENANT	(GOLD) SECOND LIEUTENANT	(GOLD) SECOND LIEUTENANT	ENSIGN	ENSIGN
(SILVER) FIRST LIEUTENANT	(SILVER) FIRST LIEUTENANT	(SILVER) FIRST LIEUTENANT	LIEUTENANT JUNIOR GRADE	LIEUTENANT JUNIOR GRADE
(SILVER) CAPTAIN	(SILVER) CAPTAIN	(SILVER) CAPTAIN	LIEUTENANT	LIEUTENANT
(GOLD) MAJOR	(GOLD) MAJOR	(GOLD) MAJOR	LIEUTENANT COMMANDER	LIEUTENANT COMMANDER
(SILVER) LIEUTENANT COLONEL	(SILVER) LIEUTENANT COLONEL	(SILVER) LIEUTENANT COLONEL	COMMANDER	COMMANDER

FIGURE 206. Comparative officer insignia of the United States Armed Forces.

SERVICE				
ARMY	AIR FORCE	MARINE CORPS	NAVY	COAST GUARD
COLONEL	COLONEL	COLONEL	CAPTAIN	CAPTAIN
BRIGADIER GENERAL	BRIGADIER GENERAL	BRIGADIER GENERAL	COMMODORE	COMMODORE
MAJOR GENERAL	MAJOR GENERAL	MAJOR GENERAL	REAR ADMIRAL	REAR ADMIRAL
LIEUTENANT GENERAL	LIEUTENANT GENERAL	LIEUTENANT GENERAL	VICE ADMIRAL	VICE ADMIRAL
GENERAL	GENERAL	GENERAL	ADMIRAL	ADMIRAL
GENERAL OF THE ARMY	GENERAL OF THE AIR FORCE	NONE	FLEET ADMIRAL	NONE
AS PRESCRIBED BY INCUMBENT GENERAL OF THE ARMIES	NONE	NONE	NONE	NONE

⅜-inch lengths of the suspension ribbon appropriately stiffened for wearing.

Awards are worn as prescribed in Chap. 10, Uniform Regulations. In general, the awards for heroism and distinguished service are worn first (above and to the wearer's right) followed by campaign medals, marksmanship medals, and foreign awards.

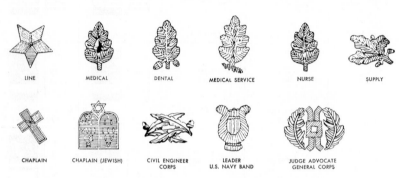

| LINE | MEDICAL | DENTAL | MEDICAL SERVICE | NURSE | SUPPLY |

| CHAPLAIN | CHAPLAIN (JEWISH) | CIVIL ENGINEER CORPS | LEADER U.S. NAVY BAND | JUDGE ADVOCATE GENERAL CORPS |

FIGURE 207. Commissioned Officers' devices.

When large medals are worn, the Medal of Honor is worn from a pendant around the neck. Other medals are worn suspended from bars above the left breast pocket. Each row of medals is 4⅛ inches wide (3 medals side-by-side or 4 or 5 overlapped). Additional medals are worn on added bars placed above the first bar. On service dress uniforms, a patch of material similar in nature to the uniform may be placed over sewed-on ribbons. The Senior Unit Citation to which entitled may be worn on the right breast. All medals to which entitled shall be worn up to 5. More may be worn if desired.

Miniature medals are worn with evening and dinner dress. The Medal of Honor, which is not made in miniature, is worn as it is when large medals are prescribed. Miniature medals are mounted on a holding bar. When the number exceeds the length of a 4⅛-inch holding bar, medals are overlapped. Medals in excess of 11 are placed on a second bar. At least 4 decorations shall be worn if earned; others may be worn.

Service ribbons are worn on service uniforms. Ribbons are worn on holding bars without interval between ribbons on bars. All shall be worn up to 6. If more than 6 are possessed, only 6 of the highest precedence need be worn, but all may be worn. Each row shall contain 3, except the top row which shall contain 1, 2, or 3 as necessary, centered above other rows. Ribbons may be sewed to uniforms or to bars which may be pinned or otherwise attached to uniforms. Sewed-on ribbons are worn on blue uniforms; pinned-on ribbons are worn on white and khaki uniforms.

Attachments such as clasps, stars, and oak leaf clusters are author-

FIGURE 208. Warrant Officers' devices.

ized for wear with certain awards. The proper wearing of attachments is set forth in detail in Uniform Regulations, Chapter 10.

Ribbons are one of the first parts of the uniform noticed. A set of clean, unfrayed ribbons goes a long way toward setting the tone of a uniform. An officer should therefore pay particular attention to his ribbons. Make sure that they are worn properly centered and squared. See that the attachments are securely fastened and centered. As with other items of uniforms, buy ribbons and miniatures from a reputable tailor or store. Large medals are presented, not bought.

Reporting

211. REPORTING TO A SHIP. If your first orders call for you to report to a ship, you will now have arrived in the port in which you expect to find your ship. You have received a letter from the Executive Officer (or from an officer designated by him to reply to you) confirming the fact that your ship is scheduled to be in Norfolk at an anchorage on the day you are reporting. You have changed into the proper uniform and have arrived at the fleet landing. Have with you your original orders and copies, qualification jacket, pay accounts and health record.

All ships in port make periodic boat trips to the regular fleet landing. Arrange to have your baggage on the landing before 0730 and you will not be far wrong. Better advice, still—if you know your ship is in port, proceed to the landing with your baggage and *take the next boat*. Dispatch orders might send your ship to sea before morning.

Even though this is your first boat trip, you may find yourself in command. Review the portions of Chapters 3 and 5 concerning boat handling and boat etiquette *before* you commence your leave.

If you report to a large ship in an officer's motorboat you will probably be "piped over the side" (see Chapter 5) for the first time in your career. Prior to debarking, have your orders in hand, but leave your baggage in the boat. The Officer of the Deck will have it brought up to the quarterdeck for you. After the boat is alongside, proceed to the top of the ladder, stop at the top grating, and salute the quarterdeck facing the colors (usually aft). After completing your salute, walk down off the grating toward the Officer of the Deck and salute him as you approach. You should report, "Ensign Jones, reporting aboard for duty, sir."

The OOD will require a copy of your orders for the Log. He will probably shake hands with you and welcome you to the ship, and then his messenger will escort you to the officer who acts as the Captain's Aide, or in smaller ships, to the Executive Officer.

After you have reported to this officer you will be told your prospective shipboard assignment. You will be given a check-in list which will require that you report to the First Lieutenant for berthing instructions, to the Mess Treasurer, to the Medical Officer, to the Disbursing Officer, and to your head of department. Most ships make a practice of having the Ship's Secretary take you to these officers and then arrange a general tour of the ship. At some time prior to reporting you should provide yourself with at least 25 certified copies of your orders, which will be needed as follows during your check-in procedure:

Two in connection with pay accounts.

Two in connection with payment of mileage.

Seven in connection with transportation of baggage or household effects.

Three in connection with travel of dependents.

Three for uniform gratuity (Reserve only).

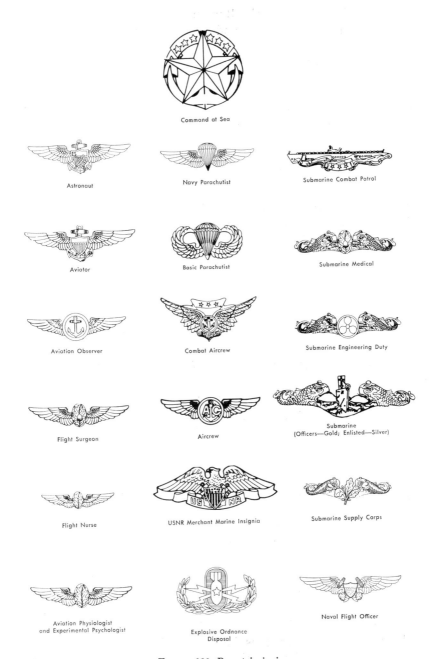

Command at Sea

Astronaut

Navy Parachutist

Submarine Combat Patrol

Aviator

Basic Parachutist

Submarine Medical

Aviation Observer

Combat Aircrew

Submarine Engineering Duty

Flight Surgeon

Aircrew

Submarine
(Officers—Gold; Enlisted—Silver)

Flight Nurse

USNR Merchant Marine Insignia

Submarine Supply Corps

Aviation Physiologist
and Experimental Psychologist

Explosive Ordnance
Disposal

Naval Flight Officer

FIGURE 209. Breast insignia.

Three for forwarding to the Bureau of Naval Personnel, the Commandant of your home district and the naval activity controlling your mobilization assignment.

Soon after you report, the Ship's Secretary will take you to the Executive Officer, who will arrange a time for you to report in person to the Captain. You will find the other activities to which you must report much more concentrated and more convenient than at a shore station.

Within 48 hours, you should make a social call upon the Captain in his cabin. To do this, ascertain that he is in his cabin. Then give his orderly your calling card and ask him to tell the Captain, "Ensign Jones would like to pay his respects to the Captain." On smaller ships, this social call is sometimes omitted. Ask the Executive Officer. He will be happy to advise you. See Section 414 for information as to making social calls on other officers ashore.

By the time you have settled into your quarters, you should have made an opportunity to meet and report to the officer who is to be your immediate superior. He will usually outline your duties and indicate when he expects you to begin carrying them out. If a complete tour of the ship has not already been scheduled, ask him to arrange one.

You should ask the Ship's Office for a copy of the Ship's Organization Book and Ship's Regulations at the earliest opportunity. Master its contents thoroughly. You will be expected to know it (see Chapter 12).

Review the information on security in Chapter 8 and when time permits, borrow the Ship's Office copy of The Department of the Navy Security Manual for a more thorough study of security.

Try to obtain a clear understanding of your duties, both primary and collateral, and consult not only the Ship's Organization Book and Navy Regulations, but also your immediate superior if you are uncertain. Your initial duties on a large ship may be relatively simple, but do not wait for someone to tell you what to do—look for something to do. You will soon find that an officer who is willing to assume responsibility will be given the requisite authority.

212. SHAKING DOWN ABOARD SHIP. After reporting to the Commanding Officer and to the head of department under whom you will serve, report to the First Lieutenant of the ship. The First Lieutenant is the head of the Deck Department in ships which are not primarily combatant. In combatant ships, he is an assistant to the Weapons Officer for deck seamanship. In this capacity, he acts as "housekeeper" for the ship. As such, he is in charge of assignment of rooms.

Staterooms aboard ship vary, but you may be sure of one thing—your room will be small. Senior officers, having greater responsibilities, are assigned the more roomy quarters. Junior officers are doubled or quadrupled up in fairly large staterooms in double-decked bunks. Some ships have bunk rooms for junior officers, which contain 6 to 12 bunks.

You will find space cramped and bathing facilities "down the passageway" adequate but not luxurious, but your quarters will be comfortable and well furnished. You will have a bunk (upper or lower according to seniority) with a comfortable mattress and springs. You will have part of a desk, which also has drawers for stowing clothing, and a chest of drawers or part of one. And you will have some hanging space for your uniforms. Some rooms have portholes, but most officers' quarters today are ventilated by vent pipes and forced ventilation.

In addition to these articles of furniture, most of which are built in, you will be supplied with towels and bedding, including blankets, sheets and pillowcases. The room stewardsman will keep your bed and your room as clean as you insist.

Get to know your roommates. It requires a nice adjustment of personality to live in harmony in a restricted space with a number of other positive individualities. This must be your aim. You cannot expect to have all the conveniences that you enjoyed at home. Life aboard ship is a matter of give-and-take. *Be sure that you give more than you take.*

You will mess in the Wardroom or junior officers' mess. In this comfortably appointed messroom, you will meet and come to know your fellow officers. *It is your task to make them shipmates.* Here in the Wardroom you will learn to enjoy their companionship and will make the early friendships which often last a lifetime (see Section 409 for information on officers' messes and Wardroom etiquette).

Stewardsmen are furnished by the Navy. They are enlisted men, and may be white, Negro, Chamorro (natives of Guam) or Filipino. These men are the source for officers' cooks and stewards. They are in charge of the Wardroom, pantries, and galley, as well as the officers' rooms. The steward administers the details of the mess (consult Section 410 for duties of the Mess Treasurer).

213. REPORTING TO A SHORE STATION. In the event your first duty station is ashore, much of the preceding advice will apply, with certain obvious exceptions.

Let us assume that you are a Naval Reserve officer reporting to a

FIGURE 210. Junior officer in his stateroom.

school of indoctrination for your first duty. It is probable that, since you are to be one student in a large class, a number of officers will be reporting. In this case, the Commanding Officer usually will arrange for several officers and enlisted men to receive the new officers. All that you need to do in this case is to present yourself at the proper place at the correct time. Your orders will be taken, endorsed and returned to you. Be sure to have several copies.

Mimeographed instructions will usually be issued. Be sure that you obtain all instructions, station regulations, etc., which should be in your possession, and that you understand what you are to do.

Should you arrive by yourself, proceed to the Executive Officer's office or to the Aide to the Commanding Officer's office. In the outer office, a yeoman will take your orders. If the Aide or Executive Officer is senior to you, stand at attention and report, "Lieutenant Gish reporting for duty as a student officer, sir."

The Aide will welcome you to the station and give you such information as to reporting or temporary quarters as you will require. He will also arrange times for you to call upon the Commanding Officer in his office and to meet the officer or head of department under whom you will work. When you leave the Aide or Executive Officer, you should have no doubt as to what you are to do and where and when you are to do it. Normally, you will be given a check-in list; if not, follow the suggestions in Section 214.

At indoctrination school, your quarters may consist of a tent, a room in Bachelor Officers' Quarters, or a bunk in student officers' barracks. It may be necessary to find quarters for yourself in the town adjacent to the station. The Public Works Officer or the First Lieutenant will inform you as to quarters available. It is a custom to allow officers ample time to get settled in their quarters.

214. PERSONAL ADMINISTRATION. As soon as possible after getting squared away in your quarters either afloat or ashore and after shaking down, you should attend to certain matters of your own personal administration. Some of these may be accomplished during a "check-in" procedure."

Ship's Office or Personnel Office. Your first stop should be at the Ship's Office (or Personnel Office ashore), where you will be required to make out a report of leave of absence, an officer's history card, an officer's preference card, and certain other forms. Collect your original orders. If you have dependents, procure a Dependents ID card.

Disbursing Office. Next, visit the Disbursing Officer, who will collect your pay accounts (or open an account for you if you do not have one) and arrange to pay you. Have your original orders in hand with all available copies. The Disbursing Officer will pay you mileage for your own transportation and will reimburse you for your dependents' transportation. Register desired allotments.

Medical Officer. Visit sick bay or sick quarters and leave your health record. A corpsman will enter your name on the records and verify that your immunizations are up to date. If you require routine medical or dental attention, make appointments.

Insurance. You should consider seriously taking out Navy Mutual Aid insurance, and you may want to consider Naval Academy Foundation and Armed Forces Relief and Benefit Association insurance. You will automatically be issued $10,000 worth of Serviceman's Group Life Insurance (SGLI) at a premium of $2.00 per month, probably the best insurance buy available. You may cancel this insurance or reduce it to $5,000.

Additional Visits Ashore. The Public Works Officer or First Lieutenant will inform you as to quarters arrangements.

The Shipping and Receiving Section of the Supply Office will have any baggage or effects that you may have shipped from home or former ship or station.

Stop by the Commissioned Officers' Mess for lunch and make arrangements to join it and get your membership card.

At the Navy Exchange, you can pick up at reasonable prices any additional items of uniform or personal clothing which you require. If married, you will wish to check in at the Commissary Store and make arrangements for your wife to patronize it.

If you own a car, obtain a station driver's license and arrange for a station sticker for your car. Liability insurance will be required. Your insurance policy will be required at most stations as proof.

215. SELF-IMPROVEMENT. You have come to your ship or station indoctrinated and educated. You will find your brother officers an honorable, friendly group who will welcome you as a shipmate and messmate, and will honor you by assuming that you know your job and intend to do it well. Your commission, your uniform, and your orders have placed you in this position. You must now seek to maintain and enchance your situation by your ability, energy, courage and personal character.

Your most important duty lies in improving your professional knowledge. Become familiar with your ship and its equipment, not only in your own division, but also in all other parts of the ship. Commence correspondence courses in professional subjects. Your attention is invited to the books listed in the Bibliography, expecially the first list. Perhaps you have already read some of these. Get them out again, read them, study them. When you have thoroughly absorbed the material in these books, commence the second list. It is never too soon to begin to learn the lessons of your profession from your predecessors in this honorable calling and from the long course of recorded history. The time to begin to orient yourself to your new life in the naval service is *NOW!*

CHAPTER 3

Military Duties of the Naval Officer

He stood steadfast by his wounded superior and friend.
—SAID OF ENSIGN JOHN R. MONAGHAN, USN, APIA, SAMOA, 1899

301. GENERAL. Each officer of the Navy should recognize that he is, first of all, a naval officer. Regardless of whether he is line, staff, or specialist, in our modern Navy each young officer must develop some specialized field of interest in which he expects to excel. For some, it may be navigation, gunnery, electronics, aviation; for others, it may be medical science, supply and logistics, religious and moral philosophies; and, for others, naval engineering, civil engineering, or ship design. Whatever his special interest and present assignment, every officer is governed by the same military rules and regulations, honors the same military principles, and performs many of the same military duties. While various officers may have different foundations in science and technology, every officer must recognize his professional responsibility for leadership of the men entrusted to his command and for the proper performance of his military duties.

Too much stress cannot be placed upon the element of service. The naval officer serves in two honored fields: as a military man—a naval leader—and in his technical specialty, whatever that may be. Competence—indeed, excellence—is expected of him in both areas.

It is important to stress again that the naval officer serves the Navy and his country in an era of new and increasing complexities. Our very existence is challenged by an increasingly successful barbarian ideology. We now operate many ships of radically new design and fight with weapons with startingly new and complicated operational problems. Our nation's responsibilities require naval operations on an heretofore unimagined global scale, employing a larger and more operational Navy in this "warless time" than in any other previously known. We must cope with the problems of four-service administrative and operational unification, which necessitates a new application of traditional methods of leadership and proven abilities and skills. The young officer will advance himself best in his profession if he will master early the intricacies of ship and staff organization; adhere to the policies laid down by higher authority; educate himself not only in leadership but also in effective administration and sound management afloat and ashore; and strive always for a levelheaded and conservative fiscal policy.

He will also do well to master the customs, practices, and traditions of the naval service, which are discussed in detail in later chapters, and serve them with honor. He should recognize that our Navy of today has many facets and therefore many specialties, each one necessary to achieve a mastery of the whole art of warfare. Not one of them can be disdained or maligned, without damaging that perfection of teamwork without which no military organization can function successfully.

Throughout the multifarious activities of the Navy, the line officer has a special purpose—the responsibility of command. Of the line officer, Admiral H. P. Smith has written:

> The dramatic technological developments of the missile age have not changed the true concept of the line officer. He is the professional military executive in peace and war. His function is to provide direction, operation and control of the entire organization and to ensure that it remains ready to defeat the enemy in combat. He "fights the fleet" in war, and in peace he is responsible for keeping the Navy strong and ready, as an instrument of national policy.
>
> The line officer's primary duty remains to fit himself with the education and experience to manage, direct and coordinate the vastly complex operation of combined land, sea and air forces. His requirement for knowledge and experience is limitless; his work is complex and vital; his reward is the authority to make ultimate decisions and to bear the responsibility for them. In the final analysis, the outstanding officer is outstanding because he possesses the properly channeled motivation and drive to excel.

Throughout all of his assignments, each officer will find that one common denominator persists: the obligation for supervision and leadership. Regardless of his link in the chain of command, be he commanding officer or junior staff, division or watch officer, he always will have supervisory authority and responsibility over others. This responsibility covers a wide range, from military performance and discipline through such difficult ponderables as morale and personal counseling, to a spirit of service and loyalty to cause. Our need to attain technological excellence is obvious; but it is becoming increasingly apparent that greater effort must be devoted to developing our human resources, if we are to continue to be able to use our technology effectively. Regardless of his special training or ability, an officer will always be obligated to exercise leadership through example, counsel and guidance. Since the unaided achievement of the individual is very meager, the most useful accomplishment the young officer can early acquire is the ability to work harmoniously with other people.

One of the first steps to be taken by an officer in shaking down after his arrival in a new ship or station is to find out about all of the duties assigned to him. Not all of the military duties described in the following sections are applicable to every category of naval officer, but the principles expressed apply to each officer, whether line, staff, or specialist.

Each officer is assigned, first of all, a *primary duty,* the duty most important to him and to his ship. Primary duty for Commanding and Executive Officers of all ships and stations and for heads of departments of the large ships and stations is assigned by BuPers orders. For other officers, primary duty is assigned by the Commanding Officer, either by letter or through the medium of the Ship's Roster.

Each officer is next assigned a *battle station,* usually based upon his primary duty and delineated in the Ship's Organization. Certain officers are assigned *emergency bill duties* such as Fire, Emergency Assistance, Landing Force, Collision, etc. These individual duties are given in the Watch, Quarter, and Station Bill.

Next in importance is *watch standing.* An officer should become promptly informed as to the type of watch to which he has been assigned. The Senior Deck Watch Officer, the Chief Engineer, the Communication Officer, and other supervising officers post watch lists for keeping the various watches required in a ship.

Each officer is also assigned certain *collateral duties,* such as Recreation Officer, Athletic Officer, Voting Officer, etc. Officers are informed as to these duties either by letter from the Commanding Officer or by listing in a Ship's Notice.

Primary Duty

302. PRIMARY DUTY. The primary duty assigned each officer stems directly from the Ship's Organization. This duty is essentially administrative and indicates the officer's position in the day-to-day administrative organization of the ship. However, since a ship of the Navy exists to fight, or to support fighting, the administrative organization of the ship closely parallels the fighting or battle organization of the ship. In most cases an officer's title as indicated by his primary duty is the same as his battle station, i.e., Weapons Officer.

The duties of the most important members of a ship's organization are set forth in Navy Regulations. An officer should have a complete grasp of these regulations, starting with the duties of the officers of his department. At first opportunity he should also study the general duties of other officers.

The Manual of Navy Officers Classification gives the basic function, duties, responsibility, and authority of all shipboard billets. See Ship's Organization and Regulations (Chapter 12) for detailed descriptions of the duties of all shipboard billets. Refer to the *Division Officer's Guide* and *The Bluejackets' Manual* for good descriptions of shipboard organization and of primary duty.

303. BATTLE STATIONS. As previously indicated, an officer's battle station may be the same as his primary duty. This is not always the case. Many junior officers in the Engineering Department are assigned to gunnery battle stations.

An officer's performance at his battle station is the most important contribution he can make to the readiness of his ship. This is particularly true in wartime. In peacetime an officer's primary duty tends to overshadow his battle station duty. Consequently, an officer will do well to remind himself frequently of the true importance of high performance at his battle station.

Find your battle station promptly after arrival aboard and master its requirements as soon, and as thoroughly, as you can. Find the shortest routes to it both by day and by night, and in both fair and foul weather.

304. WATCH, QUARTER, AND STATION BILL DUTIES. The Ship's Organization Book will contain many bills or plans for meeting emergencies. The most common of these bills are posted in conspicuous areas of the ship in a combined form known as a Watch, Quarter, and Station Bill. Study the Ship's Organization Book and this bill to find out your proper duties under each bill and the location to which you should proceed for each bill. Next, learn as much of the more important bills, such as the General Emergency Bill, as you can. Supervising the execution of these bills will be one of your duties as a watch officer. Refer to the *Division Officer's Guide* and *The Bluejackets' Manual* for good descriptions of the Watch, Quarter and Station Bill.

Watch Standing

305. WATCH STANDING. An officer is best known by the watch he keeps. Early in his career an officer should develop a proper attitude toward watch standing and should regard it as an honor and a privilege rather than an onerous chore. The Officer of the Deck while on watch is the most important person aboard under the Commanding Officer. Other officers of the watch are likewise important, but in slightly lesser degree.

The Navy Regulations state:

> The Officer of the Deck is the officer on watch in charge of the ship. He shall be responsible for the safety of the ship and for the performance of the duties prescribed in these regulations and by the Commanding Officer. Every person on board who is subject to the orders of the Commanding Officer, except the Executive Officer, and those other officers specified in article 1009, shall be subordinate to the Officer of the Deck. (NR 1008).

The *Watch Officer's Guide,* published by the U. S. Naval Institute, contains two excellent sections on the duties of the Officer of the Deck, and should be studied thoroughly. The duties of Combat Information Center watch officer will be found in appropriate Fleet Training publications and generally will be supplemented by ship's orders. Duties of Communication watch officers will be found in Communication Instructions. Duties of the Engineering Officer of the watch are generally prescribed by Type Commander's orders.

All line officers must familiarize themselves with the following publications:

1. Navy Regulations
2. Farwell's Rules of the Nautical Road.
3. General Maneuvering Instructions.
4. Signal Book.
5. Current Fleet Tactical Orders.
6. Current Type Doctrine.
7. Current Cruising Instructions and Operations Orders in effect.

Particular attention is invited to Navy Regulations, Chapter 10, which covers the duties of Watch and Division Officers, the Officer of the Deck, the Engineering Officer of the Watch, and the Deck and Engineering Logs. Familiarity with these publications can be obtained only by constant reference and careful study.

An officer is not qualified to stand a deck watch at sea or at anchor unless he knows the Rules of the Road and how to apply them. They

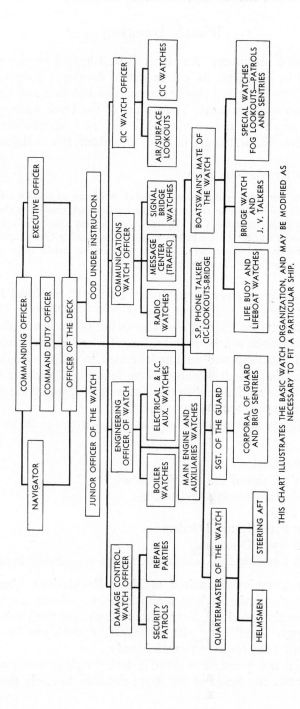

THIS CHART ILLUSTRATES THE BASIC WATCH ORGANIZATION, AND MAY BE MODIFIED AS NECESSARY TO FIT A PARTICULAR SHIP.

FIGURE 301. Watch organization under way.

may be found in Knight's *Modern Seamanship;* especially recommended for study is Farwell's *Rules of the Nautical Road.* Both are available in ships' libraries. These rules apply equally in war and peacetime, and must be scrupulously observed.

Orders and instructions pertaining to tactics and the tactical organization are available, generally, in confidential publications that may be obtained from the Technical Publications Officer. Instructions in these subjects for watch officers is conducted by the Operations Officer. All officers must be thoroughly indoctrinated in all current instructions in order to carry out their part of the operation intelligently. For the responsibility of the Officer of the Deck for honors, see Chapter 5.

306. WATCH UNDER WAY. The following notes to the young officer standing deck watch, while not intended to be exhaustive, are included to assist in keeping a proper deck watch:

1. When coming on watch, visualize the proper action to be taken in case an enemy submarine, an aircraft, a torpedo, or a surface ship is reported or seen; or what you are required to do in case of man overboard, or sighting at night a ship without lights, close aboard, or sighting a mine or suspicious object in the water, or other emergency.

2. Check the condition of readiness of the battery, the degree of closure existing throughout the ship, and the setting of the degaussing cables.

3. Know your recognition signals, challenges, and replies; know how to use current recognition devices and how to operate the ship's special lighting circuits.

4. Keep your watch alert and, at night, your bridge dark and all lights out if darken ship has been ordered. Insist that the incoming watch be visually adapted before relieving the watch.

5. Be thoroughly familiar with all instruments and voice tubes on bridge, and be able to find them quickly in the dark.

6. Check your position on the chart, and ascertain what lights or navigational landmarks to expect during your watch, with characteristics, and what they will look like on the scope of your radar PPI.

7. Personally see that the course is correctly kept. Form the habit of glancing at the PPI scope, steering repeater and steering magnetic compass every few minutes. Keep the course by both steering magnetic compass and steering repeater always in mind in order that you may detect immediately any derangement of gyro. See that Quartermaster records readings of the compasses in compass record book.

8. Before acknowledging a signal, be sure you understand and know how to execute it.

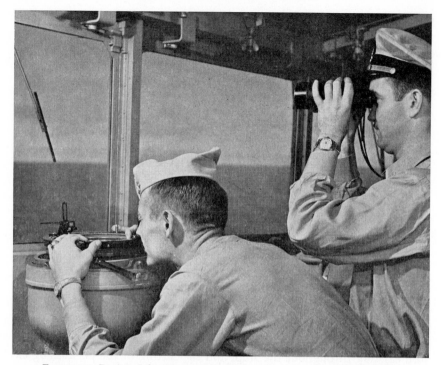

FIGURE 302. Duties of the Officer of the Deck under way are many and varied.
Constant vigilance is required at sea.

9. From time to time check the ship's position on the chart to ensure safety, making full use of radar, soundings, bearings of lights, radio beacons, and radio compass station bearings, etc. Note: Prescribed radio silence shall not be broken except by permission of the Captain.

10. Your duties at the conn, and keeping a lookout, are paramount. Your attention must not be diverted therefrom by chart work, which can be largely delegated to competent assistants. Ensure that all lookouts are awake and on the job. You have to see hazards to navigation early and see an enemy before he sees you.

11. Report immediately to the Captain all ships, land, or suspicious objects sighted or visible on radar scope with their relative bearing and approximate distance. In the case of a ship or plane, report, as soon as determined, its approximate course, whether it will pass clear, and its character, friendly or enemy.

12. Note immediately true bearings of all lights, ships, or aircraft sighted, and report promptly to the Captain if bearings of ships do not change.

13. When necessary to change course to avoid a ship having the right of way, make the change soon enough and large enough to ensure the safety of your ship and to leave no doubt in the mind of the Officer of the Deck of the other ship as to your intention. Most collisions result from a failure to take timely action.

14. Avoid crossing ahead of a ship having the right of way.

15. Satisfy yourself that you are familiar with the Rules of the Road, which will govern your actions in any emergency that may arise in your watch.

16. Show promptness and initiative in taking any required action, such as starting fog signals, using hand lead, stationing fog lookouts, etc.

17. Do not permit any negligence in reports affecting either the peacetime or wartime safety of the ship.

18. If in formation, report immediately when any ship leaves formation or gets badly out of position. Report should you get out of position yourself.

19. Report to the Navigator all navigational aids sighted and all changes in course or speed.

20. Report to the Captain any marked change in weather, sea or barometer. Report immediately indication of fog or thick weather. In case of fog, be prepared to stream towing spar and station additional lookouts; also, have spare spar ready. Have searchlights manned and ready.

21. In case of *any* doubt at *any* time, call the Captain.

22. The Captain sleeps in the sea cabin. The Officer of the Deck can communicate with him by telephone, voice tube or orderly.

23. At all times, the Officer of the Deck must assure himself that the required soundings and bearings are taken and are being plotted and noted in relation to the safety of the course. Prompt report must be made to the Captain should such plots show the ship not to be on a safe and proper course.

24. Prior to relieving the deck, the OOD shall read, *understand,* and initial the Night Orders.

25. If you have trouble remembering the details in turning over the watch, keep an OOD checkoff list similar to the one given in the next section. Turn all pertinent facts over to your relief.

26. Have your Junior Officer make frequent inspections on topside and below decks during the night watches. In particular, he should visit lookouts, lifeboat crews, lifebuoy watches, steering engine-room watches, and the various security watches.

27. Lookouts are a responsibility of the OOD. Keep them alert. Check their knowledge of their duties by asking them questions.

28. Write your Log and sign it before leaving the bridge or quarterdeck, while events are fresh in your mind. Now that the Log is not typed for submission, particular care must be taken that it is neat and complete. Be sure to check the details of the left-hand page. Too often this has been left to the Quartermaster.

FIGURE 303. CIC Watch Officer checks ship's position by radar in destroyer CIC.

29. Be selective in your use of loud-speaker systems. *Do not pass words* over a circuit that have no interest for that circuit. For example, do not pipe down dinner for the crew on the officers' circuit. Select the circuits, and tell the bos'nmate which ones to use.

30. Once each watch, it is good practice to exercise at shifting steering control to various stations.

31. Be sure lifebuoy releases are operative at the beginning of your watch. Remote controls may be tested, but first ensure that buoy is, secured by a temporary lanyard.

32. Learn and use standard phraseology in giving orders to wheel and engines.

33. Move around on the bridge. See everything. Do not settle down

in one spot. Keep a bright lookout yourself, as a check on the effectiveness of your lookouts.

34. Plan ahead beyond your watch. Do not leave your relief "hell to pay and no pitch hot." For example, if many boat trips are to be made between 1230 and 1300, feed the necessary boat crews early. In this connection, make timely preparation when entering or leaving port.

35. Become noted for keeping a smart watch. Be alert, prompt, and decisive yourself. Demand smart performance from your watch.

36. Keep a close rein on your Junior Officer. If you do not, you will find he can get you into more trouble than any other member of your watch.

37. Remember that you are in charge, temporarily, of the ship. While on watch you come next after the Captain in authority. Exercise your authority to carry out your duties. But you will be well advised to exercise your temporary authority with tact. You are on watch only four hours. The other 20 hours of the day, many officers are senior to you.

38. Finally, there is no adequate excuse that can be offered or accepted for slovenly, careless performance of duty. Be on the job. *Carry out your orders.*

307. WATCH IN PORT. Keep a list like the one given below on which to enter details of a watch in port.

OOD CHECKOFF LIST IN PORT

1. If ANCHORED: Anchor in use .... Scope of chain............
2. Depth of water .... Status of hawse ....
3. If MOORED: Swivel.............. Condition of hawse..............
4. If ALONGSIDE DOCK: Lines to dock........ Connections to dock........
5. Anchorage bearings ....
6. Weather (present and forecast) ....
7. Bad-weather preparations ....
8. State of tide............ Drift lead............ Gyro............
9. Boiler and auxiliaries in use ....
10. Ships present ....
11. S.O.P.A.............. Guard........... Medical Guard...........
12. Location of Captain, Executive Officer and Head of Department..........
    Who is CO?..
13. Location of Admiral ....
14. Who has head of department duty? ....
15. Boats in water, location, and fuel in each ....
16. Running boats .... Relief boats ....
17. Boat officers available ....
18. Special boat trips ....

19. Are absentee, prisoner and P.A.L. lists on hand?.......................
20. Are all duty lists on hand and up to date? ....
21. Ship's appearance (canvas, bedding, clothes, bunting, lights, etc.) ....
....
22. Orders for the Day and special orders, execution of ....
23. Liberty Sections .... Expires .... No. men ashore ....
24. 0800, 1200, 2000, reported to the Captain ....
25. Watch relieved ....
26. Other information ....

In Port, Reports to Commanding Officer. Among reports in port
are the following:

1. Change in weather, shifts of wind, marked barometric change.
2. Movements of all men-of-war.
3. Movements of large merchant ships.
4. Arrival and departure of own planes.
5. Serious injury to personnel or material.
6. Flag officers or commanding officers embarked in boat and headed
for the ship.
7. Dragging of anchor.
8. Winding of chronometers.
9. The hours 0800, 1200, and 2000.
10. Any change in condition of readiness of battery or closure of
ship.
11. Any aircraft-warning signals.

Reports to Executive Officer. Reports should be made of the following:

1. Execution of special orders.
2. Departure and return of special details, special boat trips, etc.
3. Compliance with dispatch requests or orders received from other
vessels and commands.
4. Movement of ship's planes.
5. Receipt and transfer of drafts of men.
6. All details of organization, police, inspections, discipline, and
exercises.

Smartness of Ship. The following items require careful checking
and may be the subject of unfavorable comment unless constant watch
is kept to see that they are in order:

1. *Clothes* should not be hung up to dry in exposed parts of the ship
instead of in drying rooms.
2. *Swab racks* should be kept against structure and not in open
exposed parts of main deck or blocking passageway.

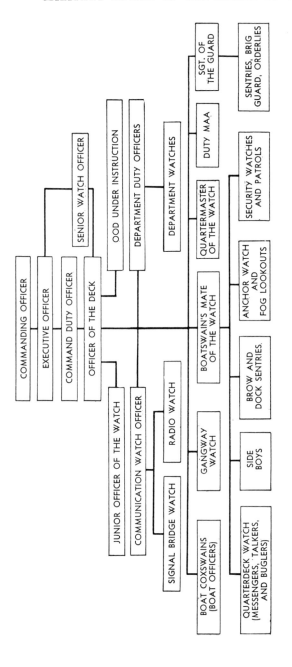

FIGURE 304. Watch organization in port.

3. *Halliards* must be kept taut throughout the ship; periodic inspection is necessary, as halliards taut at 0800 may be loose at 1000 owing to weather changes.

4. *Irish pennants*. Inspect to see there are no loose lines over side and that Irish pennants are taken up.

5. *Dungarees*. Keep men in dungarees off topside, except those authorized in Ship's Order, unless dungarees are uniform of the day.

6. *Boat Crews*. Inspect uniforms each time boats leave ship; require clean, neat uniforms and that they be properly worn. Require boat crews to conduct themselves in a military manner, i.e., no lounging in boats under way and no sitting on rails aft, etc. Require coxswains to salute when passengers enter or leave boats and when acknowledging orders. Make sure "Instructions for Boat Crews" are carried out.

7. Ensure that absentee pennants are hoisted and lowered promptly.

8. The Quartermaster of the Watch should be sent aft periodically to check the tautness of halliards and see that colors and absentee and commission pennants are clear.

9. The Junior Officer of the Watch should be required to make frequent inspections of the topside.

10. Colors should be executed promptly and smartly, following the motions of the senior officer present.

Smartness of Quarterdeck.   The Officer of the Deck in port is responsible for the general appearance of the quarterdeck during his watch. Keep unauthorized men clear; keep free of stores, motion-picture cans, and other loose gear; maintain a taut, clean quarterdeck. When stores must be handled on the quarterdeck, tarpaulins should be spread. See that no oil, food, paint, or other matter is spilled on deck. If fresh spots are noted, have the deck cleaned immediately.

Special Boat Trips.   1. The Officer of the Deck is usually authorized to grant requests for special boat trips. Care should be exercised to ensure that boats will always be available for scheduled trips, such as liberty, guard mail, and United States Mail.

2. When a special trip, such as to a repair ship, is being made, pass the word in order that all departments may take advantage of it.

3. Requests for trips for recreation parties, stores, etc., which normally require the boat to be away from the ship for a period of greater than one hour, should be referred to the Executive Officer.

Guard-Mail Boats.   Guard-mail trips should leave the ship promptly at the scheduled times. Boats should not be diverted on side trips while making the guard-mail trip. Upon anchoring or returning to port, a guard-mail trip should be made immediately to the division flagship, or, when it is absent, to the ships in port or at anchor as follows:

1. To force flagship.

2. If force flagship is absent, to senior ship of your task force present.

The Ship's Secretary will keep a corrected copy of the guard-mail schedule posted in the OOD booth.

Appearance of the OOD Booth and Navigation Bridge. The Officer of the Deck is responsible for the appearance of the OOD booth when the ship is at anchor and of the navigation bridge and pilothouse when under way. All necessary articles such as binoculars, spyglasses, logs, notebooks, order books, pencils, and file boards should be kept neatly stowed. Proper disposition should be made of unnecessary articles. Mess gear should be returned to the pantry immediately after use.

Inspection of Provisions Delivered by a Contractor. In the absence of an officer of the Supply Corps or a pay clerk, the Officer of the Deck is often designated by the Commanding Officer to inspect, for quantity, provisions delivered by a contractor. If on board, the Medical Officer should inspect fresh provisions as to quality; otherwise, this duty may be performed by a hospital corpsman.

Security. The Officer of the Deck should particularly concern himself with the enforcement of security orders, seeing that prescribed security measures are being taken, that security watches are alert, and that required reports are received. He should cause inspections to be made and see that other appropriate measures are taken to ensure that only authorized articles and materials are brought on board ship. He should be courteous but meticulous in the identification of all persons who come on board the ship.

Uniform for Quarterdeck Watch. The following information with respect to uniforms for the quarterdeck watch will be useful to officers standing deck watches:

1. Officers. Service uniform of the day with gloves. Spyglass or pistol and web belt (pistol worn outside of blouse) may be prescribed.

2. Men. Undress uniform of the day with neckerchief.

3. Quartermaster and Bos'nmate of the Watch. Web belt and pistol may be prescribed.

4. From taps to 0600 the anchor watch may wear the uniform of the day.

5. The Officer of the Deck should require all members of the watch to be in clean, neat uniforms, with shoes shined and hair neatly cut, and clean shaven.

Collateral Duties

308. COLLATERAL DUTIES. Many duties in a shipboard organization not important enough to be classed as primary duties are called collateral duties. This term covers such duties as Education Services Officer, Wardroom Mess Treasurer, Voting Officer, etc. An officer in a small ship may be assigned several such duties. Some duties may require only a small amount of time. Others are quite demanding. A commanding officer may assign any type of duty within the limits of Navy Regulations to an officer, but the more commonly assigned duties are:

Athletic Officer. Young officers are generally assigned as coaches or officer representatives for ship's athletic teams. Assignment will generally be made on the basis of the officer's athletic ability. However, if no officer aboard is skilled in a particular sport, an unskilled officer may be appointed. If you are so appointed, lack of personal skill should not stop you from carrying out your duties properly. Find out the senior chief petty officer or petty officer playing with the team. Designate him as coach. You can then carry out the purely administrative phases of the job, such as determining the schedule of games, handling the budget, arranging transportation for the team, etc. Your attendance at games, your enthusiasm, and your interest will communicate themselves to your team (see Section 619 for the importance attributed to this duty).

Training and Education Officer. The Training and Education Officers function as staff assistants to the Executive Officer in administering the ship's training and education program. They formulate, plan for and coordinate shipboard training in order to facilitate the educational and professional advancement of personnel. On smaller ships these functions are performed by one officer.

This requires that the Training Officer prepare and maintain a long-range ship's training schedule, or plan, based upon the ship's employment schedule. He assists the ship's officers in making their own plans in order to implement the long-range plan and maintain a library of lesson plans and training aids for their use. The Education Officer supervises the Ship's Information and Education Program and advises the Executive Officer and heads of departments concerning quotas at various functional schools.

Mess Treasurer. See Section 410 for a description of the duties of a Mess Treasurer.

Voting Officer. The Voting Officer maintains a compilation of the systems of absentee voting in each state, informs all hands at the proper time for procurement of absentee ballots, and gives advice and counsel to anyone seeking information on voting.

Insurance Officer. The Insurance Officer is the ship's expert on government insurance and Navy Mutual Aid. He maintains application forms, actuarial statistics, information pamphlets, and other information, and assists with any problems on insurance.

Welfare Officer. The Welfare Officer plans and executes the ship's welfare program. This includes entertainment, movies, tours, athletic equipment (other than organized teams), and the Welfare Fund. He acts as custodian of the Welfare Fund and recommends necessary expenditures from it.

The Manual of Naval Officer Qualifications lists the complete details of these collateral duties.

Temporary Additional Duty

309. TAD. Those three letters mean "Temporary Additional Duty." As its name indicates, it is temporary and is in addition to primary and collateral duties, and any other duties that may have been assigned. Instances most frequently encountered are Shore Patrol Duty (see Section 310) and being detailed as a member of a court-martial or investigative body. Such duty may also assign an officer, for a long or short period to another ship or station.

Shore Patrol Duty

310. SHORE PATROL DUTY. An assignment that an officer is frequently given is that of Shore Patrol Officer. He may be detailed as an Assistant Shore Patrol Officer or even as Senior Patrol Officer while he is a junior officer and may be called upon to be Senior Patrol Officer even when a senior officer. Such assignments usually are on a temporary additional duty basis and customarily vary from a day to a month in duration. In some ports, the Shore Patrol landed by a ship will be the only one; in others, it will be part of an over-all detail that is landed; or it may be landed to augment a permanent Shore Patrol that already is established.

Navy Shore Patrol. Good conduct ashore of naval personnel, both officer and enlisted, is of vital importance to good relations with civil governmental authorities and civilians in general in port cities and in towns and cities adjacent to naval establishments. While an officer

FIGURE 305. Shore patrol on duty.

must always regard himself as "on duty" and take corrective action whenever he observes conduct detrimental to good order and discipline or to the good name of the Armed Forces, he has especial responsibility in this regard when he is assigned to Shore Patrol. Wherever enlisted men are granted liberty, naval authority provides Shore Patrol, whose duties are:

> To assist civil authorities in dealing with the men of the Armed Forces.
> To maintain good discipline and behavior among bluejackets and Marines on shore.
> To aid and safeguard enlisted men on liberty in every way possible.

This duty is assigned to a group of Navy and Marine Corps officers and rated men established ashore for these purposes, with the officer in charge known as the Senior Patrol Officer of a port or area. In a few localities, where large numbers of enlisted personnel of all services can be expected to be on liberty, a joint patrol is organized called, "Armed Forces Police."

Navy Shore Patrol officers and men wear a blue brassard embossed with yellow letters "SP," and their uniform usually includes pistol belts and leggings, with pistol or night stick. Marine officers and men serving on shore patrol wear the regulation military police scarlet brassard, embossed with gold letters "MP," together with belt and prescribed side arms.

To carry out the stated duties, Shore Patrol generally perform the following tasks:

Patrol areas frequented by men on liberty. Noncommissioned officers work in pairs. When both bluejackets and Marines are ashore, each patrol should consist of one man of each service, so that offenders will be handled by a member of their own service.

Maintain close liaison with municipal police, prosecuting attorney, and other emergency services.

Operate medical aid stations where men may obtain emergency treatment.

Supervise fleet landings and patrol transportation centers used by military and naval personnel.

In your personal contacts as an officer with members of Shore Patrol or Military Police:

Never resist, obstruct, or fail to cooperate with an SP or MP of whatever rank or service. Joint regulations provide that SPs and MPs have all-services authority, with power to enforce any lawful regulation, instruction, or to perform necessary acts. If you have a complaint against the Shore Patrol, submit it through proper military channels.

Advice on Shore Patrol. Service as a member of a Shore Patrol requires a high degree of discipline and excellent performance of duty. Keep the following suggestions always in mind:

a. Be a model officer in every respect—outstanding in dress, irreproachable in conduct and bearing, courteous but firm in your official dealings. Take as your patrol motto, "How can we help this man?"

b. Remember that you are on *military* patrol duty. Your patrolmen and you have no authority over civilians.

c. Permit no drinking of alcoholic liquor by your detail while on SP duty. The least evidence that a member of your shore patrol has consumed alcohol on duty requires a report and means a court-martial.

d. See that the officers and men of your patrol are in conspicuous evidence to men on liberty and civilians. This will help to reduce violations and arrests and to preserve order. Demand outstanding appearance and conduct from your officers and men.

e. Provide medical assistance readily at hand. Should medical officer or corpsman not be assigned to your patrol, be sure that every member of your patrol knows where he can obtain immediate medical assistance.

f. Establish good relations with the local police. Cooperate fully with them and they will do the same for you. Ensure that your patrol is unfailingly courteous to civilians.

g. In a foreign port, obtain a trustworthy interpreter, preferably an officer or enlisted man.

h. Have your enlisted petty officers handle drunken enlisted men, so as to avoid the possibility of drunken insolence or insubordination to an officer. Have intoxicated prisoners examined by medical personnel, and obtain a written statement as to their condition.

i. Handle prisoners strictly, but by the regulations. Permit no undue force, physical violence, or abusive behavior, no matter how much a prisoner may provoke you or a member of your patrol.

j. Prevent disorderly public scenes, prolonged disputes, or brawls. Get troublemakers, loudmouthed men, or obstinate persons to headquarters, out of public view, and deal with them privately.

k. Know your orders, Navy Regulations, and Uniform Code of Military Justice.

l. Exercise common sense and tact in your dealings. You are ashore to *prevent* trouble as much as to stop it.

m. Last, but perhaps most important of all, know how to place a person under arrest or restraint—and make sure that the members of your detail know also. Consult the current official directive on that subject and follow it; otherwise you may find it impossible to prove that an "arrested" person legally broke arrest should he run away or wander off in an alcoholic daze.

Divisional Relationships

311. DIVISIONAL RELATIONSHIPS. All officers reporting aboard are assigned to a division for administrative purposes. In large ships newly assigned officers become junior division officers. In small ships newly assigned officers may be assigned as division officers. Each officer should therefore become familiar with Article 1043, U. S. Navy Regulations, and other related matter regarding the duties of the division officer. The U. S. Naval Institute publishes a handbook entitled *Division Officer's Guide* which gives in great detail the duties of division officers.

Navy Regulations state that:

> A division officer, within the meaning of these regulations, is one assigned to command a division of the ship's organization.

Capable division officers are the backbone of a ship's organization. A division officer is responsible, under the head of his department, for the organization, administration, and operation of his division, and its assigned personnel and material in support of the overall mission of the department. His most important duty is to organize and control the enlisted personnel of his division in order to maintain his division and the equipment assigned to his division at the maximum state of operational readiness. It is a time-tested theory that men who are thoroughly instructed, well cared for, and led with inspiration and aggressiveness can make any military organization work even if their equipment is not of the latest type.

The division officer is responsible for maintaining the Division Watch, Quarter, and Station Bill and for preparing Division Organization and other directives as necessary. He also maintains the Division Training Program. He administers that part of the 3-M System applicable to the equipment assigned to his division.

The division officer implements the foregoing plans by ensuring that all personnel assigned to stations are properly trained in accordance with the training program.

He controls the correspondence initiated by his division and by the individuals of his division and, in liaison with the Executive Officer's office (or Personnel Officer on large ships), oversees the administration of

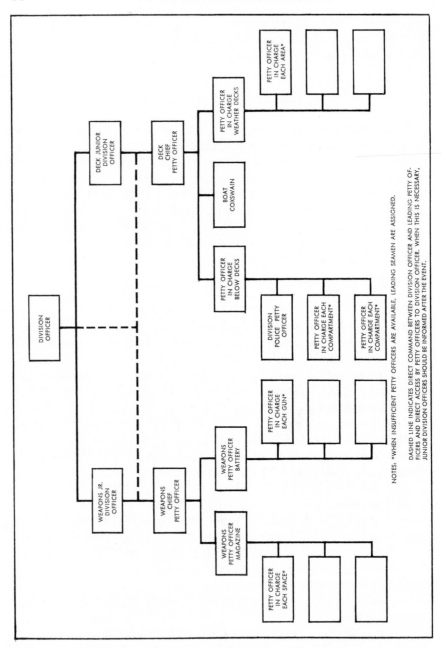

FIGURE 306. Division Administrative Organization Chart.

his personnel. In this connection he maintains records of advancement in rating, eligibility for schools and shore duty, and other pertinent data which will help him to administer the affairs of his personnel.

The division officer prepares Enlisted Evaluation Reports for personnel of his division.

He conducts inspection of material, equipment, and spaces under his cognizance for cleanliness, preservation, and safety, and supervises their cleaning and maintenance.

He recommends disciplinary action, advancements in rating, special privileges, and leave to the Executive Officer.

The Junior Division Officer is assigned to assist the division officer in carrying out his duties. He has no directly assigned responsibilities other than those delegated to him by the division officer. He is next in command in the event of the absence of the division officer and therefore must have intimate knowledge of all the petty officers of the division at all times. In addition, the division officer may delegate to him the training program or other individual duties with the necessary authority to carry them out.

Division Petty Officers. An allowance of petty officers is assigned to each division to assist the division officer in carrying out his duties. These petty officers are military members of the chain of command, as well as specialists in their fields.

Division Organization. The Division Organization should prescribe the duties and responsibilities of all principal petty officers of the division. This organization, together with the Cleaning Bill and other bills, should provide a framework for the day-to-day administration of the division.

A typical administration chart (Figure 306) shows the delegation of authority from the division officer down to the lowest petty officer. Frequently, it will be necessary for the division officer to work directly with the leading petty officers, and for the leading petty officers to make reports, and to have direct access, to the division officer. In this event, the junior division officer responsible should be kept informed by the leading petty officer concerned.

Such bypassing of the chain of command within a division is necessary because of the nature of junior officer training. The junior officer is frequently absent from the division for school, watches, and special duties designed to prepare him for more important duty as watch and division officer. A division officer must keep the division running and, therefore, must at times deal directly with his leading petty officers. Whenever possible, the good division officer will observe the chain of command in his dealings with his subordinates (see Sections 622 and 1212).

It should be noted that the foregoing section described only the administrative organization of a division in order to bring out divisional relationships. The Battle and Watch Organizations are described in Chapter 12 of this book, in the *Division Officer's Guide,* and the Naval Warfare Publication 50 (NWP 50A).

Inspections

312. INSPECTIONS. Some of your first military duties will be in connection with inspections, of which there are several different types. Not only your men and you, but also your assigned ship areas and compartments, machinery, weapons, and other equipage will be inspected; your books will be audited and your administrative procedures will be examined; and your combat readiness will be thoroughly tested. In addition to personal readiness for inspection, you must also ensure that all men and equipment assigned to you are ready for inspection—which requires that, before your division is inspected, you yourself must be an inspector *and* corrector of deficiencies.

313. CAPTAIN'S INSPECTION. Article 708, Navy Regulations, provides that, "The commanding officer shall, when circumstances permit, hold an inspection of the personnel and material of the command on such day of each week, except Sunday, as may be expedient. Normally aboard ship, and where practicable at other activities, the inspection of personnel shall be held Saturday before noon."

It is customary to hold these required inspections on Friday and Saturday. The most commonly used commencement times are 1330 Friday for the material or "below decks" inspection and 0900 Saturday for the personnel, weather deck, and living space inspections.

On large ships, the below decks area and the weather deck and living space areas are divided into zones, with the Commanding Officer inspecting a different zone each week, and the Executive Officer and heads of departments rotating through other inspection zones. On all ships, the Commanding Officer usually inspects the personnel regardless of the size of the ship.

For lower deck inspection, the word is usually passed about 1300 for all hands to stand by lower deck spaces for inspection. The uniform for this inspection is generally clean working dress khaki and dungarees. All men responsible for cleaning and maintaining spaces and equipment below decks then proceed to their stations and prepare for inspection by opening storerooms and lockers, turning on lights, and casting loose equipment. Inspection parties assemble outside the Commanding Officer's cabin or other designated space. At 1330 the Executive Officer reports to the Commanding Officer that the ship is ready for inspection. Inspection parties then proceed to their zones and conduct the inspection. The Commanding Officer is usually preceded by the Chief Master at Arms and has in his inspection party a medical officer, the chief engineer, or his representative and a yeoman. As the Commanding Officer enters each compartment, the Chief Master at Arms orders, "Attention." The man whose compartment is being inspected reports, "Good afternoon, Captain, Jones, Fireman, compartment 3-40-1-E, A Division, ready for inspection, sir." Upon completion of inspection of this compartment, the party moves on to the next compartment. After all parties have completed inspection, all hands are piped down and

FIGURE 307. Captain's personnel inspection.

the inspection is considered completed. Notes taken by the various inspectors are consolidated, written up, and distributed for corrective action.

For personnel, weather deck, and living space inspection, the crew generally assembles at inspection parade about 20 minutes before the scheduled time of inspection. This period is utilized by Division Officers and leading petty officers to inspect and instruct personnel, and to allow compartment cleaners time to finish cleaning compartments. Officers' call is sounded 5 minutes before scheduled time of inspection. Division Officers proceed to the quarterdeck or other designated parade where they form in two ranks to the rear of heads of departments. The Executive Officer issues any special instructions he may have regarding conduct of the inspection. Division Officers return to their posts.

After sounding of inspection call, the Executive Officer reports to the Commanding Officer that ship's personnel are ready for inspection. The Commanding Officer customarily proceeds to the quarterdeck and commences personnel inspection from that location, proceeding around the ship in a manner generally prescribed in the Ship's Organization Book, so as to visit each division in proper order.

Each division is formed in open order, as nearly as the configuration of its parade will permit, with junior officers and chief petty officers formed outboard. The Division Officer takes post at that end of the division to be approached by the Commanding Officer. At the latter's approach, the Division Officer orders, "Hand salute." He then salutes and greets the inspecting officer with, "Good morning, Captain." After the inspecting officer returns the salute, the Division Officer orders, "Two." The Division Officer then reports to the inspecting officer, "First Division, sir, 80 men, no (or number of) unauthorized absentees." As the Commanding Officer acknowledges the report and begins the inspection, the Division Officer falls in one pace behind the Commanding Officer.

The next phase of the inspection will vary at the will of the Commanding Officer, but generally will consist of inspecting the front of one rank and then inspecting the front of the second rank in reverse direction, so as to return to the starting point. After the division has been ordered to face about and uncover, the back of each rank is similarly inspected. Occasionally a commanding officer will ask to see socks, identification tags, or other articles. Each division is inspected in the same manner in succession.

After completion of inspection of personnel, the word is passed for divisions to fall out and all hands concerned to stand by for inspection of weather deck spaces and living compartments. After a short interval to allow these men to proceed to their stations, the inspection parties form and proceed to their zones of inspection. The procedure used is similar to that described for lower deck inspection except that the occasion is more formal, with all hands remaining in inspection uniform. Upon completion of this phase of the inspection, the crew is piped down. Again, notes taken by inspectors are consolidated and issued to appropriate officers for correction.

The *Division Officer's Guide* gives excellent advice to the division officer on methods of preparation for Captain's inspection.

314. ADMINISTRATIVE INSPECTION. Administrative inspection is generally conducted once or twice annually and is scheduled by the Type Commander. The inspection may be used to determine a unit's readiness for deployment or for general operations after shakedown, or for indicating to the Type Commander the unit's general state of administrative readiness. Usually one such inspection each year is conducted as a *surprise inspection,* with the unit inspected given notification of the event about midnight of the date of inspection.

An administrative inspection is generally conducted by the unit commander and an assisting unit from a ship of the same type as that inspected. The first day is devoted to a careful inspection of the records of the unit to determine if they are properly kept. The Type Commander usually publishes a checkoff list to be used in this inspection. On the second day a formal personnel inspection is conducted with the crew in uniform designated by the chief inspector the night before. Normally a modified lower decks, living compartments, and weather decks inspection is made after personnel inspection. Normal practice is to hold a post-inspection critique in order to apprise the inspected unit of deficiencies, including those too minor to be included in the official report.

The *Division Officer's Guide* gives some good advice on preparation for this inspection. A smart ship is always ready for such inspection.

315. OPERATIONAL READINESS INSPECTION (ORI). Annually each unit is scheduled by the Type Commander to receive an Operational Readiness Inspection. As its title implies, this inspection is designed to test and measure the over-all operational readiness of the ship. The inspection usually lasts 48 hours and is conducted by a unit commander and an inspecting party from an assisting ship. Wartime conditions are simulated as closely as possible. Battle dress, battle messing, and condition watches are used during this period. A series of exercises and battle problems is conducted in order to test the capability of the unit to use all of its equipment and to demonstrate the state of training of the crew in all aspects from first aid to abandon ship.

316. MATERIAL INSPECTION. In the 6-month period prior to commencement of a regularly scheduled overhaul, a Material Inspection is conducted. This inspection is usually conducted by the Board of Inspection and Survey, a group of experts in such matters. However, the inspection may be conducted by a specially convened board.

A unit is generally given a full week alongside a tender or pier in which to conduct this event in order to permit the unit to open and place out of commission sufficient machinery to enable the Board to determine the material state of the ship. This inspection requires several days during which the Board closely examines material records, and removes paint and preservatives as necessary to find the true condition of the hull and equipment.

Small Boat Handling

317. SMALL BOAT HANDLING. Your first chance to command will come sooner than you expect. The Navy Regulations say:

> When embarked in a boat the senior line officer (including commissioned (chief) warrant and warrant officers) eligible for command at sea has authority over all persons embarked therein, and is responsible under all circumstances for the safety and management of the boat. (NR 1331)

Only officers of the unrestricted line of the Navy (male) are eligible for command at sea. The moment you enter a boat and are the senior unrestricted line officer embarked, you are in command of that boat. Making this determination may require some diplomacy. Do not be afraid to ask an officer in civilian clothes if he is the senior officer in the boat. Keep asking until you find someone senior to you. If officers are present in uniform and outrank you, it is still permissible and logical to make discreet inquiries until you determine that there is an officer present of the *unrestricted line* who outranks you. Remember that restricted line officers wear stars on their sleeves.

If you are not in command, enjoy the boat trip, but keep your eyes and ears open. If you are in command, choose a seat where you can

FIGURE 308. Smart boat crews exemplify a smart ship.

see forward. Keep a lookout for other boats, lights, debris, etc. Do not hesitate to direct the coxswain of the boat as necessary to ensure safety of the boat, compliance with the Rules of the Nautical Road, or rendering of proper honors. You have full authority to shift trim of the boat or to order passengers to act as additional lookouts if weather closes in. You may change the coxswain's orders for good and sufficient reasons, but, if you do, be prepared to render satisfactory explanation to the Officer of the Deck upon your return to the ship (see Section 504 for Boat Etiquette).

Presumably the Boat Coxswain is competent to make a good landing and knows the Rules of the Nautical Road; if not, report any deficiency to the Officer of the Deck. Unless you are skilled at handling that particular type of boat, it is best to leave the actual boat handling alongside gangway or float to him; however, check to ensure he does not crowd in ahead of a senior, and see that he does not use excessive speed (rocking floats, wetting down occupants of other boats, swamping rowboats or canoes and other private craft). Above all, see that he observes the Rules of the Road—and by a safe margin. Some coxswains of large boats exhibit all the traits of a bully where smaller boats are concerned.

Each boat has in it, stamped on a brass plate, its maximum capacity. See that the boat is never overloaded. In case of fog or rough weather, it may be necessary for safety arbitrarily to reduce this figure and carry only a partial load. In such a situation, juniors are off-loaded first. Whenever it is necessary to leave personnel behind at a boat landing, be sure to inform the Officer of the Deck so that he may arrange another trip. There are *supposed* to be enough life jackets for all occupants; know where these are stowed. In fog or rough weather it may be necessary for safety to have all occupants wear lifejackets. San Francisco Bay and Hampton Roads are two areas where these precautions frequently are necessary.

Occasionally a motorboat's crew will lash down the canvas coverings over the entrances to the compartments to keep the interior dry. *Never permit this.* If the boat capsizes or sinks in collision, the occupants inside have no chance of getting out. Someone can easily hold the canvas covering in place and all occupants will be safer.

Do not permit any smoking at any time in a power boat. Navy personnel know this but sometimes need to be reminded. Almost invariably, civilian passengers will "light up"; if they do, tactfully point out to them that smoking in Navy boats is prohibited because of the fire hazard it entails.

General War Notes

318. GENERAL WAR NOTES. In time of war the professional duties of an officer shift in emphasis. Training becomes more important than in peacetime, instead of less, as might be presumed. Only the highest state of training of each man at his battle station is acceptable, and this state, once attained, must be kept at a high level. Cross training, to provide reliefs for important battle stations in the event of casualties, must be started. Even rate training must be accentuated, for new construction or activation will soon rob you of some of your rated men. Trained lookouts will be needed in large numbers, even in this day of radar and sonar. A satisfactory training program can be maintained with careful planning. Advantage should be taken of the long watch periods so that men are trained during these periods as readiness of the ship will permit. Upkeep and cleanliness require new approaches. Maintenance and sanitation should be foremost. Appearance must necessarily suffer somewhat, but high standards should not be forgotten. Ensure that important equipment works. Frequent sweeping and scrubbing can take the place of painting, which generally has to be reserved for preservation only.

Pay particular attention to food. It should be well prepared and well served. Soup and hot or cold beverages served on night watches will go a long way to improve the efficiency of the watch standers.

Exercise care in safeguarding sleeping arrangements for watch standers. A well-rested lookout may save the ship.

Officers and men should be kept informed, within security limits, of the general situation and of the particular mission of the ship. This can be done by ensuring wide dissemination of press news and by passing on word to the men of your division at every opportunity.

The emphasis on administrative matters will change. Many of the reports and summaries required for budgetary and legal reasons in peacetime will cease. Those reports still required, such as ammunition inventories, etc., should be carefully administered. If a report is of such importance that it is still required in wartime, then it should receive prompt and proper attention.

The following important list of general war notes summarizes the foregoing and in addition provides a few additional time-tested and experience-tested reminders:

1. Cleanliness is for sanitation only, both personnel and ship.

2. Do not worry about uniforms. Make sure that men are comfortably dressed for weather at hand.

3. Insist that men wear long sleeves and long trousers to avoid flash burns. This is especially true in the atomic age. In hot weather, regular "flashproof" clothing is not practical.

4. Insist on good food, well prepared and served; soup, sandwiches, etc., for night watches.

5. Avoid use of general alarm, loudspeakers, and shouting. Save the racket for action or probable action; at the same time, conserve everyone's nerves (including your own).

6. Insist on watches being arranged to give everyone the utmost rest and relaxation commensurate with security and safety and the ability to handle a situation. You will really need your energy, when you need it.

7. Provide the best possible relaxation aboard ship and ashore that you can arrange.

8. *Lookouts* must be well trained and continually cautioned to keep

their eyes in their own sector. Sleeper planes avoiding radar detection and approaching from the offside of an action are doubly dangerous. See that lookouts are comfortable and have the best in binoculars and filters.

9. Training must be continued eternally for guns, damage control, depth charges, etc. Take advantage of every opportunity, but *do not wear your men down.* Keep in mind the training of condition watch standers, so that they can shoot if they have to. Night training is important but hard to achieve. Coordination between OOD, lookouts, identification, recognition, and battery cannot be sufficiently emphasized.

10. *Disseminate as much information* to ship's crew as you can. They will do much better if they have an idea what they are doing and why.

11. Keep everything practical. All your men will be trying to win a war. Many will come into the service for that purpose only. There are enough hubbub and lost motion elsewhere. They will be quick to sense and resent anything which is not practical.

12. This is elementary, but *keep the mission in mind* and encourage officers, particularly watch officers, to look ahead toward the next move or next possible move. If you can keep 15 minutes ahead of what is going on, you will accomplish a minor miracle.

13. Take the reduction of paper work seriously. Avoid writing too much, and particularly avoid having your yeoman "take a letter." He can be better employed as a gun pointer. A pencil memorandum will usually suffice.

14. Be ready at all times to go anywhere north, south, east, or west. This applies to clothing, fuel, provisions, and state of mind. At the same time, *travel light* with regard to personal possessions and clothing.

15. If it will not help win *this* war, forget it.

16. Do not worry about grand strategy, etc. You will lose sleep if you do, without accomplishing anything. Concentrate on your own problems, but still *do not worry.*

17. Make sure that officers, key men, and similar ratings *do not all eat or sleep or stand watch at the same time or place.* If they do, one torpedo or bomb can wipe out much of the effective fighting, steaming, or ship control force of the ship.

18. You will have to make action reports and keep the ship's *war diary.* A small organization to help keep the diary up to date and to obtain action data is advisable. However, *this is secondary to fighting the action.*

19. You cannot put too much emphasis on recognition and identifi-cation of your own and enemy warships, airplanes, and merchant ships. Coordination of all elements of ship control, communication, and the battery is essential.

20. Passing mail and fueling at sea are tactical exercises continually used. DD's *will have to be good at coming up alongside.*

21. All watch officers must be able to handle the ship. No one can tell when a watch officer may have to take the ship out of port or bring her back without benefit of higher command.

22. Be sure that communication systems, recognition systems, etc., are up to date; this is sometimes difficult.

23. Be sure that you have plenty of charts. You never know where you are going next.

24. In posting lookouts and deck watches at night, take into account the time required to adjust men's eyes to night vision. Unless steps are taken, enlisted men will relieve *on time* whether or not they can see in the darkness.

25. Those men on watch, but not essential to the immediate situa-tion, should be permitted to rest or sleep on station. They can be roused when needed. Ensure that those needed are on the alert.

The foregoing notes are just as applicable to the future as they were in the Vietnam and Korean conflicts and in World War II. Training, forehandedness, and care of your men and equipment should be your watchwords in any era.

CHAPTER 4

Traditions and Customs
of the Naval Service

After you, Pilot.
—COMMANDER T. A. M. CRAVEN, USN,
LOSS OF THE U.S.S. *Tecumseh*, 1864

401. GENERAL. In the preceding chapter, the first few weeks of life as a naval officer and the first few days of life aboard ship were outlined. The young officer beginning his career has become aware of many customs and traditions of the naval service. Being piped aboard is a custom of many years' standing. So are many of the other customs he will encounter in his first days in a ship.

As soon as possible after reporting and as part of the shaking down process, a young officer should begin to gain a thorough understanding of all the traditions and customs of the naval service. The best source of such knowledge is the book *Naval Customs, Traditions, and Usage* by the late Vice Admiral L. P. Lovette, USN. The more immediate and common customs which the young officer will be required to know will be covered in this chapter.

Naval Traditions and Customs

402. CUSTOM AND TRADITION. Much of the *custom* in the United States Navy is based on *tradition*. Many of us have had the idea that tradition is a static influence, established by naval heroes long dead. Nothing could be further from the fact.

When Rear Admiral Isaac Kidd stayed on his flag bridge at Pearl Harbor, directing the defense of his ships against the sneak air attack of the Japanese Navy until struck down by enemy action, refusing to be succored, continuing to direct the fight until he died; when Captain Cassin Young, blown overboard by a bomb explosion from the bridge of his ship, swam back, climbed aboard, and fought his ship so successfully that he saved it for further service in the war; when Commander Gilmore told his deck watch officer, "Take her down," as he lay fatally wounded on the deck of his submarine; each and every one not only followed naval custom—he extended and enriched naval tradition by his heroic action.

But tradition is not a heritage only from the dead. It is a living force, continuously enriched and extended by the heroic actions of officers and men we know well in our service associations of today. We can be certain that it will be further enhanced by some shipmate of ours, perhaps by one least likely to be suspected of ever becoming a "maker of naval tradition."

When Captain Gehres brought home the carrier *Franklin* by dogged determination to save his ship even though that feat seemed all but impossible, he not only followed the tradition of Lawrence, "Don't give up the ship," but he illuminated and emblazoned it on a brighter banner. Many a captain of a fighting ship in Iron Bottom Sound and up The Slot in the Solomons thought of Commander Craven's words, "After you, Pilot," although he may have said, as the water washed over the deck of his ship, "You go ahead, Benny. I'll stick around till I see that all the boys are clear." Some of those officers still survive as living embodiments of naval tradition—others found a last resting place in ocean depths lined with the rusting steel skeletons of gallant ships, American as well as Japanese.

Halsey, Spruance, Leahy, Nimitz, Mitscher, Turner, King, Kinkaid, and McCain are names which add luster to pages of naval history already brightened by those of Lawrence, Perry, Decatur, Isaac Hull, Farragut, Dewey, Sampson, Sims, and their kind.

A *custom* may be defined as a form or course of action characteristically repeated under like circumstances, a whole body of usages, practices, or conventions regulating social life. A custom may be a long-established practice considered as unwritten law and resting for authority on long consent, or a usage that has by long continuance acquired a legally binding force.

Much of our daily life is governed and regulated by the force of custom. Many customs are so firmly entrenched as to have become established as law. Custom and usage, properly established and recognized, have the force of law, and cognizance may be taken of them by a court of law.

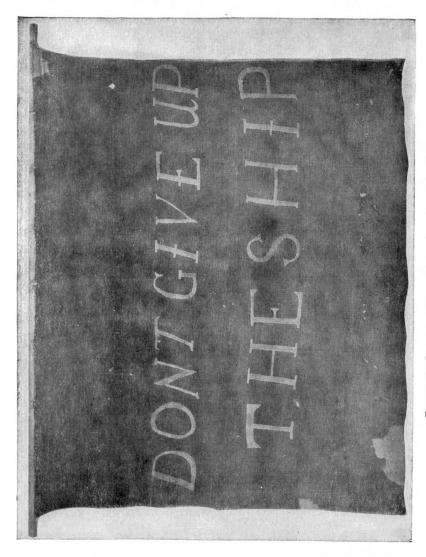

FIGURE 401. Lawrence's immortal words on Perry's battle flag.

Each community, state, and country, each trade, art, and profession, each group of people having interests in common with others regulate at least a part of their lives by customs and usages peculiar to the activities of that group. In the naval service, there are customs and usages that are peculiar to the personnel serving in the Navy. The origin of many of these is obscure, but they have the power of full authority and are conscientiously observed. Many have been incorporated into regulations that have the full force of law. Some have the form of

FIGURE 402. Rendering side honors to an admiral as he comes aboard.

"do not" rather than "do." Taboos are often more stringently enforced than customs. The breach of some Navy customs merely brands the offender as ignorant, careless, or ill-bred; but there are others the violation of which would bring official censure or disciplinary action.

403. THE QUARTERDECK. Navy Regulations require that the Commanding Officer "clearly define the limits of the quarterdeck." The sanctity of the quarterdeck should be firmly enforced, and every officer and man should take pride in observing the proper etiquette. To the Officer of the Deck and his assistants falls the duty of maintaining this discipline.

The following suggestions on quarterdeck etiquette, quoted from a Navy instruction pamphlet, give excellent advice:

1. Never appear on quarterdeck unless in uniform of the day, except in crossing to enter or leave a boat or as your duties may require.

2. Never stand around on the quarterdeck for any length of time in civilian clothes.

3. Salute the quarterdeck every time you come onto it (this applies to large ships which have a quarterdeck with defined limits).

4. Never smoke on the quarterdeck.

5. Never engage in recreational athletics on the quarterdeck unless it is sanctioned by the Captain, and then only after working hours.

6. Never walk on the starboard side of the quarterdeck except in the course of necessary official business or on invitation of the Admiral or the Captain.

7. Refrain from horseplay or any other unmilitary conduct on the quarterdeck.

The starboard gangway to the quarterdeck is used by all commissioned officers, warrant officers, and their visitors; the port gangway is used by all others. If the construction of the ship or other circumstances make a change in this rule expedient, the change may be made at the discretion of the Commanding Officer. In heavy weather, the lee gangway is used by everyone. Large ships acting as flagships are sometimes equipped with an additional starboard gangway which is used by the embarked flag officer and senior officers of his staff. Small ships have only one gangway which may be rigged on either side and is used by all hands.

404. THE CORRECT USE OF TITLES. In oral communication, officers, of and above the rank of commander are always addressed and referred to by their titles, as "Admiral," "Captain," "Commander Jones." Officers below the rank of commander are addressed as "Mister," and, in the case of officers of the Medical or Dental Corps, as "Doctor." It is generally considered improper to address a lieutenant commander as "Commander", unless he is the Executive Officer.

But note that, aboard ship or in any naval organization or on any naval station, there is only one "Captain," the regularly assigned commanding officer, regardless of his rank. Also, the phrase "the Commander" is used only to designate the Executive Officer of the ship or station and him alone. Other captains and commanders attached to the same ship or station should be addressed by rank and name, as "Captain Rogers" or "Commander Peters."

Officers of the Army, Air Force, and Marine Corps of and above the rank of captain are addressed and referred to by their titles, as "Gen-

Person Addressed or Introduced	To Military Personnel		To Civilians	
	Introduce as:	Address as:	Introduce as:	Address as:
Naval Officer (Comdr. or above)	Commander Smith	(same)	Commander Smith[1]	(same)
Marine, Army, or Air Force Officer (Capt. or above)	Major (or other rank) Smith	(same)	Major Smith[1]	(same)
Naval Officer (Lt. Comdr. or below)	Mr. Smith	(same)	Lt. Comdr. Smith[1] Doctor Smith	Mr. Smith Dr. Smith
Marine, Army or Air Force Officer (First Lt. or below)	Mr. Smith	(same)	Lieutenant Smith[1]	Mr. Smith
Woman Officer (Comdr. or above and Capt. or above in other services)	Comdr. (or Col.) Smith[2]	Miss (or Mrs.) Smith (or use rank)	Comdr. (or Col.) Smith[2]	Miss (or Mrs.) Smith (or use rank)
Woman Officer (Lt. Comdr. or below and First Lt. or below in other services)	Miss (or Mrs.) Smith	(same)	Lieutenant Smith[1]	Miss (or Mrs.) Smith
Navy Staff Corps Officer (Comdr. or above)	Comdr. Smith[3] Chaplain Smith	(same) (same)	Comdr. Smith[3] Chaplain Smith	(same) (same)
Coast Guard or Coast and Geodetic Survey Officer	Same as for rank in the Navy[4]	(same)	(same)	(same)
U. S. Public Health Service Officer (M.D. or Dentist)	Dr. Smith[4]	(same)	Dr. Smith of the Public Health Service	Dr. Smith
U. S. Public Health Service Officer (Sanitary Engineer)	Mr. Smith[4]	(same)	Mr. Smith of the Public Health Service	Mr. Smith
Chief Warrant Officer[5]	Mr. Smith or Chief Gunner Smith	Chief Gunner Smith	Chief Warrant Officer Smith or Chief Gunner Smith	Mr. Smith or Chief Gunner Smith
Midshipman[6] or Cadet or Aviation Cadet	Midshipman or Cadet or Aviation Cadet Smith	Mr. Smith	Midshipman or Cadet or Aviation Cadet Smith	Mr. Smith
Warrant Officer[6]	Mr. Smith or Gunner Smith	Gunner Smith	Warrant Officer Smith or Gunner Smith	Mr. Smith or Gunner Smith

[1] When not in uniform, an officer should be introduced as "of the Navy" or "of the Marine Corps" or of other service. Suggested phraseology: "This is Lieutenant Smith of the Navy. Mr. Smith is now stationed in the Bureau of Naval Personnel." Such a form of introduction indicates the officer's rank, service, and how to address him. See Fig. 205 for insignia of rank of the four Armed Services.
[2] When the status of a woman officer is not clear, add "of the Medical Corps," "or the Medical Service Corps," "of the Navy Nurse Corps," etc.
[3] Add "of the Medical Corps," "of the Civil Engineer Corps," or other corps, when helpful to indicate the status of officer. If a senior officer of the Medical Corps prefers to be addressed as "doctor" such preference should be honored. Some senior members of the Chaplain Corps prefer to be addressed by their rank, but it is always correct to address a chaplain of any rank as "Chaplain."
[4] In any case where there is reason to believe that the officer's insignia might not be recognized, it is correct to add, "of the Public Health Service," "of the Coast Guard," or "of the Coast and Geodetic Survey."
[5] Chief Warrant Officers (W-2, W-3 and W-4) are commissioned officers; Warrant Officers (W-1) are not.
[6] Midshipmen, cadets and aviation cadets are officers "in a qualified sense."

FIGURE 403. Introducing and addressing service personnel.

eral," "Colonel Howes," "Major," and "Captain Farrow"; others are addressed and introduced as "Mister," unless circumstances make it advisable to use their rank to inform other persons present as to their status.

A chaplain may be called "Chaplain," but the affectionate form "Padre" is often heard and is not considered lacking in respect.

Be careful of the use of the commanding officer's familiar title, "The Old Man." It is never used in his presence or as a direct form of address. When used otherwise, it is not a sign of disrespect; rather, it is a warm, respectful title of affection.

Rules for addressing and introducing women officers by rank follow those prescribed for male officers of the same service. Use of the term "Ma'am" is acceptable in speaking to women officers whenever "Sir" would be used in addressing male officers.

Enlisted men should be introduced and addressed under formal conditions such as introductions and award ceremonies, and written address in letters, orders and Correspondence in this manner, "Master Chief Smith, Chief Petty Officer Smith, or Petty Officer Smith." Enlisted men below petty officer rank are addressed as "Seaman Jones, or Fireman Jones."

Know and call your men by name. Never fall into the "Hey, Chief!" or "Hey, you!" class. Under normal working conditions, address them by their last name only. Avoid using nicknames or contractions of last name in speaking of or to enlisted men. Familiarity with enlisted persons breaks down discipline.

405. RELATIONS WITH OTHER OFFICERS. When a junior reports to the office of a senior officer, he should announce himself through the orderly, if one is stationed, or by knocking on the door. In some cases the door will stand open, and the officer is expected to enter without being told. On entering the office, he should hold his cap in his right hand, proceed directly to the officer, and state his business. If the officer knows him well, it is not necessary to state his name. If the senior officer is a stranger, the junior should announce himself as, "Ensign Joseph Doaks of the *Coral Sea,* sir."

When conducting business with a senior, maintain a military bearing. Do not lounge against his desk or otherwise relax unless asked to be seated. Undue familiarity jeopardizes a junior's standing.

Unless on watch, a junior officer always uncovers when he enters a room in which a senior is present. Such formality is not observed in the messroom, but it is good practice for all officers to uncover before entering the mess. When wearing side arms, an officer remains covered except during church services, in a chapel or church, within hallowed shrines, and while indoors at a social occasion.

It is a custom in the naval service for a junior to supplement his salute on first meeting in the morning, and frequently throughout the day, by a brief greeting. The following greeting is customary, depending upon the time of day:

From first rising for the day until noon: "Good morning, Commander (Captain, Admiral)."

From noon until sunset: "Good afternoon, Mr. ——."

From sunset on: "Good evening, Doctor ——."

It is considered proper to call a senior by his proper title and name, such as "Captain Doaks," "Chaplain," etc., rather than using the impersonal "sir."

A junior officer should be careful not to be unduly obtrusive with his greeting. For example, a junior officer would find it wise not to bother a senior engaged in conversation, working at detailed work, or concentrating on some problem. Careless insistence upon this courtesy might distract the officer from important duties.

Juniors should avoid keeping seniors waiting. When summoned by a senior, a junior should proceed to him "on the double."

When a senior officer says "I desire" or "I wish," remember that the expressed wishes or desires of a senior are, by tradition and custom of the service, equivalent to an order.

A senior presents his "compliments" to a junior when transmitting a message by a third person, such as an orderly or a messenger. A junior pays or sends his "respects" to a senior. In written correspondence, a senior may "call" attention to certain matters, but the junior may only "invite" the matter to the attention of a senior. In writing a memorandum, a senior officer subscribes it "Respectfully," a junior writing to a senior subscribes a memorandum "Very respectfully."

The signature of a gentleman is his bond. Signed to a check, it means that he stands good for the amount indicated. Signed to a letter or memorandum, it signifies that the ideas expressed come from him or that he concurs in them. The title of office is no part of a signature, but, in some forms of correspondence, it may be subscribed after the signature as a means of identification.

The place of honor is on the right. Accordingly, when a junior walks, rides, or sits with a senior, he takes position alongside and to the left of that senior. A junior opens doors for a senior and passes through the

FIGURE 404. The proper relationship between junior and senior officers
is important to the naval tradition.

doorway last. When officers are walking in company, juniors keep pace with the senior and all should be in step. When pacing to and fro, positions are not exchanged at the turnabout. On board ship, the senior is usually accorded the outboard position. When passing a senior, pass to the left; and, as you salute alongside, request, "By your leave, sir."

When you have been ordered or instructed to accomplish some task, report back promptly to the officer issuing the order upon completion of the task; or, if not completed, report as to the situation and your reasons for not being able to carry out the assigned task.

Learn to give complete, accurate, pointed answers to questions. If you do not know or cannot give a complete or correct answer, be open and direct in your reply. A frank "I don't know, sir, but I will find out and let you know" is much better received than a wandering, inconclusive, or evasive reply.

Officers must be open and direct in all their dealings. They must appreciate the meanings of "on watch," "on duty," "in charge," and "in command." They must inculcate in their subordinates an appreciation of these military virtues.

406. PHRASEOLOGY.   Certain standard forms of speech and address are in general use. Seniors may be addressed by their title, "Captain," "Commander," "Mr. Jones," or "sir." The forms "Captain, I report . . . ," "Sir, I request . . ." are correct. Note that officers go on "shore leave." Enlisted personnel go on "liberty." When preparing to leave your own ship, address your head of department (the Executive Officer in a small ship) thus, "Sir, I request permission to leave the ship." On departure from your own ship, to the Officer of the Deck, say, "Sir, I have permission to leave the ship." On your return, "Sir, I report my return on board."

Note the different procedure on a ship other than that to which you are attached. To the Officer of the Deck, say, "Sir, I request permission to come on board," and "Sir, I request permission to leave the ship."

When given an order, respond in a seamanlike manner with "Aye aye, sir," which means that you understand the order and will carry it out. Never answer "O.K." "Very well" should be used only by a senior to a junior—never the reverse—as both an acknowledgement and approval of a report.

407. ORIGIN OF MORE COMMON CUSTOMS.   Much of our phraseology and our more common customs have been handed down from the days of sail. Many strictly military terms have come to us from the

FIGURE 405. Traditionally, all naval ships and stations make colors at 0800.

British Navy. The origin of many of these is obscure, but the commonly accepted versions follow:

Anchor Watch. In days of sail when hemp anchor cables and oil burning anchor lights were in use, a ship at anchor needed an alert watch to trim the lamps and to observe the anchor cables. Today the anchor watch is available to handle the ship's ground tackle if necessary, but is also available for other duties.

Aye Aye. In old English this phrase meant "Yes, yes," and today means, "I understand your orders and will carry them out."

Binnacle List. The binnacle list was a list originally placed on the binnacle each morning by the ship's Surgeon to indicate to the Captain and watch all personnel not available for full duty. Today, it is a list of personnel not fit for full duty but not hospitalized.

Boatswain. Pronounced "Bo'sun." "*Swain,*" or "*swein,*" was the word for servant or boy in Middle English. A boatswain was therefore the servant of the entire ship. His pipe was originally used to call the stroke in a galley, but it is now a badge of office used to call attention or to pipe the side.

Chains. Chains were once used to brace the platform in the bows from which the leadsman heaved the lead. Now the area or platform where the lead is heaved has retained this name.

Dead Horse. Shipping-on pay used to be given to members of a crew as an advance pay. When this was worked off, a stuffed canvas horse was burned to celebrate the event. The custom of paying a dead horse still exists in our Navy.

Dipping the National Ensign. In days of sail a merchant vessel was required to heave to when approaching a warship on the high seas. This required clewing up most of her canvas with attendant delay. The custom of dipping her ensign as an indication of readiness to be searched developed during years of peace. The man-of-war gave permission to proceed by answering the dip. U. S. naval vessels answer dip for dip, but never dip except in acknowledgement.

Dog Watch. Corruption of deck watch, or shortened watch.

Drawing Sword in Wardroom. In earlier days, when swords often were drawn in anger, to preserve the decorum of the Wardroom, it was necessary to discourage dueling among officers by levying stiff fines upon anyone who drew a sword within its confines. The custom has come down through the ages to the modern practice of requiring any officer who unsheaths his sword in the Wardroom to stand drinks or cigars for all other officers present at the time.

Eyes of the Ship. In ancient time mariners placed carved figure-

FIGURE 406. Morning quarters aboard ship in the 1880's.

heads on the bows of ships. The forepart of the ship therefore became known as the eyes of the ship from the eyes of the figure.

Forecastle. Early ships had tall, castle-like structures fore and aft. Hence, forward castle, forecastle (pronounced fōk's'l).

Gun Salute. First salutes were rendered by firing the entire ship's batteries. Since considerable time was required to re-load, firing a salute indicated absence of hostile intent. This custom evolved into an honor.

Head. The ship's latrine in sailing days was located as far forward on the ship as possible since wind was usually from aft or abeam.

Mast. The old setting for the dispensation of justice was near the ship's mainmast.

Midshipmen. Midshipmen were originally young men serving as officer apprentices who were quartered amidships (hence midshipmen).

Piping the Side. Piping was originally done by the boatswain to control hoisting of a basket in which a visiting officer was brought aboard at sea from a small boat. Side boys were assigned to hoist the basket aboard. The more senior officers were generally stouter and required more side boys. Hence, necessity became custom and eventually regulation.

Spit-kid. In the past, spit-kid or spit-kit was a small wooden cask set about the decks for spit boxes. Today it refers to a spittoon or an ash tray. Navy men use this term derisively to refer to a small, unseaworthy vessel.

Wardroom. In the British Navy a common compartment near the officers' staterooms was used as a storage for officers' uniforms. Its title of "wardrobe" was subsequently corrupted to "wardroom." This compartment gradually came to be a room in which meals were taken and a social center.

Many other interesting customs and naval expressions can be found in *Naval Customs, Traditions, and Usage,* and *The Marine Officer's Guide.*

408. TABOOS. Do not jump the chain of command. In other words, do not go "over the head" of your immediate supervisor, without his authority. If it is necessary to confer with the Executive Officer or, in exceptional cases, with the Commanding Officer, the junior officer must first explain the case and obtain the permission of his division officer or head of department.

Excuses for failure or negligence are generally unacceptable. Accept responsibility, and freely accept the blame if the failure is yours. Improper functioning of your division or men is your failure, and the blame is yours.

A phrase in common use at the Naval Academy for many years is "greasing," indicating servility, or "bootlicking," a deliberate courting of favor. This type of currying favor finds no place in a naval officer's life and should be shunned.

Do not contract debts beyond your current ability to pay. Many likely officers' careers have been damaged by dunning letters from creditors passing through the hands of their senior officers and being filed in their "jackets." The officer who cannot regulate his own affairs is not fit to direct the affairs of others.

Be careful in your associations ashore. A man is best known by the company he keeps. Choose your friends wisely. Avoid too casual friendships with both men and women formed in public places ashore.

Learn the small customs and commonplaces of naval life that distinguish the officer, the gentleman, and the seaman from the landlubber. Whistling while in a ship is reserved for the boatswain and his mates. Keep your cap off the Wardroom table and preferably in the place provided for it. Avoid entering or walking through the crew's messing compartments during meal hours except when absolutely necessary. If you must, doff your cap while passing through.

409. WARDROOM MESS. The term "mess" is applied to those Navy groups who for convenience and sociability eat together. The word "mess" comes from the Latin word *mensa*, meaning table. Navy Regulations provide that officers shall mess in the compartments assigned therefor. Those officers entitled to the privileges of the Wardroom are therefore members of the Wardroom Mess. Similarly, junior officers entitled

FIGURE 407. Officers at mess in wardroom.

to the Junior Officers' Wardroom are members of the Junior Officers' Wardroom Mess (in large ships having such a mess). It is familiarly called the J.O. Mess.

The Executive Officer is the President of the Wardroom Mess. Navy Regulations prescribe the seating arrangement. Officers are assigned permanent seats at the table; alternately, in the order of rank, to the right and left of the presiding officer, except that the seat opposite that of the presiding officer is occupied by the Mess Treasurer. (Second ranking officer sits on the right of the presiding officer, third on the left, and so on.) Common courtesy and respect require you to be in the mess prior to mealtime so that you may sit down when the Executive Officer takes his seat. Proper etiquette also requires that officers remain in the mess, in their chairs, unless they are excused by the President of the Mess or until he rises. This custom may have fallen somewhat into disuse in some ships, but this does not excuse the junior officer from exercising ordinary politeness.

The officers' mess is organized on a businesslike basis. There is a mess fund to which each officer must contribute his share on joining the mess. As an officer receives a ration allowance from the Navy, it is a courteous gesture, within the first 24 hours aboard, to ask the Mess Treasurer for his mess bill and mess entrance fee and to pay them at once. The monthly mess assessments defray the cost of food, periodicals, other essentials, and conveniences. This fund is administered by the Mess Treasurer, who is elected by its members. He must serve if elected, but is not required to serve longer than two months consecutively. His work involves the purchase of food, preparation of menus, and supervision of service. It is recognized as collateral duty, and attention is given to his performance in the marking of an officer's report of fitness. At the close of each month, the Mess Treasurer must give the mess a statement of the mess accounts, which is audited by the ship's Auditing Board.

In general, members of the junior officers' mess address each other by their first names or nicknames in unofficial conversation. However, when a junior officer is a member of the Wardroom Mess, he addresses seniors of the rank of lieutenant commander and below as "Mister," and those above that rank by title of their rank, i.e., "Commander," "Captain," etc. The commanding officer is, of course, always addressed as "Captain." The senior officers of the Wardroom Mess will always welcome a junior officer and treat him as a full-fledged member of the mess in every respect. Nevertheless, a junior officer should not be too forward in conversation or action. An error on the side of formality is more readily pardoned than one in the other direction.

The Wardroom is your home in your ship. Make it as pleasant a place to live as you would your own home. It is also your club, where you may gather with your shipmates for moments of relaxation, a discussion of the daily problems, or just a game of acey-deucey over a cup of coffee. Remove your cap before entering and accord the Wardroom the other courtesies you would give your own family at home. All this does not necessarily mean that the quiet of a public reading room or a morgue need be maintained. One commanding officer, welcoming a new ensign on board, made the statement that his criterion of a happy Wardroom country was based on the amount of noise that filtered up to his cabin and that this outfit was the noisiest damned bunch he had ever heard. It was a happy ship.

The Wardroom country is "out of bounds" to enlisted men except in special circumstances. Do not use your stateroom as an office; keep your contacts with your men in their parts of the ship or in the regular ship's offices.

Like many other phases of naval courtesy, Wardroom etiquette of necessity undergoes many changes in time of war. In the interest of completeness, perhaps the best approach to the subject would be to take up the generally prevailing rules of Wardroom etiquette as they are in peacetime and then to give some of the variations that would be brought about by war.

In Peacetime. The Wardroom is the commissioned officers' mess and lounge room. The main peacetime rules of its etiquette are:

1. Do not enter or lounge in the Wardroom out of uniform. On some destroyers and small ships some latitude is allowed in this, but you should be certain the Commanding Officer sanctions any such variance. Be on guard against following the example of a careless or slovenly individual. The Captain may not have spoken to this individual, but his opinion has been formed, which will be reflected in the fitness report of that officer. It is best not to wear your hat in the Wardroom at any time, but it is essential that you never wear your hat in the Wardroom while your shipmates are eating. This applies to officers coming into the Wardroom after meals and finding the previous watch officers eating their late meals.

2. Never sit down to meals before the Executive or Senior Member sits down.

3. If necessary to leave before completion of meal, excuse yourself to the Senior Member at your table.

4. Always introduce your guests to the Wardroom officers, at least to those at your table.

5. All guests are guests of *all* Wardroom officers. Be friendly and sociable to guests. Do not continuously talk shop. It gives the appearance that you know nothing else and that you are showing off. In addition, you may reveal confidential information.

6. Whenever an officer from another ship enters the Wardroom, introduce yourself, extend all courtesies, and ask to help him in any way possible.

7. Never be late for meals. If you are unavoidably late, make your apologies to the Senior Member.

8. Only those on the sick list have the privilege of eating in their rooms.

9. Do not loiter in the Wardroom during working hours. You are supposed to be at work, not playing cards or drinking coffee to kill time. This will mark an officer as being of the indolent type. There is always plenty to keep you busy and ways in which you can advance yourself. When a young officer reports on board it is best that he devote most of his spare time to professional reading and getting acquainted with his Ship's Organization and Regulations. Save a certain amount of time each day for professional study.

10. Do not be boisterous or otherwise noisy in the Wardroom. This is the home of all the officers and their rights and privileges must be respected. All must share equally.

11. Pay your mess bill and all other personal ship bills promptly. Your Wardroom mess bill is payable in advance.

12. Be civil and just in all your dealings with stewardsmen. If you have a complaint, it is best to make it to the Mess Treasurer.

13. Some messes have local rules, *i.e.*, not to talk shop at meals, not to play the radio during meal hours, etc.

14. Do not abuse the use of the watch boy by sending him on long errands.

15. When entertaining aboard ship, remember the Wardroom is the other officers' home as well as your own. Be sure you entertain guests whom your messmates and their families would be happy to meet.[1]

Good manners, with a consideration for other members and their guests, constitute the first principles to which all others are secondary.

In Wartime. During a war, the routine of the Wardroom is vastly different from that just described. Regular mealtimes are out of the question when the crew is at battle stations or the ship is in Condition

---

[1] It is an old custom that, except for a Wardroom or ship's party, officers' guests aboard ship leave by 2200. Observance of this custom shows consideration for your shipmates

Two. If, before starting to eat, one always waited for the presiding officer to sit down, meals would be too irregular and delayed.

Many an officer who has served in wartime can report that, instead of dining in the Wardroom, he has eaten sandwiches and coffee served topside whenever he could snatch a hasty bite. A rule about never being late for meals is hardly binding under such circumstances.

Also, the custom of not talking shop is not practicable when war is the business of the day. Mealtime frequently provides an opportunity to exchange those items of information about experiences that increase the knowledge of all fighting men. Talking shop in wartime brightens conversation and may even help to win the next battle.

Even the seating arrangements in Wardrooms may undergo changes during a war. A ship may scatter her higher ranking officers among many tables rather than concentrate them at one place, where a chance enemy hit might wipe out all of them at once. It is for that same reason that in some ships, officers and men took their meals in shifts, cross-sectioned by rank.

In short, in peacetime, wardroom etiquette follows the old established customs; but during a war, common sense and necessity dictate changes in form but not in principle.

See also Section 416 for Mess and Club Etiquette Ashore and Chapter 26, Wardroom Life, in *Service Etiquette*.

410. THE WARDROOM MESS TREASURER. The position of Mess Treasurer is a very responsible one, particularly on long cruises and in wartime, for upon his effectiveness depends the quality of the food served and, in a large measure, the contentment of the mess. In some Wardrooms, both a Mess Caterer and a Mess Treasurer are elected and the duties are divided. The commanding officers of some ships appoint the Mess Treasurer, or the ship's Supply Officer, Commissary Officer, or Medical Officer is considered, *ex officio,* the Mess Treasurer.

Should you be appointed or elected to either of these positions, devote as much time and attention to it as you can spare from your regular duties. In general, among other things, do not overlook the following:

1. Supervise the preparation of menus. Provide variety. Most stewards have a tendency to repeat weekly menus—"beans on Tuesday, chicken on Sunday." Study the available cookbooks for ideas. Keep the quality up. Insist on the proper etiquette in serving.

2. Inspect the Wardroom, pantry, and galley at least daily. Check on the condition of food in iceboxes. Inspect stewardsmen for cleanli-

ness of person and clothing. The Medical Officer will gladly assist you with health and sanitary inspections.

3. Insist that the stewardsmen keep the officers' rooms in proper order and that they attend to them punctually. Do not permit stewardsmen to loaf in staterooms or mess rooms. The Wardroom radio is for the officers' entertainment, not a "juke box" running 24 hours a day for the stewardsmen.

4. Keep a standard form of double-entry type of books. Require receipts for all expenditures and for money advanced the steward. Never make collections or pay bills without making the proper entry immediately in your books. Keep books balanced so that you know the financial status of the mess at all times. Require prompt payment of mess bills; pay dealers' bills on receipt. Limit cash expenditures by the steward to a minimum. Some unscrupulous dealers permit the stewards a cash "cut" for their trade. It is an excellent practice to accompany the steward shopping occasionally, in order to establish direct contact with the dealers. Officers' messes are often combined to eliminate duplication of effort with respect to the procurement and preparation (not serving) of food. Messes are subsisted primarily from the general mess, but may be augmented from supplies ashore as desired.

5. Keep the bulk of the mess funds in a convenient bank, and pay by check. This system is the most satisfactory as it provides a simple accounting method. Arrange for the proper naval authority to take over this account in the case of loss of the ship; this fund is a part of the estate of each member. Keep your cash on hand in a reliable safe.

6. Close your books promptly at the end of the month and submit them, in the proper form, for audit. See that the Auditing Board completes the audit, and send your accounts to the Captain, via the Executive Officer, by the 10th of the month.

411. LIVING WITH OTHERS. The normal military courtesies expected of you will be covered in Chapter 5 and the specific customs and courtesies of the Wardroom have been outlined in Section 409. However, there are many other areas in which you can contribute in large measure to your own social stature and to your ability to live with others on a mutually pleasant basis.

Navy life is informal and pleasant. One important contribution you can make is to keep yourself well informed on current events, both domestic and foreign, and particularly on international affairs. You thus improve your education in such important matters and at the same time give yourself conversational material out of the "shop" area.

No officer can afford to neglect his personal appearance. You must be scrupulously clean in person and meticulous in your grooming. Dress conservatively when in civilian clothes and in the best quality of uniforms that you can afford to buy.

Avoid thoughtless offense. Be considerate of those with whom you associate. Ill-considered actions and unintentionally offensive conduct are usually indicative of poor manners.

When passing through the crew's quarters or chief petty officers' quarters while the men are seated at meals, uncover. This also applies, at all times, in sick bay.

Use only standard terminology in speech and writing. Every officer should be proud of his seamanlike qualities. The use of "gadget" and "gilhooly" in describing equipment on board ship brands the user as the worst kind of landlubber. Study naval terms in the back of Knight's *Seamanship* published by Van Nostrand, in the *Naval Terms Dictionary* published by the U. S. Naval Institute, and in *Naval Orientation* (NavPers 16138D).

A cheery "good morning" to seniors and juniors alike starts the day off with a smile. Cultivate an optimistic attitude. Be courteous to guests at the dinner table. Talk, but do not monopolize the conversation. Long monologues are usually exceedingly dull.

Remember that gambling, drinking, or unauthorized possession of liquor on board ship are serious offenses.

You will find that most of the older officers are just as anxious to help you as you are to learn. After all, there is a job to be done and if you can learn how to do it and do it well, they will be pleased to let you help carry the load.

Remember that the more experienced officers in your mess will respect you for your frank admission of ignorance, whereas they will soon "have your number," if you assume a presumptuous attitude and continually make blunders (see also Sections 418-419).

Naval Social Life and Service Etiquette

412. SOCIAL LIFE. As a naval officer, you, with your wife and family, are members of a special society, which possesses certain rights, privileges, customs, rules and obligations, together making up a code which most naval officers and their families observe. Somewhat formal and possessing its certain taboos, this code is not rigid and does not require strict social conformity for conformity's sake. Within the code, there is ample room for individuality, freedom of action, and the rollicking fun for which the Navy has always been notable.

Your commission made you an officer. To be called a gentleman requires understanding and considerable effort on your part. We must always remember that John Paul Jones set the standard when he wrote of the naval officer of his era, "He should be as well a gentleman of liberal education, refined manners, punctilious courtesy, and the nicest sense of personal honor."

Vice Admiral Robert B. Pirie, USN (Ret), wrote, "Naval officers have always been called upon to represent their Nation at home and abroad, officially and personally. They must navigate the shoals and deeps of good society anywhere in the world as skillfully and surely as they handle a ship in formation or combat."

As a naval officer, you must honor the ancient and valid social traditions of the naval service. For your edification, you will find interesting Lovette's *Naval Customs, Traditions, and Usage* published by the U. S. Naval Institute. Frequently recall that phrase, "An officer and a gentleman." It is current and important. It means just as much as it did in the time of John Paul Jones.

You will find officers of the Navy and Marine Corps and their families a friendly group. For a good many years, officers in the Regular Navy were, in a great measure, insulated from civil life. In recent years, they have reached out more to participate in the life of the community about them. They probably still concern themselves too much with their own little world of the Navy. New officers from civil life bring with them new horizons and interests. If there seems to be too much "shop talk" at social gatherings, do not be surprised, but try to contribute something to the discussion besides "shop" and children and "day workers."

Whatever the talk, you will have a good time, for Navy social life is informal and pleasant. A sincere desire on your part, and on the part of your family, to contribute is a sound attitude to adopt.

413. SOCIAL OCCASIONS. Within the United States and at many of our naval stations overseas, social activity is kept simple and informal. You entertain your friends both naval and civilian in your home or at the Officers' Club. A few friends for cocktails or dinner before a dance, or a larger cocktail party to repay your obligations, are about all that the married junior officer can manage. The bachelor should be careful to entertain with sufficient frequence at cocktails and dinner to keep his social obligations repaid. Be sure to include your

Captain, Executive Officer, and other senior officers in your entertainment.

For more senior officers, the scope of affairs is wider and more demanding. Books have been written covering all the ramifications of naval social life. Space can be allotted here for only a brief summary. You may be entertained or entertain at any of the following:

Receptions and Cocktail Parties. A reception is a ceremony of receiving guests, usually honoring someone and usually formal. A reception may be held during daylight hours or in the evening. It is ordinarily severely limited as to time and the limitations should be observed. Tea, coffee, or alcoholic punch may be served. Receptions vary in size from a few friends to a large number of guests. If a reception is given in the garden or on a terrace, it may be called a garden party. At the "at home" of a senior officer, "calls are considered made and returned."

The cocktail party differs from the reception in that it is informal, there is no receiving line, usually no honored guest, cards are not left, and a variety of alcoholic drinks are served. The cocktail party is a useful affair for the low-salaried officer to entertain a large number of guests. Guests may arrive at any time during the customary two hours stated in the invitation. Some guests may stay on afterward for buffet supper or to spend the evening, but do not do so unless invited or unless you are certain your host and hostess really wish you to stay. In Washington, cocktail parties usually end near the stated hour.

Balls and Dances. The function most frequently attended by naval families is the Officers' Club dance. In later years, an officer and his family will engage in more formal social activity of this type at embassies, the White House, or charity affairs, such as the Navy Relief Ball.

Dinners and Buffet Suppers. These will be as simple as the family dinner, with the lady of the house doing the cooking and serving, or a larger buffet supper, or a formal dinner for 30 guests. For the young officer, his first experience at managing a formal dinner will be as mess caterer for a shipboard mess dinner or as personal aide to a flag officer (see *Service Etiquette,* Chapter 11).

For the young officer, servants are very nearly a memory of the past. Older officers may have a part-time maid, may bring in servants from the Club, or employ a caterer.

Enough space can not be allotted to this subject to do it justice. For ample information on the subject of entertaining, consult a good book on etiquette. Specially recommended for naval officers and their wives are *Welcome Aboard* and *Service Etiquette.*

For *Military Weddings* see the excellent description and advice given in both of the previously cited books.

414. CALLS. One obstacle in the way of enjoying Navy social life is meeting and getting to know your fellow officers and their families. An old custom takes care of this. Begin your naval career correctly. Make the customary social calls.

Both civil and military customs require the exchange of social calls under certain circumstances. The Navy Regulations formerly stated that "an officer joining a ship or naval station shall, in addition to reporting for duty, make a visit of courtesy to his commanding officer or commandant within 48 hours after joining." As previously pointed out in Section 211, this call is made on board ship, in the Captain's cabin. Ask the Executive Officer when it will be convenient for the Captain to receive you. This call is made, even though you have previously reported to the Captain. On large shore stations, the Commanding Officer (or senior officer) will generally designate certain periods when he is "at home," and calls should be made at that time. Social calls ashore, in wartime, are generally discontinued. However, in peacetime, the newly arrived officer should call in turn at the homes of the Commanding Officer, the Executive Officer, and his own head of department. These calls should be made within two weeks. If you are married, your wife should accompany you on these "must" calls.

It is necessary to differentiate between a bachelor and a married officer with wife present. A bachelor may, and should, as expeditiously as possible call on all the married officers and their families. His calls will not be returned, but he may expect to be invited to dinner or have his courtesy repaid in a similar way. Once having called, he is socially eligible to be invited to dinner, a party and other social functions—at which he is *not* acceptable until he has called. You can learn a lot about a man by visiting him in his home and meeting his family. Don't be afraid to call on a tough old sundowner—he may be delighted to see you ashore. You may leave his home with a better understanding of him, may even discover that you have mutual interests, hobbies or friends. Don't plunge into the "Who-do-you-know-that-I-know?" routine; develop it gradually if at all.

If you are married, your wife, of course, should accompany you on all calls on married officers. After you have made your "must" calls, sit back and wait. The "must" calls will be returned within two weeks (or some explanation offered). It is up to the other officers, married and single, regardless of rank, to call on you, the newcomer, first. Return these within two weeks. You have a similar obligation to call on any married officer and wife who reports after you, regardless of his rank. If your wife is not with you, make the calls required of a bachelor, explain that your wife is not at the moment with you; when she arrives, make the "must" calls with her. File your shore address and phone number with the proper ship or station office, which, by the way, is an excellent place to obtain addresses and phone numbers. Large stations usually publish a directory giving also such data as marital status and official duties. At some large stations, such as the Naval Academy, each department is considered a unit in itself so far as calling is concerned, but most officers call on the new heads of departments or attend their "at homes." The usual calling hours in naval social life are from 1600 to 1800; the times for "at homes" are always specified, usually are from 1700 to 1900. Always make discreet inquiries about local calling hours for there may be local "ground rules."

If you are assigned to a ship, you are not required to call upon the embarked flag officer or other unit commander, if there be one, or his staff; however, a social call at the home of the flag officer or unit commander, his Chief of Staff or Chief Staff Officer, after you have made your "must" calls, is very much in order. Consult the Flag Lieutenant, as individual preferences vary. Similarly, if you are assigned to a staff, social calls at the homes of the flagship's Captain and Executive Officer will be regarded favorably.

Civilian calling practice differs somewhat from naval custom: there is no rank, command structure, no "must" calls. The hours are generally the same, but it is the longer established residents who make the first call on the newcomers. The newly arrived family has ample opportunity to select their new friends. In any case, a call made on you should be returned within two weeks, unless you definitely want nothing further to do with the persons who called—failure to return their call so signifies.

It is considered that a call is made if you call and leave cards, regardless of whether or not you find the family at home. If the family is found to be out, it is considered friendly to make another call within a reasonable length of time. Calling at a time when it is obvious that the family will not be at home (as when an officer has the duty) is exceedingly discourteous, and this discourtesy will not be readily overlooked.

Calls are sometimes regarded as a bore by junior officers, but they are the basis of all social life of the Navy. Careful adherence to these social duties will go a long way toward making you a well-liked officer in your ship. Try to arrange your calls, especially those on the Captain's,

Executive Officer's, and your own immediate superior officer's families, so that you *will* find them at home.

Remember that small ships are more intimate than large ships and that most officers' families will appreciate your making a friendly call at reasonably frequent intervals. A strictly duty call requires that you remain 15 to 20 minutes. A friendly call may last longer; but be careful not to overstay your welcome, and be quick to sense a situation when you have called at the wrong time. It is always possible that another couple that has just come in has been invited for some special engagement or that the family may be wishing to go out. Through a social sense and an unselfish attitude, you will quickly detect these situations. Do not do *all* the talking, but do *some*. Acquire a friendly, sociable attitude. Do not talk too much about yourself or air your own opinions. Talk about something other than "shop" or where you came from.

On sea duty, in wartime, many of the social niceties of the service have had to be abandoned. Families have been evacuated from many advance bases. At home yards and bases, ships are in port for such short periods that officers are principally concerned with seeing their families and getting a little rest from the sea.

For complete information on making calls, dress, calling time, leave-taking, calls on foreign station, and proper calling cards, see *Service Etiquette,* Chapter 5; *Welcome Aboard,* Chapter V; and *Social Usage and Protocol.*

The special circumstances of wartime do not diminish in the least the pleasures and advantages of calling in the Navy. Where the old customs can be carried out, on shore and afloat, they should be observed. "You cannot like your fellow man save that you know him." Happy is the ship whose officers work and fight and play together well.

415. CLUBS AND MESSES ASHORE. Each base or station has a commissioned officers' mess, which is the center of social activity for officers and their wives.

The Commissioned Officers' Mess (Open), often referred to as "The Club" or "The Officers' Club," has as its primary mission providing social and recreational facilities, meals, and refreshments to officers of the Navy on active duty. Where facilities permit, the privileges of the (Open) Mess are frequently extended to officers of the other Armed Services and to reserve officers, as well as to officers' dependents. At large activities the Commissioned Officers' Mess (Open) may consist of a dining room, snack bar, cocktail lounge, lounge areas, and rooms for private parties. In some instances there are swimming pools, golf courses, and tennis courts. Packaged liquor stores may be operated by overseas Messes and Messes inside the United States at activities specifically approved by the Secretary of the Navy.

The Commissioned Officers' Mess (Closed) has as its primary mission furnishing essential lodging and subsistence to bachelor officers of the Navy on active duty. To accomplish this mission, the Mess ordinarily consists of galley and dining room, bedrooms, lounge areas, and recreational spaces. If there is no Commissioned Officers' Mess (Closed) readily accessible to residents of the Bachelor Officers' Quarters, a bar and cocktail lounge may be operated in the B.O.Q. Station officers not resident in the Mess often take their lunch here. Occasionally (Closed) Mess members schedule social functions with the approval of the Commanding Officer and of course may invite guests.

Private Clubs. In the various ports you visit, at home and abroad, you will often be offered the facilities of men's clubs and country clubs. Accept these opportunities to meet the local people and make yourself agreeable to them, but do not "take over" or be otherwise objectionable. Show your appreciation of the privileges granted by a courteous and gentlemanly demeanor.

When extended the privileges of a club, leave a card for the secretary. A note of appreciation on departure is also welcomed.

In addition to officers' clubs and service messes in the Washington area, two of the outstanding private military and naval clubs in the country offer excellent services to members. The Army and Navy Club, located on Farragut Square, is the town club and provides all the facilities of a men's club, including rooms for members. The Army and Navy Country Club, in nearby Arlington, Virginia, is a family country club for service personnel offering the widest variety of club and sport facilities.

Both clubs offer officers newly commissioned in the lowest grades of their service an opportunity to join at reduced entrance fees, the town club with no entrance fee, the Country Club with an entrance fee of 15% of the regular. In both clubs, the young officer living away from the Washington area would pay the equivalent of one month's dues per year in a nonresident status. In addition to the bargain rate on entrance, the officer would also have available the facilities of the Clubs on visits to the Capital and immediately upon assignment to duty in Washington. The new officer is strongly advised to take advantage of this opportunity.

416. MESS AND CLUB ETIQUETTE ASHORE. The club or mess belongs to its members. Assume responsibility for *your* mess and support it. As a guest, observe the local rules and customs.

Participate in meetings, campaigns, and elections. Be ready to assume responsibility as an officer, treasurer, or committee member.

At the club or mess, dress conservatively and correctly. Except when engaging in athletics, or if club rules permit other variations, you will be correct if you wear full uniform of the day or complete civilian clothes, with coat and tie.

Pay your club bills promptly. Be sure your checks are bankable. Honor your obligations.

When guest of a member of a club or mess, do not try to be host— at the bar or in the dining room. But be sure you reciprocate promptly. If you see a stranger in your mess, introduce yourself and make him welcome.

In private club or service mess, when in doubt as to proper action or local ground rule, do the gentlemanly thing. You will never go wrong.

417. WASHINGTON SOCIAL LIFE. The White House is the center of Washington social life. Young bachelor officers, on duty in the Washington area, are sometimes detailed to additional duty as White House Naval Aides and participate extensively in the White House social activities and in Washington social life. The more senior officers may expect occasional invitations to the White House for large receptions.

A White House invitation is considered a Presidential command. It takes precedence over all other social commitments. If you have questions about uniform or other matters, consult one of the aides to the Chief of Naval Personnel for briefing.

White House Aides and many other officers will be invited to official parties of the diplomatic corps. The invitation will indicate the dress. Active officers will always wear appropriate uniform at embassy or legation functions.

On Washington duty, learn foreign badges and insignia of rank and the national anthems of the countries represented. Be alert at diplomatic parties to be courteous and helpful. Be certain that not only your uniform but also your dignity, smartness, and conduct set you apart as a naval officer and a representative of the United States.

Calling Etiquette. Make your customary call upon your reporting senior. The dress is civilian clothes. Flag officers do not require calls as elsewhere, but many of them hold periodic "at homes," where attendance is considered a call made and returned.

If "at homes" are not held, the new arrival "leaves cards" for the Chief and Assistant Chief of Bureau or office at his home. His other associates then leave cards for him, the officer who has been in Washington longest being the first to "drop cards." There is sound reasoning behind this custom, for the bureaus and offices are so large that the leisure time of any senior officer would be almost entirely consumed in making calls.

Officers of the grade of captain and above should leave cards at the White House once a year. It is permissible to leave cards on the Secretary of Defense, the Secretary, Under Secretary, and the Assistant Secretaries of the Navy. Flag officers leave cards on the Chief of Naval Operations. Officers returning from foreign duty should call at the embassies of the countries where they have served, making arrangements with the social secretary in advance.

In addition, call on your particular friends and acquaintances, following the procedures which obtain elsewhere.

418. ETIQUETTE. *Etiquette* embodies the forms required by good breeding, social conventions, and good manners to be observed in social or official life.

There is more to being well-bred than knowing table manners or rules of decorum. Good manners require an innate sense for saying and doing the right thing in any social or official situation. Essential ingredients are consideration for others, kindliness, and courtesy. A long treatise could be written on this subject. Fortunately, several excellent books are available. Specifically for the officer and his wife, the Naval Institute has published a definitive book, *Service Etiquette,* by Rear Admiral Bruce McCandless, USN (Ret.), Captain Brooks J. Harral, USN, and Oretha D. Swartz. Also excellent for the Navy wife and published by the Naval Institute is *Welcome Aboard,* by Florence Ridgely Johnson. Every naval officer and his wife should acquire these.

419. HINTS ON SOCIAL CUSTOMS AND ETIQUETTE. In all social contacts whether within the bounds of service society or among civilians, the naval officer is expected, of his own initiative, to observe the highest standards of gentlemanly conduct. Such conduct arises from innate qualities of the individual and from a knowledge and acceptance of social customs.

Social customs have been defined as the forms, fashions, and manners observed in the society of educated and cultivated people. They constitute a code of conduct which fosters grace and courtesy and eliminates the coarse and offensive. They are extremely practical, for they help to facilitate good living, to get things done quickly and agreeably, to smooth the course of social gatherings, and to eliminate all possible friction from our daily contacts with one another.

With experience in living, a knowledge of social customs comes slowly but inevitably, an ofttimes unpleasant and costly procedure. How much better to make a study of recorded experience in social intercourse, learn the forms, fashions, and manners, and save yourself much unhappiness and trouble.

Since the aforementioned books are available, no attempt will be made to cover these subjects exhaustively here. What follows are a few briefly stated observations. They should be regarded, not as definitive, but only as elementary.

1. Be courteous to fellow guests at the dinner table, manifest a kindly attitude toward *all* guests, and especially toward the ladies in your near vicinity, paying not too much or too little attention to any one, no matter how attractive she may be. Talk, but do not monopolize the conversation. Long monologues are usually exceedingly dull.

2. Toward the ladies, you should have an attitude of special consideration and attention and so conduct yourself as will most contribute to their pleasure and happiness. The social relations between ladies and gentlemen must be based upon individual dignity and mutual respect. Special consideration should always be extended to elderly ladies. You rise in the presence of ladies, remove your hat when talking to them, offer your arm to assist them, and endeavor never to keep a lady waiting.

3. Learn the correct social actions for entering a living room or a home for a social call, for the receiving line, for leaving a party, for a tea or dance, for the formal dinner and dinner dance, etc.

4. A gentleman renders appropriate acknowledgement for every courtesy and kindness extended to him. It is rude to accept hospitality without expressing appreciation. It is both rude and selfish not to attempt to reciprocate social favors accepted. Persons of moderate circumstances are not expected to meet social obligations on the same monetary standard as wealthy friends, but, within the limits of their resources, they must discharge those obligations.

5. If invited to dinner, you are not necessarily expected to remain all afternoon or evening. A visit of a half to one hour after the meal is all that courtesy demands. If a guest of honor is present, it is good manners to wait, when possible, until his or her departure, then take your leave.

6. Correct and dignified speech, coupled with a capacity for interesting and intelligent conversation, constitutes one of the finest assets

of a lady or gentleman. While a limited use of slang adds salt and flavor to American speech, the incessant use of slang or colloquial expressions leads to a narrow and deficient vocabulary. He who swears or indulges in obscene language usually does so because he is unable to express himself forcefully in proper language. In ordinary conversation, even where only men are present, foul language is ill-bred and undignified.

7. Interesting conversation requires a broad contact with literature and familiarity with current events. Devote a part of each day to reading and study. Reading is a habit. Like all good habits, it must be practiced to be useful.

8. Be meticulous about your personal correspondence. Be prompt in answering all letters. Answer invitations immediately. You can find the proper form for a letter, acknowledgement, or thank you note on a social occasion in the books mentioned in Section 418. Whenever an invitation of any sort includes an R.S.V.P., it must be answered the same day.

9. As a house guest, a gentleman must be exceedingly thoughtful of his hostess. Be punctual to meals, and do nothing to upset the routine. Never stay longer than the period for which invited. On leaving the home of a friend after a visit of a weekend or longer, tip the servants moderately and in keeping with your financial status. If there are no servants in the household, do not be afraid to help out in an unobtrusive way, particularly if you know the family well. Promptly after departure, write a note of appreciation to your hostess. While not mandatory, an inexpensive present, such as a book, flowers, or candy, is always appreciated.

10. Obtain a good quality of engraved calling cards, and learn to use them in accordance with social custom.

11. In making introductions, except when a man is an exceedingly important dignitary, gentlemen are introduced to ladies. Very young ladies are properly introduced to gentlemen of advanced years or who combine advancing years with high civil or military rank. When introducing your close relatives, state the relationship. Avoid the use of elaborate phrases. "Allow me to . . .," "May I . . .," or "I would like you to meet . . ." are ample. When being introduced, a simple acknowledgement is "How do you do." "Pleased to meet you" is *not* considered in good form. If seated, rise to acknowledge an introduction. At the dinner table, rising may inconvenience others and you remain seated during introduction to ladies and other gentlemen.

12. If a bachelor accepts an invitation, he is obligated to make a "party call" (preferably within 10 days or 2 weeks). If a hostess has

been exceptionally kind to a bachelor, he may express his appreciation by flowers, candy, or a book. But a friendly note is just as effective.

13. If you leave a port before you have had an opportunity to express your appreciation for hospitality received, either write friendly, informal notes or send p.p.c. (*pour prendre congé*) cards. Also, send p.p.c. cards to clubs that have extended their privileges.

14. It is not necessary to put yourself under obligation to persons whom you do not like. If you are invited by a hostess for whom you do not care, it is quite proper to decline the invitation and then omit your call of appreciation. Such a gesture says, "I do not care to be friends."

Your study of social tact, courtesy, and agreeable conduct must go far afield and must be exercised in "practical work" on all social occasions, before you can consider yourself fully qualified as the sort of gentleman who "never gives unintentional offense."

420. ACCOMMODATION. As elsewhere noted, a genius probably would not fit well into our modern naval organization. Long ago, recognizing the dearth of genius in naval tactics, our Navy set out to have in its officer corps, instead of genius, a high average of intelligence and initiative. The officers of the Navy form a closely knit organization, which you now have joined. There is ample room for the normal variation in personality encountered among the ordinary run of men, but there is little patience with the eccentric and the abnormal.

The new officer is expected to accept his fair burden of responsibility cheerfully and willingly. Life in the Navy will be new and strange. You must be adaptable, ready to conform. The problems which you will encounter will present you with a distinct challenge.

The path to glory and to fame lies ahead along one of those tracks across the restless sea. How well you take advantage of your opportunities will depend on how well and how quickly you find your place in the organization. Remember, it is *you* who must orient *yourself* with respect to the new horizons of your naval career.

If you are able to put the foregoing observations to your own use, you will avoid the most common pitfalls of living with others. One last and probably the most important observation of all—live by the golden rule.

> For all your years prepare,
> And meet them ever alike:
> When you are the anvil, bear—
> When you are the hammer, strike.

CHAPTER 5

Military Courtesy, Honors, and Ceremonies

The colors must never be struck.

—LIEUTENANT WILLIAM BURROWS, USN,
U.S.S. *Enterprise*, 1813

Courtesy

501. COURTESY implies a courtly politeness, a graceful and considerate behavior toward others, acts of kindness performed with politeness, a favor or indulgence as distinguished from a right. "Military courtesy" is the term used to classify or include those special acts and ceremonial procedures which are required between members of the service or which are habitually observed because of the equally strong force of custom and usage. In addition to the required formalities, there are those many acts of civility and good breeding which are the requisite of a gentleman in civilian or military life.

502. MILITARY COURTESY. The rules for military courtesy are soundly based on custom and tradition, and their strict observance forms an important factor in the maintenance of discipline. It must be appreciated that these evidences of respect and courtesy are observed equally by all officers and men in the naval service. Like loyalty, military courtesy operates from senior to junior, as well as from junior to senior. Consideration and respect for the junior are necessary attributes of the senior.

503. THE SALUTE. This is an act of courtesy which has been handed down to us through the ages and which forms an integral part

FIGURE 501. The hand salute.

of the military life. And, as such an act, the officer receiving the salute is as responsible for returning it as is the junior to render the salute. Learn to salute properly. A sloppy salute is more discourteous than a failure to salute. Nothing gives a better indication of the state of discipline in a ship than the observance of the forms of military courtesy (see Figure 501).

Navy Regulations Regarding Salutes. The hand salute is the long-established form of greeting and recognition exchanged between persons in the armed services. All persons in the naval service shall be alert to render or return the salute as prescribed in the Regulations. The salute by persons in the naval service shall be rendered and returned with the right hand, when practicable; except that, with arms in hand, the salute appropriate thereto shall be rendered or returned.

Juniors salute first. All salutes received when in uniform and covered shall be returned; at other times salutes received shall be appropriately

FIGURE 502A. When to salute. Enlisted men salute officers, and junior officers salute senior when meeting, when passing near. when addressing or when being addressed. Men and officers salute all senior U. S. and allied officers they may encounter. When several officers are saluted, all shall return it.

FIGURE 502B. When to salute. Officers and all enlisted men not in formation salute during honors to the national ensign or playing of national anthem. In overtaking a senior, the salute shall be given when abreast, with "By your leave sir."

FIGURE 502C. When to salute. Guards salute all officers passing close aboard. On every occasion salute the captain, officers senior to him, senior officers from other ships. On first daily meeting enlisted men salute all officers. Junior officers salute senior.

FIGURE 502D. When to salute. Sentries at gangways salute all officers going or coming over side and passing close aboard. When officer meets detail ashore or afloat, man in charge salutes for detail. When no man is in charge, first man who sees officer calls attention; then all salute.

acknowledged. Persons uncovered shall not salute, except when failure to do so would cause embarrassment or misunderstanding.

Civilians may be saluted by persons in uniform when appropriate, but the uniform hat or cap shall not be raised as a form of salutation.

A person in the naval service not in uniform shall, in rendering salutes or exchanging greetings, comply with the rules and customs established for a civilian; except that, when saluting another person in the armed services, the hand salute shall be used. (NR 2110)

Salutes shall be rendered by persons in the naval service to officers of the armed services of the United States, the Coast Guard, and foreign armed services; to high ranking dignitaries of the United States and foreign nations; and to officers of the Coast and Geodetic Survey and Public Health Service who are at the time serving with the armed services of the United States. Naval personnel must be alert to observe the passing of an automobile from which the flag of a high ranking dignitary is displayed and, when such is seen, to be punctilious in rendering a salute to the occupant who returns the salute. Passengers and driver return salute rendered if safety permits.

All persons in the naval service shall salute all officers senior to themselves on each occasion of meeting or passing near or when addressing or being addressed by such officers, except that:

1. On board ship salutes shall be dispensed with after the first daily meeting, except for those rendered to the commanding officer and officers senior to him, to visiting officers, to officers making inspections, and to officers when addressing or being addressed by them.

2. When such procedure does not conflict with the spirit of these regulations, at crowded gatherings or in congested areas, salutes shall

be rendered only when addressing, or being addressed by, an officer who is senior to them. In public places or conveyances, a salute is not rendered where considered inappropriate.

3. Persons at work or engaged in games shall salute only when addressed by an officer senior to them and then only if circumstances warrant.

Note: Persons engaged as described in (2) and (3) will stand at attention when addressed and may be called to attention to clear a gangway for a senior officer. At mess the person addressed simply sits at attention.

4. Persons in formation shall salute only on command.

Note: If addressed by an officer senior to him, a naval person should stand at attention until the conversation is finished or the officer gives him "At ease" or "Carry on."

5. When boats pass each other with embarked officers or officials in view, hand salutes shall be rendered by the senior officer and coxswain in each boat. Officers seated in boats shall not rise when saluting: coxswains shall rise unless dangerous or impracticable to do so. (NR 2111)

Note: It is customary for the senior officer in a boat to rise and salute when an officer senior to him enters or leaves the boat or when acknowledging a gun salute.

General Notes on Salutes and Other Military Courtesies. Salutes are normally exchanged at a distance of 6 paces, but 25 paces is not excessive. The junior remains at salute until his salute is returned or the senior is well past him. Habitually to accompany your salute with a greeting, such as "Good morning, sir," is a good practice.

When overtaking a senior, if for any reason it becomes necessary to pass him, the salute should be given when abreast the senior and you should ask, "By your leave, sir?"

If escorting a lady, on meeting another officer or officers, the customary exchange of salutes should be made. If seated, rise and salute.

If not wearing headdress, or both hands are burdened, you should greet your senior officer orally with, "Good morning, sir"; "Good evening, Mr. Jones"; "Good afternoon, Admiral"; or other appropriate remark. When your right hand is engaged and cannot be used, salute with the left hand.

The custom at Air Force and Army posts is to salute when uncovered as well as when covered. Follow their custom when at the bases of these other armed services.

A salute is rendered to a senior officer whenever he is recognized, whether covered or not, in uniform or in civilian clothes. Be zealous in recognizing your seniors. A junior, uncovered, stands at attention until a senior has passed. A senior, uncovered, usually bows to a junior or speaks to him, to acknowledge the salute.

When formally addressing, or being addressed by, a senior officer, stand at attention. If covered, salute when first addressed and again upon conclusion of the instructions or conversation. If uncovered, stand at attention throughout the conversation, unless otherwise directed by the senior officer. While saluting and before entering upon a conversation, give your name, as "Ensign Joseph Doaks, sir."

Whenever a senior officer visits your room or office officially, rise, stand at attention and salute giving your rank and name. If the senior's visit is not official, rise, uncover if covered and stand at attention. If you are unknown to the senior, state your rank and name.

The command "Gangway" should be given by anyone who observes an officer approaching a gangway where his passage is blocked. Attention should be paid to extending this courtesy to important civilians as well. Enlisted men should not use this word to clear a passage for themselves or other enlisted men, but should say "Coming through" or use some other expression which will not indicate that an officer or other important personage is seeking passage. There must be no doubt that the gangway is properly cleared. The senior officer or petty officer in the immediate vicinity is responsible for seeing that this is promptly done.

The requirements of the command "Attention" should also be carried out, when practicable, when officers are escorting visitors through their own ship. The requirements of "Attention" and "Gangway" must be strictly obeyed, whether the visitors are officers or civilians. If the party does not intend to pass on promptly, the passing dignitary should give the order "Carry on" without unnecessary delay.

"Sir" is a military expression, which is always used in connection with "Yes" and "No," when conversing with senior officers or with officers on duty. Many senior officers use it when addressing their juniors as a matter of "courtesy downward." "Sir" is customarily added in such routine statements as "The watch is relieved, sir"; "I request permission to leave the ship, sir"; and "I am ready to relieve you, sir."

Women officers and enlisted personnel are, in general, governed by the same regulations and customs with regard to saluting as are the male members of the naval service.

It should be remembered that women in the Navy are not an auxiliary group but have been integrated into the Regular Navy and the Naval Reserve and so are an integral part of the Navy. Navy women are proud of the distinction thus conferred upon them, proud to inherit the customs and traditions of the Navy.

Women in the Navy, therefore, render to officers and other officials salutes in accordance with established customs and rules of military courtesy. Out-of-doors, when a woman officer or enlisted person is wearing her hat, she will always salute an officer senior to her. It should be noted that the rendering of official salutes takes precedence over the usual social customs established between ladies and gentlemen. The only exception is that women do not *always* salute when wearing a hat. Indoors, where men customarily remove their officer's cap, women do not salute.

From this exposition, officers and enlisted men will understand that the usual military courtesies extended from juniors to seniors are the privilege of women officers and should be rendered to them on all proper occasions.

504. BOAT ETIQUETTE. Figure 503 illustrates some of the more common rules of boat etiquette. You should master all the rules of boat etiquette thoroughly. As a junior officer you will be called upon frequently to act as a boat officer, and through the years you will make many boat trips both in command and as a passenger. The following general rules will help you when you are a passenger:

1. Juniors board boats *first*. Move forward as necessary to give following seniors room astern. Do not sit in stern sheets unless invited to

FIGURE 503. Boat etiquette. Enlisted men rise and salute when an officer enters or leaves. When an officer passes near, officer or petty officer in charge salutes; if none is present, all men salute. Officers rise and salute when a senior enters or leaves.

do so. Do not make a last-minute dash for the boat. Board boat before last boat-gong.

2. Rise when seniors embark.

3. Leave *after* seniors unless senior gives orders to contrary.

4. Keep your hands and arms inside the boat.

5. Step carefully on spaces provided and avoid walking on thwarts, decks, and other varnished areas.

6. Do not change a coxswain's orders except in an emergency and then be prepared to substantiate your decision to the Officer of the Deck on your return to the ship.

When you are in command you should ensure that your boat coxswain observes the following rules of etiquette and good seamanship:

1. Do not cross bow, crowd, overhaul and pass or otherwise disregard the presence of a senior.

2. Ensure that you and coxswain salute passing seniors first. Return salutes promptly.

3. When approaching a ship or landing, give way to seniors.

4. When officers are in a boat, require enlisted men to maintain appropriate silence, particularly when approaching ships or landings.

5. Require coxswain to haul clear of ship or landing while waiting and do not permit crew to leave boat.

6. Do not allow crew to lounge in boat when running. Keep all members of crew in same uniform.

Boat Salutes. Boats salute in passing much the same as military men do. The junior salutes first. However, only the coxswain and the

senior officer, if officers are embarked, render or return the salute. Others do not salute but sit at attention, facing in the direction of their seats. Those saluting do not rise when saluting, but face in the direction of the boat saluted if practicable. The coxswain rises if seated and rising is not dangerous.

When the boat is not under way, rules are the same except that the coxswain salutes officers entering or leaving boat, if safe to do so.

During colors the boat lies to, and the senior officer, boat officer, or coxswain stands at attention and salutes. Others remain seated at attention. During colors, passengers in a vehicle also remain seated at attention.

During gun salutes, boats not carrying the person saluted observe the same courtesy as for colors. The boat carrying the person saluted stops, disengages clutch, and heads parallel to saluting ship. Only the person honored rises.

Boat Appearance. A ship is known by the appearance of its boats and their general smartness. An alert, well-uniformed crew is the first step in this direction. A good crew will keep a good boat. Chrome and fancywork help, but they are not substitutes for cleanliness, preservation, and neatness.

Boat Hails. All boats approaching a ship at night should be hailed as soon as within hearing distance. The proper challenge is "Boat ahoy!" The coxswain will answer to indicate the rank of the senior passenger as follows:

Officer or Official	Reply
President or Vice-President	"UNITED STATES"
Secretary of Defense, Deputy or Assistant Secretary of Defense	"DEFENSE"
Secretary, Under or Assistant Secretary of the Navy	"NAVY"
Chief of Naval Operations	"NAVAL OPERATIONS"
Fleet or Force Commander	"FLEET" or abbreviation of title
General Officer	"GENERAL OFFICER"
Chief of Staff	"STAFF"
Flotilla, Squadron, or Division Commander	"(type) FLOTILLA (number)," etc.
Marine Officer Commanding Brigade	"BRIGADE COMMANDER"
Commanding Officer of a Ship	"................" (name of ship)
Marine Officer Commanding Regiment	"REGIMENTAL COMMANDER"
Commissioned Officer	"AYE, AYE"
Other Officers	"NO, NO"
Enlisted men	"HELLO"
Boat not intending to come alongside	"PASSING"

During hours when honors are rendered, the Officer of the Deck should challenge the coxswain by raising his arm with closed fist in the direction of the approaching boat. The coxswain should answer by raising the number of fingers corresponding to the number of side boys rated by the senior passenger. A clenched fist indicates no officer passengers.

Boat Flags. A boat displays the personal flag of an officer officially entitled to the boat when he is embarked officially in uniform. The ensign is also displayed. If he is embarked in uniform, but not officially (i.e., en route to or from an official visit) the ensign only is displayed. If he is embarked in civilian clothes, a miniature personal flag or pennant is displayed in the cockpit.

Boat Gongs. When officers arrive unexpectedly and the proper officers of the ship and embarked staff have not been properly notified, boat gongs usually are sounded, corresponding to the number of side boys. The officer's organization, as taken from the boat hail, is then announced. In some ships this custom is extended to every arrival and departure, but best opinion holds that this is improper usage and is a poor substitute for proper watch standing.

505. THE NATIONAL ANTHEM. The National Anthem of the United States of America is "The Star-Spangled Banner." When played by a naval band, it shall be played through without repetition of any part not required to make it complete; except for the necessary measures which are repeated to accommodate the words when the anthem is sung.

The playing of the National Anthem of the United States, or of any other country, as part of a medley is prohibited. (NR 2105)

Whenever the National Anthem of the United States is played, persons in the naval service shall stand at attention and face the music, except at colors, when they shall face the ensign. When covered they shall come to the salute at the first note of the anthem and shall remain at the salute until the last note of the anthem. Persons in ranks shall come to the salute together, by command. Persons in vehicles or in boats shall remain seated or standing. Only the boat officer or the coxswain stands and salutes.

The same marks of respect prescribed during the playing of the National Anthem of the United States shall be shown during the playing of a foreign national anthem. (NR 2106)

When uncovered, in uniform, it is customary to stand at attention during the playing of the National Anthem of the United States or a foreign nation. If in civilian clothes and covered, remove the hat with your right hand and place it over your left breast.

506. NAVY REGULATIONS ON OTHER MARKS OF RESPECT. Juniors shall show deference to seniors at all times by recognizing their presence and by employing a courteous and respectful bearing and mode of speech toward them.

Juniors shall stand at attention, unless seated at mess, or unless circumstances make such action impracticable or inappropriate:

1. When addressed by an officer senior to them.

2. When an officer of flag or general rank, the commanding officer, or an officer senior to him in the chain of command, or an officer making an official inspection enters the room, compartment, or deck space where they may be.

Juniors shall walk or ride on the left of seniors whom they are accompanying.

Officers shall enter boats and automobiles in inverse order of rank and shall leave them in order of rank, unless there is special reason to the contrary. The seniors shall be accorded the more desirable seats.

Note: A "special reason to the contrary" exists when the senior indicates his wish that other arrangements shall obtain.

507. VISITING MEN-OF-WAR. A member of the naval service wishing to visit a man-of-war anchored out in the stream should obtain permission at the landing to embark in one of her boats. He should ask the senior officer using the boat or the coxswain if he may have permission to go off to the ship in the boat.

The starboard accommodation ladder is reserved for commissioned officers.

Observe proper boat etiquette (see Section 504).

Do not land over another boat without permission. Ordinarily, such permission should not be requested.

All officers and men, whenever reaching the quarterdeck of a man-of-war from a boat, from a gangway, from the shore or from another part of the ship, shall salute the national ensign. In the event that the ensign is not hoisted, this salute is rendered only when leaving or coming on board ship. This salute is entirely distinct from the salute to the officer of the deck. When coming on board a ship, stop at the top of the accommodation ladder or gangway, face the colors, render the salute, after which the officer of the deck should be saluted. In leaving the quarterdeck to go ashore, the same salutes are rendered in the reverse order.

In ships having a quarterdeck which is set apart for ceremonies it is customary to salute the national ensign when entering the limits of the quarterdeck from any part of the ship.

When visiting a man-of-war, after saluting the officer of the deck, say, "I request permission to come aboard, sir." Before leaving, salute the officer of the deck and say, "Sir, with your permission, I will leave the ship."

Honors, Official Visits, and Calls

508. THE OFFICER OF THE DECK AND HONORS. It is the duty of all officers standing deck watches to be entirely familiar with any situation that might arise during his watch. Although wartime requirements eliminate many of the honors and ceremonies obtaining in peace, certain occasions may arise where knowledge of the procedure is required.

In the first place, the officer must have a working knowledge of the honors. A copy of honor tables is generally posted on the quarterdeck for reference; and, when time permits, this may be consulted in planning the ceremony. It is the "surprise" visit that the Officer of the Deck must guard against.[1]

Constant vigilance is required by the entire watch. The signal bridge watch must be alert to note flag officers leaving and returning to other ships and must report the movements of barges and gigs flying personal flags that may approach. The watch on deck is equally responsible. Side boys, guard, and band (when required) must not be permitted to wander or be absent from station. Promptness and smartness are requisites.

If attached to a flagship, maintain a close liaison with the Flag Lieutenant. Know where the Admiral, Chief of Staff, Staff Duty Officer, and Commanding Officer are at all times. Inform the responsible officer at the earliest possible moment. Nothing is more embarrassing to the visitor than not to be met properly on the occasion of a ceremonial visit. And such a situation is usually quite unpleasant for the Officer of the Deck, too.

Make your preparations in advance. Determine in your own mind what is required in any contingency. Be sure that the bandmaster (or buglers) and the officer in charge of the guard know exactly what their duties are. Instruct the bos'nmate in his duties. Rehearse the side boys. Inspect all participating for neatness of person and equipment. And, in that connection, be above reproach yourself. The Officer of the Deck represents the Commanding Officer and sets the example to be followed by the entire watch.

509. PASSING HONORS are those honors, other than gun salutes, rendered on occasions when ships or embarked officials or officers pass, or are passed, close aboard. "Close aboard" shall mean passing within 600

HONORS RELATIVE TO OFFICIAL VISITS OF NAVAL AND MILITARY OFFICERS

Except as modified or dispensed with by Navy Regulations, the honors prescribed in this table shall be rendered by a ship or station on the occasion of the official visits of the following United States officers (ashore, the single gun salute, when prescribed below, shall be fired on arrival instead of on departure):

Officer	Uniform	Gun salute Arrival	Gun salute Departure	Ruffles and flourishes	Music	Guard	Side boys
Chairman, Joint Chiefs of Staff.....	Full dress..	19	19	4	General's or Admiral's march.	Full.......	8
Chief of Staff, U.S. Army............	.....do.....	19	19	4	General's march....	.....do.....	8
Chief of Naval Operations...........	.....do.....	19	19	4	Admiral's march....	.....do.....	8
Chief of Staff, U.S. Air Force.......	.....do.....	19	19	4	General's march....	.....do.....	8
Commandant of the Marine Corps...	.....do.....	19	19	4	Admiral's march[1] ...	.....do.....	8
General of the Army.................	.....do.....	19	19	4	General's march....	.....do.....	8
Fleet Admiral......................	.....do.....	19	19	4	Admiral's march....	.....do.....	8
General of the Air Force............	.....do.....	19	19	4	General's march....	.....do.....	8
Generals...........................	.....do.....	17	17	4	........do.[1]........	.....do.....	8
Admirals...........................	.....do.....	17	17	4	Admiral's march....	.....do.....	8
Naval or other Military Governor, commissioned as such by the President, within the area of his jurisdiction.	.....do.....		17	4	General's[1] or Admiral's march.	.....do.....	8
Vice Admiral or Lieutenant General..	.....do.....		15	3	........do.[1]........	.....do.....	8
Rear Admiral or Major General.....	.....do.....		13	2	........do.[1]........	.....do.....	6
Commodore or Brigadier General...	.....do.....		11	1	........do.[1]........	.....do.....	6
Captain, Commander, Colonel, or Lieutenant Colonel.	Of the day..				....	Of the day..	4
Other commissioned officers.........	.....do.....				....	.....do. ...	2

[1] Marine Corps general officers receive the Admiral's March.

HONORS AND CEREMONIES

Table of Honors for Official Visits of United States Civil Officials. Except as modified or dispensed with by these regulations, the honors prescribed in this table shall be rendered by a ship or station on the occasion of the official visit of the following United States civil officials (ashore, the single gun salute, when prescribed below, shall be fired on arrival instead of on departure):

Official	Uniform	Gun salute Arrival	Gun salute Depart-ure	Ruffles and flourishes	Music	Guard	Side boys	Crew	Within what limits	Flag What	Flag Where	Flag During
President	Full dress	21	21	4	National anthem.[1]	Full	8	Man rail[4]		President's	Main truck.	Visit.
Ex-President or President-elect.	do	21	21	4	Admiral's march.	do	8	Quarters		National	do	Salute.
Secretary of State when acting as special foreign representative of the President.	do	19	19	4	National anthem.	do	8	do		Secretary's	do	Visit.
Vice President.	do		19	4	Admiral's march.	do	8	do		Vice President's.	do	do.
Speaker of the House of Representatives.	do		19	4	do	do	8			National.	Fore truck.	Salute.
Governor of a State of the United States	do		19	4	do	do	8		Area under his jurisdiction.	do	do	do.
Chief Justice of the United States	do		19	4	do	do	8			do	do	do.
Ambassador, High Commissioner, or special diplomatic representative whose credentials give him authority equal to or greater than that of an Ambassador.	do		19	4	National anthem.	do	8		Nation or nations to which accredited.	do	do	do.
Associate Justices of Supreme Court.	do		19	4	Admiral's march.	do	8			do	do	do.
U.S. representative to the U.N.	do	19	19	4	do	do	8			do	do	do.
Secretary of Defense.	do	19	19	4	Honor's march.[3]	do	8	Quarters		Secretary's.	Main truck.	do.
Deputy Secretary of Defense.	do	19	19	4	do	do	8	do		Deputy Secretary's.	do	do.
Cabinet Officer[2] (other than Secretary of Defense).	do	19	19	4	Admiral's march.	do	8			National.	Fore truck.	Salute.
Secretary of the Army.	do	19	19	4	Honor's march.[3]	do	8			do	do	do.
Secretary of the Navy.	do	19	19	4	do	do	8	Quarters		Secretary's.	Main truck.	Visit.
Secretary of the Air Force.	do	19	19	4	do	do	8			National.	Fore truck.	Salute.
Director of Defense Research and Engineering.	do	19	19	4	Admiral's march.	do	8			Director's.	do	Visit.
President pro tempore of the Senate.	do		19	4	Honor's march.[3]	do	8			National.	do	Salute.
Assistant Secretaries of Defense.	do	17	17	4		do	8	Quarters		Assistant Secretary's.	Main truck.	Visit.

	Music	Guns	Ruffles and flourishes	March	Side boys	Piped	Flag displayed over	Flag displayed	Position	Honors
General Counsel of the DOD	do	17	4	do	8			National	Fore truck	Salute.
Under Secretary of the Army	do	17	4	do	8			do	do	do.
Under Secretary of the Navy	do	17	4	do	8	Quarters		Under Secretary's	Main truck	Visit.
Under Secretary of the Air Force	do	17	4	do	8			National	Fore truck	Salute.
Assistant Secretaries of the Army	do	17	4	do	8			do	do	do.
Assistant Secretaries of the Navy	do	17	4	do	8	Quarters		Assistant Secretary's	Main truck	Visit.
Assistant Secretaries of the Air Force	do	17	4	do	8			National	Fore truck	Salute.
Governor General or Governor of a Commonwealth or possession of the United States, or area under United States Administration.	do		4	Admiral's	8		Area under his jurisdiction.	do	do	do.
Other Under Secretaries of Cabinet, the Solicitor General, the Deputy Attorney General, and the Deputy Postmaster General.	do	17	4	do	8			do	do	do.
Members of Congress	do	17	4	do	8			do	do	do.
Envoy Extraordinary and Minister Plenipotentiary	do	15	3	do	8		Nation to which accredited.	do	do	do.
Minister Resident	do	13	2	do	6		do.	do	do	do.
Charge d'Affaires	do	11	1	do	6		District to which assigned.	do	do	do.
Career Minister, or Counselor of Embassy or Legation.	do	11	1	do	6		do.	do	do	do.
Consul General; or Counsul or Vice Counsul when in charge of a Consulate General.	do	11	1	do	6		District to which assigned.	National	Fore truck	Salute.
First Secretary of Embassy or Legation.	Of the day			Of the day	4		Nation to which accredited.			
Consul; or Vice Counsul when in charge of a Consulate.	do	7		do	4		District to which assigned.	National	Fore truck	Salute.
Mayor of an incorporated city.	do			do	4		Within limits of mayorality.			
Second or Third Secretary of Embassy or Legation.	do				2		Nation to which accredited.			
Vice Counsul when only representative of United States, and not in charge of a Consulate General or Consulate.	do	5		Of the day.	2		District to which assigned.	National	Fore truck	do.
Consular Agent when only representative of the United States.	do				2		do.			

1 See Article 2161 regarding musical honors to President.
2 In the order of precedence as follows:
Secretary of State—Secretary of the Treasury—Attorney General—Postmaster General—Secretary of the Interior—Secretary of Agriculture—Secretary of Commerce—Secretary of Labor—Secretary of Health, Education, and Welfare—Secretary of Transportation.
3 32-bar melody in the trio of "Stars and Stripes Forever."
4 Not appropriate on shore installations.

TABLE OF HONORS AND CEREMONIES—*Continued*

FALLING IN AT SEA OR ELSEWHERE WITH SHIP FLYING PERSONAL FLAG

Flag	Salute	Remarks
President.. Or standard of President of foreign republic, sovereign or member of reigning royal family.......	21 guns 21 guns	All ships in company fire salute. National ensign of foreign nation at main during salute. All ships in company fire salute.
Secretary of Defense and Secretary of Navy................ Secretary of State (when representative of President)........ Under Secretary of the Navy.......................... Assistant Secretary of Navy..........................	19 guns 19 guns 17 guns 17 guns	Senior ship only (if two or more in company) fires salute. By each ship. Senior ship only (if two or more in company) fires salute. Senior ship only (if two or more in company) fires salute.

SHIPS PASSING OR BEING PASSED

Foreign or U.S. man-of-war flying flag of President of U.S., president of foreign republic or a foreign sovereign, or member of reigning royal family.	Uniform as prescribed by SOP. Man rail unless otherwise ordered by SOP. Full guard and band. Attention by bugle. National anthem. Hand salute. 4 ruffles and flourishes.	
Secretary of State when special foreign representative of the President.	Same as above, except crew at Quarters.	
Vice-President.	Uniform of the day. Crew at Quarters. Full guard and band. Attention by bugle. National anthem. Hand salute.	
Foreign or U.S. man-of-war flying flag of Secretary of Defense, Secretary of the Navy, Under Secretary of the Navy, or Assistant Secretary of the Navy.	Crew at Quarters. Full guard and band. Attention by bugle. National anthem. Hand salute. Uniform of the day.	

GUN SALUTES—GENERAL

1. The interval between guns in all salutes shall be five seconds.

2. During the firing of a salute all officers and men on the quarter deck, or in the ceremonial party if ashore, shall render the hand salute; other persons on deck, or in the vicinity of the ceremonial party if ashore, shall stand at attention.

3. No salute shall be fired between sunset and sunrise. As a general rule, salutes shall be fired between 8:00 A.M. and sunset. Salutes shall not be fired on Sunday, unless required by international courtesy.

4. The national ensign shall always be displayed during a salute.

5. In the case of a salute at 8:00 A.M., the first gun shall be fired at the last note of the last national anthem or at the end of morning colors.

6. Whenever a salute is fired, following the motions of the flagship or ship of the senior officer present, each ship shall begin its salute with the first gun from the flag or senior ship.

Foreign or U.S. man-of-war with or without personal flag.	Attention by bugle. Hand salute.	(Add guard of the day and foreign national anthem for a foreign man-of-war.)
Vessel of own formation not on detached duty.	(Attention by bugle—hand salute.) (In tactical evolutions outside of port—none.)	

NOTES: Out of port, no honors shall be rendered between vessels while they are engaged in tactical maneuvers or evolutions. When two or more ships are in company, whether at anchor or underway, coming to anchor, or getting underway, they shall be considered as a part of the same formation and as engaged in maneuvers or evolutions, so far as concerns salutes. In case of a ship or ships joining such formations, honors shall not be rendered unless such ship or ships have been or are on detached duty. The term "detached duty" in this case does not apply to a ship or ships temporarily out of formation, but only to ships which have been, or will be, absent for at least 6 months from the vicinity of the ships which they are joining or leaving. U.S. Coast Guard ships and U.S. Naval Stations are rendered passing honors.

PASSING IN BOAT, CLOSE ABOARD, WITH FLAG OR PENNANT FLYING

President of U.S.	Man rail, if ordered by SOP.
President of foreign republic.	Full guard and band.
Foreign sovereign.	Attention by bugle and salute by all persons in view.
Member of reigning royal family.	4 ruffles and flourishes.
*Secretary of State when en route to foreign country in the capacity of representative of the President.	National anthem (U.S. or foreign). *All except to man the rail.
Vice-President.	Full guard and band.
Secretary of Defense.	Attention by bugle.
Secretary of Navy.	4 ruffles and flourishes.
Under Secretary of Navy.	March.
Assistant Secretary of Navy.	Hand salute from "present arms" until end of flourishes. Sentries, men on watch on deck, in view, salute.
Other civil official entitled to honors on official visit. Officer of an armed service.	Attention by bugle, and salute by all persons in view on deck. do.

NOTES: For all officers passing close aboard, when recognized, whether in uniform or not, it is customary for officer of the deck, boat keepers, and sentries to salute.
By "close aboard" is meant within 600 yards for passing ships, 400 yards for boats. For high personages and foreign ships, interpret the term liberally. In any case, be careful not to render less honor than may be due.

7. In the official presence of the President of the United States or of the president or sovereign of any other nation, no gun salute shall be fired by vessels of the Navy to any personage of lesser degree.

8. a. No salutes shall be fired in the presence of a senior without his permission, except it be one in honor of such senior.

b. In the presence of a senior flag officer, salutes to junior flag officers shall not be fired except in the following cases (the senior flag officer's permission must first have been obtained):

(1) Flag officer relinquishing command.

(2) Flag officer inspecting ship of his command on arrival and again on departure if his flag is hoisted on board.

(3) On departure of flag officer visiting officially for the first time a ship of the Navy not under his command.

(4) Flag officer as president of Board of Inspection and Survey on arrival and again on departure.

c. If flag officer assumes command in the presence of another flag officer his senior, the flag of former shall not be saluted, but he shall salute the flag of his senior, which salute shall be returned according to number of guns to which junior is entitled. If flag officer assumes command in presence of one or more flag officers his junior, salute is fired by his own flagship, and in addition he is saluted by flag officer next in rank and by him only.

TABLES OF HONORS FOR OFFICIAL VISITS OF FOREIGN OFFICIALS AND OFFICERS

Except as modified or dispensed with by these regulations, the honors prescribed in this table shall be rendered by a ship or station on the occasion of the official visit of the following foreign officials and officers (ashore, the single gun salute, when prescribed below, shall be fired on arrival instead of on departure):

Official or officer	Uniform	Gun salute		Ruffles and flourishes	Music	Guard	Side boys¹	Crew	Flag		
		Arrival	Departure						What	Where	During
President or Sovereign.	Full dress.	21	21	4	Foreign national anthem.	Full...	8	Man rail.¹	Foreign ensign.	Main truck.	Visit. Visit.
Member of reigning royal family.	..do....	21	21	4	..do....	..do....	8	..do....	..do....	..do....	Salute.
Prime Minister or other cabinet officer.	..do....		19	4	Admiral's march.	..do....	8		..do....	Fore truck.	do.
Officer of armed forces, diplomatic or consular representative in country to which accredited, or other distinguished official.	*Civil officials:* Honors as for official of the United States of comparable position. For example, foreign civil officials, occupying positions comparable to U.S. Department of Defense civil officials, shall receive equivalent honors. *Officers of Armed Forces:* Honors as for officer of the United States of the same grade, except, that equivalent honors shall be rendered to foreign officers who occupy a position comparable to Chairman JCS, CNO, Chief of Staff Army, Chief of Staff Air Force, or CMC.										
Official not herein provided for.	Honors as prescribed by the senior officer present; such honors normally shall be those accorded the foreign official when visiting officially a ship of his own nation, but a gun salute, if prescribed, shall not exceed 19 guns.										

¹ Not appropriate on shore installations.

yards for ships and 400 yards for boats. These rules shall be interpreted liberally, to ensure that appropriate honors are rendered (NR 2130). Passing honors between ships of the Navy and Coast Guard consist of sounding "Attention" and rendering the hand salute by all persons in view on deck and not in ranks.

Passing honors are not rendered after sunset or before 0800 except when international courtesy requires.

Passing honors are not exchanged between ships of the Navy engaged in tactical evolutions outside port.

The senior officer present may direct that passing honors be dispensed with in whole or in part. They are usually suspended in time of war.

The passing honors rendered to military officers and government officials are given in the table of honors and ceremonies. They are rendered by a ship of the Navy passing close aboard a ship, boat, or naval station displaying the flag of the official. These honors are acknowledged by rendering the same honors in return.

Passing honors prescribed in the table for the President of the United States are rendered by a ship of the Navy being passed close aboard by a ship or boat displaying the flag or standard of a foreign president, sovereign, or member of a reigning royal family, except that the foreign national anthem is played instead of the national anthem of the United States.

Similar passing honors shall be exchanged between foreign warships passed close aboard, to consist of parading the guard of the day, sounding "Attention," rendering the salute by all persons in view on deck, and playing the foreign national anthem.

The crew is normally paraded at quarters entering or leaving port in daylight, so as to be prepared for passing honors.

Persons on the quarterdeck salute when a boat displaying a miniature of a flag or pennant passes close aboard.

Procedure. "Attention" is sounded on the bugle or by other means when the bow of one ship passes the bow or stern of the other, the junior saluting first. If a senior is embarked in a boat, "Attention" is sounded before the boat is abreast, or nearest to abreast, the quarterdeck.

The guard, if required, presents arms, and all persons in view on deck salute.

The music, if required, sounds off.

"Carry on" is sounded by bugle or other means when the prescribed honors have been rendered and acknowledged.

510. OFFICIAL VISITS AND CALLS—DEFINITIONS.

Official Visit: A formal visit of courtesy which requires special honors and ceremonies.

Official Call: An official but informal visit of courtesy which requires no more than side honors. Do not confuse official calls with personal calls, which are discussed in Sections 211 and 414.

Guard of the Day: Not less than one rifle squad from the Marine detachment or the seaman guard.

Full Guard: Not less than one rifle platoon.

Guard of Honor: On shore stations, a guard, not part of the interior guard, which is paraded for rendering honors.

Compliment of the Guard: On shore stations, interior guard turns out and presents arms, as a compliment to visiting officers or civilian dignitaries.

Shipboard Compliments: Include honors by a guard and the following, which are not rendered ashore:

Man the rail on weather decks or crew at quarters

Pipe boats alongside and dignitary over the side

Side boys

These compliments are rendered by naval officers and enlisted men.

511. PREPARATIONS FOR OFFICIAL VISITS OR CALLS.   The Admiral's Aide or Flag Lieutenant makes arrangements for visits and calls. In ships or on stations where there is no flag officer, the Executive Officer or the Ship's Secretary functions in this regard. If full honors are involved, close liaison between the maker and recipient of an official visit is indicated to coordinate the following details:

Exact time and place visit is to be made

Uniform

Transportation (by whose boat or car?)

Use of calling cards

Refreshments or not

Arrangements to break or haul down personal flags

Gun salutes

On shore, arrangements as to entrance to station and whether guard of honor is required.

Insofar as possible, ashore or afloat, the same salutes, honors, and ceremonies are rendered.

512. WHEN TO MAKE OFFICIAL VISITS AND CALLS.   *By Officers of the Naval Service.* Official visits and calls are paid only by officers in command, and are distinct from the personal calls described in Sections 211, 213, and 414. Generally speaking, official visits are made more often by commanders afloat. Official calls are usually made on shore.

An officer assuming command shall, at the first opportunity thereafter, make an official visit to the senior to whom he has reported for duty in command and to any successor of that senior; except that for shore commands a call shall be made in lieu of such official visit.

Unless dispensed with by the senior, calls shall be made:

1. By the commander of an arriving unit upon his immediate superior in the chain of command, if present; and, when circumstances permit, upon the senior officer present.

2. By an officer in command upon an immediate superior in the chain of command on the arrival of the latter.

3. By an officer who has been the senior officer present upon his successor.

4. By the commander of a unit arriving at a naval base or station upon the commander of such base or station; except that when the former is senior, the latter shall make the call.

5. By an officer reporting for duty upon his commanding officer.

When arrivals occur after 1600, or on Sunday, or on a holiday, the required calls may be postponed until the next working day. (NR 2144)

Officers of Other Armed Services. When in the vicinity of a command of another armed service of the United States, the senior officer present in the naval service shall arrange with the commander concerned for the exchange of official visits or calls, as appropriate. (NR 2145)

Diplomatic and Consular Representatives. Upon arrival in port where United States diplomatic or consular representatives accredited to that foreign government are present, the senior officer present shall, if time and circumstances permit, exchange official visits with both the senior diplomatic representative and the senior consular representative. When practicable, prior notice of his arrival in port and the probable duration of stay shall be given to such representative. A suitable boat shall be furnished for making official visits.

Officers of the naval service shall make the first visit to the chief of a diplomatic mission of or above the rank of chargé d'affaires. (NR 2146)

In the exchange of visits with consular representatives, officers in the naval service shall make or receive the first visit in accordance with their relative precedence as given in the following table.

Official	Takes precedence
Chief of a United States diplomatic mission, including a Chargé d'Affaires*	Over any officer of the armed services of the United States; and over any United States civil official, except the Secretary of State, whose official salute is less than 21 guns
Career Minister	With, but before, Commodore or Brigadier General
Counselor First Secretary, when no Counselor is assigned Consul General; or Consul or Vice-Consul, when in charge of a Consulate General First Secretary, when a Counselor is assigned	With, but after, Brigadier General or Commodore
Consul, or Vice-Consul, when in charge of a Consulate Second Secretary	With, but after, Captain in the Navy
Vice-Consul Third Secretary Consular Agent	With, but after, Lieutenant in the Navy

Governors of United States Territories and Possessions. See the Navy Regulations, Article 2147.

Foreign Officials and Officers. The senior officer present shall make official visits to foreign officials and officers as custom and courtesy demand.

When in doubt as to what foreign officials and officers are to be visited, saluted, or otherwise honored, or as to the rank of any official or officer, or whether a gun salute involving a return will be returned, the senior officer present shall send an officer to obtain the required information.

The following rules, in which the maritime powers generally have concurred, shall be observed by officers of the naval service, and their observance by foreign officers may be expected:

1. The senior officer present shall, upon the arrival of foreign warships, send an officer to call upon the officer in command of the arriving

* An acting chief of a United States diplomatic mission, when holding the title of Chargé d'Affaires, takes precedence as specified in this table, but shall be accorded the honors specified for a Chargé d'Affaires on the occasion of an official visit.

FIGURE 504. Rendering honors after a change-of-command ceremony.

ships to offer customary courtesies and exchange information as appropriate; except that in a foreign port such call shall be made only if the officer in command of the arriving ships is the senior officer present of his nation. This call will be returned at once.

2. Within 24 hours after arrival, the senior officer in command of arriving ships shall, if he be the senior officer present of his nation, make an official visit to the senior officer present of each foreign nation who holds a grade equal to or superior to his; and the senior officer present of each foreign nation who holds a grade junior to his will make an official visit to him within the same time limit.

3. After the interchange of visits between the senior officers previously specified, other flag officers in command and the commanding officers of ships arriving shall exchange official visits, when appropriate, with the flag and commanding officers of ships present. An arriving officer shall make the first visits to officers present who hold grades equal or superior to his and shall receive the first visits from others.

4. It is customary for calls to be exchanged by committees of Wardroom officers of the ships of different nations present, in the order in which their respective commanding officers have exchanged visits.

5. Should another officer become the senior officer present of a nation, he shall exchange official visits with foreign senior officers present as prescribed in this article. (NR 2148)

513. PROCEDURE FOR RENDERING HONORS AFLOAT. The honors prescribed for an official visit shall be rendered on arrival as follows:

1. When the rail is manned, men shall be uniformly spaced at the rail on each weather deck, facing outboard.

2. "Attention" shall be sounded as the visitor's boat or vehicle approaches the ship.

3. The boat or vehicle shall be piped as it comes alongside.

4. The visitor shall be piped over the side, and all persons on the quarterdeck shall salute and the guard shall present arms until the termination of the pipe, flourishes, music, or gun salute, whichever shall be the last rendered.

5. The prescribed flag or pennant shall be broken as the visitor reaches the quarterdeck and salutes the colors.

6. The piping of the side, the ruffles and flourishes, the music, and the gun salute shall be rendered in the order named. In the absence of a band, "To the Colors" shall be sounded by bugle in lieu of the National Anthem, when required.

7. The visitor, if entitled to 11 guns or more, shall be invited to inspect the guard upon completion of the gun salute or such other honors as may be rendered.

The honors prescribed for an official visit shall be rendered on departure as follows:

1. The rail shall be manned, if required.

2. "Attention" shall be sounded as the visitor arrives on the quarterdeck.

3. At the end of leave taking, the guard shall present arms, all persons on the quarterdeck shall salute, and the ruffles and flourishes, followed by the music, shall be rendered. As the visitor enters the line of side boys, he shall be piped over the side. The salute and present arms shall terminate with the pipe, and, unless a gun salute is to be fired, a flag or pennant displayed in honor of the visitor shall be hauled down.

4. The boat or vehicle shall be piped away from the side.

5. If a gun salute is prescribed on departure, it shall be fired when the visitor is clear of the side and the flag or pennant displayed in honor of the visitor shall be hauled down with the last gun of the salute.

The same honors and ceremonies as for an official visit to a ship of the Navy shall be rendered, insofar as practicable and appropriate, on the occasion of an official visit to a naval station. (NR 2151)

514. RETURNING OFFICIAL VISITS OR CALLS. An official visit shall be returned within 24 hours, when practicable.

A flag or general officer shall, circumstances permitting, return the official visits of officers of the grade of captain in the Navy or senior thereto and of officials of corresponding grade. He may send his chief of staff to return other official visits.

Officers other than flag or general officers shall personally return all official calls.

Flag and general officers may expect official visits to be returned in person by foreign governors, officers, and other high officials except chiefs of state. Other officers may expect such visits to be returned by suitable representatives.

Calls made by juniors upon seniors in the naval service shall be returned as courtesy requires and circumstances permit; calls made by persons not in the naval service shall be returned.

515. SIDE HONORS, SIDE BOYS, AND GUARD AND BAND. On the arrival and departure of civil officials and foreign officers, and of United States officers when so directed by the senior officer present, the side shall be piped and the appropriate number of side boys paraded.

Officers appropriate to the occasion shall attend the side on the arrival and departure of officials and officers. (NR 2153)

Side boys shall not be paraded on Sunday, or on other days between sunset and 0800, or during meal hours of the crew, general drills and evolutions, and periods of regular overhaul, except in honor of civil officials or foreign officers, when they may be paraded at any time during daylight.

Except for official visits and other formal occasions, side boys shall not be paraded in honor of officers of the armed services of the United States, unless otherwise directed by the senior officer present.

Side boys shall not be paraded in honor of an officer of the armed services in civilian clothes, unless such officer is at the time acting in an official civil capacity.

The side shall be piped when side boys are paraded, but not at other times.

The guard and band shall not be paraded in honor of the arrival or departure of an individual at times when side boys in his honor are dispensed with. (NR 2154)

Display of the National Ensign, Personal Flags, and Pennants

516. NATIONAL ENSIGN AND JACK, AFLOAT. When not underway, the national ensign and the union jack shall be displayed from 0800 un-

The flag on a crossed staff.   The flag on a horizontal staff.

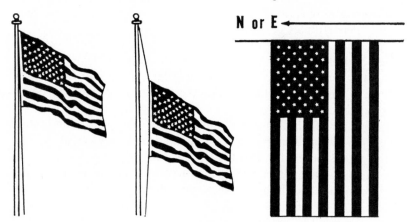

The flag at half-mast.   The flag over a street.

FIGURE 505. Correct methods of displaying the National Ensign.

til sunset from the flagstaff and the jack staff, respectively. The union jack shall be the size of the union of the national ensign.

A ship which enters port at night shall, when appropriate, display the national ensign from the gaff at daylight for a time sufficient to establish her nationality; it is customary for other ships of war to display their national ensigns in return. The national ensign, union jack, and personal flags and pennants shall be displayed from ships and craft of the Navy, in or out of service or commission, in accordance with rules laid down in Navy Regulations, Article 2163.

The national ensign shall be displayed during daylight from the gaff of a ship underway under the following circumstances, unless or as otherwise directed by the senior officer present:

1. Getting underway and coming to anchor.
2. Falling in with other ships.
3. Cruising near land.
4. During battle. (NR 2163)

On board ship or at a command ashore, upon all occasions of hoisting, lowering, or half-masting the national ensign, the motions of the senior officer present shall be followed, except as prescribed for answering a dip or firing a gun salute (NR 2169). It is customary for the senior officer present, at 0745, to make a preparatory signal, giving the size of the colors to be hoisted.

517. AT COMMANDS ASHORE. The national ensign is displayed from 0800 to sunset near the headquarters of every command ashore, or at the headquarters of the senior commander when the proximity of head-quarters of two or more commands makes the display of separate ensigns inappropriate. When an outlying activity of a command is so located that its government character is not clearly indicated by the display of the national ensign as prescribed, the national ensign shall also be displayed at that activity. (NR 2164)

518. IN BOATS. The national ensign shall be displayed from water-borne boats of the naval service:

1. When underway during daylight in a foreign port.
2. When ships are required to be dressed or full-dressed.
3. When going alongside a foreign vessel.
4. When an officer or official is embarked on an official occasion.
5. When a flag or general officer, a unit commander, a commanding officer, or a chief of staff, in uniform, is embarked in a boat of his command or in one assigned to his personal use.
6. At such other times as may be prescribed by the senior officer present afloat (SOPA). (NR 2166)

519. DURING GUN SALUTES. A ship of the Navy shall display the national ensign at a masthead while firing a salute in honor of a United States anniversary or official, as follows:

1. At the main during the national salute prescribed for February 22 and July 4.
2. At the main during a 21-gun salute to a United States civil official, except by a ship which is displaying the personal flag of the official being saluted.

During a gun salute, the national ensign shall remain displayed from the gaff or the flagstaff, in addition to the display at the main or fore. (NR 2165)

520. DIPPING THE NATIONAL ENSIGN. When any vessel, under the United States registry or the registry of a nation formally recognized by the government of the United States, salutes a ship of the Navy by dipping her ensign, it shall be answered dip for dip. If not already being displayed, the national ensign shall be hoisted for the purpose of answering the dip. An ensign being displayed at half-mast shall be hoisted to the truck or peak before a dip is answered.

No ship of the Navy shall dip the national ensign unless in return for such compliment.

Of the colors carried by a naval force on shore, only the battalion or regimental colors shall be dipped in rendering or acknowledging a salute. (NR 2167)

521. HALF-MASTING THE NATIONAL ENSIGN AND THE UNION JACK. In half-masting the national ensign it shall, if not previously hoisted, first be hoisted to the truck or peak and then lowered to half-mast. Before lowering from half-mast, the ensign shall be hoisted to the truck or peak and then lowered.

When the national ensign is half-masted, the union jack, if displayed from the jack staff, shall likewise be half-masted.

Personal flags, command pennants, and commission pennants shall not be displayed at half-mast except as prescribed in the Regulations for a deceased official or officer. (NR 2168)

522. MORNING AND EVENING COLORS. The following ceremonies are observed at colors on board ships in commission:

The guard of the day and the band are present, if available. At morning colors, "Attention" is sounded on the bugle. This is followed by the playing of the National Anthem by the band, at the beginning of which the ensign is started up and hoisted smartly to peak or truck. All officers and men face the ensign and render the salute required, and the guard of the day and sentries under arms come to the position of present arms while the National Anthem is being played. In the absence of a band, "To the Colors" is sounded on the bugle. In the absence of a bugle, "Attention" is sounded by other appropriate means and the procedure prescribed is followed during the raising or lowering of the ensign. Subsequent to "The Star-Spangled Banner," honors to

FIGURE 506. Morning colors aboard the *USS Josephus Daniels* (DLG-27).

foreign ensigns are rendered, at morning colors only, by the band playing the appropriate foreign national anthem. The salute and present
arms terminate with the sounding of "Carry on."

The same ceremonies are observed at sunset, the ensign being started from the peak or truck at the beginning of the National Anthem and the lowering so regulated as to be completed at the last note. In the absence of a band, "Retreat" is sounded on the bugle.

The same ceremonies are observed, insofar as may be practicable, at naval stations.

523. DISTINCTIVE MARK OF A NAVAL VESSEL. The distinctive mark of a ship or craft of the Navy in commission shall be a personal flag or command pennant of an officer of the Navy, or a commission pennant. The distinctive mark of a hospital ship of the Navy, in commission in time of war, shall be a Red Cross flag. Not more than one distinctive mark shall be displayed by a ship or craft at one time, nor shall the commission pennant and the personal flag of a civil official be displayed at one time. (NR 2163)

524. PERSONAL FLAGS AND PENNANTS AFLOAT. Except as otherwise prescribed in the Regulations, a flag officer or a unit commander afloat shall display his personal flag or command pennant from his flagship. At no time shall he display it from more than one ship.

When a flag officer eligible for command at sea is embarked for passage in a ship of the Navy, his personal flag shall be displayed from such ship, unless there is already displayed from such ship the flag of an officer his senior.

When a civil official, in whose honor the display of a personal flag is prescribed during an official visit, is embarked for passage in a ship of the Navy, his personal flag shall be displayed from such ship.

A personal flag or command pennant may be hauled down during battle or at any time when the officer concerned, or the senior officer present, considers that it is desirable thus to render a flagship less distinguishable. When hauled down, it shall be replaced with a commission pennant.

An officer of the Navy commanding a ship engaged otherwise than in the service of the United States shall not display a personal flag, command pennant, or commission pennant from such ship, or in the bow of a boat. (NR 2170)

For further information on the display of personal flags and pennants afloat, ashore, and in boats and automobiles, consult Navy Regulations, Articles 2171 to 2179.

Ceremonies

525. TYPES OF CEREMONIES ASHORE. The Navy and Marine Corps have eight military ceremonies in which the young officer may become

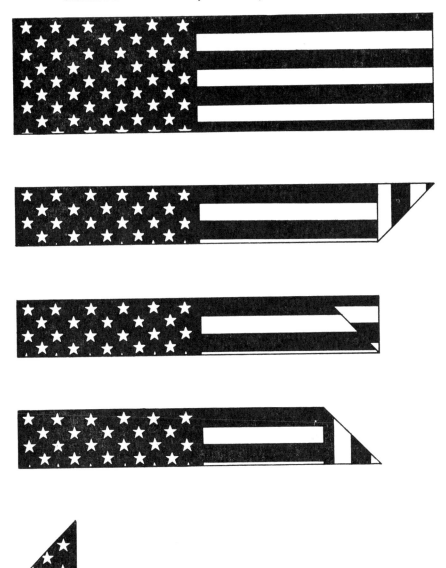

FIGURE 507. Folding the National Ensign.

involved when serving at shore stations. These ceremonies are conducted in the manner described in appropriate articles of the Landing Party Manual. See also paragraphs 1822-25 of the *Marine Officer's Guide,* published by the United States Naval Institute.

A Review is a ceremony at which a command parades for inspection in honor of a senior officer other than its commander.

Presentation of Awards follows, in part, the procedure prescribed for a review, except that the individuals being decorated receive the review.

A Parade is the ceremony at which the commanding officer of a battalion or larger unit forms and drills his entire command, and then has them pass in review. The battalion parade is the most common form of ceremony on shore.

Escort of the National Colors is known in the Marine Corps as "Marching on (or off) the Colors." When the colors are to take part in a ceremony, they are ceremonially received by a picked escort and escorted from their place of safekeeping, and similarly returned.

Escort of Honor is the ceremonial escorting of a senior officer or other dignitary during an official visit, or upon arrival or departure.

Military Funeral ceremonial is probably the most ancient in the profession of arms.

FIGURE 508. A military funeral at Arlington.

Inspection of Troops is a ceremony having as its object the determination of the general military appearance and condition of the individual uniform and equipment of a command.

Guard Mounting is the ceremony in which a guard is organized, is inspected before assuming the guard, and relieves an outgoing guard.

Morning and Evening Colors have been described in Section 522.

526. PRECEDENCE IN PARADES OR CEREMONIES. Members of the armed forces of the United States shall take precedence in the following order during formations in which the members may participate:

1. Cadets, United States Military Academy.
2. Midshipmen, United States Naval Academy.
3. Cadets, United States Coast Guard Academy.
4. Cadets, United States Air Force Academy.
5. United States Army.
6. United States Marine Corps.
7. United States Navy.

FIGURE 509. Pass in review.

8. United States Air Force.
9. United States Coast Guard.
10. Army National Guard of the United States.
11. Army Reserve.
12. Marine Corps Reserve.
13. Naval Reserve.
14. Air National Guard of the United States.
15. Air Force Reserve.
16. Coast Guard Reserve.
17. Other training organizations of the Army, Marine Corps, Navy, Air Force, and Coast Guard in that order, respectively.

Notes: 1. During any period when the United States Coast Guard is operating as a part of the United States Navy, the Cadets, U. S. Coast Guard Academy, the United States Coast Guard, and the Coast Guard Reserve shall take precedence, respectively, next after the Midshipmen, U. S. Naval Academy, the United States Navy, and the Naval Reserve.

2. Veterans and other patriotic organizations follow after item 16 or 17 in the order prescribed by the grand marshal of the parade.

3. The place of honor is the head of column or right of line. When a ceremony is conducted by U. S. forces or on U. S. territory, foreign units should be assigned that post of honor in alphabetical order of nationalities ahead of U. S. forces.

527. COMMISSIONING AND ASSUMING COMMAND. The commissioning ceremony is not prescribed specifically by Navy Regulations, but custom has established a uniform procedure which is formal and impressive. By the appointed time, the crew is assembled on the quarterdeck, stern or other open area, usually in two ranks facing inboard. Officers assemble in two ranks athwartship facing aft. A band and Marine or seaman guard forms to starboard of the ceremonial area. Distinguished guests and principal participants are seated aft facing forward. If space permits, guests of the officers and crew are seated behind the distinguished guests, otherwise in other appropriate nearby areas or in seats placed on the adjacent pier. The first watch, including the Officer of the Deck, is assembled on the quarterdeck. Quartermasters are stationed at national ensign, jack, and commission pennant or flag officer's flag halliards.

The Naval District Commandant or other officer effecting the transfer opens the ceremony by reading his orders for delivery of the ship. "Attention" is then sounded on the bugle, the National Anthem is played, and the ensign, jack, and commission pennant or flag officer's flag are hoisted simultaneously. The ship is officially commissioned with this act.

The Commandant or other officer effecting the transfer delivers the ship to the Commanding Officer by saying, "I hereby deliver the U.S.S. *Blake*." The officer ordered to command the ship reads his orders from the Chief of Naval Personnel and states, "I hereby assume command of the U.S.S. *Blake*," and orders the Executive Officer to "set the watch." The Executive Officer in turn directs the Officer of the Deck to set the watch, and the ship's Boatswain (or Chief Boatswain's Mate on small ships) pipes the watch. The Officer of the Deck and the other members of the watch take stations.

The Commanding Officer customarily makes a short speech touching on the work of the building yard, the name of the ship, the history of any previous ships of the same name, and other items of interest.

If the state, city, or sponsor has a presentation of silver, or other gift to make, this portion of the ceremony then takes place, and the

Commanding Officer makes an additional speech of appreciation on behalf of the Navy Department, himself, and his officers and men. This may be followed by a speech by the special guest of honor. The ceremony is completed with a benediction by the ship or yard chaplain.

It is usually customary, particularly in peacetime, for the officers and crew to be provided with formal invitations which they may use to invite family and friends to the ceremony. After the ceremony, a reception, or lunch, is usually held simultaneously in the Wardroom, C.P.O. mess and crews' mess to entertain the guests.

The entire ceremony is a very impressive occasion and serves as a fitting entry of the ship into the United States Navy as a living entity.

528. CEREMONY OF TURNOVER OF COMMAND. The Navy Regulations provide that "A commanding officer about to be relieved of his command shall, at the time of turning over command, call all hands to muster. The officer about to be relieved shall read his orders of detachment and turn over the command to his successor, who shall read his orders and assume command."

FIGURE 510. Change of command ceremony for an embarked flag officer aboard an aircraft carrier.

In a large ship, this ceremony is quite formal; in the small ship, the ceremony is relatively simple. All hands are called to Quarters at the appointed hour. The crew usually forms in two fore and aft ranks, equally divided on either side of the fantail or weather deck as far outboard as possible, and facing inboard. Officers form in a rank or ranks athwartships as far aft as possible, facing forward. Chairs are placed for distinguished guests and others in the area enclosed by these ranks. A lectern and suitable public address facilities are provided. A quartermaster mans a telephone at some location where he can observe the ceremony and can still communicate with the signal bridge. The uniform should be full dress, blue or white, with swords. Officer guests usually wear service dress, blue or white, without swords.

When the Executive Officer reports the crew at Quarters, the retiring Commanding Officer and his relief proceed to the area together. If the retiring Commanding Officer wishes to say a few words to the crew that he is leaving, this is the proper time. After a *brief* speech, he should publish his orders of detachment to the officers and crew. He should then step back. The new Commanding Officer steps forward and publishes his orders to command, after which it is appropriate to face about, salute the retiring Commanding Officer, and say, "I relieve you, sir."

At this time a new commission pennant is hoisted and broken, and the old pennant is lowered, brought to the area, and presented to the retiring Commanding Officer by the Chief Quartermaster.

The retiring Commanding Officer should then step back an appropriate distance so as to be able to observe the remainder of the ceremony, but to take no further part in it. At this point, some new commanding officers like to state briefly their policies. The best opinion holds that this is not a good time for him to make a speech. It is better to let his actions speak for him. It is not inappropriate for him to state that, for the present, he intends to carry out the policies of the former commanding officer and that all orders issued by him remain in full force and effect until canceled or modified. He should then turn to the Executive Officer and order "Pipe down." The ceremony is over, and he is now Commanding Officer of the good ship *Blake*.

In the event there is no permanent commanding officer for you to relieve, the ceremony should be conducted in just as formal and official a manner as described above with certain necessary modifications.

529. PRESENTATION OF AWARDS. For this ceremony the crew is usually formed as for change of command ceremony. Those receiving awards form in a single rank in front of the lectern. The Executive Officer usually calls each recipient forward by announcing his name. The recipient then marches to a point one pace in front of the lectern and salutes. The Commanding Officer then reads the citation or letter. The Executive Officer hands him the medal, if one is involved, and the Commanding Officer then pins it on the recipient. The Commanding Officer hands the original copy of the citation to the recipient with his left hand and shakes hands with the recipient with his right hand. The recipient then salutes and returns to his place in rank. Some commanding officers prefer to make a few informal remarks either before or after reading the citation, and flag officers may have an aide read the citation.

Upon completion of the last award the ceremony is completed and the crew is piped down. On shore stations the awards ceremony is usually made a part of a parade ceremony.

CHAPTER 6

Leading the American Bluejacket

Naval Leadership

601. LEADERSHIP. *Naval Leadership* is the art of accomplishing the Mission of the Navy through its people, both officer and enlisted; it embodies those qualities of intellect, human understanding and moral character which enable a man to inspire, to lead, and to manage successfully a group of other persons. Being a highly personal accomplishment, effective leadership is soundly based on personal example, an understanding and execution of good management practices, and moral responsibility of the leader.

The naval profession, which you have joined, is an honorable one which has long commanded the respect and affection of our fellow countrymen. To maintain and extend this regard, as well as to meet the requirements of his own conscience, a naval leader must always exhibit in himself an example of the high military ideals of our Navy.

The United States Navy has long been distinguished for the high quality of its officers and men, a quality which we must never let dim or lose its luster. In difficult times of war or quasi-war, as well as in peace, the opportunity is ever with us to maintain and to raise the standards of naval leadership. With the infinitely more powerful weapons which science is giving us, how much more important becomes the character, the moral spirit, and the determination of the men who man those weapons!

The eternal verities of leadership have always been recognized and

140

honored in the United States Navy. From the earliest days of the Continental Navy, officers have been exhorted to exhibit the essential military qualities of loyalty, tact, patience, justice, firmness, simplicity, self-control, and charity. In his relations with his subordinates, the naval commander has ever been advised to maintain such an attitude of proper reserve as will protect his dignity and authority, and yet will not inhibit a natural cordiality or discourage his juniors from expressing their views freely or from asking his opinion without reserve. Thus will he promote good discipline and an elevated spirit in the command.

On the character of the naval officer, Commodore John Paul Jones wrote:

> None other than a Gentleman, as well as a Seaman both in Theory and in Practice is qualified to support the Character of a Commission Officer in the Navy, nor is any Man fit to Command a Ship of War, who is not also capable of communicating his Ideas on Paper in Language that becomes his Rank.

John Paul Jones was himself given the following excellent advice by Benjamin Franklin:

> Hereafter, if you should observe an occasion to give your officers and friends a little more praise than is their due, and confess more fault than you can justly be charged with, you will only become the sooner for it, a great captain. Criticising and censuring almost everyone you have to do with, will diminish friends, increase enemies, and thereby hurt your affairs.

The traditionally high standards of behavior and performance of duty in the Navy must be maintained. The naval leader must dominate the many factors which complicate handling personnel today and, despite all other distracting obligations, he must accomplish the proper training and indoctrination of his men.

He must never forget that the *purpose* of every ship and organization in the Navy is to prepare for combat and to engage in combat successfully. To accomplish this purpose, a true leader must exert his influence upon his men so as to reduce boredom and fatigue, relieve hunger and physical discomfort, and inspire personal pride in the organization, to the end that his officers and men will produce as a team in combat.

602. THE NAVAL OFFICER AS A LEADER. In any military organization, a leader will always be one who goes before to show his followers the way he wishes them to proceed, succeeds in endowing them with his spirit by his sincere interest in their welfare and by the qualities of his leadership, so that they will execute his will, comply with his demands, be eager to learn his wishes, and carry out his orders cheerfully, willingly, even blindly.

As Ensign George Gay said, of his Skipper of Torpedo Squadron Eight at the Battle of Midway, "I know that, if I had it to do all over again, I'd follow him through exactly the same thing. We did the things he wanted us to do, not because he was our boss, but because we felt that, if we did the things he wanted us to do, it was the right thing to do."

His Skipper, Commander J. C. Waldron, had acquired those touchstones of leadership—enthusiasm, a desire for service, a selfless devotion to duty—which inspired his officers and men to follow him to the end of the road because they knew instinctively that it would be "the right thing to do." By the study of the lives of effective leaders and of the teachings of psychology and sociology, it is the task of the naval officer to acquire that inspirational quality of good leadership which causes men to follow along in his wake and to work enthusiastically for the ultimate goal of all military organizations—victory in combat.

Leadership among all ranks and ratings is a very personal thing. Some men have naturally winning personalities, which draw others to them as if by magnetic attraction. Other personalities vary all the way from magnetic to repellent. If your personality is not so very winning, you can work on it, try to change it. Some men succeed. More often, you are apt so to confuse yourself that you will end up not knowing *what* you are. If you do not have a magnetic personality, there is not much use trying to create a synthetic one. Accept your personality as it is, an inherent part of you, and try to work with it on that basis. A straightforward, consistent sundowner is much better to work for than an officer who is saintly sweet reason one day and the devil incarnate the next. As far as possible, adopt a calm, judicious manner in all your official contacts, meeting all of your associates with the same quiet, impartial attitude.

Through the centuries, certain attributes of personality and character have appeared over and over again in the persons of the great military leaders. Perhaps leadership cannot be taught, *but it can be learned.* Study leadership earnestly, not only as a junior officer, but all your life in the service—study the lives of great leaders, the psychology of human behavior, leadership in industry and in the military services. Study always in the great school of experience—so that you will *acquire an understanding* of the attributes which men have always admired in their leaders and *recognize* the basic stimuli which move men to proper action. These are the bricks with which you can build your military character.*

Combat readiness requires that all persons in authority observe in themselves the standards of moral behavior and devotion to duty which will "guard against and suppress all dissolute and immoral practices" and, in the words of the Navy Regulations, "promote and safeguard the morale, the physical well-being, and the general welfare of the officers and enlisted persons under their command or charge." The key to successful naval leadership is personal attention and supervision based on moral responsibility.

603. MORAL RESPONSIBILITY. The most essential ingredient of leadership is the maintenance of moral standards and the teaching of moral values. Leadership in this sense is that aspect of personnel management which involves ethics as related to behavior. It stresses responsibility of the individual to the Navy, to our country, and to himself, and the adherence to those standards of conduct and behavior which have always been inherent in our civilization. Of moral responsibility, Admiral Arleigh Burke has said:

> America's most important role in the world, almost from the day our country was born, has been the role of moral leadership. . . . Teach our young people to believe in the responsibility of one to another; their responsibility to God; to the peoples of the world. Teach them to believe in themselves; to believe in their worth as human beings; to believe in their place in leading the world out of the darkness of oppression. Teach them to believe that no one owes us a living, but that we owe much to others. Teach them to believe in the priceless heritage of freedom, and that it must be won anew by every generation. And teach them to believe in the United States of America. The hope of the world lies here, in our physical power, our moral strength, our integrity, and our will to assume the responsibilities that history plainly intends us to bear.

Vulgarity and cheapening of moral standards inevitably result in the lowering of the morale of a command and lead to the undermining of legitimate authority. The protection and enhancement of moral standards is the responsibility of the commanding officer of every ship and station, but other officers and petty officers must assume their fair share of this essential responsibility. A leadership program has been instituted which has as its aim to build leadership on its real foundation, moral responsibility, and to forge on that base a tool which will improve combat readiness. Although this program for improvement

* See Professional Reading (page 548) for a list of recommended books on leadership.

FIGURE 601. The Navy Chaplain is the moral and religious teacher
for the Navy and Marine Corps.

of moral leadership and character education was originally developed
by Navy Chaplains, it is actually a Line Officer program and a very
personal and individual responsibility for every officer and petty officer. The program includes command attention to:

  a. The personal example of behavior and performance set by officers.

  b. The moral atmosphere of the command.

  c. The current standards of personal supervision of men, both in
regard to management effectiveness and the development of moral
responsibility.

  The Command Responsibility. The Commanding Officer of a ship
or station has been given the responsibility—

to *protect* moral standards by suppressing all influences detrimental to the moral and spiritual welfare of personnel;

to *develop* moral standards through group instruction and personal interview;

to *promote* the realization of moral, spiritual, and religious values, consistent with the religious beliefs of the individual concerned;

to *be concerned* with the off-duty and recreational activities of personnel;

to *cooperate* with agencies which may contribute to the moral and spiritual welfare of personnel.

The Commanding Officer is charged with carrying out his responsibility by exhibiting in himself the traditional good characteristics of virtue, honor, patriotism and subordination so that he may by his own example influence his subordinate leaders to set a good example for their men.

Subordinate Officers' Responsibility.   Certain subordinate officers are specifically charged with important responsibilities for contributing materially to the establishment and conduct of an adequate program.

The Chaplain is the chief adviser to the Commanding Officer on moral and religious matters. He is recognized as a key officer in promoting the advancement of moral, spiritual, and religious values among the officers and enlisted personnel.

The Special Services Officer has the major responsibility for the off-duty activities of all personnel. In carrying out his duties in this regard, he must recognize that he works with the "free time" of military personnel and, like the Chaplain, he must depend upon making a voluntary appeal with his program.

The Educational Services Officer, in addition to his duties of assisting the planning board for training, has a large share of the responsibility for carrying out specific parts of the commanding officers' continuing program to promote improvement in moral standards and in the advancement of character education. He does this by organizing and supervising off-duty classes in subjects germane to the over-all plan. He should also provide cultural leadership in the command so as to help the individual to become aware of that dimension in his life in which he gives expression to certain of his spiritual capacities.

The Medical Officer, in addition to his particular concern for the physical health of personnel, must also concern himself with the mental, emotional, moral and spiritual problems of all personnel of a command. He will carry out these responsibilities in formal lectures, informal discussion, in general dissemination of information, and in treatment, advice, and counsel.

The Personnel Officer, Legal Officer, and Public Affairs Officer are in key positions to keep the Commanding Officer informed on the special responsibilities of their offices and to take a personal interest in the needs of all personnel as individuals within the areas of their specialized duties.

Division Officer's Responsibility. The Division Officer, and indeed each of his junior officers, has a paramount and direct responsibility in the line channel of command. It follows that he also has personal responsibility to develop the moral responsibility of his men. In constant association with his men as he supervises their work, he is, as well, the bridge between the command and its men. His prime responsibilities in this area march along closely with his duties of education, training, supervision, and correction of his men, but must be accompanied by a keen personal interest in each individual of his unit and a personal example of living in accordance with the highest principles in his own moral and spiritual life. If the Division Officer and his enlisted leaders fail in this respect, the morale, indeed the *moral tone* of the whole command, will correspondingly suffer.

President Eisenhower, in an address to the graduating class at the Naval Academy, has said:

> Because of the threat imposed by a militant and aggressive atheism, I believe that the strengthening of all phases of our moral and spiritual foundations has a profound significance for the actual security of our nation.
>
> Basic to our democratic civilization are the principles and convictions that have bound us together as a nation. Among these are personal liberty, human rights, and the dignity of man. All these have their roots in deeply held religious faith—in a belief in God. . . . The stronger we become spiritually, the safer our civilization.
>
> Each must truly understand these spiritual values, and have the will to nurture and strengthen them—to defend and protect them against all enemies, foreign and domestic. Nothing can be more effective in assuring our ability to continue to live the lives of a free people.

Much of what follows in this chapter will deal with the moral responsibility of the young officer. He should also become familiar with his duties in this regard by a thorough study of the United States Naval Leadership Manual (NavPers 15934A).

604. PERFORMANCE OF DUTY. In our Navy, the only acceptable standard is performance of duty to the limit of one's ability. The standards, which we strive to maintain with integrity, are very high, but they are attainable and they are equitable. Not all may become outstanding leaders, but perfection is a goal for which you must strive.

Learn to accept responsibility. With experience, your capacity will increase. By degrees, you will be given more important duties. Your responsibility for your current assignment is a continuing function. Only with death, or passing on to the inactive list, can you, as an officer, ever feel wholly free from responsibility and the problems, worries, and care which it brings in its train.

You will find your brother officers an honorable, friendly group. When you join a new ship, they will welcome you as a shipmate and a messmate. They will honor you by assuming that you know your job and intend to do it well. Your uniform will gain you an entrée into this body, but it will be your character and personality, your ability and energy and courage which will earn you the friendship and esteem of these officers, your new shipmates, and the respect and admiration of the bluejackets with whom you will work.

What you need to know is the way to go about becoming a naval officer whom your shipmates, both officer and enlisted, will esteem. This depends in some measure upon your personality, but to a greater extent upon your character. There is a healthy competition among naval officers for recognition as an able officer and for the respect of their brother officers. Whether you strive for it or not, there is one thing you will soon acquire, a *service reputation*. Be sure that yours is one of which you will be proud! To ensure this requires energy, intelligence, and courage—courage not only in battle, but also the courage to do your everyday tasks well.

Do not become impatient. Like other important careers, the naval profession requires a long apprenticeship. Only to a few, favored by opportunity, do recognition and promotion come early. There is much to learn, and the time is short. Therefore, do not be afraid of work. Look for things to do. Do not count as wasted the time spent on any small task from which you learn something of value. Good leadership is made up of a lot of little things. The capacity for hard work and the willingness to perform it are important among them.

Do not expect to be told how to do each little task. In the Navy, you can expect to be told *what* to do but not *how* to do it. You will be receiving *orders*, not *instructions*.

Act on your own initiative. *Do not wait to be told.* Lord Nelson wrote from Egypt, "To do nothing was disgraceful; therefore I made use of my understanding." So should you look for things to do, within the field of your own operations. Do something. The junior officer who early acquires a good service reputation is not afraid of work. He makes himself useful to his immediate superiors

Yet this is not enough. You must keep on producing. Your seniors are not interested in your past. Your antecedents, your fine reputation from previous duty, your good connections in the Navy are of concern to your seniors only insofar as they indicate your probable future performance of duty in your present assignment. The best advice that can be given is: Do your job well. Let results tell your efficiency. Do not talk about your accomplishments any more than you can help. The fitness reports will take care of themselves (see Chapter 7).

Remember that your Navy is administered on the theory that there are few geniuses in the field of modern naval warfare. Most naval officers are ordinary men. Some are brighter than others. There is no penalty for brilliance. But even if you are an ordinary man of ordinary intelligence, hew to the line, concentrate on the attainment of your specific objective, put aside all distracting considerations, work hard, and you will help achieve your goal.

Do not set yourself above your fellows. When an officer concludes that he is something special, above and beyond his shipmates, it is exceedingly difficult to keep this opinion to himself. There is a wide gap between the proper self-confidence of an able officer and the self-pride of a fool.

A disciplined ambition, an accurate evaluation of your capabilities, self-confidence, skill in the use of the tools of your craft, a reasoned intelligence, daring without rashness—these are characteristics that you are encouraged to develop. *But avoid a foolish conceit*. Thus you can win through to that fine service reputation for which you strive, but you can acquire it only if you truly earn it.

605. POSITIVE LEADERSHIP. The effective naval leader is one who inspires his men to constructive effort through a thorough knowledge of his job and a knowledge and understanding of his men. He is loyal both to his subordinates and to his seniors, and is impartial in his dealings with his men. He can accept responsibility and also delegate authority to his juniors. He uses initiative to accomplish what needs to be done and makes necessary decisions promptly. He constantly exhibits a concern for his men and looks out for their welfare. And finally, he possesses a high level of individual moral courage.

When faced with a problem, a good leader first obtains a clear understanding of the nature of the problem; remains mentally calm so that he can use his understanding to decide how to solve the problem; and finally uses his talents of communication to put his objective across to his men so clearly that each individual of his command will identify himself with his leader's wishes as their common goal. It is this last quality of leadership that is so vitally important. So conduct yourself that the men of your outfit will *want* to do what they have been told. The skill of positive leadership is so to apply your knowledge and talent that your orders, commands, even your unexpressed wishes are carried into effect with a maximum of effectiveness and a minimum of confusion. Of a really effective leader, it can be said, "His every suggestion was to his men as if they had been given a command."

Man is impressed or convinced principally by what he hears or sees. In your speech, your orders, commands, or suggestions, be concise and positive, without pompousness or condescension. Don't shout. Don't be common. Vulgarity, profanity, obscenity are the mark of the deficient personality, incapable of expressing himself in other than the most ordinary and inadequate terms.

During World War II, a young officer was overheard to say about his Executive Officer in a destroyer, "Just look at him! He always looks as if he had just come out of a shower, freshly shaved, and put on clean khaki. As for me, I melt down into a mess five minutes after I change my shirt."

That lieutenant commander had a reputation for always looking neat, even under the most difficult operating conditions "in a sealed-up tin-can" in the tropics. His junior was impressed by his ability to maintain a fine military appearance under all conditions.

Another destroyer had just been through a series of harrowing experiences in a dark night up the Slot. The Skipper had quietly done the things that had to be done and was relaxing on a wing of the bridge. One of his young officers came up on the bridge and reported a serious casualty that endangered the safety of the ship. The Skipper took it quite calmly, called the Officer of the Deck and told him in a low tone of voice what to do. The younger officer stared at his Skipper's hunched form for a long moment. "I don't see how you can take it so calmly. I really don't."

The Skipper smiled to himself in the darkness, for he was really shaking inwardly from his recent experiences, but his outward manner had convinced the younger officer that all was well. "Go down and shore up the collision bulkhead, Joe," he said, softly. "We've got to contain that flooding."

The younger officer muttered something under his breath. "I don't see why the Boss sent us up the Slot tonight—we didn't have a chance."

"He had his reasons—good reasons," the Skipper replied. "Go on down now. You can do it. We'll make it home all right."

The Skipper was a leader, demonstrating almost unconsciously his belief in the work he was doing, the rightness of his cause, and his trust and confidence in his senior and his subordinates. He richly deserved the relationship of mutual loyalty, confidence, and respect which he had built up within his command.

While such a captain confidently accepts the word of his subordinates, he would be ruthless in relieving them from duty or having them disrated if he learned that they were undeserving of his trust. Doubtless he delegated to his subordinate officers and petty officers the full authority they required to carry out their duties and gave them the privileges of their positions. He could be friendly enough to call the young officer, Joe, but he was not so close to him that he could not correct his criticism of the Boss. And there was never any doubt in the minds of the younger officers in that ship who was in command. They admired their Skipper, not only for his professional competence, but also for his moral courage. They recognized him as a man of integrity. They knew that they could depend on him to make the right decisions when the going was rough. When it came time to turn over his command to his successor, he could honestly feel that he was presenting him with a fully combat-ready ship.

606. FOLLOWERSHIP. A good leader must have good followers. You cannot be a good leader unless you are willing also to follow enthusiastically the precepts and mandates of your senior officers. A good follower must have the capacity to be inspired, must understand his leaders so well that he can anticipate their every wish, and must know the place of his job in the over-all scheme of things so that he can produce effectively with a minimum of supervision. He must have a capacity for loyalty to his leaders and develop a discriminating partiality for them. He must be ever ready to accept delegated authority and responsibility. He must look for things to be done within his own area of responsibility and accept decisions and carry out orders instantly and without question. He will appreciate the concern that his leaders show for his welfare but will come to understand the limitations of service life and will not complicate the problems of his leaders with unreasonable demands and endless griping. He will attempt to follow the example of his leader in his moral and spiritual life and to pass his standards along to his subordinates, so that the moral tone of the whole organization will benefit.

Nearly all of the officers and enlisted personnel in the naval service are followers as well as leaders. Each leader, as a follower, has responsibilities to his senior, failure in the execution of which will bring the best of leadership to nought. It is our duty *as both leaders and followers* to implement the policy of our senior so that we may meet his standards of performance and efficiency, or exceed them, if that be necessary.

There is too much of the spirit of "What's in it for me" in American life and in the military services today. The Navy—indeed, any military service—exists for the single-minded purpose of *service* to the country, of preparation for combat and the support of national policy in combat, if that be required. Within the Navy, there must be a reemphasis of *the spirit of naval service.* In short, as leaders we must be prepared to *follow* where we are led by *able leaders.* And our leaders must be able to inspire us to follow them, willingly and effectively.

To be a good follower is as demanding, in its way, as to be a leader. The ability to follow is developed by an able leader who can direct and inspire the motivation of his subordinates so as to demonstrate clearly to them that following his lead is worth the effort that it requires. The follower early in his naval service must be imbued with the will to succeed.

At all levels in the service, if we are to become good leaders, we must first become effective followers. Until we learn to subordinate our personal welfare to the good of the service, we will not be good followers. The man who aspires to be a chief petty officer must first be an outstanding seaman; the captain of a ship, a fine executive officer; the admiral in command of a task force must first have demonstrated his ability not only to command a ship and men, but to follow the lead and carry out the wishes of his appointed leaders.

Without good followership, there can be no effective leadership.

607. CONFORMITY. A fundamental feature of any military organization is the conformity of its members to its code, its rituals, and its taboos, and their pride in the organization. The pride of members in an organization is most often exhibited by the proper wearing of the distinctive symbols of the organization. In the military services, this pride is exhibited not only in the wearing of the uniform and its insignia, but in *how* the uniform is worn and in the *manner* in which members of the organization observe the prescribed recognition of other members. These external signs are an indication of the real internal strength of the organization.

Conformity is exemplified by a sincere belief in the code of ethics of the organization, by a willingness to observe its rituals and to protect the prestige of the leader, and to indicate respect for his authority by following his orders and honoring his suggestions. As nonconformity is undesirable, members of a strong organization will try to punish violators of the code. Since many years have been required to establish an organization such as our Navy and to indoctrinate its members, it is important that all members know its background and comply with its rules.

Conformity strengthens an important aspect of a military organization—the respect and deference shown its leader. Let the leader give an order, express a wish, make a suggestion, and the members comply, willingly and eagerly. The code was adopted to state the need for prompt obedience of the leader. The traditions are based on respect for the leader; the customs enhance that respect; the taboos prevent its deterioration.

You must be ready to accept your fair share of the burden of responsibility, cheerfully and willingly. You must be adaptable. You must conform. You must be quick to learn new duties, with very little instruction. You must become expert in the operation of new equipment with only an operating manual to guide you. You must learn to direct the overhaul and maintenance of complicated machinery and weapons systems, the like of which you could not even imagine. You will daily encounter problems which will give you a constant challenge.

At the Naval Academy, the scholastic policy of instruction is survival of the scholastically fit. In effect, the student is told, "It's all in the book—don't expect your instructors to lay it out for you on a silver platter. Dig it out for yourself." The student is also given limited time in which to solve a problem.

This policy is no happenstance; it is not designed merely to cram much work into a little time, but also to develop the power of prompt decision. On the bridge at sea, in the engine-room of a destroyer, at the "pushbutton" of a guided missile in a submerged submarine, you do not have quiet and leisure in which to study your problem. Frequently, a nearly correct solution quickly determined is more valuable than an exact answer deliberately arrived at. *To be effective, decision must be prompt.*

You must know your men. You must know your material; on your expert knowledge may depend the ability of your ship to carry on, long after your commander has any right to expect that it could. In the words of Fleet Admiral King, you must "make the most of what you have."

How well you take advantage of your opportunities in the Navy will depend on how well and how quickly you find your place in the organization. It is *you* who must orient *yourself* with respect to the new horizons of your naval career.

Opportunity has a strange, almost uncanny way of abiding where it knows it will find a fitting home.

608. CHARACTER DEVELOPMENT. It is a common human trait to desire popularity. Everyone would like to have a winning personality, to be welcomed wherever he goes with affection, respect, and esteem. Some officers attempt to take a short cut to popularity by giving to everyone everything he wishes. Such an officer inevitably becomes a weak character, one few men can admire.

Personal popularity is desirable, but the development of a sound military character is an essential to good leadership. It is fortunate that the Naval Academy has clung tenaciously through its more than 100 years to two fundamentals, discipline and the development of character, for it is principally out of these two elements that the art of leadership grows. The young officer cannot begin too early to think seriously about the problems of his career. By the time he reaches his first ship or station, an officer's characteristics as an individual have become pretty well fixed. But his military character is yet in the formative stage. His qualification for leadership to a preponderant degree will depend upon his development of the mental and moral factors of his character.

Character is formed by the blending of many complex and opposing elements. An officer's duty is to lead wisely, kindly, efficiently, and with human understanding. What are the characteristics which a young officer should attempt to cultivate?

Seek to lead a healthy and normal life in all of its phases. Cultivate a healthy mind in a healthy body. Take plenty of recreation. Take an interest in some sport which you can follow all your life. *Seek the company of the best in men and women.*

Cultivate a proper humbleness and unaffectedness of spirit. It is futile, often disastrous, to burden yourself and confuse your subordinates by complexity, abstruseness, or subtlety. Be direct and unpretentious. Friendliness is one of the great levers of leadership. You can be friendly with your men, without, however, permitting any lowering of discipline or destroying in any way the officer-man relationship.

The great leaders were always simple men. No man can come close to his fellowman unless he is simple and direct. A leader who acts simply, thinks clearly, and is human need never cloak himself in an artificial mantle of reserve.

The naval leader must practice *self-control*. No man can aspire to lead and govern other men until he has first learned to govern himself. If you have a temper, acquire complete control of it, loosing it upon your men only when temper will serve the ends of military discipline. Cultivate the virtues of restraint, calmness, and a proper reserve.

Tact is the essential lubricant for the machine of human relationship. Tact has been said to be the nice discernment of what (and when) to do or say. It enables an officer to operate in difficult situations without loss of good will and to conduct his affairs without giving unintentional offense to others.

You can mean well, but have a knack for talking out of turn, of offering unsolicited advice and assistance without knowledge whereof you speak. If you have something to say, pick your time, place, and attendant circumstances. Above all, think before you speak. Be sure you are right. Don't rush in with ill-considered advice and unwanted comment.

A disciplined ambition, if not misdirected, is a good characteristic. It *can* lead an officer to high places, but if it degenerates into too strong a *personal ambition*, it can wreck an officer's career on the shoals of selfishness and vanity. Let a man be humble, not vain, when he holds high place; let him be grateful that opportunity has given him his chance to serve. To a man of the right sensibility, rank, honors and privilege are only the badges of office; he regards himself as the servant of the office which he holds.

Be unselfish. Persuade rather than coerce; cooperate rather than command; think of others before you think of yourself. Eschew selfishness, for selfishness of character leaves an evil trail in its wake. Place service above self throughout your whole career.

Do not concern yourself with unnecessary problems. Do the task before you the best you know how. Whatever your job, aim to do it better than the officer preceding or following you. Let no duty, because it is small, cause you to neglect it. The meaner the work, within reason, the more you should seek it.

Think ahead, plan for the future; when you are perplexed, seek out the facts, and analyze them in your own mind and own way, but do not let this interfere with your present, normal duties.

The complete *loyalty* of every subordinate is a vital necessity to success in naval operations. But loyalty cannot be demanded; it must be earned.

Loyalty is a two-way street—to be expected upward, it must be freely given downward.

Of Lord Nelson, Southey wrote, "Never was any commander more beloved. He governed men by their reason and their affections; they knew that he was incapable of caprice or tyranny; and they obeyed him with alacrity and joy, because he possessed their confidence as well as their love. 'Our Nel,' they used to say, 'is as brave as a lion, and as gentle as a lamb.' Severe discipline he detested, although he had been bred in a severe school." Of a slight to himself and his officers Lord Nelson once wrote, "Yet, if I know my own thoughts, it is not for myself, or on my own account chiefly, that I feel the sting of disappointment. No! It is for my brave officers, for my noble-minded friends and comrades. Such a gallant set of fellows! Such a band of brothers! My heart swells at the thought of them!"

No sensible commander expects or desires blind, unreasoning loyalty. Our system in the Navy is built upon the reasoned, intelligent execution of orders. Every commander worthy of his command welcomes advice and suggestion. At some point, however, the time for discussion is past. The decision must be taken. However you may disagree with the commander's decision, it is your duty, and it should be a matter of personal honor, to fulfill his orders, to go beyond his orders and carry out his wishes as you know he would wish them carried out.

If you hope to win the loyalty of your men, you must deserve it by giving loyalty upward. Never let them hear you criticize your seniors. In little matters and in the big important ones, let your men know that you honor the orders and policies of your commander.

Be sure that you are just as loyal to your men. Show them in many ways that their welfare is your concern, that you are always looking for ways to better their condition. Acquire a genuine interest in their welfare.

A young engineering division officer learned that two of his men were in jail in Los Angeles for disturbing the peace. He made a special trip from Long Beach to the county jail, sought them out, arranged bail, and provided a lawyer when their case came up two weeks later in court. The men probably did not get off any easier than if he had stayed aboard ship, but he had two very loyal supporters in his division. Look out for your men and they will look out for you, will give you a loyalty that you could never hope to command.

As you avoid conceit, so you will refrain from idle and thoughtless criticism of your seniors. Careless comment on the orders and decisions of your commander will give the impression that you are disloyal. If you quarrel with the decision of your senior, keep it to yourself. It is just as easy to say something nice about your associates as something unpleasant. Avoid the reputation of being a Wardroom grouser. Cooped up together in a small space aboard ship, many things irritate. But remember this—whatever the issue, *you can be wrong.*

Give loyalty upward. Earn the loyalty of your men. And let no man have reason to doubt your loyalty.

Learn to accept responsibility. Learn prompt decision, *and practice it.* There is no greater detriment to an organization than a vacillating officer, who cannot make up his mind. It is highly important to be able to say NO at the proper time, but the attitude of mind which prompts one to say NO rather than YES is negative. Some officers seem to take an unholy delight in saying NO and thereby destroy the morale of their command. He who inclines to say YES when he can is mentally constructive and progressive.

In wartime and in many situations in peacetime, you cannot take the time to explain your decisions. You must say, briefly and even abruptly, "Go there. Do that. No, carry out my orders." Any reasonable man in a subordinate position will recognize the pressure of events and unhesitatingly comply.

When there is more leisure, it is the part of wisdom to temper your NO with an explanation. With experience, an officer learns how to do this, without opening the way to bootless discussion and argument. He states his reasons briefly and then gives his decision. Some officers become so adept at presenting unpleasant decisions that hardly ever does a person leave their presence unhappy or resentful.

Be sure that your reasons are valid, not capricious. Be certain that your decision is based on the case in hand, not on some incident that has upset you. With experience, you will come to command that happy combination of wisdom and courage which will enable you to say NO at the right time and place.

Know your men. Know their jobs and how to do them better than they do. Know your own job better than any of your subordinates. While you are learning, do not be afraid to ask questions of anyone, whatever his rank or rate. Learn, also, the job of the next officer ahead of you. Detachments are frequent, and promotions are coming along. Be sure that you will be ready when your turn comes.

Character is the stamp of the aggregate of an individual's distinctive qualities impressed by nature, education and habit, which can be strengthened by moral vigor and firmness acquired through self-discipline. An officer with an intelligent and urgent purpose will soon possess the character to enable him to bear up under the most challenging situations. Without good character, an officer will not inspire the full trust of those who follow him and success in an undertaking cannot be assured. With character, an officer will develop the skill and determination to lead his followers where opportunity abides.

609. THE POWER OF EXAMPLE. Of all tools of good leadership, none is more important than personal example in setting the tone of a command. This is particularly true in this age when the bluejacket observes his officers more shrewdly and with less awe than ever before. An officer can be a power for good or a power for evil. As you learn to set a proper example for your men, as you live the kind of life you would have them lead, so you will promote good discipline in your organization. Nothing is more destructive of good discipline than the attitude of an officer who, by every word and deed, says to his subordinates, "Don't do as I do. Do as I say." Ensure that you are an example of all you advocate and enforce.

R.H.I.P. (rank has its privileges) is a well-known phrase in military circles. Rank does have its privileges, and many of them are properly set by law and custom. It also has its responsibilities. Rank, however, never permits the officer to disregard the rights and privileges of those serving under him. A proper discipline can be maintained only by a good example set by the leader. Remember, the bluejacket forms his opinion of you by what he observes. His reactions to your orders will reflect that opinion. So conduct yourself that your men will be proud of you, and proud to maintain the correct disciplinary standards which you set.

Leadership by example sets a proper standard for good discipline and encourages cheerful cooperation and compliance with orders. Leadership by driving promotes bad discipline; it is not regarded with favor in our Navy. The American bluejacket has a right to expect good treatment and fair play. Beyond a certain point, he cannot be driven. Be chary of threats. Lead; do not drive. Show your men the advantages of good behavior by example. Soft-pedal fear of punishment, and accent the hope of reward.

If you chew gum in uniform, you present a slack, slovenly appearance, which your men will copy. How can you expect your men to wear hats topside if you go bareheaded, or be clean and neat in uniform, if your socks have holes in them, your shoes are seldom shined, your linen is dirty, your hair is long, and your face unshaved? Can you expect your men to render snappy salutes and have a military bearing if you are sloppy in rendering honors and drape your torso loosely over the lifeline? Will your men jump to your orders if you give them in a listless, halfhearted, uncertain tone?

The men in your outfit form a mirror in which you can inspect yourself.

If you expect your men to be brave in battle, you must show them that you are unconcerned and confident. Everyone is afraid at times. That is no disgrace. Regardless of how frightened he may be, the leader must have so disciplined himself that he can rise above fear and lead his men with an outward appearance of courage and fearless-

FIGURE 602. The capable leader always sets a good example for his men.

ness. It is not fear that is shameful; it is succumbing to panic and not conquering fear of which you will inevtitably be ashamed. Particularly, when the going is most difficult and the danger greatest, must the officer, by example, set the standard of resolute courage which will lead his group through the peril of panic and fear of disaster.

The most insignificant acts and omissions sometimes cause men to loose faith in their leaders. That is why Navy Regulations state that commanders "are required to show in themselves a good example of virtue, honor, patriotism, and subordination." As the leaders act, as they inspire the confidence and esteem of their subordinates, so will the men follow.

Set a good example to your petty officers by leading your men in the tasks you give them. Get to know their jobs and teach them how to do them better. By your intelligence, accomplishment, character, and example make them proud of you, proud to follow wherever you may lead.

If habitually displayed by the officers, such qualities as smartness, neatness, alertness, pride of military bearing, and confidence soon permeate the crew of a ship and set a tone which promotes outstanding performance.

610. KNOW YOUR JOB. There is no substitute for professional competence. All the talk in the world, all the reading of good books on leadership cannot make you into an effective leader overnight. But you can abbreviate your period of apprenticeship if you will learn to avoid some of the more obvious pitfalls and if you will profit by the mistakes that others have made before you. Read, learn, and apply your knowledge so as to save yourself some of that soul searching and uncertainty which all young officers at first experience.

Know your stuff! First, learn your own job. Know the place of the naval service in the general plan. Then learn the missions of the other services. If you are going to be a successful leader, you can't know too much. Know the jobs of the men under you. Learn from the firemen and seamen, from the painters and side cleaners, from the firecontrolmen and missilemen and machinist mates. *Do not be too proud!* Learn from anyone who can teach you the things you need to know.

Know the yesterdays of history—the signposts of the future. Justice Oliver Wendell Holmes used to say, "Young man, *make the most of the scraps of time.*" Learn to organize yourself, to make good use of your days and hours and minutes. To know your job better than the next man, you've got to spend more time studying it. Not that you shouldn't allow time for recreation, but there are days and weeks wasted around the coffee pot in the Wardroom, on the quiet night watches, in the minutes between exercises.

Don't become merely bookish. Keep it practical. Know the background of military history. Know your men, what makes them behave as they do. Know your specialty. Know it so well that, if a man asks you, "What am I supposed to do with this machine, or that missile, under these conditions," you can show him. But if you don't know, tell him honestly, "I don't know," and then add, "But I'll find out." You will never lose the respect of your men if you frankly admit your ignorance, but don't try to bluff! The bluejacket, today, is too intelligent not to spot the hollow fraud.

There is no substitute for experience. Do the immediate task as well as you know how, but seek out experience to teach you how to do it better. Be observant. Cultivate the habit of observation. Let no detail, however small, escape your attention.

When you are confronted with your first group of enlisted men, you will be possessed by an initial uncertainty. Only by study and experience can you acquire the confidence of the "know what" and "know how." The Navy has become so mechanized that many officers are inclined to forget the human element. Our naval machinery, electronics, guns, missiles, aircraft and ships are wonderful, but they cannot run themselves. No matter how advanced we may become in science, the Navy will always require *men* to operate the *machines*. We will always need officers to *lead the men*.

Know your most important job—handling the American bluejacket. He will be your especial care. No scientific knowledge you may possess, no research you may perform, no mechanical experience you may acquire can ever be of as much importance to you and of as much value to the Navy and your ship as expert knowledge and practicing proficiency in the handling of men.

Such knowledge cannot be acquired overnight. There is no substitute for plain hard work. Channel your effort, organize your time, so that you will achieve a mastery of the myriad details of your job. As a by-product you will acquire that confidence in yourself and your men which comes only from knowledge and experience. *If you know your job, you can be sure of yourself.*

611. ISSUING ORDERS. The most important element of an order is that it be just and proper. Nearly as important is that you learn how to give an order effectively. At first, you may be pretty uncertain of yourself, but do not let this become apparent to your men. An order, given hesitatingly, will be doubtfully received.

Learn and use the proper naval phraseology. Think about your orders before you issue them. Incorporate the idea of collaboration, of working together. Phrase your orders to be short, snappy, and incisive. Give them in a strong, firm, authoritative tone of voice, with only enough volume to be heard by the men affected. Do not let your voice trail off at the end uncertainly. Be calm and decisive, without brusqueness or an appearance of anger.

Make sure that an order is clearly stated and that the man who receives it knows exactly what you mean to say, and that *you* mean what you say. Insist upon immediate and unquestioned obedience. As Admiral Carney, former Chief of Naval Operations, once said, "I have served in many ships in which the need for discipline was understood by all hands from top to bottom . . . where an order was obeyed with alacrity and without question because of a great mutual confidence that existed among the members of the ships' companies . . . and those ships were inevitably proud and happy organizations in which serious breaches of discipline were almost unknown."

When there is time, the importance of obedience, to the man and to the unit, should be explained. Whenever you can, explain briefly the *why* of an order. Thus, you inspire cooperation and develop the comprehending kind of discipline that will make instant obedience unquestioned when circumstances so require.

Insofar as may be possible, issue your orders through your division petty officers. Leave it to them to assign the men and to give them detailed instructions. Thus, you will build up the importance of your petty officers and promote a smooth-functioning organization, which will operate effectively in your absence. Tell your petty officer *what* you want done. Except in unusual circumstances, where a technique is unfamiliar or a specific procedure must be followed, leave the *how* up to him.

Follow through! It is not enough to issue an order. The weakest excuse you can offer is, "I told the bos'nsmate." You must follow up and *see that your orders are carried out!* There can be no excuse for slovenly work or a job not fully accomplished on time. Train your junior officers and your petty officers to understand quite clearly that following through comprises several phases—issuing the order, seeing that the work is commenced, ensuring that the work is being expeditiously accomplished, inspecting the completed job (with properly high standards), and requiring further work until the job is satisfactory.

You should not have to check on all of the details, personally, but only when *someone in your organization* has done so can you feel that the leadership in your division has properly followed through.

The American Bluejacket

612. KNOW THE AMERICAN BLUEJACKET. The present demands upon the leadership of the junior officer are vastly more extensive and complex than they were between the World Wars. The problems of handling the modern American bluejacket sometimes seem almost more than the inexperienced junior officer can carry. Solving them is his creative responsibility and requires the knowledgeable and strong support of his seniors.

Mahan has said, "Good men with poor ships are better than poor men with good ships." It is your job to make our bluejackets good men in good ships. One of your first tasks in preparing yourself to handle modern American bluejackets is to discover who and what they are.

Who are the American bluejackets? First of all, the vast majority of American bluejackets, the nonrated seamen, are better educated and more intelligent than in former years. A high percentage have completed a course in a Class-A service school before reporting to their first ship or station.

They have been taught to use their minds constructively. When properly trained, they can troubleshoot and repair complicated equipment aboard ship which would baffle many college-trained engineers. On the other hand, many of them are more demanding of their rights and insistent on "democratic treatment"—some of the less well-adjusted even deny the necessity of military authority as a concept. Many exhibit the attitude of "What's in it for me?" before commencing any task. Few of the new seamen and firemen on arrival aboard ship recognize and honor the age-old military need for "immediate and unquestioned obedience to orders."

In the 1930's, the high ratio of applicants to those enlisted at recruiting stations screened out many undesirables. Today, the waiting lists are small or nonexistent, the Navy has had to resort at times to the draft in peacetime, and the severe screening process before enlistment no longer exists to help the division officer with his job. Many nonrated men are in the Navy "just for the ride"—to perform their required service, and no more. These men are often cynical of the traditional forms of motivation—patriotism, service to country, religious fervor, pride in their work, identification with, and pride in, the reputation of their organization. Though their greater intelligence makes them easier to instruct and train, the young bluejackets are much harder to handle. The challenge to the junior officer is with him every moment of his working day. He must employ all of the tools of good leadership and develop to the maximum his skill in human relations.

Secondly, the American bluejackets are more sophisticated than in former years. They know their "rights" and they feel the equal of any other man in the world. They are representative *young* Americans, who are willing (but not eager) to do their bit, are ready to follow sensible direction and accept necessary privations, but will resist autocratic regimentation with democratic fervor. They are too intelligent to follow blindly wherever they may be led, too imbued with a sense of rightness to be driven.

Being young, many of them, their character is as yet unformed, their moral development incomplete. The naval officer has a serious responsibility to ensure that character building and moral development proceed together in the naval training of these youths so that they may continue their progress toward normal, ethical maturity. They must be led with enlightened leadership toward effectiveness as bluejackets and as men.

In wartime or in periods of naval expansion, the average of education and intelligence may decrease. During World War II, the average educational level of enlistees dropped to between the sixth- and seventh-grade levels.

The education and intelligence level of your enlisted men are important points for your consideration. Recruits with lower IQs are harder to instruct and train. The General Classification Tests of recruits may go up or down; it is your job to find the brighter young man and assign him to a billet where his quick mind is needed. Thus, you not only give him an opportunity to get ahead, but also remove the disciplinary problem of frustration and boredom in an insufficiently challenging assignment.

Do not expect the American bluejacket to follow in a blind, unreasoning fashion. The vast majority respond well to discipline, expect leadership, orders, and supervision. They have been trained to follow expert leaders. If they fail, it is because they do not receive the proper kind of direction. Not only must they be told what to do, they must also be told the reason why.

If discipline is lax, fumbling, or inadequate, your enlisted men will take advantage. What they want and need, what they have a right to expect, is expert guidance and firm supervision, executed with wisdom and understanding.

Military discipline and the autocratic authority of a military society are foreign to our democratic American youth. Some young men react favorably to discipline; others do not. Some bluejackets resent officers, but by far the vast majority accept officers and expect them to take charge and issue the proper orders. They need direction; they want to respect authority and the officers placed over them. But they also expect their officers to show an interest in them as individuals. In the strongest terms, they feel a need for personal identification—a sense of belonging and of importance to their organization.

Whether a bluejacket resents an individual officer or not depends upon the officer, his personality and character, his competence and attainments. What the bluejacket dislikes in an officer is the incompetent, the unreasonably irascible, the hollow bluff. Most bluejackets want to look up to their officers, to respect them. If an officer is recognized as able, energetic, and possessed of an understanding heart, he will be respected and accepted as a good boss.

The bluejacket is a keen critic. He soon knows the intrinsic worth of the various officers placed over him. *It is the man behind the gold braid who counts.*

The modern bluejacket is a more complex character than formerly. Serving in a period of quasi-peace, in a twilight zone between the peace we all seek and total war, the stresses and strains of naval discipline and unnatural shipboard life at sea often induce in him strange characteristics. But basically, he is little different from yourself had you taken another route to the naval service. He resents the same injustices, hates the same oppressions, knows the same fears, responds to the same stimuli. He is a cross-section of America, which produced both you and him.

Here is your raw material—young American manhood!

Yours is the task to cultivate in them the proper military attributes. It should be your desire to have your men develop a seamanlike and military spirit, so that everything they do is accomplished in a smart and snappy fashion. You must also train them to have a proper sense of duty and honor, so that, when they are given important assignments or assigned battery, lookout, radar, and other war watches, they will know their importance and devote their full attention and intelligence to them. You should educate your men thoroughly in naval customs, so that they will maintain a careful observance of naval etiquette. Your ultimate objective is to develop them into well-rounded man-of-war's men, thoroughly acclimated to life aboard ship and well trained and indoctrinated for the verities of combat.

613. Recruit training. Successful applicants are enlisted at one of the many recruiting stations located in various centers throughout the nation. Enlistees are then sent to one of the several training centers distributed about the country. The regular peacetime training centers are located at Great Lakes, Illinois, Orlando, Florida and San Diego,

California. In wartime, additional centers are established to accommodate the larger number of recruits. The period of training in peacetime is generally three months and in wartime three to eight weeks, depending upon the immediate demands of the fleet and of the previous experience of the recruits in vocations readily adaptable to the Navy.

During the recruit training period, enlistees are outfitted with full equipment at government expense and schooled in the elements of infantry drill, naval customs and procedure, boat handling, and seamanship. They observe a strict disciplinary routine and physical-conditioning program, which serves as a foundation for further training afloat. During this period, all recruits are given classification tests to determine their aptitude and potential abilities in connection with selection for further training in service schools prior to joining the fleet.

614. EDUCATION AND TRAINING ABOARD SHIP. Your primary duty with respect to your men is so to train and indoctrinate them that they will become good man-of-war's men. The primary purpose of shipboard training is to develop the willingness and ability of your men to engage in combat. Set properly high standards and insist on their attainment. Frequently evaluate the training of your men to ensure that they are learning the things necessary for them to know.

Your responsibility for training extends to all the men entrusted to your command, but you will pay especial attention to the training of new recruits. Nearly every recruit reporting aboard ship is in a profound state of bewilderment. Perhaps you can recall the difficult period of adjustment during your first week aboard ship. Your difficulties as an officer were mild compared to the confusion of a new recruit when he is herded aboard a crowded man-of-war, and is dropped into the maelstrom of military life. The importance of his first 10 days aboard ship cannot be exaggerated. If he is thoughtfully and carefully handled, if he is properly indoctrinated on resentment, regimentation, fear, and adjustment to life in the service, if he is shown about the ship and taught how to live in harmony with many other men in its limited spaces, if he is instructed in the importance of subordinating himself to the aims of military discipline, the advantages of proper conduct, the necessity for instant and unquestioning obedience, the ship will have taken a decisive step toward solving the problem of making him into a successful man-of-war's man.

In many ships, it is the policy of the Commanding Officer to place a draft of new recruits in a special division for 10 days, an excellent practice. In one cruiser, all of the men of a new draft, recruits or seasoned man-of-war's men, are assigned to the X Division, with the Assistant to the Executive Officer as Division Officer. Aided by the ship's police petty officers and experienced enlisted men of the draft, he musters the men, assigns them temporarily to vacant bunks in various parts of the ship. Bags and ditty bags are stowed adjacent to their bunks. These will be the new men's billets for 10 days.

Recruits sometimes arrive on board dirty, unshaven, with dirty bedding and a bag half full of dirty clothes. The Division Officer sees that the men bathe and shave, put on clean clothing, and obtain regulation

FIGURE 603. Afloat or ashore, the naval leader is always a teacher.

haircuts. Periods of 1 to 2 hours at the barbershop are reserved exclusively for the draft.

Bag inspection is held on the fo'c'sle to check condition of clothing and make out requisitions for articles needed. If the ship is operating in the tropics, blue clothing is ignored, for blues already provide the First Lieutenant with a serious stowage problem. Bags are stowed and the Division is marched to Small Stores, where a special issue is held for them. Clean from the skin out, hair neatly cut and close shaved, properly uniformed, the new men of the ship's company are ready to face the future with head up and chin out. So effective has this system proved that a draft has been received aboard on Thursday afternoon and been commended by the Captain for appearance at Saturday inspection.

The draft is broken up into small groups and conducted throughout the ship by petty officers thoroughly familiar with the various parts of the ship. Lectures are scheduled at frequent intervals. The Chaplain gives the men a talk on life aboard ship and explains to them the relationship between religion and ethics and the Navy. It is a great comfort to a deeply religious man to learn that he can usually attend a service conducted by a minister of his faith, either in his own ship or in another in the harbor. A weapons department officer tells the men about the armament and its functioning. Engineers describe the plant and damage control. An officer in the deck department lectures on shipboard seamanship and kindred subjects. A medical officer discusses personal and social hygiene, and also mental, emotional, and moral problems which they may encounter. The X Division Officer instructs the men on watch standing, security, censoring, leave, liberty, and a wide variety of other subjects.

Careful and thoughtful assignment of a new man is very important to the man and to the ship. A personnel board studies the records of recruits, particularly their qualification cards on which are recorded the results of expert tests, interviewing, and classification at the training station. School graduates are earmarked for billets in their specialties. A painstaking study of the records of each man in the draft and consideration of the recommendation of the X Division Officer based on his personal interview bring improved performance of duty by a man properly assigned to a job in which he can take a personal interest and at which he can excel.

At the end of 10 days in the X Division, the new seaman or fireman is partially acclimated. For the new men of the draft, the first few days in your division are very important. Take care to see that each man is well settled in his locker and bunk, that he knows what his job is, where his battle station is located, how and when to get there, what the bells and bugle calls mean, where and how to get something to eat (have you ever considered the confusion of a recruit's first trip through a ship's chow line?), and which head and washroom he is supposed to use. This is also the time to show your personal interest in him as an individual. Be sure that you speak to each new man by name in his first two or three days in your division.

Such thoughtful attention will prevent a Mast case such as this one where a new man was reported by his Division Officer for twice failing to man his battle station. At the preliminary investigation the Executive Officer asked, "Were you shown your battle station, Thomson?"

"Oh, yes, sir. A fellow took me topside and pointed out one of the little guns and told me that was my station when GQ blew."

"Why didn't you get there?"

"Didn't know the bugle call, sir. Then, I couldn't get to the gun, sir.

Everybody was going the opposite direction. Took me twenty minutes to get there."

"What happened the next time?"

"Well, sir, Mr. Bradshaw cussed me out, so I got up early yesterday morning and went topside and sat on a bitt and waited. Some sailors come running by. I asked one, 'Is that GQ, mate?' He says, 'Hell, no, it's chow call.' I went down to get in chow line. No chow line. I asked another sailor, and he said, sure, it was GQ. I ran topside to my gun, but I was late again."

The Executive Officer excused the young seaman, but he had some severe words to say to the Division Officer in his cabin afterward.

A few days spent in properly settling a new man into your division will bring you dividends in better performance of duty. Study his qualifications card and record. Mistakes in assignment have been and can be made. In a large division, you have an opportunity to make proper placement. The small, highly educated and intelligent seaman can be put in training for such jobs as computer, tracker, firecontrolman, electronics striker, etc. Put the husky lad with a third-grade education on the business end of a loading machine or in training for deck seaman.

Show a definite interest in your new men. Get to know them. Talk to them; ask them questions about their past lives and their families, their education and their hopes and ambitions. Find out what they are thinking about—what makes them run. From the beginning, make your new men feel wanted and recognized. Give them a feeling of personal identification with the division—a sense of importance and of belonging. From such understanding of your men, you can employ the skills of human relations necessary to inspire them to loyalty to the division and a determination to excel.

Division School. Get out of the Wardroom or office! The proper place for the division officer is with his men. He must personally supervise and engage in every phase of their training and instruction. It will be impossible to convince your men that training is important if you turn it over completely to your junior officers and petty officers. You must convince them by personal participation that training is important to you.

Most well-managed ships set aside at least three 1-hour periods a week for school. Division officers, junior officers and petty officers should instruct the men of their division in their individual duties, seamanship, watch standing, honors, customs of the service, and a dozen other subjects. The men should also have an opportunity to ask questions about their training courses. Training films applicable to the subject should be employed, but they must be *carefully selected to fit in with the planned course.* Once or twice a month, divisional officers can employ these school periods to conduct progress tests and examinations for the training courses. Consult Shipboard Procedures (NWP-50 series) for guidance.

The Navy provides excellent training courses for the ratings to which men may aspire. Assign a junior officer as division training officer and require him to keep proper records of training course progress and other phases of your men's training. Keep dated records of progress and urge the laggards to be industrious. As division officer, take a keen interest in the training courses and ensure that good men are not held back from promotion because they have not completed required courses, schools, and practical factors (see also Section 616).

Ensure that special attention is given to the individuals with lower mental levels, so that they acquire sufficient understanding not to become confused and fail to function adequately. Instruct the mentally slow group separately so as not to hold back those of quicker mentality. Where there are only a few of the mentally slow in a division, the junior officer can give them special attention after the others are dismissed. With such recognition of their importance to the division, they will exert extra effort and become more conscientious about meeting the demands of their leaders.

An incident occurred recently in one of the repair ships. An excellent striker for shipfitter could not be recommended for promotion because he had not completed his training courses. On investigation, his Division Officer discovered that this man read haltingly and wrote so poorly that he was ashamed to take a progress test. The Division Officer arranged to enroll him in courses in reading and writing under the supervision of the Chaplain. A shipmate volunteered to read the courses aloud to him. The Division Officer gave him progress tests and course examinations orally. Four months later, he passed a service-wide written examination for shipfitter with a mark of 3.65.

Hints for Shipboard Instructors. Many young officers and some petty officers overuse the lecture to the virtual elimination of the demonstration method. Be enthusiastic! Carefully prepare your instruction so as not to waste the brief time available.

Do not assume that your men know more than they do. Pitch your instruction to the level of your class comprehension. Differentiate among the individual capacities and state of advancement of the various students. Separate the slower mentalities from the more advanced so that they can be given specialized instruction and the quicker mentalities can progress.

Give reasonable study assignments, test for advanced study of the material assigned, and give each member of the class an opportunity to recite. Prepare in advance for use of blackboard illustrations, training films, and film strips to work in well with your assigned topic.

Phrase your questions to your men to be understandable. Encourage questions from your students. Evaluate their performance fairly. Prepare written tests with care to cover the assigned material.

Keep your oral instruction brief and to the point. Talk slowly and loudly enough to be heard by the lad at the rear of the class. Emphasize a number of key points at the conclusion of each instruction period.

Learn and use the last names (but not the first names) of the members of your class. When addressing a petty officer or non-rated man directly, use of the last name only, is appropriate. When addressing a chief petty officer directly, "Chief" or "Chief Jones" is correct. When introducing a petty officer or a non-rated man to civilians or to a group of enlisted men, use the rating group and last name, as "Fireman Smith" or "Petty Officer Jones". Do not ridicule the man who does poorly or makes a silly answer. Do not engage in arguments with your students. Do not use the class as a forum for discussing personal problems or specialized points of view.

Irresponsible sarcasm will destroy the value of the instruction.

As a final admonition, take a real and sincere interest in the training of your men. Give encouragement to those who need it. Make the information available to those who need to learn. Keep yourself always ready to assist the good man who wants to get ahead.

615. YOUR PETTY OFFICERS. The organizations of the Navy, both ashore and afloat, require competent and well-trained enlisted men to act as petty officers in various specialties or ratings and to perform the diversified skilled trades necessary for the proper functioning of modern naval ships. By petty officer is meant, not only good technicians, but also *leaders* who take charge and accomplish results *without supervision*. In recent years, the "old line" petty officer—the kind of chiefs and P.O.'s who ran the show and ran it well in the "old Navy" of between wars—has been pitifully scarce. The responsibility for this deplorable condition rests squarely upon the officers of the Navy. The senior officers are definitely responsible for *permitting* such a condition to exist, but the *ultimate* responsibility rests upon those officers who have (or should have) daily and intimate association with the petty officers and the men—the division officer and his junior officers.

The Navy has nearly 70 petty officer ratings, many of which, such as sonar technicians, journalists, electronics technicians, missile technicians and communications technicians, were established during or since World War II. The petty officers having these ratings comprise the skilled technicians in every field of naval science and endeavor, both ashore and at sea. The technical competence of these petty officers in their duties to a large degree determines the fighting capacity and effectiveness of our fleet—but, unless they are leaders as well as technicians, no division, no ship, no shore establishment can function at full efficiency.

If the division officer must know his men, how much more important it is to know his petty officers. He must work with them so closely that he knows the stimuli to which they will respond. With good petty officers, hope of reward is by far the best stimulus. The division officer

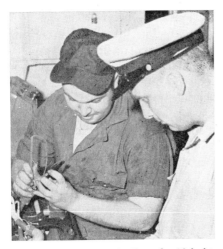

must make the position of his petty officers a respected and privileged office. He must seek out special privileges to set them apart from the nonrated men— consideration can be given to special liberty, 72-hour liberty, relief from assignment to working parties, to the more desirable watches, lockers, and bunks.

The division officer must back up his petty officers. Permit no insolence or disrespect. The men must be made to understand that an order from a petty officer must be obeyed as promptly and unquestioningly as if it came from the division officer.

FIGURE 604. The naval officer should insist that his petty officers closely supervise the work of the men.

Assign each petty officer in a division to specific duties with charge over specific equipment and part of the ship, and requisite authority over the men assigned to work for him. Make him responsible to the leading petty officer of the division and to yourself for his assignment and insist on proper standards of performance. Thus, you will build up in your petty officer and in his men a pride in their work and in the division.

Show your confidence and trust in your petty officer. Check up on him, but do it in such a fashion that he will not feel that you are interfering in the details of his job. Give him a job to do and leave the "how to" up to him. Correct him when he falls down on the job—but praise him when commendation is deserved.

Insist that your petty officer set a proper example in appearance, courtesy, and honors to the men of the division. In the "Old Navy," as we mentioned earlier, it was the snappy, neat, properly uniformed, meticulously correct and courteous leading petty officer who always had the outstanding division in the ship.

Selecting Your Petty Officers. One of the most important duties of a division officer is the selection of his petty officers. In considering your men for advancement to a petty officer rating, it is not enough that they have fulfilled all the basic requirements (see Section 616). Your petty officers must also have excellent military characters.

Always select your petty officers on merit. Do not let your personal likes or dislikes influence your recommendations for advancement. If you promote an incapable lad who yet has a likable personality and good service manners, you inflict as serious harm upon the service as if you hold back a capable man whose characteristics and mannerisms are displeasing to you. Before advancing a seaman or fireman to a petty officer rating, give him a job, such as leading compartment cleaner or fireman in charge of detail, where you can observe how he exercises those qualities of leadership necessary in a petty officer. Do not carry along to higher ratings those third class petty officers who are ineffective leaders or are inefficient in their specialties. If, by admonition, encouragement, instruction, and leadership, you cannot make them into good petty officers, recommend them for disrating.

Your nonrated men must be able to look up to their petty officers, and, correspondingly, your petty officers must possess to a high degree the military characteristics of a leader. The petty officers have always been the backbone of the Navy. For the good of the service, in your selection of petty officers, try always to be wise.

616. REQUIREMENTS FOR ADVANCEMENT. Certain general requirements for advancement in ratings must be fulfilled. The detailed requirements are too voluminous and change too frequently to be given here. They may be found in the BuPers Manual, Part C, and in the Bureau of Naval Personnel Instructions, 1400 Series. Officers should keep themselves thoroughly familiar with these sources.

There are, also, seven basic requirements for advancement. These are briefly stated here and should be checked before each man is recommended:

First, is there authority to advance the man?

The BuPers Manual grants authority to commanding officers to advance men in rating by three methods, in accordance with,

a. Specific instructions issued in Instructions and Notices.

b. A letter issued to each Commanding Officer in specific cases.

c. An advancement letter issued by the Commanding Officer, U. S. Naval Examining Center, at the direction of the Chief of Naval Personnel following service-wide examinations.

Second, has he served sufficient time in his present rating and in the service?

The Manual gives the basic service requirements, but these are frequently modified by BuPers Instructions, and commanding officers are authorized further to reduce these requirements in the cases of specially deserving men.

Third, has he completed the practical factors of the rating to which he is to be recommended?

These practical factors are listed under each rating in the Manual of Qualifications for Advancement in Rating (NavPers 18068). Aboard ship, the division officer should satisfy himself that each man can actually do the work of the rate for which he is striking and ensure that his practical-factors qualification is noted in his service record. It is folly to recommend a man for a rate at which he cannot function effectively.

Fourth, has he satisfactorily completed a course of instruction at a service school, if such be required?

See BuPersInst. P1430.7 series for list of rates for which graduation from a service school is a requirement for promotion.

Fifth, has he completed the required training courses?

It is your responsibility to see that he has taken and passed the proper general training course and also the training course for the rating for which he is striking. Ensure that completion of these training courses has been recorded in his service record.

Sixth, can he pass the prescribed examination in general and technical subjects?

The requirements are briefed under the Military Requirements and Professional Qualifications for each rate in NavPers 18068.

Seventh, if being recommended for a petty officer rating, is he petty officer material?

See discussion under *Selecting Your Petty Officers* (Section 615).

If your man passes muster on all these basic requirements, recommend him for advancement in rating to the Executive Officer at the proper time. For rates E-7 and below, the Executive Officer will set the date, time, and place for conducting the examinations. If service-wide examinations are required, the Executive Officer will inform you of the next scheduled examination period.

617. LOOK OUT FOR YOUR MEN. One important aspect of leadership is too often neglected—*Look out for your men!*

Take a personal interest in your men. Collectively and as individuals, see that they are made aware of your interest and concern for their welfare. Reprimand, as you must, but never miss an opportunity to commend. After each operation, recommend men with outstanding performance to the Captain for Meritorious Mast.

FIGURE 605. Looking out for your men includes night rations for the Black Gang.

Leave and Liberty. Liberty and the thirty days' annual leave authorized for every officer and enlisted person is an entitlement, not a right. Frequently in war or quasi-war, months will pass when the Commanding Officer can grant no leave. In the advanced operating areas, it is often impossible to grant any kind of liberty. After a severe operating period, when leave can be granted, try to arrange for all your men to get at least a few days. There is nothing so beneficial to officer or man as the rejuvenating effect of getting completely away from the ship and the job for a little while.

Do things for and with your men. At advanced bases or in other ports where liberty cannot be granted at all, recreation of various sorts can usually be arranged. Plan hunting parties, and go along with your men—the whole division can probably be taken care of in three parties. Baseball, softball, volleyball, swimming, and other sports help to enliven a dull port. Fishing from ship's boats or over the side is a popular means of recreation. If you can only arrange to take your men to an isolated beach for a swim and picnic, the change will be helpful; general mess food acquires an unusual savor when cooked over an open fire.

See that your junior officer goes on recreation parties which you cannot attend.

A good leave and liberty program under arduous operating conditions includes the following:

a. Commence liberty immediately upon arrival in U. S. or foreign liberty port, regardless of time of arrival.

b. Hold a "rope-yarn Sunday" every Wednesday.

c. Grant regular liberty on Saturday morning as early as possible.

d. Grant 72-hour liberty liberally.

e. Promulgate the long-range leave program well in advance.

f. Maintain a policy of emergency leave for any man with personal or family matters to attend.

g. Encourage exchange of duty between men with similar responsibilities.

h. Send petty officers on liberty 30 minutes in advance of rest of crew.

i. Run liberty boats all night.

Make every effort to see that your men have good, hot food. The Supply Officer has much more experience at feeding large numbers of men than you, but some of his subordinates sometimes slack off. Show up at the mess lines of your division frequently enough to learn just what the men are being fed and to correct unsatisfactory messing conditions. Eat their food—not just a pecking sample, but a whole meal. In combat, during long sieges at General Quarters in peacetime, and immediately afterward, provide the men with hot food.

The living conditions of your men should be one of your principal concerns. Our ships, large and small, are crowded. Your suggestions may be instrumental in improving the general livability of a compartment. Do not accept unsatisfactory conditions as necessary merely because they exist. Ask yourself: Can more ventilation be provided? Can bunks and lockers be rearranged to give more room? Can some bunks and lockers be moved to unused space in another compartment? Investigate, plan, then recommend improvements.

All such activities on your part comprise a proper interest in the welfare of your men. Your interest in, and close association with your men, will help to keep you better informed on their capabilities and potentialities, the contributions that they can make to your division and the ship. But be sure that you do not go too far. Upstanding men do not want to be looked after as if they were children. You must maintain a proper balance between a sincere interest and an overzealous concern. Look out for your men, but *do not coddle them.*

618. RELATIONSHIP WITH YOUR MEN. The nature of your relationship with your men is the surest measure of your success. A new officer is at first likely to be fumbling and uncertain. His new station and authority are strange to him. The democracy under which he has been reared makes foreign to his nature the sharp cleavage between officers and men required by military discipline.

Avoid undue familiarity with your men. First, you must earn their respect by your knowledge and competence. Then, you must insist that your men always maintain the proper attitude of subordination and military courtesy.

Within the bounds of discipline, be approachable and friendly. *Begin by learning the names of your men.* As long as a man is just a number, or "Hey, you!" to an officer, there can be no feeling of mutual trust. Fitting names to the faces in your organization is not difficult. Tests show that the average officer can learn the names of 40 men in a week, know 125 men by sight and name in a month of daily contact. As a student of leadership and human relations, the laboratory is as near as the fo'c'sle or outside your office door. Get out of your room or office. Do not hang out in the Wardroom! Direct personal supervision brings acquaintance, and acquaintance breeds knowledge of your men. Be available in your part of the ship during working hours.

Some young officers feel that they promote friendliness between their men and themselves by calling them by their first names or by nicknames. Nothing could be more false. Call your men by their last names, and by their last names only. See Section 614 for the proper method of address and introduction.

If you do not know a man's name, call him by his rate, or an abbreviation thereof, such as bos'nmate, steward, firecontrolman or machinist. But immediately find out his name. Do not be a "Hey, you!" officer.

Just as important, insist that the men address you by your proper tag handle—"Mister" and your last name, for every young officer. Insist that your men properly address and refer to all other officers, correcting them firmly when you hear them do otherwise.

When a new man comes to the division, meet him with a friendly handshake and a word of welcome. In your need to get to know your men, do not presume upon your position. On first acquaintance, you are not privileged to conduct an inquisition into a man's private affairs. Longer association will develop into an acquaintance in which the information you need to know about the man will develop naturally. You must expect that you will be asked questions as well. Within proper bounds, encourage this free play of informal conversation. To be natural, informative and useful, such conversation must be a two-way exchange. The chief value of such interchanges is that they permit the enlisted man to see his officer as a man.

Irony is a dangerous tool in the officer-man interchange. *Sarcasm* is a two-edged sword which cuts both the receiver and the giver. Do not feel that you have to sprinkle profanity into every sentence. Vulgar talk is the crutch of an inadequate vocabulary.

On meeting one of your men in a public place, greet him personally and in a friendly manner. If his family is with him, be gracious to his wife and children. You lose nothing in stature and grow in your man's esteem.

An officer does not drink with his men. This time-honored proscription should be observed with good judgment. If you are offered a drink at a division or ship's party ashore, where it would be discourteous to decline, take a glass for comradeship. But always remember that no officer ever *gets drunk* with his men. Exercise of common sense and human understanding will always resolve successfully such difficult situations.

Visit your sick men. A man never forgets the officer who exhibits the human kindliness to come to see him when he is ill. Find out if there is anything that he needs and if there is anything you can do to advance his recovery.

Inspire collaboration by your interest in your men. When you get to know your men individually, you not only give them a feeling of belonging, but also develop in them a desire to serve the organization thoughtfully and helpfully. To ask for suggestions in solving a problem is pleasing to a petty officer or nonrated man. Never let doubt develop that you are the boss, but a good leader never has to "fly his stripes."

Give credit where credit is due—and give it publicly. Make the presentation as formal as possible.

Do not pass the buck. You are responsible for every action in your organization. Give a deserved reprimand to any subordinate who falls down on the job, but in minor discrepancies "take the rap" for him as far as senior authority is concerned.

Do not issue orders which you cannot enforce. On the other hand, promise nothing which you cannot deliver. Your word must be as good as your bond.

In all your dealings with your men, avoid extremes of laxness and tautness. Be sure that your men know their place, but to firmness bring kindliness and courtesy. Try to be the same at all times, so that you can avoid confusion to your men and they may always know what to expect from you.

619. MORALE. The morale of a military organization is of the utmost importance and is the constant concern of its leader. The morale of a ship may be said to be the state of mind of the crew with reference to confidence in its leaders, to courage, and to fidelity of purpose. Like the character of a ship, the standard of morale is set in the Wardroom. The morale of a crew is nourished, promoted, and sustained by the character and professional competence of the ship's officers.

There is considerable confusion in the thinking with respect to morale. Why does one ship have an excellent morale, when a ship in the same division, with very nearly the same sort of officers and men and similar operating and living conditions, has a low morale? This is a question to which no one knows the complete answer. The following suggestions have been tried in a number of ships during peace and war and have helped to improve the morale and spirit of the crew.

Keep the men informed. Once you are at sea, tell the men as much about future operations as you can. They will react differently to information that they are out for gunnery and tactical exercises or that contact with the enemy is probable. Nothing is feared as much as the unknown. When battle is in prospect, *put out the dope!* A good effect will result not only in the spirit of the men, but also in the manner in which they will perform their duties. Post charts of the operating areas on bulletin boards about the ship and keep them up to date. If the ship should be sunk, the men will know where they are and what to do about it.

See that orders are promulgated to your men. Publish the Executive Officer's memorandums and Ship's Orders to your division at Quarters. Keep a file of effective orders available for your petty officers and insist that they read them.

Insist that your men get enough rest. When the ship is on a watch-in-four schedule, ship's work can be conducted in a normal manner. But when the crew is on watch and watch, it is a good plan to abandon any ambitious schemes of cleanliness and upkeep and to do only the most necessary work. In slack times in operations under wartime conditions, let men not immediately required sleep on their stations, but insist that men on lookout, telephones, and other important watches maintain a war alertness.

With service of ships in combat areas for long months without any adequate liberty and recreation, the most effective means of preventing a lowering of morale is to keep the men busy at sea, and in port when at dull and uninteresting advanced bases. At sea, greater effort should be expended toward intensive training of the crew at their battle stations. In port, the cleanliness and upkeep of the ship and crew should be given the careful attention of all officers.

All ships nowadays have motion-picture projectors, and there is hardly a place in the world where programs cannot be obtained. Frequently, blackouts and dimouts prevent showing movies on topside, but with a careful investigation of local conditions, you will usually find that if several showings are arranged during the afternoon and evening nearly every person who wants to see the picture can do so. Newer ships have closed circuit television that can be used for entertainment as well as for training.

There are many other ways to promote the amusement and contentment of the crew. Boxing meets and other happy hours not only provide entertainment for the audience, but give an outlet to the talented members of the crew for their excess energy. Many ship's companies have worked up simulated radio shows, comprising excellent music and clever skits. In smaller ships, quiz programs after the pattern of "Information, Please" have proved to be very popular with the crew. Even small ships have organized glee clubs, hillbilly bands and string quartets.

Of primary interest and concern to all sailors is their personal mail.

It should be the concern of all officers to promote the expeditious forwarding of mail and its rapid distribution. As Officer of the Deck, see that the mail orderly gets off promptly on his regular trips and is sent immediately to the Fleet Post Office on receipt of information that mail has arrived in the harbor.

Initiate a regular training program in consonance with schedules promulgated by higher authority—and stick to it.

Create a positive atmosphere in your division. No good performance of even a routine job should go without public commendation. Performance not up to standard should be the subject of constructive criticism and instruction, not reprimand. Give commendation and criticism to and through your petty officers. Use the proper chain of command.

Neither you nor your petty officers have authority to restrict a bluejacket to the ship. If the offense is serious enough for such punishment, take your man to Captain's Mast.

See that messmen are always clean in their person, wear clean whites, keep their tables and mess gear spotlessly clean and sanitary, and police up promptly after each meal. Rotate mess duty frequently among the nonrated men.

Insist that your men present a seamanlike appearance in dungarees—articles properly marked, sleeves and trouser legs rolled down, except when scrubbing decks or paintwork. Require your men to be in the proper uniform-of-the-day on watch, in port, and on Sundays and holidays. Inspect your men for personal appearance at each Quarters formation.

If permitted by Ship's Regulations, promote a television set for your division. See if music can be played over the loud speaker system during the noon hour.

Arrange for an advance payday to meet liberty or leave requirements and provide checks for any men who desire them.

Counseling. Learn how to counsel your men when they face a personal problem or some difficulty which they cannot resolve without assistance. Since your man's problem is important to him as a person, it should be handled personally and privately. Let *him* talk. Listen carefully to his explanation, review the facts he has presented, think the problem through aloud, and then advise him. Help him to help himself.

Indicate your willingness to help by your attitude and sympathetic manner of asking questions. Recognize your limitations. Seek assistance from your seniors, refer the man to the Chaplain, or take him to see another appropriate officer. Remember that, as a counselor, whatever you learn is given in confidence, and respect such confidence. After counseling, keep in touch with your man and follow through.

Religion. Many of your men are of a deeply religious nature. See that they have an opportunity regularly to attend a service conducted by a minister of their faith. In port, a chaplain in another ship will be happy to hold service in your ship, if asked. Insist that improper activities be suspended during church services. You will find that, during action, a strong religious belief will calm the fears of the men and help them to perform their duties effectively.

Do not leave religious activity exclusively to the chaplains. Be broad-minded—regardless of your personal affiliation, set a good example by attending Divine Services when held in your ship and by living according to the highest moral and ethical principles. Encourage your men to attend religious services. Active participation in the religion of their choice will elevate their moral standards, contribute to a high morale in the ship, and help to raise the moral tone of the whole command.

Develop a team spirit in your division. Give each of your men a feeling of identification with the group. It will be necessary to pay especial attention to the backward member of your group so that he will feel

FIGURE 606. Church service aboard ship.

that he belongs and is recognized as an integral part of the group. One way to accomplish this is to encourage him to go out for athletics, for ship or division baseball, football, basketball team, or boat crew. When he becomes a participator in an athletic team, he will be easier to incorporate into your division team. He will gain a feeling of loyalty to your division and a spirit "not to let the other fellow down."

Division and ship competition help to develop a team spirit. Whenever the ship or division participates in a competition, the whole organization off watch should attend and cheer for their team. Thus the individual will tend to lose that uncooperative attitude of "What's in it for me?" and acquire instead a feeling that the reputation and performance of the division is more important than the safety and rewards of the individual.

Team spirit can also be fostered in talks by the division officer. In idle moments while waiting at Quarters, he can impress upon his men his enthusiasm for the division and the ship and his confidence that his men and his outfit are *the best*. This will help to make his men want to

FIGURE 607. Commendation is a strong lever of leadership. The Admiral awards the Bronze Star.

belong to his organization, and lead them to appreciate that the intangible but greatest reward a service man can expect comes from a feeling of satisfaction for man's service well rendered to other men.

To build up a good morale in your division and in your ship, take a real interest in your men. Instruct and train them until they are good workers. Develop in them a confidence in themselves and in their leaders. Thus you build up within them a profound conviction of excellence, until you hear them saying about the decks, "The *Blake* is the best damned ship in this or any other Navy." That is the sort of spirit which makes for a happy ship and wins battles under any conceivable circumstances.

Perhaps you may ask again, at this point, "What is morale?" A ship with a good morale is a taut, efficient, well-organized ship, in which the officers are capable leaders who *at all times* display a fine example of fairness, loyalty, and consideration for their subordinates and who thus exhibit in themselves and inspire in their men a conviction of military excellence.

620. DISCIPLINE AND PUNISHMENT. Discipline has been defined as training or a course of training that corrects, molds, strengthens, or perfects. There, in a few words, is your directive for handling your men. Guide and direct their efforts along the correct channels to good discipline.

Admiral Arleigh A. Burke has written, "Discipline is the art of synchronizing human relationships so that each individual knows and does his part in order that all parts will work well together. Good discipline gives each man confidence that the man next to him will do his very best, that he will uphold the honor and the duty of his unit."[1]

Punishment may be defined as the infliction of a penalty by one in authority in retribution for an offense. Note the word "retribution." It implies the violation of certain rules, laws, or orders, issued by competent authority, for violation of which the offender must pay a fair and just penalty.

Discipline in our Navy is not synonymous with *punishment*. When the men are properly directed, there is little need for punishment.

Discipline can be generated by the officer who has first disciplined himself. Confidence in the leader promotes good discipline. Cheerful, spontaneous cooperation and compliance with orders are results of proper discipline under a respected leader. The discipline of fear, of driving, of "cracking the whip," of threats of punishment is neither encouraged in our service nor desirable.

Poor discipline results in ineffective operations and lowered combat efficiency. Many military authorities believe that the worst influence on discipline in the services has been the extensive introduction of civilian standards of performance since World War II. In a reversal of

[1] *Selected Readings in Leadership*, page 14, U. S. Naval Institute, Annapolis, Md.

statistics, 65 percent of naval personnel are now on shore instead of at sea. Like their civilian counterparts, many junior officers and petty officers live "off-base" and commute to work each day, tending to resent any interference with their normal 8-hour day. The sense of integration, of close association, of belonging to an organization as a "band of brothers" is apt to get lost under such operating conditions.

When men, who have been accustomed to such shore duty are ordered to sea, with long periods in European waters or in the Orient, with much time at sea and little leave or liberty, the resentment tends to increase, but the voice of the majority must never be permitted to become the voice of authority. Leadership under such operating conditions has never been more challenging for the junior officer.

Admiral Burke has listed four major factors materially disrupting good discipline:[2]

1. Lack of information. Subordinates must be kept informed as to problems and the *why* of certain actions.

2. Lack of interest. Seniors must affirmatively indicate that they are interested in their juniors and their problems.

3. Slackness in command. The old saying that "a taut ship is a happy ship" is still valid. The officers and men know where they stand and what is expected of them.

4. Instability of personnel and operating schedules. With foresight and careful planning, reasonable permanency of personnel in ships and on shore stations can be established. Longer enlistments will reduce in-transit time. While operating schedules probably never can be completely stabilized, better planning can reduce the inconvenience of too frequent changes in schedule to ship-based personnel.

Most of the problems of poor discipline can be corrected by a general tautening within the divisions of a ship. Tautness requires absolute fairness. No "soft billets" can exist. The officers and men must be on the job and require others to be on the job. Only in this way can each man place absolute dependence upon his division mates and shipmates. Men who fail to meet these standards must be promptly called to account. A smart, happy ship and clean, alert men are the *results* of good discipline and effective leadership, not the *cause* thereof.

An ideal state of discipline in a ship's company is attained when there is a maximum of efficiency and contentment, combined with a minimum of punishment. However, the fact that there have been but few punishments in recent months in a ship does not necessarily indicate that discipline is at a peak; it may indicate that the disciplinary

[2] *Ibid.*, pp. 86-93.

system is faulty. To be effective, punishment must be prompt and just.

Discipline in Your Division. The supervision and guidance which the division officer, his junior officers, and petty officers daily give to the men are the key factors in achieving a high standard of discipline in a ship. Junior officers and petty officers have a tendency to be too lenient with minor infractions of discipline. Direct personal action by the division officer on the first appearance of such an attitude will correct such discrepancies, eliminate charges of favoritism, prevent later courts-martial, and greatly increase the effectiveness of the command. To have the required knowledge of incipient trouble, senior officers and division officers must place more emphasis on handling men and less on paper work. This necessitates close supervision and considerable time spent with subordinates.

To promote good discipline in your division, you must set high standards by example and precept and insist that your standards be maintained. A well-disciplined division exhibits smartness in every activity. The routine evolutions run like clockwork, the men are military and snappy in their movements, and present a pleasing appearance at all times. Each duty is performed with smartness and precision.

To build up such a spirit in your division, you must spend the time with your men adequately to supervise, guide, and counsel them and thus develop a feeling of mutual respect and understanding. Foster in your men a feeling that they are superior. When you hear them saying about their parts of the ship, "The Fighting Fifth is the best damned division in the ship," you possess an *esprit de corps* which is beyond price.

You will always have a small percentage of backward, inefficient, sloppy, virtually useless men. Procedures are available to rid the service of those undesirables and misfits who succeed in getting into the Navy despite the screening efforts of the recruiting officers. Where a good man has taken a sudden slump, it is your duty to discover the reason. Get him off by himself where you can talk together uninterrupted and not overheard. Sometimes his trouble is personal—illness in his family, loss of a dear relative, marital or financial difficulties, family insecurity. Sometimes his difficulty is aboard ship, possibly right in your division. Sometimes, he is a dog with a bad name. Often, a mere airing of his difficulties will resolve them. Use your understanding and authority. Talk to him. Admonish him as to the probable results of slovenly or vicious behavior. Point out the advantage of good behavior —advancement in rating, increase in pay, and honor and distinction among his shipmates.

If such discussions are not effective, take corrective measures which will not infringe upon your commanding officer's prerogative to administer all punishment. If a man is shiftless, does not turn-to well, or is hard to keep on the job, you are well within your authority to require him to complete his work after working hours. However, you must keep a close check on your bos'nmate and other leading petty officers. Be sure you know what is going on below decks. Most leading petty officers are right thinking, conscientious men, but a careless or brutal petty officer can ruin the spirit and discipline in a division.

Some men are just not amenable to discipline. If you cannot straighten out a man, put him on the report when he has committed an offense in violation of the UCMJ. The Executive Officer and the Captain will always back you up. Investigate each case thoroughly, especially when a petty officer makes the report. Know the facts and be ready to support at Mast your recommendation for punishment.

Whether you have put a man of your division on report or someone else has, always go to Captain's Mast with your man. If he is a good man, step forward and say a good word for him. If you feel that you can say nothing favorable for him, your mere presence at Mast is helpful. Your man will feel, "There's the Division Officer standing up with me, anyhow, even if he can't say anything for me." But remember, your frequent appearance at Mast with your men reflects discredit upon your division and, therefore, upon your performance of duty.

Measures of Discipline. Admiral Burke has said: "A well-disciplined organization is one whose members work with enthusiasm, willingness, and zest as individuals and as a group to fulfill the mission of the organization with expectation of success." He has stated that, in addition to the criterion of combat ability, good discipline is exemplified by the following:

1. A dignified pride and self-respect—pride in the Navy, in the unit, and in oneself.

2. A willingness to work for and make personal sacrifices for the group good.

3. A smart appearance—a sloppy ship or slovenly man will be so in action.

4. A respect for fellow men, exemplified by courtesy and consideration.

5. A cheerful optimism, liveliness, and exhilaration.

In handling your men, never forget the great stimulus of praise given for work well done. Commend your men publicly. When you must reprimand, do so privately. *Avoid ridicule of your men,* for ridicule is one of the most vicious weapons in existence for breaking a man's spirit and ruining the morale of a division or a command.

621. THE AMERICAN BLUEJACKET. We have examined at some length into the character and motivation of the American bluejacket and have arrived at the conclusion that he is superior to the enlisted man in any other Navy. The American bluejacket cannot be driven, overawed, browbeaten, or abused. He must be *led* by able leaders, who by example, ability, consideration, and fair play promote in their men the will to excel and a resolute loyalty to their leaders and to their cause.

The deeds of the enlisted men in World War II and the Korean conflict reaffirmed again and again their high quality and great ability. They came ashore on Guadalcanal from sinking ships in Savo Sound and asked, "How in the hell do they expect us to fight battle wagons with tin cans?" But they did just that—and won!

It is your grave responsibility as an officer to measure up to the excellent standard necessary to lead and inspire such men to proper action. Most important among all the qualities which promote efficiency and encourage good morale and a fighting spirit in your ship is a sincere and conscientious interest in the personal welfare of your men.

622. NOTES FOR THE DIVISION OFFICER. 1. In a certain ship which was well known for its appearance and efficiency and in which discipline had reached a high state, an unwritten order required that the Division Officer be in his part of the ship at 0800 each working day. He was not to interfere with the petty officers, supervising the work of cleaning up before Quarters, but his mere presence indicated to all hands his interest in the work going on. He maintained close touch with his men, and this interest was well repaid. When anything is going on in your part of the ship, be there. Keep the same hours that you require your men to keep.

On the other hand, in this same ship, officers were not required to remain on board after their work had been completed. It was unnecessary to "gun deck" the appearance of working furiously and accomplishing nothing. When an officer requested permission to leave the ship—at any hour—it was understood by his head of department that his work was completed for that day.

2. Utilize your leading petty officers as junior division officers. Give them responsibility. Outline what is to be done, and leave the "how" up to them. Restrict your dealings with lower ratings to a minimum.

And, in that connection, do not use the Wardroom or your stateroom as a place of business, in which to interview your men or issue directions. See them in their own parts of the ship or in an office if provided.

3. Again, set the example for your men. Be neat and clean. It has been said that no officer (and gentleman) who has any self-respect would appear before his shipmates in the morning unshaven. You cannot expect obedience to custom or orders unless you abide by these yourself.

4. Salute the Admiral, Captain, and Executive Officer whenever you meet them about ship, except when standing watch on bridge. Then, salute when making reports.

Salute other officers your senior when you first meet them for the day. Give them a cheery "Good morning," return their greeting pleasantly. Do not ignore them.

Find out the local custom as to permission to leave the ship. On many ships, you must obtain permission from both your division officer and the head of department. On some ships, permission to go ashore is presumed to be granted out of working hours, *when your work is done.* In wartime, shore leave is severely curtailed and hours ashore are few.

Boat etiquette is designed to expedite loading boats. It is neither polite nor sensible to stand back for a senior when it is your turn to embark. Nor is it courteous to leap out of a boat to get clear of the gangway unless told to do so. Observe proper boat etiquette.

5. The new officer should realize that his situation is very much like being "plebes again"—with important variations. Listen well, but talk little. At first, you will be given all the dirty little odd jobs. Do them well.

6. Get around the ship. The Wardroom is no place for a junior officer, except during meal hours and out of working hours.

7. No matter how late you went to bed, always be up early on the job. Your Executive Officer will not be pleased to see junior officers breakfasting late and luxuriously at 0900, or even at 0830. When you really feel bad in the morning, try a shave. It often makes you feel better, and it always improves your appearance.

8. *R.H.I.P.* Just because you saw a senior officer do something, it is not necessarily permissible for you. With increased responsibility come higher rank and correspondingly greater privileges.

9. The proper attitude toward your seniors is deferential friendliness. Remember, jokes and "wisecracks" travel a one-way path from senior to junior. Some seniors can "take it," but no one seems to like a "smart aleck." Although your Captain and Executive Officer may be

somewhat reserved and unapproachable, they are human and want to be friendly. Remember, they have been through it all, and so they know what you are thinking about, while you have but an imperfect knowledge of their problems, cares, and troubles. But always remember —*the senior officers of your ship are on your team, too.*

10. In peacetime, the new ensign is kept under instruction for a considerable period because he has so much to learn. In wartime, heavy responsibilities are immediately thrust upon him. *He must grow up quickly.* So make work for yourself. Ask your division officer if you can handle certain details for him. Then, *handle them well.*

11. Always follow through on a job. If there is any criticism or complaint, you probably have not used your full intelligence or worked hard enough at the job.

12. Consult your division officer or other immediate senior frequently with regard to your work. Do not be afraid to ask his advice.

13. Keep yourself and your men busy with useful work, keep your men fully informed, exhibit and express a positive optimism, and cultivate the saving grace of a good sense of humor.

14. All of us make mistakes. Your seniors have. You will. Do your utmost to be right; but, when wrong, do not be afraid to admit it. Both your seniors and juniors will respect you the more for an honest admission of error. When reprimanded or when your attention is called to an error, take it in the proper spirit of cooperation. We are all striving for perfection. A cheerful "Aye, aye, sir" turns away wrath.

623. LEADERSHIP. A number of thoughts on leadership have been examined. But what is good leadership? Unfortunately, a definition is difficult to contrive. But this is known. You will be a good leader when your men look up to you with confidence in your leadership; when they are eager to know your wishes and to see them fulfilled; when they are unhappy at your censure and are eager to win your praise; when they are ready to jump at a word from you, whether they think you are right or wrong.

Most important is the power of example. Before everything, you must *practice what you preach!* You must be what you want your men to be. In your person, in your every act and speech, you must be military, smart, and decisive. If you expect your men to work hard and effectively, you must be active, energetic, and enthusiastic—and *you must be cheerful!* Such an example is contagious. By such example, you are practicing what you preach.

At the risk of redundancy, the importance of knowing your job must be stressed. Of course, you must know your own specialty; you must know your own bailiwick, inside and out; but, also, be a *seaman!* Know more about the ship and your part of the ship than any of your blue-jackets know. Ask yourself these question—now:

Where are the fireplugs? How do I get into the magazines at anchor at night?

Could I veer the anchor chain, unassisted by the chief bos'nmate? Could I let go the anchor with only a seaman to help? Could I slip the buoy and go to sea if left senior officer on board? Could I get back again if I did? How do I connect up and heave in on the chain?

If an engineer, can I get the plant underway? What does the chief engineer do to get underway? Could I handle low steam pressure and tell inexperienced men what to do? Could I show them? If the boilers lost suction, what should I do?

Do I know my stuff?

Do not forget that your character is expressed by your every act. Your words, expressions, habitual gestures, and subtle actions are the book by which your character is read. Therefore, avoid careless criticism. *Any fool can criticize.* If the situation in your ship is bad, *do something* about it. Do not just sit and gripe and whine. Keep always in mind that "the character of a ship is set in the Wardroom." Whatever happens, however grim the circumstances, *keep cheerful.*

CHAPTER 7

Personal Administration

Although I can not insure success, I will endeavor to deserve it.
—COMMODORE JOHN PAUL JONES, 1780

Your Official Record

701. YOUR PERSONAL FILE. Make a point of keeping a personal file of your official and semiofficial records and correspondence. The day of your arrival at your first station is the best time to start your file. Commence your file with your first set of orders and attachments. To these papers, add important official or semiofficial letters which you write or receive. It is suggested that you break this single file down into subject files as time increases the bulk of your official papers.

Keep a scrap book of photographs and other memorabilia. Twenty years from now, you will be happy to refresh your memory of the stirring events of your early naval career. Not infrequently, you will find these personal records of inestimable value in establishing facts and dates of importance to you.

Keep a journal or at least a date book. It may seem laughable to you now, but officers do write their memoirs and many of them are important sources of historical material. Jot down in brief form important happenings each day or once a week.

702. PURPOSE OF AN OFFICER'S OFFICIAL RECORD. Upon first commissioning you were suddenly removed from the routine of academy, college, or school, which exercised a careful guidance of all your affairs, and thrown very much upon your own. Suddenly released from regimentation, many a young officer, without intent to be lax in conduct or indifferent to the demands of duty, has failed to accept his new station and responsibilities with full seriousness and industry or has neglected to observe the proper code of conduct of a naval officer. Before he realizes it, a considerable body of unfavorable material collects in the "books which are kept in Washington," which, taken in the aggregate, could be as detrimental to his future as trial and conviction by general court-martial.

Whether favorable or unfavorable, matter rightfully placed in an officer's record cannot be removed without special authorization of the Secretary of the Navy. Such permission is rarely granted. Each day of his naval career, an officer accumulates material of record, which continually adds to the evidence which will become the basis for his personal and professional "service reputation."

FIGURE 701. USS *Warden* (DLG-18) exemplifies the speed and fire power of the modern fleet.

An officer's official record, kept in the Bureau of Naval Personnel, consists of a number of separate files. Chief among these are:

The Fitness Report Jacket, which contains:

• Reports of fitness.

• Letters attached to, and officially submitted as part of fitness reports.

• Photographs.

• Statements regarding unsatisfactory fitness reports and acknowledgment of any unfavorable matter therein.

The Officer's Miscellaneous Correspondence and Orders Jacket contains all correspondence to, from, and affecting an officer of a general nature, such as reports of leave, beneficiary slips, home address, request for and orders to duty, etc.

The Confidential File includes correspondence pertaining to an officer from any source which must be retained in a confidential status. In the majority of officers' cases, there is no confidential file. It may be seen only on authorization of the Chief of Naval Personnel on each occasion. Matter of an unfavorable nature is referred to the officer before it is filed.

Professional Examinations of officers to promotion, when given, are filed in the office of the Judge Advocate General and may be examined by the individual officer there.

Records of Proceedings of courts and boards affecting an officer are also filed in the office of the Judge Advocate General.

The Selection Board Jacket is presented to the selection board which is considering an officer for promotion. It contains:

• Certificates: Birth, citizenship, education and training. Commissions, appointments, acceptances, waivers, oaths of office, classification changes, records of emergency data, statements of personal history, certificates of security clearance and documents certifying completion of security investigative requirements.

• Copies of citations, awards, and letters of commendation or censure.

• Reports of physical examination, medical surveys, personal biographies, transcripts of service, applications for commissions, notices of separation, requests for change of duty and tenders of resignation, retirement requests, and other voluntary applications for separation from active duty.

• Written communications from the officer concerned inviting attention of the selection board to matters of record.

• Statements of the officer in reply to adverse matter in his selection board jacket.

• Extracts from the findings and recommendations of courts and boards concerning the officer. These include statements of disciplinary action and promulgating letters of general courts-martial. Complete records of proceedings of courts-martial, inquiries, investigations, etc., are filed in the office of the Judge Advocate General.

Correspondence of a confidential nature pertaining to an officer's record is filed in the personal custody of the Head, Officer Records Branch, BuPers and cross-referenced in the record. In the majority of cases, there is no confidential matter pertaining to the officer and, consequently, no confidential file. Access to an officer's confidential file is allowed in the same manner as the rest of his record.

In addition to the officer's official record as described, correspondence of a general administration nature pertaining to an officer is filed in his Officer's Miscellaneous Correspondence and Orders File. This file, which does not go before selection boards, includes such matter as copies of orders, officer order memoranda, home addresses, the enlisted record of an officer who was given a permanent initial appointment or warrant subsequent to 1 January 1948, and other material not needed in his official record for performance evaluation.

Certain records you must have filed in your ship or at your duty station or always with you when in transit:

Your *Service Record* contains a summary of your military service; your military and civilian background, education, and skills; a record of emergency data (see Section 1706); and similar personal information. This record enables your commanding officer to give you a proper assignment in line with your experience and ability.

Your *Pay Record* is a card on which your pay and allowances are credited, and which shows a paymaster the amount of pay to which you are entitled at any time. Your pay record is filed with the disbursing officer of your ship but should be carried with you when in transit or on authorized leave. Upon presenting your orders or leave papers with your pay record, you can draw pay due you from any armed forces disbursing officer.

Your *Health Record* is kept in the Bureau of Medicine and Surgery and a copy is furnished you, entered up-to-date, when you are detached or ordered to temporary duty. It contains your physical description and the medical history of every ailment you have had during your military service. An important function of your health record is to record the inoculations and vaccinations which you are required to have current.

703. ACCESS TO OFFICIAL RECORD. An officer himself, the clerk of a court of competent jurisdiction in response to a valid order of that court, the officers of the Navy Department for use in official business, and the representative of the officer upon presentation by him of written authorization from the officer, may have access to an officer's official record. If the officer desires his representative to see his confidential file, he must so state in his letter of authorization.

704. PURPOSE OF FITNESS REPORTS. A performance evaluation or Fitness Report of some kind is an utter necessity. In an organization as large as the Navy, without Fitness Reports it would be impossible to pass upon the relative merits of officers of the same experience when considering them for promotion or assignment to duty. Imperfect as it may be, owing to human faults and frailties in its preparation, the Fitness Report has evolved down through the years and is one of the best records of its type in existence today.

At its best, the Fitness Report, properly prepared by a commanding officer afloat or ashore, gives an objective evaluation of the officer reported on. Practically, it represents the well-considered opinion of a senior as to the performance of duty during a specific period of one of his subordinates. With the years, a collection of such reports accumulates in the officer's file in the Bureau of Naval Personnel in Washington. These reports are made by a number of senior officers, who may be presumed to be impersonal in their actions and to have the best interests of the service at heart. Taken together, the reports give a running record of an officer's performance of duty under varying conditions and make possible an accurate estimate of the individual's capabilities by a selection board, when one is convened to consider officers of his grade for promotion. They also provide guidance to the detail officer in the Bureau of Naval Personnel in assigning the officer to duty which he can best perform.

Fitness Reports serve the following specific purposes:

• To inform the bureau as to duties performed by an officer during a specific period and the manner in which those duties were performed.

• To furnish information on the degree to which an officer has exhibited the qualities of leadership during a certain period.

• To obtain a record of the current qualifications of an officer in several types of duty.

• To obtain opinions as to the officer's all-around ability and value to the service and his qualification for promotion.

• To indicate the professional qualifications of the officer.

• To indicate commendatory or censorious material received about him and any disciplinary action taken.

• To indicate the general state of his health.

• To indicate his personal characteristics.

705. FITNESS REPORTS. The basic rules for submission of Fitness Reports are given in Navy Regulations, Article 1701, as implemented and supplemented by BuPers Instruction 1611 Series. These rules and instructions are too lengthy to quote in full but should be carefully studied by every officer, particularly by those required to report upon the fitness of other officers under them.

A Fitness Report must be submitted covering each day of an officer's service from date of initial commission until retirement or death, usually by his next senior in the chain of command. The commanding officer of a ship or aviation squadron reports on the fitness of all officers under his command. When he is on temporary additional duty or deployed under an operational commander, an officer may be concurrently reported on by the officer under whose immediate command or control he comes, if significant duties are performed, as well as by his regular commanding officer. These concurrent reports are forwarded to his record in BuPers via his regular commanding officer tc inform him of what and how well his subordinate has performed for another commander. When an officer reports for additional or operational duty to an officer who is junior to him, his concurrent fitness reports are made out by the first officer in this chain of command who is his senior. The authority to prepare Fitness Reports in the Navy Department and in large commands is sometimes delegated, with the concurrence of the Chief of Naval Personnel, to responsible juniors in principal subordinate administrative divisions within these organizations where the number of officers to be reported on warrants such action.

Periodic Fitness Reports are submitted annually on lieutenants and more senior officers who have accumulated sufficient performance record for selection and assignment purposes. Semi-annual reports are made for junior officers to ensure more frequent performance evaluation as well as to accelerate the development of adequate performance records for selection and assignment purposes. Reports are also made whenever an officer or his reporting senior is detached. Officers under instruction are reported on upon completion of the course of instruction and at least once a year when undergoing courses of longer duration.

Special reports are submitted when an officer (1) distinguishes himself in battle; (2) performs an outstanding act of valor or devotion to duty; (3) displays extraordinary courage, ability, or resource in time of peril or great responsibility; (4) is guilty of serious misconduct or marked inefficiency; or (5) when requested by the Chief of Naval Personnel for specific purpose.

Fitness Reports are mailed direct to the Bureau of Naval Personnel by the reporting senior (except that concurrent reports are forwarded via the regular reporting senior) and are considered confidential in nature. To speed up forwarding and handling, they are not marked confidential but are mailed in double envelopes, the inner envelope marked "Report of Fitness, For Official Use Only." When papers of a classified nature are attached, the report must be handled in the same manner as the classified material concerned.

To promote complete freedom of expression, reporting officers are not *required* to show a report to an officer, unless an item or remark is unsatisfactory or unfavorable, in which case he refers it to the officer privately (officially) for such statement as he cares to make. A reporting officer *may,* however, show his Fitness Report to an officer. Some commanding officers make this a practice, feeling that they promote the efficiency of the individual and the ship by indicating to their officers in what ways they are considered to be excellent and in what particulars they can improve themselves. A reporting officer is required to indicate on the form whether or not the officer reported on has seen the report.

Sometimes it is not possible, but when it is, a Fitness Report must "say something." In most ships, it is customary for heads of departments to submit rough reports to the Executive Officer, who indicates any changes he may think advisable and forwards them to the Captain for his information. Under this procedure, an officer can feel assured that his performance of duty has been carefully considered by at least two senior officers besides the Captain, one of whom, at least, must have a considerable knowledge of his abilities. With good advice, a commanding officer can make his reports significant and meaningful, both to the individual officer and to the Navy.

706. PREPARATION OF FITNESS REPORTS. The officer who is called upon to report on the performance of his juniors bears a heavy responsibility. The Navy Regulations say, "Reports of fitness are decisive in the career of the individual officer and have an important influence on the efficiency of the entire service. The preparation of these reports is, therefore, one of the most important and responsible duties of superior officers."

The task of making out these reports should not be entered upon lightly. The preparation of a report should begin sufficiently in advance of the due date to insure its arrival in the Bureau of Naval Personnel within 15 days following the terminal date of the report. Being so closely geared to selection board convening dates, any delay in the submission of reports after the due date could result in the board not having the most recent performance evaluation. Careful consideration should be given to each officer by the reporting officer and by the officers who submit rough reports to a commanding officer for consideration. A reporting officer should have complete knowledge as to the standards currently in use; otherwise he may, unwittingly, do serious damage to an officer he really admires.

The reporting officer must keep before him constantly the necessity for presenting an accurate and concise picture of the officer reported upon. As one captain expressed it:

> When you are making out Fitness Reports, you are alone with a piece of paper, God, and your own conscience. I make it a practice to throw out all partisanship, insofar as is humanly possible, and try to evaluate the officer concerned as accurately as I can, keeping in mind the standard of marks and remarks that prevail in the service today. I consider making out these reports the most important single duty that I perform. If I allow myself to be influenced by friendship, because an ineffective young lad has a likable personality, I do the Navy an injustice. If I allow my personal antipathy for some officer to influence me against him, when he is doing a superior job, I am doing that officer an injustice. I honestly attempt to be impartial. On how well other reporting officers and I succeed depends, in a large measure, how effective our officer corps will be. It is our duty to do this job well.

It is in filling out the remarks section that the reporting officer must do the soul searching to which the captain referred above. When filled out, this statement should constitute a complete, but brief, estimate of the character and abilities of the officer reported upon. Comments under this paragraph might read as follows:

> This officer has a pleasing personality and a fine military character. He is adept at handling personnel, getting along particularly well with enlisted men. Under exceptionally difficult conditions, he has repeatedly exhibited the finest attributes of leadership. See section 13 for commendation by Commander Task Force 8. He is an efficient control officer for antiaircraft batteries of any kind and is well qualified for gunnery officer of any type of ship up to heavy cruiser. He is well qualified for promotion.

Not all officers will merit such a glowing summation of their military virtues, but all should strive to deserve it.

707. WHAT THE FITNESS REPORT MEANS TO YOU. If you are a young officer, you will be interested principally in receiving reports rather than making them. As previously pointed out, they constitute an accurate evaluation of your merits and demerits. Not all commanders believe in letting officers know how they are doing, but there is a way you can find out. If you will present yourself at the Bureau of Naval Personnel the next time you are in Washington, you will be granted permission to examine your Fitness Reports and the rest of your record. Most officers feel that thus they gain a knowledge about themselves which is invaluable. If the same unfortunate traits are commented upon time after time, once you know about this you can take steps to correct your deficiencies. But avoid the obvious pitfall—do not feel resentment against the reporting senior. Except in very unusual cases, he is perfectly sincere. Remember, *you* can be wrong. You want to improve your performance of duty. Learn about yourself by looking at *you* through *his eyes*. In very few professions is this opportunity to see yourself as others see you presented. If you take a constructive view of your reports, you can determine your own weaknesses and "pull yourself up by your own bootstraps."

But the best advice about Fitness Reports is—do not worry about them. Do the job given you to the best of your ability. Do it even better than you know how. Go out and look for opportunities to help. In the words of a wise captain of the old school, "The Fitness Reports will take care of themselves."

Promotion

708. GENERAL. The Navy goes through periods of cutback and periods of great expansion. In the cutback phase, promotion is very slow. In expansion periods, there are frequent opportunities for advancement. But promotion does not come automatically—it must be earned. While it is essential that an officer perform the duties of his current rank conscientiously, diligently, and effectively, he must also demonstrate his capacity for carrying the added responsibilities of the next higher rank.

As has been demonstrated in peace and war, able young officers will drive upward through sheer merit. Courage, foresight, and ingenuity will bring their reward in steady and certain advancement.

709. SYSTEM OF PROMOTION. The Officer Personnel Act of 1947, now codified in Title 10, United States Code, provides the basis for the post-war promotion system in the Army, Navy, and Air Force. Promotions are accomplished by selection to grades above lieutenant (jg); the eligibility requirements, selection board procedure, etc., being the same, whether for temporary or permanent promotion, as outlined. So long as temporary promotions are permitted under the act, however, selection boards for permanent promotions will not be convened. The number of permanent appointments allowed in each grade in the line and in those grades of the staff corps where distribution is prescribed will be based upon the distribution applied to the total number of permanently commissioned line officers or staff officers of the corps concerned, on active duty, subject to the finite numerical limitations on permanent rear admirals. The total number of officers serving in a grade in the line or in a staff corps where distribution is prescribed, under both temporary and permanent commissions, will be based upon the distribution applied to the total number of line officers, or staff officers of the corps concerned, on active duty, including Regulars, Reserves, and temporary officers, subject to reduction by the Secretary of the Navy if he finds that a lesser number than the computed number for a grade will meet the needs of the service. For the Regular officer, selection for temporary promotion and failure of selection for temporary promotion have a permanent effect.

For example, a Regular line officer whose permanent grade is lieutenant commander and temporary grade commander, when the distribution percentages place him in the permanent grade of commander, would be permanently commissioned in that grade without further selection. If temporarily promoted to captain, he would later be permanently commissioned as a captain when the distribution of Regular officers permitted, without further selection. If he failed of selection for temporary promotion to captain twice or more, he would be retired upon the completion of 26 years of total commissioned service.

A Reserve or temporary officer reaching a promotion point will be temporarily promoted if recommended by the selection board as qualified for continued active duty in the higher grade. It is not required that such officers be recommended as best fitted for promotion to the next higher grade. Reserve and temporary officers not recommended for promotion are not mandatorily retired or discharged and may be retained on active duty.

Aeronautical engineering duty and special duty categories were created by the OPA of 1947. Designation of officers for special duty in fields such as communications, law, hydrography, photography, public affairs, psychology and intelligence was provided.

Admirals and Vice Admirals. Of the Officers who may be designated for the rank of admiral or vice admiral the law provided that only the Chief of Naval Operations and seven others may have the rank of admiral. However, that restriction has been dispensed with for the present by Executive Order. If the Chief of Staff to the President or the Chairman of the Joint Chiefs of Staff is a naval or Marine officer, the rank of admiral or general is authorized for those offices.

Relative rank of flag and general officers is provided by statute so that brigadier generals of the Army, Air Force and Marine Corps rank with rear admirals of the lower half of the Navy list and major generals with the rear admirals of the upper half. The date of rank of an officer appointed as major general continues to date from the same date as that of his appointment as brigadier general.

Distribution. Of the total number of officers serving on active duty in the line of the Navy in the grade of ensign and above, excluding fleet admirals and officers carried as additional numbers in grade, the number of officers who may serve in each of the grades above lieutenant may not, except as otherwise provided, exceed a number appropriate to the total number as set forth in a table in the Code.

The Secretary of the Navy, whenever the needs of the service require but at least once annually, shall compute the number of officers authorized for each grade above lieutenant. The number so computed is the number of line officers on active duty, excluding officers carried as additional numbers in grade, prescribed for the grade concerned. However, if the Secretary determines at the time of making these computations that the number of officers required to meet the needs of the service in any grade above lieutenant is less than the prescribed number for that grade as computed, the lesser number becomes the prescribed number for the grade and the reduction may be applied as an increase in the prescribed number for any lower grade.

At the time of making the computations, the Secretary shall also determine the numbers of line officers on active duty, excluding officers carried as additional numbers in grade, that will be required to meet the needs of the service during the ensuing year in the grades of lieutenant, lieutenant (junior grade), and ensign. The numbers so determined are the prescribed numbers for these grades.

The total number of rear admirals designated for engineering duty, aeronautical engineering duty, and special duty may not exceed a number equal to 13 per cent of the authorized number of other line rear admirals.

The number of officers designated for engineering duty, aeronautical engineering duty, and special duty in the combined grades of captain, commander, and lieutenant commander may not exceed numbers equal, respectively, to 9, 5, and 5 per cent of line officers, exclusive of ED, AED, and SD officers and limited duty officers, in those grades.

Running Mates. In general, distribution for the staff corps is that resulting from the operation of the running mate principle. Since the number of line officers not restricted in the performance of duty forms the basis on which grade limitations and the control elements function, it is necessary that staff corps officers be related in some manner to this line structure. The running mate principle is simply the means of relating the individual staff corps officer to a line officer not restricted in the performance of duty with whom he shares eligibility for consideration for promotion and with whom he is appointed after being selected. This is to insure that line officers and officers of each staff corps are afforded the same rates and opportunities for promotion.

Except in time of war or national emergency, the following numerical limits are prescribed for permanently commissioned rear admirals, line and staff: unrestricted line, 150; ED, AED, and SD, combined, 19; Medical Corps, 15; Supply Corps, 13; Chaplains, 2; Civil Engineer Corps, 4; Dental Corps, 4.

Eligibility for Selection. Line officers will be eligible for consideration for selection when they will have completed, on June 30 of the fiscal year in which the selection board is convened, the following years of service in the grade in which serving: captains, 3; commanders, as prescribed by SecNav; lieutenant commanders, 4; lieutenants, 4; lieutenants (jg), 2.

Ensigns of the line and staff corps are promoted to lieutenant (jg) after 18 months as ensigns. Officers of the Chaplain Corps, some officers of the Civil Engineer Corps and Medical Service Corps will originally be appointed in the grade of lieutenant (jg). All staff officers will be assigned running mates after appointment to the grade of lieutenant (jg).

Officers of the Medical and Dental Corps will be originally appointed in such grade as their constructive service dictates.

Staff corps and reserve officers will become eligible for selection and will fall into promotion zones with their line running mates.

Normal Terms of Service. The years of service in grade and total commissioned service shown in the accompanying table are prescribed for line officers not restricted in the performance of duty as normal terms of service:

Grade	Service in grade	Total commissioned service
Captain	5	30
Commander	7	25
Lieutenant commander	6	18
Lieutenant	6	12
Lieutenant (jg)	3	6

For the purposes of eligibility for continuation on the active list and separation from the active list, the total commissioned service of any Regular commissioned line officer appointed upon graduation from the

Naval Academy or from civilian or enlisted status is computed from June 30 of the fiscal year in which he accepted his appointment; and any Regular commissioned officer appointed from other sources is deemed to have, for these purposes, as much total commissioned service as the Naval Academy or the former civilian or enlisted appointee who is or was junior to him at the time of appointment. For the same purposes staff corps officers, except those transferred from a Reserve or temporary status under the act of April 18, 1946, whose original appointment to the Regular Navy was in the grade of lieutenant (jg) or ensign will compute their total commissioned service from June 30 of the fiscal year in which they accepted their appointment, any other staff corps officer will be deemed to have for these purposes as much total commissioned service as any of the foregoing staff officers in his corps who are junior to him.

Exceptions to the foregoing are Medical Service Corps officers appointed under the Act of April 18, 1946, who are allowed to have total commissioned service for these purposes equivalent to that of their running mates and Nurse Corps officers whose service is based on a total of active service as commissioned officers in the Nurse Corps and active service under appointment as Navy nurses.

Promotion Zone, Accelerated Promotion, and Failure of Selection. The Secretary of the Navy will determine the number of line officers on the eligible list who must either be selected or be deemed to fail of selection in order to maintain a flow of promotion consistent with normal terms of service and to assure equality of opportunity for promotion of officers in succeeding years. Eligible officers not previously failing of selection down to this point will be in the promotion zone, All officers senior to and including the junior officer in the promotion zone will be deemed to fail of selection, if not selected, regardless of how far down the list the board goes. Even though eligible, and considered by the board, no officer junior to the junior officer in the promotion zone will be deemed to fail of selection. The board can therefore select an outstanding eligible officer below the promotion zone for accelerated promotion without "passing over" a large number of good officers. Except in selections for promotion to the grade of rear admiral, the number of officers holding permanent commissions in the Regular Navy which a board may select from below the promotion zone may not exceed 5 percent of the number of officers to be selected.

Line officers are ordinarily required to have 2 years' sea or foreign service in grade or on the promotion list for that grade before being promoted to the next higher grade. However, this requirement is temporarily suspended by Executive Order. Further, this does not apply to the officers designated for engineering duty, aeronautical engineering duty, or special duty.

Brief Summary of Promotion System. Officers of the Navy of the grade of lieutenant (jg) through captain are recommended for promotion by boards convened by the Secretary of the Navy. The names and records of all eligible officers are furnished these boards, who are sworn to perform their duties without prejudice or partiality, "having in view both the special fitness of officers and the efficiency of the naval service."

Thus evaluation of officers is within the discretion of the members of the selection boards, subject to approval by the President and confirmation by the Senate. If a selectee is not acceptable to the President, the board is so informed and makes another selection.

Selection boards recommend for promotion those eligible officers whom they consider best fitted for promotion, except that, for promotion to lieutenant and lieutenant commander in certain staff corps and for promotion of women officers to lieutenant, officers need only be considered qualified for promotion.

The number and grade of officers serving as members of selection boards are prescribed by law. For promotion of captains or rear admiral the grade must be rear admiral or above. In practically all other cases, it is captain or above. Members of line boards, except for continuation of rear admirals on active duty, must be officers of the active list. No officer may serve on two successive boards for the same grade. When officers designated for engineering duty, aeronautical engineering duty, or special duty are eligible for consideration, the law requires that membership include three officers of such category, who, however, cannot act in the cases of officers other than their own category.

Officers attain the grade and rank of admiral or vice admiral, by and with the advice and consent of the Senate, upon designation by the President, and continue in such grade and rank while serving in the designated position (see also Officer Fact Book (NavPers 15898) Chapter 6).

Professional Examination for Promotion. At present, written professional promotion examinations are not required. Professional qualifications are determined by selection boards acting as naval examining boards.

Temporary and Permanent Promotions. All promotions in the Navy or Naval Reserve are made by temporary appointments in the higher grade with the exception of promotion of women officers. Temporary appointments are made from approved promotion lists as vacancies in the temporary grade structure occur after selectees have established qualifications as prescribed, or in the cases of ensigns and warrant officers, when they become eligible for promotion upon the expiration of the prescribed service in grade.

Permanent Appointments. A permanent appointment is not normally a promotion, except in the cases of women officers who are issued permanent appointments from a promotion list to fill vacancies. Other permanent appointments are made by seniority, without selection, as vacancies occur in the permanent grade structure of the Navy or Naval Reserve. Permanent warrant officers advanced temporarily will be issued a permanent appointment to their new grade when they have completed the terms of service specified by law (three years for warrant officers W-1 to W-2 and six year for warrant officers W-2 and W-3 to W-3 and W-4, respectively). Usually a permanent appointment lags a temporary appointment by several years. It bears the same date of rank but a later effective date. An officer's precedence and pay are not affected by a permanent appointment issued subsequent to a temporary appointment to the same grade.

A permanent appointment may not be revoked, suspended or cancelled except by formal legal proceedings. A temporary appointment may be terminated by the President and an individual reverted to the grade of his permanent appointment. This would normally occur only in the event of drastic reductions in the size of the Navy which would reduce the authorized numbers within each grade. An officer does not normally serve in a grade more than one higher than his permanent one.

During the war or declared periods of National Emergency provisions of Title 10, U.S. Code (formerly temporary promotion Act, P.L. 188) authorize temporary appointments to all officer grades for temporary service. Such appointments include first or initial appointments to commissioned status, and those resulting from regular promotion. They are subject to termination six months following the declared end of the war or emergency by the President and, at that time, the individual concerned is reverted to whatever permanent status held. Such appointments made during World War II and subsequent thereto until 1954, which were not first or original appointments, were confirmed by the Congress as having been made under permanent legislation and are not now subject to revocation.

710. EFFECTING APPOINTMENTS AND PROMOTIONS. A line officer becomes due for promotion after selection and passing any required promotion examination when a vacancy is found to exist in the rank in which he is qualified for promotion. Staff officers are promoted contemporaneously with their running mates.

Oath of office is required for original appointment but is no longer required by law for subsequent promotions.

After the appointment or promotion has been made, the appointee will acknowledge receipt by form letter of acceptance to the Bureau of Naval Personnel. (Original to Bureau of Naval Personnel; two certified copies to the Disbursing Officer for adjustment of pay accounts.)

711. PROMOTION FOR HEROISM. Prior to November, 1959, officers could be advanced in grade upon retirement for heroism in action. The so-called Hump Bill of August, 1959, abolished such promotion after 1 November 1959.

712. EARLY INVOLUNTARY RETIREMENT. Title 10, U.S. Code contains authority for early involuntary retirement of rear admirals who were not selected by a selection board for continuation on the active list after five years service in grade and 35 years of total commissioned service. This provision is temporarily suspended by Executive Order. Rear admirals are currently retiring with less service following consideration by retirement selection boards.

In August, 1959, Congress passed the so-called Hump Bill, designed to apply the non-continuation process to the grades of captain and commander. This legislation was required to create early retirements in order to achieve sufficient vacancies to permit the promotion system to operate for the future well-being of the Navy.

Under this legislation the Secretary is authorized to convene selection boards for the purpose of recommending captains for continuation on the active list.

The Secretary is required to convene selection boards, or to direct selection boards convened for promotion, to recommend, among commanders who have failed two or more times of selection to captain, officers for continuation on the active list. Officers so recommended in the approved report of a board would not be subject to forced retirement until the completion of 26 years of total commissioned service, and would not be subject to later continuation boards.

Normally, this duty will be performed by the membership of the selection board convened for the selection of commanders for promotion. The field will include officers who, having failed of selection for promotion the previous year, again fail of selection by the current board. Under the present schedule of promotion zones, therefore, some officers will be considered for continuation before the completion of 20 years of total commissioned service. Notwithstanding this early consideration, retirement is not required prior to the completion of 20 years' total commissioned service.

The term "total commissioned service," as used in the law and in this discussion, is the service defined in the Officer Personnel Act to determine when mandatory retirements occur. For line officers who were originally commissioned as Regular permanent ensigns and have served continuously on active duty ever since, it is almost equal to actual commissioned service. For former Naval Reserve officers whose commissioned service includes some inactive time, "total commissioned service" may be different—it is based on the commissioned service of officers originally commissioned in the Regular Navy who had the same seniority at the time of the Naval Reserve officer's transfer to Regular Navy. In addition, other factors determine the "total commissioned service" of some specialist officers and staff corps officers.

The year from which each officer's "total commissioned service" is computed is carried in the Navy Register in the column headed "Service Date."

Captains considered by a continuation board who are not recommended as best qualified for continuation are required to retire on June 30 of the fiscal year in which considered. Twice failed commanders, who have not been recommended as best qualified for continuation, are required to retire on June 30 of the fiscal year in which considered for continuation, or, if they will not have completed at least 20 years of total commissioned service in that year, on June 30 of the fiscal year in which they complete 20 years of total commissioned service.

Retired pay will be computed at 2.5 percent of the active duty pay at time of retirement times the number of years' service creditable for pay purposes at that time. For the purpose of determining this multiplier, a period of six months or more is counted as a full year. If this multiplier is less than 20, an officer retiring on the mandatory date will nevertheless have his retired pay computed at 50 percent of his active duty pay.

A lump-sum payment of two thousand dollars is authorized for each officer retiring under the Act if all of the following conditions exist in his case:

(a) he is retired in the grade held on the date of enactment, or in the grade for which he was on a promotion list prior to the date of enactment; and

(b) he has not been selected for promotion; and

(c) His name has not been reported as an officer whose retention would not be warranted in any circumstances.

The lump-sum payment is payable on retirement even though the officer elects to retire voluntarily prior to the required retirement date.

Officers who are recommended as best qualified for continuation on the active list will not be subject to retirement under the "Hump" law while serving in the same grade, but will be subject to the mandatory retirement points for their grade in the normal promotion law (30 or 31 years if captain, depending on category, and 26 years if commanders.)

Retirements under this Act will be considered to have been voluntary. This provision of law is intended to prevent any notation in records available to the public which would identify any retirement as a mandatory retirement.

The Act expired on June 30, 1970.

713. REQUIREMENT FOR STAFF DUTY. Department of Defense Directive 1320.5A established a requirement for a tour of duty with a Joint, Combined, Allied, or Secretary of Defense Staff to qualify for general or flag officer rank. A normal tour of duty must be served in such a staff. Generally, service with any Joint, Combined, Allied, or Secretary of Defense Staff is considered qualifying and, in addition, certain service with Military Assistance Advisory Groups, or staffs which in fact plan for or conduct joint, combined, or allied operations. Only unrestricted line officers are required to meet this qualification, although others are encouraged to do so.

Leave and Liberty

714. LEAVE. An officer is granted "shore leave" as distinct from "liberty," which is granted to an enlisted man. The legal term as defined by the Armed Forces Leave Act of 1946 is "liberty." The use of the term "shore leave" is a custom of long standing in the Navy and signifies an officer's temporary absence from ship or station not chargeable as leave under the Armed Forces Leave Act of 1946. Briefly, shore leave begins at the end of working hours and ends at the commencement of working hours the next working day. Sundays and holidays are included. Shore leave can be extended by a commanding officer up to 96 hours if a national holiday falls on Friday or Monday and may be further extended until expiration of shore leave on the following day (see NR 1284).

Leave, or leave of absence, is authorized absence from duty for a period longer than shore leave or in an area away from the general vicinity of ship or station.

Accrued leave is the unused leave accumulating at the rate of 2½ days per month which stands to the credit of an individual at the beginning of the fiscal year; it may not exceed 60 days.

The amount of leave that an officer is granted is contingent upon the exigencies of the service, the need for mental and physical relaxation, the nature of the services he performs, and the desirability of affording him additional time to permit adjustment of personal affairs when a change of permanent station is involved. The necessities of the service always come first. Although a leave-of-absence allowance of 30 days per year has been established, officers should realize that frequently it will be impossible to take all of their leave in any one year. It is advisable to let some leave accrue against the day of retirement, as up to 2 months' pay will be paid on retirement for accrued leave. Under the present law and rulings, no more than 60 days can accrue, any accumulated over that amount being cut off at the end of each fiscal year. All leave over 60 days not taken on your retirement day is lost.

For these and other definitions, see BuPers Manual, Articles C6201-6212.

Taking Leave of Absence and Delay in Reporting. A leave of absence begins on the day following that on which an officer departs from his station or duty. The day of departure, whatever the hour, is counted as a day of duty; the day of return as a day of absence, except when such return is made before the regular hour for forenoon Quarters on board ship or for beginning work at a shore station, in which case it shall not be counted as a day of absence. Leave for 1 month beginning on the first day of a calendar month shall expire on the last day of the month, whatever its number of days. Beginning on an intermediate day, the leave will expire on the day preceding the same day of the next month. To illustrate:

AMOUNT OF LEAVE	DEPARTURE	RETURN
10 days	June 10	June 20
10 days	June 10	June 21 (prior to forenoon Quarters or beginning of work)
1 month	February 1, 1960	February 29, 1960
1 month	April 4	May 3
1 month and 10 days ...	September 10	October 19

Frequently in orders the Bureau of Naval Personnel authorizes an

FIGURE 702. In Hong Kong, the Chief shows his men on liberty a good buy on Thai silk.

officer to delay in reporting from one station to a new one. This authorized delay is counted as leave, except for proceed and travel time. It is to be noted, however, that in the Bureau's orders for a change of station, where a specific number of days is authorized to count as leave, an officer may not exercise the privilege of returning prior to forenoon Quarters on ship or the beginning of work at a shore station, inasmuch as the officer is not returning from leave but is reporting for duty after being granted a delay in such reporting (BuPers Manual, Articles C6307 and 6311).

If an officer is on duty abroad, or on a foreign station, and is granted leave for the purpose of visiting the United States, his leave begins from the date of his arrival therein and expires on the date of his departure therefrom, and the dates of such arrival and departure must be reported to the Navy Department (BuPers Manual, Article C6310).

Address To Be Furnished. When leave of absence is obtained while on duty at a station, the officer must furnish his address or addresses while on leave to the officer authorized to grant leave. In orders involving a change of station issued by the Bureau of Naval Personnel, where leave or delay in reporting is authorized, officers should carefully note that the Bureau of Naval Personnel is to be advised of the address or addresses while on leave. When more than 15 days' leave is granted, a copy of approved request is forwarded to the Bureau.

Return. Every officer to whom leave is granted shall promptly report in writing his return therefrom to the officer who granted it and to the Bureau of Naval Personnel, giving the date of its commencement and stating the number of days of absence from station or duty, inclusive of travel time (BuPers Manual, Article C6403).

Sick Leave. Sick leave is leave granted to officer and enlisted personnel while under treatment in a naval hospital within the continental United States, provided that the following conditions prevail:

1. The individual is no longer in need of actual treatment in the hospital but has not recovered to the extent of being fit for duty.

2. A period of convalescence at home can be expected to hasten recovery and return to active duty, as determined either by the medical officer in command or by a board of medical survey.

Sick leave is not chargeable against accrued or earned leave.

Leave Records. Leave record forms have been established for officers and are kept in each officer's service record which accompanies him with each change of duty. The individual is responsible for proper upkeep of his record even though it is kept in the custody of and authenticated by the commanding officer or other duly designated officer. See BuPers Manual, Article B-2213 on keeping leave record.

CHAPTER 8

Oral and Written Communication

War is an affair of getting news, interpreting, disseminating, and acting upon it.

Oral Communication

801. THE OCCASION. In your everyday work about the ship, you will constantly be using the medium of speech for instruction purposes. Many officers are detailed to instruction duty, at the Naval Academy, at War Colleges, at OCS or a service school, or at one of the universities or colleges which has an NROTC unit. Civic organizations and patriotic societies frequently request naval officers to address their members.

On any and all of these occasions, an officer's objective is to get his message across to his listeners. Regardless of the importance of the occasion, how well you put across your ideas depends, to a large extent, on how well you have mastered the elements of good public speaking.

802. INSTRUCTION. In talking to a small number of men in your organization, your talk can and should be informal. One requisite of a good instruction talk is that it must be carefully prepared to the extent that you have a firm mastery of the material you are going to discuss and a fair conception of the order of presentation you intend to use.

An instructor should *not* speak from notes, unless his material is too difficult to remember or is composed of detailed figures and facts. The delivery should be one of easy informality. Most good instructors break up their instruction into subjects and provide an opportunity after each subject for questions to clear up difficult points.

If you use blackboard illustrations, draw the diagrams beforehand with some thought and care. Sketches drawn during a lecture are usually hastily and poorly done. For larger groups, slides or slide films, made with considerable care, are often indicated. If training motion-picture films on your subject are available, use them, but be sure they fit in with your planned instruction. Sixteen-millimeter films can be stopped and examined in detail or run back to a frame which illustrates a point with which your students are having difficulty.

Demonstrate the problem or machine under discussion. After the lecture, give the students practical work on the machine or on similar problems. Thus, you use all the known processes of learning—through the ears by listening, through the eyes by seeing, and through the hands and mind (reasoning process) by doing.

At the end of the period, sum up the principal points made during the period. Thus, you clinch the subject matter in the student's mind. See Division School in Section 614 for further suggestions on conducting instruction periods.

Remember, *to be effective, instruction must be brief.*

803. THE ELEMENTS OF A GOOD TALK. Whether you are instructing a small class of seamen or making an important policy speech before a distinguished audience in Town Hall, every good talk has four simple requirements. In his course in public speaking for senior naval officers, Professor Henry G. Roberts[1] states them as follows:

> The first characteristic of a good talk is—it must have *a message!* The speaker must have something to say. What he says must be worth saying—and worth listening to. In every speech class, I get this question—"What on earth shall I talk about?" To that question, I have one answer—"Talk about the two things you know best. Talk about the Navy and talk about your work in the Navy."
>
> Tell them what goes on in your naval activity. Tell them of your own work, afloat and ashore, of your officers and men and women and civil employees. Show them how your ship or activity fits into the larger picture of the Navy. . . .
>
> The second characteristic of every good talk is *naturalness.* The audience wants to hear *you.* Make it your own talk. Don't try to copy some good naval speaker. Don't paw through the files for a canned speech. Say what *you* have to say. Say it in *your own way.* The audience wants to hear *you.*
>
> The next characteristic of an effective talk is that it must be *sincere.* Nothing can possibly be more disillusioning than to hear a naval officer talk about the Navy in such a way that you wonder whether he actually believes a word that he is saying. . . . The only way to succeed in giving an impression of sincerity is *to be sincere.* Believe in what you say; say it as if you believed it.

[1] Formerly training consultant at the Navy Department and instructor in public speaking at the Naval Ordnance Laboratory, the Naval Engineering Experiment Station, the Naval Postgraduate School, the National War College, and the Industrial College of the Armed Forces.

Finally, a really good talk must radiate *enthusiasm*. An enthusiastic speaker is one who shows great eagerness to have his ideas understood, believed, and acted upon. He must demonstrate their importance both in its larger aspects and to his immediate audience. If you want your audience to be enthusiastic about the Navy, radiate enthusiasm yourself.

Every good talk has a message. It must have naturalness—it must reflect the man who is making it. It must have sincerity and enthusiasm. Keep those principles in mind, don't lose your nerve, and you'll get along fine. Remember these four—*message, naturalness, sincerity, enthusiasm*.

804. BRIEFING AND PRESENTATION. As you advance in the service, you will be making more important presentations. The occasion may be as simple as briefing the Captain on some phase of a coming operation or, as a staff officer, you may be required to brief all of the officers of a task force or task group. In conference at high and low levels, you will be using the methods of speechmaking to present your views and persuade their acceptance. Early in your career, learn to organize your thoughts clearly and concisely and to present them effectively.

805. SPEECHMAKING. For naval officers to make good speeches is of critcal importance to the Navy because it provides an opportunity for the American public to meet and get to know the professional naval officers who direct the Navy. When you speak to a local service club in a small town, you *are* the local embodiment of the Navy. Your coming is an event. The filling-station operator who shakes your hand may have a son in the Navy, and he sizes up the sort of man under whom his son is serving. The local editor of the county paper, who sits next to you at lunch, is carefully evaluating you. If favorably impressed, the Navy and you will get a good report in his columns. The car salesman, who introduces you, *may* spend the week-end telling his friends what fine men we have as naval officers. It will depend on you. Every person you impress favorably is one more friend for the Navy. It is work worth doing well, for it pays great dividends for the Navy.

This places a definite responsibility upon you—the officer, young or old, who makes speeches. Can you measure up? Surely you can, as well or better than those who have had to accept this duty before you. By careful application, it is quite possible for you to learn to do a good job of speechmaking. It will not be easy, but it can be done.

806. PRELIMINARY SPADEWORK. Before you complete your speech and before you leave for the place where you will make it, you or the Public Affairs Officer responsible must lay certain groundwork for your appearance. Check carefully to see whether or not your speech needs to be forwarded to the Navy Department for clearance. As a general guide, clearance is required only for very senior officers, or when your speech discusses foreign policy, or government policy or security is involved.

Well in advance make available to newspaper and radio outlets and to the sponsoring organization a copy of your speech or a brief outline of the major points to be covered. The sponsor usually has excellent relations with the local press and radio and can give you valuable publicity assistance.

Remember that the press and radio will be looking for quotable leads

and excerpts of real local news value. Obtain such information as will enable you to incorporate local allusions into your text.

A good photograph (or a negative) and biographical material should also be made available to the sponsor and local news outlets. Advise them as to your time of arrival, where you will stay, and what arrangements will be made for meeting press and radio representatives.

FIGURE 801. Maintenance of good public relations is essential to the naval support of our foreign policy.

Arrive half a day or a day in advance of time scheduled for your speech. Meet your sponsors and other local people, and learn what you can about the community and its affairs.

After your speech, make yourself available to the audience for informal discussion and questioning, if appropriate. Give the press and radio representatives another opportunity to interview you.

807. PUBLIC ADDRESSES.   In making public addresses to civilian audiences, you will, in a measure, be employing the methods of instruction. Presumably, you know something that the audience wants to hear. Some such occasions are impromptu and require only a few words—an adherence to the old rule of the Duke of Wellington, "Say what you have to say, don't quote Latin, and sit down."

Keep it brief!—The maximum length for a speech should be 15 to 20 minutes, unless specifically requested to cover a subject at greater length. You will be applauded for your brevity, if not for your wit.

The author recalls a dinner given in honor for the late Admiral Laning. It was a pleasant affair in the Wardroom of the *Pennsylvania,* full of warm friendliness for a beloved Captain. Everything went well, until one of the ladies arose and delivered herself of an original poem in celebration of the occasion.

The Executive Officer called upon Captain Laning to say a few words in response. We settled back expecting to hear him make one of the distinguished speeches for which he was noted. But not so. Obviously, the tribute had thrown him into a momentary state of confusion. He said a few words of appreciation and asked that we excuse him from any further remarks. "You see," he said, "my impromptu speeches are always very carefully prepared." His remark might well be the guiding precept for anyone who aspires to become a public speaker.

The author's brother, who was an able orator and after-dinner speaker, once gave him a thumbnail outline for a speech that has proved to be equal to nearly every occasion—particularly when you are suddenly called upon without warning and have to get up and say something coherent. This was his advice:

> Look your audience firmly in the eye, meanwhile considering the subject that has been suddenly thrust upon you. Ask yourself, *What is it?* Then answer that question. State what you are going to talk about very briefly.
>
> Next ask yourself, *What do you know about it?* If you are talking about the Navy, you will know a great deal about it and take a long while telling what you know, which is not desirable. Confine yourself, say, to *Standing Watch in a Blow Off Iceland*. Here is the dangerous part of your speech. *Stick to facts.* Save your feelings and thoughts and impressions for later. If they pop into your mind, sternly repress them, but keep them in mind, if they are good, because you will need them in a few moments.
>
> And next ask yourself, *What do I think about it?* Here you can let yourself go for as long as the occasion seems to demand. If you've stood watches in the North Atlantic off Iceland, you're pretty apt to have some very definite feelings and thoughts and impressions of the experience.
>
> Then, at the last, ask yourself, *What am I going to do about it?* Here is your chance to tie up the loose ends, make recommendations, draw lessons, or whatever your desires may be. This should be very brief. This is P. T. Barnum's *grand egress*. When you finish it, you will find yourself outside your speech. Your impromptu speech is ended.
>
> Then, sit down!

This outline is also useful in preparing a more formal address. You will note the similarity to the recommendations for drafting a letter given in Section 815.

808. SHALL YOU USE NOTES OR WRITE YOUR SPEECH? If you can do it effectively, a much better speech results when it is given apparently offhand, or from a brief outline and notes. There is nothing more destructive of an otherwise excellent speech than to read it. Some speeches are so important that you must be sure you say exactly what you intend. In this case, they must be written, and they usually are read.

Many good platform speakers make it a practice, while always apparently delivering their talks extemporaneously, to outline and write their speeches out completely beforehand to achieve facility of phrasing and smoothness of diction. They find, after they have dictated and read a speech over to themselves a few times, that the outline upon which it was constructed sticks in their minds, while the smooth phrases that they hewed out by writing and rewriting—*and rewriting*—come back to them as if they were bright and sparkling from a fresh mind.

Some speakers prefer to use notes. If your memory is not good, this is an excellent plan. Even when using notes, it is a good plan to write your speech and read it over to yourself or your long-suffering wife a few times.

Do not neglect to use a tape recorder, which is available in most large ships and at most naval stations. Record your speech and play it back; you will have the benefit of hearing yourself as others will hear you—you can also use the recorded speech as a first draft for revision and improvement of phraseology and delivery.

If you must read a speech, try to memorize a few of the better passages, strategically spaced throughout the speech, so that you can frequently look up and meet the eyes of your spellbound listeners.

Keep to an informal style of delivery, even when reading a speech. This can be accomplished by reading the written text over aloud so many times that, when delivering it, you can look down at your script occasionally, absorb the idea of the next paragraph, look up at your audience, and speak it verbatim.

This will contribute to the naturalness of your delivery and will help to slow down the usually too rapid delivery of a speech that has to be read. The pauses, for the listeners, will create an effect of dramatic emphasis. You will find as you acquire expertness, that you can be looking at the audience about 90 per cent of the time, even when delivering a written speech that must be textually accurate.

809. ANECDOTES. Intersperse the "dull, dead facts" of your speech with illustrative examples. Make them as interesting and gripping as you can from your experience. If you can leaven your talk with humor, you will promote the sustained attention of your audience. Most people will listen attentively to the dullest stretch of fact if they feel that you are apt to reward them with a laugh as hearty as that last one.

Take care that your anecdotes are pertinent to the speech. Do not drag in a story just because it is funny at the risk of confusion to your listeners. Use exciting anecdotes to illustrate the points you are making to achieve both *interest* and *emphasis*.

Try to select an anecdote that will teach a lesson. And do not fail to point this out, after the laughter has died down.

810. THE PREVIEW. By all means, rehearse your important speeches. Arrange a critical audience, but do not get angry with her (as some do). She is interested in your successful accomplishment, too. She can tell you whether or not your speech is clearly expressed, convincing, properly arranged, too little or sufficiently anecdotal, whether the jokes are funny, and whether or not your meaning can be misunderstood.

Most important of all, you will find that you will achieve a facility of expression with rehearsal which you did not imagine you possessed. If you are one who faces each audience with uneasiness, you will find that the confidence you will build up during several rehearsals will go a long way toward quieting your platform nervousness.

811. THE ENDING. To your audience, your speech should *seem* to be brief, even though long. This is accomplished by good organization and interesting delivery. If given an hour to talk, be sure that you fill that hour with enough facts, discussion, and anecdote so that you do not have to repeat yourself. It is far better to *run short* of the time allotted than to *run over*.

Your speech should be brief; your conclusion should be even briefer. When you finish telling *what you think about it,* your speech is practically done. Sum up the points you have made. Close on a colorful phrase or a delightful bit of imagery if you can. But *end your speech*. Do not let it drag on to an anticlimactic ending. When you have reached the *grand egress,* open the door, and, without waiting on ceremony, step outside.

812. Do's AND DON'T'S. In his classes in speechmaking, Professor Roberts presented five Do's and five Don't's for naval officer speechmakers. Briefed down, as they must be here, they provide excellent guidance for the young, as well as for the mature and experienced officer, who has to make a speech on any naval occasion.

The Do's.—1. When asked to make a speech, *Do it!* This is the most difficult decision to make. Doubtless you can think up many excellent reasons and excuses for declining. You know that you should make it, but you just don't want to. It's work. It takes time. You are busy enough at your regular duties. But no duty could possibly be more important than your share of the proper relations of the Navy with the American public. The next time an invitation comes to you, resist that temptation to say, "No." Call in your yeoman or pick up the phone and say, "I shall be happy to be your guest and to speak to you briefly on the subject you have selected."

That is the first Do—*Do it!*

2. *Do it yourself!* Don't palm the job off on one of your juniors. Some one of your officers may be a much better speaker than you, but the Chamber of Commerce wants to hear *you*, the head man. The more gold you have on your sleeve, the more they want *you* as a speaker and as an authoritative representative of the Navy. So don't send your Executive Officer or some junior officer. Even more important, don't call in one of your public information specialists and tell him, "Write me a speech." Do it yourself. You probably can do a better job of writing a speech *for yourself* than any officer in your command. So figure out your own speech, write it, say it, rewrite it, and say it again. *Do it yourself!*

3. *Do keep it simple!* The major difference between conversation and speech-making is that, with a speech, one person does all the talking. Don't think that a good speech has to be an elaborate oration. Don't worry about fancy words to use. Keep it simple. The people who will listen to you are interested in a plain recital of facts and your ideas in simple language. Give it to them that way, and you can't go wrong.

4. *Do keep it short!* You may get invitations to talk for an hour. No group of adults should be required to sit and listen to one man talk that long! The vast majority of talks should be 10 or, at the most, 15 minutes in length. Some chairmen will ask you to "take as much time as you like." To you, that should mean 10 minutes. Respect the attention limitations of your listeners. *Keep it short!*

5. *Do what you would do in conversation—look at the man you're talking to.* If you look continuously at your notes or script or up at the ceiling, your listeners begin to squirm and to wish to heaven that you would get through and let them go about their business. And so, *talk to one person in your audience at a time—look him straight in the eye.* It's as simple as that. Take one man at a time and talk to him for a moment. Then, pick out another and look him straight in the eye, man to man. Then on to another. If you want to increase your effectiveness in public speaking 100 per cent overnight, do exactly what you would do in conversation—look at the man you are talking to.

The Don't's.—1. *Don't apologize!* You are not expected to be a professional spellbinder. If you have shortcomings as a speaker, it is unnecessary to advertise the obvious. Approach your task with confidence and do the best you can. Don't make it any harder by telling the audience how bad you think you are. You might be better than you think.

2. *Don't put too much reliance on the supposedly funny story!* A good speech must be more than a collection of Navy jokes. Use a really humorous story. It must be sure-fire; it should have an obvious application to the point of the speech; and it should be well told. Before you use a story in a public speech, try it out in private conversation a few times to be sure it sparks. And be certain it is in good taste.

3. *Don't open your speech by announcing your subject!* The fellow who in-

troduced you has probably covered that subject, sometimes to the point of boredom. Your opening words are of vital importance. Your audience begins to judge you in the first 30 seconds of your speech. If your beginning is dull, uninteresting, and colorless, you may lose ground with your listeners which you will never regain. And so work hard on your opening sentences to make them striking, interesting, challenging and attention-compelling. Your audience will be on your side, eager to hear what else you have to say.

If, as infrequently happens, the chairman neglects to announce your subject, don't let that upset you. Launch into your planned introduction. If you have prepared a good, interesting speech, they will soon find out what it is about. But don't let your introduction begin with "The subject of my speech tonight is . . ."

4. *Don't attempt the impossible; you can't be effective with a speech manuscript in front of you.* In other words, don't read your speech. Getting up to read a speech manuscript is like going swimming with an anchor secured around your neck. With your eyes tied down to the script instead of meeting the eyes of individuals in the audience, you cannot hope to be fully effective.

So prepare your speech adequately as previously suggested. If you have practiced it enough, you will find that you don't need a script, that having to refer to one is an unbearable nuisance.

Do it the easy way. If subject matter permits, you will have a great advantage when you stand up to speak without a manuscript. You will be talking ideas, not words. You will find that you will be able to look at individuals in the audience—and talk to *them*—not mouth a sequence of words from a paper, which have but little meaning to you, and less to them. If the requirement for clearance necessitates that you use a written and cleared text, practice it enough to give the impression that you are delivering it extemporaneously.

5. *Don't forget the man in the back row!* He came to hear you, too. Make it easy for him. Speak up!

There might well be added another *Don't*. When you accept an invitation to make a speech, don't forget that you are representing the Navy. Do more than make your speech. Do a full job of public relations. Remember, what you do, what you say, and how you do and say it constitute a very real and important part of the public's impression of the Navy. Public relations cannot be left to the public relations experts. It is a 24-hour-a-day job for every officer in the Navy.

813. RANDOM NOTES. The following points should be kept in mind:

1. Begin your speech with something vital, striking, or thought-provoking. Then get to the main point at once.

2. Speak to—not "down to"—your audience.

3. If you read your speech, look up from your paper at your audience from time to time. Let them know *you* are present as well as your voice. Don't read *from* your paper; read *to* your audience.

4. Look pleasant. Don't rock back and forth on your heels or prome-
nade up and down the rostrum. Keep your hands out of your pockets.

5. Employ appropriate gestures that come naturally to you.

6. Use the full range of your voice for emphasis and other effects.

7. Speak loudly enough to be heard by the last man in the last row—
but do not shout your speech.

8. An audience cannot turn back the pages to see what you said. So
repeat points frequently. Summarize succinctly at the end.

9. Public-address systems that function are a great assistance. But
do not "kiss the microphone." Keeping your lips a few inches from the
"mike" gives much better results. The correct distance varies with different installations. If you shout at a microphone, what you say is completely unintelligible. The type of "mike" that hangs about your neck
is excellent, but be careful about lowering your head. The resultant
blast from the loud-speakers will rupture the eardrums of your listeners.

10. Avoid long words and Navy jargon which will be unfamiliar to
your audience. Keep your language simple, yet as colorful as you can
manage.

11. Avoid clichés, such as the conventional apology for lack of experience or thanking the audience for their attention.

12. If you are using slide illustrations, procure a "spotlight" pointer.
It is much more effective than a long fish pole.

13. When you are through, do not say, "Well, I guess that's all." Sit
down.

Official Correspondence

814. NAVAL CORRESPONDENCE. The term "correspondence" includes letters, endorsements, speedletters, and memoranda, and is
divided into two general classes, classified and unclassified. The originator of the letter is responsible for the initial classification (see Section 819).

Unclassified matter requires no special safeguarding, or the safeguarding can be entrusted entirely to the discretion of the custodian.

Classified matter must be carefully safeguarded and be permanently
or temporarily limited in circulation; it is classified, marked, handled,
transmitted, and filed in accordance with specific naval instructions.

Specific instructions for letter correspondence are given in Navy

Regulations, Chapter 16. The Navy Correspondence Manual gives detailed instructions and examples of typing practices, form letters, assembling correspondence, writing practices, forms of address and salutation, and a useful chapter on developing and writing an official letter. Correspondence is filed in accordance with the Navy-Marine Corps Standard Classification System (SECNAVINST 5210.11 series).

815. WRITING THE NAVAL LETTER. Official naval correspondence differs so markedly and in so many ways from commercial and civil practice that suggestions for improvement of the preparation of such correspondence and a few examples have been included here. Until familiar with the prescribed forms, keep the Navy Correspondence Manual and a good dictionary close at hand.

The following letter might have been prepared by an inexperienced officer and is included here as a "bad example."

                              PC 832
                           Operating Area
                           Jan. 3, 19—

To—Lt. Jones at Repair Base
From—Captain of PC 832
Dear Sir,

   When we were in the yard in December, you remember, a job was done on our starboard propeller and shaft. Well when we were on patrol on 1 Jan. in the search area 30 miles east of Cape Charles Light we contacted the destroyer Green in accordance with plan and started a search for the downed plane reported there. At noon that day the Green made contact and we maneuvered to search for survivors. Upon backing, the starboard shaft froze and we haven't been able to move it since.

   I'd like to get this fixed when we come in at 4 P.M. 6 Jan.

                              Very truly yours,
                              JOE BLOKE
                              Lt. jg USNR
                              Commanding Officer
                              PC 832

P.S.
   We didn't find any survivors.
        J. B.

Among the many errors in style and tone in this letter, the following are particularly important:

1. Incorrect margins and spacing.
2. Nonstandard letterhead.
3. Date incorrectly arranged (should be "3 Jan 19—").

4. Misplaced "To," "From."

5. Incorrect address (official correspondence must not be sent to the individual).

6. Incorrect office of origin (should be "From: Commanding Officer").

7. Courtesy forms "Dear Sir" and "Very truly yours" are not used in official correspondence.

8. No subject, references, or official routing.

9. Most important of all, *confidential* information of a detailed and vital nature (area, rendezvous, ship concerned, operations, and time of arrival) is compromised by use of nonclassified letter.

10. Entire letter is a rambling account giving no specific information that would assist the repair officer in planning repairs.

11. "4 P.M." irregular (should be "1600").

12. Rank and station should not follow signature.

The Navy Correspondence Manual specifies the form and arrangement of official letters. Construction of a competent, understandable letter within the official framework necessitates some knowledge of good usage and considerable competence in the organization of thought and material.

Where possible, the body of a letter should be divided into three paragraphs, with appropriate subparagraphs lettered *a, b, c,* etc., as required. The subject matter of these paragraphs in general should be as follows:

Paragraph 1. Facts. In this paragraph, state the facts of the case under discussion. For instance, in a letter reporting an engineering casualty, state the facts involved, time, date, material damaged, extent of casualty, etc.

Paragraph 2. Discussion. In this paragraph, discuss the subject matter of the letter and the facts stated in paragraph 1. For instance, in an engineering-casualty letter, this paragraph would discuss causes, reasons, extenuating circumstances indicating that no penalty should be applied, etc. *This paragraph is often omitted from short letters,* which are no more than a report of facts and a recommendation for future action.

Paragraph 3. Action. Here at the end of the letter, state action *taken* or *recommended.* Be brief, clear, concise in this paragraph.

Tabulate recommendations in subparagraphs for clarity.

In your letters, use "recommended" rather than "requested" or "suggested" in paragraph 3 when addressing seniors. Use "directed" rather than "suggested" or "ordered" when addressing juniors.

The "bad example" has been rewritten in the proper form shown here:

USS PC 832
Care of Fleet Post Office
New York, N.Y.

In reply refer to:
JB:DAF:cj
E6-4/5
Ser: 0134
3 Jan 19—

CONFIDENTIAL

From: Commanding Officer
To: Commander Norfolk Naval Shipyard

Subj: Repairs, starboard engine shaft, request for (U)

Ref: (a) NSYNOR Job Order PC 832-543-1 #24, dated 10 Dec 19—
      (b) Art 0727, U. S. Navy Regulations

Encl: (1) Sketch of estimated damage

1. While this ship was conducting routine operations in connection with search and rescue, a casualty occurred on the starboard engine shaft which rendered the shaft inoperative. The report required by reference (b) has been made. During last overhaul, modifications were made to this installation in accordance with reference (a).

2. While the damage can be estimated only, it is believed that the shock of a sudden reversal of the engine displaced the steady block (Dr. No. 113846) as indicated in enclosure (1).

3. It is recommended that an inspection be made immediately upon the return of this ship and that repairs be instituted at this time.

J. BLOKE

DOWNGRADED AT 3 YEAR INTERVALS
DECLASSIFIED AFTER 12 YEARS
DOD DIR 5200.10

CONFIDENTIAL

As an individual, you will originate official correspondence. It may include requests for duty, replies to requests for information, or any suggestions you may have for improvements in methods or equipment. These letters should be prepared in the official form.

816. NOTES FOR NAVAL LETTER WRITERS. The following general notes are included to supplement those contained in official publications of the Departments of Defense and Navy:

1. Forward all correspondence through the prescribed official channels.

2. Separate letters should be written on separate subjects, unless the subjects are of a very similar nature.

3. As a general rule, a letter should be answered by a separate letter and not by endorsement.

4. Minimize correspondence as much as is compatible with the public interest, as regards both the number of letters written and their length.

5. Use accurate, simple, and concise sentences. Arrange the paragraphs of a letter in logical sequence. Confine each letter to the subject at hand, without omitting any essential details. Maintain a courteous tone.

6. Official correspondence between subordinate officers of ships or naval stations is forbidden by the regulations. Therefore, any interoffice correspondence should be in the form of a memorandum. In memorandum communications, custom dictates that the junior subscribe himself, above his signature, "Very respectfully," while the senior addressing a junior uses "Respectfully." Abbreviations are commonly used.

7. When official business is conducted by telephone or orally, the substance of any communication or order that should be made a matter of record should be reduced to writing without unnecessary delay.

8. All communications, orders, bills, requisitions, and papers that by law or regulation are to be signed, approved, or forwarded by an officer in command must be actually signed by such officer in his own handwriting or, in his absence, by the officer next in command at the time. The name of the officer should be typewritten under his signature.

9. An officer signing for another in whose absence he is in command or in charge should have the word "Acting" after his signature; in this case the title of the official from whom the communication emanates, as indicated after the word "From" at the beginning of the letter, should not be modified. Thus, in the absence of the Commandant, the words "From: The Commandant, Third Naval District" would still appear in the heading, the acting Commandant would sign, and his name would be typewritten, followed by "Acting."

10. When an officer is writing on his own account, his rank is indicated after the word "From" in the heading of a letter and his file number and numerical designator are included after his name. Therefore, only his signature is necessary in conclusion. This, however, should include the typewritten name, which should also appear on all copies.

11. The only time an officer's rank appears after his signature is in

letters addressed to officials and civilians who have not adopted the official form of naval correspondence. These letters are prepared in the regular business style; and, in order that the recipient of the letter may know the rank and office held by the sender, after the complimentary close of the letter the writer's signature is typed, together with his rank, title, or position. Full instructions for writing this sort of letter are given in the Navy Correspondence Manual.

12. Be temperate and courteous in all correspondence. With civilians or with other Government agencies, your correspondence should be especially prompt, courteous, complete, and accurate.

13. Avoid pointless letters. Confine your correspondence with seniors to specific requests, reports, and recommendations.

14. The Navy-Marine Corps Standard Classification System (SEC-NAVINST 5210.11 series) gives instructions for filing official correspondence. To prevent confusion, see that your yeomen follow the system established by that publication.

Security

817. SECURITY. Security may be described as the process of keeping classified information confined to channels where it belongs and preventing the dissemination to unauthorized persons of confidential, secret, or top secret information regarding any phase of naval operations or research or scientific development. It includes the admonition *not to talk* to anyone except authorized officers and officials about publications, codes, ciphers, or classified information. The Department of the Navy Security Manual for Classified Information covers in great detail all aspects of security including classification, dissemination of information, custody and stowage, security control, and personnel investigations and security clearances. Adequate security is vital to naval operations. All officers should frequently and carefully consult the Security Manual for details of the foregoing aspects.

818. NEED FOR SECURITY AND SECURITY-CONSCIOUSNESS. In this era when our potential enemy has declared that he will make every possible effort and use all available devices, honest and dishonest, to penetrate our security measures, it behooves all naval personnel to be particularly aware of security measures.

819. CLASSIFICATION CATEGORIES. No discussion of security can proceed without a clear understanding of the various classification categories. Classified matter is designated as follows:

1. *Top Secret.* The use of Top Secret shall be limited to defense information or material which requires the highest degree of protection. The Top Secret classification shall be applied only to that information or material the defense aspect of which is paramount, and the unauthorized disclosure of which could result in exceptionally grave damage to the nation, such as:

a. Leading to a definite break in diplomatic relations affecting the defense of the United States, an armed attack against the United States or its allies, or a war.

b. The compromise of military or defense plans, or intelligence operations, or scientific or technological developments vital to the national defense.

2. *Secret.* The use of the classification Secret shall be limited to defense information or material the unauthorized disclosure of which could result in serious damage to the nation, such as:

a. Jeopardizing the international relations of the United States.

b. Endangering the effectiveness of a program or policy of vital importance to the national defense.

c. Compromising important military or defense plans, or scientific or technological developments important to national defense.

d. Revealing important intelligence operations.

3. *Confidential.* The use of the classification Confidential shall be limited to defense information or material the unauthorized disclosure of which could be prejudicial to the defense interests of the Nation, such as:

a. Operational and battle reports which contain information of value to the enemy.

b. Intelligence reports.

c. Military radio frequency and call sign allocations.

d. Operational and tactical doctrine.

e. Mobilization plans.

Classified material is downgraded with the passage of time. An automatic time-phased downgrading and declassification marking system is used. Each classified document must bear a special notation which identifies its status in this system. Normally the writer of each letter will assure that it bears the date or event subsequent to which it will be downgraded or declassified (OPNAVINST 5510.1 series). One of the following notations will be used:

Downgraded to Secret on (date or other specified event).

Downgraded to Confidential (or when appropriate, Confidential-Modified Handling Authorized) on (date, or after specified event).

When it is not possible to assign a specific date or event, one of four automatic time-phased downgrading and declassification groups may be used as follows:

Group 1—Excluded from automatic downgrading and declassification.

Group 2—Exempted from automatic downgrading.

Group 3—Downgraded at 12-year intervals; not automatically declassified.

Group 4—Downgraded at 3-year intervals; Declassified after 12 years.

The appropriate downgrading and declassification notation is placed on the first page of each separate part of the document 1 inch from the bottom of the page.

820. DISCLOSURE OF CLASSIFIED INFORMATION. Dissemination of information in classified matter should be carefully restricted. Classified matter shall be divulged only to those persons and to the extent required by circumstances and in accordance with the degree of its classification. Naval personnel, whether officer or enlisted, are not entitled to knowledge or possession of classified matter solely because of rank, position, or office. There must also be a real necessity to know.

The Department of the Navy Security Manual for Classified Information specifically provides that information as to the existence, nature, content, or whereabouts of classified matter shall, except as specifically authorized by the Secretary of the Navy or the Chief of Naval Operations, be disclosed only as follows:

In the absence of specific exceptions authorized in accordance with the Security Manual for Classified Information, dissemination of classified information shall be limited strictly to those persons whose official military or other governmental duties require such access in the interest of promoting national defense and who have been properly cleared for access thereto. Responsibility for determining whether a person's official military or other governmental duties require that he possess or have access to any classified information and whether he is authorized to receive it rests upon the person who has such knowledge and not upon the recipient.

In processing top secret and secret matter, use enlisted persons and civilians only to the minimum extent necessary, and such persons must be specially tested and designated for their reliability and integrity. When you are required by competent authority to divulge classified matter to persons outside the naval service, inform them in writing as to the classification of the matter and direct their attention to their liability to prosecution under the Espionage Act or the Atomic Energy Act.

Never release information or discuss the past or present status, techniques, or procedures in cryptanalysis or the degree of success attained or specific results achieved by any cryptanalytic unit operating under the authority of our government or any department thereof.

Never discuss classified matter in the presence of persons not authorized to have knowledge thereof—this includes naval personnel, officer or enlisted, senior or junior.

As division officer, you must impress upon your men the importance of not divulging confidential information in bars, cafes, and restaurants. A few seemingly innocent remarks dropped here and there may be just the information an espionage agent is looking for to "complete the picture." See that security in all its phases is observed diligently aboard your ship, bearing in mind that space limitations in small ships and craft sometimes make certain undesirable practices necessary as a matter of expediency.

Never discuss classified matter over the telephone, since telephone lines are susceptible to invasion by modern-day listening devices. Attempts to paraphrase or use code words to conceal the classified nature of your subject, should not be utilized. BE SAFE—don't discuss "anything" which is classified, over the telephone.

821. HANDLING OF CLASSIFIED MATERIAL. Make sure that all classified publications and devices in your custody are given the proper degree of security stowage while not actually being used by you. The Navy Security Manual prescribes the several degrees of security stowage; it is extremely unlikely that any *top secret* material will be entrusted to your care as a newly commissioned officer and should perchance it be, you will be elaborately instructed; it is probable—almost certain—that you will have custody of a few *secret* items and much that is *confidential*. *Secret* and *confidential* matter must be kept in your stateroom safe when not actually being used.

Registered publications not only are classified but are numbered; they are inventoried by actually sighting them periodically and on change of command. The Communication Officer is signed for these; when you draw one from him, he will require you to sign a card for it. Check the short title and serial number against the receipt you sign; also, make sure there are no missing pages by checking it page by page against the list of effective pages in the front; if it is defective *don't sign for it* and *don't take it*. Ascertain also if it is corrected to date by looking at the "list of corrections" page and asking if it is corrected to date.

Once you sign for it, and until you return it and are relieved of charge by the Communication Officer's countersignature on the card, you are responsible. When you no longer require it, return it and get off charge. If a fellow officer wants to borrow it, decline; both of you should go to the Communication Officer with the publication, have him sign you off charge and your friend on charge—then it becomes *his* responsibility. Don't be a nice fellow and let your friend sign directly to you—do it the prescribed way, then you are completely clear of any unpleasantness that might later develop.

Losing a registered publication is a soul-searing experience, involving legal proceedings—certainly an investigation, perhaps a court-martial. If you cannot give a publication the proper security stowage, so state and don't draw or accept it. If you should lose classified matter, report the loss immediately to the Classified Material Control Officer. Not only are you required to do so, but the sooner a search for it can be instituted the better are the chances of recovering it. "But Captain, I left them on my desk while I took a quick shower and when I got back they were gone," is most unimpressive.

822. SAFE STOWAGE. Learn promptly how to set (or change) the combination of your safe; it really is quite simple. Several cautionary remarks are in order: (1) If you have a three-combination safe, set *all* three rings; if you set only one or two, you have only a one- or two-combination safe, which does not meet the requirements for a *three-*combination safe; (2) Do not set easily ascertainable numbers such as 10-20-30, your serial number, birth date, automobile license number, home phone number—they are among the first even an amateur safe-cracker would use; (3) Try the new combination several times *with the safe door open* to make sure it is set properly; then try it with the door closed but the safe empty; if these attempts are successful, stow your safe, close the door, twirl the combination knob at least three times—and hope that you can reopen your safe when you need to do so.

Most important is to remember the combination. You are required to file with the Communication Officer the current combination of your safe in a double-sealed envelope, the outer one to be marked with the necessary data, such as "Ens. J. W. Gish—Stateroom 110, inboard safe." If for any reason the Communication Officer has to open your safe in your absence, he is required to report that fact and the circumstances to you promptly upon your return. If another person knows the combination to your safe, change it—for your security and out of fairness to him. The U. S. Navy Security Manual for Classified Matter requires all safe combinations to be changed at least once every six months. Remember to file the new combination with the Communications Officer.

823. PERSONNEL SECURITY INVESTIGATIONS AND CLEARANCES. Personnel security investigations are of two types, National Agency Checks and Background Investigations. A National Agency Check consists of the investigation of records and files of appropriate governmental investigative agencies. A Background Investigation makes inquiry into the birth record, education, employment, references, neighborhood reputation, criminal record if any, military service, foreign connections, citizenship status, credit record, foreign travel, and organizations of an individual to develop whether or not access to classified information is clearly consistent with the interests of national security.

If it is evident that the full investigation cannot be expeditiously completed, an *interim clearance* may be granted. Upon completion of all investigative requirements, a *final clearance* may be granted.

The granting of clearance is the responsibility of competent authority, either the commander or administrative senior in the chain of command. The authority concerned issues a Certificate of Clearance which is made a permanent record of the command and of the grantee's personal record. The Certificate of Clearance does not of itself authorize access to classified information, but establishes eligibility provided the commander then determines such information should be given the individual on a need-to-know basis. When an individual is transferred to a new station, the new commander or administrative senior must reestablish the individual's clearance.

824. THE SHIP'S SECRETARY. In small ships, the Ship's Secretary is responsible for the care and routing of all ship's correspondence, for the stowage and custody of secret and confidential matter issued to him, and for the operation and maintenance of material used in connection therewith.

He keeps informed of the progress of correspondence from officer to officer and maintains a follow-up system to ensure that letters are returned to the Ship's Office within a reasonable length of time.

825. MAIL LOG. The Ship's Secretary keeps the classified and registered-mail logs. All confidential and secret mail and all registered mail

(guard mail and otherwise) must be logged, along with pertinent data —originator, date mailed, serial number, date received, subject, number of copies, ship's serial number.

Classified mail must be accorded stowage as required by Navy Regulations, Article 1517. The Security Manual gives information on classification and handling of classified correspondence. See Navy Regulations, Article 1504, and Section 819 of this book for definition of top secret, secret, and confidential.

826. NAVY POSTAL CLERKS. Navy postal clerks are enlisted men who handle mail aboard ship—sell stamps, make up and dispatch mail, receive and open all pouches addressed to the ship, deliver mail and perform other postal duties. Postal clerks are no longer bonded as such. The Navy Department makes reimbursement to the Postal Department for any losses which may occur in a postal clerk's accounts.

The following discuss qualifications, duties, and responsibilities of Navy mail clerks: Navy Regulations, Article 0722; Manual for Navy Mail Clerks; BuPers Manual, Articles B1201-1209, C7417; and United States Navy Postal Instruction (OPNAVINST 2700.14 series).

CHAPTER 9

The Armed Forces of the
United States

It is not enough that we be good naval officers. That is expected of us, of course. But of infinitely greater importance, we must also be good citizens. Ask yourself, "Is this for the good of my country?" and act accordingly. That will demand a higher loyalty than the finest devotion to any party, sect or service.

—FLEET ADMIRAL CHESTER W. NIMITZ. USN

The Organization for National Security

901. THE COMMANDER IN CHIEF. The President of the United States is, by provision of our Constitution, Commander-in-Chief of the Armed Forces. The President is advised in national security matters by several agencies which are part of the Executive Office of the President. These agencies are the National Security Council, the Central Intelligence Agency, the Office of Emergency Planning, and the Bureau of the Budget (see Figure 901).

902. THE NATIONAL SECURITY COUNCIL. Established by the National Security Act, as amended, the Council has as members the President, Vice-President, Secretary of State, Secretary of Defense, and Director of the Office of Emergency Planning. The act provides that the Secretaries and Under Secretaries of other executive departments and of the military departments may serve as members of the Council, when appointed by the President with the advice and consent of the Senate. The Council staff is headed by a civilian Executive Secretary appointed by the President. The staff includes officers and civilian officials from the Departments of State and Defense and the four military services. This secretariat conducts the routine business of the Council.

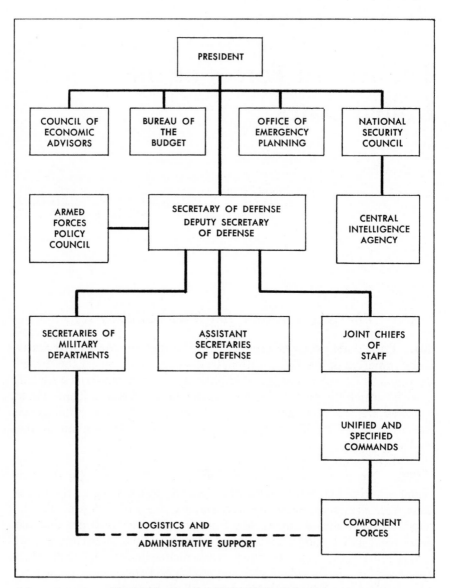

FIGURE 901. Organization for National Security.

The Council's function is to advise the President on domestic, foreign, and military policies and problems relating to national security, so as to enable the military services and other departments and agencies of the government to cooperate more effectively in matters involving national security. The duties of the Council include the following: to assess and appraise the objectives, commitments, and risks of the United States in relation to the actual and potential military power of the nation; to consider policies on matters of common interest to the departments and agencies of the government concerned with national security; and to make recommendations to the President on subjects which may affect the national policies of the government.

903. THE CENTRAL INTELLIGENCE AGENCY (CIA). This agency is administered under direction of the National Security Council by a Director appointed by the President with the advice and consent of the Senate. The Director may be either a military officer or a civilian. If an officer, while serving as Director he is completely separated from his service.

The Agency coordinates all intelligence activities of the government. CIA advises the National Security Council concerning intelligence activities of the government which relate to national security, makes recommendations to the National Security Council for coordination of these intelligence activities, correlates and evaluates intelligence, and disseminates such intelligence within the government—using, where appropriate, existing agencies—performs additional intelligence services of common concern which the National Security Council determines can be more efficiently accomplished centrally, and performs such other functions related to intelligence as the National Security Council may direct.

904. THE OFFICE OF EMERGENCY PLANNING (OEP). The Office of Emergency Planning, a successor agency to the Office of Defense Mobilization, was established as the Office of Civil and Defense Mobilization within the Executive Office of the Presdent by Reorganization Plan 1 of 1958, as amended by act of August 26, 1958. Executive Order 10952 of August 1961, transferred to the Department of Defense major civil defense operating functions of OCDM, following which the Office was redesignated the Office of Emergency Planning by act of September 22, 1961. The responsibilities of the Office of Emergency Planning are prescribed by Executive Order 11051 of September 27, 1962.

The Director of the Office of Emergency Planning assists and advises the President in coordinating and determining policy for all emergency preparedness activities of the Government and sits as a member of the National Security Council. He develops plans, conducts programs, and coordinates preparations for the continuity of Federal, State, and local governments under emergency conditions.

905. BUREAU OF THE BUDGET. Established in 1921, this Bureau is administered by the Director of the Budget. The functions of the Bureau are: to help the President prepare the Budget and formulate the fiscal program of the government; to supervise administration of the Budget; to improve government administrative management; to help the President bring about more efficient and economical conduct of government service; to clear and coordinate departmental advice on proposed legislation and make recommendations as to Presidential action on legislative enactments; to assist in consideration, clearance, and preparation of Executive orders and proclamations; to improve, develop, and coordinate Federal and other statistical services; and to inform the President of the progress of government work proposed, initiated, and completed.

The Department of Defense

906. THE MISSION. The Department of Defense was created to provide for the future security of the United States through the establishment of integrated policies and procedures for the departments, agencies, and functions of the government relating to the national security. The Department of Defense provides for the authoritative coordination and unified direction under civilian control of three military departments for the operation and administration of the Army, the Navy (including naval aviation and the United States Marine Corps), and the Air Force, with their assigned combat and service components. It provides for the effective strategic direction of the Armed Forces, for their operation under unified control, and for their integration into an efficient team of land, naval, and air forces.

The Secretary of Defense. The Secretary of Defense is the principal assistant to the President in all matters relating to the Department of Defense. He is appointed from civilian life by the President with the consent of the Senate. Under the direction of the President, and subject to the provisions of the National Security Act, the Secretary exercises direction, authority, and control over the Department of Defense.

The Deputy Secretary of Defense. The Deputy Secretary of Defense is responsible for the supervision and coordination of the activities of the Department of Defense as directed by the Secretary of Defense. He acts for, and exercises the powers of, the Secretary of Defense during his absence or disability.

The Armed Forces Policy Council, composed of the Secretary of Defense (chairman), the Deputy Secretary of Defense, the Secretaries of the Army, Navy, and Air Force, and the Service Chiefs advise the Secretary of Defense on matters of broad policy relating to the administration and operation of the Department of Defense, and on such other matters as the Secretary of Defense may direct.

907. THE OFFICE OF THE SECRETARY OF DEFENSE. Various agencies, offices, and positions created under the National Security Act, together with certain other agencies which assist the Secretary of Defense, are referred to collectively as the Office of the Secretary of Defense. They constitute the primary staff of the Secretary of Defense on matters within their cognizance.

The Director of Defense Research and Engineering takes precedence after the Deputy Secretary of Defense and the Service Secretaries. He performs such duties with respect to research and engineering as the Secretary of Defense may prescribe including the direction and control of research and engineering activities requiring central management.

The Assistant Secretary of Defense (Manpower and Reserve Affairs) is responsible for manpower and personnel matters, domestic security programs, and reserve affairs.

The Assistant Secretary of Defense (Comptroller) supervises preparation of Defense budget estimates; fiscal, cost, operating, and capital property accounting; progress and statistical reporting; internal audit; expenditure and collection of funds administered by the Department; and establishes uniform terminologies, classifications, and procedures in such matters.

The Assistant Secretary of Defense (International Security Affairs) is responsible for the coordination of activities relating to international affairs, psychological policy affairs, intergovernmental conferences, and

FIGURE 902. USS *Long Beach* (CGN-9).

other politico-military matters. He also represents the Department of Defense on interagency and international organizations relating to international security affairs.

The Assistant Secretary of Defense (Public Affairs) advises the Secretary of Defense on public information and other public affairs.

Other *Assistant Secretaries* perform staff functions for the Secretary of Defense in the areas of responsibility designated here:

• Administration
• Installations and Logistics
• Systems Analysis

The Assistant to the Secretary (Atomic Energy) is responsible for atomic energy matters within and involving the Department of Defense and for representation of the Department on such matters. He may also serve as Chairman of the Military Liaison Committee to the Atomic Energy Commission if appointed by the President.

The Assistant to the Secretary (Legislative Affairs) develops the over-all legislative program for the Department of Defense.

The General Counsel is the chief legal officer of the Department of Defense.

908. BOARDS, COMMITTEES, AND AGENCIES OF THE DEPARTMENT OF DEFENSE. The following principal organizations are included in the staff for administering the Department of Defense:

Armed Forces Policy Council
National Security Agency
  (NSA)
Joint Strategic Planning Staff
Office of Management Engineering
Reserve Forces Policy Board
Military Liaison Committee to the
  Atomic Energy Commission
Weapons System Evaluation Group
Military Traffic Service
Armed Forces Medical Policy Council
Office of Public Information

Defense Agencies for:
  Advanced Research Proj-
    ects (ARPA)
  Atomic Support (DASA)
  Supply (DSA)
  Intelligence (DIA)
  Communications (DCA)
  Contract Audit Agency

909. THE NATIONAL SECURITY ACT. The National Security Act of 1947, as amended in 1953, 1958, and 1962, is the basic military legislation of the United States.

The policy section of the act reads: "It is the intent of Congress to provide a comprehensive program for the future security of the United States; to provide for the establishment of integrated policies and procedures for the departments, agencies, and functions of the Government relating to the national security." In so doing, the act:

1. Provides three military departments, separately administered, for the operation and administration of the Army, the Navy (including naval aviation), the United States Marine Corps, and the Air Force, with their assigned combatant and service components;

2. Provides for coordination and direction of the three military departments and four services under the Secretary of Defense;

3. Provides for strategic direction of the Armed Forces, for their operation under unified control, and for the integration of the four services into an efficient team of land, naval, and air forces, but not for the establishment of a single Chief of Staff over the Armed Forces nor an Armed Forces general staff.

Unification has been accomplished by giving the Secretary of Defense authority, direction, and virtual military control over the four military services. He also has authority to eliminate duplication in procurement, supply, transportation, storage, health, and research.

910. FUNCTIONS OF THE ARMED FORCES. After enactment of the National Security Act of 1947, the Secretary of Defense called a meeting of the service heads at Key West, Florida, at which agreement as to the functions of the services was reached in a document known as the Key West Agreement, later modified and amplified at a conference in Newport, Rhode Island.

After the Reorganization Act of 1958, the Secretary of Defense promulgated Department of Defense Directive Number 5100.1 of December 31, 1958, which set forth the functions of the Department of Defense and its major components and cancels the Key West and Newport Agreements.

The Joint Chiefs of Staff

911. THE JOINT CHIEFS OF STAFF—HISTORICAL. The authority of the President as Commander-in-Chief of the Army and Navy formerly was exercised through the Secretaries of War and Navy. During World War II, however, a need was felt for a more personal control. To promote this end, to make certain of direct access by his chief military advisers to the President, and to improve coordination between the Army and Navy, organization of the Joint Chiefs of Staff was ordered. With the appointment of Admiral William D. Leahy, USN (Retired), as Chief of Staff to the President, a new billet, this distinguished officer became the senior member and presiding chairman of the Joint Chiefs of Staff. At first, the members were General George C. Marshall, Chief of Staff of the Army, and Admiral Ernest J. King, Commander-in-Chief of the United States Fleet and Chief of Naval Operations. Feeling the need for experience and counsel on air warfare, Lieutenant General H. H. Arnold, Chief of the Army Air Corps, was added to the agency as a full partner. These four officers, all of them subsequently promoted to Fleet Admiral or General of the Army, composed the Joint Chiefs of Staff which conducted the global warfare of World War II.

During the war, the Joint Chiefs functioned as a part of the Combined Chiefs of Staff, an Anglo-American military agency consisting of the United States Joint Chiefs of Staff and two senior British Army general officers, one British admiral, and one British air vice-marshal.

At meetings, often held twice a day, the Joint Chiefs discussed the grand strategy of the war and planned and formulated directives. The Chief of Staff of the Army and the Commander-in-Chief of the United States Fleet acted as executive agents for the Joint Chiefs in carrying out their plans and directives.

Meetings of the Combined Chiefs of Staff integrated the plans and operations of the United States Armed Forces into the broad scheme of strategy of the Allied Powers in that truly global war.

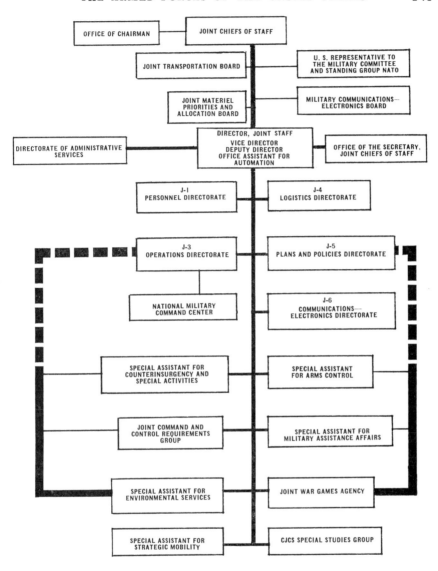

NOT A COMPLETE OR OFFICIAL JCS ORGANIZATION CHART

FIGURE 903. Organization of the Joint Chiefs of Staff.

With the coming of peace and the return to retirement of Fleet Admiral Leahy, considerable difficulty was found in reaching unanimous decisions on important issues on which there were serious disagreements between two or more of the Chiefs. Accordingly, when the Security Act came up for amendment in 1949, a Chairman was authorized, specifically designated to preside at the meetings of the Joint Chiefs in order to expedite the business of that agency, but he was not to be considered Chief of Staff to either the President or the Secretary of Defense or of the Armed Services. The act also provided that he should have no vote in the meetings and deliberations of the Joint Chiefs.

912. THE JOINT CHIEFS OF STAFF (JCS)—COMPOSITION AND FUNCTIONS. As reconstituted by the National Security Act (Amended), the Joint Chiefs of Staff consist of a Chairman appointed from one of the services by the President, the Chiefs of Staff of the Army and Air

FIGURE 904. The Joint Chiefs of Staff, 1969.

Force, the Chief of Naval Operations, and the Commandant of the Marine Corps when matters concerning the Marine Corps are under consideration. Figure 903 shows the organization of this important body and the flow of authority.

It should be noted that the *JCS organization* includes not only the Chiefs themselves, but the Joint Staff, the Secretariat, and various boards and organizations.

The organization of the Joint Staff, composed of about 400 officers of all services, is shown in Figures 903 and 905.

The functions of the JCS are set forth in Department of Defense Directives number 5100.1 and 5158.1 of December 31, 1958, and in the National Security Act of 1947, as amended. These are:

1. To serve as advisers and as military staff in the chain of operational command with respect to unified and specified commands, to provide a channel of communications from the President and Secretary of Defense to unified and specified commands, and to coordinate all communications in matters of joint interest addressed to the commanders of the unified or specified commands by other authority.

2. To prepare strategic plans and provide for the strategic direction of the armed forces, including the direction of operations conducted by commanders of unified and specified commands and the discharge of any other function of command for such commands directed by the Secretary of Defense.

3. To prepare integrated logistic plans, which may include assignments of logistic responsibilities to the armed forces and the Defense Supply Agency in accordance with such plans.

4. To prepare integrated plans for military mobilization.

5. To provide adequate, timely, and reliable joint intelligence for use within the Department of Defense.

6. To review major personnel, material, and logistic requirements of the armed forces in relation to strategic and logistic plans.

7. To review the plans and programs of commanders of unified and specified commands to determine their adequacy, feasibility, and suitability for the performance of assigned missions.

8. To provide military guidance for use by the military departments, the armed forces and the defense agencies, as needed in the preparation of their respective detailed plans.

9. To participate, as directed, in the preparation of combined plans for military action in conjunction with the armed forces of other nations.

10. To recommend to the Secretary of Defense the establishment and force structure of unified and specified commands in strategic areas.

11. To determine the headquarters support, such as facilities, personnel, and communications, required by commanders of unified and specified commands and to recommend the assignment to the military departments of the responsibilities for providing such support.

12. To establish doctrines for (a) unified operations and training and (b) coordination of the military education of members of the armed forces.

13. To recommend to the Secretary of Defense the assignment of primary responsibility for any function of the armed forces requiring such determination and the transfer, reassignment, abolition, or consolidation of such functions.

14. To prepare and submit to the Secretary of Defense for information and consideration in connection with the preparation of budgets, statements of military requirements based upon United States strategic considerations, current national security policy, and strategic war plans. These statements of requirements shall include tasks, priority of tasks, force requirements, and general strategic guidance for the development of military installations and bases and for equipping and maintaining military forces.

15. To advise and assist the Secretary of Defense in research and engineering matters by preparing: (a) statements of broad strategic guidance to be used in the preparation of an integrated Department of Defense program, (b) statements of over-all military requirements; (c) statements of the relative military importance of development activities to meet the needs of the unified and speci-

fied commanders, and (d) recommendations for the assignment of specific new weapons to the armed forces.

16. To prepare and submit to the Secretary of Defense for information and consideration general strategic guidance for the development of industrial mobilization programs.

17. To prepare and submit to the Secretary of Defense military guidance for use in the development of military aid programs and other actions relating to foreign military forces, including recommendations for allied military force, material, and facilities requirements related to United States strategic objectives, current national security policy, strategic war plans, and the implementation of approved programs; and to make recommendations to the Secretary of Defense, as necessary, for keeping the Military Assistance Program in consonance with agreed strategic concepts.

18. To provide United States representation on the Military Staff Committee of the United Nations, in accordance with the provisions of the Charter of the United Nations, and representation on other properly authorized military staffs, boards, councils, and missions.

19. To perform such other duties as the President or the Secretary of Defense may prescribe.

913. THE JOINT CHIEFS OF STAFF—OPERATION. Not much is generally known in the naval service about the methods of operation of the JCS. Its procedures and activities, little changed since the war, are briefly outlined here.

A problem for the Joint Chiefs of Staff may be presented to them by the President or the Secretary of Defense; it may be brought up by one of its members; it may be forced upon them by the exigencies of war operations or international emergency; it may come to them through its representation on the Military Staff Committee of the United Nations; or it may come up in the course of making basic or emergency war plans. However it may originate, it is usually presented to the Joint Chiefs on paper through their Secretary.

The JCS Secretary then usually routes this paper to each Chief in his capacity as a Service Chief and to the Commandant of the Marine Corps when the subject under discussion concerns the Marine Corps. The Chiefs refer the paper to their service staffs. The views of each service are then transmitted to the other services via the JCS Secretary and compromises are effected if possible. If agreement is obtained, the agreed paper is then forwarded to the Secretary of Defense.

If the Chairman had disagreed with the decision he would have so advised the Secretary of Defense.

Had agreement not been reached before or during a formal meeting of the Chiefs on the subject, a vote would have been taken and if a split decision resulted, each Chief would then write his recommendations

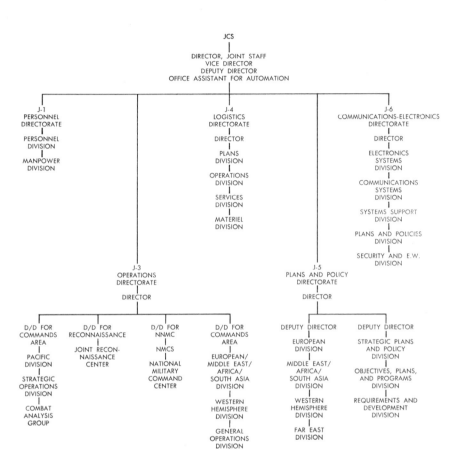

FIGURE 905. Organization of the Joint Staff.

to the Secretary of Defense and the Chairman would forward them to the Secretary of Defense with his recommendations in the matter.

If this paper had presented a problem which had to be studied by JCS planners, it would go through a somewhat different routine. From the JCS Secretariat, it would be referred to the appropriate directorate of the Joint Staff.

The completed paper would be returned to the Joint Chiefs of Staff Secretary whose Secretariat transforms the "study" into a JCS document for consideration by the Chiefs. Each Service Chief passes it on

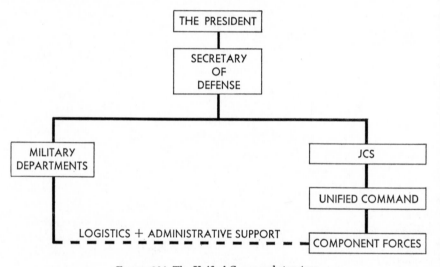

FIGURE 906. The Unified Command structure.

to his staff agency which handles JCS documents for him. It is forwarded to the proper offices in the Department for comment and then back to the Chief. Concurrences are made by telephone to the JCS Secretary. Minor comments are held for discussion at a JCS meeting. Major comments are written and circulated to the other Chiefs. By the time the issue gets before a meeting of the JCS, the subject has had a very lengthy and thorough study. If the paper is one on which there are important disagreements, the JCS Secretary puts it on the agenda for the next meeting.

Two or three times a week in peacetime, as many times a day in war or national emergency, the Joint Chiefs of Staff meet in the JCS conference room in the Pentagon. Usually present are the Chiefs and one principal assistant for each, the Director of the Joint Staff, and the Secretary of the JCS. Other officers and civilian officials of the government are invited to attend meetings for consultation on matters of especial interest to them. The Joint Chiefs may discuss the subjects on the agenda informally among themselves, or elaborate presentations of the various service views may be made for their consideration.

It is important to understand that the majority of JCS decisions are unanimous, even though some disagreements receive enough publicity to give the opposite impression.

Unified Commands

914. THE UNIFIED COMMAND STRUCTURE. Unified commands were established during World War II. These commands came directly under the Joint Chiefs of Staff, who appointed an officer of the service having dominant interest as Commander and assigned forces to that commander. One of the three services was assigned as "Executive Agent" to furnish support to the command. A variation of the unified command is the specified command, where the forces are all of one service, but are under the direct command of the Joint Chiefs of Staff. The Strategic Air Command is an example of a specified command.

The Reorganization Act of 1958 altered the command arrangements of the Unified Command structure. This change was made to streamline the structure. Figure 906 illustrates the present system.

The executive agency system has been abolished. Orders now go from the President to the Secretary of Defense and then to the commander of the unified or specified combatant command through the Joint Chiefs of Staff acting as a corporate body (see Figure 907).

All forces not assigned to a unified or a specified command remain in their departments as does the administration of forces assigned to unified and specified commands.

The Unified and Specified commands are:
1. U. S. European Command.
2. U. S. Southern Command.
3. Atlantic Command.
4. Pacific Command.
5. U. S. Strike Command.
6. Continental Air Defense Command.
7. *Strategic Air Command.
8. Alaskan Command.

* Specified Command.

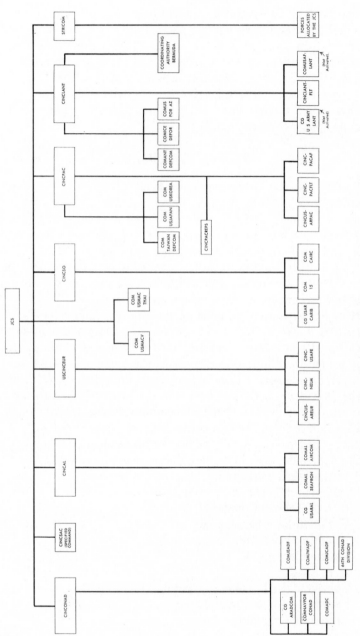

FIGURE 907. Commands established by the Secretary of Defense.

FIGURE 908. USS *Forrest Sherman* (DD-931).

The Department of the Army

915. THE MISSION OF THE ARMY. The Department of the Army is charged with the responsibility of providing support for national and international policy and the security of the United States by planning, directing, and reviewing the military and civil operations of the Army Establishment.

The United States Army includes land-combat and service forces and such aviation and water transport as may be organic therein. Of the three major services, the Army has primary interest in all operations on land, except in those operations otherwise assigned to other services.

916. THE FUNCTIONS OF THE ARMY. The functions of the Department of the Army are set forth in Department of Defense Directive 5100.1 of December 31, 1958, as follows:

The Department of the Army is responsible for the preparation of land forces necessary for the effective prosecution of war except as otherwise assigned and, in accordance with integrated mobilization plans, for the expansion of the peacetime components of the Army to meet the needs of war.

The Army, within the Department of the Army, includes land combat and service forces and such aviation and water transport as may be organic therein.

Primary Functions of the Army

a. To organize, train, and equip Army forces for the conduct of prompt and sustained combat operations on land—specifically, forces to defeat enemy land forces and to seize, occupy, and defend land area.

b. To organize, train and equip Army air defense units, including the provision of Army forces as required for the defense of the United States against air attack, in accordance with doctrines established by the Joint Chiefs of Staff.

c. To organize and equip, in coordination with the other Services, and to provide Army forces for joint amphibious and airborne operations, and to provide for the training of such forces, in accordance with doctrines established by the Joint Chiefs of Staff.

(1) To develop, in coordination with the other Services, doctrines, tactics, techniques, and equipment of interest to the Army for amphibious operations and not provided for in this document.

(2) To develop, in coordination with the other Services, the doctrines, procedures, and equipment employed by Army and Marine Forces in airborne operations. The Army shall have primary interest in the development of those airborne doctrines, procedures, and equipment which are of common interest to the Army and the Marine Corps.

d. To provide an organization capable of furnishing adequate, timely, and reliable intelligence for the Army.

e. To provide forces for the occupations of territories abroad, to include initial establishment of military government pending transfer of this responsibility to other authority.

f. To formulate doctrines and procedures for the organizing, equipping, training, and employment of forces operating on land, except that the formulation of doctrines and procedures for the organization, equipping, training, and employment of Marine Corps units for amphibious operations shall be a function of the Department of the Navy, coordinating as required by this document.

g. To conduct the following activities:

(1) The administration and operation of the Panama Canal.

(2) The authorized civil works program, including projects for improvement of navigation, flood control, beach erosion control, and other water resource developments in the United States, its territories, and its possessions.

(3) Certain other civil activities prescribed by law.

Collateral Functions of the Army
To train forces:

a. To interdict enemy sea and air power and communications through operations on or from land.

917. THE ORGANIZATION OF THE ARMY. Command flows through the Secretary of the Army and military channels to Army units and installations throughout the world (see Figure 909).

In the field the Army is divided into armies which are made up of corps and divisions, all of which contain a balanced organization of combat arms and administrative services to make them effective fighting units. Commencing at the lower echelons, the units of an Army organization can be described as follows:

Company. The smallest administrative unit, usually commanded by a captain, made up of squads and platoons.

Troop and Battery. The same as company in the infantry for the armor and artillery.

Battalion. Made up of three or more companies. A battery of artillery might be attached to an infantry battalion.

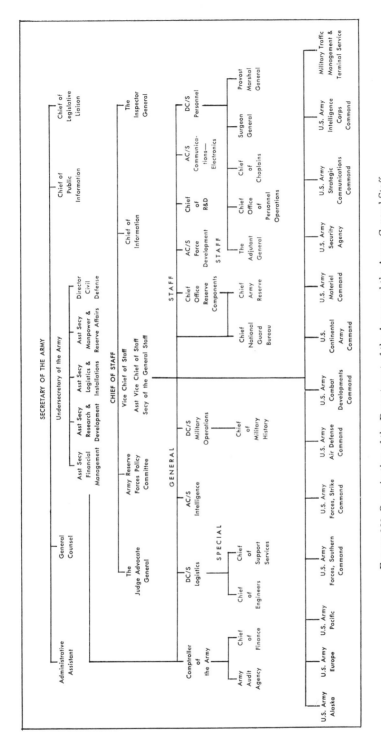

FIGURE 909. Organization of the Department of the Army and the Army General Staff.

Regiment. To be an effective combat team, the infantry regiment usually includes three battalions, attached artillery, and frequently armor.

Division. The infantry division includes three infantry regiments, the division artillery, and supporting service units.

Corps. Corps headquarters; two or more infantry, airborne, or armored divisions; the corps artillery and supporting troops of the various arms and services.

Army. Army headquarters, two or more corps, and supporting troops of the arms and services.

The Army is made up of the following basic and special branches:

Basic Branches	*Special Branches*
Infantry	Judge Advocate General's Corps
Armor	Chaplains
Artillery	Army Medical Service:
Corps of Engineers	Medical Corps
Signal Corps	Dental Corps
Adjutant General's Corps	Veterinary Corps
Quartermaster Corps	Army Nurse Corps
Finance Corps	Women's Medical Specialist Corps
Ordnance Corps	
Chemical Corps	
Transportation Corps	
Military Police Corps	

918. THE SECRETARY OF THE ARMY AND HIS ASSISTANTS. The Secretary of the Army heads the Department of the Army. He is responsible for all affairs of the Army Establishment. In addition, the Secretary of the Army has certain quasi-civil functions, such as: maintenance and operation of the Panama Canal, the Alaska Communications Service, and the Corps of Engineers' civil works program; supervision of U.S. battle monuments; and direction of the civilian marksmanship program.

Immediately under the Secretary of the Army are the following assistants and major agencies:

Under Secretary of the Army
Assistant Secretaries of the Army (Financial Management, Research and Development, Installations and Logistics, Manpower and Reserve Affairs)
General Counsel
Chief of Legislative Liaison
Chief of Public Information
Director of Civil Defense
Special Assistant for Civil Functions

Administrative Assistant
Army Policy Council

919. ARMY STAFF. The Army Staff is the staff of the Secretary of the Army and includes the Chief of Staff and his immediate assistants, the General Staff and the Special Staff Agencies.

Duties of the Army Staff include: preparing plans for national security, both separately and in conjunction with the other military services; investigating and reporting on questions affecting the efficiency of the Army and its state of preparation for military operations; execution and supervision of approved plans and instructions; and acting for the Secretary and the Chief of Staff in informing all officers and coordinating the Army Establishment.

The Chief of Staff. The Chief of Staff is the principal military adviser of the Secretary of the Army and is charged by him with the planning, development, and execution of the Army program. The Chief of Staff, under the direction of the Secretary of the Army, supervises all members and organizations of the Army, performs the duties prescribed for him by the National Security Act of 1947 and other laws, and performs such other military duties not otherwise assigned by law as may be assigned to him by the President or by the Secretary of the Army. Except as otherwise prescribed by law, by the President, or by the Secretary of Defense, the Chief of Staff performs his duties under the direction of the Secretary of the Army. The Chief of Staff, by virtue of his position, takes rank above all officers on the active list of the Army, Navy, and Air Force, except the Chairman of the Joint Chiefs of Staff, and except the Chief of Naval Operations and the Chief of Staff, United States Air Force, if those latter two officers' appointments, as such, antedate his. The Chief of Staff presides over the Army Staff, transmits to the Secretary of the Army plans and recommendations prepared by the Army Staff, advises him in regard thereto, and upon the approval of plans or recommendations by the Secretary of the Army, acts as his agent in carrying the same into effect.

920. THE GENERAL STAFF. Under the Chief of Staff, the General Staff renders professional advice and assistance to the Secretary of the Army; provides broad policies and plans for major Army commanders and the heads of other Department of the Army staff agencies; and prepares and issues directives, in the name of the Secretary of the Army, to implement approved plans and policies. The General Staff is made up of all commissioned officers assigned to the offices of the Chief of Staff,

Vice Chief of Staff, Deputy and Assistant Chiefs of Staff, Army Comptroller, and Secretary of the General Staff. The Deputy Chiefs of Staff also supervise and control the various Technical Services and the Special Staff.

921. SPECIAL STAFF. The Special Staff advises the Secretary of the Army and Chief of Staff, through the cognizant Deputy Chief of Staff, on specialized matters within its several fields. The following officers comprise the Special Staff:

Chief of Personnel Operations	Chief of Support Services
*Chief of Finance	*The Adjutant General
Chief of Engineers	*Chief of Chaplains
Chief of Army Reserve	Chief of Information
Chief, National Guard Bureau	*The Provost Marshal General
Chief of Military History	The Inspector General
Chief of U. S. Army Audit Agency	Chief of Communications-Electronics
The Judge Advocate General	The Surgeon General

922. MAJOR ARMY COMMANDS. *Material Command (MC)* performs material development, procurement and supply functions, as well as service tests and evaluation functions.

Army Combat Developments Command (ACDC) performs all combat development functions for the Army, that is to say, research, development, and early integration into the Army of new doctrine, new organization, and new material to obtain greatest combat effectiveness. The Command also produces the Army's comprehensive library of field and training manuals.

923. CONTINENTAL ARMY COMMAND. The Continental Army Command controls the army areas and undertakes and coordinates such functions as the following: general direction of training objectives, organization, and equipment utilized by the Army in the field; development of doctrine for tactical and technical employment of individuals and units in the field, and of materiel needed in performance of their missions; also training of the Army National Guard, the Reserve Officers' Training Corps (ROTC), and units established under Section 55c of the National Defense Act.

924. ARMY AREAS. The Department of the Army is organized, in the Zone of the Interior, into six army areas and the Military District of Washington.

* Also serve as chiefs of their respective branches.

FIGURE 910. Army troops in action.

Except for certain activities specifically exempted, the commanding general of each area commands all units, activities, and installations within his area.

925. THE UNITED STATES ARMY. The United States Army provides for the security of the United States within its area of responsibility and particularly within the Zone of the Interior. Part of the Army is on full-time duty. Other components are ordinarily inactive in peacetime. All components may be called to active duty during an emergency declared by Congress or in the event of war.

Regular Army. The Regular Army for over a century and a half has been the framework upon which we have built up our wartime armies.

It is the duty of the Regular Army to:

1. Perform occupation duties;
2. Garrison the United States and oversea possessions and bases;
3. Train the National Guard, Organized Reserve, and ROTC;
4. Provide an organization for the administration and supply of the peacetime military establishment;

5. Provide educated officers and men to become leaders, in event of war, of the expanded Army of the United States;

6. Expand and record the body of military knowledge so as to keep this country up to date and prepared;

7. Constitute, with the National Guard and units of the Organized Reserve, a covering force in case of a major war;

8. Cooperate with the Marine Corps, Navy, and Air Force in carrying out their missions.

National Guard. The National Guard is the civilian militia of the United States. In time of peace, the National Guard of any State can be called to active duty by the governor of that State to perform emergency duties. Units or individual members of the National Guard can be called to active duty by the Federal government only during war or national emergency, or with their own consent in time of peace. In addition to augmenting the Regular Army, the Guard trains additional volunteers and assigned selectees; supplies instructors for schools and training centers; furnishes cadres of experienced officers and men for new units; and furnishes enlisted men who qualify for officer commissions.

Ready and Standby Reserve Corps. Like the National Guard, Army Reserve units train in local armories and are subject to orders to active duty under similar conditions. Individual members are assigned to Army Reserve organizations in or near their home towns. The Organized Reserve, however, is not subject to State control of any kind.

926. WOMEN IN THE ARMY. Women have served in and with the United States Army for many years and in a number of wars, at first as civilian nurses, then as Army nurses, and finally as members of the Women's Army Corps and the Women's Medical Specialist Corps.

927. EDUCATION OF OFFICER CANDIDATES. Three school systems train candidates for commissions in the Army—the Military Academy, Officer Candidate Schools, and Reserve Officers Training Corps.

The United States Military Academy, West Point, New York, was established in 1802 for the purpose of training young gentlemen as commissioned officers. Duty, Honor, Country—superb motto of the Corps of Cadets—have long served to set West Point's high standard.

The Military Academy is commanded by a Superintendent, an Army general officer. The four-year curriculum includes cultural subjects as well as military science. The cadet graduates with a B.S. degree and, if physically fit, is usually commissioned as a second lieutenant in the Army. However, at his own request, he may be commissioned in one of the other services.

Officer Candidate Schools are conducted for men at the Army General School, Fort Riley, Kansas, and for women at the WAC Training Center, Camp Lee, Virginia. The course is usually six months. Most candidates for the former are chosen from enlisted men of the Regular Army, the Reserve, and the National Guard.

Reserve Officers' Training Corps (ROTC) units are located at over 250 civilian universities and colleges. Long a major source of officers for our Army, the first unit was established in 1862.

Army and Air ROTC are basically similar to the Naval ROTC.

The Department of the Air Force

928. MISSION OF THE AIR FORCE. The Department of the Air Force and the United States Air Force were established in 1947 by the National Security Act. The Air Force includes air combat and service forces. It is organized, trained, and equipped for prompt and sustained offensive and defensive combat operations in the air.

929. THE FUNCTIONS OF THE AIR FORCE. The functions of the Air Force, as set forth in Department of Defense Directive 5100.1 of December 31, 1958, are:

The Department of the Air Force is responsible for the preparation of the air forces necessary for the effective prosecution of war except as otherwise assigned and, in accordance with integrated mobilization plans, for the expansion of the peacetime components of the Air Force to meet the needs of war.

The Air Force, within the Department of the Air Force, includes aviation forces, both combat and service, not otherwise assigned.

Primary Functions of the Air Force

a. To organize, train, and equip Air Force forces for the conduct of prompt and sustained combat operations in the air—specifically, forces to defend the United States against air attack in accordance with doctrines established by the Joint Chiefs of Staff, to gain and maintain general air supremacy, to defeat enemy air forces, to control vital air areas, and to establish local air superiority except as otherwise assigned herein.

b. To develop doctrines and procedures, in coordination with the other Services, for the unified defense of the United States against air attack.

c. To organize, train, and equip Air Force forces for strategic air warfare.

d. To organize and equip Air Force forces for joint amphibious and airborne operations, in coordination with the other Services, and to provide for their training in accordance with doctrines established by the Joint Chiefs of Staff.

e. To furnish close combat and logistical air support to the Army, to include air lift, support, and resupply of airborne operations, aerial photography, tactical reconnaissance, and interdiction of enemy land power and communications.

f. To provide air transport for the armed forces, except as otherwise assigned.

g. To develop, in coordination with the other Services, doctrines, procedures, and equipment for air defense from land areas, including the continental United States.

h. To formulate doctrines and procedures for the organizing, equipping, training, and employment of Air Force forces.

i. To provide an organization capable of furnishing adequate, timely, and reliable intelligence for the Air Force.

j. To furnish aerial photography for cartographic purposes.

k. To develop, in coordination with the other Services, tactics, techniques. and equipment of interest to the Air Force for amphibious operations and not provided for in this directive.

l. To develop, in coordination with the other Services, doctrines, procedures, and equipment employed by Air Force forces in airborne operations.

Collateral Functions of the Air Force
To train forces:

a. To interdict enemy sea power through air operations.
b. To conduct antisubmarine warfare and to protect shipping.
c. To conduct aerial mine-laying operations.

930. ORGANIZATION OF THE AIR FORCE. Command Organization in the Air Force provides clearly defined command channels from the President through the Secretary of Defense and the Secretary of the Air Force to the squadron and the individual plane commander. As a result of experience during and after World War II, Korea, and Vietnam, the Air Force has evolved the following basic organizational structure (see Figure 911).

Flight. The lowest tactical echelon recognized in the Air Force structure. Flights are not formally designated in the structure, but are subdivisions of combat squadrons. They provide the basis for combat formations, and are used for training purposes.

Squadron. The basic unit in the organizational structure of the United States Air Force. A squadron is manned and equipped to best perform a specific military function such as combat, maintenance, food service, and communications.

Group. A flexible unit composed of two or more squadrons whose functions may be either tactical or administrative in nature.

Wing. The smallest Air Force unit manned and equipped to operate independently in sustained action until replacement and resupply can take place.

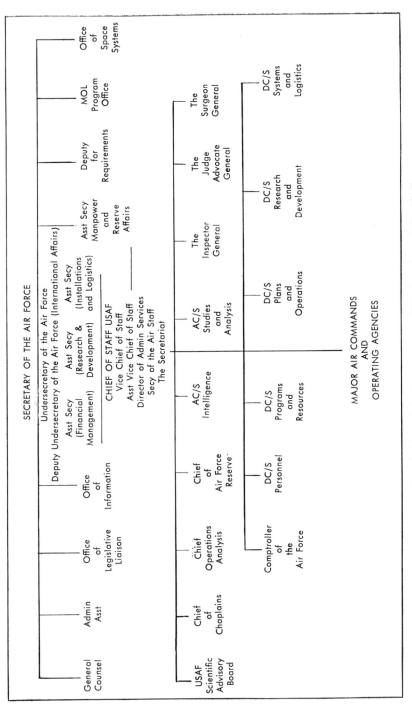

FIGURE 911. Organization of the Department and Headquarters of the Air Force.

Air Division. An air combat organization normally consisting of two or more wings. Divisions are operational in nature with minimum administrative or logistics responsibilities.

Numbered Air Force. The intermediate command echelon designed to control and administer a grouping of combat wings. It is flexible in organization and can vary in size. Usually, a Numbered Air Force has one of three missions—strategic, tactical, or defensive. Its wings may be grouped for operational control under Air Divisions, or be directly under the Numbered Air Force.

Major Command. A functionally titled command echelon directly below Headquarters USAF, charged with a major responsibility in fulfilling the Air Force mission.

931. THE SECRETARY OF THE AIR FORCE AND HIS ASSISTANTS. The Secretary of the Air Force heads the Department of the Air Force and is responsible for all matters pertaining to its operation.

Under the Secretary of the Air Force are the following assistants:
The Under Secretary of the Air Force
Assistant Secretary of the Air Force (Financial Management)
Assistant Secretary of the Air Force (Installations and Logistics)
Assistant Secretary of the Air Force (Research and Development)
Assistant Secretary of the Air Force (Manpower and Reserve Affairs)
Administrative Assistant
General Counsel
Director, Office of Legislative Liaison
Director, Office of Information
Military Assistant
Vice Director, MOL (Man Orbiting Laboratory) Program
Director, Office of Space Systems
Deputy Undersecretary of the Air Force (International Affairs)
Director, Air Force Personnel Council
Chairman, Air Reserve Forces Policy Committee

932. HEADQUARTERS, U. S. AIR FORCE. The Chief of Staff supervises all elements of the United States Air Force, and exercises command over the major air commands; he is responsible for policies and plans to accomplish the Air Force mission, and serves as principal military adviser and executive to the Secretary of the Air Force.

Under the Chief of Staff, the following assistants and agencies perform staff functions:

Vice Chief of Staff
Assistant Vice Chief of Staff
Secretary of the Air Staff
Scientific Advisory Board
Chief Scientist
Chief Operations Analysis
Surgeon General
Inspector General
Judge Advocate General
Chief of Chaplains
Director of Administrative Service

Assistant Chiefs of Staff for
  Intelligence
  Studies and Analysis
Deputy Chiefs of Staff for
  Personnel
  Programs and Resources
  Plans and Operations
  Research and Development
  Systems and Logistics
Comptroller of the Air Force
Chief of Air Force Reserve

The Air Staff. The Air Staff is organized about the offices of five Deputy Chiefs of Staff: Personnel; Programs and Requirements; Research and Development; Plans and Operations; and Systems and Logistics.

933. MAJOR AIR COMMANDS. The Air Force is divided into a number of continental and overseas commands:
  Air Defense Command
  The Air Force Logistics Command
  The Air Force Systems Command
  The Air Training Command
  The Air University
  Continental Air Command
  Headquarters Command, USAF
  Strategic Air Command
  Tactical Air Command
  Military Airlift Command
  USAF Security Service
  Air Force Communications Service
  Air Force Component Commands in Overseas JCS-established
    commands.

In addition to the foregoing, the Chief of Staff of the Air Force has operational responsibility over the Military Airlift Command (MAC), which provides world-wide air transportation for the Department of Defense (MAC).

FIGURE 912. Air Force B-52's, Strato Fortress, heavy bombers.

Continental Air Defense Command is a joint organization which coordinates Air Force, Navy, and Marine fighter units, as well as all air warning services, and Army anti-aircraft, for the continental United States.

934. THE UNITED STATES AIR FORCE (USAF). Composed of the Regular Air Force, Air National Guard, Air Force Reserve, and Air Force ROTC, the U. S. Air Force provides for the air security and defense of the United States. These component organizations are similar to those of the Army.

935. WOMEN IN THE AIR FORCE. After the separation of the Army Air Force from the Army to become the U. S. Air Force, women of the Women's Army Corps (WAC) serving with Air Force units were transferred to the Women in the Air Force (WAF). Army nurses also transferred to the Air Force Nurse Corps. The Women's Armed Services Act of June 1948 provided for women in the Air Force as in the other services. The procedure for promotion, pay, retirement, and separation from the service are similar to those for WAC's.

936. EDUCATION OF AIR FORCE OFFICER CANDIDATES. Officer candidates for Air Force commissions receive their training in a number of different institutions: the U. S. Air Force Academy, Air Force ROTC units, Aviation Cadet Program, and Officer Candidate School.

The United States Air Force Academy, Colorado. This newest of the service academies provides the main input of regular officers for the Air Force. The curriculum includes both cultural and military subjects, and leads to a B.S. degree and a commission as a second lieutenant in the Air Force. However, at his own request, a graduate may be commissioned in one of the other services.

Aviation Cadet Program. In addition to the Air Force Academy the Aviation Cadet Program provides many of the young officer pilots. The normal course lasts about a year. Commissioned officer student-pilots also receive flight training at schools forming part of this program. Most of the bases concerned are located in Texas.

Officer Candidate School. Located at Lackland Air Force Base, San Antonio, Texas, the Air Force Officer Training School is coeducational; male and female officer candidates attend the same classes. The curriculum includes administration, organization, supply, military law, and field sanitation. Successful graduates are commissioned in the Air Force Reserve, with an opportunity to apply for regular commissions.

The Air Force ROTC is similar in purpose and organization to the Army and Navy ROTC.

The Airman Education and Commissioning Program provides undergraduate education, followed by officer training and a commission for selected career-minded airmen serving on active duty.

CHAPTER 10

The Department of the Navy

Each man must do all in his power for his country.
—COMMODORE ISAAC HULL, USN,
U.S.S. *Constitution*, 1813

Mission and Functions

1001. THE MISSION OF THE NAVY. The fundamental Naval Policy is: "To maintain the Navy and Marine Corps, as a part of the Department of Defense, in sufficient strength and readiness to fulfill its responsibilities as set forth in the National Security Act of 1947 as amended and the Functions of the Department of Defense and its major components issued by the Secretary of Defense on 31 December 1958."

The Section of the National Security Act of 1947 (Amended), which applies to the Department of the Navy, reads as follows:

Section 206. (a) The term "Department of the Navy" as used in this Act shall be construed to mean the Department of the Navy at the seat of government; the headquarters, United States Marine Corps; the entire operating forces of the United States Navy, including naval aviation, and of the United States Marine Corps, including the reserve components of such forces; all field activities, headquarters, forces, bases, installation, activities, and functions under the control or supervision of the Department of the Navy; and the United States Coast Guard when operating as a part of the Navy pursuant to law.

(b) In general the United States Navy, within the Department of the Navy, shall include naval combat and service forces and such aviation as may be organic therein. It shall be organized, trained, and equipped primarily for prompt and sustained combat incident to operations at sea. It shall be responsible for the preparation of naval forces necessary for the effective prosecution of war except as otherwise assigned, and, in accordance with integrated joint mobilization plans, for the expansion of the peacetime components of the Navy to meet the needs of war.

All naval aviation shall be integrated with the naval service as part thereof

264

within the Department of the Navy. Naval aviation shall consist of combat and service and training forces, and shall include land-based naval aviation, air transport essential for naval operations, all air weapons and air techniques involved in the operations and activities of the United States Navy, and the entire remainder of the aeronautical organization of the United States Navy, together with the personnel necessary therefor.

The Navy shall be generally responsible for naval reconnaissance, antisubmarine warfare, and protection of shipping.

The Navy shall develop aircraft, weapons, tactics, technique, organization, and equipment of naval combat and service elements; matters of joint concern as to these functions shall be coordinated between the Army, the Air Force, and the Navy.

(c) The United States Marine Corps, within the Department of the Navy, shall include land combat and service forces and such aviation as may be organic therein. The Marine Corps shall be organized, trained, and equipped to provide Fleet Marine Forces of combined arms, together with supporting air components, for service with the fleet in the seizure or defense of advanced naval bases and for the conduct of such land operations as may be essential to the prosecution of a naval campaign. It shall be the duty of the Marine Corps to develop, in coordination with the Army and the Air Force, those phases of amphibious operations which pertain to the tactics, technique, and equipment employed by landing forces. In addition, the Marine Corps shall provide detachments and organizations for service on armed vessels of the Navy, shall provide security detachments for the protection of naval property at naval stations and bases, and shall perform such other duties as the President may direct: Provided, That such additional duties shall not detract from or interfere with the operations for which the Marine Corps is primarily organized. The Marine Corps shall be responsible, in accordance with integrated joint mobilization plans, for the expansion of peacetime components of the Marine Corps to meet the needs of war.

The mission of the Navy was further interpreted by the delineation of the functions of the United States Navy in Department of Defense Directive 5100.1 of December 31, 1958, which is given below:

FUNCTIONS OF THE DEPARTMENT OF THE NAVY

The Department of the Navy is responsible for the preparation of Navy and Marine Corps forces necessary for the effective prosecution of war except as otherwise assigned and, in accordance with integrated mobilization plans, for the expansion of the peacetime components of the Navy and Marine Corps to meet the needs of war.

Within the Department of the Navy, the Navy includes naval combat and service forces and such aviation as may be organic therein, and the Marine Corps includes not less than three combat divisions and three air wings and such other land combat, aviation, and other services as may be organic therein.

PRIMARY FUNCTIONS OF THE NAVY AND THE MARINE CORPS

a. To organize, train, and equip Navy and Marine Corps forces for the conduct of prompt and sustained combat operations at sea, including operations of

FIGURE 1001. USS *Forrestal* (CVA-59).

sea-based aircraft and land-based naval air components—specifically, forces to seek out and destroy enemy naval forces and to suppress enemy sea commerce, to gain and maintain general naval supremacy to control vital sea areas and to protect vital sea lines of communication, to establish and maintain local superiority (including air) in an area of naval operations, to seize and defend advanced naval bases, and to conduct such land and air operations as may be essential to the prosecution of a naval campaign.

b. To maintain the Marine Corps, having the following specific functions:

(1) To provide Fleet Marine Forces of combined arms, together with supporting air components, for service with the Fleet in the seizure or defense of advanced naval bases and for the conduct of such land operations as may be essential to the prosecution of a naval campaign. These functions do not contemplate the creation of a second land Army.

(2) To provide detachments and organizations for service on armed vessels of the Navy, and security detachments for the protection of naval property at naval stations and bases.

(3) To develop, in coordination with the other Services, the doctrines, tactics, techniques, and equipment employed by landing forces in amphibious operations. The Marine Corps shall have primary interest in the development of those landing force doctrines, tactics, techniques, and equipment which are of common interest to the Army and the Marine Corps.

(4) To train and equip, as required, Marine Forces for airborne operations, in coordination with the other Services and in accordance with doctrines established by the Joint Chiefs of Staff.

(5) To develop, in coordination with the other Services, doctrines, procedures, and equipment of interest to the Marine Corps for airborne operations and not provided for in Section V, paragraph A 1 c (2).

c. To organize and equip, in coordination with the other Services, and to provide naval forces, including naval close air-support forces, for the conduct of joint amphibious operations, and to be responsible for the amphibious training of all forces assigned to joint amphibious operations in accordance with doctrines established by the Joint Chiefs of Staff.

d. To develop, in coordination with the other Services, the doctrines, procedures, and equipment of naval forces for amphibious operations, and the doctrines and procedures for joint amphibious operations.

e. To furnish adequate, timely, and reliable intelligence for the Navy and Marine Corps.

f. To organize, train, and equip naval forces for naval reconnaissance, antisubmarine warfare, and protection of shipping, and mine laying, including the air aspects thereof, and controlled mine field operations.

g. To provide air support essential for naval operations.

h. To provide sea-based air defense and the sea-based means for coordinating control for defense against air attack, coordinating with the other Services in matters of joint concern.

i. To provide naval (including naval air) forces as required for the defense of the United States against air attack, in accordance with doctrines established by the Joint Chiefs of Staff.

j. To furnish aerial photography as necessary for Navy and Marine Corps operations.

COLLATERAL FUNCTIONS OF THE NAVY AND THE MARINE CORPS

To train forces:

a. To interdict enemy land and air power and communications through operations at sea.

b. To conduct close air and naval support for land operations.

c. To furnish aerial photography for cartographic purposes.

d. To be prepared to participate in the over-all air effort as directed.

e. To establish military government, as directed, pending transfer of this responsibility to other authority.

Certain specific collateral functions of the Navy and Marine Corps are listed below:

1. To interdict enemy land and air power and communications through operations at sea.

2. To conduct close air support for land operations.

3. To furnish aerial photography for cartographic purposes.

4. To be prepared to participate in the over-all effort as directed by the Joint Chiefs of Staff.

1002. HISTORY. With all the wealth of tradition from operation in war and peace since 1774, a complete history of the United States Navy is not only inappropriate but impossible here. Every officer should be thoroughly familiar with the Navy's history from its early glorious days. A few important highlights from the early days of the Revolution to our Navy's present status as one service of our nation's military establishment will be recorded. See also the Bibliography for recommended reading.

1003. THE CONSTITUTION. The United States of America is founded upon a single document, the Constitution. The provisions of the United States Constitution governing the Armed Forces have never been changed since the original was written.

When commissioned as an officer, you took an oath to support the Constitution, as the essential core of our national structure.

In 1798, the Navy Regulations had this to say on the subject:

> There shall be at the seat of government an executive department, to be known as the Department of the Navy, and a Secretary of the Navy, who shall be the head thereof. (Section 415, R.S.)

A Board of Naval Commissioners of three members was created by the act of February 7, 1815.

On August 31, 1842, the "bureau system" was established by Congress. The original bureaus were the Bureau of Yards and Docks; Bureau of Construction, Equipment, and Repair; Bureau of Provisions and Clothing; Bureau of Ordnance and Hydrography; and Bureau of Medicine and Surgery.

The acts of Congress on July 11, 1890, March 3, 1891, and June 20, 1940, provided for an Under Secretary and an Assistant Secretary.

On March 3, 1915, the Office of the Chief of Naval Operations was provided for by an Act of Congress.

On July 12, 1921, Congress created the Bureau of Aeronautics, "which shall be charged with matters pertaining to naval aeronautics as may be prescribed by the Secretary of the Navy."

On June 24, 1926, Congress authorized an Assistant Secretary of the Navy for Air.

FIGURE 1002. Jet attack bomber (A-6A) prepares to touch down on the deck of an aircraft carrier.

By 1942, Navy Regulations read:

The business of the Department of the Navy not specifically assigned by law shall be distributed in such manner as the Secretary of the Navy shall judge to be expedient and proper among the following bureaus:

First, a Bureau of Yards and Docks.
Second, a Bureau of Naval Personnel.
Third, a Bureau of Ordnance.
Fourth, a Bureau of Ships.
Fifth, a Bureau of Supplies and Accounts.
Sixth, a Bureau of Medicine and Surgery.
Seventh, a Bureau of Aeronautics.

The National Security Act of 1947 (Amended) established the new Department of Defense in 1949 as an *executive* department of the government to include the military departments of the Army, Navy, and Air Force. The Secretary of the Navy was demoted from Cabinet rank. Only the Secretary of Defense is now a member of the President's Cabinet. The reorganization act of 1958 established the number of Assistant Secretaries as three. The Secretary of the Navy re-designated the Assistant Secretary of the Navy for Air as the Assistant Secretary of the Navy for Research and Development and continued the Assistant Secretaries for Material and Personnel and Reserve Forces.

On December 1, 1959, the Bureaus of Ordnance and Aeronautics were combined as the Bureau of Naval Weapons.

In 1965 and 1966 the Assistant Secretaries were re-designated for Financial Management, Research and Development, and Installations and Logistics and a Deputy Under Secretary for Manpower was created.

In 1966 the Bureaus of Naval Weapons, Supply, Yards and Docks, and Ships were re-organized as integral parts of the Naval Material Command.

In 1968 the Office of the Assistant Secretary for Manpower and Reserve Affairs was established.

1004. CONGRESS AND THE NAVY. *Responsibility of Congress.* Since Congress is the major legislative body of the United States Government and since it has the sole power to appropriate funds, it derives from these functions the power to determine the nature of the Navy and the amount of money which may be made available for ships, men, equipment, training, etc. Congress thus has major control over the size and power of the Navy. Both the Senate and House of Representatives have committees on Armed Services. These committees, as well as the committees on appropriations, study the needs of the naval and other military establishments and make recommendations, which find their way into the appropriation bills of the Department of Defense, on the basis of which money is appropriated from the National Treasury for naval and military purposes.

Responsibility of the Navy Department to Congress. The Navy Department provides several officers on full-time duty for liaison with the two Houses of Congress. They have their offices in the congressional office buildings on Capitol Hill.

The Assistant Comptroller of the Navy Department, who is the Director of Budget and Reports, under the supervision of the Assistant Secretary for Financial Management who is also the Comptroller of the Navy Department, directs the preparation of the Navy Budget and supplementary appropriation requests which are forwarded to the Comptroller of the Department of Defense. The Budget is based on requirements carefully screened by the Joint Chiefs of Staff and interpreted in the form of detailed requirements for the Naval Material Command and for the Bureaus or Offices of the Navy Department by the Chief of Naval Operations.

Proposals for legislation affecting the Navy may be originated by members of Congress, by the Navy Department, or by other departments or offices of the Department of Defense. No matter where they originate, such requests are referred to the appropriate committees of both Houses.

The Naval Establishment

1005. THE ORGANIZATION OF THE NAVY DEPARTMENT. The term "Department of the Navy" is construed to mean the Department of the Navy at the seat of government; the headquarters, United States Marine Corps; the entire operating forces of the United States Navy, including naval aviation, and of the United States Marine Corps, including the reserve components of such forces; all field activities, headquarters, forces, bases, installations, activities, and functions under the control or supervision of the Secretary of the Navy; and the United States Coast Guard when operating as part of the Navy pursuant to law.

The term "Department of the Navy" is synonymous with the term "Naval Establishment."

The Department of the Navy consists of three principal parts, as follows:

1. The Operating Forces of the Navy, which comprise the several fleets, seagoing forces, sea frontier forces, district forces, Fleet Marine Forces and other assigned Marine Corps forces, the Military Sea Transportation Service, and such shore activities of the Navy and other forces and activities as may be assigned to the Operating Forces of the Navy by the President or the Secretary of the Navy.

2. The Navy Department, which is the central executive authority of the Department of the Navy, is located at the seat of government. These organizationally comprise the Office of the Secretary of the Navy, the Office of the Chief of Naval Operations, and the headquarters organizations of the United States Marine Corps, the Naval Material Command, the Bureau of Naval Personnel, the Bureau of Medicine

and Surgery, the Office of the Comptroller of the Navy, the Office of the Judge Advocate General, the Office of Naval Research, and the offices of Staff Assistants to the Secretary. The United States Coast Guard operates under the Department of Transportation during peacetime.

3. The Shore Establishment comprises all activities of the Department of the Navy not assigned to the Operating Forces of the Navy and not part of the Navy Department. This includes those Operating Forces of the Marine Corps which are not assigned to the Operating Forces of the Navy or to a unified or specified combatant command.

Policy of the Department of the Navy. It is the policy of the Department of the Navy, as part of the Department of Defense, to maintain the Navy and Marine Corps as an efficient, mobile, integrated force of multiple capabilities, and sufficiently strong and ready at all times to fulfill their responsibilities, in conjunction with our other Armed Forces, to support and defend the Constitution of the United States against all enemies, foreign and domestic; to ensure, by timely and effective military action, the security of the United States, its possessions, and areas vital to its interest; to uphold and advance the national policies and interests of the United States; and to safeguard the internal security of the United States. The effectuation of this policy imposes upon the executive administration of the Department of the Navy four principal tasks:

First, to interpret, apply and uphold the national policies and interests in the development and use of the Department of the Navy. This task may be described as the "policy control" of the Department of the Navy.

Second, to command the operating forces and, with respect to those Navy and Marine Corps forces assigned to unified and specified combatant commands, to exercise such command in a manner consistent with the full operational command vested in their unified and specified combatant commanders; to maintain the operating forces in a state of readiness to conduct war; and to promulgate to the Department of the Navy directives embracing matters of operations, security, intelligence, discipline, naval communications, and similar matters of naval administration. This task may be described as the "naval command" of the Department of the Navy.

Third, to coordinate and direct the effort of the Navy Department and the Shore Establishment, in order to assure the development, procurement, production and distribution of material, facilities and personnel to the operating forces. This task may be described as the "logistics administration and control" of the Department of the Navy.

Fourth, to develop and maintain efficiency and economy in the operation of the Department of the Navy with particular regard to matters of organization, staffing, administrative procedures, the utilization of personnel, materials, and facilities, and the budgeting and expenditure of funds. This task may be described as the "business administration" of the Department of the Navy.

The Executive Organization. Supervision and direction. The executive administration of the Department of the Navy consists of:

1. The Secretary of the Navy, who is responsible, under the direction, authority, and control of the Secretary of Defense, for the op- eration of the Department of the Navy as well as its efficiency, including the policy, administration and control of all matters within the Department of the Navy.

2. The Civilian Executive Assistants to the Secretary, who are the Under Secretary of the Navy, Assistant Secretaries of the Navy, and the Special Assistant to the Secretary, and the Deputy Under Secretary for Manpower.

3. The Naval Professional Assistants to the Secretary, who are:

(a) The principal Naval Professional Assistant and the Naval Command Assistant, who is the Chief of Naval Operations.

(b) The Marine Corps Command Assistant, who is the Commandant of the Marine Corps.

(c) The Commandant of the Coast Guard, when the Coast Guard is operating as part of the Navy pursuant to law.

(d) The Naval Technical Assistants, who are the Chief of Naval Material, the Chiefs of Bureaus, the Comptroller of the Navy, the Chief of Naval Research, and the Judge Advocate General.

Assignment of Tasks. The four principal tasks of the executive administration of the Department of the Navy are assigned among the Secretary, his Civilian Executive Assistants and his Naval Professional Assistants, as set forth in the following paragraphs. For greater detail of duties consult General Order No. 5.

1. *The Secretary of the Navy* is responsible for the policy, administration and control of the Department of the Navy, and for its operating efficiency. In the discharge of this broad responsibility:

2. *The Civilian Executive Assistants,* all of whom shall function under the supervision, coordination and direction of the Under Secretary, are responsible to the Secretary of the Navy for the supervision and management of the work, and operating efficiency, of the Department of the Navy in meeting requirements of the Operating Forces of the Navy and of the Marine Corps.

3. *The Naval Professional Assistants.* The Chief of Naval Operations is the senior military officer of the Department of the Navy, and is responsible to the Secretary of the Navy for the command, use and administration of the Operating Forces of the Navy. With respect to those Navy and Marine Corps forces assigned to unified and specified combatant commands, this responsibility shall be discharged in a manner consistent with the full operational command vested in their unified and specified combatant commanders. He is the principal naval adviser to the President and to the Secretary of the Navy on the conduct of war, and the principal naval adviser and naval executive to the Secretary on the conduct of the activities of the Department of the Navy. He is the Navy member of the Joint Chiefs of Staff, and is responsible for keeping the Secretary of the Navy fully informed on matters considered or acted upon by the Joint Chiefs of Staff.

The Commandant of the Marine Corps is the senior officer of the United States Marine Corps. He commands the Marine Corps, and is directly responsible to the Secretary of the Navy for its administration, discipline, internal organization, unit training, requirements, efficiency, and readiness, and for the total performance of the Marine Corps. When performing these functions, the Commandant of the Marine Corps is not a part of the permanent command structure of the Chief of Naval Operations. However, there must be a close cooperative relationship between the Chief of Naval Operations, as the senior military officer of the Department of the Navy, and the Commandant of the Marine Corps, who has command responsibility over that organization. The Commandant of the Marine Corps has an additional direct responsibility to the Chief of Naval Operations for the readiness and performance of those elements of the operating forces of the Marine Corps assigned to the Operating Forces of the Navy. Such Marine Corps forces, when so assigned, are under the command of the Chief of Naval Operations.

From the Secretary stems Policy Control; from the Chief of Naval Operations, Naval Command and Consumer Logistics; and from the Civilian Executive Assistants, Business Administration and Producer Logistics.

The Navy Department

1006. GENERAL. One of the principal components of the Naval Establishment, the Navy Department is composed of the offices of the

Secretary of the Navy, the Civilian Executive Assistants, the Chief of Naval Operations, the Chief of Naval Material, and the bureaus and offices headed by the Naval Technical Assistants including the Headquarters of the Marine Corps and the Coast Guard (when serving under the Navy Department).

1007. THE SECRETARY OF THE NAVY. The Secretary of the Navy has the general superintendence of construction, manning, armament, equipment, maintenance, and employment of vessels of war and performs such other duties as the President, who is Commander-in-Chief, may direct. He has direct cognizance of commissioned and enlisted personnel and public relations.

The Staff Assistants to the Secretary are the Administrative Officer, Navy Department; the General Counsel; the Chief of Industrial Relations; the Chief of Information; the Chief of Legislative Affairs; the Director, Office of Management Information; the Director, Office of Naval Petroleum and Oil Shale Reserves; the Director, Office of Program Appraisal; and the heads of such other offices and boards as may be established by law or by the Secretary of the Navy for the purpose of assisting the Secretary or one or more of his Civilian Executive Assistants in the administration of the Department of the Navy. Each of the foregoing shall supervise all functions and activities internal to his office and assigned shore (field) activities if any. Each shall be responsible to the Secretary of the Navy or to one of his Civilian Executive Assistants for the utilization of resources by and the operating efficiency of all activities under their respective supervision. The duties of the individual Staff Assistants and their respective offices will be as provided by law or as assigned by separate directive of the Secretary of the Navy.

The Executive Office of the Secretary (EXOS)

1008. GENERAL. The various boards and offices reporting to, and performing staff functions and services for, the Secretary and his Civilian Executive Assistants are collectively referred to as the Executive Office of the Secretary. Administratively, these agencies are regarded as a single organizational entity of the Navy Department.

The Civilian Executive Assistants. The responsibilities of the Civilian Executive Assistants for Business Administration and Producer Logistics have already been discussed in Section 1005.

1009. THE OFFICES AND BOARDS OF THE EXECUTIVE OFFICE OF THE SECRETARY. *The Office of the Judge Advocate General* has cognizance of all major phases of military, administrative, legislative, and applied law incident to the operation of the Naval Establishment.

With respect to military law, it reviews the records of proceedings of all courts-martial, courts of inquiry, and boards of investigation.

It advises and prepares opinions on questions of administrative law concerned with the administration of naval affairs, including legal questions arising on pay and allowances for naval personnel. Matters of international law are also reviewed and opinions prepared thereon.

The Office of the Comptroller. Subject to the authority of the Secretary of the Navy, the Comptroller is directly responsible for budgeting, accounting, progress and statistical reporting, internal audit, and for administrative organizational structure and managerial procedures relating to such responsibilities within the Department of the Navy and for coordination and correlation of matters under his cognizance with the Comptrollers of the Departments of Defense, Army, and Air Force, and other departments and agencies of the government.

Office of the General Counsel is responsible for providing throughout the Department of the Navy legal services in the field of business and commercial law.

Office of Information initiates, stimulates, and develops within the Naval Establishment information to be used to further the information mission of the Navy.

Office of Legislative Affairs assists the Secretary and all other principal civilian and military officials with legislative affairs and Congressional relations.

Office of Management Information operates a management information center which serves the Navy Department and coordinates the Navy's management information system developments.

Office of Naval Petroleum and Oil Shale Reserves advises the Navy Department on all matters relating to oil shale, crude petroleum and associated hydrocarbon resources.

Office of Program Appraisal is a personal staff office of the Secretary and provides him with appraisals of Navy and Defense Department plans, studies and proposals.

The Office of Naval Research is charged with duties of encouraging, planning, initiating, and coordinating naval research.

The Administrative Office, Navy Department, is responsible for the general administration and business management of the Department

ORGANIZATION of the DEPARTMENT of the NAVY

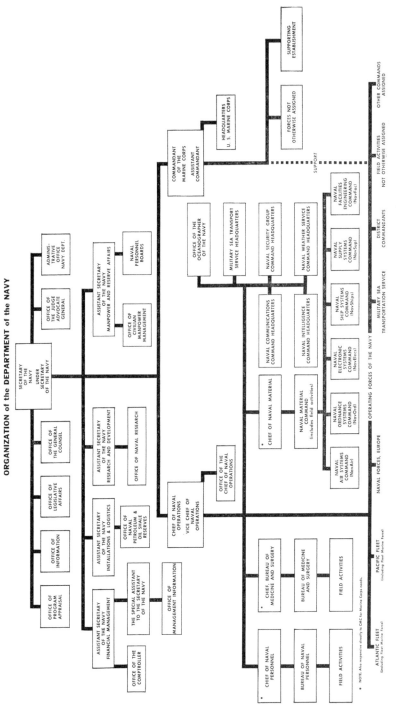

FIGURE 1003. Organization of the Navy Department.

and administers certain management programs and appropriations, applying to the Naval Establishment.

The Office of Industrial Relations is responsible for the development of the Navy's industrial relations program concerning civilian employees and for advising and assisting bureaus, offices, and shore activities in the application of the program throughout the departmental and field services.

Navy Department Boards. The following boards have been established for the purpose of representing and advising the Secretary of the Navy on matters which come under their cognizance:

The Armed Services Board of Contract Appeals.

The Facilities Review Board.

The Material Review Board.

The Navy Department Board of Review, Discharges, and Dismissals.

Naval Personnel Boards. Certain Naval Personnel Boards and Councils are established either by law or by administrative action of the Secretary to assist him in the discharge of his responsibility to promote the welfare of the officer and enlisted personnel of the Navy. The purpose and duties of most of these Boards are indicated in their title. Details as to their charters can be obtained by reference to such publications as *The United States Navy*, issued by the Secretary's Office, or by application to the Management Engineer of the Navy Department.

Joint Boards and Committees. To promote joint action, joint boards and committees are established either by law or by order of the Secretary of Defense or the President. A number of these have already been mentioned under the discussion of the duties and procedures of the Joint Chiefs of Staff.

One other in effect is the *Air Coordinating Committee,* which examines international and domestic aviation problems and development affecting more than one department or agency, to coordinate their activities.

The Office of the Chief of Naval Operations (OPNAV)

1010. GENERAL. The various offices, boards, and agencies reporting to, and performing staff duty for, the Chief of Naval Operations are collectively referred to as the Office of the Chief of Naval Operations. Under the authority exercised by the Chief of Naval Operations, they assist him in executing two kinds of duties: Naval Command of the Naval Establishment and Consumer Logistics. These duties were previously discussed in Section 1005 (see Figure 1004).

1011. THE CHIEF OF NAVAL OPERATIONS (CNO). *The Naval Command Assistant* is the Chief of Naval Operations, who acts as the principal naval adviser to the President, the Secretary of Defense, and the Secretary of the Navy on the conduct of war and as the principal naval adviser and naval executive to the Secretary of the Navy on the conduct of the activities of the Naval Establishment. He is a member of the Armed Forces Policy Council and the Joint Chiefs of Staff.

The Chief of Naval Operations has responsibility for the command, use, and administration of the Operating Forces, and is responsible to the Secretary of the Navy for their use in war and for plans and preparations for their readiness for war. With respect to those Navy and Marine Corps forces assigned to unified and specified combatant commands, this responsibility is discharged in a manner consistent with the full operational command vested in their commanders. He is charged, under the direction of the Secretary of the Navy, with the preparation, readiness, and logistic support of the Operating Forces and with the coordination and direction of effort to this end of the Naval Material Command and the bureaus and offices of the Navy Department.

During the temporary absence of the Secretary of the Navy, the following, in the order named, are next in succession: the Under Secretary of the Navy, the Assistant Secretaries of the Navy, the Chief of Naval Operations, and the Vice Chief of Naval Operations.

1012. THE VICE CHIEF OF NAVAL OPERATIONS (VCNO). The principal assistant and adviser to the Chief of Naval Operations in his duty as *Naval Command Assistant* exercises executive authority with respect to the Naval Establishment as delegated by CNO and performs the duties of CNO in that officer's absence. He directs the activities of the Navy Program Planning Group and coordinates the efforts of the Deputy Chiefs of Naval Operations, and the following offices and officers:

Office of Naval Intelligence—collects, processes and disseminates intelligence of naval interest and maintains liaison with other intelligence agencies.

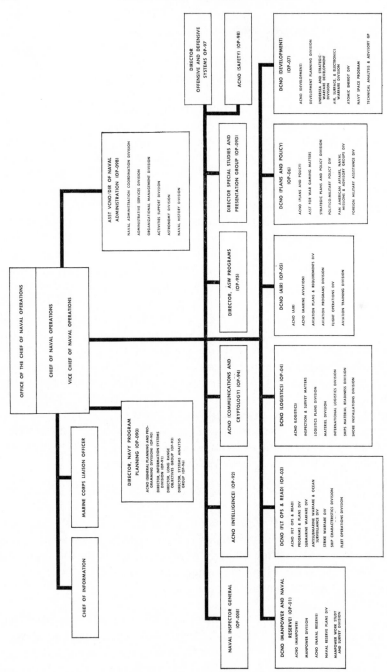

Figure 1004. Organization of the Office of the Chief of Naval Operations.

Office of Naval Communications—Maintains and operates the Navy Communications System and Security Group.

Office of Antisubmarine Warfare—exercises central supervision and coordination of all antisubmarine warfare matters.

The Chief of Information, as principal adviser to the Secretary of the Navy and to CNO on matters of policy relating to public understanding of the Navy and Marine Corps, coordinates the public information and civil-relations policies and programs of the Navy.

The Naval Inspector General (NIG), while coming directly under CNO, is also responsible directly to the Secretary of the Navy for inspection of activities coming within his jurisdiction.

Special Studies and Presentation Group—analyzes matters pertaining to conduct of war, readiness, and command.

Marine Corps Liaison Officer—maintains liaison for the Commandant of the Marine Corps with CNO.

1013. ASSISTANT VCNO (OP-09B). *Director of Naval Administration,* a rear admiral, maintains liaison with other government departments and conducts the general administration of the Office of the Chief of Naval Operations.

The following two field activities are under the management control of the Director of Naval Administration:

The Office of the Oceanographer of the Navy, under the Oceanographer of the Navy, is charged with the execution of hydrographic surveys in foreign waters and on the high seas; the collection and dissemination of hydrographic and navigational information and data; the preparation and printing by its own personnel and with its own equipment of maps and charts relating to and required in navigation, including confidential, strategical, and tactical charts for naval operations and maneuvers; the preparation and issue of sailing directions (pilots), light lists, pilot charts, navigational manuals, periodicals, and radio broadcasts for the use of all vessels of the United States and for the benefit and use of navigators generally; the furnishing of the foregoing to the Navy and other public services, and the sale of charts and publications to the mercantile marine of all nations and to the general public at the cost of printing and paper. The Office of the Oceanographer of the Navy directs the Oceanographic Program, including, in addition to the foregoing, responsibility for the promotion of ocean science and ocean engineering and development.

Naval Observatory, under the Superintendent, determines and transmits for broadcasting throughout the world at frequent intervals the correct time. These signals establish standard time for the United

States and are also used by navigators at sea to determine their chronometer errors and astronomical positions and by surveyors, engineers, scientific workers, and commercial laboratories for the determination of position, measurement of gravity, calibration of radio frequencies, and other purposes requiring exact time.

The Nautical Almanac Office of the Observatory compiles and publishes astronomical publications required for safe navigation and fundamental positional astronomy, such as *The American Nautical Almanac, The American Air Almanac,* and *The American Ephemeris and Nautical Almanac.*

1014. PERSONNEL (OP-01). *The Deputy Chief of Naval Operations* (Manpower and Naval Reserve), a vice admiral, prepares and implements personnel plans and policies for the Chief of Naval Operations. He maintains a close liaison with the Bureau of Naval Personnel, the same officer often serving both as Chief of Naval Personnel and DCNO (Personnel).

Among his duties and responsibilities, he is required to formulate personnel plans and policies for military personnel of the Naval Establishment; to prepare implementing directives therefor and to control the over-all allocation of naval personnel.

The Assistant Chief of Naval Operations (ACNO) (Naval Reserve), also called Director of Naval Reserve, is a Flag Officer of the Navy, whose duty it is to prepare, in coordination with the bureaus and offices having cognizance over components of the Naval Reserve, the plans of the Naval Reserve.

1015. FLEET OPERATIONS AND READINESS (OP-03). *The Deputy Chief of Naval Operations* (Fleet Operations and Readiness), a vice admiral, implements the command functions of the Office of CNO by preparation and dissemination to the Operating Forces of approved policies, plans, orders, and necessary operational information. He has three Assistant Chiefs of Naval Operations, one for operations, who advises him on matters of policy pertaining to operations of the fleets and forces, one for readiness, who advises him on matters of policy pertaining to readiness as they relate to undersea warfare, fleet operational readiness, and atomic energy, and one for training.

1016. LOGISTICS (OP-04). *The Deputy Chief of Naval Operations (Logistics),* a vice admiral, plans for and provides logistic support for the Operating Forces and Naval Shore Establishment, including such logistics of naval aviation activities as are not assigned to DCNO (Air); and exercises this mission and objective for the Naval Reserve the same as, but separately from, the regular Naval Establishment.

1017. AIR (OP-05). *The Deputy Chief of Naval Operations (Air)*, a vice admiral, plans and provides for the naval aeronautical elements of the Operating Forces, including their preparation, training, readiness for war, and their logistic support; and supervises the Naval Air Reserve.

1018. PLANS AND POLICY (OP-06). *The Deputy Chief of Naval Operations (Plans and Policy)*, a vice admiral, develops and disseminates plans and policies, and serves as the principal adviser to the Secretary of the Navy and the Chief of Naval Operations on international politico-military matters, including foreign military assistance.

1019. DEVELOPMENT (OP-07). *The Deputy Chief of Naval Operations (Development)*, a vice admiral, implements the responsibilities of the Chief of Naval Operations in respect to over-all planning and direction of the Navy research and development program.

Naval Technical Assistants

1020. GENERAL. The Naval Technical Assistants—the Chiefs of Bureaus, the Chief of Naval Research, the Chief of Naval Material, the Judge Advocate General—are directly responsible for the discharge of all the duties assigned to their respective organizations, in accordance with the orders and directives of the Secretary, the Civilian Executive Assistants, and the Chief of Naval Operations and are the technical advisers and assistants in their special fields to the Secretary, the Civilian Executive Assistants, and the Chief of Naval Operations.

1021. THE NAVAL MATERIAL COMMAND AND THE BUREAUS. In 1966 the Navy was reorganized to change its traditional bilinear structure into a unilinear framework by placing the Navy's material, medical and personnel supporting organizations under command of the Chief of Naval Operations. The Naval Material Support Establishment became the Naval Material Command. The Bureaus of Naval Weapons, Supplies and Accounts, Ships, and Yards and Docks were re-structured to

FIGURE 1005. USS *Brooke* (DEG-1).

produce six functional commands, Air Systems, Ship Systems, Electronic Systems, Ordnance Systems, Supply Systems, and Facilities Engineering. The Bureaus of Naval Personnel and Medicine and Surgery remained as separate organizations but also were placed under the command of the Chief of Naval Operations.

The Ship Systems Command—is responsible for the design and integration of all displacement type ships, ground effect machines and hydrofoil craft. This includes construction, overhaul, modernization and conversion and covers propulsion, navigation, habitability, ship-mounted sonar, search radar, Naval Tactical Data System, degaussing, minesweeping, and salvage equipment.

The Air Systems Command—is responsible for aircraft, air-launched weapon systems, airborne electronics, air-launched underwater sound systems, airborne pyrotechnics, astronautics, catapults and arresting gear, airborne minesweeping equipment, aircraft drone and target systems, and photographic and meteorological equipment.

The Electronic Systems Command—is responsible for shore electronics, the Sound Surveillance System, material support of certain Air

Systems Command electronics equipment, certain space programs, shore-based strategic data systems, data link systems external to ships and aircraft, radiac equipment and electronic test equipment.

The Ordnance Systems Command—is responsible for shipboard weapon systems, ship-mounted sonar, air-launched underwater weapons, explosive safety, small arms, demolitions, harbor defense, ship pyrotechnics and seaborne targets.

The Supply Systems Command—is the new title for the Bureau of Supplies and Accounts. Responsibilities, which remain the same, are for the procurement, custody, cataloging, inventory control, shipment, warehousing, issue, sale of and accounting for all supplies including food, fuel, clothing, general stores, retail store stock, and other property and services.

In connection with fiscal matters, the Supply Systems Command has responsibility for the procurement and disbursement of money. It also prepares and serves food in all general messes except at naval hospitals, and administers a centralized storage-operating organization for the control of all storage facilities of the Naval Establishment.

The Bureau of Naval Personnel (BuPers) is charged with, and is responsible for, the procurement, education, training, discipline, promotion, welfare and morale, and distribution of officers and enlisted personnel of the Navy.

The Bureau of Naval Personnel has responsibility for the maintenance of all records concerning medals and awards.

It supervises and controls naval places of confinement and prisoners, including prisoners of war.

The Bureau of Naval Personnel supervises the welfare and recreational activities of the naval service, except those under the cognizance of the Marine Corps, and the libraries for the naval service and Marine Corps.

The Bureau of Medicine and Surgery (BuMed) (headed by the Surgeon General) is composed of appropriate administrative and professional divisions and is responsible for the maintenance of the health of the Navy and Marine Corps. Its duties include the care of its sick and injured and the professional education and training of the officers, nurses, and enlisted men and women of the Medical Department. The Bureau maintains health records of all officers and enlisted personnel of the Navy.

The Facilities Engineering Command—is the new title for the Bureau of Yards and Docks. The responsibilities of this command comprise all that relates to the design and construction of public works and public utilities of the Naval Shore Establishment, and during wartime it supervises the construction of private plant facilities and extensions financed with naval funds. The scope of its functions includes structures and improvements located within the United States, various island possessions, in Panama, British islands in the Atlantic, and temporary advanced bases, wherever they may be.

Its work embraces such major engineering categories as drydocks, both graving and floating, marine railways, shipbuilding ways, harbor works, quay walls, piers, wharves, landings, dredging operations, floating and stationary cranes, power plants, fuel plants, fleet facilities, shops and industrial buildings, turret and erection shops, machine and electric shops, foundries, structural shops, and assembly and repair shops for aircraft.

The principles established and the experience gained by BuDocks throughout its early history laid the foundation for its extraordinary expansion in World War I and again in World War II.

Like all other branches of the armed services, the Civil Engineer Corps (CEC) mushroomed during World War II. The fact that about 98 percent of all its officers were Reserves presented a sizable training problem. In the early part of the war, the need for Naval Construction Battalions overseas was so great that officers received correspondence course instruction in naval regulations and command functions while serving at advanced bases.

The increasing complexity of warfare has made the logistics problem enormous, both because of the enlarged scale and scope of war and because of its accelerated pace. For this reason, the World War II job of the Bureau of Yards and Docks as an administrative component and of the CEC as an operational force was tremendous. Fueling and docking facilities had to be established; food and equipment depots were needed to handle supplies for the combat areas; hospitals were necessary to receive the wounded and sick; and repair facilities for ships had to be equipped and ready for instant action. Most pressing of all was the need for airstrips.

Many CEC officers were engaged in supervising the work of Naval Construction Battalions, Special, which performed stevedoring; others supervised the specialized work of construction battalion maintenance units which took over the maintenance of advanced bases, thereby releasing construction battalions for participation in new landings; some were in charge of pontoon detachments, smoke generation units, malaria control units, and underwater demolition teams.

The CEC was ready for the two-ocean task imposed by World War II. In the interval between world wars, some of its alert officers had devoted their best thought to the construction problems the Navy would face in the event of war. An outstanding example of this planning was the floating drydock program. As late as July 1940 the Navy had only three such structures, and these had been designed for use in quiet harbors where outside facilities existed for power and for crew accommodations. It was apparent that if war came there would be sea fighting on a scale previously unknown and that ships would need repairs thousands of miles from home ports. To this end, the Civil Engineers prepared radically new designs for a fleet of floating drydocks that could repair ships close to the scene of battle, making it possible for the damaged ships to return quickly to the fight. In some cases, ships that otherwise would not have been able to make the long voyage to the United States for repairs were salvaged.

Hardly less spectacular was the development of the Navy pontoon. Pontoon causeways, launched from ship-side at full speed ahead, enabled allied forces to bridge the shallow waters along the southern coast of Sicily, to the surprise of the Germans who had considered those waters a natural barrier. Some 10,000 Army vehicles rolled from ship to shore over the steel pontoon bridges, setting the pattern for every ensuing invasion in the war.

Establishment of the Seabees. Naval Construction Battalions, popularly known as the Seabees, were established during World War II under the cognizance of the Bureau of Yards and Docks to meet the need for uniformed men to perform construction work in combat areas. They served as an adjunct of the seagoing Navy, under officers of the Civil Engineer Corps.

With the advent of World War II it became apparent that the services of contractors and their civilian workers engaged in building naval projects at numerous overseas points could not be employed for construction work in combat zones. In the first place, under military law, their status as civilians prevented them from offering resistance to an enemy without becoming liable to summary execution as guerrillas in the event of capture. Further, civilian workers lacked the training necessary to defend themselves. This was grimly demonstrated at Wake, Cavite, and Guam, where some civilian construction workers were killed and many more captured.

A construction battalion, as initially established, was composed of four companies, which included the necessary construction skills for any job, plus a headquarters company consisting of yeomen, storekeepers, cooks, and so on. As a complete operating unit a battalion could be sent into the field on its own. The complement of a battalion was set at 34 officers and 1,083 men.

Seabees participated in every major amphibious operation conducted by American fighting forces. Their job was to assist in the unloading of combat equipment and supplies. Later they undertook the rehabilitation of existing airfields and the construction of new fields.

The Seabees were assigned the construction of shipbuilding and ship repair plants; port and harbor works; aviation training and operating stations; ammunition depots and ordnance production facilities; supply depots, hospitals, fleet operating bases, and fuel depots; housing for officers, enlisted men, and civilians; and floating and graving docks of all sizes and characters.

They constructed bases in the United Kingdom, Iceland, Newfoundland, Bermuda, the Caribbean area, Panama, South America, Africa, Alaska, and wherever the fighting forces went in the Pacific. The Seabees constructed more than 300 advanced bases of various sizes, kinds, and characteristics in the first two years of the war—some accommodating 50,000 men and containing industrial and hospital storage and other facilities required in cities several times that population.

Seabees proved to be excellent defensive troops. General MacArthur awarded the Presidential Unit Citation to the 40th Seabees for action against the enemy on Los Negros Island in March 1944.

The advanced bases, which served as stepping stones to the final defeat of Japan, were built by the regular construction battalions just discussed. But, as the war progressed, new needs developed and specialized types of battalions and detachments became necessary. The new specialized units ultimately grew into a sizable force, the largest of which was called Naval Construction Battalions, Special. This group functioned as stevedores. They were recruited from the country's leading steamship and stevedoring companies and were taught Navy methods on a mock Liberty ship built on land.

Because their outstanding contribution had clearly established the need for such a force, the Seabees were made a permanent part of the Navy in 1946, but were reduced to a peacetime level of less than 5,000. Just before the Korean crisis in June 1950, there were 3,300 Seabees on active duty. These men were being trained to serve as a nucleus for the force which would be necessary in an emergency. They participated in the Korean conflict, including the Inchon and Wonsan landings; they helped restore port facilities for the unloading of vitally important supplies and worked on airfields.

Early in 1947 the primary concept of the Amphibious Construction Battalion was outlined in the tentative plans for a naval beach group prepared by CNO.

In 1951 the type command, Naval Construction Battalions, Atlantic Fleet, was established under the Commander, Service Forces, Atlantic, to coordinate and control the deployment of construction battalions in the Atlantic area.

1022. THE UNITED STATES MARINE CORPS. The Continental Marines, based on a similar organization in the Royal Navy of Great Britain, were established by resolution of the Continental Congress, November 10, 1775. The Marine Corps was established by act of Congress, July 11, 1798. The authorized strength of the Corps is 20 percent of that authorized for the Navy.

The Missions of the Corps, as defined *by law,* are as follows: To provide Fleet Marine Forces of combined arms, together with supporting air components, for service with the fleet in the seizure or defense of advanced naval bases and for the conduct of such land operations as may be essential to the prosecution of a naval campaign; to develop, in coordination with other services, those phases of amphibious operations which pertain to the tactics, techniques, and equipment employed by landing forces; to provide detachments and organizations for service on board naval vessels; to provide security detachments for protection of naval stations and bases; and to perform such other duties as the President may direct.

In addition to the foregoing missions, which have been stated in the National Security Act of 1947, succeeding directives by the Secretary of Defense have given to the Marine Corps primary responsibility within our defense establishment for development of amphibious techniques, material, and doctrine pertaining to landing operations, thus ratifying the pioneering role established by the Corps in this field since before World War I (see also Section 1001).

Tradition in the Marine Corps demonstrates probably to a greater degree than in any other military organization in the world the power of pride in Corps to unify and motivate a fighting force. Almost as soon as he enlists, a recruit Marine learns that the Corps' traditions are as much a part of his equipment as his pack or rifle. These traditions have many facets: devotion to duty and to discipline, loyalty to country and to Corps, self-sacrifice, versatility, and dependability. Tradition is fostered by the distinctive uniforms and insignia of the Marines, their excellent equipment, their readiness to fight in peace or war, the sentiments of their "Marine's Hymn," and in the nicknames they have earned.

Headquarters. The Commandant of the Marine Corps is responsible directly to the Secretary of the Navy for the procurement, discharge, education, training, discipline, and distribution of officers and enlisted men of the Corps, including the Marine Corps Reserve, and its equipment, supply, administration, and general efficiency. The Commandant is one of the Naval Professional Assistants to the Secretary and a principal adviser to both the Secretary and the Chief of Naval Operations.

The Headquarters is the staff of the Commandant. It is composed as follows:

The Chief of Staff, the Commandant's execution officer.

FIGURE 1006. Marine amphibious landing in Vietnam.

The Deputy Chief of Staff (Plans and Programs)—coordinates staff action with regard to JCS matters, planning, programing and budgeting.

The Deputy Chief of Staff (Research, Development and Studies)—supervises staff activities in these fields.

The Deputy Chief of Staff (Air)—plans, coordinates, and formulates policy concerning Marine aviation.

The Director, Marine Corps Command Center is supervisor of a continuously manned, secure command facility.

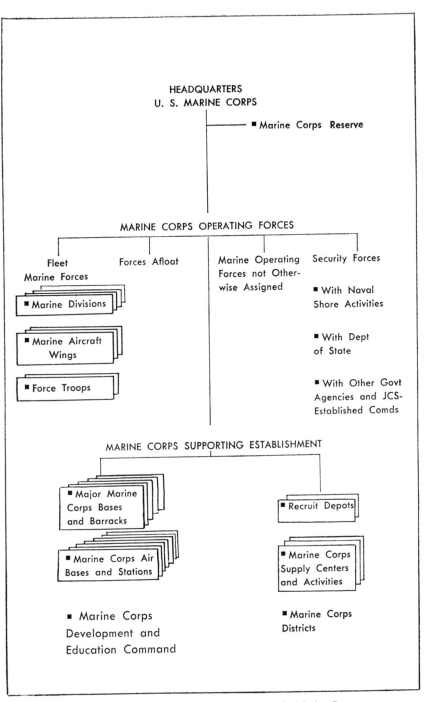

FIGURE 1007. Organization of Headquarters of the Marine Corps.

The Assistant Chief of Staff (G-1)—handles matters concerning personnel administration in the area of requirements and distribution.

The Assistant Chief of Staff (G-2)—formulates plans and policies pertaining to intelligence.

The Assistant Chief of Staff (G-3)—is responsible for joint plans for operations, doctrines, tactics and techniques employed by landing forces.

The Assistant Chief of Staff (G-4)—formulates logistic plans, programs, and policies.

The Director of Personnel is responsible for personnel procurement, promotion, retirement, and accounting.

The Quartermaster General is responsible for the management of the Marine Corps Supply System.

The Director, Marine Corps Reserve, the Fiscal Director, the Inspector General, the Director of Information, the Director of the Policy Analysis Division, the Director, Administrative Division, the Director, Data Processing Division, the Legislative Assistant, the Counsel, the Director of Women Marines, the Staff Medical, Dental officers, the Staff Chaplain, and the Sergeant Major of the Marine Corps all serve on the Commandant's staff with duties approximately described by their titles.

The Shore Establishment of the Marine Corps includes two Recruit Depots; Parris Island, North Carolina; and San Diego, California, where recruits receive their basic training. The major continental bases are at Camp Lejeune near Jacksonville, North Carolina, and the Marine Corps Air Station, Cherry Point, North Carolina, for the East Coast; and Camp Pendleton, near Oceanside, California, and the Marine Corps Air Station, El Toro, near Santa Ana, California, for the West Coast.

The Marine Corps Schools are located at Quantico, Va. The Basic School trains and indoctrinates new officers taken into the service as second lieutenants from the Naval Academy, from among civilian university graduates, or from the ranks. The 8-month course places emphasis on individual and crew-served weapons, small-unit tactics, basic administration and military law, and small-unit leadership. Upon graduation, the young officer is ordered to duty in the Fleet Marine Force or in a Marine Detachment aboard ship. Another source of Marine officers is the Naval Aviation Cadet Program.

After 10 years of service, an officer becomes eligible for the Junior Course of the Amphibious Warfare School, which trains him for action and command on the battalion and regimental levels. After about 18 years, the officer becomes eligible for the Senior Course at the Amphibious Warfare School, which trains officers in staff and command duties at the division and corps levels. Naval officers and officers from the other services attend these schools on a quota basis.

Marine Corps Reserve. Making allowance for functional differences, the Marine Corps Reserve organization parallels that of the Naval Reserve and is, in fact, governed by the same basic legislation. The preponderance of the organized ground units of the Reserve is composed of infantry battalions, although an adequate number of specialist units, such as artillery, tracked vehicle, engineer, and communication organizations, are likewise operating. More than 30 squadrons are included in the Aviation Reserve of the Corps.

Women's Reserve. The Marine Corps Women's Reserve, with an authorized strength of 1,000 officers and 18,000 enlisted women, was established on February 13, 1943.

The Operating Forces of the Marine Corps consist of two Fleet Marine Forces (FMF), integral units of the United States Atlantic and Pacific Fleets. The Fleet Marine Force, which includes the air and ground tactical units of the Corps, was organized in 1933. Its mission of conducting overseas amphibious operations for the seizure and defense of advanced bases as part of a naval campaign requires that the FMF be kept in a high state of readiness for action. Its units—infantry, artillery, armor, communications, engineer, and logistic troops, and aviation organizations to provide close air support of ground troops— are kept continuously trained and highly mobile.

The Commanding Generals of the FMFs, wearing the three stars of a lieutenant general while so assigned, occupy the status of type commanders in the fleets of which the FMFs are a part.

1023. THE UNITED STATES COAST GUARD. *Purpose.* The functions of the Coast Guard embrace, in general terms, maritime-law enforcement, saving and protecting life and property, providing navigational aids to maritime commerce and to transoceanic air commerce, promoting the efficiency and safety of the American merchant marine, and readiness for military duty.

History. Created by act of Congress on August 4, 1790, at the request of the first Secretary of the Treasury, Alexander Hamilton, the Coast Guard has been variously known as the Revenue Marine, Revenue Service, and Revenue Cutter Service. As early as 1799, Congress provided that the cutters should, whenever the President directed, cooperate with the Navy. An act of Congress in 1915 consolidated the

Revenue Cutter Service and the Life Saving Service into the Coast Guard, which operates under the Treasury in peacetime and as part of the Navy under the Navy Secretary in time of war or whenever the President directs.

In addition to its peacetime service to the country, the Coast Guard has given effective and ofttimes heroic service in wartime. It participated with the Navy in the quasi-war with France in 1798, the War of 1812, the Seminole War, the Mexican War of 1846-1849, and is credited with firing the first shot in the Civil War when the revenue cutter *Harriet Lane* fired across the bow of the steamer *Nashville* just before the bombardment of Fort Sumter. The *Harriet Lane* also participated in the bombardment of Hatteras Inlet and of Vicksburg.

In World War I, the Coast Guard not only hunted submarines and raiders, but also performed convoy duty in the transport of troops overseas. Peace after World War I brought the Coast Guard its greatest expansion and most onerous duty—enforcement of Prohibition. With repeal of the Eighteenth Amendment, the Coast Guard was drastically cut back in size. In 1939, the Lighthouse Service of the Department of Commerce was transferred to the Treasury and Coast Guard. In 1940, the Coast Guard established an Atlantic Weather Observation Service, patrolling weather stations for protection of transatlantic air commerce. The Coast Guard Reserve was established as a civilian auxiliary in 1939 and became a military organization in 1941. By November, 1941, the entire Coast Guard was operating as a part of the Navy.

In World War II, in addition to guarding our continental coastline, the Coast Guard Regulars and Reserves manned 351 vessels of the Navy.

Headquarters. The Commandant of the Coast Guard directs the administrative affairs of the Coast Guard and maintains his office in Coast Guard Headquarters, Washington, D.C. The Headquarters is organized on a functional basis.

The Commandant is assisted by a Headquarters organization consisting of an Assistant Commandant, a Planning and Control Staff, and Offices of Engineering, Finance and Supply, Merchant Marine Safety, Operations, and Personnel.

Law Enforcement. The Coast Guard is charged with the enforcement, or assistance in enforcing, of all applicable Federal laws upon the high seas and waters subject to the jurisdiction of the United States.

Through its captains of the ports, it enforces rules and regulations governing the anchorage and movement of vessels in territorial waters.

Saving Life and Property and Assistance to Marine Commerce. In carrying out its responsibilities with respect to search and rescue (saving of life and property) and in rendering assistance to vessels and aircraft in distress, the service maintains an established organization of inshore and offshore rescue surface vessels, aircraft, lifeboat stations, and radio stations, together with rescue-coordination centers in each Coast Guard district.

The Coast Guard operates and maintains ocean stations in both the North Atlantic and North Pacific oceans, for the purpose of providing search and rescue, communication, and air-navigation facilities and meteorological services in such ocean areas as are regularly traversed by aircraft of the United States.

Safety and Efficiency of Merchant Marine. The functions of the Coast Guard which relate to the merchant marine include the following: the investigation of marine disasters and the collection of statistics relating thereto; the approval of plans for the construction, repair, and alteration of vessels; the approval of materials, equipment, and appliances; the issuance of certificates of inspection and of permits indicating the approval of vessels for operations which may be hazardous to life and property; the regulation of the transportation of explosives and other dangerous articles on vessels; the administration of loadline requirements; the control of logbooks; the numbering of undocumented vessels; the licensing and certificating of officers, pilots, and seamen; the enforcement of manning requirements, citizenship requirements, and requirements for the mustering and drilling of crews; the suspension and revocation of licenses and certificates; the licensing of motorboat operators; the shipment, discharge, protection, and welfare of merchant seamen; and the promulgation and enforcement of rules for lights, signals, speed, steering, sailing, passing, anchorage, movement, and towlines of vessels.

Navigation Aids. The Coast Guard established and maintains aids to maritime navigation.

Aviation. The Coast Guard maintains aviation stations along the coasts and on the Great Lakes engaged in search and rescue work, in aerial reconnaissance, and in cooperating with other Federal agencies in such matters as law enforcement and mapping.

Coast Guard Academy. The Coast Guard Academy is maintained at New London, Connecticut, for the professional instruction of cadets, who become eligible to receive commissions in the service upon graduation from a 4-year course.

Coast Guard Reserve and Auxiliary. The Coast Guard Reserve, as established on June 23, 1939, and the Coast Guard Auxiliary established on February 19, 1941, are administered by the Commandant of the Coast Guard, pursuant to act of Congress.

Publications. The Coast Guard publishes Light Lists and Loran and radio-beacon system charts, which give information on aids to navigation, and various pamphlets.

Coast Guard Districts. For the purpose of administration, the United States and its territories and possessions are divided into 12 Coast Guard districts, each under a district commander.

The Shore Establishment

1024. GENERAL. The Shore Establishment comprises the field activities of the bureaus and offices of the Navy Department and includes all shore activities not assigned to the Operating Forces. The function is to supply, maintain, and support the Operating Forces. The responsibilities of the Civilian Executive and Naval Professional Assistants for *Producer Logistics* here reach culmination through furnishing or delivering the materials, services, and personnel which the Operating Forces require for their operations in peace or war.

Administration. The system of administration of the Shore Establishment and the shore activities assigned to the Operating Forces of the Navy is established and defined in detail in General Order No. 19. The *Catalog of Naval Shore Activities, SNDL* (OpNav P09B3-105) lists all shore and field activities by type, area, echelon of command, and area coordination. Direction is exercised through military command and management control. These terms are defined as follows:

Command is the exercise of authority and responsibility for shore activities for: (1) matters which are responsibilities of the Chief of Naval Operations or, as appropriate, the Commandant of the Marine Corps, such as operations, security, intelligence, discipline, naval communications, and similar matters of naval operation and administration; (2) coordination of the efforts of shore activities as is necessary to ensure that direct support and services are furnished to operating forces of the Navy and Marine Corps in a timely and effective manner; (3) continuous evaluation of the capabilities and readiness of shore activities for furnishing support direct to fleet units, consistent with their requirements; and (4) matters related to the customs, traditions, and usage of the naval service. Military command includes also matters related to defense, and, under conditions of emergency or disaster, when normal exercise of management control is impractical, shall include the power and duty to exercise authoritative direction as circumstances may require. The function of inspection and the responsibility for appropriate coordination are inherent in military command.

Support is the provision of resources to a command or activity to enable it to carry out its mission. It complements command, and includes administrative, personnel, and material support, guidance and assistance in and evaluation of such matters as organization, procedures, budgeting, accounting, and utilization of personnel, funds, material, and facilities.

Area Coordination insures that the total efforts of all shore activities support the combatant forces. It includes command and support relationships with combatant forces, common support services, emergency planning, disaster control, and defense, and similar activities.

Administrative and Technical Guidance is furnished by Bureaus and Offices to shore activities in accordance with their assigned functional responsibilities.

Sea Frontiers are part of the Operating Forces but have military command of certain naval districts for logistic support of the Operating Forces. They are more fully discussed in Sec. 1105.

Naval Districts. The United States and its island possessions are divided into Naval Districts with limits and headquarters as shown in Figure 1008.

1025. ORGANIZATION OF THE NAVAL DISTRICTS. Each naval district is commanded by an officer designated "Commandant," a flag officer of the line, eligible for command at sea, who is the direct representative of the Secretary of the Navy and the Chief of Naval Operations for all matters pertaining to the maintenance of high standards of naval performance and discipline and in all matters which affect area standardization, coordination, defense, and security. He is the direct representative of the bureaus and offices of the Navy Department for such matters as may be specifically assigned by the bureaus and offices, for all matters concerning relations with the public and with other departments of the government within his district.

The organization of a naval district establishes, between the Commandant and the commanding officers of the groups and units included in the district, relations similar to those which exist between the commander-in-chief of a fleet and the various units of his command (see Figure 1009 for command relationships).

District craft, including vessels, aircraft, and small boats, directly under the Commandant, are administered by him. Craft assigned to specific units are under the immediate jurisdiction of the commanding

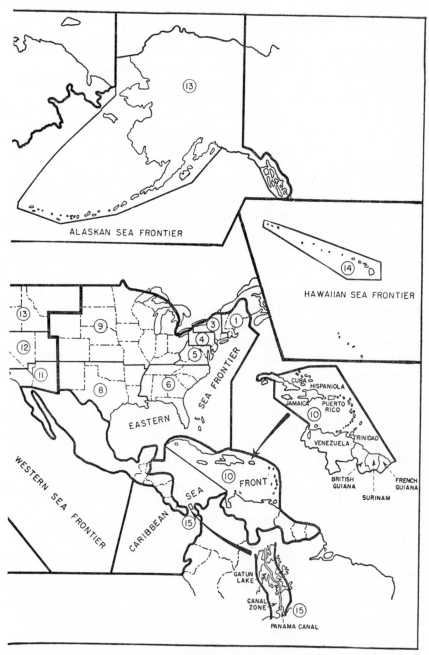

FIGURE 1008. Sea Frontiers and Naval Districts.

1st ND—Hq., Boston
3rd ND—Hq., New York
4th ND—Hq., Philadelphia
5th ND—Hq., Norfolk
6th ND—Hq., Charleston

8th ND—Hq., New Orleans
9th ND—Hq., Great Lakes
10th ND—Hq., San Juan
11th ND—Hq., San Diego
12th ND—Hq., San Francisco

13th ND—Hq., Seattle
14th ND—Hq., Pearl Harbor
15th ND—Hq., Balboa
Naval District Washington

officers of the naval bases, shipyards, or stations to which they are assigned.

Exceptions. Certain activities within the geographical limits of a naval district may, for good reasons, not be under the command of the Commandant or may be under his control only in a limited sense. Examples of these are fleet bases such as Guantánamo, Cuba, the Amphibious Bases at Little Creek, Virginia and Coronado, California, and air stations under the Naval Air Training and Naval Airship Training and Experimental Commands.

Within the geographical confines of the Fifth Naval District, the Naval District, Washington, D.C., has the same relationship to shore activities and to the Navy Department as set forth for numbered naval districts.

Functions of the Commandant. Among the functions exercised by the Commandant are logistical and operational support of the Operating Forces, the defense of the district and control of local disasters or emergencies, public relations, maintenance of industrial mobilization plans for the district, control of Naval Reserve matters except for the Naval Air Reserve, intelligence, communications, collaboration with the Army and Air Force, and others too numerous to mention here.

1026. NAVAL BASES. A naval base is a group of shore activities in the same area, which furnish direct logistic support to ships of the Operating Forces, with a naval base commander in military command of the group. A typical naval base includes a naval shipyard (commanded by an officer professionally and technically qualified in industrial matters), a naval station, a naval supply center or depot, a navy fuel depot, a naval ammunition and net depot, and a naval degaussing station. Frequently, a naval air station and a fleet training center or fleet schools are further assigned in accordance with General Order No. 19.

It should be noted that the naval district commandant—who is an *area* commander—is in the military chain of command of the components of the naval base; through the naval base commander he discharges his duties relative to direct logistic support of ships of the Operating Forces and such other of his responsibilities as may be appropriate.

The commanding officers of the several component activities under the military command of a naval base commander receive direction on matters involving administrative and technical guidance direct from the responsible bureaus and offices of the Navy Department, except where otherwise specifically delegated.

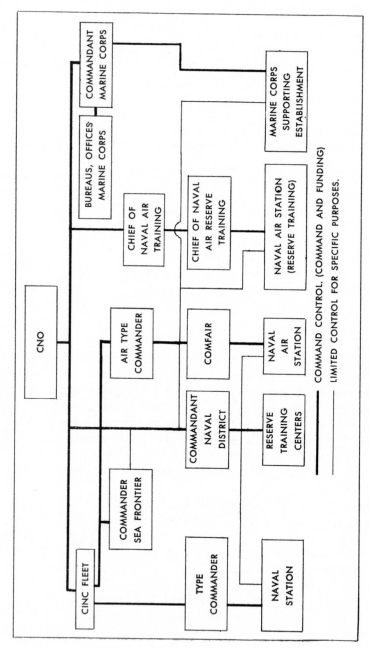

FIGURE 1009. Naval command relations ashore.

1027. NAVAL AIR BASES. Naval Air Base Commands comprise those activities of the Shore Establishment furnishing aviation logistic support to the Operating Forces.

The commander, naval air bases, of a naval district, as in the case of the commander of a naval base, is under the command of the district commandant. Activities assigned to a naval air base command are under the command of the naval air bases commander and are coordinated by him with other air activities of his command. Administrative and technical guidance of such activities stems from the responsible bureau or office of the Navy Department, except where otherwise specifically delegated.

It should be pointed out that other air activities within naval districts, performing functions unlike those above noted, are not assigned to the commander, naval air bases. These include:

1. The Naval Air Training Command, and Naval Airship Training and Experimental Command. Activities of these commands are under their respective functional chiefs, subject to the control of the district commandants in disaster or emergency.

2. The Commanders, Marine Corps Air Bases Eastern Area, Cherry Point, North Carolina, and Western Area, El Toro, California. These

FIGURE 1010. USS *Von Steuben* (SSBN-632).

are under the command of the Commandant, Marine Corps, and co-ordinate their work with and are guided by measures of coordination of the district commandants.

3. The Pacific Missile Range and the Naval Air Rocket Test Station. These, like other activities of the Shore Establishment not a part of a naval base, a naval air bases command, or a functional command, are under the command of the district commandant.

The Operating Forces

1028. FORCES AFLOAT. The Operating Forces are the several fleets, seagoing forces, sea frontier forces, district forces, and such shore activities and other forces and activities of the Navy as are assigned to the Operating Forces by the President or the Secretary of the Navy. Chapter 11 gives a detailed account of the organization of the Operating Forces.

Components of the United States Navy

1029. COMPOSITION. The United States Navy consists of the Regular Navy and the Naval Reserve. Together, these two components, the military and the civilian elements of the Navy, have long provided for the first line of defense of our country and for the security of the vital sea lanes so that our sea transport and our commerce could proceed upon their lawful pursuits.

Each element of the Navy has its own important function. The Regular Navy and the Naval Reserve are dependent upon one another, and each, in turn, must work closely and harmoniously with all elements of our sister services if the Armed Forces of the United States are to achieve the truly magnificent teamwork of which they are capable and which they must have if they are to win through to victory in modern war.

1030. THE REGULAR NAVY. Consisting of officers and enlisted personnel who have elected to make the naval service a lifetime career, the Regular Navy is our permanent professional naval force. These are the officers and enlisted men and women who form the nucleus for training and expansion of the Navy into such a vast organization as fought the naval campaigns of World War II.

In such a troubled world as we now have, a good many officers and

FIGURE 1011. A-6A Intruder with a display of its entire arsenal inventory.

enlisted men and women of the Naval Reserve have also been retained on active duty to keep the Navy up to the strength required to carry out its mission.

Officers of the Regular Navy and the Naval Reserve are divided among the line and seven staff corps.

Line. Officers of the line exercise the military command of the Navy. The senior line officer present anywhere at any time is accountable for the exercise of his authority and cannot divest himself of this responsibility. Only line officers can exercise command at sea. In general, only line officers exercise command ashore, except that members of certain corps, such as Medical, Supply, and Civil Engineer Corps, command shore activities under the technical control of their respective bureaus or Systems Commands.

Among officers of the line are certain officer specialists who have been designated to perform engineering duty only, such as naval constructors and naval engineers, and others who perform limited duties in specialized fields, such as hydrography, communications, and law. These officers may not command at sea, but some of them will have command of shore stations which come under their specialty.

Line officers, therefore, are the officers who command, administer, train, and fight the ships and larger units of the fleet. The unrestricted line officer specializes, but his specialty is command in war.

Medical Corps. The officers of the Medical Corps are composed exclusively of graduate and practicing doctors of medicine. Under the Bureau of Medicine and Surgery, they are charged with the administration of members of the Nurse Corps and Medical Service Corps.

Dental Corps. The officers of the Dental Corps are composed exclusively of graduate and practicing doctors of dentistry. Their service and opportunities for further education and specialization are similar to those offered to medical officers. Although a separate corps, the Dental Corps comes under the administrative control of the Bureau of Medicine and Surgery of the Navy Department. At naval hospitals, the dental service and dental officers are under the command of the medical officer in command of the hospital.

Nurse Corps. See Section 1031.

Medical Service Corps. The officers of the Medical Service Corps are composed of men and women who, in civilian life, have acquired specialized competence in the fields of optometry, pharmacy, or such allied medical sciences as bacteriology, biochemistry, psychology, sanitation engineering, or medical statistics. Officers, both men and women, are appointed from civil life, usually in the grade of ensign. The Medical Service Corps is under the administrative control of the Bureau of Medicine and Surgery, and, at naval hospitals, members of the Corps are part of the organization of the hospital under the command of the medical officer in command.

Supply Corps. Officers, chief and warrant officers of the Supply Corps administer the services of supply for the Navy and receive and disburse appropriated naval funds for supply and for pay, subsistence, and transportation.

The Supply Corps is the business branch of the Navy. Its duties in the business field include providing the food, fuel, clothing, general stores, spare parts, and innumerable services required by the Navy and its personnel. It receives, warehouses, ships, issues, and accounts for naval supplies. Its officers pay all public bills incurred by naval activities and make payroll disbursements—both afloat and ashore. Its officers command the naval supply depots and naval supply centers.

Chaplain Corps. Officers of the Chaplain Corps are ordained ministers of various denominations. They serve under a Chief of Chaplains with the rank of rear admiral who has his office in the Bureau of Naval

Personnel. The officers of the Chaplain Corps conduct religious services aboard Navy ships, at Navy and Marine shore stations, and with the Marines in the field. Although their duties are primarily religious, their scope of activities is far wider than falls to the lot of a civilian clergyman. They live in close daily contact afloat and ashore with the young men of the Navy and Marine Corps, and thus are afforded an opportunity not only to promote their spiritual and moral growth, but also to guide and counsel them in their studies, their recreational pursuits, and in the multitude of problems that beset youth.

The authorization for chaplains in the United States Navy dates back to the Act of March 1794, which provided for the beginnings of our present-day Navy.

From the beginning, the chaplain's major duties were primarily religious. It was and is his responsibility, working under the direction of his commanding officer, to conduct divine services, to administer the sacraments of his church, to teach the principles of his religion, and to officiate at religious ceremonies. But the Navy has usually given the chaplain collateral duties.

Navy chaplains through the years have frequently taken the initiative in introducing reforms in the naval service. Chaplains introduced libraries aboard ships and sponsored choirs and bands. They continued to be teachers for many years even after the Naval Academy was founded at Annapolis.

In 1914 Congress established a quota of one chaplain for every 1,250 naval personnel. In 1947 this quota was changed to one chaplain for every 800. Some 5,000 chaplains are known to have served in either the Continental Navy or the United States Navy to April 1968.

Through the years, a number of clergymen have made history both for the Chaplain Corps and for the Navy. During the War of 1812 several unordained men who served for a short time as chaplains actually participated in fighting. Among these was Samuel Livermore (in whose honor a destroyer was named), who served as chaplain on the *Chesapeake* under Captain James Lawrence.

Chaplain Jones was influential in introducing coffee in the Navy. On February 10, 1842, Jones wrote to the Secretary of the Navy offering to buy coffee if the Navy "would furnish conveniences for having it prepared." His offer was accepted. Chaplain Jones was the first head of the Department of English Studies at the Naval Academy and also its first chaplain.

During World War II, Navy chaplains engaged in a great variety of collateral duties. They served as educational officers, insurance officers, editors of papers, and secretaries of Navy Relief. Some were in charge of theaters and others led orchestras and bands. Chaplains often found that as much as 80 percent of their time was taken up with consultations.

Navy chaplains made history in World War II. Only 192 chaplains, including 87 reserves, were on duty on December 7, 1941. Before hostilities came to an end in August 1945, a total of 2,934 chaplains had been on duty.

Never before in the history of our nation did our Government do so much to assist chaplains of both the Army and the Navy as during World War II. Material aids, such as hymn books, altar equipment, and chapels, were provided. Millions of dollars were thus spent, and by the time the war was over the Navy had 111 chapels at various naval installations within the United States and several at overseas bases. In addition to these, hundreds of temporary chapels were built from native materials on the islands of the Pacific, often by the men themselves in off-duty hours.

A Chaplain's School for the indoctrination of Reserves was conducted during the war, first at Norfolk and then at the College of William and Mary, Williamsburg, Virginia. Here enlisted personnel, both men and women, also were trained as chaplains' assistants. A slogan used at the school read: "Cooperation Without Compromise." Chaplains of all of the major faiths proved that it was possible to work together and still permit each chaplain to remain true to the fundamental tenets of his faith. Protestant, Catholic, and Jewish chaplains often took turns in conducting divine services in the same chapel, using much of the same equipment. In countless ways, chaplains found that they could minister to men and women of religious denominations other than their own.

All accessions to the Corps during the war entered as Reserve chaplains. Before the war ended, the Reserves numbered 96 per cent of the entire Corps. Upon the shoulders of the small group of older Regular Navy chaplains fell the chief responsibility of administration. Since the Marine Corps and Coast Guard have no chaplains, these units fell within the responsibility of the Navy chaplaincy. When the war was over, most of the Reserves returned to civilian life. However, even before the war ended, the transfer of Reserves to Regular Navy had begun and the Corps was soon up to authorized strength.

Civil Engineer Corps. The officers of the Civil Engineer Corps consist of graduates of the Naval Academy, the NROTC Program, or graduate civil engineers. Officers of this Corps are normally restricted to shore duty. They perform such duties as supervision of buildings and grounds and plant establishments at naval shipyards and naval stations, supervision of construction of buildings on shore, survey of property, and layout of naval stations. See Section 1021 for Seabees.

Judge Advocate General Corps. In 1968 the lawyers of the Navy were formed into the JAG Corps. Nonlawyers, however, still perform many legal duties within the military judicial system.

Warrant Officers. In 1960 the procurement of additional warrant officers was terminated but was resumed in October, 1965. Warrant officers possess detailed practical knowledge of their specialty and include in their ranks many of the finest specialists in the Navy.

Enlisted Men. Basic legislation enacted since World War II allows 500,000 enlisted men in the Regular Navy. Expansion during emergency is accomplished by calling to active duty many naval reservists and by enlisting and sometimes by drafting greater numbers of recruits. Cutbacks, when necessary, are made both by returning reservists to inactive duty and by slowing down procurement of regulars. The actual number of enlisted men in the Navy during any fiscal year depends upon the operating forces and shore establishment to be maintained and upon the current appropriations for pay and allowances of enlisted men.

1031. WOMEN IN THE NAVY AND ITS COMPONENTS. *Nurse Corps.* The Navy Nurse Corps was established by an act of Congress in 1908 to serve as a nursing unit in the Medical Department of the Navy. In 1942, Congress enacted legislation giving members of the Corps relative rank to that of commissioned officers of the Navy. By an act of Congress in April, 1947, the Nurse Corps was established as a staff corps of the Navy within the Medical Department of the Navy and the Nurse Corps Reserve was authorized. While so serving, the Director of the Corps has the rank of captain. Nurses appointed into the Navy hold permanent commissions in the Regular Navy.

Female Yeomen. During 1917, as the United States was reaching her final decision to enter World War I, the Civil Service Commission could not meet the need of naval shore stations for clerical assistance occasioned by the increased activities incident to preparation for war. It was found that the act of August 29, 1916, which established the Naval Reserve Force, did not use the term "male" and women were declared eligible for enrollment.

Immediately after the United States went to war against the Central Powers, the enrollment of women was taken up on a large scale in order to release enlisted men for active service at sea. As a result a total of 11,275 yeomen (F) were in service at the time of the armistice. These women served, in addition to clerical duties, as translators, draftsmen, fingerprint experts, camouflage designers, and recruiting agents. They were stationed in Guam, the Panama Canal Zone, and Hawaii, in addition to the United States and France. All yeomen (F) were released from active duty by July 31, 1919.

WAVES. The Women's Reserve of the United States Naval Reserve was authorized by the Congress July 30, 1942, in order to permit women volunteers to serve at shore stations within the continental United States and release Navy men for duty at sea. The full name of the Women's Reserve at its inception was "Women Accepted for Volunteer Emergency Service," from which it derived its briefer name, the WAVES. Restrictions on the ranks held by officers specified that there could be but one lieutenant commander, 35 lieutenants, and that no more than 35 percent of the total number of officers could be lieutenants (jg).

Subsequent legislation in November, 1943, provided for one officer of the Women's Reserve in the rank of captain and removed limitations on the lower ranks.

An act of Congress, September 27, 1944, enlarged the area to which WAVES could be assigned by redefining the American Area to add the Territories of Hawaii and Alaska. The Women's Reserve was an integral part of the naval service and in no sense a separate corps. The women were trained and assigned to duty as direct replacements for men or to fill new jobs in expanding activities which would otherwise have required the services of men.

The Regular Navy. Women in the Navy do not comprise a separate organization or a separate corps. In 1946, recognizing the excellent performance of duty of the female members of the naval service during World War II, the Navy Department sought legislation to continue women in the Navy as a part of the regular establishment. The Women's Armed Services Integration Act of 1948 provided that all laws or parts of laws which now or hereafter authorize commissioned and warrant officers in the Regular Navy, subject to the provisions of the act, shall be construed to include authority to enlist and appoint women in the Regular Navy and the Naval Reserve.

The number of enlisted women may not exceed 2 percent of the authorized enlisted strength of the Regular Navy, and women officers may not exceed 10 percent of the enlisted woman strength. Enlisted women have the same opportunities for advancement as enlisted men. Women officers are selected for promotion and are advanced in a manner similar to male officers, but are not permitted to have a permanent commission higher than commander. Retirement benefits are the same as for male officers and enlisted men. Pay and allowances, leave, liberty, and other benefits applying to male personnel are applicable to women, except that husbands of women are not considered to be dependents unless they are in fact dependent upon the woman for their chief support.

Training. Recruit training for enlisted women is of 10 weeks' duration. Upon completion, approximately 60 percent are sent to advanced training schools. The remaining 40 percent are ordered to duty stations for on-the-job training. At the advanced schools, the training is co-educational. Men and women compete for class standing. Competition also holds throughout the woman's naval career for advancement in rating. Women are eligible for all ratings, except those the duties of which are beyond their physical strength and those of a strictly seagoing nature. Training of women officers, conducted at the U. S. Naval Woman Officer School, Newport, Rhode Island, consists of an 8 week officer candidate orientation phase and an 8 week commissioned officer indoctrination course.

Women Marines. In August, 1918, Secretary of the Navy Josephus Daniels granted authority "to enroll women in the Marine Corps Reserve for clerical duty." The records show that 305 were enlisted, the highest rank to which they were promoted in World War I being sergeant. The women reservists wore a uniform similar to the enlisted men's, and were subject to the same rules and regulations as applied to enlisted men. After World War I, Women Marines were transferred to inactive duty and subsequently were discharged from the Marine Corps Reserve.

To meet the recognized need for full mobilization of human resources in World War II, in February, 1943, the Marine Corps Women's Reserve was activated.

The Regular Marine Corps. Women Marines in the Regular Marine Corps were authorized by the Women's Armed Services Integration Act of 1948. They are not a separate organization but are integrated into the regular establishment.

Women in the Marines are directed by a colonel who is Director of Women in the Marine Corps Headquarters. She is selected from among women officers of the grade of major or lieutenant colonel.

With a nucleus of veteran officers and enlisted women, the recruitment and appointment of Women Marines into the regular establishment now goes forward. Enlisted women are given recruit training at Parris Island. Women candidates for commissions in the Regular Marine Corps, selected from among qualified college graduates and under-graduates and enlisted Women Marines, are trained at the Women Officers' Training Class at Quantico. Their training closely parallels the training of male officer candidates, except that combat training is omitted.

The Coast Guard SPARS. The Women's Reserve of the Coast Guard Reserve called the SPARS, from the Coast Guard motto, "Semper Paratus," was established by the same amendment to the Naval Reserve Act of 1938, passed in July, 1942, that authorized the WAVES and Women Marines. Identical in composition and basic duties as the WAVES, they served the Coast Guard and the Navy with distinction during World War II.

The Regular Coast Guard. The place of the SPARS in the regular establishment of the Coast Guard was assured by the same legislation that integrated women into the other military services. Their procurement, training, and duties are comparable to those performed by the women in the Navy.

Significance. Women came into the component organizations of the naval service to serve their country by replacing officers and enlisted men trained for combat. By their perseverance, loyalty, intelligence, and efficiency, they contributed much to the prosecution of World War II. The Regular Navy, Marine Corps, and Coast Guard have welcomed the Women of the Naval Services into the regular establishment, confident that their continued excellent performance of duty will make substantial contribution to the effectiveness of the Navy of the United States in peace and war.

The United States Naval Reserve

1032. MISSION. The mission of the Naval Reserve is to provide qualified individuals and trained units to be available for active duty in time of war or national emergency, and at such other times as the national security may require. The Naval Reserve is designed to meet the requirements of the Navy in excess of those of the regular component during and after the period needed for the procurement and training of additional qualified individuals and trained units to achieve the planned mobilization.

The Secretary of the Navy has established the policy that the administration of the Naval Reserve shall be integrated into the Regular Naval Establishment so completely that all agencies of the Navy will function for, and provide for, the Naval Reserve in all respects as they do for the Regular Navy.

1033. OBLIGATED SERVICE. Each male person who was initially enlisted, appointed or inducted into the naval service, including the Naval Reserve, prior to attaining the 26th anniversary of his birth is required to serve on active duty in the Navy and/or in some active status in the Naval Reserve for a specified period of time. His length of obligated service will depend upon the initial date of entry into naval service. There are three general groups: those who entered prior to June 19, 1951; those who entered during the period from June 19, 1951 to August 10, 1955; and those who entered subsequent to August 10, 1955. Each group is governed by a different Reserve Act. In general, under the Reserve Forces Act of 1955, those men entering the naval service subsequent to August 10, 1955, acquire a 6-year obligation with 2 years of active duty.

1034. RESERVE CATEGORIES AND STATUS. Within the Naval Reserve each Reservist is placed in one of the following categories:

1. Ready Reserve: A Ready Reservist is liable for active duty either

FIGURE 1012. A Terrier is fired at a drone target.

in time of war, in time of national emergency declared by Congress or proclaimed by the President, or when otherwise authorized by law.

2. Standby Reserve: A Standby Reservist is liable for active duty only in time of war or national emergency declared by the Congress or when otherwise authorized by law, and is subject to call through the Selective Service System.

3. Retired Reserve: A Retired Reservist is liable for active duty only in time of war or national emergency declared by the Congress, or when otherwise authorized by law upon determination by the Secretary of Defense that adequate numbers of qualified members of the Naval Reserve are not readily available from the Ready and Standby Reserves.

The Armed Forces Reserve Act of 1952 provided that all Reservists be in an active, inactive, or a retired status.

While on the inactive status list, members of the Naval Reserve are not eligible to participate in training for pay, retirement credits, or to be considered for or to effect a promotion or advancement. Such Reservists may take correspondence courses; however, no retirement points may be credited for any otherwise creditable portion of a correspondence course completed while on the inactive status list.

Reservists on the inactive status list may be removed therefrom upon application, in accordance with regulations prescribed by the Secretary of the Navy. Normally, the minimum retention on the inactive status list is for a period of one year.

1035. METHODS OF TRAINING. There are three methods by which training is accomplished in the Naval Reserve:

1. *Drilling* by organized units in training centers or other designated places weekly, monthly or semimonthly on designated nights or weekends according to the nature and scope of the training prescribed;

2. *Active duty for training,* which consists of one period of two or more weeks of continuous training on active duty taken each year; this duty is performed in ships, at schools and at other activities ashore;

3. *Correspondence courses* are taken at home and cover all areas and levels of technical training for both officer and enlisted personnel.

These methods of training may be used either singly or in combinations by Naval Reservists according to their needs, desires and availability. Members of non-pay units and of the Active Status Pool (officers and men who are not members of organized units) may perform active duty for training within the limits of funds available. All Reservists are encouraged to pursue correspondence courses.

1036. NAVAL RESERVE PROGRAMS. The Reserve Programs are pay or non-pay depending upon the intensity of the training, the priority of mobilization needs for the personnel, and the standards of performance required. Most of the non-pay programs are primarily for officer training.

All paid drilling units of the Naval Reserve, i.e. the Selected Reserve, are organized into five components. Those individuals who are receiving pay and who are not drilling members of Selected Reserve units are placed in the Program Support Personnel Component. The mission and composition of these components may be summarized as follows:

1. *Anti-Submarine Warfare Component* which provides trained ASW forces capable of immediate employment at full war complement in time of war, national emergency, or when otherwise authorized by law. It consists of Reserve Crews with assigned DD/DE type ships and ASW Air Squadrons with assigned aircraft.

2. *Mine Warfare Component* which provides trained Mine Warfare forces capable of immediate employment at full war complement in time of war, national emergency or when otherwise authorized by law. It consists of Reserve Crews (BLUE) with assigned ships (MSC/MSCO).

3. *Active Fleet Augmentation Component* which provides trained personnel for immediate active duty in time of war, national emergency or when otherwise authorized by law to raise the manning level of afloat units of the active fleet to full war complement, and for requirements to meet specific needs of other programs in certain rates not being trained therein. It is composed of the following programs:

Naval Reserve Destroyer Division Commander/Staff units
Naval Reserve MINE Division and Squadron Commander/Staff units
Mine Warfare Reserve Crews (GOLD)
Naval Reserve Group Commander/Staff units
Surface Program (Surface and Fleet Divisions)
Submarine Program (Divisions and Sections)
Military Sea Transportation Service Program
Naval Control of Shipping Organization Program

4. *Fleet Support Activities Component* which provides urgently needed personnel for immediate active duty in time of war, national emergency or when otherwise authorized by law for the limited augmentation or formation of first priority activities or units, serving with

or directly supporting the fleet. It is composed of the following pro-grams:

Advanced Base Command Program
Amphibious Beach Group Program
Construction Battalion Program
Inshore Undersea Warfare Program
Ships Supply Officer Program
Ship Activation, Maintenance and Repair Program

5. *Shore Establishment Component* which provides urgently needed personnel for immediate active duty in time of war, national emergency or when authorized by law for limited augmentation of various first priority activities of the shore establishment. It is composed of the following programs:

Intelligence Program
Mobilization Team Program
Naval Security Group Program
Selective Service Program
Telecommunications Censorship Program
Transportation, Traffic and Terminal Management Program

6. *Program Support Personnel* which provides support for the drilling programs in recruiting, training, administration, and special services, such as medical and dental examinations, and assistance by chaplains. It consists of all Naval Reservists in paid drilling status in Specialist Programs, Naval Reserve Officers' Schools, and Composite Companies; all Naval Reservists in paid appropriate duty status.

7. *Schools and Special Programs* which include the Naval Reserve Officers School and special programs as the Chaplain, Medical, Law, and Composite programs.

8. *Aviation Programs,* which include programs for the Air Wing Staffs and Squadrons; for Auxiliary Air and Ground Units; the non-pay program; and certain specialized training programs.

The following are descriptions of a few of the typical programs:

Naval Air Reserve. The mission of the Naval Air Reserve is to main-tain selected reserve aviation personnel in a state of training, readiness, and availability for immediate employment as aviation squadrons, with aircraft, and as personnel augmentation of the active forces in the event of mobilization.

The Naval Air Reserve Training Command, in the chain of command under the Chief of Naval Operations and the Chief of Naval Air Train-ing, administers the training of aviation units divided among Naval Air Reserve activities spread geographically across the United States.

These units provide the Navy with an M-Day capability of increasing its air ASW forces. Their Fleet Logistic Support Squadrons provide the Navy with a much needed airlift capability. A corps of specialists in areas such as Air Intelligence, Aerology, Medicine, Supply, Communications, and Administration ensure that fleet units will have a capability of accelerated operations in wartime. In addition, Air Reserve units furnish the necessary trained personnel to augment fleet squadrons from allowance to complement, thus providing these squadrons with the capability of sustained operations at wartime levels.

The training of Naval Air Reserve squadrons closely parallels that of active fleet squadrons. Much of this training is conducted under the supervision of the fleet commanders at fleet bases while the squadrons are performing periods of active duty for training, at which time readiness inspections are conducted on each squadron. In addition, fleet commanders on both the east and west coasts periodically conduct fleet exercises in which Naval Air Reserve squadrons and crews participate along with their fleet counterparts.

Naval Reserve Officers Schools (NROS). Established throughout the nation in the centers of population are a number of Naval Reserve Officers Schools. These schools are established to provide a means of continuing and increasing the professional proficiency of Naval Reserve officers.

They are for the most part located at Naval Reserve Training Centers or at colleges and universities.

The schools run on a 40-drill basis, corresponding with an academic year, with 2 weeks' active duty for training normally provided. The curriculum is designed to fit the needs of officers of various ranks and designators.

Enrollment is open to any inactive Naval Reserve officer in good standing in the Naval Reserve. Likewise, officers in another drilling unit in a pay or non-pay status may participate in the NROS program. Pay for officer students is not authorized.

1037. STRUCTURE OF RESERVE UNITS. Except for the Aviation Program as described in Section 1036, the basic unit of the Reserve organization in pay units is the *division,* while in the non-pay program, the basic unit is the *company.* Both the commanding officer of a division and of a company are issued orders as Commanding Officer by the Commandant of the Naval District.

The Naval Reserve Group Commander exercises broad military command of all Naval Reserve pay and non-pay units attached to or supported by the training center where he is located. In addition, he directs, monitors, and promotes the professional development of all Naval Reserve officers on inactive duty assigned to Naval Reserve units under his command or who live in the area served by his command.

The required billet structure of pay and non-pay units is specified by the Chief of Naval Personnel and is designed to accomplish the training and administration of the unit. Associate billets for various types of pay units may be authorized by the Chief of Naval Personnel to provide specialized personnel for the training and administration of the unit.

1038. INSTRUCTION AND TRAINING OF THE NAVAL RESERVE. *Correspondence courses* in professional naval subjects are available to officers of the Naval Reserve on active or inactive duty. These courses cover a broad scope ranging from basic courses to highly specialized courses. The general areas covered are Naval Orientation, Navy Regulations, Chaplains, Communications, Deck, Engineering, Electronics, Law, Medical, Naval Aviation, Supply, and Transportation.

The majority of the officers' correspondence courses are administered by the Naval Correspondence Course Center, Naval Supply Depot, Scotia, New York. The following bureaus and activities also offer correspondence courses as indicated:

Bureau of Medicine and Surgery
  A series of specialists courses for medical personnel

Naval War College, Newport, Rhode Island
  Strategy and Tactics
  International Law (Regular Course)
  International Law (Advanced Course)
  Logistics

Naval Intelligence School, Washington, D.C.
  Naval Intelligence

Naval Submarine School, New London, Connecticut
  Basic Submarine Course
  Advanced Submarine Course

Chief of Naval Operations (20-2), Washington, D.C.
  Communications Supplementary Activity

See also Section 1408.

Regular drills consist of training in duties pertaining to the Navy, as designated from time to time by the Bureau of Naval Personnel in separate training instructions.

Regular drills must be:

1. Prescribed by the Chief of Naval Personnel for the designated division, squadron, or other authorized organization.

2. Performed under competent orders in accordance with instructions issued by the Bureau of Naval Personnel.

3. Designated in advance for each organization as a whole by its commanding officer.

4. Of not less than 2 hours' duration.

5. Attended by officers and men in uniform.

6. Conducted on days other than legal holidays.

7. Drills for aviation units are usually conducted on weekends, in order to provide necessary consecutive hours for training in aircraft.

Active duty for training is prescribed for personnel of the Selected Reserve Program and authorized for a limited number of personnel in other programs. The Bureau of Naval Personnel issues instructions for training while on active duty for training.

Reserve Training Facilities. Approximately 300 Naval Reserve Training Centers are provided at locations where pay units of the Naval Reserve have been authorized. These centers provide the office space, drill halls, classroom space and equipment needed for the training and administration of the Reserve units meeting at the center. The training centers vary in size depending upon the number of organizations sharing the facilities. In some cities, centers are shared with the Marine Corps Reserve and other services.

Ships and other floating equipment are assigned by the Chief of Naval Operations to the Commander, Naval Reserve Training Command, for use by the naval districts in the training of the Naval Reserve. In addition, units of the fleet provide billets for Naval Reservists to accomplish active duty for training.

1039. ADMINISTRATION OF THE NAVAL RESERVE. Prior to World War II, the Naval Reserve Program was administered as a single section of the Bureau of Navigation, predecessor of the Bureau of Naval Personnel. Since the war, with obvious need for integration of the Naval Reserve with the Regular Navy, the Naval Reserve Program has been completely integrated into the offices and bureaus of the Navy Department.

Office of the Chief of Naval Operations.   In addition to over-all responsibility as "expediter" and plans coordinator to ensure effective integration of the Naval Reserve Program, the Assistant Chief of Naval Operations (Naval Reserve) determines the number of officers and men to be maintained in the various classes of the Naval Reserve, determines the number of stationkeepers and shipkeepers and the number of reservists required on active duty for other Reserve activities, and supervises the procurement and equipment of Naval Reserve Training Centers and other facilities for training reservists.

The Bureau of Naval Personnel.   Having primary responsibility for personnel and training of personnel in the Navy Department, the Bureau of Naval Personnel is responsible for procurement, education, training, discipline, and distribution of officers and men of the Naval Reserve and their organization, administration, and mobilization.

The Air Systems Command.   Because the Air Systems Command has certain functions in support of the Regular Establishment, it also performs similar functions for the Naval Reserve, for the Naval Air Reserve, which comes under the Deputy Chief of Naval Operations (Air) for plans for logistic support and for supervision of training.

Other Bureaus and Offices.   Technical bureaus of the Navy Department are responsible for furnishing technical equipment under their cognizance needed for training reservists, for the cost of major repairs to such equipment, and for supervision of technical training of reserve specialists in programs under their sponsorship. For example, the Seabee Program is under technical control of Facilities Engineering Command; Cargo Handling under Supply Systems Command; and ship repair under Ships Systems Command; etc.

Commandants of Naval Districts.   Except for reservists who are members of, or are associated with, the Naval Air Reserve, all naval reservists who live within the boundaries of a naval district come under the jurisdiction of the Commandant of that district.

Subject to the supervision of the Bureaus and Offices of the Navy Department, the Commandant is charged with the procurement, administration, training, and readiness for war of the Naval Reserve under his jurisdiction; and for the maintenance, operation, and repair of material, training centers, training facilities, and floating equipment assigned for this purpose.

In addition, the Bureau of Naval Personnel details Regular Navy and Naval Reserve officers on active duty as Commanding Officers of the training centers, and they are directly responsible to the Commandant for their performance of duty.

The Chief of Naval Air Reserve Training. Under the Chief of Naval Operations, the Chief of Naval Air Reserve Training is responsible for the coordination and training of technical units and other activities of the Naval Air Reserve Program. He administers his activities through the Chief of Naval Air Training, located at the Naval Air Station, Glenview, Illinois. He also supervises and furnishes logistic support for the Marine Corps Air Reserve Training Command.

Naval Reserve Flag for Merchant Vessels. A suitable flag or pennant has been prescribed by the Secretary of the Navy which may be flown from the mainmasthead as an emblem of the Naval Reserve on seagoing vessels documented under the laws of the United States, under a warrant issued for each vessel by the Secretary of the Navy.

Naval Reserve Yacht Pennant. A suitable pennant has been prescribed by the Secretary of the Navy which may be flown as an emblem of the Naval Reserve from the foremasthead on yachts and similar vessels documented under the laws of the United States, under a warrant issued for each such yacht or similar vessel by the Secretary of the Navy.

1040. WOMEN IN THE NAVAL RESERVE. Women, both officer and enlisted, may participate in most Naval Reserve programs. Their training requirements and eligibility for benefits are the same as those prescribed for male members. With the exception of a few Recruit Training Divisions, there are no separate reserve drilling units for women.

CHAPTER 11

The Operating Forces, Fleet Organization, and Operations

Whatever else you are, be a seaman. Know the ways of the sea and of the men who go down to the sea in ships.

1101. THE OPERATING FORCES. The Operating Forces of the Navy comprise the several fleets, seagoing forces, sea frontier forces, district forces, Fleet Marine Forces and other assigned Marine Corp forces, the Military Sea Transportation Service, and such shore activities of the Navy and other forces and activities as may be assigned to the Operating Forces of the Navy by the President or the Secretary of the Navy. (Consult General Orders No. 5 and 9 if complete details are desired.) Command of the Operating Forces is assigned to the Chief of Naval Operations (CNO), subject to the authority vested in the President by the Constitution and the Secretaries of Defense and Navy by law. The Chief of Naval Operations is responsible for executing the directives of the Joint Chiefs of Staff insofar as they affect the Navy.

Ships of the Operating Forces are organized under three different organizational systems. First, the majority of forces are assigned to Type Commanders for administrative control and for operational control during primary and intermediate training phases. Second, these same forces are assigned to Fleet Commanders, for advanced training and operations. Third, some elements of these forces are further assigned to Task Force Organizations for specific operations and missions.

Organization

1102. TYPE ORGANIZATION. The first system of organization with which the young officer will come into contact is the Type Organization.

FIGURE 1101. The USS *Carpenter* (DD-825) pulls away from the USS *Constellation* (CVA-64) after refueling at sea.

All ships are organized into broad categories under commanders whose titles are self-explanatory, such as Amphibious, Destroyer, Mine, Submarine, Air, etc. Some Type Commanders command two types, as Commander Cruiser-Destroyer Force, Pacific Fleet. Each type command contains further administrative sub-divisions such as Flotillas, Squadrons, and Divisions or Air Wings, Air Groups, and Squadrons. Normal administration is carried on by this organization, and a ship or unit is always under the administrative control of the appropriate Type Commander, even though under the operational control of a Fleet or Task Force Commander. Normally a ship or unit remains under the operational control of its Type Commander during primary and intermediate training and upon completion of these phases of its training cycle is shifted to the operational control of a Fleet Commander.

1103. FLEET ORGANIZATION. There are four regularly constituted fleets—the First and Seventh Fleets in the Pacific under the Commander in Chief, Pacific Fleet, and the Second and Sixth Fleets in the Atlantic under the Commander in Chief, Atlantic Fleet. Under normal peacetime procedures the Commander First Fleet exercises operational control over all forces on the Pacific Coast and the Commander

Seventh Fleet exercises operational control over certain forces in the Far East. Similarly in the Atlantic, Commander Second Fleet exercises operational control over all forces in the Atlantic and Commander Sixth Fleet exercises operational control over certain forces in the Mediterranean.

1104. TASK FORCE ORGANIZATION. Only rarely does the task to be performed by the Navy lend itself to the use of the foregoing organizations. In order to provide flexibility of organization and ease of communications, the Task Force Organization (or more properly the Task Fleet Organization) was formed during World War II. Under this system a flexible structure is provided consisting of Fleets further divided into Forces, Groups, Units and Elements. Each sub-division has a numbered designation and appropriate communication call signs. When a Task Fleet Commander is assigned a task by higher authority, he can then assign necessary forces under his command to accomplish the task. He assigns the officers to command an appropriate block of the Task Organization. The Task Commander reassigns the forces assigned to him to appropriate sub-divisions of the organization and he then has a flexible, immediately ready organization. The Task Organization is adaptable to any magnitude of organization.

A typical Task Fleet numbering system would be one in which the Commander of the Sixth Fleet would assign his major forces to numbered forces, such as his striking forces to TF 60, his amphibious forces to TF 61, his service forces to TF 62, and so forth.

Within each force he would then assign logical sub-divisions of that force to Task Groups; for example, within Task Force 60 would be TG 60.1, Carrier Group; TG 60.2, Heavy Support Force; and so forth.

Within each Task Group, further sub-division produces Task Units. Task Group 60.1, the Carrier Group, would then be sub-divided into TU 60.1, Carrier Unit, and so forth.

Each Task Unit may be divided into Task Elements. In this case TU 60.1.2, Destroyer Screen Unit, would become TE 60.1.21, Advanced Screen Element, and TE 60.1.22, Rescue Destroyer Unit. Note that elements are formed by adding a second number to the unit number without using a decimal.

The chain of command can be determined at a glance. Changes, additions, and deletions can be made easily by dispatch.

1105. HIGHER COMMAND ARRANGEMENTS. Superimposed upon the

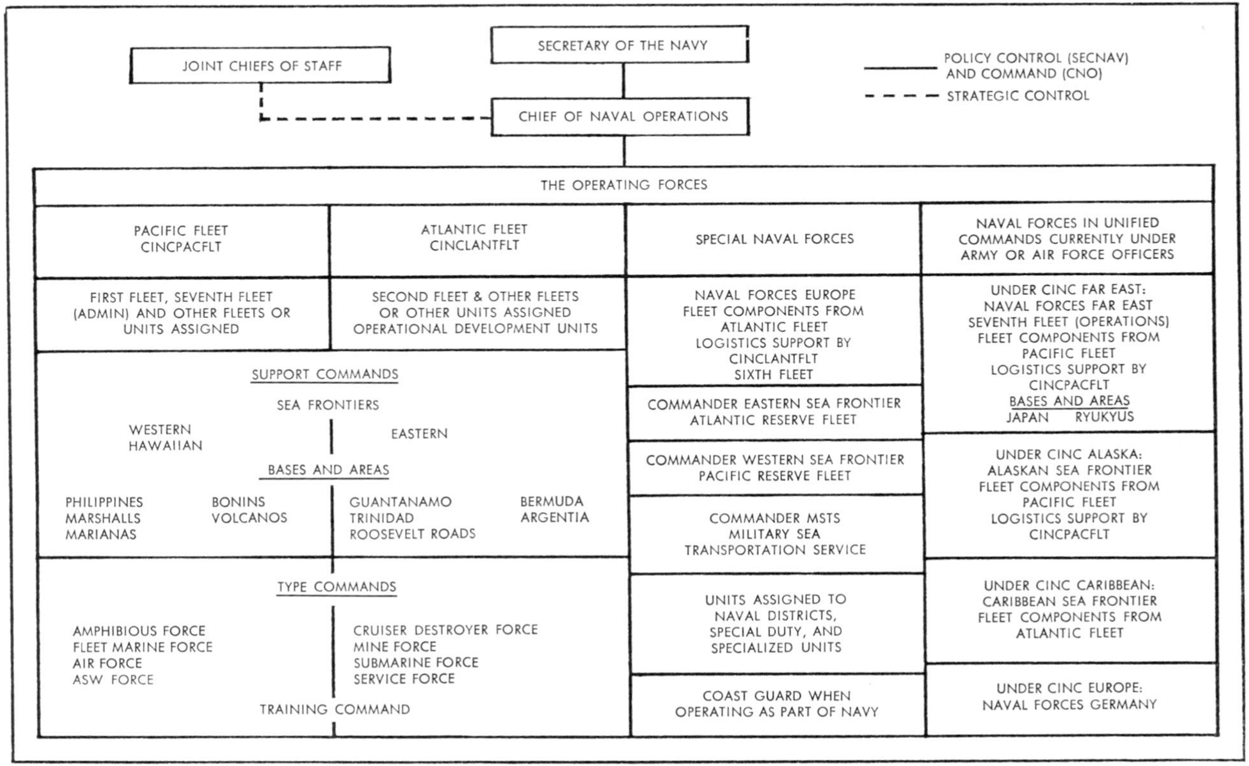

JOINT CHIEFS OF STAFF

SECRETARY OF THE NAVY

CHIEF OF NAVAL OPERATIONS

POLICY CONTROL (SECNAV) AND COMMAND (CNO)
— — — STRATEGIC CONTROL

THE OPERATING FORCES

PACIFIC FLEET CINCPACFLT

FIRST FLEET, SEVENTH FLEET (ADMIN) AND OTHER FLEETS OR UNITS ASSIGNED

SUPPORT COMMANDS

SEA FRONTIERS
WESTERN
HAWAIIAN
EASTERN

BASES AND AREAS
PHILIPPINES
MARSHALLS
MARIANAS
BONINS
VOLCANOS
GUANTANAMO
TRINIDAD
ROOSEVELT ROADS
BERMUDA
ARGENTIA

TYPE COMMANDS
AMPHIBIOUS FORCE
FLEET MARINE FORCE
AIR FORCE
ASW FORCE
CRUISER DESTROYER FORCE
MINE FORCE
SUBMARINE FORCE
SERVICE FORCE
TRAINING COMMAND

ATLANTIC FLEET CINCLANTFLT

SECOND FLEET & OTHER FLEETS OR OTHER UNITS ASSIGNED OPERATIONAL DEVELOPMENT UNITS

SPECIAL NAVAL FORCES

NAVAL FORCES EUROPE FLEET COMPONENTS FROM ATLANTIC FLEET LOGISTICS SUPPORT BY CINCLANTFLT SIXTH FLEET

COMMANDER EASTERN SEA FRONTIER ATLANTIC RESERVE FLEET

COMMANDER WESTERN SEA FRONTIER PACIFIC RESERVE FLEET

COMMANDER MSTS MILITARY SEA TRANSPORTATION SERVICE

UNITS ASSIGNED TO NAVAL DISTRICTS, SPECIAL DUTY, AND SPECIALIZED UNITS

COAST GUARD WHEN OPERATING AS PART OF NAVY

NAVAL FORCES IN UNIFIED COMMANDS CURRENTLY UNDER ARMY OR AIR FORCE OFFICERS

UNDER CINC FAR EAST: NAVAL FORCES FAR EAST SEVENTH FLEET (OPERATIONS) FLEET COMPONENTS FROM PACIFIC FLEET LOGISTICS SUPPORT BY CINCPACFLT BASES AND AREAS JAPAN RYUKYUS

UNDER CINC ALASKA: ALASKAN SEA FRONTIER FLEET COMPONENTS FROM PACIFIC FLEET LOGISTICS SUPPORT BY CINCPACFLT

UNDER CINC CARIBBEAN: CARIBBEAN SEA FRONTIER FLEET COMPONENTS FROM ATLANTIC FLEET

UNDER CINC EUROPE: NAVAL FORCES GERMANY

FIGURE 1102. Organization of the Operating Forces of the Navy.

basic organizations heretofore described are certain higher command arrangements. The young officer first reporting will not need to know them in detail. However, these arrangements are presented here for information. Figure 1102 gives the basic structure of these arrangements.

The assignment of Sea Frontier Commanders to higher echelons of command is as follows: Commander Eastern Sea Frontier is assigned to the Command of CinCLantFlt; and Commanders Hawaiian and Western Sea Frontiers to the command of CinCPacFlt. However, CNO retains command of Commanders Eastern and Western Sea Frontiers for the purpose of exercising military command over component naval districts for uniformity and, currently, for command of the two reserve fleets. Additionally, ComWestSeaFron is directly under CNO for the operational control of assigned Military Sea Transportation Service units (MSTS and Navy allocated or chartered merchant vessels). Under the Unified Command Plan, Commanders Caribbean and Alaskan Sea Frontiers are assigned, respectively, to the Commanders in Chief, Caribbean and Alaska.

Subject to the authority and direction of CNO, the Commander, MSTS, exercises direction, authority, and control over the Military Sea Transportation Service.

Units assigned to naval districts and river commands, and a few on independent duty not otherwise assigned, are under CNO directly, or in the case of naval districts, through the Commandant.

Under the Unified Command Plan, the Naval Forces Europe are under the operational control of the Commander in Chief Europe, at present an Army officer so designated by the Joint Chiefs of Staff.

As CNO directs, naval components are assigned from the Pacific Fleet to the Seventh Fleet, to the Naval Forces Far East, and to the Alaskan Sea Frontier. These are logistically supported by CinCPacFlt. CNO similarly directs the assignment of naval components to the Naval Forces Europe, to the Southern Command and to the Caribbean Sea Frontier from the Atlantic Fleet. CinClantFlt provides logistic support to Naval Forces Europe.

1106. ALLIED ORGANIZATIONS. The United States is a member of the United Nations Organization and is a signatory to numerous pacts and agreements. Many of our agreements commit us to the use of armed force in the event of attack on our allies. Under some agreements we have committed ourselves to provide components of armed forces in advance of armed attack. Obviously, a naval officer in this age must have a thorough understanding of international politics and must be conversant with our agreements and obligations. While a full study of all our agreements is impracticable here, a summary of the most important is given.

Rio Pact, 1947.—The Inter-American Treaty of Reciprocal Assistance was signed with certain Latin American republics. All members agreed that an armed attack against an American state shall be considered an attack against all American states. All signatories are committed to meeting the attack.

NATO Pact, 1949. The North Atlantic Treaty was signed by the United States, Canada, Great Britain, France, Italy, Norway, Denmark, Belgium, the Netherlands, Luxembourg, Portugal, and Iceland. Greece and Turkey acceded to the pact in 1952 and Germany joined in 1955. Signatory parties agreed to come to the aid of any party attacked and that an attack against one or more parties either in Europe or North America shall be considered an attack against all parties. Since this pact requires the largest U. S. effort to implement, it will be considered further at the end of this section.

Philippine Pact, 1951. Under this pact the United States and the Philippine Republic agree to stand together if attacked.

Japanese Pacts, 1951, 1954, and 1960. In 1951 the United States and Japan signed an agreement providing for the stationing of certain U. S. forces in Japan, and in 1954 a mutual defense pact was signed for the purpose of assisting Japanese rearmament. In 1960 a Treaty of Mutual Cooperation and Security was signed. This 10-year treaty placed United States-Japanese relations on a basis of complete equality and mutual understanding. Japan continued to grant the United States the use of bases in Japan, but with the requirement that the United States consult with Japan prior to making major changes in equipment based in Japan or in the use of bases for the conduct of military combat operations undertaken from Japan.

Korean Pact, 1953. This pact provides for United States armed aid to Korea in the event of attack and provides for stationing of U. S. forces in Korea.

Spanish Pact, 1953. The Spanish pact provides for development and use by the U. S. of certain bases on Spanish soil.

Southeast Asia Collective Defense Treaty, 1954 (SEATO). This pact provides for mutual aid in order to develop resistance to subversion or attack. It was signed by the United States, Great Britain, France, Aus-

SUPREME HEADQUARTERS ALLIED POWERS EUROPE
Casteau, Belgium

Allied Forces Northern Europe
Kolsaas, Norway
Allied Land Forces Norway
Oslo, Norway
Tactical Air Force
South Norway
Homenkollen, Norway
Naval Forces
Scandanavian Approaches
Stavanger, Norway
Allied Forces
Baltic Approaches
Karup, Denmark
Naval Forces
Kiel-Holtenau, Germany
Air Forces
Karup, Denmark
Land Forces Jutland
Rendsburg, Germany
Allied Task Forces
North Norway
Bodö, Norway
Tactical Air Force
Bodö, Norway
Naval Forces
Bodö, Norway
Land Forces
Oslo. Norway

Allied Forces Central Europe
Brunssum, Netherlands
Northern Army Group
Munich, Germany
Central Army Group
Seckenheim, Germany
Second Allied Tactical
Air Force
Munich, Germany
Fourth Allied Tactical
Air Force
Ramstein, Germany
United Kingdom
Air Defense Region
Stanmore, England
Ace Mobile Force Land
Seckenheim, Germany

Allied Forces Southern Europe
Naples, Italy
Allied Land Forces
Southeast Europe
Izmir, Turkey
Allied Land Forces
Southern Europe
Verona, Italy
Naval Striking and
Support Forces
Southern Europe
Naples, Italy
Allied Air Force
Southern Europe
Naples, Italy
Fifth Allied
Tactical Air Force
Vicenza, Italy
Sixth Allied
Tactical Air Force
Izmir, Turkey
Allied Naval Forces
Southern Europe
Malta
Gibraltar-Mediterranean
Area
Gibraltar
Western Mediterranean
Area
Malta
Central Mediterranean
Area
Naples, Italy
U.S. Fleet Air Wing
Mediterranean
Naples, Italy
Eastern Mediterranean
Area
Athens, Greece
Southeast Mediterranean
Area
Malta
Northeast Mediterranean
Area
Ankara, Turkey
Submarines—Mediterranean
Malta

FIGURE 1103. Organization of the Supreme Allied Command Europe.

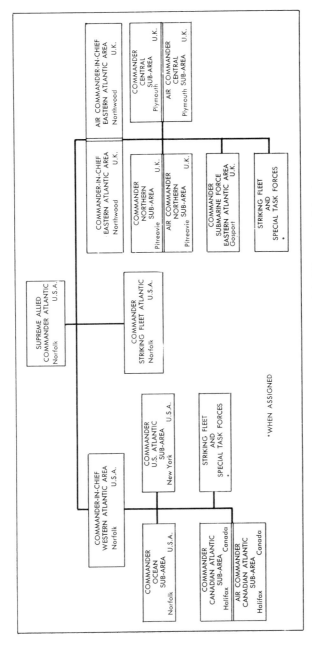

FIGURE 1104. Organization of the Allied Command, Atlantic.

tralia, New Zealand, the Philippine Republic, Thailand, and Pakistan.

Other Agreements. The United States is a party to many other agreements providing military assistance to various countries.

NATO. As stated previously, our largest international commitment as far as armed forces are concerned is to the North Atlantic Treaty Organization. All naval officers should study the book *NATO, The First Five Years, 1949-1954,* by Lord Ismay, for a complete understanding of the complexities of this organization. Figures 1103 and 1104 give the organizations of the Allied Command Europe and the Allied Command Atlantic. The United States contributes heavily to the Staffs of these organizations and provides armed forces as components of these commands.

Employment

1107. EMPLOYMENT SCHEDULES. We have reviewed the several organizational systems through which the Chief of Naval Operations exercises command. Obviously it is not practicable for the Chief of Naval Operations to direct the movements of several hundred naval units on a daily basis. He therefore delegates authority to subordinate commanders to direct necessary movements. He issues an over-all general employment plan which lists the major exercises, deployments, and other commitments expected. He issues a Fleet Operating Policy which gives general procedures and policy to be followed by subordinate com-

FIGURE 1105. A task unit engages in antisubmarine warfare training.

manders in implementing this schedule, and he further promulgates an overhaul schedule.

With the foregoing information in hand, the Fleet Commanders are able to promulgate annual employment schedules which list major categories of assignments for ships of their fleets for an entire year. Quarterly schedules are customarily issued which incorporate the latest known changes and additional details.

Type Commanders are then able to promulgate their own annual employment schedule and quarterly employment schedules using the schedules of their superior commanders as guides. The Type Commander's employment schedule is generally quite detailed and constitutes authority for unit commanders and commanding officers to make required movements.

In summary, each descending echelon implements the schedule of the senior echelons in such a manner that an over-all training schedule is carried out for advanced fleet training, and so that units of the fleet will progress through primary and intermediate stages of training in such a manner as to be prepared for advanced training at the proper time. Thus, highly trained units of the fleets are prepared for deployment and for meeting the Navy's many commitments. The detailed methods whereby this is accomplished will be discussed in succeeding sections.

1108. FLEET TRAINING CYCLES. Ships and squadrons of the Navy deploy to meet overseas commitments in regular cycles. The periods of

FIGURE 1106. Fleet training involves flight operations from carriers.

deployment are chosen so as to be long enough to take fullest advantage of the unit's advanced state of training, but not so long as to constitute undue hardship upon the unit's personnel. The cycle is based on the unit's overhaul schedule and commences with this period. Upon completion of overhaul the unit commences refresher training, a period of progressive elementary training during which the new personnel acquired during overhaul can be shaken down and integrated into the ship's company. This period usually lasts about 6 weeks and is followed by a brief post-shakedown overhaul. The unit then commences a period of intermediate training under its Type Commander followed by an advanced training period. Upon completion of this phase, the unit is given a short period to prepare for overseas movement and is then deployed for a period ranging from 4½ to 7 months. After deployment the unit is given a leave and upkeep period during which many new officers and men will probably be received. This change requires that additional primary and intermediate training be scheduled again before advanced training. The unit is then sometimes deployed for a second time, and sometimes is used to meet local advanced exercise commitments. At the conclusion of this phase of the cycle, yard overhaul is again scheduled. Aviation units follow generally similar cycles but do not, of course, require yard overhauls, and conduct most of their primary and intermediate training from shore bases.

A typical training cycle for a destroyer is given here:

MONTHS OF CYCLE	EMPLOYMENT
0-3	Shipyard overhaul. Ready for sea period last 10 days
4-5	Refresher training
6	Post-shakedown availability
7	Type training
8	Advanced training (on defense exercise)
9-13	Transit; deployment
14-15	Return transit; post-deployment leave period
16	Type training; services
17-19	Hunter-killer force
20	Prepare for overseas deployment
21-25	Transit; deployment; return transit
26	Post-deployment leave
27	Material inspection; upkeep
28-30	Shipyard overhaul

1109. SHIP OVERHAULS. Shipyard overhauls are controlled by two factors. *First,* the ship's need of a regular, periodic overhaul. The Chief of Naval Operations has determined that there is an ideal interval between successive overhauls. This interval must be short enough to ensure that major items of maintenance and alterations and improve-

FIGURE 1107. Fleet oiler refueling destroyers at sea.

ments do not go too long without accomplishment and long enough to assure that maximum use is made of the ship's capability before expenditure of overhaul funds. *Second,* economical use of all naval shipyards and repair facilities must be planned so that repair activities are neither overcrowded nor partially idle. These two factors are reconciled in an annual overhaul schedule published by the Chief of Naval Operations. For each type, a length of overhaul is fixed and a maximum period between overhauls is determined. For example, a destroyer has a 3-month overhaul with a 24-month period between overhauls. Larger ships have correspondingly longer periods. During wartime or peacetime emergencies, these periods are lengthened as necessary. An attempt is made to give smaller ships priority for overhaul near home ports.

During an overhaul period, essential maintenance is accomplished, major repairs are undertaken, and alterations and improvements are made. The number of these items undertaken depends on time and money available for the ship. Planning for such an event commences long before entry to the shipyard and involves all ship's officers.

The ship's routine is altered considerably in a naval shipyard. Many officers and men are ordered away to schools and training activities on temporary additional duty. Much of the ship is uninhabitable and it often becomes necessary to move some of the officers and crew to barracks ashore.

After completion of overhaul a period of approximately 10 days, known as a "readiness for sea" period, is scheduled to enable the ship to re-load equipment, make necessary calibrations, and otherwise to prepare for sea.

1110. TYPE COMPETITIONS. A competitive system of conducting and scoring certain exercises and inspections has been traditional in our Navy for many years, except for war periods. Such a system provides a competitive stimulus for individual ship personnel, a morale booster in the form of awards, a convenient measurement for unit and type commanders to use in assessing readiness of their ships, and an over-all indicator to the Chief of Naval Operations as to readiness of the fleets. The current form of competition is organized on a basis of intra-type competition. Each class of ship competes only with the other ships of its type. The Chief of Naval Operations has promulgated basic rules for

FIGURE 1108. In joint operations the naval task force lands the Army assault troops at Kiska.

the competition together with a standard scoring system, certain standard exercises for each type, and a system of awards.

Scoring. All phases of the competition are scored on a "word" basis, such as Outstanding, Excellent, etc., with a corresponding numerical system prescribed for convenience in calculation. A weighting system is used to give each exercise and each department proper weight. Using this system, each ship of a type can be described simply by the use of a word, and can be compared in detail with other ships, using a numerical score.

Exercises. General standards and scoring rules and methods of conducting, observing, and reporting exercises are prescribed by the Chief of Naval Operations. Each Type Commander then prescribes certain preparatory noncompetitive exercises followed by a series of competitive exercises to be completed by each ship each competitive (fiscal) year. The scheduling and conducting of these exercises is then carried out by unit commanders.

Awards. At the end of the competitive year, awards are presented to those ships standing highest in the competition. Normally about 10 per cent of all ships are awarded the right to display a Battle Efficiency Award pennant and a white block "E" on the bridge structure. Additional "E" awards are authorized for certain outstanding departments regardless of the over-all standing of the ship concerned. Awards are made at a suitable ceremony and are displayed until the end of the next competitive year.

The young officer should keep well informed of all aspects of the type competition. Knowledge of methods of scoring is important. As

FIGURE 1109. The Fleet Marine Force is an essential part of the Operating Forces of the Navy.

in computing income tax, a ship is supposed to take advantage of benefits in the scoring system to the fullest extent possible. Naturally, no form of sharp practice should be used, but you should know in what part of a prescribed range band your ship can shoot best if you are in the weapons department, and what bearings give you best radar coverage if you are in the operations department. You would need to have and would use this knowledge in war; determining it and using it in competition is therefore a part of readiness.

1111. DEPLOYMENTS. "The battle is the payoff." Deployment of naval units is a peacetime form of preparation for battle. In the present age, the first overt military moves of war may be made close to or over our own borders—by long-range air attack, submarine-launched guided missile attack, or by long-range missile attack. In these cases, for adequate defense it would be necessary to have all naval units as nearly ready for war as possible, whether located in coastal waters or overseas.

FIGURE 1110. USS *Hammerberg* (DE-1015) fires Weapon Alfa.

While highly desirable, such a procedure is not completely feasible. Some units must be reduced in readiness for overhaul, personnel changes, etc. These units normally remain in coastal waters. Since the probable area of international trouble is limited attack or war at overseas locations, the United States keeps armed forces deployed in areas as close as possible to probable trouble areas. The Navy's part in this over-all plan calls for keeping certain numbers of units deployed overseas. Some few units have their home ports changed to the deployment area and spend the 2-year period between overhauls in that area, with families transported overseas at government expense. The majority of deployed units move to deployment areas either once or twice in a training cycle. Deployment periods vary with area and type.

When deployed, most units operate as part of the Sixth Fleet in the Mediterranean or the Seventh Fleet in the Far East. About 60 per cent of a deployment period is spent in operations, generally of an advanced nature; the remaining 40 per cent is spent in making visits of courtesy to foreign ports in the area, using these visits to provide leave and upkeep time.

Units transiting to overseas areas are generally sailed in a group for training.

Successful completion of a deployment should be a great source of satisfaction to a naval officer. He will have participated in the execution of foreign policy by his very presence overseas, and will have taken part in naval exercises of the most advanced nature. In addition to these professional attainments, he will have added to his personal education and experience and will have enjoyed travel and visits to foreign lands.

1112. THE IMPORTANCE OF SEA DUTY. The United States Navy is responsible for maintaining freedom of the seas in peacetime and control of the sea in wartime. This prime responsibility requires that its commanders, its officers and its men have intimate, up-to-date knowledge of both the sea and the ships which sail upon it. Such knowledge comes only from the constant practice of the art of going to sea.

While it is true that senior naval officers bear heavy responsibility in matters of grand strategy, planning, and the budget while ashore, the average naval officer of the lower and middle grades *does not belong ashore.* Periods of shore duty for these officers are for functional training, formal education, teaching, and other kindred types of duty. Shore duty is therefore not an end in itself, but a form of preparation for added responsibility *at sea.*

To perform effectively at sea, a naval officer must first be profession-

FIGURE 1111. Fleet amphibious landings are an integral part of naval operations afloat.

ally skilled in leading men, using technical equipment, and in handling ships and aircraft. He must spend many years learning how to apply these basic skills to ships and aircraft at sea.

He must know the purpose of his ship's employment and, when deployed, the reason for his deployment. Further, he must know the reason for his visits to foreign ports and the tensions and difficulties to be expected in the areas to be visited. He must thoroughly comprehend the larger aspects of fleet and area organizations and operations, so that, in his more limited field, he can contribute to the over-all mission of his ship, his unit, and the Navy. This contribution he can make best *at sea*.

CHAPTER **12**

Ship's Organization and Regulations

Organization is more than arranging officers in blocks and drawing policy and command control lines on a "flow chart." Organization must include the living embodiment of the principles of the "flow chart" in the daily affairs of the personnel of the command.

1201. GENERAL CONSIDERATIONS. One of your first tasks will be to learn all about the organization of your ship. Each ship prepares and publishes its own Ship's Organization Book, based upon the provisions of Shipboard Procedures (NWP-50) and the type organization published by the type commander. Ship's organizations vary in detail from ship to ship, even among sister ships. The following notes provide general information on which to base your study of the organization of your own ship.

The usual organization of a combatant ship provides for the organization of all hands for the following purposes: battle, emergencies and other general evolutions, administrative purposes, operation of the ship, sufficient force on board at all times to care for the safety, operation, and maintenance of the ship, and various subsidiary or special purposes.

The basic organization is that for battle. The organization for emergencies and other general evolutions and the organization for administrative purposes correspond as nearly as practicable to the organization for battle.

A ship's organization is issued to the end that, through the assignment of duties and responsibilities to individuals and to activities of the ship, coordination, precision, and smartness will follow; uncertainty and waste of time and effort will be avoided; and efficiency, high

337

morale, and loyalty will result. The basic principle of this organization and its administration is expressed in the three words: *organize, deputize, supervise.*

The first requisite, to organize, is attained by the assignment of specific duties to departments, divisions, and individuals for the accomplishment of all usual ship's tasks and for the handling of emergencies.

A good organization will provide organized responsibility. Such responsibility rests finally and unequivocally in the commander and is expressed by him through his executive officer. This ultimate responsibility cannot be shifted to another by orders, organization, or oral quibbling. It is continuous and only ceases upon death or detachment.

A good organization will be of the utmost simplicity consistent with the necessities of the command it administers. Its provisions should not be so definite as to limit the scope of subordinates, but rather should be general and flexible enough to provide for any possible contingency. Too many organizations run into many pages on a subject where 25 words would suffice. But an organization must be complete enough to lay down general principles by which members of the command may govern themselves without having to resort frequently to higher authority for minor decisions.

A command should be so organized as to provide ease of administration. In a correctly organized unit, administration should become a routine matter handled mainly by subordinates, leaving the Captain and Executive Officer free to give their thought and efforts to major considerations.

The second requisite, to deputize, is provided through the echelon of command, by which the authority necessary to vitalize the organization proceeds from the Captain down through subordinate officers to the lowest seaman. A good organization must be decentralized. The command, that lives and breathes only in the personality and forcefulness of a dynamic and vigorous captain, will fall apart upon his death, disability, or detachment to other duty. A good naval organization contemplates such changes as routine and provides for a continuity of administration.

In a well-organized naval unit, a considerable part of a commander's responsibility and authority will be delegated. His subordinates will be held responsible to the captain for affairs in their subdivisions and they will be provided by him with all the authority necessary to carry out their duties. It is the function of a ship's organization to state clearly and concisely the fields of responsibility of the subordinate and his commander and to delineate between the spheres of responsibility of the various subordinate officers.

A good organization also provides for, and encourages, initiative in subordinate leaders. Initiative follows naturally in an organization that affords proper decentralization. An over-organized, one-man administration stultifies the initiative. Where every possible contingency is provided for in a written organization or in ship's regulations and every minor decision is reserved to higher authority, the subordinate leader becomes a mechanical executor of the decrees of his seniors. Zeal and initiative are restricted and helpful suggestions are cut off at the source.

The third requisite, to supervise, must be met by all those in authority down through the echelon of command to ensure controlled functioning of the organization in its tasks.

Finally, an organization must be so constructed that it will seem to run itself, so that it will function in the absence or disability of its commander, and so administered that every member will receive a square deal. If this be accomplished, loyalty, zeal, earnestness, devotion to duty, and all of the other prime virtues so necessary in subordinates will follow in its train.

Departments and Activities. Under the Executive Officer, as the representative of the Captain, the tasks of the ship are assigned to the following departments and activities and by them further subdivided by divisions as described under this Division Organization:

Weapons Department.   Supply Department.
Operations Department.   Communications (in some ships).
Navigation Department.   Reactor Department (in some
Engineering Department.   ships).
Medical Department.

In appropriate types of ships, there may also be Air, Repair, Deck, and Dental Departments or a hospital.

1202. The commanding officer. Regardless of his rank, the Commanding Officer of a naval ship has full command and exercises authority and precedence over all officers and persons serving within his ship. The Navy Regulations direct the Commanding Officer to set a good example of virtue, honor, patriotism, and subordination. By the Regulations, he is also charged with the supervision of the conduct of all persons attached to the ship under his command or temporarily embarked therein. Should the Commanding Officer fail to suppress unlaw-

COMMANDING OFFICER

| Aide
Personnel Officer
Educational Services Officer | Legal Officer
Transport Quartermaster or Transportation Officer (if applicable) | Ship's Secretary
Chaplain
Chief Master at Arms |

Operations Department	Weapons (or Deck) Department[1]	Navigation Department	Air Department[3]	Engineering Department	Supply Department	Medical Department
Operations Officer Communication Officer Reg. Pub. Officer Signal Officer Radio Officer CIC Officer Intelligence Officer Radar Assistants Lookout & Recognition Officer Antisubmarine Warfare Officer (in ships not having AS armament installed) Aircraft Control Officer Electronic Repair Officer Meteorological Officer Communication, Lookout, and CIC Divisions	Weapons Officer[1] Assistant Weapons Officer, Assistant Fire Control Officer and other Assistants First Lieutenant[2] Assistants Aviation Officer in other than carriers & tenders Antisubmarine Officer (in AS ships) Marine Officer Main, Secondary & A.A. Battery Divisions Marine Detachment Aviation Division (if no Air Department)	Navigator Assistant Navigators Navigation Division	Air Officer Assistant Air Officer Flight Deck Officer Landing Signal Officer Aircraft Maintenance Off. Ordnance Off. Shops Officer Air Divisions Air Groups Aircraft Squadrons	Engineer Officer Main Propulsion Officer Damage Control Officer Electrical Officer Auxiliary, Repair Boiler, Main Engines, Divisions	Supply Officer Disbursing Officer Stores Officer Mess Officer Ship's Store Officer Supply Divisions	Medical Officer Medical Officers as required Medical Division

				Repair Department[4]	Dental Department	
				Repair Officer Assistant Repair Officers for Machinery, Hull, Instruments, Electronics, etc.	Dental Officer Dental Officers as required	

[1] Head of Department in ships whose offensive weapons are primarily ordnance or aircraft.
[2] Head of Department in other types.
[3] In aircraft carriers.
[4] In repair ships and tenders.

FIGURE 1201. Typical ship's organization of a large ship.

ful activities or conduct, he is liable to such punishment as a General Court-Martial may adjudge.

The Commanding Officer is required to maintain his ship in material readiness for war. To accomplish this, he should exercise his authority through his Executive Officer, who, with the assistance of the various heads of departments, prepares the organization of the ship and schedules and conducts exercises and drills designed to bring the ship to a high state of efficiency.

The Navy Regulations state that heads of departments should consult frequently with the Commanding Officer concerning the activities of their departments and he, in turn, should communicate to them and the other officers of the ship his plans for battle, in order that his subordinates may carry out his intentions intelligently and, in the event of his death or incapacitation, can follow the general plan. Such indoctrination of subordinates promotes unity of action.

When action is imminent or when engaged in battle, the crew are called to general quarters and the ship is made ready for action. The Commanding Officer should, in such circumstances, take his battle station in such a position in the ship as will enable him to fight the ship to the best advantage. Should the ship be lost, both custom and regulation require that the Captain of the ship be the last to leave.

Among the many responsibilities placed in the hands of the Commanding Officer are the following:

The punitive articles of the Uniform Code of Military Justice should be published monthly to the crew. This is designed to bring to the attention of the officers and men the provisions of law with respect to discipline and punishment under which the Navy operates.

The welfare and living conditions of the crew are a direct responsibility of the Commanding Officer. The Medical Officer of the ship assists the Commanding Officer to maintain the ship in a sanitary condition and provides for proper care of the sick. The Commanding Officer should ensure that provisions and stores are maintained and properly stowed.

Safety of the ship is at all times a primary consideration. Handling, stowage, and use of ammunition are special concerns of the Commanding Officer, as is the watertight integrity of the ship and the efficiency of the crew at damage control.

Although the Navigator is specifically charged with the safe navigation of the ship, the Commanding Officer cannot delegate his responsibility for the safety of the ship. He will cause the draft of the ship to be taken and recorded. Proper lookouts must be stationed to meet the existing conditions of weather and to provide the necessary alert for war conditions. The Commanding Officer should present in himself not only a capable naval officer but a competent mariner conversant with the necessities for safe navigation, the Rules of the Nautical Road, and, in wartime, he must possess complete information with regard to mine fields, wrecks, submarines reported, changes in lights and buoyage, and other information which affect the safety of the ship.

Under the direction of the Commanding Officer, the Executive Officer is charged with the training and instruction of the officers in his ship. The Educational Services Officer assists the Executive Officer in this regard through the planning board for training. The Commanding Officer should concern himself that all officers improve themselves by specific study, using assignments and notebooks as required to ensure that officers are preparing themselves for their duties. Whenever possible the Commanding Officer should encourage his Executive Officer and other officers to handle the ship, in order to further their training for command.

For further discussion of the duties of the Commanding Officer, see Chapter 15.

1203. THE EXECUTIVE OFFICER. As the title indicates, the Executive Officer is the executive arm for the Commanding Officer of the ship. In order to carry out his Captain's wishes, the Executive Officer must be thoroughly informed as to his policies and see that these policies are put into effect. In exercising his executive duties, the Executive Officer works through and with the heads of departments, who assist him in the organization, administration, operation, and fighting of the ship. The Executive Officer derives his authority from the Commanding Officer. When aboard ship, he is always on duty.

In order to perform his duties effectively, the Executive Officer must be familiar with every part of the ship. With the advice and assistance of heads of departments, he schedules and coordinates all ship's work, drills and exercises, organization, inspection of the ship, and is the chief police officer of the ship.

As personnel officer, the Executive Officer is assistant to the Commanding Officer for the morale of the crew. The Executive Officer investigates and reports to the Commanding Officer on all matters of discipline and conduct within the ship. In his office, the Executive Officer supervises the preparation of leave and liberty lists and the proper entries in all service records of the enlisted men.

To be alert to the changing state of affairs within the ship, the Executive Officer must keep in close touch with all the activities of the ship. He supervises and directs the heads of departments in the performance of their duties, taking special interest in the training and instruction of junior officers. Subject to the direction of the Commanding Officer, he is authorized to supervise and direct the officer of the deck in the performance of his duty and with regard to the general routine and duties of the ship.

Responsibility for the personnel and for the ship's routine, efficiency, and discipline lies mainly with the Executive Officer. He is responsible for the morale, welfare, and discipline of the crew and the assignment of officers and men and their records. With the Chaplain as his assistant, he must have an interest in religious matters and see that religious services and advice and counsel are available to the crew. He coordinates the work, training, and exercises of the ship and manages the routine. He supervises the ship's correspondence and legal matters affecting the ship and crew.

All matters of discipline and conduct of the crew are investigated by him and reported to the Commanding Officer. He approves the liberty list and leave papers of the crew.

When all hands are called for any evolution, except Quarters or General Quarters, he relieves the deck, but he is not required to stand a regular watch, although he may relieve the officer of the deck for short periods as a matter of accommodation.

Whenever the ship is cleared for action, the Officer of the Deck receives reports from the primary battle control stations and reports to the Commanding Officer that the ship is ready for action. Should the Captain be incapacitated, the Executive Officer is his relief. For this reason, his battle station should be in a location remote from the bridge or coning tower where he would escape a casualty disabling the Captain. In Destroyers, his battle station is normally in the Combat Information Center where he performs the functions of evaluator assisted by the Operations Officer; in larger ships, it is normally in the secondary ship-control station.

Assistants to the Executive Officer. In the smaller ships, the Executive Officer may have no assistants. In the larger ships, he usually has several to assist him in the performance of his varied duties.

Among these are an *Aide,* who is an Administrative Assistant, and a *Personnel Officer,* who relieve the Executive Officer of administrative details, the assignment of enlisted men, and record keeping. The *Educational Services Officer* assists the Executive Officer to discharge his duties with regard to the education and training of the crew. The *Ship's Secretary* assists with the ship's correspondence and maintains the office files. The *Chaplain* helps the Executive Officer with his responsibilities with regard to religious matters and moral leadership. He conducts divine services; arranges for participation of the crew in divine services on other ships and stations; officiates at baptisms, marriages, and funerals; visits the sick and imprisoned; and provides religious instruction and counsel to ship's personnel. He is often assigned additional duties which tend to promote the mental, moral, and physical welfare of the personnel. He assists in educational, athletic, and recreational programs; is available for counsel in personal or domestic matters; may supervise the ship's paper and library. During battle, he is usually assigned to a battle dressing station but is free to move about the ship to various battle stations.

1204. HEADS OF DEPARTMENTS. In the larger ships, heads of departments are detailed by the Chief of Naval Personnel by name. In smaller ships, the Commanding Officer makes such assignments. A head of department is the representative of the Commanding Officer in all matters pertaining to his department. All persons assigned to his department are subject to his orders.

As necessary, a head of department has a right, on all proper occasions, to communicate and confer with the Commanding Officer and receive orders directly from him. The condition of machinery and equipment and the need for major repairs are reported to the Captain by him. He is also required to keep the Executive Officer informed of all such matters.

The head of department assigns personnel to stations and duties within the department and supervises their work and training. He is responsible for their observance of security measures and safety precautions.

The proper operation, care, preservation, and maintenance of department equipment are his responsibility as are cleanliness and upkeep of spaces assigned. He frequently inspects both personnel and equipment and takes action to correct any factors that may interfere with the department's effectiveness.

He prepares bills and orders for the organization and operation of the department. He manages the allotments made to his department and must be zealous that these funds are wisely and economically expended. He must anticipate personnel and material needs and submit timely requests for fulfillment of his department's requirements. He keeps the records and submits the required reports of his department. Most important of all is full cooperation with other heads of departments in order that the work, training, and exercises of the ship may proceed smoothly and efficiently.

A head of department takes his battle station where he can best supervise and control the performance of action duties and responsibilities of his officers and men.

1205. THE OPERATIONS DEPARTMENT. The head of this department is entitled the *Operations Officer*. He is responsible, under the Commanding Officer, for the duties of a department head as described and especially for the collection, evaluation, and dissemination of combat and operational information required for the assigned missions and tasks of the ship. Except for responsibilities assigned to another officer, he is responsible for all other matters related to the operations of the ship and designated airborne aircraft.

Functions for which the Operations Officer is responsible include the conduct of visual and electronic exterior communication and search and electronic warfare. Assisted by the Communication and Intelligence Officers, control of registered publications and the collection and analysis of intelligence information come under the Operations Department. So do the collection, interpretation and dissemination of meteorological information.

The normal battle station of the Operations Officer is in the combat information center as evaluator or assistant evaluator of the information fed into that center, but the Commanding Officer may station him elsewhere if he feels that he can, there, better perform his battle duties.

As assistant to the Operations Officer, the *Communication Officer* is responsible for visual and electronic exterior communications and for related internal systems. Through his assistants, the *Signal Officer*, the *Radio Officer* and the *Registered Publication Officer*, he is responsible for the operation, care, and maintenance of visual and electronic exterior communication equipment and the procurement, care and handling of classified registered publications and devices issued to the ship. The Communication Officer acts as head of the coding board and is responsible for training of its members.

The *Combat Information Center Officer* assists the Operations Officer by collecting and disseminating combat and operational information and by the operation and care of such equipment as radar and underwater search gear on ships not having antisubmarine armament installed. The Meteorological Officer when assigned, is delegated the responsibility of providing information concerning present and anticipated weather conditions, sonar and radar propagation conditions, and sea and surf conditions. The Electronic Warfare Officer is responsible for the organization, supervision and planning of electronic warfare, both active and passive.

1206. WEAPONS (OR DECK) DEPARTMENT. Ships whose offensive characteristics are those primarily relating to ordnance or aircraft have a Weapons Department headed by the Weapons Officer whose responsibilities also embrace those pertaining to deck seamanship; the Weapons Officer in such case is assisted by the First Lieutenant. Other ships have a Deck Department whose head is the First Lieutenant; in such case the Weapons Officer is his assistant.

FIGURE 1202. Gunnery drill during training operations.

In small ships, the duties of the Weapons Officer and First Lieutenant may be combined.

Organized aviation units regularly attached to and embarked in a ship not having an Air Department are assigned to the Weapons Department and comprise the aviation division; such units retain their basic organization even when so assigned. Other divisions of the Weapons (or Deck) Department are the Marine detachment, and the main, secondary, and antiaircraft battery divisions.

Weapons Officer. In general, the Weapons Officer is charged primarily, under the Commanding Officer, with supervision and direction of the employment of the ordnance equipment and the equipment associated with deck seamanship.

Like all department heads, he is charged by Navy Regulations with a variety of duties peculiar to his department, in addition to those regularly assigned to department heads. Some of his most important tasks, as might be expected, are in connection with safety precautions necessary in the handling and stowage of ammunition. He must ensure that safety orders are posted in conspicuous places and that personnel adhere strictly to them. Thorough instruction and frequent drills in pertinent safety measures are required of him. Inspections and tests of ammunition and ammunition spaces as prescribed by the Commander of the Ordnance Systems Command are his responsibility as are the procurement, care, handling, stowage, accounting for and use of explosives.

In ships that do not have an Air Department, operations, such as launching and recovery, connected with assigned planes are functions of the Weapons or Deck Departments and are delegated to the Aviation Officer.

Operation, care, and maintenance of armament, electronic equipment, mine warfare equipment, and antisubmarine equipment when not otherwise assigned are functions of the Weapons Department. Deck seamanship, loading, and unloading operations, and any care or maintenance in connection with such operations are within the province of the Weapons Officer. He has charge of operation and upkeep of the ship's boats, except the engine and engine compartment, which are the responsibility of the Engineer Officer.

His battle station is as control officer of the ship's batteries or as directed by the Commanding Officer.

He may have as assistants, in addition to the First Lieutenant, the following: Antisubmarine Officer, Missile Officer, Nuclear Weapons Officer, Torpedo Officer, Ordnance Officer, Commanding Officer of the Marine Detachment and OinC of the DASH Detachment when embarked. The ship's function and operating condition determine the type and number of assistants assigned.

First Lieutenant. As previously stated, the First Lieutenant is the head of the Deck Department on ships not primarily concerned with offense through ordnance or aircraft. He is charged basically with the supervising and directing of the employment of equipment associated with deck seamanship and of ordnance equipment. Like all department heads he is responsible for the training, direction, and coordination of personnel assigned to his department, for the maintenance and submission of reports required, and for the care and upkeep of allotted spaces.

The remainder of his duties are similar to those described in the preceding section as belonging to the Weapons Officer, except that his main responsibilities are those concerned with deck seamanship, while those related to ordnance are of secondary importance, and are delegated to his assistant, the Weapons Officer, if assigned.

Other assistants may include a Cargo Officer and Boatswain. He may also have the assistants listed as assigned to the Weapons Officer in the previous section.

The battle station of the First Lieutenant is where he may best supervise the performance of deck functions; his assistant, the Weapons Officer, acts as control officer of the ship's batteries.

Marine Officer. The commanding officer of the ship's Marine detachment, although not a head of department, occupies a somewhat similar position with respect to the internal administration and security responsibilities of the Marines aboard. In a dual role, he is also one of the division officers of the Weapons Department, inasmuch as the Marine detachment is a regular part of the ship's company.

The Marine detachment commander is responsible to the ship's Captain for the efficiency of his detachment and for the phases of ship's internal administration that are applicable to the detachment. He is responsible to the department head for training conducted under his supervision and operation of such equipment, supplies, and spaces as are assigned to the Marine detachment by the head of department.

Marine Detachments Afloat. Marine detachments aboard larger ships form a separate division. In wartime, Marine detachments of varying size serve in many types of ships—battleships, carriers, heavy and light cruisers, and troop transports. Each Marine must volunteer, work, and train for the privilege of becoming a seagoing Marine.

Marines serve as orderlies for the ship's commanding officer or for other high-ranking naval officers aboard, and they also act as security guards at sea or in port. Marines may be detailed to other duties afloat, including but not limited to communications staff, liaison, guard, and aviation duty when so ordered by competent authority. Except as otherwise prescribed by law or regulation, the authority and responsibility of Marines so detailed are the same as for naval personnel serving in similar positions.

The functions of a Marine detachment in a Navy ship are as follows:

1. To provide a unit organized, trained, and equipped for operations ashore, as part of the ship's landing force, as part of a landing force of Marines from ships of a fleet or task force, or as an independent force for limited operations.

FIGURE 1203. A Marine detachment in a ship forms an integral part of the ship's company.

2. To provide gun crews.

3. To provide internal security for the ship.

In battle, the Marine detachment normally mans guns and fire-control stations of the anti-aircraft battery. The detachment is usually employed as a complete division in the battle organization of the ship.

Marines perform such all-hands evolutions as taking ammunition and provisioning ship, and maintain their own parts of the ship. In port, Marine sentries guard the ship gangways and the piers, as required.

Marine officers may be assigned as officer or junior officer of the deck in port. Underway, junior Marine officers may act as junior officers of the watch and specially qualified Marine officers may take the deck, although this is not usual.

1207. THE NAVIGATION DEPARTMENT. As head of the Navigation Department, the *Navigator* is directly responsible to the Commanding Officer for the safe navigation and piloting of the ship. He makes reports directly to the Commanding Officer and keeps the Operations Officer informed as to the position of the ship and other navigational matters. He advises the Commanding Officer and the officer of the deck as to the ship's movements and, if the ship is running into danger, as to a safe course to steer.

In order to carry out this phase of his duties effectively, he must maintain an accurate plot of the ship's position by astronomical, visual, electronic, or other appropriate means; study all available sources of information, prior to entering pilot waters, regarding navigation of the ship in such waters; give careful attention to the course of the ship and the depth of water when approaching land or shoals; maintain record books of all observations and computations made for the purpose of navigating the ship, with results and dates involved; report in writing to the Commanding Officer, when underway, the ship's position at stated intervals, and at such other times as the Commanding Officer may request; and procure and keep corrected and up to date all hydrographic and navigational charts, sailing directions, light lists, and other publications and devices for navigation as may be required.

He has responsibility for the operation, care, and maintenance of the navigational equipment. To this end he is required to determine daily, when the ship is underway and weather conditions permit, the error of the gyro and standard compasses and report the result in writing to the Commanding Officer. He also compensates the magnetic compasses and prepares tables of deviations, copies of which are posted at the appropriate compass stations. Accuracy of ship's chronometers and clocks is his responsibility also, and he is required to ensure that electronic navigational equipment used by him is kept in proper adjustment and that calibration curves or tables are maintained and checked at prescribed intervals.

The Navigator is responsible for the care and proper operation of the steering gear in general (except the steering engine and steering motors).

Daily, and oftener if necessary, the Navigator inspects the deck log and the quartermaster's notebook. He is required to take corrective action if necessary to ensure that they are properly kept. He also prepares such reports and records as are necessary in connection with his navigational duties, including those pertaining to the compasses, hydrography, oceanography, and meteorology.

He relieves the officer of the deck as authorized or directed by the Commanding Officer.

1208. THE AIR DEPARTMENT. Aircraft carriers and seaplane tenders have an Air Department. Ships that do not have such a department may have an aviation division, which is a part of the Weapons or Deck Department, and the title of the head of this division is Aviation Officer. The title of the head of the Air Department is the *Air Officer*. This department may be composed of air divisions, air wings, air groups, and aircraft squadrons.

The Air Officer is charged primarily with launching and landing operations. He is also responsible for the servicing, maintenance and repair of aircraft. Other aircraft and airborne electronic equipment assigned to the Air Department must also be maintained and repaired by his personnel. His operation and maintenance duties extend to all aircraft-handling equipment such as elevators, cranes, catapults and arresting gear, and seadrome equipment.

Not only servicing but also arming of assigned aircraft must be ensured by the Air Officer. Launching, landing, and handling operations of planes are his responsibility as are any visual traffic-control measures necessary for safe, effective performance of these operations. The fuels and lubricants and the operations, maintenance, and security of the related systems are in charge of the Air Officer, who also maintains any records in connection with fuel and submits them daily to the Commanding Officer.

The Air Officer must undertake aircraft-salvage operations in case of crash and may on occasion have opportunity to put into operation his knowledge of fire fighting. Safety precautions must be enforced by him and he must ensure that, in those parts of the ship where aircraft are stowed and handled and where inflammables or explosives assigned to his department are stowed, such precautions are posted. Drill and instruction in safety matters affecting his personnel must be carried on by him.

Normally, the Air Officer's battle station on a carrier is in a location where he can best control flight-deck operations; in a seaplane tender, he is located where he can control aircraft and servicing and maintenance operations.

His assistants may include the following: Assistant Air Officer, Flight Deck Officer, Catapult Officer, Arresting Gear Officer, Hanger Deck Officer, Aviation Fuels Officer and Aircraft Handing Officer.

1209. THE ENGINEERING DEPARTMENT. The head of the Engineering Department is designated the *Engineer Officer* and is called the Chief Engineer. He performs the duties regularly assigned to a department head; and in addition is responsible under the Captain for the operation, care and maintenance of all propulsion and auxiliary machinery, for the control of damage and, upon request from the head of the department concerned, for the accomplishment of any repairs that are beyond the capacity of the repair personnel or equipment of other departments.

Specifically, Navy Regulations charges him with the operation, care, and maintenance of all machinery, piping systems, and electric and electronic devices not otherwise assigned. Hull and machinery repair are within his province as are the furnishing of power, light, ventilation. heat, refrigeration, compressed air and water. Maintenance of underwater fittings is assigned to the Engineering Department. Any fuels and lubricants not assigned to other departments for care, stowage, and use are the responsibility of this department. The engineering log and the engineer's bell book are also kept here.

Various assistants may be assigned to help the Chief Engineer carry on the functions of his department. These may include the Main Propulsion Assistant, Damage Control Officer and Electrical Officer.

In battle, the Engineer Officer is usually stationed in main control.

Assistants. Main Propulsion Assistant. The Main Propulsion Assistant, when assigned, is responsible under the Engineer Officer for the operation, care, and maintenance of the ship's propulsion machinery, its auxiliaries, and any other auxiliaries assigned.

By Navy Regulations this officer must ensure the effective operation of the main engines and boilers and assigned auxiliaries. Frequent examinations must be made of machinery and of equipment, and repairs and adjustments must be effected, subject to required authorization.

Supervision and operation of the main engines are his responsibility when getting underway or at other times when unusual care is required. He must ensure that boiler fires are not lighted or secured without permission from the Captain, except in cases of emergency. He must ensure that main engines are not turned except in obedience to a signal from or by permission of the officer of the deck.

His responsibilities also extend to the care, stowage, and use of bunker fuels, except those for aircraft, and to the operation, maintenance and security of the related systems.

To him the Chief Engineer delegates the duties connected with keeping the engineering log and the engineer's bell book and those pertaining to various other engineering records.

The Main Propulsion Assistant's battle station is normally at the secondary main-propulsion control station.

He may be assigned officer and other assistants.

Damage Control Assistant. When a Damage Control Assistant is assigned, he is responsible, under the Chief Engineer, for establishing and maintaining an effective damage control organization, and for supervising repairs to the hull and machinery, except when they are otherwise assigned.

His responsibilities in the prevention and control of damage include control of stability, list, and trim. He is required to supervise placing the ship in the condition of closure ordered by the Captain and must ensure that appropriate closure classifications are assigned and conspicuously marked upon or adjacent to the objects to which they apply. He coordinates and supervises the carrying out of prescribed tests of compartments and spaces for tightness. He prepares and maintains bills for the control of damage and stability and ensures that correct compartment check-off lists are posted. Further, the training of ship's personnel in damage control is assigned to him; this includes instruction in emergency repairs and nonmedical defensive measures against gas and similar weapons.

The operation, care, and maintenance of auxiliary machinery, piping, and drainage systems not otherwise assigned are in his charge. Similarly, he is responsible for the ship repair facilities and the repair of hull and boats.

He may be assigned officer assistants to aid him in the performance of his duties.

The Damage Control Assistant's battle station is usually at the main damage-control station.

1210. THE MEDICAL DEPARTMENT. The head of the Medical Department is the *Medical Officer.* He is normally the senior officer of the Medical Corps attached to and serving on board a ship.

The Medical Officer is directly responsible, under the Commanding Officer, for maintaining the health of the personnel of the command and must make the necessary inspections to ensure it. He also acts in an advisory capacity to the Commanding Officer in matters pertaining to sanitation and hygiene.

Not only must the Medical Officer furnish medical care and treatment to personnel assigned to the command, he must, when directed by the Captain, provide these services to such other persons of the United States Armed Forces as may require them.

When circumstances require, he cooperates with local health authorities in matters affecting the health of the community. He assists such authorities in quarantine inspections and also advises the Commanding Officer regarding the medical aspects of pertinent quarantine regulations.

Although the Supply Officer receives, delivers, and ships medical and dental supplies, the Medical Officer is charged with procuring, inspecting, stowing, issuing, and transferring of medical supplies. (Dental supplies are similarly handled by the Dental Officer.)

In addition to performing the usual instructional responsibilities of department heads, the Medical Officer must ensure that all ship's personnel are adequately trained in administering first aid.

He works in close cooperation with the Dental Officer. If, in the course of a physical examination, he notes dental conditions that need attention, he refers such matters to the Dental Officer.

The Medical Officer is stationed in battle where he can best serve and supervise attendance of the wounded.

The Dental Department. The head of the Dental Department is the *Dental Officer.* He is the senior officer of the Dental Crops attached to and serving on board and is directly responsible to the Commanding Officer for all professional, technical, and administrative matters connected with dental services. He and his subordinates may in emergency situations and in other circumstances prescribed in the organization of the command for battle, perform such duties for the care of the sick and wounded as the Commanding Officer may direct.

In those commands that have a Dental Department, the Dental Officer serves as department head. He is responsible, under the Commanding Officer, for preventing and controlling dental diseases and supervising dental hygiene within the command. He also serves as adviser to the Commanding Officer in such matters.

His duties in dental affairs parallel those of the Medical Officer in medical matters. He collaborates with the Medical Officer, informing him of any adverse physical conditions that he may have discovered in the course of a dental examination.

1211. THE SUPPLY DEPARTMENT. This department handles such matters as procurement, receipt, stowage, issue, and accounting for equipment, repair parts, and consumable supplies required to support the ship's employment. Supply responsibilities normally include disbursing, stores, mess, and ship's store.

As head of the Supply Department, the *Supply Officer,* under the Commanding Officer, has responsibility for fulfillment of the purpose and functions of the Supply Department, including receiving, delivering, and shipping of authorized baggage and medical and dental supplies and equipment. Material received under orders and contracts must be inspected by him or by qualified technical inspectors.

He has responsibility also for the proper operation of the general mess, its commissary records and returns, storeroom spaces, issue rooms, etc. Ships' Stores afloat and Navy Exchanges ashore are under Supply Corps supervision. Clothing and small stores are operated by Supply Department personnel.

Accounting duties include allotment, cost, appropriation, and property accounting. He maintains stock records for accountability and to facilitate replenishment of stocks. In a large ship, his assistants may include the Disbursing Officer, the Stores Officer, the Ship's Store Officer and the Mess Officer.

In battle, the Supply Officer and his assistants are assigned such duties as preparation and distribution of battle rations, stations on gun batteries, in CIC, on damage control stations, or on the coding board.

The *Assistant for Disbursing,* when assigned, is responsible for maintaining pay records and for paying the crew, and for making general disbursements.

1212. DIVISION ORGANIZATION. The ability of the ship to accomplish its task with the requisite smoothness, precision, and smartness is determined finally by the soundness of each division's organization and administration, for which its respective division officer is responsible, together with thorough indoctrination of personnel effected through constant instruction and coordinated training (see Figure 1204).

The personnel of each division are so detailed, under the immediate supervision of assigned petty officers where possible, to cover all duties, material, and spaces assigned to the division. To this end, the Division

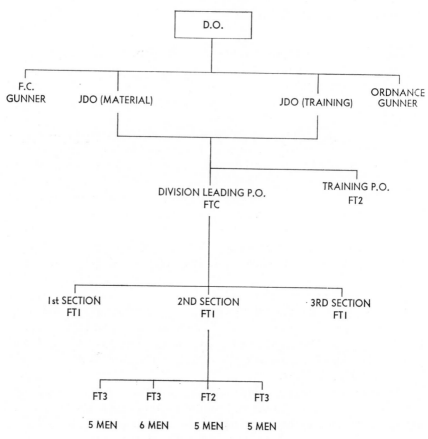

FIGURE 1204. Division structural organization.

Officer must maintain the Watch, Quarter, and Station Bill[1] in an up-to-date condition.

Division officers must see that the functions of their divisions are carried on at all times, even during their temporary absence. Because of this fact and because they are frequently engaged in other duties, division officers must insist that their junior officers and petty officers accept responsibility within the division. To the end that this acceptance of responsibility may be developed and maintained, division officers should

[1] The bill detailing the men of the division to watches and to specific duties at such evolutions as fire and collision quarters, abandon-ship stations, and fire and rescue parties, and to various cleaning stations.

normally accomplish division tasks by working directly through their officers and petty officers, bearing in mind the undermining effect of habitually exercising authority directly over a petty officer's subordinates in tasks for which the petty officer is held responsible. Petty officers are further required to accept the responsibility, common to all petty officers, for maintaining discipline and enforcing compliance with orders, regulations, instructions, and customs of the service of the personnel under their direction or in the part of the ship to which they are assigned. Any tendency to consider this solely the responsibility of the ship's Master-at-Arms[2] must be avoided.

In order to maintain at all times the ability of the division to accomplish its tasks, not only when all division personnel are in the ship, but also when part of the personnel, either officer or enlisted, is absent, each division officer must keep up to date, in addition to the Watch, Quarter, and Station Bill, a division book. In the preparation of his division book, each division officer should analyze the duties of his division as set forth in the Ship's Organization and should maintain standing orders in his division book covering his division's responsibilities under each of the bills and chapters of the Ship's Organization. The division book should further contain such division officer's orders as are necessary to ensure continuing compliance with orders and instructions issued by his head of department or other authority that are of a continuing nature. Copies of these orders should be in a division standing-order file available at all times to duty and other petty officers of the division.

Refer frequently to the *Division Officer's Guide* for excellent suggestions and advice on division leadership, organization, administration, training, discipline, inspections, welfare and recreation, material and maintenance, and the human factor in handling men (see also Section 311 on Divisional Relationship, and Section 622, Notes for the Division Officer).

1213. THE BATTLE BILL. Usually a confidential supplement to the Ship's Organization Book, this Bill lists the stations manned in all conditions of readiness and provides for the manning of these stations. Assignments in the Battle Bill are indicated by a specific rate and thereby take into account the necessary qualifications to place men where they are best fitted to serve in battle. The Bill also provides for occasions anticipating battle when lesser numbers are required on battle stations. In its preamble, it states the fighting doctrine and the action doctrine.

Conditions of Readiness. Condition 1.—The maximum state of readiness for battle, with the entire crew at battle stations.

[2] Members of the "police force" of the ship.

Condition 1 E.—Condition assumed when enemy forces of comparable strength may be encountered, with all battle stations manned but not on the alert. Useful as a rest condition during long periods at Condition 1.

Condition 2.—Condition assumed when major action is improbable but surface encounter with enemy light forces, submarines or air is possible.

Condition 3.—Condition assumed when only prospect of surprise is by aircraft or submarine.

Condition 4.—Condition assumed in normal peacetime cruising.

Condition 5.—Condition assumed in port during peacetime.

1214. WATCH, QUARTER, AND STATION BILL. Based on the Battle Bill, watches, berthing, messing, battle stations, emergency stations, and routine assignments are set forth in a Watch, Quarter, and Station Bill. In translating the Battle Bill to the Watch, Quarter and Station Bill, several men of the same rate may be available for a specific job indicated in the Battle Bill. Before making a specific assignment, the responsible officers must carefully weigh the degree of military qualifications and personal attributes possessed by the men available for assignment.

Watches. The assignment of officers and men to watches and sections within a division is carried out in a manner which ensures proper manning of battle stations required to meet prescribed conditions. The personnel on watch are temporarily removed from their regular stations and duties and devote their entire attention to their watch duties. There are three watch sections.

Watch officers are put in charge of a watch. The Commanding Officer may assign to such duty any commissioned or warrant officer (or a petty officer, when conditions so require) whom he considers qualified (see also Sections 305-7).

Engineering Officers of the Watch are in charge of the ship's main propulsion plant and of associated auxiliaries. He may be directed in the performance of his duties by the Engineer Officer or the main propulsion assistant. During his watch, he is responsible to the Officer of the Deck and to the Engineer Officer for the proper operation of the Engineering Department machinery and the keeping of required records.

Watchkeeping at sea rotates among the watches on a normal 4-hour basis. Watches not on steaming or battle stations engage in ship's work, drills, recreation, and rest.

Watchkeeping in port rotates among watch sections which have the

24-hour port detail. General practice is to have at least one-third of the ship's personnel on board at all times.

1215. OTHER SHIP'S BILLS. We have been considering administrative bills. The functional organization of a ship includes operational and emergency bills and ship's procedures.

These ship's bills provide a method for establishing assignments of ship's personnel to duties or stations for the purpose of executing specific evolutions or accomplishing certain functions. In general, a bill includes a statement of purpose, general information, assignment of responsibilities, statement on organization, assignment of personnel, and procedures. The responsibility for a bill includes maintaining the processes and organization of the bill current with respect to directives of higher authority and lessons from experience, maintaining current and accurate master muster lists of personnel assigned to the bill, and furnishing copies of these muster lists to the Officer of the Deck at sea and in port.

Operational Bills. Included in most Ship's Organization Books are bills for Special Sea Detail, Replenishment at Sea, Rescue and Assistance, Landing Party and a multi-purpose bill titled "Visit and Search, Prize Crew and Boarding and Capture Bill."

Emergency Bills. These bills are composed of the General Emergency, Nuclear, Biological and Chemical Defense and the Man Overboard Bills.

Ship's Procedures are written statements of a series of coordinated steps to be taken by an office, department, or division for the accomplishment of a specific function. These procedures are usually developed by the department responsible, are published as ship's instructions, and included in the ship's directives binder.

Lack of space prevents description of these bills and procedures. The young officer should study them thoroughly in his own Ship's Organization Book,

FIGURE 1205. A man-overboard drill.

especially as they apply to the duties and responsibilities of his division.

1216. Ship's regulations. The Ship's Secretary will issue you a copy of the Ship's Regulations. Make a careful study of them. They contain indispensable information. They will answer your questions on many subjects and save you much embarrassment. If other questions come up, ask your shipmates—they will be glad to help you.

Ship's Regulations are enforceable under the UCMJ which gives to the Commanding Officer of a ship or station authority to punish persons who are guilty of violating them.

The foreword to the Ship's Regulations usually states the persons who are subject to those regulations and their duty to obey them.

Ship's Regulations include requirements as to the use of alcohol and narcotics, arrest by civil authorities, berthing, card games and gambling, crew's heads and washrooms, divine services, government property, haircuts, health and sanitation, leave and liberty, mail and postal matters, uniforms and clothing, pecuniary dealings, property and passes, Quarters and muster, reports of offenses, security of classified matter, tipping, unauthorized entry, watches, patrols and sentries and many other subjects. Safety regulations are usually included as a separate section.

In connection with your study of the Ship's Organization and the Ship's Regulations, study also the Ship's Plans. A copy of this blueprint volume may be obtained from the Engineering Log Room.

This brief summary of the many facets of Ship's Organization should serve to impress upon you the necessity for becoming thoroughly acquainted with the organization and regulations of your own ship. When knowledge is power, it is folly to be ignorant of the requirements which will govern every moment of your waking day.

CHAPTER 13

Staff Organization and Functions

Nothing succeeds in war except in consequence of a well arranged plan.
—NAPOLEON

1301. GENERAL. Although a young naval officer may pursue his career for several years before serving on a staff, he can expect at an early time in his career to come in contact with the members of a staff. It is therefore necessary that he have knowledge of the organization of staffs and of their functions. An excellent outline of these requirements is given in The Navy Staff (NWP 12). If you are assigned to a staff, study this publication and the Staff Instructions issued by your Commander carefully. The ensuing outline of Staff Organization and the functions of members of a staff will serve as a general guide.

Every Commander, in high echelon or low, performs administrative and operational functions aimed at achieving his mission. He must make decisions, formulate plans, issue directives to subordinates to carry out the plans, and ascertain that his orders are carried out in accordance with his intentions. He must set the policies and supervise the day-to-day activities which mold the men and equipment of his command into an effective fighting or supporting force. He must plan for future requirements as well as attend to the present requirements of the command.

The Commander is responsible to his superior for everything his organization does or fails to do. *He may delegate his authority, but never his responsibility.* He assigns tasks to subordinate commanders who are responsible to him for the accomplishment of these tasks and who, in turn, assign duties to their subordinates. In this way, authority is delegated, responsibility is definitely fixed, and the chain of command is established. The tasks assigned to subordinate commanders should contribute directly toward accomplishing the over-all mission of a command, not toward relieving the Commander of duties which he and his staff should perform.

In the lowest echelons, a Commander may himself perform all the functions of command. His decisions and plans are controlled largely by directives from above, his orders to subordinates usually are oral, and his supervision is confined to the limits of his own ship or small command. As he rises in the chain of command, his command increases in size and in the scope of the operations it will conduct. To control such an organization, a commander must have assistants to furnish him information and advice, to help him prepare estimates and develop plans, to write and transmit directives and instructions, to supervise and evaluate the execution of planned actions, and, in short, to relieve him of numerous administrative details. These assistants, formally organized, are known as the *Staff*.

1302. The staff and its relation to the commander. The command of a naval task force, large or small, is vested in the Task Force Commander, whose rank will depend upon the size of his force and the importance of its mission. The Commander of most task forces will usually be a flag officer. Regardless of the personnel involved, as long as they are waterborne, the Task Force Commander is, properly, a naval officer. Upon him rests the entire responsibility for loading his vessels for the task assigned, the safe conduct of the force to the action area, the final attack (up to the shore line in the case of a landing), and the safe withdrawal of the naval vessels after the attack is completed. It is obvious that, with the many details involved, the Task Force Commander must be assisted by a competent staff of officers.

One of the first and most important lessons that a staff officer must learn is his relation to the Commander. As was pointed out, all responsibility is the Commander's; none of it can be assumed by his staff. Every order and command is his, not theirs. The staff is assigned to the Commander in the capacity of additional eyes to see and ears to hear in order that reports may be timely and accurate; additional legs to move over the extensive administrative field; additional brains to study, analyze, and organize; and additional hands to prepare the reams of paper work necessary in every large command. The members of the staff serve the Commander, serve the task force through the Commander, and never in the conduct of their duty do they appear in any capacity other than that of an aide, or an officer assigned to an office, or a section devoted to carrying out the command mission. A staff officer going on board a ship other than the one carrying the flag of his Commander would introduce himself, not as "Lieutenant Jones of the U.S.S. *Turner*," but as "Lieutenant Jones, Communication Officer for Commander Task Force 47." The personal identity of each member of a staff is merged in the identity of the Commander.

1303. GENERAL FUNCTIONS OF A STAFF. A Navy staff exists for one purpose: to assist the Commander in carrying out the functions of command for which he is responsible. These include operational functions and supporting functions. *Operational functions* lead directly to the determination of tasks and accomplishment of the missions assigned to the command: decision, evaluating intelligence, formulating plans for and directing the execution of missions assigned, and providing means by which command can be exercised. *Supporting functions* provide for the physical and mental welfare, and for the morale and training of the command, as well as for the supply and allocation of personnel, material, bases, and fighting equipment.

The magnitude of the functions of command will vary with the type and size of the command. For instance, an administrative or type commander is concerned mainly with support to the fleet as a whole—personnel administration, basic type training, and the initial conditioning of ships and aircraft. These support tasks then form the basis for the operational functions. On the other hand, an operational or tactical commander is more directly concerned with the purely operational functions: over-all training for combat; and planning for, supervising, and evaluating the execution of combat operations. However, regardless of the size and type of an organization, the basic functions of command are common to all commands.

If a staff is to furnish maximum assistance to the Commander, it must be organized to function effectively. Efficient staff work, no less than effective management, depends upon sound organization. For this reason, much emphasis is placed on the formulation of a *basic plan* for dividing the work of the staff, for assigning personnel to positions on the staff, and for delegating authority and assigning duties within the staff.

1304. LIAISON WITH OTHER COMMANDS. Coordinated teamwork is the essence of successful military operations and of the efficiency of the staff functions of a command. The nature of the operations of a naval task force, involving, as it does so frequently, joint operations of elements of all the armed services of the United States and allied powers, requires of an operational staff extensive liaison between members of the staff and with commanders and staff members of other armed services. Liaison must be conducted in a courteous and cooperative manner, so as to reflect credit, not only on the Navy in general, but on the admiral's command in particular. In conducting such liaison, the Commander must be kept fully informed. It must be thoroughly appreciated by every good staff officer that tentative agreements reached on lower staff levels do not constitute decisions binding upon the Commander. *Tentative agreements must be presented to the Commander for approval or revision before becoming finally effective.* The vast scope of naval and joint operations, particularly of amphibious warfare, and the complex interrelation of forces and types makes this procedure essential to proper staff service to your Commander.

1305. COMPLETED STAFF WORK. A tendency occasionally develops on the part of a staff officer to feel that, when he has presented a problem in general terms and recommended a solution to his chief, his full duty has been performed. Such action is not fully effective and does not promote efficient teamwork.

The writer recalls a young head of department on a destroyer who went into the cabin to see the Captain about a problem of supply within his department. The matter was discussed fully with the Captain and a course of action recommended to him, which the Captain approved. "I think you ought to write a letter to the Naval Supply Depot about that, Captain," the young officer finished up his discussion.

The Captain looked at him soberly. "I never write letters," he said. "I just sign them."

It is the function and duty of subordinate staff officers to present to their chief in adequate detail the facts and figures on which he can base decisions and to implement those decisions in the form of "completed staff work." *Never attempt to "pass the buck" upward to your boss in matters of detail.*

Completed staff work includes the study of a problem *and* the presentation of a solution by a staff officer in such form that all his chief has to do is to sign or initial the letter or directive. A good staff officer never presents his solution in segments or bothers his chief with long explanations or informative memorandums.

As a staff officer, resist the natural impulse to ask your boss what to do; it is your job to advise your chief what ought to be done. He needs acceptable solutions, not questions. You are a better staff officer when you work out all the details of a problem, no matter how complicated or perplexing they may be, without consulting your boss. It is also wise to consult with your fellow staff officers, so that you can indicate their agreement or state the area of disagreement to your chief when you present what you hope will be a final solution.

To accomplish this you will generally have to study, write, restudy, and rewrite until you have found the best possible solution to your problem. If junior to a section chief, your solution may be a rough draft, but such a rough draft as you feel can immediately be written up in final form. Never use a rough draft to shift to your chief the responsibility for editing your paper into final form for policy or action. In most instances, completed staff work results in a document that is ready for the signature of the Commander without oral presentation or accompanying memorandum. A proper solution will be recognized by the Commander. If he wants further comment or explanation, he will ask for it. But if that happens very often, you can feel pretty certain that you are not following through on your job to full completion.

As a final test of your work, when you have finished a job, ask yourself, "If I were the boss, would I sign this order and stake my professional reputation that it is a feasible, and the most acceptable, solution to the problem?" If your answer is "No," then you had better work the paper over again. It is not yet *completed staff work*.

1306. ORGANIZATION OF A NAVAL STAFF. The basic organization of an "Operational Navy Staff," based on functional divisions, is shown in Figure 1301. It adheres to the principles of unity of command and span of control. The functions of command should be homogeneously assigned to each of the five divisions in accordance with their relationship to the division titles.

Before considering in detail the assignment of functions and duties to the staff divisions, certain characteristics of the organization plan should be stressed. The fact that the five divisions are shown in Figure 1301 on the same level has no significance as far as the rank of a division head is concerned. The head of the administration division, for instance, may be junior to the officers in the operations and plans division. The chain of staff authority extends from the Commander to the Chief of Staff, to the division heads, and down through each division, but it does not cross from one division to another. The head of one division normally exercises no control over personnel of another division, except when designated by the Chief of Staff to coordinate staff work on a specific project.

It should be noted that the divisions are numbered N-1 through N-5.

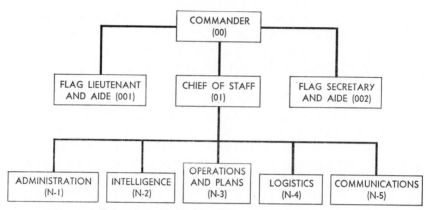

FIGURE 1301. Typical organization of a naval staff.

If a sixth division be required, it will be numbered N-6. The first four divisions of this typical Navy staff resemble generally the Army's and the Marine Corps' G-1, G-2, G-3, and G-4, and S-1, S-2, S-3, and S-4; and the Air Force's A-1, A-2, A-3, and A-4. In those services, the four staff sections represent a division of the command functions or duties which a Commander must perform, as follows: 1—Personnel, 2—Intelligence, 3—Operations and Plans, and 4—Logistics. Structures for Army and Marine Corps staffs at the various echelons of command are generally fixed. An Air Force commander has more freedom in organizing his staff because the Air Force, like the Navy, must mold its task organizations for particular situations, and the staff must meet the requirements of the command.

In the Navy, every function of command, except decision, is assigned to a staff division. The function of decision, as mentioned previously, must be performed by the Commander himself. The Navy does not have a "Special Staff" group (Signal Officer, Engineer Officer, etc.) as do the command organizations of the Army, Marine Corps, and Air Force. In the Navy, all officers—line, staff corps, or specialist—are fully integrated into the five staff divisions. However, the *specialist officers* may have direct access to the Commander and to the Chief of Staff because of the special nature of their particular duties, and the Commander will often seek information from them directly. Nevertheless, they are under their respective division heads for administrative purposes, and their estimates and plans are included in the division estimates and plans.

On the other hand, the Special Staff officers in command organizations of services other than the Navy provide technical and special advice and assistance to the Commander and to the General Staff (or co-ordinating or executive) divisions. They may also command subordinate units in the Commander's organization. For example, a division engineer may command the division's Engineer Combat Battalion, thus serving both on the staff and in the chain of command.

The question often arises as to why communications (N-5) is given divisional status on a Navy staff. Rapid communications (electronic transmissions, flashing lights, and signal flags, rather than correspondence or hand-carried messages) play a vital role in every naval operation. Actually, they are the means by which command is exercised and should be considered as a major function of command. A communications division does more than send and receive messages; it is responsible for other functions. By their nature, the functions performed by the communications division require direct access to the Commander and to the Chief of Staff, and they affect all other divisions of the staff as well as subordinate commanders. The Communications Officer on a Navy staff assists the other divisions of the staff with their day-to-day rapid communications, prepares the communications for the plans they formulate, and coordinates communication planning with other sections of the staff. In behalf of the Commander he ensures that the responsible section of the staff expedites the incoming rapid communications and coordinates action with other sections before an order is issued or a reply is dispatched.

1307. DUTY OF STAFF MEMBERS. Ordered as a personal aide to an admiral, the *Chief of Staff* (or *Chief Staff Officer* to a commodore or lower ranking officer) is the senior officer of the staff. It is his responsibility to keep the Admiral informed of the condition and situation of command, of subordinate commands, and of other commands in the same theater of operations; and to advise the Admiral on administrative matters, exercise general supervision of administrative work, and coordinate the activities of the staff.

With regard to correspondence, the Chief of Staff signs routine papers not involving questions of new policy and not involving approval or disapproval of a previous recommendation or action of a flag officer, action on legal papers, or leave requests of flag officers. All such correspondence is signed by the Admiral. The Chief of Staff also signs papers concerning matters on which the policy of the Admiral is known, action on requests for repairs and alterations, endorsements forwarding letters from higher authority quoted for compliance or guidance, and orders to all officers except flag officers.

Another personal aide is the *Flag Secretary,* who on many staffs also acts as Assistant Chief of Staff for Administration. He is responsible for intra-staff administration and receives dispatches, maintains records, routes, and files, and assumes responsibility for the control and security of all official correspondence. He authenticates and distributes copies of plans, orders, and multiple-address correspondence; is responsible for the correctness of form of correspondence originated by the staff and for the expeditious handling of correspondence which requires action; and is Top Secret control officer. He arranges for handling and use of United States and Guard Mail, administers the Flag Office and supervises the performance of duty of the Flag Division Officer, and handles matters pertaining to printing. He is also responsible for the preparation of the War Diary, for keeping a chronology of events during combat operations and peacetime exercises, for the preparation of Fitness Reports for the Admiral, and for the assignment of staff quarters.

The *Personal Aide and Flag Lieutenant* looks out for such matters as salutes, honors, presentation of awards, official calls, uniforms, entertainments, invitations, and liaison to promote cordial relations with local organizations, both governmental and civilian. He is responsible for the Admiral's calls and call book; is the staff boarding officer and maintains the boarding book; arranges for transportation to be available for the Admiral, afloat and ashore; and keeps the Chief of Staff, Staff Duty Officer, Officer of the Deck of the flagship, and other interested persons advised as to the prospective movements of the Admiral.

He tends the side upon the arrival and departure of the Admiral, visiting flag and general officers, and other important dignitaries. He also acts as Flag Signal Officer. As such, he is responsible to the Staff Communication Officer for his communication duties. In many flagships, he takes over and is responsible for all visual signaling to and from the flagship and for the performance of all signal personnel, whether assigned to the ship or staff.

The *Administration Division* (N-1) is under the *Assistant Chief of Staff for Administration,* who is often the *Flag Secretary.* In addition to the duties already enumerated for that officer, he is responsible for advising the Admiral on the formulation of command administrative policies; for publication of command letters and their yearly compilation and consolidation; for the compilation of a quarterly command administrative organization book and staff roster and directory; for the compilation of all data for reports and other papers as to enlisted personnel within the command; and for the procurement, classification, assignment, pay, promotion, transfer, and replacement of all officer and enlisted personnel.

In conjunction with the *Legal Officer*, he supervises rewards and punishment and oversees the individual training of enlisted personnel for advancement in rating, as coordinated by the Training Sub-Section in Operations. He prepares plans for, and reviews reports on, administrative inspections. He prepares the quarterly command summary.

The *Intelligence Division* (N-2) is headed by the *Assistant Chief of Staff for Intelligence*. This division is responsible for groundwork on the formulation of policies pertaining to all sorts of combat intelligence, counterintelligence, propaganda, psychological warfare, and public information, and for the implementing of these policies, as far as staff cognizance is concerned.

The *Intelligence Officer* also keeps the Admiral and staff informed as to the capabilities of present and potential enemies by the collection, evaluation, interpretation, and dissemination of information regarding the enemy, including hydrography, terrain, and weather. Through liaison with subordinate, parallel, and higher commands, and by use of all existing sources of intelligence, including aviation and submarine visual and photographic reconnaissance, he strives to keep his intelligence of an actual or potential enemy current and accurate.

He supervises counterintelligence, propaganda, counterpropaganda and psychological warfare. He prepares intelligence studies of prospective operating areas, strategic estimates, and the intelligence annex of all operation orders and plans for the force. He keeps the Intelligence Journal and maintains situation maps during combat operations or training exercises. He supervises the photo-lab, photographic interpretation, cartographic work as required, and map, chart, and photographic reproduction. He collects, sifts, and interprets information obtained from prisoners of war and from the examination of captured enemy material, supplies, equipment, and documents. He supervises the training of intelligence personnel under the coordination of the Training Sub-Section of Operations.

The *Operations Division* (N-3) headed by the *Assistant Chief of Staff for Operations, or Operations Officer,* is the primary executive element of the staff and is charged with those staff functions which relate to organization and command, training, planning, making preparations for, and issuing, directives in connection with combat operations and training exercises, the execution of such operations and exercises, and the correlation of reports thereon. The *Operations Officer* has specific responsibility for making a continuous study of the existing situation and for the preparation of tentative plans for consideration of the Admiral; and for the preparation of operation plans and orders, including the annexes dealing with task organization, general concept, movement plan, the attack or order of combat plan, and protective measures for the force at the objective. He supervises and coordinates the preparation of other annexes.

The *Operations Officer* prepares the command employment schedules, issues the necessary movements orders, and keeps track of the location and movements of ships and units of the command. He advises the Admiral as to organization and command and the assignment of

FIGURE 1302. An admiral and part of his staff planning operations in flag plot.

ships, air wings, air groups, and other elements of the armed services to task forces or task groups for special or specific tasks.

He prepares and keeps current the type doctrine and procedures and initiates action in other sections concerning standard operating procedures and techniques which are indicated by observation, investigation, battle or exercise reports, or casualties to personnel or equipment. He is responsible for readiness inspections and reviews readiness reports.

Based on operational experience, he recommends alterations to current types of ships and aircraft and suggests improved characteristics in new design which concern operational efficiency.

All matters relating to the training of individuals, ships, divisions, squadrons, forces, and special task organizations, and the maintenance of records thereon, come under the *Operations Officer's* cognizance, including, in amphibious commands, all aspects of the ship-to-shore movement and all training therefor.

The *Logistics Division* (N-4), headed by the *Assistant Chief of Staff for Logistics,* is responsible for advising the Admiral on all matters relating to logistics, maintenance, and material. An essential element of strategy and the execution of operations, which was too often ignored in wars before World War I, the importance of logistics was finally recognized in World War II in its local, theater of war, national and world-wide implications. Since the last war the logistic element of war has been emphasized in the planning and operational considerations of all services of all nations.

The *Assistant Chief of Staff for Logistics* prepares logistics studies for proposed operations and the logistics annex for all operation orders and plans, in connection with which he must maintain full liaison with subordinate, parallel and senior commands with respect to material, repair, supply and service of all units and forces assigned to the command. This includes the supervision of maintenance and alterations of ships, craft and aircraft of the force, arranging availabilities for overhaul, screening work requests, and administering funds available for repairs. He conducts and supervises engineering competitions and training, material inspections, damage-control practices and competitive exercises and reports on the same. In consultation with the *Operations Officer,* he recommends alterations to ships and craft and improved characteristics for new design. He is responsible for ordnance and electronics maintenance and material in the command.

He examines captured enemy material and equipment and advises the *Intelligence Officer* with respect to its features.

The *Communication Division* (N-5) of a naval staff is headed by the *Assistant Chief of Staff for Communications.*

This division is responsible for providing adequate rapid communications within the command and with other commands; for the custody and supervision of publications distributed through the Registered Publication system; and for communication security, communication discipline, electronic communication material requirements, communication intelligence and postal matters. The communications division may operate a staff message center or crypto-center.

Other officers, formerly known as members of the Special Staff, are now assigned to one of the five divisions. The Legal Officer, Medical Officer and Chaplain all are usually assigned to the Administration

Division, although on some Amphibious Staffs, the Medical Officer is in the Logistics Division.

1308. THE STAFF DUTY OFFICER. Certain line officers of the staff in sufficient number and of proper seniority are designated by the Chief of Staff to take turns as Staff Duty Officer, and to take a day's duty in port and a regular watch on the flag bridge at sea. Specific authority to exchange duties must usually be obtained from the Chief of Staff.

In port, the Staff Duty Officer receives routine reports and acts on routine matters and on other matters as necessary in the absence of the staff officer having cognizance. Upon the return of any officer for whom he has acted in his absence, the Staff Duty Officer must inform him of action taken. He regulates the use of staff boats and tends the side on all occasions of ceremony or to meet visiting officers of command or flag rank.

He sees all dispatches, initials them, and takes action if the proper action officer is not aboard. In the absence of the Flag Secretary, he examines mail received and decides what action is to be taken on it.

The duties of the Staff Duty Officer assume special importance when, in the absence of the Admiral, Chief of Staff, or other staff officer, he is called upon to make decisions in an emergency or on matters which cannot be delayed. For this reason, it is imperative that officers taking a day's duty keep informed as to the existing situation, the policies of the Admiral, and the usual and proper manner of taking action on the various matters which may arise.

Underway, the Staff Duty Officer is on the bridge at all times during his watch. He represents the Admiral in much the same way that the Officer of the Deck represents the Captain of a ship. It is necessary that he inform himself of the formation, the location of ships and units, land or lights in sight or to be sighted, and of any other particular or event which may be of interest to the Admiral.

In an emergency, in the absence of the Task Force Commander or Chief of Staff, he makes such signals as are required, reporting his action immediately to the Admiral, Chief of Staff, and Operations Officer. The best advice is—*Act first, report afterward.*

He makes reports to the Admiral as to the safe navigation of the formation, the flagship's position, and the usual hazards to navigation such as are customarily made to the commanding officer of a ship. He keeps the staff log, which is submitted daily to the staff member detailed to additional duty as Staff Navigator, who examines it and submits it to the Operations Officer and the Chief of Staff for checking and approval.

The Staff Duty Officer underway must have complete general information on the operation or movement underway, the prospective events during his watch, hazards from the enemy in a wartime operation, hours at which condition of readiness will be changed, the Admiral's plans for defense of the formation if attacked or challenged, hours for launching and recovering aircraft, joining or detaching any units, etc. He must be completely on the alert at all times, not letting his attention be distracted from his duties by any consideration.

1309. RELATIONSHIP BETWEEN FLAG AND FLAGSHIP. Staff officers embarked in a ship must always be most careful to preserve the unity of command of the flagship. Requests to the ship in the name of the Admiral should always be made direct to the Captain or Executive Officer and should be prefaced, "The Admiral desires that you. . . ."

It should be remembered that *all* officers and enlisted personnel, with the exception of the flag officer or unit commander, who serve in a ship, are subject to the authority of the Commanding Officer and to his discipline and punishment. The staff officer does well to realize that he has no separate authority of his own, that all his authority stems from the Admiral, and that in all things he is acting for the Admiral. Not uncommonly, pleasant relationships between staff and flagship have been jeopardized by the thoughtless actions of some junior staff officer or by the antagonistic attitude of some senior officer in staff or ship toward junior officers of ship or staff.

The following notes may be helpful to young officers serving on staffs:

1. Leave and liberty for men assigned to duty with the flag must conform as closely as possible to that of the flagship. The Flag Division Officer must be extra zealous in regard to routine personnel reports, individual requests, liberty lists, disciplinary matters, uniform, proper parade at Quarters, etc.

2. Marines assigned to the flag muster with the flagship Marine Detachment and are administered and trained by the Commanding Officer of the flagship Marine Detachment.

3. Keep your Watch, Quarter, and Station Bill up to date. Give your division chief petty officers and leading petty officers an opportunity to perform their divisional duties with their men.

4. Flag personnel, unless excused by proper authority, should ob-

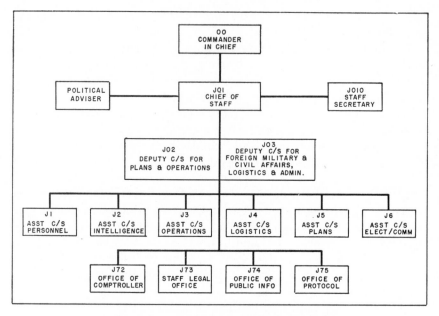

FIGURE 1303. Typical Joint Staff organization.

serve the calls to general drills in as prompt and snappy a manner as any other member of the ship's company.

5. Maintain the staff compartments, lockers, bedding, and messing facilities assigned on a par with or better than those of the ship's company.

6. The Flag Lieutenant is in charge of staff boat crews, chauffeurs, stewardsmen of the Admiral's and other flag messes, automobiles, and boats. The flagship is responsible for the maintenance and upkeep of flag vehicles and boats, including the observance of all safety precautions.

7. The flagship normally maneuvers in obedience to signal from the flag in the same manner as other vessels. However, the Admiral may direct the flagship orally, and the flagship may be directed to act independently of the formation.

8. The Captain is responsible for the position and station keeping of the flagship. As Staff Duty Officer, do not heckle the flagship, unless directed to take action by the Task Force Commander or Chief of Staff, or unless you see that the ship is running into danger. And then speak in the name of the Admiral.

9. When the Admiral has retired, all reports to him are made to the

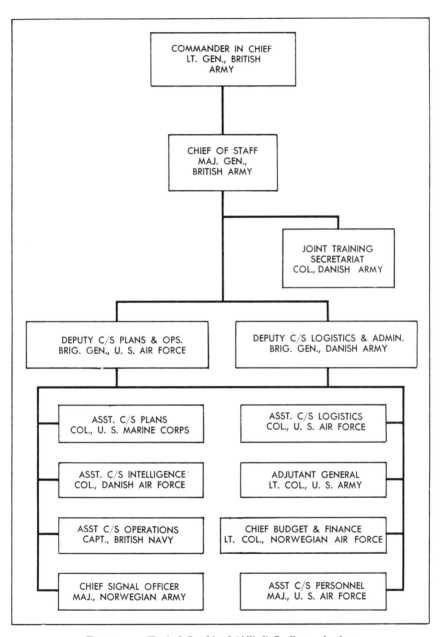

FIGURE 1304. Typical Combined (Allied) Staff organization.

Staff Duty Officer, who decides which reports warrant the Admiral's attention. The Officer of the Deck of the flagship should err on the side of too many rather than too few reports to the Staff Duty Officer and the Admiral at night.

10. The flagship navigator reports the flagship position to the staff navigator at 0800, 1200 and 2000.

11. Underway, the Admiral's Night Order Book is shown to the flagship commanding officer for his information and initialing and then is turned over to the Staff Duty Officer for his guidance and compliance.

12. In your relations with the flagship, endeavor always to be considerate of the officers and enlisted men of the ship, that your cruise in the ship may be pleasant and that close working harmony between the Admiral and his staff and the commanding officer and crew of the flagship is promoted by your every contact with ship personnel.

1310. JOINT, COMBINED, AND ALLIED STAFFS. The young naval officer will only rarely have opportunity to serve on other than a naval staff. However, he may have occasion to deal with higher echelon staffs and for this reason should at least be familiar with nomenclature and purposes of these staffs. In later years a more thorough knowledge of the organization and functions of Joint and Combined or Allied Staffs will be necessary.

Joint Staff. A Joint Staff is the staff assigned to the Commander of a Joint Command. A Joint Command is made up of forces from more than one U. S. service. The Commander may be of any U. S. service, and his staff generally includes officers from all services furnishing components of his command. A Joint Staff is usually organized along the lines of the naval staff (see Figure 1301) except that additional

FIGURE 1305. NATO is comprised of men from many different nations.

staff divisions are sometimes added and the *Plans Division* is sometimes separate. The letter "N" is usually replaced by "J" in the designations of Staff Organization. A typical Joint Staff Organization is shown in Figure 1303.

Combined or Allied Staff. A Combined Staff is the staff assigned to a Combined Commander. This staff is also referred to as an Allied Staff. A Combined Commander may be an officer of any armed service of any country of a group of allies. The NATO complex consists of many such commands. A typical Combined Staff Organization is illustrated in Figure 1304.

CHAPTER 14

Education for Command

*It is the man you are capable of making, not the man
that you have become, that is most important to you.*

—MAXIM

1401. CAREER PATTERNS OF OFFICERS OF THE NAVY. From the day
he steps aboard his first ship until the day he assumes his highest
command, an officer is continuously in training. At sea he is in training
to assume the duties of the next senior billet in his organization. Ashore
he is educated in the broader aspects of command responsibilities. In
both areas, his training and education are for the purpose of enabling
him to advance up the ladder of responsibility.

The career pattern of each category of officer is very carefully
planned by the Officer Distribution Division under the Chief of Naval
Personnel. Typical patterns for a surface line officer (category 1100),
an aviation line officer (category 1300) and a submarine line officer
(category 1120) are shown in Figures 1401 through 1406. The Officer
Fact Book (NavPers 15898), from which these plates were reproduced,
contains additional career patterns for other categories of officers. An
individual career may differ considerably from these ideals and still be
properly planned. If doubt exists, the Officer Fact Book should be consulted for additional information. If doubt persists, an inquiry should
be addressed to the Director of Officer Distribution in BuPers via official
channels.

Each officer has a major share in planning his own career. He is responsible for his own professional competence, his performance record
and his education, and should take the initiative in making known the
types of duty and education that he feels will best suit his capabilities
and desires. To accomplish this, consider carefully and submit promptly (on August 1 annually and when changes occur) your Officer's

GRADE	YRS.	PERIOD	PHASE	SEA			SHORE
ENS	1			**FIRST TOUR**			
			First Operational	Amphibious, Auxiliaries, Carriers, Cruisers, Destroyers, Minecraft	May attend functional school during tours		Newly commissioned officers normally are not assigned ashore. Officers volunteering and qualified for special programs may have shorter first operational tour.
	2	FUNDAMENTAL PROFESSIONAL DEVELOPMENT					
LTJG	3			**SECOND TOUR**			
				Destroyer School			NGLO
				Destroyer Type Head of Dept	Type/Billet other than that served in during first tour.		EOD UDT SEAL *Phase in with contemporaries*
	4						
	5		Educational	**DUTIES ALLIED TO TRAINING**			**PROFESSIONAL**
LT	6			There is no fixed dividing line between the 1st operational tour and first subspecialty and/or educational tour. The duration of the initial sea tour is determined primarily by the attainment of basic sea qualifications in one or more of the functional areas.			Instructor, NROTC, USNA, OCS, ASW, ENG NavDist, bases, staffs, technical bureaus and offices, OpNav, etc Postgraduate education
	7		Second Operational	**DUTIES WHICH ROUND OUT QUALIFICATIONS**			
	8			CO: AOG, LST(S), ATF XO: LST(L), APD, DE Head of Dept: DD types, Amphibs, Auxiliaries Dept Asst: CA, CAG, CLG, CV Afloat Staff: MinRon, DesFlot, DesRon			NGLO EOD UDT SEAL
	9		Subspecialty and/or Educational	Officers trained in specialist areas return to sea and phase in with contemporaries			Increased responsibilities in the shore establishment (U. S. & foreign) Research and development activities Instructor duty Subspecialists normally assigned to subspecialty field.
	10						
	11	INTERMEDIATE DEVELOPMENT	First Advanced Operational	CO: DE, DER, APD, AGS(S), MSO, ARS, LST(L) XO: AE, DD, AF, ARG, AO, LSD, AGTR Afloat Staff: Flt, Tycom, CruDesFlot, CarDiv Head of Dept: CA, CLG, CAG, CG, DLG Ops: AKA, APA, LSD(L), AGC Repair: AD			
LCDR	12			*Note: Some officers may be short-toured to attend service colleges.*			EOD UDT SEAL
	13						
	14		Subspecialty and/or Educational	Officers trained in specialist areas return to sea and phase in with contemporaries			PG education Service Colleges Subspecialists normally assigned to subspecialty
	15						

* Indicates average promotion points. Actual promotion point will vary within each promotion zone and will shift according to required promotion flow.

FIGURE 1401. Typical professional development pattern for surface line officer.

GRADE	YRS.	PERIOD	PHASE	SEA		SHORE
CDR	16	Second Advanced Operational, Subspecialty and/or Educational	Second Advanced Operational	Unit Commands: CortRons, LanShipRons, MinDivs CO: DD types, AGS, AK, ARC(L), ARG, LSD(S), AGTR, MCS(S) XO: Cruiser, Amphibs, Auxiliaries Head of Dept: Carriers, Cruisers Afloat Staff: Flt, Tycom, DesFlot, CarDiv *NOTE: Commanders may anticipate a three year sea tour during this time frame.*	Assignments varied as necessary to round out qualifications and meet service needs.	Planning and admin positions in NavDists, Navy Dept offices, Dept of Defense and Bureaus Research and development activities Training activities PG education and service colleges Overseas staff, stations, and missions
	17					
	18					
	19					
	20					
CAPT	21	ADVANCED PROFESSIONAL DEVELOPMENT	Third Advanced Operational	Captain selectees and captains eligible for: CO: APA, AKA, AD, AE, AGC, AGS, AO, AR, AKS, AVM, LPD, LSD, DL-1, C/S CruDesFlot, HukGrp, PhibGru, Subflot	Eligible for selection for: Major Commands: CA, CC, CAG, CLG, CG, DesRon, PhibRon, ServRon, Sub-Flot, SubRon, MinFlot, DLG-16 & 26 Class, AGMR2, FLtSupp NavSta C/S Numbered Fleets C/S Tycom C/S CruDesFlot, HukGrp, PhibGru, SubFlot	Policy planning and managerial duties in OpNav, Bureaus, technical offices, shore commands and naval districts (may be allied to subspecialty field.) Service colleges Research and development activities Joint staffs CO of shore activities
	22					
	23					
	24					
	25		Final Development			
	26					
	27					
	28					
	29					
	30					

* Indicates average promotion points. Actual promotion point will vary within each promotion zone and will shift according to required promotion flow.

FIGURE 1402. Typical professional development pattern for surface line officer.

Personal History Card (NavPers 765) and the Officer's Preference Card (NavPers 2774). These cards form part of your official record and are filed at the detail desk for your rank and category, where they are carefully consulted before each assignment. Although the Officer Preference Card is normally the best way for an officer to indicate his duty preferences, circumstances of a personal nature sometimes arise which are not appropriate for inclusion in that form. When this occurs, write an unofficial, personal letter direct to your detail officer. These letters are read by no one but the detail officer and do not become a part of an officer's official record. This suggestion should not be construed, however, as an invitation to violate regulations governing correspondence on official matters. Personal letters from individuals should be confined to personal matters and therefore may be considered merely amplification of information contained on Officer Preference Cards. Although personal letters will not always be answered, the information will be noted in all cases and will receive consideration whenever possible. If your preferences change, submit a new preference card, not a personal letter.

Officers desiring special courses of instruction, changes of duty, clarification of orders or date for release from active duty, extensions of

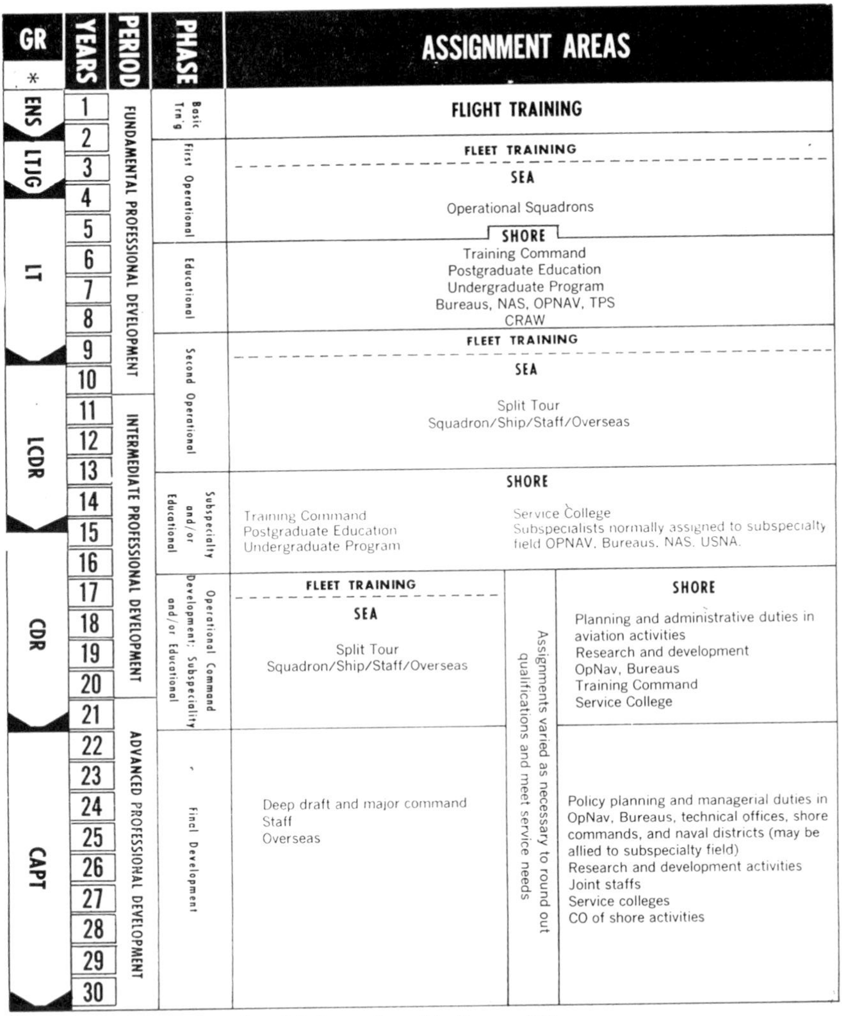

FIGURE 1403. Typical professional development pattern for naval aviators.

GR * | **YEARS** | **PERIOD** | **PHASE** | **ASSIGNMENT AREAS**

ENS — Year 1 — FUNDAMENTAL PROFESSIONAL DEVELOPMENT — Basic Trng — **FLIGHT TRAINING**

LTJG — Years 2, 3, 4 — First Operational — **FLEET TRAINING** / **SEA** / Operational Squadrons

LT — Years 5, 6, 7, 8 — Educational — **SHORE** / Training Command / Postgraduate Education / Undergraduate Program / Bureaus, NAS, OPNAV, TPS / CRAW

Years 9, 10 — Second Operational — **FLEET TRAINING** / **SEA**

LCDR — Years 11, 12, 13 — INTERMEDIATE PROFESSIONAL DEVELOPMENT — Second Operational — Split Tour / Squadron/Ship/Staff/Overseas

Years 14, 15, 16 — Subspecialty and/or Educational — **SHORE** / Training Command / Postgraduate Education / Undergraduate Program — Service College / Subspecialists normally assigned to subspecialty field OPNAV, Bureaus, NAS, USNA.

CDR — Years 17, 18, 19, 20, 21 — Operational; Subspecialty and/or Educational — **FLEET TRAINING** / **SEA** / Split Tour / Squadron/Ship/Staff/Overseas — **SHORE** / Planning and administrative duties in aviation activities / Research and development / OpNav, Bureaus / Training Command / Service College

CAPT — Years 22–30 — ADVANCED PROFESSIONAL DEVELOPMENT — Operational Command; Subspecialty / Final Development — Deep draft and major command / Staff / Overseas — Policy planning and managerial duties in OpNav, Bureaus, technical offices, shore commands, and naval districts (may be allied to subspecialty field) / Research and development activities / Joint staffs / Service colleges / CO of shore activities

(Assignments varied as necessary to round out qualifications and meet service needs)

* Indicates average promotion points. Actual promotion point will vary within each promotion zone and will shift according to required promotion flow.

duty in present assignment, transfer to or retention in the Regular Navy, extensions of active duty beyond expiration of obligated service, etc., should submit such requests by official letter. These requests become a permanent part of each officer's record and are readily available for review within the Bureau of Naval Personnel.

When in the area of Washington, D.C., it is advisable for the officer

GRADE*	YEARS	PERIOD	PHASE	ASSIGNMENT AREAS
ENS	1	FUNDAMENTAL PROFESSIONAL DEVELOPMENT	Basic Trng	FUNCTIONAL TRAINING / FLEET TRAINING
	2		First Operational	OPERATIONAL SQUADRON
LTJG	3			
	4			
	5		Educational	TRACOM SHORE STAFF/STATIONS SCHOOLS STUDENT OR INSTRUCTOR
LT	6			
	7			
	8		Second Operational	FLEET TRAINING
	9			OPERATIONAL SQUADRON (SPLIT TOUR) SHIP, CVA, CVS, AV, AVP, LPH FLEET STAFF/OVERSEAS
	10			
	11			
LCDR	12	INTERMEDIATE PROFESSIONAL DEVELOPMENT		
	13		Subspecialty and or Educational	SHORE
	14			Training Command / Postgraduate Education / Undergraduate Program — Service College / Subspecialists normally assigned to subspecialty field OPNAV, Bureaus, NAS, USNA.
	15			
	16		Operational Command Development; Subspecialty and or Educational	FLEET TRAINING
	17			SEA — SHORE
CDR	18			Split/Tour Squadron/Ship/Staff/Overseas — Assignments varied as necessary to round out qualifications and meet service needs — Planning and administrative duties in aviation activities / Research and development / OpNav, Bureaus / Training Command / Service College
	19			
	20			
	21	ADVANCED PROFESSIONAL DEVELOPMENT		
	22		Final Development	
	23			
	24			Deep draft and major command (Proposed Legislative change) / Staff / Overseas — Policy planning and managerial duties in OpNav, Bureaus, technical offices, shore commands, and naval districts (may be allied to subspecialty field). / Research and development activities / Joint staffs / Service colleges / CO of shore activities
CAPT	25			
	26			
	27			
	28			
	29			
	30			

FIGURE 1404. Typical professional development pattern for Naval Flight Officers (NFO's).

to review his fitness report and correspondence jacket in the Bureau of Naval Personnel. Officers are encouraged to visit their respective detail officers or corps sponsor to review and plan their careers, obtain the latest information concerning promotions, postgraduate instruction, etc., and exchange information of benefit to both the officer and the detail officer.

1402. EDUCATIONAL PROGRAM FOR NAVAL OFFICERS. The educa-

GRADE STD	WV	YRS.	PER.	ROTAT N	CONUS/OVERSEAS						SCHOOLS	SPECIALT'S
					PERS	ADMIN	ED & TNG	OP & LOG	INFO	COMM		
EN	EN	1	Fundamental Professional Development		AST	AST REC PHYS EVAL'BD	TNGO		AST TIO	CUST CLASS MAIL	Basic, Functional (See Fig. 7-2)	Aerology
LTJG	LTJG	2			SPEC SER		AST IE	MRC OFF				
		3			AST PERS	ASST TO ADMINO	STAFF INSTR		AST PIO	TOP SEC CONT		
		4										
LT		5			SPEC SER		OINC USAFI	AST HAR DEF	TIO	HEAD CRYPTO CEN		Comptroller
		6										
	LT	7			PERS OFF	REC PHYS EVAL BD	EDUC OFF		PIO	CEN		
		8			RATE CONTROL		I & E					
		9		NORMAL LIMIT OF DUTY IN ANY BILLET 3 YRS.						RPIO		
LCDR		10			DIST CLAS	ADMINO OFF	STAFF INSTR	AST PLANS	SIO	CWO	PG COURSES	
		11										
		12										
	LCDR	13	Advanced Professional Development		DIR SPEC SER	STAFF ADMINO AST	ASST TO DIR TRNG	AST OPER & PLANS	RADIO, TV PRO OFF AST DIST PIO	AST COMM SUPT OINC CRYPTO CEN		AVERAGE TOUR OF DUTY IN SPEC'LTY 3 YRS.
		14			MOB PLAN							
		15										
CDR		16				AC/S ADMIN	OINC OFF OR CRUIT TRNG	PLANS OFF			Available to LTJGs & above on Selective Basis	Intelligence
		17										
		18										
	CDR	19	PLANNING LEVEL		DIR CIV PERS			AST DIST PLAN OFF				
		20										
		21							DIST PIO	COMM SUPT		
		22					DIR TNG					
CAPT		23										
		24			DIR NAVPERS	DIST TRANS		SHIP CONT				Legal
		25										
		26										
		27										
	*	28										
		29										
		30										

*CAPT - APPOINTIVE FOR TENURE OF OFFICE
** Indicates average promotion points. Actual promotion point will vary within each promotion zone and will shift according to required promotion flow.

FIGURE 1405. Typical professional development pattern for women line officers.

tional program for naval officers can be divided into three major educational or training periods.

The period of fundamental professional development comprises the first six to 10 years of an officer's career—while he is in the grade of ensign to lieutenant. This first duty provides practical experience and rounds out the education he received as an officer candidate in the "college level."

The period of intermediate development occurs between the 11th and 12th years of commissioned service, which is normally served in the grades of lieutenant commander and commander. This period includes, for most line officers, command of a surface ship, submarine or aircraft squadron, possibly a staff assignment, a shore tour of duty and attendance at a post graduate course or war college.

The period of advanced development includes the 20th to 30th years of a line officer's career—in the grade of captain. As a captain, he will have a deep draft command and, if selected therefor, a large combatant ship or surface ship squadron command. Submarine or aviation

SUBMARINE OFFICERS

GRADE *	YRS	PD	PHASE	DIESEL ELECTRIC SUBMARINES SEA AND SHORE	
ENS	1			SURFACE SHIP	SUB SCHOOL
ENS	2			SUB SCHOOL	1st SS TOUR (a) ROTATE IN DEPTS QUALIFIED IN SS
LTJG	3		1st Operational	1st SS TOUR (a) ROTATE IN DEPTS QUALIFIED IN SS	(b) SS DIFFERENT TYPE
	4			(b) SS DIFFERENT TYPE	
	5				
LT	6		Prof. Educ. Tech.	1st SHORE DUTY (SAME AS NON SS 1100 OFFICER) AND PG SCHOOL	
LT	7				
	8		2nd Operational	2nd SS TOUR THIRD OFFICER QUALIFIED FOR COMMAND EXECUTIVE OFFICER	
	9				
	10				
	11			INCREASED RESPONSIBILITIES SHORE DUTY 2nd SUBSPECIALTY	
	12				
LCDR	13	ADV. & FINAL PROF. DEV.	1st Op. 1st Adv.	3rd SS TOUR CO	
	14				
	15			COMMAND OF A SUBDIV MAY BE SUBSTITUTED FOR COMMAND OF DD	

(FUNDAMENTAL PROFESSIONAL DEVELOPMENT)

* Indicates average promotion points. Actual promotion point will vary within each promotion zone and will shift according to required promotion flow.

NUCLEAR SUBMARINE OFFICERS

GRADE *	YRS			
ENS / LTJG	1	SUB SCHOOL AND NUCLEAR SCHOOL	OR	SURFACE SHIP
	2			SUB SCHOOL AND NUCLEAR SCHOOL
	3	SSN OR SSBN		
	4		SSN OR SSBN	
	5			
	6			
LT	7	DEPT HEAD SSN OR SSBN	OR	SHORE SEA STAFF OR PG SCHOOL
	8			
	9	SHORE SEA STAFF OR PG SCHOOL		DEPT HEAD SSN OR SSBN
	10			
	11		SSN XO OR DEPT HEAD	
LCDR	12			
	13	SSN CO	OR	SSBN XO
	14			
	15		SERVICE COLLEGE	
	16	SSN CO		SSBN CO
CDR	17		OR	SUB DIV
	18	SSBN CO		
	19	SUB DIV OR SEA STAFF		SEA STAFF
	20			
	21		SHORE OR STAFF	
	22			
	23	SENIOR SERVICE COLLEGE		
CAPT	24	DEEP DRAFT CO		
	25	MAJOR COMMAND		
	26			
	27	SHORE		
	28			
	29			
	30			

* Indicates average promotion points. Actual promotion point will vary within each promotion zone and will shift according to required promotion flow.

FIGURE 1406. Typical professional development pattern for submarine line officers.

line officers may be given these types of commands or large aviation or submarine commands of equivalent importance. He may also attend a service war college and have a tour of duty in Washington or be assigned to a large staff afloat, foreign or ashore.

The college level (or officer candidate training period) is the first step in the broad education which extends throughout the career of a naval officer, in which the complexity of the modern Navy and the probabilities of future scientific developments demand an adherence to that which is basic. A navy in these modern days is a highly complicated, highly technical machine for which, in addition to a great number of administrative personnel, an enormous number of technicians, both officer and enlisted, are required. In fact, all officers and men must now be specially trained and educated in order that, *in addition* to knowledge and skills common to seamen the world over, they must prepare themselves to serve, supervise, and employ effectively for the defeat of an enemy the complicated, powerful mechanisms assigned to their use in battle.

Before World War II, the system of education and training officers and enlisted men was well designed and functioned efficiently to provide the Navy with trained personnel in sufficient numbers to form a nucleus from which to expand in wartime. Throughout the Navy's postwar educational system, the vital difference between training and education has been recognized. Both are essential to the development of Navy personnel. Training searches out more immediate objectives and may be termed tactical. The scope of education is broader and more profound, more basic; it is strategic in its long-range effects and indispensable to the continuing development of an officer. Through a synthesis of theory and practice, the college level of Navy education builds a solid foundation on professional attitiude, competence in small things, and objectivity in the large ones. Thus, it makes available for further education and training the career officers upon whom the country will rely and around whom the Navy may build when it comes time to mobilize for war.

In his long-range planning for a naval career, an officer must seek for a thorough understanding of the fundamentals of the successful conduct of war before he comes to the exercise of high command. In the course of his career, every naval officer should continuously read and study to further his understanding of strategy, logistics, and naval, air, and land tactics and their application in the field of joint operations. To accomplish this, he must acquire a thorough knowledge of world geography, international politics, world history and economics, international law, and technology. He must be equipped to interpret *correctly and without bias* the lessons of the past in the light of new developments and trends in the techniques of present and future warfare. Finally, and of ultimate importance, he must develop his ability to think and to write clearly, to interpret correctly the directives of his superiors, to solve military problems and arrive at sound decisions, and to transmit his will and his intent to his subordinates.

Fundamental Professional Development

1403. TRAINING. For 4 to 6 years after first being commissioned, officers of the line are normally assigned to sea duty or foreign service and are engaged principally in being trained for their current duties or for their prospective duties. By far the most important training of both officers and enlisted men is conducted in the ships of the fleets, in the amphibious teams and air groups in active service, and in ship, unit, type, and fleet tactical and gunnery exercises and operations.

An ensign's first assignment in a ship provides the sound basis of experience needed for career planning. In his first few years at sea, still under intensive training, he receives "on-the-job" training, learning to apply his basic education plus education through correspondence courses, required reading and study, and the preparation of junior officers' journals. Satisfactory progress in these educational requirements is fully as important as the accomplishment of routine shipboard duties.

The young ensign is assigned duty in rotation in various departments of the ship, which develops a balanced understanding of, and capability in, the work and organization of the ship. This basic period also usually provides a variety of duty in different types of ships and in various parts of the world.

Courses in Navy schools for education and training in basic requirements for specific duties are also available. While officers are taking courses at such schools as Submarine School, Flight Training School, Optical School, Gunnery Officers' School, etc., enlisted men are taking education and training courses at various fleet and service schools to prepare them for the duties of their prospective ratings as technicians or for the more technical general ratings, where special knowledge is required or special skills must be acquired before they can engage in on-the-job training.

1404. FLIGHT TRAINING. Application for Flight Training is covered by Bureau of Naval Personnel Instruction 1520.20, which is revised annually. Applicants should check the current instruction carefully for exact details for qualification. The following is a brief summary of prerequisites for flight training:

a. Be less than 26 years of age.

b. Have completed 4 semesters undergraduate work at an accredited college or university.

c. Be physically qualified and aeronautically adapted for the actual control of aircraft.

d. Agree to serve 3½ years' active commissioned service after completion of flight training.

Line officers undergo a brief preflight training period at Pensacola and then move on to basic flight training and advanced training before designation as naval aviators. Preflight and basic flight training is conducted by the Basic Training Command at Pensacola, Florida. Advanced training is conducted by the Advanced Training Command at

Figure 1407A. Educational program for surface line officer

GRADE	YRS	PERIOD	PHASE	SEA	SHORE
*ENS LTJG	1–3	FUNDAMENTAL PROFESSIONAL DEVELOPMENT	First Operational	Assignment to provide experience in one or more of the three basic technical areas in order to provide opportunity for most responsible billets within individual's capacity and to undertake initial-sub-specialization. Basic and Functional Courses (See Fig. 7-2)	
LT	4–8		Educational		Selected PG Courses (See Fig. 7-3) Undergraduate College Program if Required (See Sect. 711)
			Second Operational	Assignment to Duties in One of the General Areas in which Previously Experienced, with increased utilization of subspecialist abilities.	
LCDR	9–13	INTERMEDIATE PROFESSIONAL DEVELOPMENT	Subspec. and/or Educational		
			First Advanced Operational		Selected PG Education as Appropriate Operational, Staff & Command Courses at Service Colleges (See Fig. 7-4)
			Subspec. and/or Educational	Command & Staff Experience Head of Department Afloat	
CDR	14–20		Second Advanced Operational/ Subspecialty and/or Educational		Courses at Service Colleges (See Figs. 7-4, 7-5) Selected PG Education as Appropriate
	21–24	ADVANCED PROFESSIONAL DEVELOPMENT	Third Advanced Operational	Command & Staff Experience Afloat	Higher Command & Staff courses at Service Colleges (See Fig. 7-5)
CAPT	25–30		Final Development	Major Command & Staffs Afloat	

FIGURE 1407A. Educational program for surface line officer.

Figure 1407B. Educational program for aviation line officer

GR *	YRS	PERIOD	PHASE	SEA	SHORE
ENS	1–2	FUNDAMENTAL PROFESSIONAL DEVELOPMENT	Basic Training	Pre-commissioning Education. USNA, NROTC, OCS & AOC Grads 18 mo. Flight Trng. Pensacola then Designated 13xx Such officers may be as much as 18 mo. behind that indicated on this chart.	
LTJG	3–4		First Operational	Assignment to Fleet Aircraft Duties in Executive, Operations, & Maintenance Depts. Basic, Technical & Functional Courses (See Fig. 7-2)	
LT	5–9		Educational		Selected PG Courses (See Fig. 7-3) Undergraduate College Program if Required (See Sect. 711)
			Second Operational	Assignment to Senior Duties in Fleet Squadrons and Billets in Ships Basic Tech. & Funct. Courses (See Fig. 7-2).	
LCDR	10–14	INTERMEDIATE PROFESSIONAL DEVELOPMENT	Subspeciality and/or Educational		Operational, Staff, & Command Courses at Ser. Coll. (See Fig. 7-4) Selected PG Courses (See Fig. 7-3) Undergraduate College Program if required (See Sect. 711)
CDR	15–20		Operational Command Development, Subspeciality and/or Educational	Command and Staff Development Assistant Department and Department Head Afloat Higher Command and Staff Courses at the Service Colleges (See Figs. 7-4, 7-5) Selected PG Education as Appropriate Basic, Technical & Functional Courses as Required (See Fig. 7-2)	
CAPT	21–30	ADVANCED PROFESSIONAL DEVELOPMENT	Final Development	Major Command & Staffs Afloat	

FIGURE 1407B. Educational program for aviation line officer.

Corpus Christi, Texas. Technical training is carried out by the Technical Training Command at Memphis, Tennessee. Total time for this training averages 18 months.

1405. SUBMARINE TRAINING. Application for submarine training at the Submarine Base, New London, Connecticut, is covered by Bureau of Naval Personnel Instruction 1520.6, revised annually.

An intensive course, both classroom and practical, approximately 6 months for officers and approximately 2 months for enlisted men, provides the students with basic knowledge of propulsion and auxiliary engineering installations with which they will be shipmates, of torpedoes and torpedo gunnery, and of other details of the operation and upkeep of submarines which are different from those of surface craft. The course includes considerable training at sea in submarines attached to

FIGURE 1408. Training officers for duty in submarines at New London, Conn.

the school to acquire an understanding of the operation of a submarine on the surface and submerged and of the strategy and tactics of the employment of submarines in war.

Officers of the grades of lieutenant or lieutenant (junior grade) may request training in the submarine nuclear power training program, provided they are qualified in submarines and otherwise meet the requirements of BuPers Instruction 1301.28 covering assignment of officers to nuclear-powered submarines. The Nuclear Power Course at the Submarine School at New London lasts for six months, and is followed by an additional six-month course of instruction at the prototype sites at Arco, Idaho, and West Milton, New York.

1406. FUNCTIONAL SCHOOLS. Functional schools are those schools which provide training in the various technical functions performed by officers and men in the Navy. These schools are usually of short duration (1 week to 4 months) and are usually conducted by forces afloat or by the training commands. Some examples of functional schools follow:

Optical and Gunnery Officers' Schools train officers and men in the upkeep and operation of the fire-control installations to which they are currently assigned.

Fleet Sonar and Electronics Schools train officers and men in the techniques of operating modern electronic equipment and in the tactical employment of it.

Naval Amphibious Training Commands at the Naval Amphibious Bases at Coronado, California, and Little Creek, Virginia, conduct a variety of training courses for land, sea, and air elements of all four military services, both officers and enlisted men, in the basic elements of the conduct of amphibious joint operations and in actual operational training at sea and ashore. Among the schools operated for such training are:

Gunfire Support	Communication
Air Support	Naval Beach Group
Landing Craft Control	Underwater Demolition
Intelligence	

Fleet Air Defense Training Centers train officers and men in the techniques of Air Defense.

Attendance at Functional Schools is usually arranged on a temporary additional duty basis with the Commanding Officer requesting a quota for the particular school from the activity charged with administering it. Occasionally officers attend Functional Schools en route from one station to another. The Bureau of Naval Personnel will arrange quotas for this type of schooling.

1407. SPECIALIZATION. An officer may desire to specialize permanently by entering a Staff Corps or by requesting designation as a Special Duty Officer. The following programs are available to line officers:

Engineering Duty Categories

a. *Transfer to Engineering Duty, Ships (Category 1400):*

1. *Through 3-year Naval Construction and Engineering Postgraduate Course.* This is a NavShips sponsored course. Normally, three years prior sea duty is a requirement. Students are given opportunity to specialize in Basic Hull and Design, Nuclear Propulsion, Marine Electrical, Electronics, and Ship Propulsion. Successful completion of the course at the Massachusetts Institute of Technology or Webb Institute usually leads to designation for engineering duty (category 1400). Students taking the course need not officially indicate their intent to request such designation after successful completion of the course. Approximately 25 new EDs are obtained annually from this source. (See BuPers Notice, 1520 series, for information as to applications for this course.)

2. *By Line Transfer Board Selection.* Regular and Reserve (both active and inactive) applicants for a code 1400 designator are considered by a line transfer selection board convened annually in February in the Bureau of Naval Personnel. (See BuPers Notice, 1120 series, issued annually for information as to eligibility and other data for applying for a code 1400 designator.) About 40 officers are obtained annually from this source. The majority of officers applying have 8 to 10 years of commissioned service with considerable engineering experience at sea and have usually completed a postgraduate engineering course at the Naval Postgraduate School, Monterey, California. Reserve officers selected by the board will be given further sea duty, as required, to round out their background, and will be eligible to apply for postgraduate training, if they have not had such education but are otherwise eligible.

b. *Transfer to Aviation Engineering Duty (Category 15XO).* Regular and Reserve male applicants for a code 15XO designator are considered by a line transfer selection board convened annually in February in the Bureau of Naval Personnel. See BuPers Notice, 1120 series, for information as to eligibility and other data in applying for a code 1510 (Weapons Engineering) or 1530 (Meteorology) designator. The annual selection rate is about 25-30 officers for code 1510 and about 2-4 officers for code 1530.

1. Desirable qualifications in applying for a code 1510 designator are:

(a) Grade of lieutenant commander or a lieutenant commander selectee.

(b) Designated naval aviator.

(c) Demonstrated performance as a capable naval officer.

(d) A sound and extensive background of operational experience in the Fleet.

(e) A Bachelor of Science degree from the U. S. Naval Academy or other accredited college or university in the fields of engineering or science.

(f) Satisfactory completion of graduate study at the Naval Postgraduate School or other accredited college or university culminating in a Master's degree (or its equivalent) in the field of engineering.

2. Desirable qualifications in applying for a code 1530 designator are:

(a) Grade of lieutenant or lieutenant commander.

(b) Demonstrated performance as a capable naval officer.

(c) A sound and extensive background of operational experience in the Fleet.

(d) A Bachelor of Science degree from the U. S. Naval Academy or other accredited college or university in the field of engineering or science.

(e) Satisfactory completion of graduate study in meteorology at the Naval Postgraduate School or other accredited college or university culminating in a Bachelor or Master's degree, or equivalent.

Special Duty Officers

a. Communication (code 161X), legal (code 250X), intelligence (code 163X), and public affairs (code 165X) specialists are of the utmost importance to the naval service. Their professional development is geared to ensure that they have ample opportunity to become familiar with all aspects of their specialty and expert in some particular phase of it.

Method of Transferring to Special Duty Officer Categories. Officers are selected annually by a special board convened by the Chief of

Naval Personnel from among male Regular Navy and Reserve applicants. Annually issued BuPers Notices of the 1120 series give eligibility requirements, method of application, and other pertinent details.

Supply Corps

a. Regular Navy line officers may, if meeting prescribed eligibility criteria, apply for transfer to the Supply Corps of the Regular Navy. (See BuPers Notice 1120 series, issued annually in regard to eligibility criteria, obligated service required and other data in submission of such applications.) Applications submitted are reviewed by an appropriate selection board convened annually about February in the Bureau of Naval Personnel and applicants will be informed of their selection or non-selection. NROTC (Regular) officers, on applying for a change from line to Staff Corps and who are selected for such change, are issued a new appointment in the Supply Corps of the Regular Navy. Such officers acquire a permanent Regular Navy status and will no longer be subject to selection for retention. Reserve officers can request transfer to the Supply Corps of the Regular Navy through the augmentation program.

Civil Engineer Corps

a. Officers may transfer to the Civil Engineer Corps by four separate methods. An officer of the Naval Reserve, either active or inactive, is eligible under BuPers Instruction 1210.6 series, to request a change of designator. Criteria for approval of requests are specified in Qualification Standards for Administrative Assignment of USNR Officer Specialists Designators (NavPers 18282). Approval of such requests is given on the merits of individual applications, consistent with the need of the naval service, both for CEC officers and officers of the category from which transfer is requested. An officer of the Naval Reserve, of other than the CEC (code 5105) category, is eligible, under the Augmentation Program, for a simultaneous selection for change of designator and career status. Approval of applications for transfer into the Civil Engineer Corps under this program is subject to action of a selection board. Selection is contingent upon the need of the Regular Corps for officers, upon the applicant's seniority and his degree of qualification. A line officer of the Regular Navy, who is a graduate of the Naval Academy, may be transferred into the Civil Engineer Corps through selection board action upon his application for postgraduate instruction in Civil Engineering. BuPers Notice 1520 series prescribes eligibility and method of submission of official requests. A line officer of the Regular Navy who possesses a baccalaureate degree in engineering may request transfer to the Civil Engineer Corps. An annual 1210 series BuPers Notice advertises this opportunity and requests applications. Approval of requests is subject to selection board action. Regular NROTC graduates, selected under this program, acquire permanent U. S. Navy status and are no longer subject to selection for retention.

1408. EDUCATION BY CORRESPONDENCE COURSES. Correspondence courses conducted by a number of naval activities in a wide variety of professional and educational subjects provide preliminary education for officers who may later attend resident courses in the same field. These courses extend the facilities of the school or college conducting them to officers at an earlier stage in their career and to many officers who may be unable to attend resident courses.

The Naval War College, Newport, Rhode Island, offers correspondence courses in National and International Security Organization, Military Planning, International Law, International Relations and Counterinsurgency.

Naval War College correspondence courses are graduate level courses requiring considerable time and research to complete. Typewritten solutions to the essay type questions and problems are required.

Since officers may be confronted with a situation requiring a knowledge of international law at almost any stage of their career, they should complete the basic course in that subject as early as practicable.

The Defense Intelligence School offers a graduate level correspondence course in Intelligence.

The Industrial College of the Armed Forces offers a graduate level correspondence course entitled, The Economics of National Security.

The Naval Correspondence Course Center, Scotia, New York, conducts a variety of courses for both Regular and Naval Reserve personnel including:

Naval Regulations	Practical Damage Control
Leadership	Diesel Engines
Elements of Naval Machinery	Naval Communications
Naval Ordnance and Gunnery	Marine Navigation
Engineering Administration	Naval Electronics
Personnel Administration	Air Navigation
Foundations of National Power	Investigations

The U. S. Armed Forces Institute provides armed forces personnel with educational opportunities in subjects normally taught in civilian institutions. USAFI accomplishes this through making available correspondence courses, group-study course materials and tests, and by reporting results for military and civilian accreditation purposes.

The principal USAFI is at Madison, Wisconsin. Overseas are four other USAFI's set up to provide prompt service to areas remote from Madison. Overseas USAFI's are in Alaska, the Caribbean, Europe, and Hawaii.

USAFI offers a wide choice of courses in business education and administration, English, literature, languages, mathematics, science, social studies and technical-vocational subjects. Enrollees study by correspondence, written lessons being submitted to the nearest USAFI for grading and comment. USAFI provides all necessary texts, study guides, lesson sheets, and envelopes. USAFI also provides opportunity to enroll in correspondence courses offered by leading colleges and universities under contract with the Government. Service men and women get these courses on a cost basis.

USAFI's testing service offers a variety of tests, including end-of-course tests for USAFI courses, subject examinations, and general educational development tests on both high school and college levels. USAFI scores the students tests, makes a permanent record of the score, and reports the results to naval authorities and upon request to civilian authorities.

Intermediate Professional Development

1409. TUITION AID PROGRAM. Under the Tuition Aid Program, officers may take off-duty courses in nearby accredited colleges, universities or junior colleges, and the Navy will defray part of the cost of tuition. The courses must be taken for credit and must contribute to:

(1) The improved performance of duties or the professional capabilities of the officer or (2) qualifications for a baccalaureate degree. Maximum participation under this program is seven semester hours during any semester. The Navy's contribution is 75 percent of the tuition cost. (See BuPers Instruction 1560.10 series for further information).

1410. EDUCATION AT POSTGRADUATE SCHOOL. Following his first tour of sea-duty an officer may be selected for assignment to any one of a number of postgraduate courses conducted at the Naval Postgraduate

School at Monterey, California, or at certain cooperating civilian colleges and universities.

The Superintendent of the Naval Postgraduate School supervises the education of all officers assigned to postgraduate study. An annual BuPers Notice 1520 describes the selection procedure for the postgraduate program and lists all postgraduate courses that are available. Among the postgraduate curricula offered are:

Electronics Engineering	Environmental Sciences
Civil Engineering	Naval Management
Aeronautical Engineering	Business Administration
Naval Engineering	Ordnance Engineering
Communications Engineering	Operations Analysis

Requirements of service and educational backgrounds vary with the course. Usually, five to seven years of commissioned service and a baccalaureate degree or its equivalent are considered to be minimal requirements. Officers assigned to the postgraduate program must agree to serve two years on active duty in the Navy after completion of the course, for each year of instruction.

1411. OTHER OFFICER SPECIAL SCHOOLS AND COURSES. A number of officer special schools and courses are conducted for the purpose of providing specialized training required by junior officers and refresher instruction to meet the needs of the service. These courses range in length from one week to five months. The number and variety are subject to change in accordance with the new requirements and developments within the Navy. Details concerning these and other special courses are published in the Bureau of Naval Personnel Formal Schools Catalog, NavPers 91769 series. Typical courses are as follows:

U. S. Naval School, Civil Engineer Corps Officers. Offers courses of instruction for CEC officers, Regular and Reserve, through which they may become acquainted with the specialized administrative and technical engineering information, over and above their basic knowledge of engineering, required to equip them for duty in billets assigned to them in the Navy.

U. S. Naval School, Officer Indoctrination, Chaplains. The course offered at this school is designed to give newly commissioned chaplains a broad understanding of the Navy, including the organization for national security, courtesies, customs, and other aspects of the Naval Service; to acquaint them with Naval leadership and Military Law, and to prepare them to perform their assignments as Naval Chaplains.

U. S. Navy Supply Corps School. The Basic Qualification Course of 26 weeks offered at this school qualifies newly commissioned Supply Corps Officers to perform their duties ashore and afloat in a manner which will reflect credit upon themselves, the Corps, and the Naval Service. The course is shortened to 14 weeks for officers who have received a part of their basic training in supply and fiscal matters at one of the 12 NROTC Units which conduct Supply Training.

The basic qualification course is conducted in three phases: The administrative phase which includes naval orientation and personnel administration; the supply phase which includes organization and logistics, supply afloat, commissary, ship's stores and supply management; and the disbursing phase which covers instruction in disbursing and travel.

U. S. Naval Justice School. Provides instruction in the principles of military law and procedures to officers and enlisted personnel, as well as practical application of these principles to problems which inevitably arise within every command, in order to attain a high standard in the administration of the naval disciplinary system.

1412. MARINE CORPS SCHOOLS. The Marine Corps conducts two schools at Quantico, Virginia, at this level, to which naval officers of appropriate rank may be assigned.

Marine Corps Amphibious Warfare School. This school offers an Amphibious Warfare course which prepares selected officers for the duties of field grade officer in the Fleet Marine Force; including command at the battalion/squadron level and staff duty at the regiment/group level.

This course emphasizes command and staff duties in the employment of Marine ground and aviation units in amphibious operations in an environment of cold, limited, or general war, and in all phases of counter-insurgency. The instruction is at the level of the reinforced infantry battalion and regiment and the aircraft squadron and group. The employment of the Marine division and aircraft wing is treated only to the extent necessary to provide a thorough understanding of command and staff functions within the regiment and group.

Communication Officers School. The course conducted by the school provides professional education for selected Marine Corps officers in communication command and staff duties in order to qualify them for assignment to appropriate communication billets in the Fleet Marine Force.

The scope of instruction is as follows:

FIGURE 1409. U. S. Marines come in under the atomic cloud during the maneuver at the AEC Nevada Proving Grounds.

1. Provide the student with a general knowledge of the organization of the Fleet Marine Force, ground and aviation, staff functioning, preparation of military plans and orders, offensive and defensive tactics including employment of supporting arms.

2. Provide the student with a working knowledge of the operational characteristics of all communication-electronics equipment organic to the Fleet Marine Force, the technical aspects being limited to that which is necessary to provide a general knowledge for intelligent supervision and employment of the equipment.

3. Provide the student with a working knowledge of communication security procedures, publications, and the various systems employed by ground and air elements of the Fleet Marine Force.

4. Provide the student with a working knowledge of the communication systems and requirements in the planning for and conduct of force-in-readiness operations.

5. Provide the student with a general knowledge of amphibious operations, waterborne and helicopterborne assault, and a working knowledge of the communication requirements at the MEU, MEB, MEF, and MEC level.

1413. ARMY AND AIR FORCE BRANCH SCHOOLS. Certain officers are selected for short courses at Air Force and Army schools conducted by their branches. These courses and their Navy quotas are published

FIGURE 1410. At the Naval War College, an instructor delivers a critique on a problem dealing with the Middle East.

from time to time in BuPers Notices. An individual request for a specific school is required.

Advanced Professional Development

1414. GENERAL. Normally, after 20 years of commissioned service, an officer has completed his third tour of sea duty. His small ship command has prepared him for advanced training in the duties and responsibilities of command and higher staff work. In the ensuing years, his duties involve constantly increasing responsibilities and greater authority. In his deep draft and combatant command and staff periods, his training and education must stress leadership, command and administration.

The Navy Department considers it desirable that one or two years of his shore duty during either the intermediate or advanced periods, be spent under instruction at advanced schools of the Navy, Air Force and

Army. The major schools and courses available and the intended flow of officers through them is illustrated in Figure 1407A and B.

1415. THE NAVAL WAR COLLEGE. Resident courses are conducted by the Naval War College at the following schools:

School of Naval Warfare. The Naval Warfare course, conducted at this school, is designed to further an understanding of the fundamentals of warfare, international relations and inter-service operations in order to prepare officers for higher command. This course emphasizes the integrated employment of all the elements of naval power including weapons systems and logistics in the accomplishment of the Navy's missions and upon the optimum employment of sea and naval power in furtherance of national objectives. The roles of the other military services are studied, as well as the principles and methods of participation in joint and combined operations. Officers with 16-23 years of commissioned service, usually in the grade of Captain, are eligible to attend this 10 month course.

School of Naval Command and Staff. This school conducts the Command and Staff Course which provides students with an opportunity to further their understanding of the fundamentals of warfare. The Command and Staff course emphasizes the operational functions of command, including operations planning and command decisions; and the organization, functions and procedures of operational staffs, together with participation in planning for joint and combined operations. The course is 10 months long and is available to officers with 10-16 years of commissioned service, usually in the grade of Lieutenant Commander.

In addition to the resident courses conducted at the two schools listed, a third resident course for specially selected foreign officers is conducted at the Naval War College as follows:

Naval Command Course. This 10 month resident course is designed to prepare selected foreign officers for higher command responsibilities in their own navies, and to familiarize them with U. S. Navy methods, practices and doctrines. The course provides students with a knowledge of command at fleet level and an understanding of naval warfare and weapons and of U. S. concepts for their employment, with emphasis upon operational and logistical command functions and planning.

1416. MARINE CORPS SCHOOLS.

The Marine Corps Educational Center. This center offers a professional educational course for Marine Corps officers and officers of the other services at the following school:

Marine Corps Command and Staff College. This school conducts a Command and Staff Course 10 months in length for the purpose of preparing selected officers for command at the regiment/group level; for staff duty at the division/wing and higher Fleet Marine Force levels, and for duties appropriate to the grade of lieutenant colonel/colonel with departmental, combined, joint and high level service organizations.

This course is presented in the setting of a "Field Grade Officer's Workshop," emphasizing situations requiring the student to solve problems of the type he can expect to encounter in service both in and outside of the Fleet Marine Force. Stress is placed upon planning for the conduct of force-in-readiness operations in cold, limited, or general war and in all phases of counterinsurgency. The role of the Marine Corps landing force in amphibious operations as a component of the balanced fleet within a unified command is emphasized; covering all tactical and logistical aspects of the employment of the landing force in the amphibious assault.

1417.   U. S. AIR FORCE SCHOOLS. The following two colleges are operated as components of the Air University, Maxwell Air Force Base, Montgomery, Alabama:

Air War College. The objective of the Air War College course which is conducted at this college is to prepare senior officers for high command and staff duty. The course is also designed to develop a sound understanding of the elements of national power to ensure the most effective development and employment of aerospace power.

The Air War College is the senior professional school in the U. S. Air Force educational system. Its student body is composed of a highly selected group of officers of widely diverse backgrounds who are brought together for 10 months of graduate study. The college environment is oriented toward a free expression of ideas and an opportunity for independent, analytical and creative thinking. Naval officers ordered to this college have 16 to 21 years of commissioned service.

Air Command and Staff College. The Air Command and Staff course which is conducted at this school is 10 months long. It is designed to improve the professional ability of selected officers for command and staff assignments normal to the field grades and to the development of sound Air Force command and staff doctrine and practices. The curriculum is designed to accomplish the mission of the college by achieving four primary objectives. These are: (1) to improve the students managerial skills and cultivate attitudes and habits appropriate for military officers of his grade and experience level; (2) to increase his understanding of the international environment, the institutions and instruments of national policy which have an effect on his role as a military officer; (3) to expand his knowledge of the military forces, their capabilities and alternative strategies, and to improve his ability in the employment of his own military force; and (4) to develop a stimulated, imaginative attitude toward his future and that of the Air Force. Naval officers attending this school are in the group which have 10 to 15 years of commissioned service.

1418. U. S. ARMY SCHOOLS. The Department of the Army offers advanced professional education at the following two colleges:

Army War College. This college conducts a 10 month course which prepares selected officers for command and high-level staff duties with emphasis upon Army doctrine and operations and to advance inter-departmental and inter-service understanding.

The curriculum of the U. S. Army War College comprises eight courses and an individual study and writing program. Consideration is given to the varied factors of military, political, economic, psycho-social, scientific, and technological elements of power which influence the attainment of national objectives within the international environment. Analysis is made of the nature and interdependence of these factors of national power of the United States in relation to other nations, groups of nations, and supra-national organizations, with emphasis on the use of military power in support of national security policy. Military planning and programming for and budgeting of defense resources and the development of military strategy are studied in their relationship to domestic and foreign policy as part of a national strategy. Science and technology are studied in terms of the future military power required to attain U. S. objectives in the mid- and long-range periods. Within this context, military coverage in the curriculum stresses the Army in joint, combined, and allied operations. The substance of the curriculum is interwoven upon a framework or theme—the design of a national strategy and a supporting military program. Naval officers selected for attendance at this college are in the year groups having 16 to 23 years of commissioned service.

Army Command and General Staff College. This school provides officers with a working knowledge for wartime and peacetime duty, to include the joint aspects thereof, as commanders and general staff officers at division, corps, field army, and army groups (introduction only) to include their combat service support systems.

The scope of instruction includes fundamentals of combat, including principles of war; fundamentals of leadership; legal basis of command; international law; status of forces agreements; organization, responsibilities, techniques, action and supervision in planning and execution of command and general staff and director staff; activation or mobilization and training of Army divisions; integrated Army information program; maintenance planning and supervision; civil defense; foreign special weapons; future developments in special weapons; tactical employment of stockpile special weapons; Army Command Management System; selected management control techniques including systems analysis, PERT, and automatic data processing systems; nature of communism, pattern of communist aggression; military systems of communist bloc; instruction and practice in effective military writing and speaking; planning and supervision of training in USAREUR; geographic, psycho-social, economic, military and political elements of national power; national security policy planning; strategic area studies; legal controls of international conflict; joint and combined organizations and operations; amphibious operations; airborne operations; air-ground operations; integrated airmobile operations; anti-airborne operations; anti-airmobile operations; counterinsurgency operations; unconventional warfare operations; special forces organization; psychological warfare; air defense operations; current overseas air defense operations; MAAGS and missions; Army Attaché System; organization, missions, capabilities, and limitations of division, corps and field army, including combat, combat support and combat service support operations; operations phase of army group; logistical commands; fundamentals of CONUS logistics; current overseas combat service support systems; map maneuvers; organization, doctrine, and missions of U. S. Air Force, U. S. Navy and Marine Corps; support of U. S. Army by other U. S. Services. Prominent military and civilian guests speak on selected topics to support and extend the resident instruction. Naval officers selected for this instruction are in the year groups having 10 to 15 years of commissioned service.

1419. HIGHER COMMAND AND STAFF SCHOOLS.   Recent wars have demonstrated that various Federal agencies, both civil and military, must have a more thorough appreciation of each other's problems. The factors that enter into the relationships between these agencies require integrated and coordinated effort. Attendance at the various educational institutions, previously discussed, provides opportunity for a wider acquaintance among officers and officials, for a free exchange of ideas, information, and experience, and for an appreciation of each other's problems.

Officers who are graduates of the Army Command and General Staff College, the Air War College, the Industrial College of the Armed Forces, or the Naval War College may be assigned to the staff of one of the institutions of the other services. Such representation on the staffs of the various service schools and colleges promotes a further healthy exchange of ideas and viewpoints.

While such interchange among the officers of the military services and civilian officials was advantageous, during World War II the Joint Chiefs of Staff felt a need for better understanding among the higher echelons of the armed forces and the other agencies of the Federal government which contribute an essential part to the national war effort. Accordingly, three colleges were established by the Joint Chiefs of Staff:

The Armed Forces Staff College. The Armed Forces Staff College course is five months long and two courses are conducted each year. Naval officers attending this course are included in the year groups having 10-16 years of commissioned service in the grades of commander and lieutenant commander.

The scope of instruction includes:

(a) Characteristics, organization, and employment of the armed forces and the relationships of those forces to each other with adequate exposition of their respective capabilities and limitations.

(b) Principles involved in the U. S. unified command organization and the organization of joint and combined commands and staffs and their responsibilities and procedures.

(c) Organization, composition, and functions of joint and combined commands with respect to the following: strategic, tactical, and logistic responsibilities of the commanders, with emphasis upon major war conditions, and the organization and composition of current major combined commands in which the United States participates.

(d) Aspects of joint and combined operations, including command relationships, organization, and planning.

(e) Trends of new weapons and scientific developments and their effects on joint and combined operations.

(f) Military, political, geographic, historical, economic, psychological, ideological, and other factors affecting U. S. national strategy and U. S. allied security including the threat to that security.

The Armed Forces Staff College Course is 5 months long and two courses are conducted each year. Eligibility for the Navy quota is limited to those officers included in the year groups having 10-16 years of commissioned service. Normally input will be restricted to officers in the grades of commander and lieutenant commander.

The Industrial College of the Armed Forces. The Industrial College of the Armed Forces conducts courses of study in the economic and industrial aspects of national security and in the management of resources under all conditions, giving due consideration to the interrelated military, political, and social factors affecting national security, and in the context of both national and world affairs, in order to enhance the preparation for command, staff, and policy making positions in the national and international security structure.

The scope of the studies includes:

Orientation in the broad aspects of national and world economic, political, and social conditions and trends.

Study and analysis of the structure and operations in the Department of Defense involving the management of manpower, money, and materials and its interrelationship with other government organizations concerned with these aspects of national security.

Study of the organization and processes for determining total requirements for national security, for balancing them against study and analysis of any other economic, industrial, or related factors considered significant to national security.

The Industrial College of the Armed Forces course is ten months long. Eligibility for the Navy quota is limited to those officers included in year groups having 16-25 years of commissioned service. Normally the input will be restricted to officers in the grades of Captain or senior Commander.

The National War College. The mission of the National War College as prescribed by the Joint Chiefs of Staff is, "To conduct a course of study of those agencies of government and those military, economic, scientific, political, psychological and social factors of power potential, which are essential parts of national security, in order to enhance the preparation of selected personnel of the armed forces and State Department for the exercise of joint and combined high-level policy, command and staff functions and for planning of national strategy."

The scope of instruction of the National War College course includes:

(a) Analysis of the nature and interdependence of the several factors of national power of the United States and other nations.

(b) Study of the integration of military and foreign policy; study of the role of the United Nations and other means designed to avoid armed conflict between nations.

FIGURE 1411. The National War College, top school of the Armed Forces of the United States at Fort Lesley J. McNair, Washington, D.C.

(c) Determination of the influence of the possession or deficiency of economic, scientific, political, psychological and social resources upon national security.

(d) Study of the national interests and objectives of significant nations with respect to their international relations, areas of disagreement and conflict, and policies designed to prevent war.

In addition, the following studies are made:

(a) The military force necessary to implement national policy in peace and war.

(b) Strategy and war planning.

(c) The impact of science and technology upon the armed forces.

(d) Departmental and interdepartmental problems which concern national security.

(e) The employment of joint and combined forces as related to national and coalition objectives and policies.

The National War College course is 42 weeks long. Eligibility for the

Navy quota is limited to those officers included in the year groups having 16-25 years of commissioned service. Normally, however, the input is restricted to officers in the grade of captain or a senior commander.

1420. THE FUTURE. Two important historical facts must be recalled: between World Wars I and II, the Army, including the Air Corps, never exceeded 140,000 officers and men; and the Navy at its lowest ebb had only 78,000 officers and men. With such limited numbers in our regular armed services, it was impossible to maintain organized units immediately ready for combat, which possessed any significant influence in world affairs. It was the prewar school systems in the Army and Navy which enabled our regular services to expand rapidly to the enormous and effective combination of ground, sea, and air force which won World War II.

At the Army's Command and General Staff School and Air Corps Tactical School, Army officers learned the techniques of handling the large air and ground units employed in battle in World War II. At the Army and Navy War Colleges, officers learned the principles of land, sea, and air warfare, and the exercise of command and staff functions at fleet, field army, air force, theater, Department of War and Navy, and Joint Chiefs of Staff and Combined Chiefs of Staff levels.

The postwar reorganization of the educational system for officers of the armed forces was sound and has already proved effective. As students of economics, diplomacy, national policy, and the strategy and tactics of modern global warfare and counter-insurgency, these officers apply this knowledge in time of peace, mobilization, and war.

CHAPTER 15

Command at Sea

When principle is involved, be deaf to expediency.
—COMMANDER MATTHEW FONTAINE MAURY, USN, 1849

1501. GENERAL. In peacetime, the line officer of the Navy may expect with considerable certainty that, with the passing of time, he will be ordered to command of a ship, usually a small patrol or amphibious craft as a lieutenant, a destroyer escort as a lieutenant commander, or a destroyer as a commander. As a captain, an officer will have a deep draft command and, if selected therefor, a large combatant ship or surface ship squadron command. Submarine or aviation line captains may be given these types of commands or large submarine or aviation commands of equal importance. If he has the experience of many years of sea duty behind him, the new commanding officer is adequately prepared for his new assignment and knows the steps he should take on reporting to his new command. In wartime and under cold war conditions, the line officer, both Regular and Reserve, may anticipate command early in his career and in any rank.

The responsibility that goes with command is in no way lessened by lack of experience; rather, the very lack of experience demands that the new commanding officer shall bend every effort to learn his job rapidly and perform it efficiently. The Navy expects that the men selected to be officers will be able to bear the heavy burden of responsibility immediately upon accepting their commissions. In peace or war, assignment to command of any type of vessel is a great honor. Be sure that you are prepared for it.

Orders to command, issued normally by the Bureau of Naval Personnel but occasionally by fleet and task force commanders on the spot, will usually introduce the new commanding officer to one of three possible situations:

407

1. *Ordered to command a ship not yet in commission.* This is a special situation which comes to a relatively small percentage of line officers. The specific requirements for this situation are given in considerable detail in Navy Regulations, Articles 0743 to 0747. Study of the provisions of Article 0739, which will be discussed later, will also be of value.

2. *Ordered to command a ship without a permanent commanding officer.* This situation is also relatively rare. The specific instructions for

FIGURE 1501. Command of ships at sea is the goal to which every line officer aspires.

this case are given in Navy Regulations, Article 0744. Articles 0739 and 0743 are also applicable.

3. *Ordered to command a ship already in commission.* This is the situation usually encountered.

All officers ordered to command a ship should carefully study Chapter 7 of Navy Regulations, particularly the first and second sections. They should carefully consider the admonition of the Regulations that their responsibility as commanding officer for their command is absolute, unless relieved therefrom by competent authority. Accordingly, the authority of a commanding officer is commensurate with his responsibility. While he may delegate authority to his subordinates, such delegation in no way relieves him of his continuing responsibility for the safety, well-being, and efficiency of his command until he is relieved.

Ordered to Command a Ship Not Yet in Commission

1502. REPORTING. In putting a ship into commission, as prospective commanding officer, you will probably be ordered to report to the Commandant of the Naval District, the Commander of the Naval Base in question, and then to the Commander, Naval Shipyard, or the Supervisor of Shipbuilding of the private shipyard, where your ship is being commissioned. Usually you will find that a nucleus of experienced officers and men of your crew, including your future Executive Officer, have reported to the commissioning detail before you. While, as prospective commanding officer, you have no independent authority over the preparation of your ship for service until the ship is commissioned and transferred to your command, you can and should immediately institute measures for the training of your crew. With the Executive Officer, hold conferences with key officers and decide upon the prospective assignment of those not assigned to specific duties by Bureau of Naval Personnel orders.

Officers and men can then be ordered to fleet and service schools which will prepare them for their future duties. Instruction in the new equipment to be installed in the ship, its maintenance and operation can frequently be carried on at the shipyard. Rifle-range firing, swimming and survival qualifications, open- and close-order drill can be carried on prior to taking command of the ship. All such training and other like it should be instituted by the Executive Officer at the earliest possible moment.

Upon reporting, procure the general arrangement plans of the ship and all pertinent information relative to its general condition and the work going forward on the hull, machinery, and equipment. See that your heads of departments closely follow up the details of completion of the ship. Encourage them to make, through you, suggestions for improvement of the operability of the ship and the health and comfort of the crew. By inspection of the ship soon after reporting to the yard, frequent personal inspection thereafter, and reports by your officers, you can keep yourself well informed as to the progress of the work in preparing the ship for service. Follow up on tests of equipment. Make reports to the commander of the shipyard or supervisor of shipbuilding which you consider appropriate, but be sure that the reports are not contentious, ill-considered, or unnecessary.

Through the Executive Officer, see to the preparation and printing of the Ship's Organization Book and the Ship's Regulations. Helpful in this work will be Shipboard Procedures (NWP 50), the type commander's Standard Ship's Organization and Regulations Manual, and similar publications from sister ships which have been in commission for a year or more.

Ensure that your heads of departments and your supply officer submit requisitions for articles to complete the outfitting of the ship, which are not being otherwise provided.

If you do not consider the ship to be in proper condition to be commissioned on the date set by the commander of the shipyard, report in writing such a conclusion to that commander and to the appropriate authority higher than the commander of the shipyard (usually the Chief of Naval Operations) setting forth your reasons.

If your ship is commissioned at a private shipyard or elsewhere than a naval shipyard, your relationship with the Supervisor of Shipbuilding or other naval authority will be the same as with the commander of a naval shipyard. See Section 527 for Ceremony of Commissioning and Assuming Command.

Refer also to Navy Regulations, Article 0743.

1503. PREPARING FOR SEA AND FOR DUTY IN THE FLEET. As Commanding Officer, once you have assumed command of your ship, you have full responsibility for her, and the necessary authority over all "officers, seamen, landsmen, and marines embarked in her." In preparing your ship for sea, you should take great pains to discover and correct any defects and inadequacies in crew and ship and in her installations, equipment, ammunition, and stores, before putting to sea. To ensure that all installations and equipment can be operated satisfactorily by the crew, you should also make certain that the officers and crew have been properly organized, stationed, and trained to cope effectively with any emergency that might arise in the normal course of scheduled operations.

During the outfitting and shakedown period, prepare for and conduct the prescribed trials and tests of the ship and any additional ones you may consider necessary. Take the first opportunity after leaving your outfitting yard to determine the ship's tactical characteristics, periods of rolling and pitching, and to check tactical and maneuvering data supplied you. Further advice contained in this chapter is just as applicable to the first commissioning as to transfer of command and should be carefully observed.

Ordered to Command a Ship Without a Permanent Commanding Officer

1504. PROCEDURE. Taking command under these circumstances contains elements of both the situations preceding and following this section. While there is no permanent commanding officer, the Executive Officer or one of the other officers has succeeded to temporary command of your new ship. He should, therefore, be relieved in just as official and formal a manner as if he were regularly in command. Therefore, while the situation will be unusual, the advice preceding this section and following it have full effect should you ever be confronted with the prospect of relieving of command the officer who will be executive officer or one of the heads of departments of your new command.

Ordered to Command a Ship Already in Commission

1505. REPORTING. Orders to your first command will usually require that you report to the senior officer present afloat and to your type, division or task force commander or other prospective senior in the chain of command. In reporting, in turn, aboard your new ship, you will report to the Commanding Officer, whatever his rank, just the same as before. The Commanding Officer will place the usual reporting endorsement on your orders.

If the retiring Commanding Officer has had an opportunity, he will probably be packed and as nearly ready to leave the ship as may be possible. Retiring commanding officers often move into other quarters to leave the commanding officer's cabin empty and ready for the prospective Commanding Officer, so that he may get settled promptly.

1506. INSPECTION OF THE SHIP. In Navy Regulations, Article 0739, you will find these instructions and others quoted hereafter in this chapter.

"A commanding officer about to be relieved of his command shall inspect the command in company with his successor before the transfer is effected."

In small ships, this inspection customarily follows the pattern of an ordinary weekly inspection of crew and upper decks, lower decks, and living and engineering spaces. It is advisable for the new Commanding Officer to make as thorough an inspection as circumstances permit. The retiring Commanding Officer "shall point out any defects and peculiarities of the command and account for them to his relief." It is a good plan to note important defects and check them against the records that you will examine later.

FIGURE 1502. Relieved and relieving commanding officers conduct a thorough inspection of the ship when turning over a command.

Study carefully the reports of recent inspections, work requests, and letters pointing out material deficiencies, and ascertain what steps have been taken to correct them. In wartime, you probably will have little time to correct defects. Therefore, the only course of action is to comment, in your letter on assumption of command, on defects noted.

Your orders are to *take command of the ship*. Regardless of conditions, you will take command, but you would be very foolish not to comment on unsatisfactory conditions noted. If the condition of the ship, propulsion machinery, armament, or crew is bad, take command and *do the best you can with what you have!*

1507. GENERAL DRILLS. "A commanding officer about to be relieved shall cause the crew to be exercised in his presence and in the presence of his relief at general quarters and general drills, unless conditions render it impracticable or inadvisable." Insist upon thorough and complete drills. Carefully watch the performance of the men. Do not remain on the bridge or quarterdeck. Move about the ship and observe several different stations at each drill. The experienced officer will recognize a smart, well-trained crew. There should be a minimum of noise and confusion. The drills can be carried out with the utmost efficiency without shouting and running fore and aft. Individual men should demonstrate expert knowledge of their stations and duties.

There is sometimes an inclination to gloss over or make perfunctory these drills on turning over command. Do not yield to this tendency through inexperience. In wartime, on the day after you take command, your ship and the lives of your officers and men may depend upon the efficient performance of the crew in battle or in other emergency situations. If their execution is not effective, note the fact in your turnover letter. But, more important, take immediate steps to bring the crew, by well-planned training, to a high state of efficiency.

1508. UNEXECUTED ORDERS. "A commanding officer about to be relieved shall deliver to his relief all unexecuted orders. . . ." Be sure you ask your predecessor for his unexecuted orders. In wartime, orders for operations are so secret that no one but the Commanding Officer may know about them. Ascertain to whom their contents have been divulged on board and who knows about them in the organization with which you will be operating. If the operation is continuing, obtain a clear understanding as to the part so far completed and as to your function in the future phases.

In your endorsement of the letter of turnover, note the unexecuted orders delivered to you by your predecessor.

1509. DOCUMENTS. "A commanding officer about to be relieved shall deliver to his relief . . . all regulations and orders in force, and all official correspondence and information concerning the command and the personnel thereof, as may be of service to his relief. He shall not remove the original records of his official correspondence, original letters, documents, or papers concerning the command and the personnel thereof, but he may retain authenticated copies thereof." The retiring Commanding Officer will leave, on the book-shelves in his cabin and in the ship's offices, the usual allowance of manuals and other official publications. Make sure that you receive a copy of fleet, force, and squadron standing orders and regulations. The official correspondence of the ship will be found in the ship's files, usually in the Executive Office on a small ship and in the Captain's Office on a larger ship. Booklets of ship's plans, the damage control book, and logistic and tactical data should be aboard and must be turned over.

"A commanding officer about to be relieved shall deliver to his relief all documents required by these regulations to be either kept or supervised by the commanding officer. If a Navy post office is established within the command, he shall deliver to his relief a current audit of postal accounts and effects." Be sure you check up on these documents and have a thorough understanding of the situation with respect to the post office or mail orderly in the command. It is a good plan to have a number of conferences with the officer whom you are about to relieve on these and other matters, utilizing such time as may be available. You should also discuss with him the officers and leading CPO's who will be in your new command. He knows them from close association and can give you information as to their characteristics, intelligence, abilities, and effectiveness under varying conditions, which will be of invaluable assistance to you in administering your command. Do not be afraid to ask for his views. *Take notes on each officer for future reference.*

1510. OFFICIAL KEYS. "A commanding officer about to be relieved shall deliver all magazine and other keys in his custody to his relief." Certain keys to important storerooms and restricted spaces, as well as magazine keys, are required to be kept in the custody of the Commanding Officer. In larger ships, these are locked in a small cabinet in the captain's cabin and guarded by the captain's orderly. In smaller ships, safeguarding these keys has often been rather haphazard.

Check to make sure that an effective system of stowing, issuing, and safeguarding such keys is in effect in your ship. The captains of many small ships carry the key to the key locker with them at all times, surrendering it only to open the locker in their presence or in the presence of a designated and responsible officer or to the senior duty officer or officer of the deck when the captain leaves the ship.

1511. SECRET AND CONFIDENTIAL MATTER. "A commanding officer about to be relieved shall cause an audit to be taken of all registered publications charged to the command, in accordance with the Registered Publication Manual." There is one most important piece of advice as to this material—*in a small ship, take the inventory yourself,* and personally check each book and see each serial number and short title. Be sure that the smooth list checks with the rough list made on inventory; or, better still, check the books against the typed inventory that you are going to sign and forward. Secret letters and orders should be read before assuming command. Inspect secret and confidential stowages, and ensure that they are adequate, in accordance with existing regulations on the subject. In small ships, they often are not. In this case, make sure you have a letter in the confidential files, authorizing the ship to use a less secure stowage.

A report on secret and confidential publications, on the appropriate form, to the Chief of Naval Operations (Registered Publication Section) or other fleet or force commander issuing the publications is required. A receipt for letters in the secret files should be given to your predecessor. Also, you must give him a receipt for miscellaneous forms and restricted pamphlets, carried in the ship's safes, such as honorable discharge buttons, honorable discharge certificates, damage control books, confidential charts, etc.

Remember, in taking over these publications and files, you will sign this statement: "Transfer receipt—Received the above from Samuel P. Hale. /s/ J. P. Dole." The only way you can be sure that you have received them is to *see them yourself*. After you have once done that, you can feel free to turn them over to the custody of your officer in charge of Registered Publications, who will be responsible to you for them.

While, in the largest ships, the actual inventory of secret and confidential publications is left to the officer in charge of Registered Publications and another officer not responsible for the custody and security of classified publications, this is not a good practice in smaller ships, where the corresponding officers are less experienced. The inventory serves as an inspection of the Communication Department and an introduction to current orders and doctrine under which you will operate. Your unequivocal statement that you have each of the publications listed on the inventory should be based on your own eyesight. Failure to ensure that the publications are on board on assumption of command would be a very serious omission on your part.

1512. RECORDS SIGNED. "A commanding officer about to be relieved shall submit reports of fitness of officers and sign all logbooks, journals, and other documents requiring his signature up to the date of his relief." The only caution here is to make sure, by inspection and questioning, that the records are complete, before you relieve your predecessor.

1513. DUTIES OF THE COMMANDING OFFICER. The regulations so far quoted are taken from Navy Regulations, Chapter 7. After you assume command, get out your regulation book and carefully read it over again. You will find that the responsibilities and duties that it details have a much more personal meaning. Of particular interest, you will discover, is Section 2 of that chapter, which includes such material as safe navigation, pilotage, anchoring, ship handling, entering port, customs inspections, quarantine, relations with merchant seamen, marriages on board, and loss of a ship (for Ceremony of Turnover of Command, see Section 528).

1514. THE GENERAL MESS. The Commanding Officer's duties and responsibilities with respect to the general mess and the Commissary Department of a ship are given in Navy Regulations, Chapter 18, and the Supply Systems Command Manual. The duties, responsibilities and accountability of the Commanding Officer of a small ship without a Supply Corps officer are involved and difficult and are covered in detail in the Supply Systems Command Manual, Chapter VIII. Of particular interest on taking command is the inventory of provisions, which, while not specifically mentioned in the Navy Regulations, should be a matter of special concern to the new commanding officer. It is probable that more trouble has been caused to the commanding officers of small ships by the general mess than by any other single activity in a ship. It is to your interest to ensure that the inventory on taking command is absolutely correct. *The only way to be sure of this is to participate in the inventory yourself.*

You will quite probably be assured that this is entirely unnecessary. Since it is a laborious task, you will probably be inclined to let the Commissary Officer do it. Be smart. Do it yourself. Many a commanding officer has awakened months after taking command to find his Commissary Department short of supplies, and checking back only assured him that *he had signed for provisions he did not have on board.*

Conditions may make personal inventory impossible. But, remember, these are the statements your predecessor and you will sign on the day you take command:

> I certify that this inventory covers all provisions actually on board this date and that I hold myself accountable for them.
>
> /s/ S. P. HALE
> Commander, USN
> Commanding

> I hereby acknowledge receipt of the provisions listed on this inventory.
>
> /s/ J. P. DOLE
> Commander, USN

If, owing to operations against an enemy, you are unable to take this inventory on assuming command, seize the first opportunity personally to check the monthly inventory of provisions. If shortages should exist, it is much better that *you* discover and report them, rather than have them discovered for you during an administrative inspection by the type commander.

A reference to court-martial orders of the past will show you what has happened to careless or dishonest commissary officers and stewards.

1515. SHIP'S STORE. Another prolific source of worry and trouble to a commanding officer is the Ship's Store, especially in a small ship when a Supply Corps officer is not regularly assigned. While he does not receipt for the stores on the inventory of the Ship's Store on taking command, he should concern himself that an accurate inventory has been taken. Make sure that the Ship's Store Officer and the member of the Auditing Board conducting the inventory *actually see* each item and that they open cases so as not to be fooled by the old "empty-case" fraud.

A case illustrative of this point occurred in a destroyer. The Ship's Store Operator (the enlisted man detailed to run the store) had for months informed the Ship's Store Officer and a member of the Auditing Board that he had 10 cases of cigarettes stowed in the afterhold. Both officers blithely accepted his statement, although the key to the afterhold was kept by a seaman rather than by the operator. When the true state of affairs came to light, the operator was discovered to be short stores valued at more than $200. Every officer in the ship except the Engineer Officer, who had not been a member of the Auditing Board, got into trouble as a result of the series of careless inventories and audits.

You cannot check the administration of your Ship's Store too carefully. Be sure of the following:

1. That Ship's Store Operator is bonded. That Ship's Store Officer, if not an officer of the Supply Corps, is bonded.

2. That you have impressed upon the members of your Auditing Board, personally, the importance of their duties, particularly the duty of accurate and complete inventory, and that *cash on hand is cash* (not the checks of members of the Ship's Store organization).

3. That checks are promptly banked. No checks older than 10 days should be carried as cash.

4. That you carefully check the monthly audits.

5. That you have impressed upon the Ship's Store Officer the importance of his duties.

6. Become thoroughly conversant with Supply Systems Command Manual, Chapters III and VIII and require strict compliance therewith.

1516. REPORT OF ASSUMPTION OF COMMAND. "A report of a normal, routine transfer of command and of the inspection referred to in this article [NR-0739] shall be prepared and signed by the officer being relieved and shall be endorsed by the officer succeeding him. . . . A report of the transfer of command that contains statements indicating the possible existence of unsatisfactory conditions, or adverse comments with respect to the state of readiness of the command, or its ability to perform its assigned mission, or any other nonroutine information of direct concern to higher authority, shall contain the opinion of the succeeding officer in regard thereto, and such explanation by endorsement as the officer being relieved may deem necessary. This report shall be forwarded to the Chief of Naval Operations via the chain of command with a copy direct to the commander in chief of the fleet concerned in the case of a command attached to the Operating Forces, or to the appropriate bureau or office of the Navy Department in the case of a command attached to a shore establishment, and to such other commands, bureaus, or offices as may have a direct interest. One copy shall be retained by each of the officers between whom the transfer of command takes place."

Regulations change, and forms for reporting change of command change with them. One form of letter report that has, in the past, proved to be adequate is given here.

U. S. Pacific Fleet
Destroyer Squadron Five
USS BLAKE (DD-510)
c/o Fleet Post Office
San Francisco, California

In reply refer to:
DD510/SPH:jco
Ser: 032
30 July 19—

CONFIDENTIAL

From: Commander Samuel P. HALE, USN, 357624/1100
To: Commander Destroyer Squadron FIVE
Sub: Relieving of Command of USS BLAKE (DD-510)
Ref: (a) U. S. Navy Regulations, 1948, Article 0739
      (b) BUPERS orders Pers-B1123 of 20 May 1968
      (c) BUPERS orders Pers-B1123 of 25 May 1968

1. In accordance with reference (a), I report having been relieved this date of command of the USS BLAKE (DD-510) by Commander John P. DOLE in accordance with references (b) and (c).

2. A thorough inspection of the USS BLAKE has been made by me in company with my relief.

3. The crew was exercised at general quarters and general drills.

4. The following have been turned over to my relief:
   a. All unexecuted orders.
   b. Corrected copies of Fleet, Force, and Unit Instructions, including letters.
   c. Audit of postal accounts and effects.
   d. The combination to the confidential locker and all keys normally kept in the Captain's cabin.

e. Censorship stamps number 10036 through 1139.

5. All registered publications have been audited, inventoried, the report signed, submitted and filed in accordance with RPS 4(G), Article 383.

6. I have signed the log, fitness reports of officers and other papers requiring signature to date, and have submitted my fitness report to the reporting senior.

7. Upon completion of the inspection, the crew was mustered at quarters and the orders turning over the command were read.

8. The present status of the general mess as of the date of relief indicated that the ship has an unused balance of $234.62.

9. The status of the ship's operating allotment is as follows:

Obligations outstanding	$10,324.45
Unobligated balance	$123,456.22

SAMUEL P. HALE

On inspection of the USS BLAKE (DD-510), I found conditions as reported above.

JOHN P. DOLE

Copy to:
CNO
CINCPACFLT
COMCRUDESPAC
COMDESFLOT ONE

DECLASSIFIED 1 July 19—

1517. STATUS OF COMMANDING OFFICER RELIEVED. "The officer relieved, though without authority after turning over the command, is, until his departure, entitled to all the ceremonies and distinctions accorded him while in command."

1518. FIRST OFFICERS' CONFERENCE. At the earliest possible moment, the new Commanding Officer should hold a conference with all officers. At this conference, he should lay down his policies in broad, but definite, terms, so that the officers will know how to conduct their departments to suit him.

The Commanding Officer should tell the officers something about himself, his characteristics, what annoys him, what pleases him, his receptiveness to suggestion, and other pertinent facts about his personality that will affect the discipline and happiness of the ship. A number of points might be mentioned here that a new commanding officer might take up at this conference, but these cannot better be expressed than by quoting the speech of the new Commanding Officer of the U.S.S. *Clark*,[1]

[1] Courtesy of Vice Admiral L. H. Thebaud, USN, (Ret.)

which is of such outstanding excellence as to have become a classic of our modern Navy.

At this time when we are commissioning a new ship and all starting fresh on a clean slate practically strangers to one another, it may be of value to you to have some idea of the point of view, likes and dislikes, desires and peculiarities of your Commanding Officer.

Accordingly I have set forth below a few observations, some original, some not, in the hope that they may give you a helpful insight into my philosophy of naval life.

A ship cannot be imagined without organized leadership. It is obvious that the first essential in any military body is an established system of controlling men. We have the benefit of the system as it exists in the Navy. We are backed up by all the machinery of law, regulations, and custom. They help a lot, but such things are only externals—means to an end. Obedience itself is not the object. It is only a step toward the end—a necessary step, but it should be a demonstration of willingness and not an evidence of compulsion. The end sought is the coordination of individual strength to produce the maximum concentrated effort toward the accomplishment of the object in view.

We shall never be leaders as long as our men are giving only the measure of obedience *compelled* by law. We shall be leaders only when our men look up to us with confidence, when they are anxious to know our wishes, eager to win our praise and ready to jump at a word from us in the execution of our orders regardless of whether they think them right or wrong.

How is this to be done? How can we arouse this sentiment in the men of this ship? The answer is simple, but the practice is difficult.

By setting the example. By practicing what we preach.

In the morning when we appear on deck, let us think what we would like every man in the crew to be and then let us try to be that man ourselves. Men unconsciously imitate their officers. We stand before them constantly as examples. If we are military, smart, decisive in our bearing, they will brace up and try to be like us. But if we are sloppy, careless and seem congenital sufferers from that "tired feeling," no amount of nagging will make the men otherwise. If we are active, energetic, enthusiastic, and perhaps best of all, *cheerful,* our example will be contagious.

A ship, like a navy, is as good as the men in that ship—*no better.*

Officers can guide, can influence, can mould men. But whether their efforts are successful depends upon the officers setting the very best example in everything and of *"Practicing what they preach."* There is scarcely anything more infamous, more destructive of discipline and loyalty, than the officer whose philosophy of life is based on the principle of "Don't do as I do, do as I say."

Know the practical business of going to sea. The examination papers of many officers reveal the fact that while they are able to make a diagram of a radio set or sketch of a Diesel engine, they are often deplorably deficient in elementary seamanship, in Rules of the Road, the different kinds of buoys, and how to lower or hook on a boat in a seaway. Whatever your other technical qualifications, you must be a good sailorman. I want you to know more about every man and everything in your department or part of the ship than any man in it. Know where the fire plugs are, the spanners, nozzles, magazine floods, water-tight doors, and how to handle them. Know where everything is stowed. I want every officer in the ship personally and without assistance to be able to veer chain, let go an anchor, put on a stopper, and heave in. In case of fire, collision or other emergency, lead your men through knowledge acquired beforehand. Be *able* to take charge, and when you are in charge, then *be* in charge. You know theoretically far more than any enlisted man. The same is true of all graduates of the Naval Academy. Yet you have seen, as I have seen, a lot of officers standing around like tailors' dummies, afraid they might be mistaken.

If your powers of general observation are not of the best, develop them by conscientious training. When you go up topside or walk about the decks learn instinctively to look around. Drill yourself constantly until you notice without effort and make a mental note of such things as the direction of the wind, whether or not it is freshening or the sky becoming overcast, the absence of the Admiral's flag from the ship where it usually flies, that some ship has gone alongside the tanker, that another is painting or preparing to weigh, etc. And in this process don't forget the *Clark*. If you see lines or swabs hanging over the side or the colors are foul, don't pass it all up because you are not on duty—*do* something about it. We are all on duty 24 hours a day, although not necessarily at all times engaged in executive duty. And in this connection if you return aboard at 0311 and fail to see the O.O.D., don't turn in and forget it because you're not on watch and it's not your pigeon anyhow. If you do, you're infinitely more remiss in your duty than was the O.O.D. in being in the fireroom or on the bridge over a bowl of coffee.

It is *not* how much ability an officer *has*, but *how well he uses* what he *does* have that determines his value to the Navy.

A man's character expresses itself in everything he does.

It is said that "responsibility makes cowards of us all." How many of us are but too inclined to criticize and hold forth on what *we* would do were we in so-and-so's billet. Yet when we actually do step into his shoes and shoulder the responsibility for the success or failure of operations which seemed so simple from the outside looking in, we find this responsibility so discouraging to our dash and conceit that we only too frequently follow the path of least resistance—excessive caution.

Any fool can criticize. Most fools do.

Don't nag your men; don't neglect them; don't coddle them; don't play the clown.

Almost any man with brains can run a reasonably well-designed piece of machinery. But it takes a lot more than brains successfully and continuously to run the human machine.

In matters of personal bearing, uniform, etc., I shall expect you to be guided by my example. There are certain practices to which I strongly object. They are:

1. Failing smartly to return salutes rendered you.

2. The wearing of unstarched collars with blue uniforms in port.

3. The wearing of dirty, spotted, torn, or frayed uniforms at any time except when working on greasy machinery.

4. Lounging in the Wardroom in dungarees or out of uniform.

5. Pacing or lounging on the weather decks with hands in trouser pockets. If your hands are cold put them in your blouse or jacket side pockets. It does not look unseamanlike and that is what the jacket pockets are for.

6. Chewing gum at any time in uniform.

7. Leaning over or against the life lines or against anything on the weather decks, thereby telling the world that one is a victim of that "tired feeling."

8. Needing a shave after 0800.

9. Any kind of cheap, vulgar, uncultivated talk, especially to or in the presence of an enlisted man.

10. Pencils and fountain pens in sight in uniform outside breast pockets.

11. He who suddenly bursts into a frenzy of energy and zeal when unexpectedly he finds himself under the eye of the Captain.

At sea in matters of uniform take your cue from me.

Avoid, as you would the plague, hostile criticism of authority, or even facetious or thoughtless criticism that has no hostile intent. Our naval gunnery instructions state that "Destructive criticism that is born in officers' messes will soon spread through the ship and completely kill the ship spirit."

Admiral Lord Jervis said: "Discipline begins in the Wardroom. I dread not the seamen. It is the *indiscreet* conversations of the officers and their *presumptuous* discussions of the orders they receive that produce all our ills!"

1519. OFFICIAL CALLS. Prior to taking command of your ship, you will have reported to the various commanders as directed in your orders. If putting a ship into commission, you should also make courtesy calls on the naval officials present in the area immediately adjacent to the shipyard or naval base. Now that you have assumed command, there are certain official calls you are expected to make.

Whether at a shipyard or base for commissioning or anchored out in the stream for turnover of command, immediately after taking command, make official calls on the following officers, if present in the area, or as soon as you fall in with them:

Senior officer present afloat
District commandant
Naval base commander
Fleet commander
Task force commander, if so assigned
Type commander
Division commander

See also Sections 414 and 510-515.

Many senior officers set great stock on these calls. It gives them a chance to meet you and size you up. When your name comes up, they know what you look like and something about you. It will also be helpful to you to get to know the senior officers with and for whom you

will be working. More important, it is the correct thing to do and it gets
you off to a good start in your new command billet.

1520. Succession to command. In the event of incapacity, death,
relief from duty, detachment without relief, or absence of the officer
detailed to command a ship, he shall be succeeded by the line officer,
eligible for command at sea, next in rank and regularly attached to and
on board the ship, until relieved by competent authority or until the
regular Commanding Officer returns. It is the responsibility of this
temporary Commanding Officer to endeavor to carry on the routine and
other affairs of the ship in the same manner as his predecessor. In carrying out his duties, the officer in temporary command has the same authority and responsibility as the regular Commanding Officer and receives the same reports. No ceremony is involved in such a temporary
change.

1521. The opportunity and your own policies. Command of a
man-of-war is a very personal responsibility. The policies and methods
of your predecessor may not have been the sort that will suit you.
Doubtless you will wish to make changes. Be advised, however, and
move slowly. Let the regulations and organization stand for a month or
so before you institute changes. Perhaps you will decide, with better
acquaintance, that they are not so very far from what you desire.

Never let fall the hint that in your opinion the previous regime was
ineffective. While this is sometimes the case, such an attitude constitutes an underhanded attack upon your predecessor, who can, in his
absence, make no rebuttal. Furthermore, on the part of a new Commanding Officer, this attitude will inevitably build up resentment among
the members of the command.

Study the organization and orders in effect. When an opportunity
for improvement presents itself, do not hesitate to seize it.

The morale of the crew of a ship is of the gravest concern to the
Commanding Officer (see Section 619). The following notes for the
new Commanding Officer have proved to be effective in both large and
small ships to elevate the morale of the crew:

The wise Captain does not gather too much power into his own hands.
While reserving unto himself all final authority, responsibility, and
power of decision, he will distribute as much responsibility and authority among his various subordinates as they can conceivably accept.

The Commanding Officer must at all times demonstrate a sincere interest in his officers and men. Visit all personnel on the sick list and in hospital. Insist on a regular training program for all officers and men and that division officers and leading petty officers actively supervise and participate in divisional training.

After each operating period, hold meritorious mast for deserving men. Encourage division officers to recommend for commendation those men who have performed capably during operations.

One of the most effective methods of achieving good order and discipline in a command is not a formal method of discipline at all, but the utilization of nonpunitive measures. A commanding officer may utilize "nonpunitive measures," such as administrative admonitions, reprimands, exhortations, disapprovals, criticisms, censures, reproofs, and rebukes, either written or oral. These nonpunitive measures may also include, subject to any applicable regulations, administrative withholding of privileges. These are to be utilized as corrective measures, more analogous to instruction than punishment.

Keep in personal touch with performance of ship's police force to ensure that they are properly performing their duties and are not exceeding their authority.

See that the crew is kept informed. Publish ship's schedule as far in advance as possible. Have the Navigator post charts in various parts of the ship to inform crew as to ship's movements during extended cruises and local operations. During antisubmarine warfare, gunnery, tactical, and other exercises, explain activities to crew over loudspeaker system. Post or publish evaluations of all exercises.

Take an active interest in the crew's mess. Cause studies to be made to ensure that the mess line is being served at full speed and efficiency. Have a supply officer or chief commissary steward supervise the serving of each meal.

Insist that mess men serve in clean whites and are clean and sanitary in their persons. Change mess men at least once a quarter.

Consider establishing separate tables for first class petty officers to build up their prestige.

Insist that garbage cans be removed inside the screened scullery immediately after each meal.

Sample the crew's chow frequently. At least once a month, take a meal with different divisions of the crew.

Ensure that firm plans are made for leave, liberty and recreation. See Section 617 for suggestions on leave and liberty programs.

Scrupulously avoid direct interference in the details of administration within the sphere of responsibility of a subordinate. If such action should become necessary, either the Captain is meddling or the subordinate is incompetent. If the subordinate be incompetent, he should be reprimanded, either through the Executive Officer or in his presence, or be removed from his position of authority. He should not be subjected to the public humiliation of interference in his affairs and the conse-

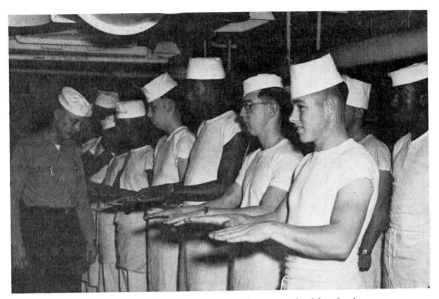

FIGURE 1503. Clean mess men will prepare healthy food.

quent loss of respect and ridicule of his younger officers and men.

The most successful Captain is he, who becomes the best coordinator, not only of the activities of the departments of his command, but also by ensuring that his command maintains its proper relationship to the larger organization of which it is a part.

While the Executive Officer must supervise the over-all activities of the heads of departments, give full authority and complete freedom to each to operate his own department; heads of departments in turn, should be required to delegate similar authority and responsibility to their division officers and leading petty officers. Insist that all hands follow the chain of command.

Any request not approved on any level must be forwarded to the Executive Officer. Requests for transfer from the ship not approved by the Executive Officer must be forwarded to the Commanding Officer.

Continually stress through Executive Officer, First Lieutenant, Officer of the Deck, and at Captain's Inspection the need for the smart, shipshape appearance of ship and crew on topside. See that the men of the crew are daily inspected for personal appearance at Quarters.

Administer strict and prompt justice, with kindliness and understanding. An otherwise excellent organization can be disrupted by poorly administered discipline. Officers and men must be held up to a high standard of performance. Errors in judgment and inadequate performance of duty must be corrected and infractions of good discipline must be punished, but the Captain, in acting as judge and jury at Captain's Mast, must be certain that his disciplinary actions are taken as corrective measures and not as a means of venting personal spite.

In your relationship with your officers, be firm, but also be kindly and courteous. By your example, set a high standard of performance and insist that it be maintained. Demonstrate your belief in the correctness of your cause. Show your trust and confidence in your officers. As you will accept the word of your subordinates, so must you be ruthless, stern, even severe, when one of your officers fails to deserve that trust. Thus will you build up a relationship of mutual loyalty, confidence, and respect within your command.

The problems of leadership are greater for one in command. The Commanding Officer must inform himself as to the individual peculiarities, characteristics, and dispositions of the officers and of as many of the men under him as may be at all possible. He must endeavor to cultivate in his subordinates a seamanlike and military spirit, a proper sense of duty and honor, and a careful observance of professional etiquette, so as to develop them into well-rounded naval officers and men.

1522. THE SHIP HAS A PERMANENT IDENTITY. You might say she has a definite personality. With normal good fortune, many commanding officers will guide her destiny down through the years. Among them will be a few outstanding officers who will impress upon her personality the indelible mark of their genius. As one of these many commanding officers, you should try to leave behind you a unit of the fleet, a ship, that is a little better for your service in her. If you can accomplish that, your accomplishment will be its own reward.

The following lines express in verse the author's feelings about a ship better than they could ever be expressed in prose.

THE SOUL OF A SHIP

Now, some say that men make a ship and her fame
    As she goes on her way down to sea;
That the crew which first man her will give her a name—
    Good, bad, or whatever may be.
The recruits coming after them soon fall in line.
    And carry tradition along—
If the spirit was good, it will always be fine—
    If bad, it will always be wrong.

The soul of a ship is a marvelous thing,
    Not made of its wood or its steel,
But fashioned of mem'ries and songs that men sing,
    And fed by the passions men feel.
It's built of ambition, of jealousy, strife,
    Of friendship, of love, and of fear;
It includes almost all of the makings of Life;
    It's nurtured on grumble—and cheer.

The soul of a ship is a molder of men—
    Her spirit lives on through the years.
As she started her life, so she is to the end;
    She shares each recruit's hopes and fears.
And each man who joins feels the breath of her life—
    As he stands up and takes heart again—
So he takes to himself the old sea as his wife,
    And the ship's made a man among men.

CHAPTER 16

The Naval Officer Ashore

Seek the company of only the best in men and women.
—ADMIRAL WILLIAM V. PRATT, USN

1601. GENERAL. As shore duty is but one phase of an officer's career pattern, it is necessary to consider it in relation to foreign-shore duty, sea duty, and rotation between sea duty and shore duty.

Shore duty comprises all duty on shore within the United States and at desirable locations overseas; service in the reserve fleets and in ships of the reserve fleets; in most district vessels and craft; and in ships and craft assigned to the Naval Reserve for training purposes.

Foreign shore duty is duty ashore at all overseas stations. For rotational purposes it is divided into two classes:

(a) Desirable locations are considered the same as shore duty in the United States.

(b) Other locations are designated as "foreign shore duty" and may be combined with sea duty in one cruise (tour of sea duty) for rotational purposes. Inasmuch as localities and total personnel requirements vary for this type of duty, it is not practicable to give a list of stations or assignments so classed. Rotation to and from foreign shore duty is examined in the light of conditions at each station and the balanced career assignment for the officer involved.

Sea Duty. A tour of sea duty is called a *cruise*. It comprises service in seagoing ships of the fleet and some other services which have been specifically designated as sea duty by the Navy Department. Included is duty at some overseas stations not considered as desirable for shore duty as those in the United States. *Sea duty* commences on date of reporting on board ship and continues until date of detachment. For officers ordered to seagoing ships of the active fleet and to foreign shore

428

duty, sea duty for rotation purposes commences with date of reporting on board or sailing from a port after detachment. Service on all ships commissioned in the Navy is considered sea duty for record purposes. So are periods of a month or more of temporary duty on board a vessel in commission during a normal tour of shore duty. For further details, see BuPers Manual, Article C5102.

Rotation Between Sea Duty and Shore Duty.—Normal *cruises* for line officers are:

(A) Male:

1. Two years for commanders and above.

2. Three to five years for officers below the grade of commander, except warrant officers. Cruises for warrant officers vary by category as determined by the number of "sea" and "shore" billets within each category. Various Bureau of Naval Personnel directives are published from time to time reflecting current tour practices as dictated by changing needs of the service.

(B) Women:

1. Normally 18 months minimum for all ranks. Ensigns will not normally be assigned to duty outside the continental limits of the United States.

Normal tours of shore duty for line officers are:

(A) Male:

1. Three years for captains and above.

2. Two and one-half to three years for commanders.

3. Two to four years for officers below the grade of commander depending on the current needs of the service.

(B) Women:

1. Two and one-half to three years for lieutenants and above.

2. Two to two and one-half years for ensigns and lieutenants (junior grade).

For male officers of the Staff Corps, a regular alternation between sea and shore cannot always be effected. Normal sequence generally will be: shore-sea-shore-foreign shore. The sequence may be modified by the exigencies of the service and the necessity to equalize the character of total service performed by officers of the same grades. For women officers of the Staff Corps (including officers of the Nurse Corps) the normal tour of duty in any one locality within CONUS is three years; overseas assignments normally are for a minimum of 18 months.

Rotation of limited duty officers between sea, shore, and foreign shore duty is planned to approximate, as far as possible, the rotation of unrestricted line officers.

Sea duty is, of course, your reason for being in the Navy. At sea is the only place where the line officer can acquire the seagoing background and experience which he will require for increasing responsibility in the higher ranks. *Only* on sea duty can the staff corps officer acquire that intimate knowledge and personal experience of the fleet, ships, and seagoing life which is essential to their effective performance of duty ashore.

Shore Duty

1602. STATIONS AVAILABLE. Duty stations located on shore both at home and overseas are many and varied. A typical naval base includes a naval station, naval supply center or depot, a naval shipyard, a naval magazine or ammunition depot and other activities which furnish direct logistic support to the Operating Forces. A naval air station, although coming under the military command of the Commander, Naval Air Bases, of the district may be "further assigned" as a component of a naval base in accordance with General Order 19. A naval base component houses the naval base headquarters and often a naval district headquarters.

The Navy Department and such large special-purpose activities as the Naval Academy, the Naval Postgraduate School, the Naval War College, special postgraduate schools, the stations of the Naval Air Training Command and the Naval Missile Center provide large numbers of shore billets for officers. Other stations may be small or isolated—or both.

Overseas, there is a wide geographical range of duty stations such as naval missions, military assistance advisory groups, and naval attaché "posts."

A full listing of naval activities located ashore all over the world will be found in the Catalog of Naval Shore Activities, published quarterly by the Office of the Chief of Naval Operations.

1603. DUTY AND RESPONSIBILITY ASHORE. One of the oddities of naval service since World War II and the Korean conflict is that, not only are more naval personnel serving on shore than ever before, but also a higher percentage of the total number are stationed ashore. With officers and men in increasing numbers living off the base and "commuting to work," there is a danger that the individual will lose that sense of close identification with his organization which is so important in building up a team spirit. The result is that the capable leader on shore has to work harder and more effectively in shorter hours to accomplish as good results.

But the officers and men stationed ashore at naval stations are not the only concern of the naval officer ashore. His fellow officers and the enlisted men making liberty and leave from our ships in ports both at home and abroad have great potentials for advancement of the aims of our government and the enhancement of the reputation of our Navy— and for trouble.

Whether naval personnel are performing sea duty, shore duty, or foreign shore duty, the verities of leadership for the commander of shore-based units are unchanged, but the problems are compounded.

1604. ORGANIZATION. Naval stations are organized much the same as described for a ship in Chapter 12 (see Figure 1601). There are a number of physical differences. Instead of the high concentration of activity in a ship, sound management and military security require that the headquarters be centralized but that various units be dispersed over wide areas. In some naval bases, the shipyard may be separated from base headquarters by several miles; the naval air station may be separated from other activities for physical reasons; enlisted and officer housing is often a considerable distance from the buildings where the occupants work.

Officers and men work in offices and buildings instead of ships; single officers live in Bachelor Officers' Quarters and single men in barracks; many young married officers and men live off base at a considerable distance from their duty stations. A modification of routine and organization is required to accommodate for these differences. But the same Navy Regulations apply. The Station Organization and the Station Regulations are just as important to personnel ashore. And the same high standard of discipline must be maintained.

Resembling a small town, almost all of the facilities and services you would expect to find in such a community are available on a naval station. Like small towns, naval stations vary because of size, age, degree of isolation, and their mission. Before leaving for a new station, you should make every effort to collect full information available locally. A letter to your future head of department or the station Executive Officer will bring you information of much value to your family and yourself.

1605. HOUSING. Bachelor Officers' Quarters are often integrated physically with the Officers' Club, but may be found in a separate building. The rooms are comfortably furnished. The more senior bachelor

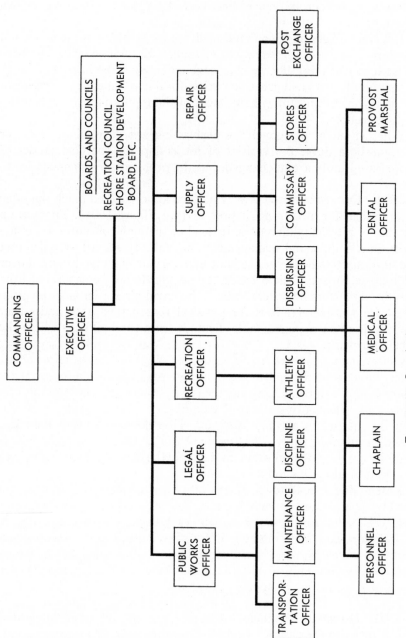

FIGURE 1601. Organization of a small naval station.

FIGURE 1602. Bachelor Officers' Quarters at Little Creek.

officers have correspondingly better quarters, frequently consisting of sitting room, bedroom, and bath.

A station may have both a "closed" Officers' Mess, where only residents of the BOQ and their personal guests may dine, and an "open" Mess in connection with the Officers' Club, where authorized members of the Mess may use all of its facilities. Excellent meals are readily available to the bachelor officers (See also Sections 415 and 416).

Married officers may live in government quarters on station, comfortable permanent residences, furnished, equipped, and maintained by the Public Works department. Others live in emergency housing developments, such as Wherry Housing units. Still others must find their own quarters, in rental residences at varying distances from the base.

Enlisted men live in barracks, if single. A few government quarters are available on some stations for married enlisted men. With increasing numbers of low-rated enlisted men married, many married sailors have difficulty finding quarters anywhere near their station which they can afford, necessitating much more "welfare work" among the enlisted men and their families than formerly. The Navy Relief Society and Red Cross workers can be helpful in times of personal crisis, but officers will find that they must take an even greater interest in the family problems of their enlisted men ashore than of those serving in ships. A man disturbed over the welfare of his family is correspondingly less efficient and useful to his organization (see also Sections 1609, 1720 and 1721).

1606. MEDICAL CARE. Medical facilities at a naval station may range from a small dispensary capable of handling routine sickness and emergencies to a large naval hospital with a capacity for caring for any medical or surgical case. Routine treatment for active duty personnel is given daily at "sick call"—emergencies are handled at any time of the day or night. Dental care for active officers and enlisted men is provided. The Medical Department of a naval station is also responsible for a continuing campaign to prevent disease and injury.

Medical care for dependents of active-duty servicemen is authorized by law (10 USC 1071-1087), originally the Dependents' Medical Care Act (1956) and now greatly expanded by P.L. 89-614, 89th Congress. By joint regulation of the Uniformed Services, the program which provides the benefits of the law has been designated the Uniformed Services Health and Medical Benefits Program. It applies to all of the Uniformed Services: Army, Navy, Air Force, Marine Corps, Coast Guard, and the commissioned corps of the Public Health Service and of the Environmental Science Services Administration (formerly the Coast and Geodetic Survey). In addition to active-duty dependents it provides benefits for retired members and their dependents, and for survivors of active-duty members and retired members.

The current issue of SecNav Instruction 6320.8 series has the up-to-date information on the benefits available and the procedures applicable. This directive is available at all naval activities.

The following general information applies only to dependents of a uniformed service member who is on active duty for a period in excess of 30 days. Benefits also apply to retired personnel and their dependents except where indicated.

Dependents are defined as:
1. Wife.
2. Unremarried widow.
3. Husband, if dependent on his wife for more than one-half of his support.
4. Unremarried widower, if he was dependent on his wife at the time of her death for more than one-half of his support because of a mental or physical incapacity.

5. Unmarried legitimate child, adopted child, or step-child who either
   (1) has not passed his 21st birthday, regardless of whether dependent upon the serviceman, or
   (2) is 21 or over but incapable of self-support because of a mental or physical incapacity that existed before age 21 and is dependent upon the serviceman (or was at his death) for more than one-half of his support.
   (3) is 21 or 22, enrolled in a full-time course in an approved institution of higher learning, and dependent upon the serviceman (or was at his death) for more than one-half of his support.
6. Parent or parent-in-law who is (or was at the death of the serviceman), dependent on him for more than one-half of his support and residing in a dwelling place provided or maintained by him.

Indentification required is DD Form 1173 (Uniformed Services Indentification and Privilege Card). Application for this card should be made on DD Form 1172 which you may obtain from the ship's office or personnel office. Other identification may be used in an emergency. Children under 10 years of age do not require cards. Their identity may be established by a parent with either the serviceman's I.D. card or the dependent parent's DD Form 1173.

Source of care. Retired personnel and their dependents are eligible for care in medical facilities of the uniformed services subject to the availability of space and facilities, and the capabilities of the professional staff. Wives and children not residing with their sponsors have free choice between armed services medical facilities and civilian medical facilities. Retired persons and wives and children residing with their sponsors will be granted inpatient civilian medical care only where there is no armed service facility in the vicinity or when required care cannot be given by such a facility. Non-availability Statements (DD Form 1251) must be obtained from the nearest uniformed service installation before seeking such care from civilian services. This statement is not required in an emergency or when the sponsor is absent on a trip. Dependents may use civilian sources for outpatient care without non-availability statements even if uniformed services facilities are available.

Treatment is authorized in service facilities on an inpatient or outpatient basis for medical and surgical conditions; nervous, mental and emotional disorders; chronic conditions and diseases; and contagious diseases. As part of or in addition to such treatment, dependents are also authorized physical examinations including eye examinations, diagnostic services, family planning services, home calls when medically necessary, ambulance service, artificial limbs and eyes, the loan of durable equipment, and limited dental care. Among those items not authorized are domiciliary or custodial care, prosthetic devices (other than artificial limbs and eyes), hearing aids, orthopedic footwear, and spectacles.

Treatment authorized at civilian sources may be either on an inpatient or outpatient basis for the same conditions, disorders and diseases as authorized in service facilities, with some exceptions. As part of such treatment, or in addition to it, the dependents may obtain family planning services, diagnostic services, insulin, drugs and medicines for which the law requires a prescription, orthopedic braces (except orthopedic shoes), crutches, artificial limbs and eyes, civilian ambulance service when medically necessary, rental of durable equipment, immunizations as part of treatment, home calls, and routine physical examinations when required by dependents who are to perform travel outside the United States under official orders as a result of the serviceman's duty assignment. Among the benefits not provided are spectacles or examinations for them, dental care except as a necessary part of medical or surgical treatment, prosthetic devices other than artificial limbs and artificial eyes, hearing aids, orthopedic shoes, routine immunizations and examinations other than indicated above, routine care of the newborn and well-baby care.

Services of Christian Science practitioners and nurses and hospitalization in a Christian Science sanatorium have also been authorized.

The seriously physically handicapped and the moderately or severely mentally retarded eligible spouses and children, as an additional feature of the program, are authorized special health services, and training and rehabilitation in civilian facilities. They may get diagnosis, inpatient and outpatient care, home treatment, training, rehabilitation, special education, institutional (residential) care in private non-profit, public and state institutions, and transportation to institutional care when appropriate. Prior approval is required before the Government can pay for any of these benefits. Further information is contained in the current directive in the Secnavinst 6320.8 series.

The charge for hospitalization in a uniformed services hospital is $1.75 a day. There is no charge for outpatient care.

The charge for hospitalization in a civilian hospital is $1.75 a day or $25 whichever is greater and for retired members and their dependents 25 percent of the hospital's charges and fees. For civilian outpatient care the patient is responsible for the first $50 of the expenses each fiscal year (1 July-30 June) and for 20 percent of the balance of all charges over the $50 (25 percent for retired members and their dependents). However, a family of two or more eligible dependents receiving care is not required to pay collectively more than the first $100 of charges each fiscal year plus 20 percent of the charges in excess of the $100 (25 percent for retired members and their dependents).

The patient's share of the expenses in the handicapped program depends upon the rank of the serviceman. The monthly payment is determined on a graduated scale running from $25 a month for the lowest enlisted grade to $250 for the highest commissioned pay grade officer. The Government will pay the balance up to $350 a month. Anything in excess of the $350 is added to the patient's share. A member who has more than one dependent receiving benefits under the handicapped program need pay only the patients share for the dependent whose charges are the least.

1607. THE NAVY COMMISSARY. The privilege of making purchases in a commissary is restricted to Regular (active and retired) armed services personnel, to Reserve personnel on active or training duty, to certain government civilians in special situations, and to their dependents. Everyone entitled to commissary privileges must have a valid identification card.

Stocks and services vary somewhat from station to station, depending upon the size of the establishment and its isolation. In some localities, one commissary is maintained by one of the armed services for the use of all the services.

The use of the naval commissary is a privilege, not a right. All purchases made by a member of the service must be for the use of himself or his household.

1608. THE NAVY EXCHANGE. A Navy Exchange is maintained at all naval bases and stations and at many smaller naval facilities. The exchange may be compared to the small town general stores. At larger bases, it carries stock as complete and varied as a small department store.

The Navy Exchange is designed to provide at reasonable prices for naval personnel, active and retired, and their dependents the articles which they require for their everyday needs. From the reasonable profits which are allowed and which are transferred to the station Welfare Fund, recreation and amusement for the station personnel are provided.

438 THE NAVAL OFFICER'S GUIDE

In addition to uniforms and accessories and other clothing, both military and civilian, the Navy Exchange stocks household supplies, many of the articles found in the corner drug store, periodicals, and tools and garden equipment. In addition, many exchanges operate soda fountains and lunchrooms, barber and beauty shops, and cobbler and tailor shops.

Eligibility for use of the Navy Exchange is the same as described for the commissary. Be prepared to identify yourself with an identification card if not in uniform.

1609. WELFARE. The activities of the Chaplain are described in Section 1030. Most naval stations have a legal assistance officer to provide legal advice to naval personnel and their dependents. American Red Cross workers and members of the Navy Relief Society do welfare work among the families of naval personnel, as required. The Navy Mutual Aid Association has a representative at many stations. The assistance provided by these groups has been more fully described in Sections 1720 and 1721.

1610. RECREATION. Most posts provide excellent recreational opportunities. Sports facilities (golf, tennis, boating, baseball, etc.) and hobby shops are open to all officers and men. The center of much of an officer's recreational activity will be the Officers' Club (see Section 415). Every naval station has a library, readily available to all personnel and their dependents.

1611. PARTICIPATION IN COMMUNITY LIFE. Naval officers stationed ashore have always been noted for their participation in the life of the community in which they live. If living in quarters on station, this is sometimes difficult, until an officer reaches the higher ranks. But those officers living in residences in the adjacent city or town have a great opportunity and an obligation. Their children are entered in the city schools. Participation in Parent-Teacher Association meetings and activities permits you to meet your neighbors and indicates an interest in the community and a willingness to contribute. Much good can be accomplished for the education of your children. Nearly all schools, public or private, require the help of the parents if the children are to have the equipment necessary for a well-rounded basic education.

Participation in church activities can be a rewarding experience. Many officers, both active and retired, become members and leaders of men's groups or vestrymen of the churches of their choice. Quite a few junior and senior officers, as a result of participation in church work, take on such responsibilities as Boy Scout Leader or members of a Scout Troop Committee, Superintendent of Sunday School or teacher therein, assistant coach for church or school teams, and many other activities which help to make a better community.

Active participation in partisan politics by naval officers while on active duty is prohibited. However, the naval officer is a citizen. He has an obligation to study and understand the political and foreign relations problems of his country. To be effective in this area when a senior officer, he must commence his apprenticeship early. There is no better arena for his earlier studies than the local politics of a community or a small city. If a homeowner (and elsewhere this is recommended), the officer and his wife should join the local homeowner's association. There, they will learn much about taxation, political problems, and political methods of the town which will be valuable information to them later. They will also more quickly come to know their neighbors and make them friends of the Navy. With residence in a community limited to two or three years, a service family can pass a lonely period upon first arriving in a community unless they are outgoing and willing to participate.

Many officers join a "service club." Membership in such an integral part of the community life at an early age gives an officer a much better understanding of the interrelation of community and service problems, with which he will have to deal officially as a senior officer.

1612. PUBLIC RELATIONS. Too many officers seem to be inclined to leave Navy public relations to the Public Affairs Officers. Good public relations is the job of every naval officer. When you walk down the street of a town or city looking snappy in a smartly turned out uniform, you are exercising good public relations. When you extend yourself to meet, to know, and to be friendly to the civilians you meet, you are establishing good relations. If you are asked to talk to a group, whether it be a Cub Scout Den about life at a naval training center or the Chamber of Commerce about an interesting experience at sea, do not beg off. Give the talk, and do a good job of it.

Like any other service, the Navy needs to be sold. Whether you try or not, you will be the Navy's salesman, good or bad. If you are sloppy or slovenly, backward and reticent, withdrawn, tending to herd only with your fellow Navy families, you will be doing a poor job of public relations. If three or four of your men stage a riot in a local bistro and land in jail, with resultant bad publicity, that is bad public relations. The opportunity for either kind of salesmanship is readily available. Be sure that your own is *good* and insist that your men be good advertising for the naval service.

Foreign Shore and Foreign Sea Duty

1613. THE OPPORTUNITY. Many of the familiar overseas bases of pre-World War II days are still active—Pearl Harbor, Guam, Subic Bay and Sangley Point in the Philippines, Panama, Alaska and Guantánamo Bay. There are also such newer bases as the fleet activities at Yokosuka and Sasebo, Japan; naval air facilities in Spain, the Azores, Sicily; naval stations at Bermuda and Argentia; naval staffs in London, Tokyo and Naples. Naval missions and Military Assistance Advisory Groups serve in many of the countries of the free world, and naval attachés are attached to embassies and legations in virtually every capital in the world.

The Seventh Fleet cruises Far Eastern waters from Japan and Korea to Taipei, Hongkong, the Philippines, and the South Sea Islands and Singapore. The Sixth Fleet patrols the Mediterranean. The Atlantic Fleet makes rendezvous with the British Fleet in exercises in Northern European waters. Elements of that fleet cruise the Caribbean and South American waters.

Before World War II, our far-flung ships in Asiatic and European waters, our fleet cruises to interesting foreign countries, afforded not only the officer but also his wife and children an opportunity to travel and to see and know foreign peoples and customs. Families usually accompanied an officer to fascinating stations in the Far East and Europe. On the Asiatic Station, inexpensive living made it possible for families to spend their winters in the Philippines and to travel north to Hong Kong, Shanghai, Peiping, and Japan during spring, summer, and fall. Many families spent pleasant summers at Tsingtao and Chefoo, where the Asiatic Fleet submarines, cruisers, and destroyers based for exercise and training.

The troubled international situation since the war, while not entirely preventing families from "following the ship," has made it difficult, costly, and fraught with some peril, as witness the experience of service families caught in Seoul at the beginning of the Korean conflict and others who had to move hastily out of Tsingtao and Shanghai as the Communist armies approached.

FIGURE 1603. International ties of friendship are made strong by good-will projects such as donating toward the building of a new school.

As hostilities worsened in South Vietnam, many families were evacuated to safer areas. Frequent rotation of ships to the various tasks fleets on foreign station has prevented authorization of transportation of dependents to the areas at government expense. The cost of private transportation and the questionable living conditions in some countries have caused many a Navy family to decide to wait out the husband's sea duty at home. Most of them have found it the best practice, looking forward to eventual retirement, to buy a home and set up a permanent establishment in a locality where the officer expects frequent shore duty, while others establish themselves at the home port of the husband's ship. The latter carry on the courageous prewar tradition of the Navy wife—*follow your man.* Under anything like postwar "normal conditions," this cannot be recommended too highly by one whose wife always "followed the ship." The rewards in shared joys, troubles, and experiences far exceed the cost in money, inconvenience, and a sometimes primitive way of living.

But a word of caution. Check up before you take your family into an unfamiliar area. *Base your decision on knowledge, not guesswork or wishful thinking.*

1614. RESPONSIBILITY. The opportunity for travel and interesting experience for naval personnel is indeed extensive. But the responsibility is also wide. Whether a tourist on shore leave from a ship of the Navy or stationed in a country, you should bear in mind President Eisenhower's admonition:

> Each of us, whether bearing a commission from his Government or traveling by himself for pleasure or business, is a representative of the United States of America. And he must try to portray America as he believes it in his heart to be—a peace-loving Nation, living in the fear of God, but in the fear of God only, and trying to be partners with our friends.

Literally, all of the seas and ports of the world are a stage, and you an actor upon it. Be sure that you play well your part.

1615. THE CHALLENGE. Because of his mission, the American navyman stationed on foreign soil is too often isolated from the people of the country in bases or stations, but he can still contribute materially to a better understanding of America. The American bluejacket going ashore in foreign ports is generally an excellent representative of his country, but he must guard against the isolated incidents which have at times created serious international crises. It would be well for our naval personnel to consider the instructions which the Department of State has issued to its representatives abroad:

It cannot be overemphasized that persons representing the United States abroad, in any capacity, and their families are the guests of the people of the countries in which they are stationed. This fact implies on their part the same sort of considerate behavior which they would expect in their own households. Their actions are scrutinized not only by the people of the country to which they are sent, but also by their compatriots traveling or residing abroad.

Throughout the world certain modes of behavior help obtain cooperation and others do not. Those that do are simply customs which through long observance have come to be accepted as necessary and useful in the society in which they are found. These customs are part and parcel of their normal behavior.

The pamphlet goes on to advise the newcomer to "adjust to his new post as quickly as possible, [but] he is not expected to adopt those local customs which would make him conspicuous or which would give offense. Usually foreign customs are properly followed only in their native environment. . . . Temporary adaptation to other modes does not supplant the ability to be at ease with your own people at home and abroad."

The presence of our naval officers and men in the ports and cities of foreign countries, many of them seeing other peoples and places for the first time, introduces special problems. Because of the differences from our home country, officers and men find their new experiences interesting but difficult—many of the conveniences of daily life are missing, and the language, customs, usages, characteristics and living habits vary widely from our own.

The naval officer ashore in a foreign country must realize that he is in a great minority—his attitudes and habits are strange and conspicuous. He is as much of an oddity to the local people as they are to him. Be tolerant of manners and customs that differ from your own. Every effort should be made to understand them—otherwise antagonism is certain to develop, which would seriously interfere with the accomplishment of your mission.

You will find that the people of most foreign countries in which you may be stationed want to be friendly and will try to make you feel welcome. They treat foreigners of any nationality as guests, with courtesy. As their guest and an American, you must reciprocate their friendliness and helpfulness. The friendship of the free and uncommitted nations of this world is important to us—it must be strengthened; this is a principal part of your mission abroad.

In many countries, Americans still have a good reputation. Strive to make it better. You will find many peoples are individualistic and independent. Many are romantic, believe that happiness is found in the sheer joy of living. They like good food, good wine, love their families and homes.

If you find it peculiar that your new neighbors take a *siesta* for a couple of hours each afternoon, in time you may also find one necessary in tropical and subtropical climates.

Given the chance for better acquaintance, most people are warm-hearted and hospitable, have quick and curious minds, and possess a deep feeling of humanity. They are ready and willing to like you. This is your challenge—give them the opportunity so to do.

1616. PREPARATION. Certain mental and psychological preparation can ease the "cultural shock" which you are almost certain to experience on your first tour of foreign duty. You can expect to be very thoroughly screened. Do not worry about damage to your career. The Navy Department recognizes the importance of duty overseas as naval attaché, member of naval missions and military aid groups, and is stressing this importance and trying to arrange for orders to officers of such seniority that their career will be advanced not hindered by good performance of their duties abroad.

It is important to such good performance that you be a professional naval officer. A professional naval attaché might possess certain advantages in language, experience in foreign living, and understanding of protocol, but the professional naval officer will always be more useful to the Navy and to our country, because of his better knowledge and understanding of naval problems. The other attributes of a good attaché can and must be learned promptly.

Do not expect too much. The tales of glamour and intrigue may be true in isolated cases and appear fascinating on television, but a great deal of hard work will be involved in the reality of a foreign situation. As one distinguished foreign service officer expressed it, "You need to be intelligent, quick thinking, contemplative. Good headwork is essential, but good footwork is important, too. I have always been afraid my feet will give out before my head."

An active and participating wife, who will be adaptable to any local situation, is vital to success in your mission. Ask yourself—and your wife—do you really want to go?

Try to obtain a frank and objective view of yourself—and your wife. Stand off at a distance and take a good look. Will you really work at the job? Or do you want to go "just for the ride?" Can you eliminate your prejudices against race, creed, or color—or at least restrain them? Will you—and your wife—give out, really mix with people of all types and social levels, and seek out ways to sell yourselves as admirable Americans? Will you both be good for our human relations with another people and their government?

Bring your wife into the discussions at the earliest stage. What she will say and do, how she will act and react, are nowhere as important to your effectiveness and to your future as on foreign duty. Will she make the extra effort to prepare herself for her duties, to study the language, to entertain often and nicely, not only your American friends, but also your associates among the people of the country and the Diplomatic Corps? Will she be ever ready to go and see and mingle, regardless of dirt, heat, humidity, and primitive back country conditions?

In many overseas situations, your wife can be much more effective than you on a day-to-day basis in advancing or improving our human relations. Will she, as well as you, feel a sense of responsibility for the foreign relations of the United States? Will such a feeling help her to survive the damage to morale of bad plumbing, flying and crawling insects, outrageous dirt and disease, strange manners and mannerisms, and the many other difficulties which she will encounter? Will your wife be your principal support and major asset to your overseas mission or a blot on the reputation of our country?

Certain areas are classified as "hardship posts." Several of the following factors, but certainly not all of them, may be present at a post: isolation from other areas involving poor transportation and inadequate postal service; lack of comfortable and sanitary housing; lack of medical personnel and facilities; lack of healthful food, such as fresh vegetables and pasteurized milk; absence of modern sanitation, such as sewage disposal, garbage collection, and control of rodents and insect pests; prevalence of communicable diseases; extreme heat or cold and humidity or excessive rainfall; frequency of natural calamities, such as earthquakes and typhoons; danger of civil disturbances, revolutions, riots or inadequate police protection.

Naval personnel are expected to have the stamina and resourcefulness to make the best of local conditions. Every assignment, however uncomfortable, offers the opportunity to advance your cultural and linguistic understanding and to meet and to know another people.

Will you and your wife be willing to stay long enough to become fully effective at your jobs?

If both of you cannot answer these questions affirmatively, stay home.

Study the country or countries to which you will be assigned. Learn all you can about their culture, history and heritage. When and in what kind of a struggle did they win their independence? What kind of men were their national heroes? Where did the people get their attitudes, values, and prejudices? What are their present social, political, and economic conditions, and for what are they now striving?

Know your stuff about the United States of America. Read up on American history. Learn as much as you can about the current issues of American foreign and domestic policy. You are certain to be quizzed on such questions as segregation, juvenile delinquency, nuclear warfare, foreign aid, import restrictions, etc. Know about such things. But don't talk about America all the time. Wait for your hosts to ask.

Find out all you can about living conditions. "Old hands" are nearly always available for consultation, but expect conditions to be worse than they will tell you. Passage of time lends enchantment. If assigned to a base or station, your comfort will be as well provided for as at home, with Officers' Club, commissary, exchange, dispensary, and recreational facilities. But if you will be with a MAAG, naval attaché or naval mission, take with you some essentials such as soap powder, soft tissues, and an air-conditioner. Navy standard anti-dysentery medicine will help to ease the initial "cultural shock." Study not only your service "post-report," but also those of the Embassy and ICA missions.

Study the language. People will say that you do not need the language, that "everybody in Purania speaks English." Do not believe them. Whether or not an official course be offered you in the months before departure, both your wife and you must commence your language study as soon as you know your destination.

President Eisenhower has said:—"Knowledge of foreign languages is particularly important in the light of America's leadership in the free world. Yet the American people are deficient in foreign languages, particularly those of the emerging nations in Asia, Africa, and the Near East. It is imperative to our national security that such deficiencies be overcome."

Experience shows that Army and Air Force officers and their wives arrive at a foreign post much better prepared to communicate with the people of a country than our naval families. Except for certain "language cripples," almost anyone with proper incentive and determination and much hard work can acquire a reasonable fluency in one of the "world languages." Some of the differently based tongues spoken by millions of people of the world are more difficult, but they, too, can be learned. Be sure that your wife and children have the requisite determination to learn.

Berlitz is available in most cities. In Washington, the Sanz 100-hour course usually certifies a modest competence on which to build. The Foreign Service Institute offers two language courses of interest to naval officers: an intensive course for four months which requires full time attendance at the Institute and which will produce a reasonable conversational competence; and part-time classes in world languages each morning from 7:30 to 8:45. Naval officers and their wives can enroll in either of these courses gratis, if recommended to the Institute by the appropriate naval authority having cognizance of their program.

The adult education course, given at the local high school or recreation center, though often maligned, can be helpful in acquiring a necessary fluency within six months after arrival on post. One year of high school Spanish has proven to be a tremendous advantage in learning the language on post.

Take advantage of any opportunity, however inadequate it may appear, to acquire a background of the language of the country before you sail. The Bureau of Naval Personnel will provide funds for lessons when requested.

Should you take your children? Certainly! School and health considerations will be one of your great preoccupations. Learn in advance what facilities will be available, but judge them on quality, not on nationality.

Be thoroughly briefed. Find out all that you possibly can about your job, its requirements, your necessary associations. Remember that, in addition to being a naval officer, you—and your wife and each member of your family—will also be an official representative. Your association with your new neighbors can be a fruitful or an unsettling experience for both parties. Since you are the intruding element, it depends pretty much on you.

Don't become self-conscious about your role as a goodwill-envoy from the American people. Nothing is so offensive, at home or overseas, as a self-important American, male or female.

1617. PERSONAL EFFECTS. When you are ordered to sea duty or foreign station, particularly in time of war or national emergency, you must realize that your duty suddenly may be changed en route. Select your wardrobe and personal effects to keep down weight and bulk and at the same time provide for any contingency—from Alaska to the Philippines, Japan to North Africa.

When possible, dispense with a trunk—it is heavy and hard to stow. Use a sea bag or a box which can be knocked down for the lumber. An

Army or Marine Corps bedroll has proved valuable under many circumstances, where adequate housing is questionable, and permits stowage of considerable gear, as well. Keep the probability of air travel in mind; pack by categories in priority: (1) toilet articles, towel, change of clothing, flashlight, orders and other papers in an air handbag; (2) urgently needed clothing and other articles in a sea-bag; (3) reserve clothing and uniform gear in bedding roll; (4) last priority uniform and civilian clothing in a locker trunk. If ordered part way or all the way by air, you can drop off the lower priorities to come later, by freight or with your family.

High-topped or field shoes are necessary in cold climates. Two suits of woolen underwear and foul-weather gear should be included if cold-weather operations are in prospect. Your bedding roll will give you the nucleus of "safari gear" for your excursions into primitive areas. Carry an extra pair of glasses and your prescription for same. Athletic gear is a necessity at many posts or stations, but should be sent in follow-up echelon of gear.

Regardless of destination and advice from "old hands," never be without: a complete suit of blues and accessories; one suit of working uniform; regulation raincoat with liner. See also Chapter 2 for further advice as to uniform equipment for sea duty and how to pack.

1618. OVERSEAS TRAVEL ADVICE. *Passports and Visas.* For any foreign country, each member of your family will require a passport. The Bureau of Naval Personnel or your sponsoring office will help you. If in or near Washington, apply in person, with your family, at the Passport Office, Department of State. Passport agencies of the Department of State are also located in New York, Chicago, New Orleans, Boston, Los Angeles, and San Francisco. In other localities, apply to the clerk of the nearest U. S. District Court. Notify the Bureau of Naval Personnel and your sponsoring office when you apply. Have the following documents with you:

Original orders
Birth certificates of all members of your family
Evidence of naturalization, if required
Old passports or their numbers
Identification card and other identification
Three (3) passport size photos, full face and uncovered, for each member of your family. Your photo should be in uniform. Color photos are now acceptable.

Obtain or ask your sponsoring office to obtain visas on all passports for all countries in which you will stop en route (other than stops while ship or aircraft is in port). Bureau of Naval Personnel or sponsoring office will advise you on request.

Physical Examinations and Immunizations. All members of your family must have physical examinations and certain immunizations before going overseas. Requirements for your destination and countries where you will stop or go ashore en route can be obtained from the nearest naval dispensary or hospital. Have *all* of your immunizations recorded on an *International Certificate* and also carry in your wallet a *Navy Immunization Card.* This will prevent a second round of immunization "shots" when going ashore en route. Physical examination and necessary "shots" can be obtained from the nearest Armed Forces dispensary or hospital without cost.

Dependent medical service overseas is often inadequate and dental service is available only in case of emergency. Have your family and yourself in the best possible physical and dental condition before going overseas.

Accompanied Baggage. Ascertain what restrictions are in force as to weight allowances, how much baggage may accompany you in staterooms and the ship's hold, date and time of sailing, time gear must be at dockside or Navy check-in point, and the address to which baggage may be shipped. See the following paragraphs for information on government transportation. Mark and tag your gear clearly and indelibly. Put one copy of your basic orders in each piece of baggage.

Government Air and Sea Transportation. Since the Navy Department uses to the fullest extent the transports and aircraft of the Military Sealift Command (MSC)[1] and the Military Airlift Command (MAC) you will usually travel in one of their craft. Some MSC ships are manned by Navy crews, some by civilian crews. Both types have a "military department" which deals with the desires and needs of all passengers, both military and dependents. MAC aircraft are manned by Air Force crews, but MAC also charters civil aircraft to carry passengers.

MSC ships provide comfortable quarters for officers, their dependents, and for enlisted men of certain top ratings and their accompanying dependents. Enlisted men traveling without dependents are berthed in troop quarters. The passengers' mess is commodious, and pleasantly equipped. Meals are generally excellent.

MAC transport flights are usually made in combination passenger-

[1] Policies vary from time to time. During the Vietnam conflict, all MSC passenger transports were laid up and all passenger traffic was handled by MAC and civil airlines.

freight air transports. The seats are fairly comfortable. Box lunches are provided whenever the aircraft is expected to be airborne during a meal hour. Baggage limitations are severe.

If traveling either by MSC or MAC, instructions and information will be furnished you. You will be completely briefed before and after embarkation by a pamphlet and by personnel of the service as to safety rules, clothing and uniform, articles which can be purchased in the ship, mess bills, recreational facilities, etc. When traveling with either service, carry enough money in cash or traveler's checks to pay your shipboard or air base expenses, including mess bills, and to meet immediate expenses at your destination.

In both a MSC ship and a MAC aircraft, the captain or commander of the aircraft (be he military officer or civilian master) is still the Captain, invested with paramount authority. The head of the military department of a ship represents the Department of Defense so far as your family and you are concerned. Give appropriate attention to his advice and instructions.

Mail. Determine in advance your new mailing address, and dispatch change-of-address cards to all your usual correspondents, business firms and publications. Your unit mail clerk and local post office have a supply of such cards. When possible, have magazines, parcels, dutiable articles addressed to you via the nearest Fleet, Air Force or Army Post Office. This will enable you to obtain low domestic prices for your magazine subscriptions and to receive parcel post without the trouble of going through foreign customs. Leave a forwarding address at every place where you stop en route.

For other travel advice, see Sections 204-5 and Appendix 4.

1619. SHORE LEAVE. If on foreign sea duty, the considerations expressed in Sections 1611-12 are still valid, but the necessity for superior conduct of both officers and men is intensified. In foreign ports, not only the reputation of our Navy is at stake, but also thoughtless and irresponsible conduct by either officers or men is offensive to the local people and damaging to our good relations with their government. Whether or not on Shore Patrol, take prompt action to prevent any breaches of good manners and discipline that may come to your attention. It may be kindly to say "Boys will be boys" in ports of the United States—in foreign ports it is serious dereliction of duty .

In every port you visit, seek out the features of special historical or cultural interest. Bars, *bistros,* and night clubs have their place, but observe the Department of State's advice to its employees, "Get to know the country by traveling widely. There is something of interest in every corner of the world."

Meet the people of the country, not only in hotel lobbies and cabarets, but also in the markets, the workers' sections, and in the country lanes. Practice the language if you have acquired some knowledge of it. During stays of long duration, get to know some of the more influential citizens, military officers, officials of the government, members of the press, leaders of the community.

Senior officers are expected to visit the American consulate—others will find it useful to do so, especially when your ship is based on a foreign port. The consular officials can often be helpful with the problems of yourself and your men and can advise you as to interesting trips, places to see, and many other activities.

1620. ON FOREIGN SHORE DUTY. Since you will be traveling under orders with a special passport, you will probably have little difficulty with local customs or immigration authorities. Your embassy or mission will assign a representative to meet you and to help you get settled. Keep the officer you are relieving advised as to your progress and present location.

Housing. If assigned to a naval base or station, you will probably have housing assigned to you, either in BOQ or in married quarters. If you have to find local quarters in the city, seek the help of those who have experienced the problem. Proper location, especially in the capital, is very important. Often you will discover that the best quarters you can find are much more expensive than you expected and much less desirable than you have been accustomed to have. Find the best accommodations you can afford for your family and then do the best you can with what you have. Take particular pains to inquire into the potability of the water and the adequacy of disposal facilities. These will both be very important to the health of your family.

Schooling. Inquire further into the facilities available. If your child will be with you two years or more, for the first year, seek out a school that teaches in English, or better, half in English and half in the language of the country. Put him in a local school the second year so that he may perfect his knowledge of the language.

If your child is of high school age, put him in a school teaching in the language of the country. He will lose in English grammar and American history, but his gain in mastery of the language of the country will overbalance this loss.

By association with the children of the country, both your younger and your older children will learn the value of difference and acquire a sounder basis for democratic tolerance.

Sanitation. Sanitation may not be up to the standard to which you have been accustomed. Find out from your medical officer the local sanitary situation and ask him to advise you as to what you can live with and what to avoid. Guard against insect-borne and enteric diseases. Keep up your immunizations, pasteurize or boil the local raw milk or use milk powder. Have your water tested and boil your drinking water, if your supply is polluted. Avoid raw vegetables and fruits. Make your own ice with boiled water or buy only from a locally certified dealer.

Know your restaurants, for sanitation and (hopefully) for infection-free eating.

Keep tab on your servants. Be sure your servants are cleanly and free of disease. Thoroughly check to see that they observe necessary sanitary precautions. Be sure that they properly preserve foods and don't serve you spoiled or over-ripe food.

Customs and Traditions. While customs and traditions vary widely throughout the world, depending upon the climate, locality, amount of Western influence, religion, and standard of living, certain fundamental similarities and differences must be recognized.

To understand the people of a country, you must know about their origin, history and economic background. Some people are socially conscious and possess high ideals of devotion to the common good, while, in other peoples, these characteristics are almost totally lacking. Some races are highly disciplined and have great respect for law and order, while others not only ignore these virtues but are really ignorant of them. In some countries, religion resides firmly in the heart of its people, while in others agnosticism and even atheism may be a credo of their faith.

Hospitality and courtesy are deeply rooted in the traditions of nearly all nations. In some countries, to refuse food or shelter to a person in need is considered tantamount to murder. Thus, inhospitality becomes an offense against the established mores and a sin against the local concept of the Supreme Being. Whatever their station in life, as a guest in their homes you will be treated with kindness and consideration and offered to share the little that they have. When a host tells you, "My house is your house," he means literally just that.

Many present day customs have traditional origin in the location and climate of a country. Foreign people feel as strongly as we do the in-

fluence of their history and take pride in maintaining against all challenge the validity of its traditions. You must expect to find foreign citizens sensitive about their national and personal honor and dignity.
Many people are quick to take offense at a real or imaginary slight.
Politeness in all your dealings is important because it indicates your
respect for an individual person deserving honorable treatment.

The position of women in most countries is quite different from that
accorded to women at home. In certain localities, women are kept in
complete seclusion and may not even be seen by men other than their
husbands and close male relatives. In others, women have a completely
subordinate position to men and are closely and jealously regarded by
their husbands and male relatives. It may be considered vulgar and dis-
respectful even to inquire about the health of a wife, daughter, or sister,
or, at the other extreme, it is very discourteous to commence a business
or social conversation without first making solicitous inquiry about a
man's wife and such of the female members of his family as you know.

Marriage relations vary widely from country to country and will, in
many cases, seem very strange. A man may be permitted by law to have
four wives, and to divorce any one of them by pronouncing his intentions three times in the presence of competent witnesses. Or divorce
may be virtually impossible, yet the keeping of mistresses outside the
home be the well-recognized right of any man who can afford them.
More so, perhaps, than with Americans, foreign men are extremely
jealous of the women in their household and react violently to any in-
sult or slight toward them, whether conscious or unconscious. Be sure
that you learn, understand, and observe the conventions about women
in the country.

The family unit, extending to grandparents, aunts, uncles, and third
to fifth cousins, is much more pronounced in most foreign societies than
it is at home. Many households, even among the poor, include grandparents and other relatives outside the immediate family. In some social
structures, marriage between first cousins is not unusual. In others,
when you marry a girl, you truly marry the whole family. Social life
almost exclusively consists of frequent clan meetings and family social
gatherings. Family unity extends much more into the business and political worlds than it does at home.

In many of the older societies, there is still a clearly defined social
stratification, with various degrees of importance attributed to it.
Rulers may come from only the higher strata of society, where lineage
and tradition, plus better education, prepare them for the effective exercise of authority. Even among the rural people, there are social dis-

tinctions based on birth, with every man knowing his relative rank and place.

Social discrimination by reason of race and color are by no means as uncommon overseas as you may have been led to believe. Whole tribes are sometimes regarded as social inferiors. Darker skin derogates its owner to the status of common laborer or field hand. Sons of the peasant and laboring classes are kept ignorant and submissive by denying them access to the leveling influence of education. But there are also countries in which absolutely no discrimination by reason of race or color is practised.

Even within the most rigid caste system, it must not be supposed that all opportunity is denied to the lower castes. Since World War I, many young men have availed themselves of the opportunity to better their lot through education and outstanding ability. A new class of educated elite has developed, moving into influential positions in government and business. Knowledge of the social and economic advantages of the "outside world" is filtering into many an isolated, underdeveloped country, where formerly every child was fated to be born, raised, work, and die in his father's caste.

To avoid offending, you must acquire accurate knowledge of the ancient customs and taboos in the country of your residence, and observe them conscientiously. Since religious and social customs are closely intermingled, a single error on your part might violate both. Not to observe the local customs will be considered an affront to the personal honor and dignity of your hosts, and frequent offense will damage your standing so seriously that, regardless of your other merits and accomplishments, you are certain to fail in your mission.

Meet the people. Remember that you are a representative of the American people. The Department of State advises its people abroad, "Don't stay in the capital, though it may be more comfortable and attractive."

In line of duty, your wife and you will certainly meet military officials, military attachés and members of the diplomatic corps and the capital society. Make the extra effort necessary to meet a wide cross section of your hosts—not only those pleasant, educated, sophisticated persons you meet at the Club, embassy receptions, formal dinners, and mission entertainments, but also the merchants, the lower government officials, the merchant sailors, and the workers. Get out in the country and to other cities and rural localities as often as you can, even if the trips take on the nature of a safari. Travel widely in the country and in neighboring countries.

FIGURE 1604. The naval officer on foreign duty advances foreign relations by getting to know
the people of the country.

See not only the conventional sights, but also what makes the country lag behind or thrive. Are natural resources available? Why aren't
they being developed? Why are there so many poor, a few rich, and
none in between? Is the cause poor management or lack of opportunity? The knowledge of the country and its people which you acquire
will be valuable to your seniors in your reports. It may some day be of
tremendous importance to you.

Remember that the governments of many countries are organized
and operated differently from our government. Accept the idea that
people of other nations have different problems and may develop different political solutions. They will not welcome advice on running their
country any more than we would.

As a resident in another country, always be conscious of the fact
that you are contributing to the impression that the other people will
form about all Americans. Strive at all times to reflect credit upon yourself, upon our government, and upon the people of the United States.

Language. An indispensable tool for really getting to know a foreign person is to be able to talk to him in his own language. "Old

hands" will tell you that you can probably "get by" with English in the capital. Too many captains and colonels, lieutenant commanders and majors and their wives spend three years "getting by" in foreign capitals and return home with little more language competence than they possessed when they arrived. Pay no attention to such advice. In the rural areas, you will have to speak the language or have an interpreter. Little satisfaction results from chatting or visiting through an interpreter, and you will be out to do a much better job than merely "get by."

If your unit does not provide language lessons, you will usually be able to hire a tutor for a small fee. Or you can enroll in the Embassy language classes free. However you accomplish it, arrange immediately for language lessons for your family. Talk and listen to the language on every possible occasion. Take advantage of the wonderful opportunity offered to perfect yourselves in one foreign language.

The importance of language on foreign duty could hardly be overemphasized. You cannot develop friendship with another people unless you understand them. You cannot understand them unless you can communicate with them. So get out and meet the people, and talk with them in their own language. It will be difficult at first, but you will be surprised how rapidly you will acquire a reasonable understanding and a competent fluency.

Protocol. You will find that your associates in the American Embassy and in the diplomatic corps place great importance on protocol. This should not be surprising to you, for the rules of protocol are designed to eliminate possible disagreements and unintentional slights to national prestige. Internationally recognized, the rules of protocol establish the generally accepted procedures governing the relationships and precedence, both official and social, of members of the diplomatic corps and of government officials.

Many other organizations also abide by formal customs, which establish the rules for giving special honors or deference to individuals on the basis of the positions they hold or of their seniority. In your life overseas, you will be associating with individuals, who, as representatives of sovereign nations, may have policies and ideologies in conflict with those of their associates. Rules of protocol make it possible for them, and for you, to establish a basis upon which you can enjoy amicable relationships.

For the naval officer going to overseas duty, the Office of Naval Intelligence has published "Social Usage and Protocol," the work principally of Miss Ruth Tarrant. Also useful is the Naval Institute publication, *Service Etiquette.*

Calls. Diplomatic, civil, and military customs require the usual exchange of social calls (see Section 414). Their protocol and social importance on overseas duty are much greater. The above mentioned books give complete information. The following notes accent their advice.

Do make the required calls.
Do consult your protocol officer or the protocol officer of the Embassy.
Do make calls promptly (within a week of arrival).
Do see that your wife makes her required calls.
Do promptly drop cards, where that is the custom.
Do have proper calling cards for all occasions.
Do return calls made on you (within a week).

Do not consider calls a bore. Use them to advance your acquaintance.
Do not stay long, particularly on first calls.
Do not neglect appropriate formality in dress and conduct.
Do not neglect protocol as to which person calls first.

Manners. Too many Americans on foreign station tend to herd together, as if for mutual protection. By so doing, you would not only miss a great opportunity to acquire new outlooks and a new understanding, but you would also severely limit your ability to accomplish your mission.

In most foreign countries, the local people like Americans. They take for granted that Americans like them. You will observe that they are eager to understand your initially poor attempts at their language and to be helpful. If you treat your new acquaintances as you would other Americans, you will get along with them well. A good rule for a pleasant life in any country is to relax and avoid impatience.

Most foreigners set a greater store upon gentlemanly manners and inherent politeness than do Americans. Before coming to business matters, make inquiry about the health of your visitor, his wife, and family, or studiously avoid mention of any female of the family, depending upon the local custom. Be prepared to shake hands frequently, as many as a dozen times a day with the same person. Avoid a crushing grip—most other people dislike a firm grip and a vigorous pumping action. Avoid backslapping. Let your pleasure and geniality show in your face and in your conversation. Some races resent touching or handling, consider it an offense to be struck or jostled. On the other hand, the *abrazo* is an established and warmly friendly greeting in many Latin countries.

Learn a variety of polite phrases of greeting, good wishes, and farewell. Such courtesy will please your associates and promote friendship. Do not expect your contacts with women and girls to be more than formal. Until you have been formally introduced, it may be a serious mistake to engage a woman in conversation, even at an embassy reception. Do not be surprised, in some societies, if you are not introduced to wives and daughters in the homes which you visit. Respect the privacy of women still wearing the veil.

The welcoming gesture to a guest in many a country is the serving of coffee. Tea or coffee, rather than an alcoholic drink, is the usual social beverage when people get together for visits, discussion, or good fellowship. Many officials of local governments and business houses make a great ceremony of coffee or tea. Learn to sit patiently through this ceremony, before trying to talk business with your host. Be prepared to serve coffee or tea to your visitors promptly upon their arrival and to make polite small talk during the serving and drinking. Flattery and flowerly compliments are more common in other world languages, but a friendly spirit and sincerity are pretty generally as much appreciated as among Americans.

Avoid impatience, preoccupation with other affairs, or appearance of undue haste. *Paciencia* is an honored virtue in the Latin countries. In many other countries, impatience is regarded as a sign of bad manners or lack of self-confidence.

Learn about the etiquette on dinners. In Latin countries, dinner is late and it is considered gracious by your hostess to make a compliment on her table and to linger on far into the night. In other areas, guests do not stay on, as they do in the West. After an early dinner, coffee (and perhaps liqueurs), the guests take immediate and flowery leave of their hosts.

Religion. You will encounter many different religions. Whether your new neighbors be Moslem, Jewish, Catholic, Protestant, Buddhist or any other religion, respect their faith. For example, it is courteous, during the Moslem holy month of Ramadhan, not to eat, drink, or smoke in the presence of those who are fasting. Never show undue curiosity or lack of respect when people are in the act of praying.

Learn to recognize how religion enters into the field of politics and government. In some countries, you will discover that the patriarch of the church sits as a full member of the council of state. Rulers have been overthrown and cabinet ministers caused to resign when in conflict with established religions. People are often sensitive when foreigners, coming into their country, try to convert them to another religion. To challenge or ridicule their religious beliefs will lead to serious misunderstanding. It is wise to avoid religion as a topic of conversation.

Give the same respect to their temples and shrines that you would give to your churches at home. If the custom is to cover the head or remove the shoes before entering a temple, observe it. Inquire before entering a church or temple—sometimes entry is forbidden during services. Picture taking in some mosques and temples is taboo. It is always bad manners to photograph worshipers at prayer. Do not smoke or talk loudly in a place of worship.

Entertainment. Entertain modestly and within your means but entertain as frequently as you can afford. Try to repay all of your social obligations, if with no more than an occasional small reception. But pay special attention to any social event you give to make it interesting and pleasant. The outgiving warmth of the hospitality of the host and hostess are much more important than ostentatious display. Try to bring together in your living room or at your table a group of people who will discover matters of common interest.

Your personal and official funds will be limited. Count as wasted any time or money you spend on entertainment where a goodly representation of the people of the country is not present. If you are isolated in an American community on a naval base or station, this can be difficult, but it can be arranged.

Both of the books mentioned under *Protocol* will be helpful to you in extending proper formal and informal entertainment on duty overseas.

The Foreign Service of the United States

1621. COMPOSITION. A sixth Federal service, with whose members you will become well acquainted on foreign duty, is the Foreign Service. A branch of the Department of State, it is a career corps of men and women who are specially selected and trained to carry out the foreign policy of our nation in day-to-day relations with other countries. Their specialty is *diplomacy,* the art and practice of conducting negotiations between nations. Approximately 8,000 serve abroad at nearly 300 posts in more than 100 countries.

The *Mission of the Foreign Service* is to protect and promote the welfare and interests of the United States and of the American people, to deal with the relations between peoples of nations as well as their governments, to assist friendly or uncommitted developing nations to achieve their aspirations for growth, and to represent our government before the many permanent international organizations.

Members of this Service have important responsibilities, which include: negotiating agreements in many different fields, political and economic reporting on conditions in other countries which affect U.S. interests, helping to prepare recommendations on policy formulation, and translating into action the policy decisions made by the President. The captain of your country's team is the Ambassador or Minister. Appointed by the President, by and with the advice and consent of the Senate, he is accredited to the Chief of State of the host country.

Consular posts—consulates general and consulates—are established in the important cities of a foreign country. Consular officers are not accredited to the host government and are not authorized to represent the President in negotiations with foreign governments.

The function of consular officers is the performance of such services as issuance of visas and passports, protection of American citizens and property, assistance to American businessmen, and services to American shipping and seamen.

1622. Classes of foreign service personnel. *Foreign Service Officers* are members of the Foreign Service Officer Corps, the career professionals who perform the principal work of the Service. They may be assigned to any kind of diplomatic or consular duty in any country where we maintain diplomatic or consular posts. About 300 are women.

Foreign Service Reserve Officers are specialists in some skill, appointed by the Secretary of State, or as diplomatic and consular officers by the President. They serve at home and abroad just as do Foreign Service Officers.

Foreign Service Staff Officers and Employees are the administrative officers, clerks, typists, secretaries, code clerks, and others who have technical, administrative, clerical, or custodial responsibilities. Making the Service their career, they may be assigned at home or to posts abroad.

Local Employees are recruited among foreign nationals for duties at consular and diplomatic posts ranging from janitorial or chauffeur service to translation and economic analysis. Their loyal service plays an important role in foreign activities. Carefully screened before employment, they do not deal with matters affecting the security of our country.

Consular Agents, appointed by the Secretary of State, are usually local businessmen of American or foreign nationality. Their duties, for which they receive a small salary, are related to shipping.

The Foreign Service officer holds a *title* determined by his assignment, as well as by his class. It is his *title* which establishes his status at his post, whereas his *class* establishes his relative seniority for internal purposes.

TITLES AND ADDRESS

DIPLOMATIC	HOW ADDRESS	CONSULAR	HOW ADDRESS
Ambassador	Mr. Ambassador	Consul General	Mr. Parker
Minister	Mr. Minister	Consul	Same
Counselor	Mr. Harbisen	Vice Consul	Same
First Secretary	Same		
Second Secretary	Same		
Third Secretary	Same		
Attaché	Same		

The principal officer at a diplomatic post is the *Chief of Mission*. His principal assistant is the *Deputy Chief of Mission*. The *Chargé d'Affaires ad interim* is the officer who is temporarily in charge of a diplomatic post in the absence of the Chief of Mission.

The title of *attaché* is assigned to an officer from a U.S. government agency other than the Department of State performing a specialized function.

TITLES AND POSITIONS AT AN EMBASSY

CLASS	TITLE	POSITION
Career Minister, Foreign Service Officer Class 1 to 3	Ambassador or Minister, Minister Counselor or Counselor of Embassy for Political Affairs	Chief of Mission, Deputy Chief of Mission and Chief of the Political Section (Supervises political reporting)
Foreign Service Officer Class 1 to 4	Economic Counselor, First or Second Secretary	Economic Officer (Responsible for reporting on economic affairs)

TITLES AND POSITIONS AT A CONSULAR POST

CLASS	TITLE	POSITION
Foreign Service Officer Class 1 to 3	Consul General	Principal Officer at a consulate general
Foreign Service Officer Class 3 to 5	Consul	Principal Officer at a consulate
Foreign Service Officer Class 6 to 8	Vice Consul	Visa Officer

In many of our diplomatic missions, officers of the rank of counselor and below hold diplomatic and consular titles concurrently.

For further information, see pamphlets published by the Department of State, *The Foreign Service of the United States* and *The American Ambassador*.

1623. UNITED STATES INFORMATION AGENCY. The Public Affairs Officer, although an employee of the U. S. Information Agency, is an

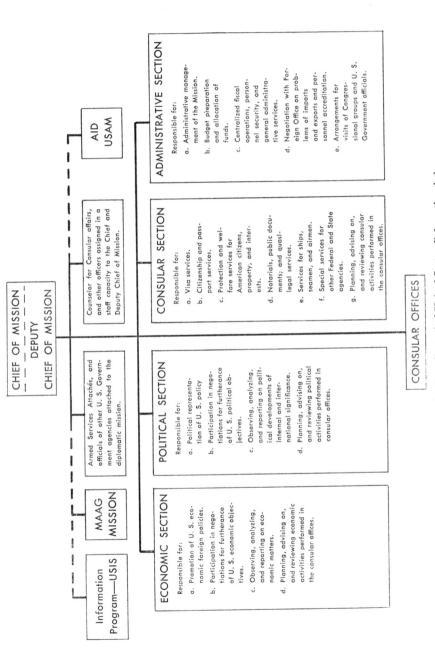

FIGURE 1605. Basic organization of a typical United States diplomatic mission.

CHIEF OF MISSION
— — — —
DEPUTY
CHIEF OF MISSION

Information Program—USIS

MAAG MISSION

Armed Services Attachés, and officials of other U. S. Government agencies attached to the diplomatic mission.

Counselor for Consular affairs, and other officers assigned in a staff capacity to the Chief and Deputy Chief of Mission.

AID USAM

ECONOMIC SECTION

Responsible for:

a. Promotion of U. S. economic foreign policies.

b. Participation in negotiations for furtherance of U. S. economic objectives.

c. Observing, analyzing, and reporting on economic matters.

d. Planning, advising on, and reviewing economic activities performed in the consular offices.

POLITICAL SECTION

Responsible for:

a. Political representation of U. S. policy

b. Participation in negotiations for furtherance of U. S. political objectives.

c. Observing, analyzing, and reporting on political developments of internal and international significance.

d. Planning, advising on, and reviewing political activities performed in consular offices.

CONSULAR SECTION

Responsible for:

a. Visa services.

b. Citizenship and passport services.

c. Protection and welfare services for American citizens, property, and interests.

d. Notarials, public documents; and quasi-legal services.

e. Services for ships, seamen, and airmen.

f. Special services for other Federal and State agencies.

g. Planning, advising on, and reviewing consular activities performed in the consular offices.

ADMINISTRATIVE SECTION

Responsible for:

a. Administrative management of the Mission.

b. Budget preparation and allocation of funds.

c. Centralized fiscal operations, personnel security, and general administrative services.

d. Negotiation with Foreign Office on problems of imports and exports and personnel accreditation.

e. Arrangements for visits of Congressional groups and U. S. Government officials.

CONSULAR OFFICES

integral member of the staff of the American Embassy. He heads the information section of the Embassy and is in charge of the country's USIA program. If there are subordinate USIA offices in the country, he is responsible for their administration. The day-by-day dissemination of information and news in support of foreign policy is one of the duties of his office.

The Public Affairs Officer supervises the operation of the USIA cultural centers in the country to which he is assigned and cooperates with the host country in the operation of the bi-national centers. The two differ in that the bi-national centers are usually organized locally by resident Americans and local citizens, with the Public Affairs Officer usually an ex officio member of the bi-national center board. These centers are frequently supplied with an American director, who may have one or more American assistants. Other members of the center staff are recruited locally. Salaries may be paid from fees collected in the English language classes and income from lectures, concerts, and other affairs for which admission is charged.

Activities of both USIA centers and bi-national centers include film showings, lectures, concerts, plays, exhibits, and other cultural programs either by local groups or visiting artists. Both centers maintain libraries with books, magazines, newspapers, and other periodicals, both in English and the language of the host country. The most important activities frequently are the classes in English and seminars or workshops for local teachers of English. All classes have heavy enrollments.

Many foreign and American observers feel that the bi-national center activity is USIA's finest operation in foreign countries. Officers and their families will find enthusiastic participation in the management and work of these centers infinitely interesting and rewarding.

USIA today is operating 182 libraries and 79 reading rooms of its own and cooperating in the operation of 154 bi-national centers. The majority of the centers are in Latin America where the first was opened in 1927, but the program has now spread to both the Near and Far East as well as Europe.

1624. AGENCY FOR INTERNATIONAL DEVELOPMENT.   The Agency for International Development (AID) is a semiautonomous unit within the U. S. Department of State. AID is responsible for coordinating all mutual defense and assistance programs.

The AID headquarters are in Washington, D.C. Overseas, AID administers assistance programs in some 81 countries in Latin America, Africa, the Near East and South Asia, and the Far East.

The field offices overseas are called United States AID missions (USAID) and, like all overseas operations of the U. S. Government, are under the control of the U. S. Ambassador. The USAID in a country is managed by a Director who usually has a Deputy and a central staff. Many of the American officials with USAID are career civil servants employed by AID or lent to it by other federal agencies. A great number are technicians and technical advisers recruited for a specific project. An increasing number are employees of American universities, businesses, and service organizations with whom AID contracts for technical assistace.

AID is responsible for the following activities:

1. *Development Assistance.* In most countries aided by the United States today, the development of human resources remains the priority need and technical assistance the heart of the development assistance program. Technical assistance trains people and helps build the wide variety of institutions needed to make trained people effective. Technical assistance projects also play a key role in assisting countries to carry out needed self help and reform measures. AID technical assistance activities are financed by Development Grant and Technical Cooperation funds.

Development lending provides needed capital for investment or to supply imports essential for economic growth. Development lending is concentrated on a limited number of major country programs. Technical assistance, on the other hand, is required in virtually all the developing countries.

In Latin America, U. S. contributions to the Alliance for Progress are administered by AID's bureau for Latin America, the head of which is also the coordinator of the Alliance for Progress.

2. *Strategic Assistance.* Both military and economic aid are used in strategic assistance programs to strengthen free world defenses and preserve the security and stability of friendly countries.

The largest element in strategic assistance is the military assistance program which provides military equipment, training and related services to help other free world nations protect themselves against external attack or subversion.

Supporting assistance is regularly programmed economic aid to countries with heavy defense burdens or other pressures that generate economic and political instability.

A third source of strategic assistance is the contingency fund, a supplement in supporting assistance to meet emergency requirements which could not be anticipated and planned in advance.

3. *Other AID programs.* AID helps promote the growth of private

enterprise in the developing countries, through its regular development programs and through special programs to encourage U.S. overseas investment, including the lending of local currencies for joint U. S.–host country ventures, participation in investment surveys, and the Investment Guaranty program. AID also administers much of the Food for Peace program overseas through which U. S. surplus food stocks are used in development. Other AID programs include contributions to international organizations, support of the work of U. S. voluntary relief agencies and support to American hospitals and schools overseas.

The naval officer abroad can contribute to these objectives of our foreign assistance programs if he knows about them and becomes familiar with the functions of AID before going abroad. He can obtain further information on AID policies and their implementation from the Agency for International Development, Department of State, Washington, D.C., 20025.

1625. OTHER CIVILIAN AGENCIES. Other agencies of our government from time to time assign representatives to our Embassies. Frequently included are attachés from the Department of Agriculture, the National Aeronautics and Space Agency, and others.

1626. THE COUNTRY-TEAM SPIRIT. Under the country-team concept, every American governmental employee, whether he be the chief of another mission or a minor technician or clerk, takes his direction from the Ambassador as captain of the team, and is responsible through his chief of mission to the Ambassador for all of his actions and activities. While the chiefs of other missions are responsible directly to their Washington agencies, they are also responsible to the Ambassador, who, in turn, is responsible to all branches of our government, through the Department of State, for the operation of the country-team under his charge. Should any person get out of line, the Ambassador has authority to have him removed from post.

With the country-team functioning in this manner, there can be no question that the policies of our government will be violated or vitiated by the ill-considered actions of representatives of any agency. The United States will present but one front, show but one face in its dealings with the officials and people of the host country.

Obviously, no Ambassador can fully comprehend all the ramifications of the duties of the members of his country-team. To arrive at sound decisions, he must receive frank and full information, advice and counsel from the members of his staff and from other missions. As with any executive, he cannot live to himself alone.

Like the Admiral or Captain of a ship, an Ambassador is never off duty. In his office, in conference with the President or Foreign Minister, at an official reception or dinner party, in visits to outlying areas of the country, he carries with him his responsibility as the personal representative of our President. He must keep himself well informed on the instructions and policies promulgated to him and also on those issued to all of the missions. He cannot procrastinate or be indecisive.

But no Ambassador can personally perform every function where a United States responsibility is involved. To operate the involved complex of activities which modern diplomacy requires, the Ambassador must delegate his authority to members of his country-team. But he must also have the effective support and complete loyalty of each member of his team.

If these tenets of good leadership and administration sound familiar, even more important is good followership on the part of subordinates in every mission which makes up the country-team. As a good naval officer, you will naturally give unstinting support to your own chief of mission. But on overseas duty, you must extend yourself even further. You must give loyal and effective support to the captain of your country-team.

The Ambassador and his wife will constantly need assistance in all fields—official, social, transportation, representation, and many others. They will rarely ask for assistance. Both you and your wife should be always on the lookout for opportunities to be helpful in any way possible.

Your contribution may be as complicated as acting as interpreter and guide for a visiting VIP or his wife, or as simple as carving a tenderloin of beef or turkey, for the Independence Day reception, which your wife roasted in her own oven the day before. You may be able to take a part in an American Community play for the benefit of charity or do a variety act for an Embassy party. If the bar boy fails to show up for an Embassy function, get behind the bar until the situation clears up. It will require a nice sense of judgment and timing to recognize the need and to fill it promptly and effectively.

In carrying out his burdensome duties, the Ambassador must lean heavily upon his political, economic, information, and military officers. If they unite to cooperate loyally as efficient members of the country-team, United States representation will be effective in that country. This is your opportunity and your principal responsibility in your tour of duty overseas.

CHAPTER 17

Personal Affairs

The road is wide,
The trails are many,
But somewhere, beyond the sunset,
Our paths will meet again.

1701. PUT YOUR HOUSE IN ORDER. Your first responsibility as an officer is to the nation and must be assumed and fulfilled without stint. But your second responsibility is to those who may be left behind. There can be no greater satisfaction to an officer than the realization that he has provided as best he could for his wife and children, mother, father, or other loved ones who depend upon him for support. The officer who fails to do this is morally guilty of neglect.

A high degree of foresight is essential. Changes of station without warning must be anticipated, and many such changes involve movement overseas or to sea duty in areas where your family cannot go. The considerate officer will make necessary arrangements to reduce the extent of confusion, hardship, shock, and privation that might otherwise attend his death in service.

Read this chapter, and have your wife read it. Take action now to place your affairs in order.

Estate Planning

1702. LIFE INSURANCE. The career of an officer in the postwar Navy presents problems of security for his family which the naval officer has not had to face before. Inflation has devalued the dollar which his bonded investments and life insurance represent. With retirement for most officers set at 52 to 54 years of age and for all at sixty-two, a naval career is shorter than that of most comparable professions. Selection further shortens the career of others. The promotion and pay laws have removed the assurance of adequate income after service, even for officers retired for physical disabilities. Officers failing of promotion to the lower grades and officers separated for physical disability with less than 8 years of active service may be given a lump-sum severance pay and no retired pay. Retirement pay for physical disability has been reduced from 75 per cent to the percentage of disability determined by the Physical Evaluation Board or to the percentage of active-duty pay otherwise authorized by law. For those who retire young enough and in fair health, the prospects for employment in civilian life at a satisfactory salary are good. For those materially handicapped or those past fifty, who have developed no special qualifications or industrial connections before retirement, the prospects for gainful employment are poor. There is a vital need for a new approach to your problem of family security after retirement and in case of death, in or out of service.

Much capital is made of the low return on life insurance compared with the same sum *regularly* invested in real estate, sound stocks, government and other bonds. A good mathematical case can be demonstrated for this viewpoint, but the value of a life-insurance program cannot be appraised on the basis of regular sums invested and safe rates of interest paid in other fields of investment.

From the moment you purchase a life-insurance policy, you have created a cash estate of the amount of that policy.

In most states, the proceeds of a policy are nontaxable under state inheritance taxes.

You can provide a modest estate while you are young and your income is low and increase it as your family responsibilities increase and your income is higher.

Your wife and family are protected during your younger years against the hazards of your profession which might otherwise leave them destitute with heavy responsibilities.

Life insurance will help to get your wife over the period between your death and the time when your children become self-supporting.

It will assist your children to acquire the education which you believe is their just due.

It provides a fair return on your investment, with as much certainty as one can expect in our world of today.

It can be so arranged as to help you maintain your accustomed standard of living after retirement in spite of reduced pay.

You will not defer payment of insurance premiums whereas you might be inclined, every now and then, to omit a "regular" investment for a month or two.

1703. YOUR LIFE-INSURANCE PROGRAM. The life-insurance program of every individual varies not only with his personality and financial condition but from year to year with income, size of family, age of children and the stage of his career. You must consider the length of your career, how long your children may reasonably be expected to be dependent upon you or your wife, the children's educational requirements, your family income outside your pay, your wife's capacity to earn money if you should die in service, your income after retirement and the responsibilities you will have then, your experience which will be useful in civilian employment, and other factors of your situation which are unique with you.

You probably have in your acquaintance a competent insurance agent for one of the many good insurance companies we have in America. You should consult him as you would your lawyer or doctor. Lay all the facts of your case before him with the fullest frankness and with assurance of integrity and discretion. Tell him what sort of needs your family have now, would have 5 and 10 years from now, on retirement, and after your children are grown and self-supporting, both if you remain alive and if you should die. If, as so many officers do, you have purchased life insurance without much plan or understanding, a really capable agent can help you to choose payment plans and to increase your insurance program, so that the minimum needs of your wife and family will be met.

Bring your wife in on your studies and discussions. Together, learn about all the types of insurance and kinds of policies available to you. While it will be an obvious fact that you obtain about twice as much insurance protection under an Ordinary Life Policy as under a 20-year Endowment Policy, do not accept the aphorism that all policies except Ordinary Life are no good. You must think of such things as retirement income, education funds for your children and cash for down payment on a house. Not all endowment policies are bad policies, nor are 20-payment and 30-payment Life, which cost more *while you are earning full pay* but are fully paid up after you are on retired pay. When you and your wife have studied the business of life insurance and your friend the life-insurance agent has studied your personal problems and your present program, you will be much better able to decide on a program over the ensuing years which will fit your income and your family needs.

Skeleton Outline of a Program. The Navy Mutual Aid Association prepares, keeps current, and will send to you upon request a copy of its folder, Suggested Life Insurance Program. The program here suggested conforms in general with those contained in that pamphlet. A combination of whole life and term policies to give the career officer the maximum coverage at the lowest possible expense, this program makes full use of all survivors' benefits and urges the active duty officer to participate in the Retired Serviceman's Family Protection Plan at the time of retirement (see Section 1814).

Social Security coverage is a fundamental feature of good estate planning. Officers retiring are urged to find employment in private industry or become self-employed in order to build up and maintain social security credits and remain currently insured (see Section 1815 for further details).

With present retirement benefits, as long as he lives, an officer can be assured of a comfortable income. A Navy captain retiring at age 53 has a substantial lifetime annuity and a lifetime expectancy of over 19 years. However, he needs a well-balanced life insurance program to supplement his Federal benefits and to provide for his wife and family in the event of death at an earlier age than might be expected.

Although each officer has individual problems, a sensible program might well include the following:

1. There are three types of U. S. Government life insurance, one currently open to all hands on active duty, and two others of earlier vintage which are still in force for those who hold, and for most but not all of those who have held, policies established under their provisions.

Servicemen's Group Life Insurance (SGLI) provides up to $10,000 term life insurance in addition to any other Government insurance carried, for all persons on active duty from 29 September 1965. Your pay is checked $2 per month for this coverage, and you are covered for the full amount until and unless you cancel all or part of your coverage, or until (as the law permits) you convert this term insurance into permanent protection with one of many fine insurance companies. Such conversion of SGLI to an individual commercial insurance policy may be effected, *without medical examination,* at any time within 120 days of your retirement or separation from the Navy.

NOTE: Under no circumstances should you cancel any part of this marvelous insurance protection; nor, however, should you cancel any other insurance you may carry. Instead, you should consider SGLI as extra protection above and beyond your permanent insurance plan.

In addition to SGLI, just described, which is current, the other two Government life insurance plans are these:

a. *United States Government Life Insurance* (USGLI) established during World War I and continued until World War II.

b. *National Service Life Insurance* (NSLI), established during World War II and continued until the Korean War.

Neither program is open except to those previously insured thereunder. If, however, you had a policy, either USGLI or NSLI, which was in force on or before 25 April 1951, which you have allowed to lapse, or surrendered for cash while on active duty before 1 January 1957, you may replace or reinstate this policy at any time while you remain on active duty or within 120 days after active duty terminates. This is a most valuable privilege and should be taken advantage of. As long as such Government insurance can be had, it constitutes by far the cheapest and the best.

In addition to the foregoing, post-service non-participating insurance for service-connected disability is still available for regulars and reservists who are disabled while on continuous active duty. It is also open to reservists disabled under certain conditions when on active duty for training.

If eligible on separation from the service, be sure to take advantage of this opportunity. *You cannot get a better insurance bargain,* unless it be SGLI previously described. For further information, write the Navy Mutual Aid for their booklet, apply to your command insurance officer or write to the nearest Veterans' Administration office for VA pamphlet 9-1 and 9-3. See also Navy Guide for Retired Personnel (NavPers 15891B).

2. Participate in the Retired Serviceman's Family Protection Plan (RSFPP). Formerly entitled the "Contingency Option Act," this plan permits you to elect to receive a reduced amount of retired pay so that your surviving dependents may receive a Government annuity following your death in retired status. Fundamentally, the disadvantage is that, upon retirement, you do not receive all the retired pay you would otherwise have, but you may now withdraw from the plan by notifying the U.S. Navy Finance Center, Cleveland; the withdrawal becomes effective six months later. Once a retiree submits a request for such withdrawal, he cannot again rejoin the plan.

At any time after 19 years service while you have two or more years' remaining service prior to retirement with pay, you may elect one of three basic options provided by the plan, and at the same time designate how much your dependents will receive per month of your retired pay after your death. Here are the options:

Option 1: Annuity for your widow—payable to her until her death or remarriage at which time payments cease.

Option 2: Annuity for a child or children—payable to a child or surviving children until there ceases to be at least one surviving child unmarried and under 18. (An unmarried child over 18 who is incapable of self-support receives the annuity until marriage, death, or recovery.)

Option 3: Annuity for both—payable to both widow and surviving children, until death or remarriage of widow, or until there are no surviving children under 18, unmarried or incapacitated.

Under all these options, if the last of your beneficiaries dies before you do, no further deductions will be made from your retired pay.

The decision to elect or not to elect the Family Protection Plan is a big one. It is not a substitute for life insurance (the annuity is taxable income to the recipients, you have no equity in the plan, and you cannot cash it in or borrow against it). Whether it is best for you depends on your personal situation. Basically, if you have a long life-expectancy on retirement, are well-fixed, with adequate life insurance and a solid estate, the plan has the disadvantages that you will probably receive reduced retired pay for many years, your widow may remarry or die soon (at which time payments cease), and she would receive little benefit. On the other hand, participating in RSFPP could be an excellent means of augmenting insurance and other survivor benefits, at a relatively small cost, for those who may be uninsurable. The law now excludes RSFPP deductions from a participant's taxable income and excludes the annuity from the deceased member's estate for Federal estate taxes.

3. By all means, join the Navy Mutual Aid Association. Its regular death benefit is $7,500, plus a substantial additional death benefit which was increased to $4,500 in June 1969.

4. Take out life insurance with a commercial company under one of the plans previously described which will provide substantial cash values at time of retirement or will be paid up before retirement.

5. From time to time, take out additional term insurance for protection of your family while the children are growing up and to ensure their education.

The Navy Mutual Aid Association recommends total insurance at various stages of an officer's career, as follows:

Ensign	$22,000 Unmarried
Lieutenant (j.g.)	$32,000 Married, one child
Lieutenant	$42,000 Married, two children
Lieutenant Commander	$57,000 Same

As a bachelor ensign, you can well afford this program. For the person who cannot or will not save this is the time to consider 20- or 30-year endowment or 20- or 30-payment life. Premiums will be lower the younger your age.

Upon reaching lieutenant commander, an officer's family responsibilities are greatest. This level of insurance should be maintained until his children are self-supporting. With less financial responsibilities, some term insurance can be dropped, but a captain after retirement may wish to maintain a level of about $47,000 to provide a reasonable support for his widow.

The Navy Mutual Aid Program Pamphlet previously mentioned gives many more interesting and useful details, with probable benefits to survivors including Social Security and Survivors' Benefits payments.

The birth of each child calls for a revaluation of your program and usually indicates an increase in life insurance. Certainly, some form of additional insurance is indicated. Consider term insurance on your own life coupled with regular investment as a first choice, ordinary insurance on your life as second choice, or finally an endowment policy on the life of the child or on your own life. If you take a policy out on the child, arrange for the type of policy which guarantees continuation of premiums if you should die. Some officers prefer to take out education policies on their own life on either endowment or retirement-income plans. If you should die before your child becomes of college age, the additional insurance on your life will help your wife to see him through school. If you find that you do not need the life-insurance money for the child's education, you can let the policy mature and receive it as either a lump-sum endowment or as retirement income at the age of sixty or sixty-five.

At least every five years, go over your current situation and your program with your agent friend. You will be surprised to find, usually, that inflation, change in income or employment, or change in family situation indicate an improvement of your program.

A few notes:

Do not buy life insurance just to be buying it. *Follow a sound program.*

Do not let your government insurance lapse if you leave the service. In service or out, it is the *best* insurance you can buy.

Check the settlement arrangements with a reliable agent periodically. They may be poorly adapted to your present circumstances. The terms of settlement may be altered. Any good agent will take care of it for you.

Be sure the beneficiary is one you want at all times. Name a contingent beneficiary. If a beneficiary (such as mother or father) dies, be sure to make a prompt change in beneficiary. Consider what would happen if both you and the beneficiary—your wife—die in the same accident. If children are designated, specify "To my children in equal shares."

See that your program provides your wife with sufficient funds immediately after your death to take care of immediate needs. The Navy Mutual Aid Association benefits are wonderful for this purpose.

Pay premiums by allotment, both for government and commercial policies. Present regulations permit indefinite allotments for payment of insurance premiums, which continue after you retire. Payment by allotment will prevent lapse of policies with resultant hardship on your survivors.

Check your policies to ensure that they protect you from all hazards of your occupation. Policies of many good companies have restrictions as to war, flying hazards, aircraft flights as pilot, crew member or as a passenger in a military airplane, etc. Know what you are buying.

Do not place all your insurance with one company, no matter how fine its reputation or how sound its financial condition may be at the present time. A safe program and full protection rest upon diversification among several good companies.

Do not overload yourself with insurance to protect yourself against doubtful hazards of an uncertain future which may never materialize. Plan a sound program with a capable agent and stick to it.

1704. LIFE-INSURANCE PROCEEDS. Every insurance policy that is offered by a reputable firm probably has a place and a usefulness. The *term* type of insurance is the lowest cost life insurance. This sort of policy builds up no cash value for the *policyholder,* only to the beneficiary, and represents what might be called "pure insurance" cost. This type of insurance is good for a temporary situation as when you have borrowed a large sum of money for a short period or as protection against certain business or other hazards of a temporary nature.

Every other policy maintains some kind of ratio between premium paid for "pure insurance" cost and benefits accorded to the policyholder; therefore, it is often possible to buy an ordinary life policy for twice as much protection as a short-term policy such as a 15- or 20-year endowment would provide and by separate investment acquire the same cash value and reserve during a comparable period, if you are sure that you can make yourself do it. It all depends on what you want to get out of your insurance program, just how much you put into it, and what kind of policies you will choose.

Endowment Policies. Premiums cease upon expiration of the 15-, 20-, or 30-year period. You may usually elect to take the face value of the policy in a lump sum, take paid-up life insurance in the same or a larger amount, or take retirement income, at the age of sixty or sixty-five, of about $10 per month per thousand of face value. Premiums are very high.

Paid-up Policies. Premiums cease at the expiration of the 20- or 30-year period (and sometimes earlier if you have left the dividends on deposit with the company), and you have fully paid-up life insurance for the face value of the policy. Premiums are not as high as for endowments, but are higher than ordinary life.

Ordinary Life Policies. Premiums usually continue until death, although some companies write policies where premiums cease at a predetermined age and still call them ordinary life. Of course, you pay higher premiums for such policies. When your children are grown and your insurance needs are less, consider taking the cash value of your policies as paid up insurance.

Naming Beneficiaries. Consider indicating a named beneficiary for each policy. A significant tax saving may result. You may wish to designate children to receive "equal shares" until family size stabilizes. (See Section 1707, *State Inheritance Tax and Federal Estate Tax.*)

Death Claims. On government insurance, death claims are submitted as follows:

Active Duty. Beneficiary of record will be mailed forms by the Veterans' Administration. The VA will be notified of an active-duty death almost as soon as the next of kin.

Proof of death is not necessary. Notification by the service is sufficient.

Death after Retirement or Separation from Service. Apply to the nearest VA office for necessary death-claim papers or see nearest Navy chaplain.

Proof of death must be furnished. The best proof is a certified copy of public death record (coroner's report). If that is not available, get an affidavit from persons who have viewed the body and who knew the deceased when he was living.

The Veterans' Administration will be glad to help all the way through this settlement.

On commercial policies, death claims are submitted as follows:

Consult local representative of the various companies, go to nearest branch office or write direct to the home office giving:

Insured's name.

Policy numbers.

State that you want them to send you the necessary forms to make a death claim.

You will then have to:

Fill out forms sent you.

Get a photostat or certified copy of death certificate or, if unobtainable, an affidavit as above. If death occurred at sea or on foreign soil, a certified copy of the Navy Department's telegram or other official notification will suffice.

Send forms and proof of death to the home office of the insurance company by *registered mail*. Hold on to your policies until the claim is paid. Do not send them in.

The local representative of the company will help you through all this quite willingly. If you are a member of the Navy Mutual Aid Association, it will wire you $1,000 (without waiting for claim) just as soon as it learns of the death of your husband, unless you advise them not to do so. They will help you with all the problems of life insurance, death benefits, etc. (see also Sections 1719-21).

1705. OTHER INSURANCE. *Automobile Insurance* will provide you protection against liability for bodily injury, property damage, medical payments, collision or upset, fire, lightning and transportation, theft, windstorm, earthquake, explosion, hail, or water damage. With the high incidence of auto accidents, the rising costs of auto repairs, the steadily increasing awards by the courts for bodily injury, a car owner is negligent if he does not protect himself with good coverage against all of the above listed liabilities.

For bodily injury, take not less than $10,000-$20,000 coverage, for property damage, $5,000. A "$50 deductible" clause for collision or upset gives you adequate coverage, but "$100 deductible" is cheaper and in the long run is usually better. Many Armed Forces posts and bases and many states require public liability and other insurance before you will be issued a permit or an auto license for your car.

Personal Property Insurance will cover your clothes, jewelry, silverware, furniture, etc. against fire, theft, and transportation hazards. "Floater policies" covering officers against such losses on a worldwide basis can be obtained for small premiums. Recommended for such a "floater policy" and for automobile insurance is United Services Automobile Association, a mutual association of officers of all the armed services with home office in San Antonio, Texas. Army Cooperative Fire Association, Fort Leavenworth, Kansas, also offers good personal property insurance. (Navy people are also covered and are represented in the management.) Should you die, your widow should contact United Services Automobile Association and ask if a percentage of premium refund is due you.

Fire insurance will protect your investment in your home and the furniture which it contains. Be sure that you carry a large enough policy to cover the cost of rebuilding the house and refurnishing. Frequent revaluation of this insurance is important.

Personal Liability Insurance will protect you against claims for injury by servants, workmen, and persons visiting your property, as well as any damage done by your pets, children, your wife or yourself and by such accidents as falling trees, a fire originating on your property, or accidents caused by sports. Such insurance is inexpensive and invaluable when trouble comes.

1706. YOUR ESTATE. *Kinds of Property.* During his lifetime, a person accumulates various kinds of property which are known collectively as his "estate." Such property may be either "real estate"—land, buildings, and improvements or fixtures erected thereon or attached thereto—or "personalty," which includes all kinds of personal property such as clothes, household furnishings, automobiles, money, stocks, bonds, jewelry, and in fact any property that is not real estate. Ask the Navy Mutual Aid Association for their excellent pamphlet, Planning Your Estate. There is also a fine discussion under Finances in Your New Career (NavPers 15895-A).

Real Estate. Give serious consideration to buying and living in your own home. Some officers reach retirement age without a home and no savings in the bank to make a down payment. Others have lived in their own homes for years, buying a house where they have duty and are not assigned quarters, and selling or renting it when they are assigned to other duty. Thus, they have arrived at retirement age with a real asset rather than rent receipts. When retirement comes, if you decide to settle in another locality than the place where you own a home, you can use your property as an asset toward purchasing a permanent home for your retirement years. If you purchase or build your new home within 18 months of the day you transfer title on your old one, you will not have to pay capital gains tax on any profit you may have made on the transaction up to the cost of the new home.

Kinds of Title. The title, or right to ownership or possession, which a person has in the separate items of his estate, may be of various kinds. He may have complete title, in which case it belongs to him alone. He may own it in "joint tenancy," i.e., he and one or more other persons may own the whole property jointly, in which case, if he dies, his interest in the property goes immediately to the surviving joint tenant or tenants and ceases to be a part of his estate subject to probate as his property. He may own the property with one or more persons in what is known as "tenancy in common," which means that he has an undivided interest in the property, which interest belongs only to him. On his death, such undivided interest is subject to probate as part of his estate and does not go to the surviving tenant or tenants.

Individual Control. During his lifetime, an individual may himself use and control his estate or he may use and control it through an agent or attorney acting under a proper power of attorney. On the individual's death, his estate is subject to probate in the courts and is distributed according to the terms of his will or, if he has no will, according to the laws of "descent and distribution" of the particular state. The personal effects of a person who dies in service are safeguarded by the government and transferred to those legally entitled thereto according to inheritance rights as established by a court of competent jurisdiction.

Advantages of Joint Ownership. The officer, who wishes to simplify the problem that would confront his widow, should consider carefully the advantages of joint ownership. Property passes to the survivor with less expense, inconvenience, and loss of time than through normal settlement in accordance with law or the terms of a will. There are also disadvantages to this. Where property of considerable value is involved or there are other complications, consult an attorney.

In order to facilitate the use and control of his property, and to provide for its disposition on his death, the individual may, in addition to executing a power of attorney and a will as discussed, arrange for the ownership of most of his property in joint tenancy with right of survivorship. By this means he may enable his joint tenant to use and control the property during his lifetime and in the event of his death to obtain full title as survivor without the property being a part of his estate subject to probate in the courts. Property held in "joint tenancy" cannot be disposed of by his will if his joint tenant survives him.

Real estate may be owned in joint tenancy with right of survivorship under proper deed. Personal property such as automobiles, machinery, and livestock, the title to which usually passes by bill of sale, may be held in joint tenancy under an appropriate instrument of conveyance. Joint bank accounts can be opened, and stocks and bonds may be issued to joint owners, with right of survivorship in each case.

United States Savings Bonds will be issued upon request to joint owners with right of survivorship. If a bond has already been issued to a single owner, it is part of his estate subject to probate on his death, but it can be reissued during his lifetime to joint owners upon proper application to the Treasury Department. Bonds can also be reissued to a single owner with designated beneficiary, which can be cashed only by the owner during his lifetime and which on death of the owner do not become part of his estate but go to his named beneficiary. A bond held by a single owner, whether a beneficiary is designated or not, can be cashed only upon a request for payment signed by him personally. A power of attorney would probably not be acceptable for such purpose.

Ownership of Automobile. A practice adopted by an increasing number of officers is the joint ownership of the family automobile. It will surprise most officers to learn that loss may occur to the owner's family if the wife or some other member of the family drives *his* car or permits another to drive it after the *owner's* death. Should there be an accident during unauthorized use of the car, the usual automobile insurance would not cover the accident. There are other hazards. This chance of loss can be eliminated by the owner instructing all concerned, in the event of his death, as to the use of the car and also by putting title to the car in joint tenancy. The certificate of title to the car must bear the names of the joint owners, and the insurance policy must be drawn up in exactly the same manner.

Advantage of Joint Account. It often happens that an officer or man who carries a bank account in his own name temporarily deprives his wife or dependents of the use of this money at a time when it is most urgently needed. Upon the husband being ordered to foreign service or upon his death, the wife or other dependents may encounter unexpected difficulties. It is possible in most states to carry joint bank accounts, and most banks have a specially prepared contract form setting out the legal status of the account in accordance with the laws of the state governing the bank.

Power of Attorney. Special advantages may be conferred on the dependents of an officer absent on duty by a power of attorney to act in his stead. The purpose of a power of attorney is to authorize another to act in the name of a person and in his stead in the same manner and to the same extent as the principal himself could act. The power may authorize another to do any acts stated in the power. It must be remembered, however, that, if the power authorizes the attorney to convey any interest in real estate, it must be executed with the strict formalities applicable to conveyances of real estate in the state in which the real property is situated. The part of the power of attorney upon which there is no uniformity in all states is that part known as the "acknowledgment." A power of attorney is void on death. Most JAG Corps officers are specifically designated as Legal Assistance Officers and can furnish necessary forms (and guidance for their execution and use) upon request.

In instances where military personnel are detailed to or are on duty at places where they cannot be reached, reimbursement may be made to near relatives for dependent travel and shipment of household effects if such relatives have a power of attorney as indicated here.

In view of the fact that naval personnel are subject to movement on short notice to duty at places where communication may be impossible or greatly delayed, such personnel are urged to take necessary steps to execute proper powers of attorney covering their affairs generally, and particularly with reference to the above specifically mentioned reimbursements from the United States, coupled with authority in said power of attorney to receive, endorse, and collect the proceeds of checks payable to the order of said personnel drawn on the Treasurer of the United States. In the event such power of attorney includes authority to transact general nongovernmental business, such personnel should consult competent civilian counsel in order to ensure that such power when executed is legally sufficient.

Such power of attorney, whether general or limited, should include *power* worded substantially as follows:

To execute vouchers in my behalf for any and all allowances and reimbursements properly payable to me by the United States, including but not restricted to shipment of household effects as authorized by law and Navy Regulations, and to receive, endorse, and collect the proceeds of checks payable to the order of the undersigned drawn on the Treasurer of the United States.

Such power, so far as it relates to the above-mentioned governmental transactions, should be executed in the presence of at least three witnesses and acknowledged before a notary public or, if executed outside the United States, before any officer of the United States authorized to administer oaths or take acknowledgments. For other purposes, each specific power must be mentioned to be effective, such as, to negotiate notes, draw checks and mortgage or sell real or personal property.

Such power for the above purposes should be executed with a sufficient number of original copies for use as follows: (1) for submission with each voucher covering payments under said power; (2) for filing with the Treasurer of the United States as authority to negotiate checks in payment of said vouchers; (3) as may be required for other uses by the attorney.

Vouchers covering pay, subsistence, rental, and travel accounts of naval personnel will not be paid by disbursing officers when executed under authority of powers of attorney. Vouchers covering transportation of dependents or expenses of shipment of household effects may be paid by disbursing officers when executed under proper powers of attorney covering specifically reimbursements of this character as indicated above. Other vouchers executed on behalf of naval personnel under powers of attorney will not be paid by disbursing officers without prior approval of the Comptroller General. Vouchers properly payable as indicated in this paragraph should be executed by the attorney in the following form: John Doe, Lieutenant, USN, by Mary Doe, Attorney in Fact.

If relatives of such personnel have but one copy of a power of attorney and the original thereof is required to be retained by the attorney, a copy thereof duly attested should be attached to the voucher covering such allowances and reimbursement, and a copy thereof likewise so certified should be filed with the Treasurer of the United States in connection with the negotiation of such checks as may be issued on said voucher. Such copies, photostatic or otherwise, should be duly attested to be true copies by a notary public, or by other civil authority authorized to take acknowledgments or oaths or to certify copies, or by a commissioned officer of the Navy, which attestation shall include, where possible, a statement by said certifying officer of the reason or necessity stated by said attorney for retention by the attorney of the original of said power.

In lieu of furnishing copies of said power of attorney to the Treasurer of the United States, the original thereof may be forwarded to that official, prior to the negotiation of the check, for examination and return if requested; or if the original of said power accompanies the voucher and no other copy is available for use in connection with negotiation of the check, the Treasury Department should be advised of that fact with sufficient information to identify the check and the character of payment that it covers.

Inquiries from dependents covering reimbursements of the character previously mentioned, will be referred to the Supply Systems Command.

Record of Emergency Data (NavPers 601-2). The purpose of this form is to provide BuPers with up-to-date information for use in the event of serious illness, injury, or death, including:

Persons to be notified in case of emergency.

Persons to receive death gratuity.

Persons (including commercial insurance companies or banks) to receive special allotments if you become missing in action, or are in any way prevented from returning to naval jurisdiction.

Names of insurance companies to be furnished a certification of casualty.

Keep this form up-to-date! You should fill out a new Record of Emergency Data:

When you first enter the service.

If you are recalled to active duty.

When you retire and periodically thereafter.

A Naval Reserve officer ordered to extended active duty.

When promoted from enlisted status to officer rank.

Whenever a change occurs in the status of your dependents or beneficiaries or persons to be notified in case of an emergency.

Change in the name of the person designated to receive death gratuity or arrears in pay.

Change in dependents to receive the special allotment of pay if you become in a missing status.

List all insurance policies in force on this form. The Chief of Naval Personnel will furnish certification of casualty to the insurance companies so named in the event of your death.

Allotments. Immediately upon receipt of your orders, for sea duty or foreign service, or notice that you are about to be ordered, see your Disbursing Officer and register allotments of that portion of your pay which you will not actually need. Be sure that allotments for the support of dependents or to a bank for the support of dependents are so designated. This is a vital necessity in the event you become a prisoner of the enemy.

In the event of your capture, BuPers, within 24 hours of official notification, informs the Casualty Assistance Affairs Officer of the Naval District in which your family lives. That officer visits your family and with BuPers is delegated, under the Missing Persons Act, the responsibility of providing for your family's welfare in your absence and of assuming your moral and legal obligations, if your family desires.

Safeguarding Your Personal Funds. Instances have arisen where, owing to loss or damage to a naval vessel, personnel attached to that vessel have suffered considerable loss of personal funds. Funds may be deposited for safekeeping with disbursing officers but, if the records are lost, you may lose the whole sum deposited.

There are several ways to safeguard your personal funds:

1. Allot most of your pay to a dependent or to a bank for the support of dependents. Even if the allotment to a bank is for your personal account, make it a joint account with your wife or other person who is actually dependent upon you for support, naming the dependent on the allotment itself, *e.g.,* First National Bank, Kalamazoo, Maine, a/c Mary Doe. Then the allotment will continue without interruption if you should be missing or become a prisoner.

2. If you have no dependents, allot the major portion of your pay for the purchase of Savings Bonds or to a bank for savings. Keep only enough money on the books of your Disbursing Officer to take care of your immediate expenses.

3. Do not allow the amount of cash in your possession to become large. Bank your surplus funds, and pay bills by check.

4. Officers and enlisted men may deposit funds for savings at 10 percent per annum with their disbursing officers while they are at sea or out of the country and for 90 days upon return to CONUS. Since copies of these records are kept in Washington, funds so deposited may be presumed to be safe if the ship is lost.

5. Officers and enlisted men can let pay "ride" on the books. Normally pay can "ride on the books" for six months. Before the disbursing officer renders his returns every six months, all claims for pay should be cleared at this time of semiannual transition.

Money. Navy, Coast Guard, and Marine Corps disbursing officers outside the continental limits of the United States are authorized, for accommodation of military and naval personnel, civilian employees of government and Navy contractors, and accredited civilians operating with Navy components, to cash United States Treasury checks or United States or foreign-currency checks drawn by military and naval disbursing officers in their official capacity on United States Treasury or on special accounts with authorized United States depositories, provided that these checks are presented by the individual in whose favor the check is drawn and endorsed and fingerprinted with the right index finger of the payee in the presence of the disbursing officer. Travelers' checks and negotiable money orders issued by the American Express Company and travelers' checks issued by the Bank of America, National Trust and Savings Association, Mellon National Bank of Pittsburgh, and National City Bank of New York may be cashed when these are presented by the payee, counter-signed and fingerprinted with the right index finger of the payee in the presence of the disbursing officer.

Disbursing officers shall not use official funds to cash checks drawn in favor of themselves.

Safe-deposit Boxes. All valuable papers, including stocks, bonds, a properly drawn and authenticated will, insurance receipts, etc., should be put in a place of safekeeping. When possible, a safe-deposit box in a reputable bank is the best place.

There are three methods of renting a safe-deposit box:

In the Name of One Individual. Only that individual can open the box. In most states, when he dies, the box can be opened only in the presence of a representative of a probate court and generally only on a court order. Since the contents are released to an executor or administrator of the estate only on order of the probate court, this will prevent access of the widow or dependents to the box, as probate proceedings take considerable time.

Joint Tenancy. Where two individuals rent a box together, either may open the box without the consent or presence of the other. In some states, the death of one results in the box being sealed and access refused to the other except on order of the probate court. Where the words in the contract with the bank are "joint tenants, with right of survivorship," most state laws permit the survivor access to the box, usually in the presence of a representative of the state taxing authority who sees if any assets are in the box which might be subject to state inheritance taxes.

Individual Ownership with Appointed Deputy. An individual who rents a box may give power of attorney to another to have access to the box. In most states, the death of the deputy does not prevent the owner from opening the box. Thus, a wife (or dependent) may rent a box and appoint her husband as deputy, giving the wife free access to the box even after the death of her husband.

In view of the differences in the laws of various states, the safe-deposit box officials of your bank should be consulted before the method of sharing a safe-deposit box is finally decided.

1707. TAXES. You may feel that you have provided adequately and even generously for your family in the event of your death, but one element of the transfer of your estate may escape your attention to the detriment of your loved ones—*taxes!*

As an owner of property, whether real estate, stocks, bonds, or other properties in any form, you want to pass on to your dependents, whose future you strive to make secure, an estate free of debt. Whether your estate is passed under your will, or by gifts or trusts during your lifetime, certain taxes must be paid to the state and Federal governments —*in cash.* If you do not provide the cash in your estate, the taxing authorities will claim liens against the estate and thus will establish, in effect, *a mortgage you did not sign,* but which is very positively a claim against your estate. Although these taxes are generally the largest single item of expense to an estate, many persons give but scant consideration to their tax problem. They do not know anything about the amount of tax which their estates will have to pay, nor do they realize that, unless liquid funds are provided, sales of securities or property will have to be made, often at a serious disadvantage to the estate.

After your death, of course, nothing can be done but sell assets or borrow on them and pay the levied tax on time. During your lifetime, though, you can, through proper planning, often arrange your estate in such a way as to make a substantial saving in the tax expense.

Executor. Most individuals who have been appointed executor under the wills of friends or relatives, or who may be asked to act as administrator, are unaware of the importance of their duties and responsibilities in settling the tax liabilities of the estates for which they will act. They do not realize that, if they close an estate and distribute the property before settling all unpaid taxes for the period of probate and for previous years, they may be held personally responsible for all unpaid taxes and penalties and may be required to make the payment from their own funds.

Before deciding to act as an executor or administrator, or to ask a friend or a member of your family so to serve, you should seriously consider the responsibilities which an unskilled individual is called upon to assume.

State Taxes. The taxes imposed upon estates vary from state to state. You should investigate the various states in which you might establish residence or own real or personal property and *know* what the provisions for that particular state are. The notes which follow may or may not be applicable to the state in which your will would, as things now stand, be probated. They are applicable to a number of states.

State Inheritance Tax. Some states impose a tax upon the inheritance of property, upon transfers without consideration made to take effect after the death of the transferor, and upon transfers made in contemplation of death. Property held in joint tenancy is taxable upon the death of one of the owners in some states unless the survivor can prove that he was the original owner.

Distinction is made in most states which have community-property laws between separate property and community property, since the right to succeed to all separate property is taxable, but succession to community property is subject to certain exemptions under the law.

On the death of your wife, should she leave no will, all the community property vests in the husband and is exempt from inheritance tax; whereas on the death of the husband, should he leave no will, the community property vests in the wife, but one-half of it is taxable. Inheritance by either spouse of the separate property of the other is taxable.

In most states, proceeds of life- and accident-insurance policies *payable to the estate or to legal representatives of the insured* are taxable, as also are such proceeds in excess of certain sums (up to $50,000 exempt in some states) payable to named beneficiaries.

The tax is usually not computed upon the aggregate amount of the whole estate. It is levied against each of the beneficiaries and is based upon the amount each beneficiary receives. It is a graduated tax and is applied by classification or relationship of the beneficiary. This varies so much between states that there is nothing for you to do but look it up for the state in which your will probably will be probated. Inheritance taxes must be paid in full by the beneficiaries or by the executor before the estate can be distributed. Payment must be in cash.

Exemptions also vary between states. For example, in California, property values exempted vary from $24,000 for your wife, to $12,000 for a minor child and $2,000 for other children, lineal ancestors, or lineal descendants. Other beneficiaries have a much smaller exemption. Tax rates commence at 2 to 7 percent and rise to 10 to 16 percent for individual bequests over $500,000.

State Estate Tax. Some states also have an estate tax, the purpose of which seems to be to ensure that the state collects as much from its inheritance tax as the taxpayer receives as a credit when paying the Federal estate tax. The difference between the state inheritance tax levied and the Federal credit is collected as a state estate tax. See the explanation of State Inheritance Tax Credit.

State Gift Taxes. In order to be sure that citizens do not escape inheritance tax by giving away their assets before their death, many states impose a gift tax. The amount of this tax depends, in general upon the value of the property transferred and the relationship which the receiver of the gift bears to the donor.

The rates and exemptions vary from state to state. In California, total property values given to any one person are exempted and taxed in the same manner as described above for inheritance taxes, except that each person may give to any person he chooses $4,000 per year and it does not count toward the total of his gifts. According to the laws in that state, a man could, in 10 years, give to his wife and three children, two of whom are minors, a total $213,000 without being subject to any state gift tax. This shows the advantage of early planning on the distribution of your estate. The annual exclusion of $4,000 does not apply if the transfer is of a *future interest* in the property donated.

Transfer for some charitable purposes are exempt in most states. Gifts to an educational institution are generally exempt.

Federal Taxes, Estate Tax. The Federal Estate Tax is imposed on the transfer of property at the death of the owner. It is based on the net value of the estate without regard to the amount of the distributive shares or the relationship of the beneficiary. The net value of the estate is determined by deducting from the total value of the estate, debts, funeral and administrative expenses, certain other items, and an exemption amounting, in the case of a citizen or resident of the United States, to $60,000. Property is valued at the date of death or one year after the decedent's death, as the executor may elect, but the sale or transfer of property during the year fixes the date of valuation.

All proceeds of insurance on the life of the decedent payable to his estate must be included in the gross estate. So also must all life insurance payable to named beneficiaries if the premium were paid directly or indirectly by the deceased, or if, at the time of his death, the decedent retained any of the rights incident to ownership. Life insurance payable irrevocably to a named beneficiary and in which decedent retains *no rights* incident to ownership—such as policy loan right or right to change beneficiary—is excluded from the gross estate.

Property held in joint tenancy and transferred upon the death of the owner is included in the gross estate unless the survivor can prove that he was the original owner. But present law provides for the allowance of a *marital deduction* for estate-tax purposes up to one-half of the property which passes to the decedent's surviving spouse. Thus, married persons may now arrange their estates so that the *marital deduction* can be used to effect substantial estate-tax savings. Also the apparent effect of present law is to exclude one-half of community property from taxation.

A *State Inheritance Tax Credit* is equal to 80 percent of what the gross Federal Estate Tax would have been under the Revenue Act of 1926, which is no longer applicable except for this one purpose. This usually operates to give a smaller credit than would be given under the 1942 act. Many states have changed their laws so that they collect at least as much from their inheritance tax as is credited to the taxpayer by the Federal government.

In most states, unless the deceased person has provided otherwise in his will, the Federal Estate Tax is prorated among the beneficiaries of the estate according to the proportion of their interest.

Federal Gift Tax.   This tax is payable by the donor in the year following that in which the gifts are made, and, if not so paid, the taxing authority will claim a lien against the property transferred.

A specific exemption of $30,000 is allowed to citizens or residents of the United States, a total specific exemption allowed to a donor during his lifetime as an aggregate value of all gifts made after June 6, 1932. The donor may take the entire exemption in one year or spread it over any number of years. Once the total $30,000 has been taken, no further specific exemption is deductible.

The law permits a donor to deduct one-half of the value of a gift made to his spouse. Where a gift is made by a married person to persons other than his spouse, the interest transferred may be considered as made one-half by each of the spouses. Gifts of community property are considered as made one-half by each spouse.

In addition to his specific exemption, a donor may deduct gifts for charitable purposes and the first $3,000 given to each of any number of persons in any calendar year. These $3,000 exclusions do not apply to gifts of *future* interests on property—the gift must be outright with no strings attached.

Federal gift tax rates vary from 2.25 percent on all gifts over $30,000 as described above after exclusions to 29.25 percent on gifts aggregating over a million dollars.

To Solve Your Estate Tax Problem. You will want to arrange your affairs so that your dependents will have the maximum protection and security that your estate can provide. You must consider the relative merits of bequests by will, by trusts under a will, by trusts created in your lifetime, and by outright gifts. Over a 10-year period, you could give to your wife $60,000, and your wife and you, under community-property arrangements, could give to each of your children $60,000 free of gift tax, a total of which you might dispose amounting to $240,000 for a family of four. A very large estate for most naval officers, but you must consider this—a gift has to be made while you are alive and such sums can be given free of tax only if gifts are consistently planned over a fairly long term of years. If the total of your estate is not more than $60,000 you will not be troubled by the Federal Estate Tax so very much, because the community-property law will let you dispose of about half of that to your wife and the exemption will take care of the rest. If you think that is a very large sum, get a commercial financial statement from your bank and fill it out. Put down everything. The total may cause you to stop and consider the taxes on your estate.

You should do the following things:

Make an analysis of your estate. Estimate your inheritance and estate taxes, and make plans to minimize them based on a study of your assets and liabilities.

Confer with the trust officer of your bank. A good trust officer can help you materially in laying out a comprehensive plan for the protection of your dependents.

Make provision for liquid assets in your estate to meet taxes. It is strongly recommended that you establish an ample reserve of salable securities and life insurance for this purpose.

Consult your attorney. His experience in making wills and trusts will be of great value to you.

Review your plan frequently. As stated above about life insurance, changes in laws, financial condition, family obligations, etc., all require that you re-evaluate your estate from time to time.

1708. Your last will and testament. *Importance.* It is highly important that officers, of whatever age and grade, prepare a will covering the disposition of their property after death. The estate of a man who dies intestate (leaving no will) is distributed by law to his next of kin. These laws vary in the different states. They but seldom fit exactly a particular case. The use of a will makes your desired distribution more certain. At least, you should ascertain the provisions of law which would control your estate and be convinced that the legal distribution will meet your wishes. In very nearly every case, a will should be made. There is considerable expense in the settlement of an estate as noted above. Possession of a will simplifies the settlement and conserves the assets of your estate.

A *will* is an instrument executed with the formalities of law whereby a person makes disposition of his property to take effect after his death. Until the maker's death, a will is alterable and revocable.

A *testator* is a person who leaves a will in force at his death.

A *codicil* is an addition to, or qualification of, a will and revokes the will only in the precise degree in which it is inconsistent therewith. The will and codicil are to be construed together. A codicil must be executed with the same formalities as the will. It is usually better to make a new will.

The *probating* of a will consists in presenting the will to the office of Register of Wills in the county where the deceased had his legal residence.

Preparing Your Will. A number of questions will arise in your mind. In order to get your ideas and estimates well organized, it is suggested that you take scratch paper and make an outline of your personal situation according to the questions asked. When you discuss your will with your attorney and the trust officer of your bank, you will have some orderly thoughts to lay before them.

What Do I Own? First, consider the property which you may not dispose freely—property limited by joint tenancy previously discussed, community property, your share of trust funds, life insurance you have already disposed to individuals, etc. Consider each of these as they affect your estate, and put down a figure opposite each as to the amount that is yours to dispose.

Consider your assets under the following headings:

Cash
Real estate
Securities
Life insurance (payable to your estate)

Business interests
Automobile, if in your name
Household furniture and furnishings (some of these will be community prop-
erty)
Personal effects
Other property

Consider now your liabilities. List your principal debts and estimates of expenses which would have to be paid from your estate. Here are the usual ones:

Expense of last illness
Funeral expenses
Unpaid household bills and expenses
Personal debts
Mortgages or notes payable (only your share, if joint)
Expense of administering your estate
Estate, inheritance, and real-estate taxes

You will probably be able to rough out most of these. For help on estimating expenses of administering estate and taxes, consult the trust officer of your bank. Federal and state taxes almost always are the biggest item on the debit side.

Who Are My Heirs and What Do I Want Them to Receive? In most families, there is little question as to whom the heirs will be. However, in making out your list of beneficiaries, bear in mind that there are several classes of persons who are entitled by law to share in your es-tate, provided that you have not previously taken care of them during your lifetime or you have not specifically excluded them in your will. Consult your attorney on this point.

You will, of course, include your wife and children. But do not forget the children of a deceased child, children still minors, aging father or mother, favorite nieces or nephews, other close relatives, close friends, business associates, servants, and, if you have a large estate, charities.

First, decide upon specific bequests of personal and real property. Be careful, next, in making cash bequests, for if your estate dwindles, you may cut off your residual legatee with very little or nothing. In cash bequests, state whether those legatees are to share in estate taxes or whether their bequests are to be tax free. In the latter case, the balance of the estate must bear the expense of all taxes. If your estate may be subject to fluctuation, it is better to make cash bequests by percentages of the estate rather than as specific amounts.

Seek advice from your attorney on such matters as specific bequests of antiques, family heirlooms, etc.; selling any part of your estate to provide ready cash; transfer of real estate with or without encumbrances; options to business associates to purchase your interest in the business out of earnings; and so on. If your marital condition changes, you should immediately make a new will to provide for your spouse.

Who Will Be My Executor? This is a problem that will give you considerable trouble. Can you impose on a business friend or close personal friend to assume such a burden? If your estate is small, it is probably best to make your wife your executor and for her to make you her executor. If your estate is large, your will complicated, give careful consideration to making your bank executor or coexecutor of your estate. The trust department of a bank is trained to handle large estates; it is a continuing institution whereas an individual eventually dies, sometimes very soon after the person who has made him executor; a bank is financially responsible; and it would receive not a cent more for its services than an individual. Go to your attorney and to your banker for advice in this matter.

Shall I Consult with My Executor? It may sound ridiculous, but individuals have suddenly found themselves named as executors in a will and thus administrators of an estate without even knowing that they had been considered for such a position. Of course, they can refuse to act, but this would seriously complicate the settlement of the estate.

After you have selected your executor and he has accepted, discuss with him your plans for your will in detail. If he is to manage your affairs successfully after you die, quite naturally he must learn a great deal about them while you are alive. Whether you choose a bank or an individual, you should take your executor into your confidence. At frequent intervals, you should go over your affairs with him and discuss changes in your will.

Shall I Consult an Attorney in Framing My Will? This is a moot question. Some do, many do not. If your estate is small, a simple holographic will (in your own handwriting) may be adequate although it is not recommended. The best advice is to consult an attorney.

Besides the simple task of expressing your thoughts and wishes in legal language, he will give you advice and recommendations that will help you to ensure a well-planned estate. From his experience in helping others, he knows what is sound, prudent, economical, and efficient. If he is also a close friend, he probably knows your family situation, has handled other legal business for you, and therefore can better give you sound advice and expert assistance. If you have never retained an attorney, select one now or seek the help of a Navy legal assistance officer or of a naval officer you know who is also a graduate lawyer.

What Should I Do with My Will? If you have chosen a bank as executor or coexecutor, the best place for your will is the file of that bank. If not, your safe-deposit box is a good place to have it. If you keep it in your desk or in a file cabinet at home, be sure that your wife and other prospective beneficiaries of your estate know where your will is and the date of your latest will. Do not hide it in secret drawers, in a grandfather's clock, or sewed into the upholstery of furniture—as has actually happened in not a few cases of disputed wills.

When Should I Review or Rewrite My Will? At frequent intervals, you must review your will, and during your lifetime you probably *should* rewrite it a number of times. Certainly not less frequently than every two or three years, you should read it over and give serious thought as to whether it still expresses your current desires. Also, certain milestones along the way of life indicate that you should reconsider your will and bring it up to date. A few of these are:

Death of a beneficiary named in your will
Your marriage, divorce, or remarriage
Change of residence
Birth or death of a child
Removal of an executor to another state or his death
Radical change in the value of your estate
Major changes in Federal or state tax laws
Sale of stock or other property mentioned in your will
Inflation causing decreased dollar values, necessitating a larger monthly in-
    come for your family

It is particularly important that you check your will on changing residence to another state. The provisions of your will may not be legal in that state, and your executor may be unable to function there. Consult your attorney whenever you change residence, and give serious consideration to a new will and to naming a new executor.

You are being considerate of your dependents when you make a will. Take the final and necessary step—*keep it up to date!*

Details of Making a Will. A will must be in writing. No particular form of words or expression is necessary to constitute a legal will if it intelligently discloses the intent of the maker respecting the disposal of his property after his death; *but the execution must be in strict compliance with the formalities required by the statutes of the state.*

A will that bequeaths personal property must be executed conformably to the law of the testator's domicile. One that devises real property must be executed conformably to the law of the state in which the real property is situated. If both realty and personalty are disposed of and these are situated in different places, the testator should conform to the laws of both places.

Nearly everywhere, a will must be attested and subscribed by witnesses. The number of witnesses required by law differs from none at all to three. Assemble *three* reliable disinterested witnesses. The testator then states, "This is my last will and testament. For its execution, will you three please be my witnesses." The testator then signs the will in their presence, so that they may clearly see him make his signature, encircles the word "seal," and inserts the date. If there is more than one page, he should sign in the left-hand margin of each page.

Witnesses must be competent, *i.e.*, be qualified to testify in court to the facts that they attest by signing the will. They should be of age, sober and sane, should not stand convicted of crime, should believe in the obligation of an oath, and should understand the testator's language. They must be disinterested—not benefited under the will, even remotely. The use of any such witnesses may result in invalidating the will, or they may lose their legacies. The witnesses should write opposite or under their respective signatures their places of residence. Since the authenticity of the signatures of the witnesses must be proved in court at the time of probating the will, care should be exercised in selecting witnesses who will be available, to simplify this legal requirement.

Officers should prepare a new will with witnesses whose presence in court can be obtained, when by reason of death or transfer a witness would be unavailable.

There are sound legal reasons for the observance of formality in the execution of a will.

Avoid duplicate signing. Two original wills invariably complicate probate. Typewritten copies, clearly labeled as such, may be prepared in the requisite number, unsigned. This is a good practice if you are filing your will with the Navy Mutual Aid Association or in your safe-deposit box. Indicate on copy where original is filed.

Avoid odious bequests, such as $1.00 to a relative whom you wish to cut off. Such bequests may serve to provoke a legal contest.

Provide for benefits under insurance policies by naming beneficiaries in the policies, not by will.

Short Form of a Simple Will. The following short form of a simple holographic will is given as an example. It is not recommended except in emergencies when an attorney is not available.

> All my estate I devise and bequeath to my wife, Mary Roe, for her own use and benefit forever, and I hereby appoint her my executrix, without bond, with full power to sell, mortgage, lease, or in any other manner dispose of the whole or any part of my estate.
>
> RICHARD ROE (Seal)

> Dated August 1, 19—.

> Subscribed, sealed, published, and declared by Richard Roe, testator above named, as and for his last will in the presence of each of us, who at his request and in his presence, in the presence of each other, at the same time, have hereto subscribed our names as witnesses this first day of August, 19—, at the city of Washington, D C.

> (Signatures and addresses of witnesses, preferably three in number.)

If you wish to make a longer or more complicated will, consult your attorney. You may need legal assistance. For samples of such wills, consult Navy Mutual Aid Association booklet and Navy Guide for Retired and Fleet Reserve Personnel (NavPers 15891B).

Form of a Simple Codicil. A codicil embracing a simple provision not materially affecting the will is safe; but if it alters the general scheme of the will, it is better to rewrite the whole will. A codicil should preferably be written on the same paper with the will, or if on a separate piece, the two should be securely annexed. The form below is given as an example:

> I, ..., of ......, make this codicil to my last will, dated August 1, 19—, hereby ratifying said will in all respects save as changed by this codicil. Whereas, by said will I gave ....., my son, a legacy of $5,000, I now give him a second legacy of $10,000, making $15,000 in all.

> (Then follows the testator's signature and the attestative clause.)

Alterations or Interlineations. Do not make alterations or interlineations in your executed will unless you have expert legal advice. Either destroy the old will and make a new one, or draw a codicil to the present will.

Effect of Marriage after Making a Will. In some states, the marriage of a man and the birth of a child, subsequent to the making of a will by him, revokes the will. But where the facts on which such revocation is ordinarily implied have been contemplated and provided for in the will, no such presumption arises and the will is not revoked. In other states, a will is never automatically revoked.

Dower Rights and Curtesy Rights. In law, *curtesy* is defined as the life estate that a husband has in the lands of his deceased wife, which by the common law takes effect where he has had issue by her, born alive, and capable of inheriting lands. *Dower* is that part of a husband's property which his widow enjoys during her life.

In many jurisdictions a husband or wife has rights in the estate of the other after death, which the survivor may elect to take despite the terms of a will. *The rights referred to are those of a wife to dower, of a husband to curtesy, and frequently, in the case of a wife, a distributive interest,* such as thirds, allowances, rights of succession, and widow's reward. These rights pertain more to the wife than to the husband; and if there is in the will no well-worded provision for the wife in lieu of them, she may in many places recover something in addition to what has been given her in the will. The safe course is to put a clear provision in the will such as "The provision made herein for my wife is in lieu of all her statutory or other rights or claims of any kind to my estate or any part thereof." It is also advisable generally to give the wife, at the least, as large an interest in her husband's estate as she would be entitled to by law if there were no will.

Payment of Just Debts. The preliminary direction to pay all the testator's just debts adds nothing to the duty imposed upon all executors by law.

Probating a Will. A will made in any part of the world, *if executed according to the law of the testator's domicile,* will be *there* admitted to probate without question.

A will should be offered for probate in the county in which the deceased had his legal residence at the time of his death. The probate of a will simply establishes its due execution by the testator. Wills may be presented for admission to probate by the executor, a legatee, a devisee, a creditor, or other person interested in the estate. The will is probated in a court having jurisdiction over such matters, called variously register of wills, probate court, or surrogate court, or in ordinary district court, county court, common pleas acting as probate court, and orphans' court.

In some states, testimony of the witnesses to the signing of the will by the testator must be produced in court at the time of probate. If, at the time of the testator's decease, one of the subscribing witnesses is dead or cannot be present, proof of the handwriting of any such absent, deceased, or insane attesting witness is admitted. *The advisability of maintaining witnesses whose presence in court can be easily obtained becomes apparent.*

Death and Burial

1709. BURIAL ARRANGEMENTS. *When Death Occurs near a Navy Shore Station.* When the death of an officer occurs at or near his station or in a Navy hospital, the local Supply Officer takes charge and arranges for local burial or shipment of the body (of an active officer) at government expense. The Commanding Officer is charged with the rendition of the required official reports.

When Death Occurs at a Place Remote from a Navy Shore Station. When an officer dies under exceptional circumstances, such as by drowning or in a train or an automobile wreck, away from a naval station or hospital, the widow should at once radio or telegraph (1) his Commanding Officer, stating necessary details and requesting instructions, and (2) the Commandant of the Naval District in which the death occurred, giving the deceased's full name, rank and branch of service; date, place and cause of death and cemetery where burial is desired; and request instructions as to burial arrangements. She should be careful to give definitely the address where the reply will reach her.

Place of Burial. The remains of an officer, active or retired, subject to local health laws and sanitary regulations, may be buried at the place of death, at his home, or in a national cemetery. During his lifetime an officer should select one of the three choices and leave written instructions on this point.

If burial is to be made in a national cemetery, the next of kin should apply by telegram to the Superintendent of the cemetery in which burial is desired.

Remains will be cremated only on written request from relatives.

1710. INTERMENT IN NATIONAL CEMETERIES EXCLUDING ARLINGTON NATIONAL CEMETERY. *Eligibility.* Any member of the Armed Forces of the United States dying in active service, or any *former* member whose last service terminated honorably, is eligible for burial in any national cemetery in which grave space is available. Widows and minor children of eligible service personnel may be buried in the same grave under the following circumstances.

Widows of Servicemen. If the service member predeceases his wife, burial is authorized in the *same* grave with the serviceman provided the widow has not remarried.

If the wife should die first, she may be buried in a national cemetery *provided* the serviceman submits a statement to the effect that upon *his* death he will be buried in the same grave.

Children of Servicemen. Minor children of an eligible serviceman may be buried in a national cemetery, but only in the same grave in which either parent has been or will be interred. If an eligible child dies before either parent, the service-connected parent must submit a signed statement that he or she will, upon death, be interred with the child.

Interment of *adult* children is not authorized in national cemeteries unless they were unmarried and in fact, up to the time of their death, physically or mentally disabled, incapable of, self-support, and consequently dependent for support upon the parents. Burial of such an eligible adult child may be made only in the same grave in which either parent has been or will be interred. No such interments will be made without prior approval of the Office of the Chief of Support Services. Requests for such interments should be submitted through the Superintendent of the national cemetery in which interment is desired, and must be accompanied by a notarized statement of data as to the marital status and degree of dependency of the deceased child and the name of the child's parent upon whose military service interment is being requested. A certificate of a physician as to the physical and/or mental disability must also be submitted.

Space Reservation. No graves are reserved in advance of immediate requirement for burial purposes—except in the case of a surviving spouse at the time of burial of the deceased, or for the parent at the time of burial of a child as provided above. There are *no* specific forms to be completed prior to burial in a national cemetery. The undertaker or person responsible for the funeral arrangements simply communicates with the Superintendent of the national cemetery in which interment is desired, furnishing complete information as follows:

Full name of decedent and veteran

Rank, organization and dates of last active service of veteran

Name and address of nearest relative

Whether military honors are desired and whether a chaplain is desired; if so, Protestant, Catholic or Jewish

Dates of birth and death of decedent

Name of state to be inscribed on government headstone (inscribed only on stone for veteran's grave)

Whether reservation of burial in the same grave is desired by surviving non-service-connected spouse.

The remains *should not be forwarded* to the national cemetery nor should the final time of the funeral services be set until the interment has been authorized and all arrangements with the Superintendent com-

PRINCIPAL VETERANS' BENEFITS

Benefits	Available to Veterans of:			
	WW II	Korea	Vietnam	Peace
Retention of Government Insurance	Yes	Yes	Yes	Yes
Civil Readjustment (GI Bill): Education	No	No	Yes	Yes[1]
Loan Guaranty	Yes[7]	Yes[7]	Yes	Yes[1]
Vocational Rehabilitation	No	No	Yes	Yes[1]
Hospitalization and Care in a "Home"	Yes	Yes	Yes	Yes
Disability Compensation (Service Connected)	Yes	Yes	Yes	Yes
Disability Pension (Nonservice Connected)	Yes	Yes	Yes	No
Burial Allowance	Yes	Yes	Yes	Yes
Burial Flag	Yes	Yes	Yes	Yes
Burial in National Cemetery	Yes	Yes	Yes	Yes
Headstone	Yes	Yes	Yes	Yes
Dependency and Indemnity Compensation	Yes[3]	Yes[3]	Yes[3]	Yes[3]
Dependents' Pension	Yes[2]	Yes[2]	Yes[2]	No
Employment: Civil Service Preference	Yes	Yes	Yes	Yes[4]
Re-Employment Following Service	Yes	Yes	Yes	Yes[5]
Out-Patient Treatment and Artificial Limbs	Yes[4]	Yes[4]	Yes[4]	Yes[6]

[1] On active duty for at least 181 continuous days, any part of which occurred after January 31, 1955.
[2] Contingent on income and not payable to parents.
[3] If death is service-connected.
[4] Service-connected disability gives added preference.
[5] Only if service is after 1 May 1940.
[6] Service-connected disability is a requirement.
[7] G.I. Loan program for World War II and Korean veterans extended to July 25, 1970.

FIGURE 1701. Principal veterans' benefits. These are subject to change at any time.

pleted. There is no charge for the grave site in a national cemetery, nor for opening or closing of the grave.

Headstones. Individual headstones in a simple, dignified style are furnished and erected without charge for both the serviceman and his widow. This is done automatically without the necessity of an application. Headstones are not furnished in the case of children but their names *will* be inscribed on the reverse side of the father's marker. When burial is in a private cemetery and a government headstone is desired, an application must be submitted to the Office of the Chief, of Support Services, Department of the Army, Memorial Division, Washington, D.C. 20315. Use of a government headstone is recommended.

1711. INTERMENT AT ARLINGTON NATIONAL CEMETERY. Burials in Arlington National Cemetery are limited to the following:

a. A member of the Army, Navy, Air Force, Marine Corps, or Coast Guard dying on active duty.

b. A retired member of one of the above services carried on a Service Retired List and eligible to receive compensation stemming from service in that Armed Force, including members of the Fleet Reserve.

c. A former member of one of the services who:

(1) Has been awarded the Medal of Honor.

(2) Is otherwise eligible by reason of honorable military service who have also held elective office in the U. S. Government or served on the Supreme Court or in the Cabinet or in an office compensated at Level II under the Executive Salary Act.

d. The spouse, minor children, and, in the discretion of the Secretary of the Army, unmarried adult children of any of the persons listed in a. through c.

e. A member of the Reserve Component of the Armed Forces, Army National Guard, Air National Guard, and a member of the Reserve Officers' Training Corps of the Army, Navy, or Air Force whose death occurred whie he was on active duty for training (includes authorized travel to or from active duty training); on inactive duty training; or hospitalized or undergoing treatment at the expense of the Government for injury or disease incurred or contracted during the periods previously mentioned.

f. The surviving spouse, minor children, and, in the discretion of the Secretary of the Army, unmarried adult children of any person already buried in Arlington National Cemetery.

g. The parents of a minor child or unmarried adult child whose remains, based on the eligibility of a parent, are already buried in Arlington National Cemetery.

The Navy Department provides an agency in Washington which is equipped and authorized to make complete arrangements with the Officer-in-Charge, Arlington National Cemetery, for the interment of the remains of members or former members of the Navy and their dependents.

The Admiral's Assistant, Chief of Naval Personnel will make the following arrangements for active or inactive duty personnel:

Making hotel reservations for family and friends; meeting trains; explaining the different types of military funerals; assisting in the selection of honorary pallbearers and furnishing transportation therefor.

Putting the widow in touch with the Navy Mutual Aid Association (if deceased is a member of that organization) or with the American Legion or other organization that will assist her in preparing an application for pension or other allowances due her from the government.

A telegram should be sent to the Bureau of Medicine and Surgery for active duty members, giving the information previously described and stating the number in the funeral party, date and hour of arrival and whether remains are to be interred at once or placed in a vault pending a later decision. Make the telegram complete and clear. In the case of inactive or former members, burial instructions should be directed to the Superintendent of the cemetery.

A telegram should be sent to the Bureau of Naval Personnel giving the information described above and stating the number in the funeral party, date and hour of arrival, and whether the remains are to be interred at once or placed in a vault pending a later decision. Make the telegram complete and clear.

Upon receipt of instructions from the cemetery, remains may be shipped to "Superintendent, Arlington National Cemetery, Arlington, Virginia" and billed to Washington, D.C. This will avoid the necessity and delay of obtaining a permit for the transfer of the body through the District of Columbia. Advise the Superintendent, Arlington National Cemetery, the exact time of arrival of remains and number of persons escorting. A representative of the Arlington National Cemetery will meet those escorting at the Military Police Booth, Union Station, Washington, D.C. When the remains are shipped direct to the cemetery, the services of an undertaker are not required to handle the body in Washington, D.C. The remains will be conveyed to the cemetery by government hearse. There is no charge for this service.

Remains are not to be shipped until after receipt of instructions from the Superintendent, Arlington National Cemetery. Remains will be met and transported to the cemetery between the hours of 0830 and 1530, Monday through Friday. Remains will not be received on Saturdays, Sundays, or holidays.

Should it be impracticable for relatives or friends to accompany the remains to this city, the body will be received, conveyed to Arlington, and interred therein with the same reverent respect and careful attention to every detail as though relatives were present.

1712. THE NAVY FUNERAL AT ARLINGTON NATIONAL CEMETERY. One of the benefits to which military personnel are entitled is burial with military honors in the national cemetery in Arlington, Virginia, a recognition of the nation's debt for the services and sacrifices of its military men and women. The size and composition of Navy military funerals vary according to the title, rank or rating of the person being buried. The policy of BuMed in providing funeral escorts is as follows:

a. The escort for flag officers, Commodore to Admiral inclusive, consists of the Navy Band; 1 company of marines, comprised of 2 platoons of 25 men each; 1 company of bluejackets, comprised of 2 platoons of 25 men each; colors and color guard; bodybearers, a separate 8-man firing squad and petty officer; personal flag bearer; and ushers.

b. The escort for a Captain, Commander, Lieutenant Commander, or Lieutenant consists of the Navy Band; 2 platoons of infantry, each platoon comprised of 26 bluejackets; colors and color guard; bodybearers; and ushers.

c. The escort for a Lieutenant (junior grade), Ensign, or Commissioned Warrant Officer, Midshipman, Aviation Cadet, or Warrant Officer consists of the Navy Band, 1 platoon of infantry, comprised of 26 bluejackets; colors and color guard; bodybearers; and ushers.

Officers are urged to leave full burial instructions with regard to type of service, whether civilian church or Navy chapel; clergy, whether Navy chaplain or civilian clergy; honorary pallbearers, whether chosen by family or left to discretion of commanding officer; ceremony, whether fraternal or patriotic organizations are authorized to conduct their ritual after the military ceremony (see also Section 1728).

If the body of the deceased has been cremated, the urn containing the ashes, together with a folded flag, is placed in a dummy casket through a trap door in the rear prior to entering the chapel. Upon arrival at the grave site the urn and flag are removed from the casket and carried to the grave.

It is earnestly recommended that the family make full use of the burial facilities which our government has provided. Aside from purely sentimental reasons, there is the practical consideration of perpetual care. Although the question of a monument is a personal one, the one provided gratuitously by the Office of the Chief of Support Services is entirely appropriate.

1713. BURIAL ALLOWANCES. *Active Duty Personnel.* All officers who die in an active duty status, and also those who are admitted to a government hospital while on active duty, retired after admission and continuously retained until the date of death, are eligible for preparation and casketing of remains, or cremation, and for transportation to the designated place of burial at Navy expense. In addition, the following allowances may be made toward funeral and burial expenses incurred by the next of kin: (1) $300 when burial is made in a private cemetery; (2) $150 when remains are consigned to a funeral home prior to burial in a national cemetery or at sea; and (3) $75 when remains are consigned directly to a national cemetery or to a naval activity for burial at sea. Claim for the interment allowance should be submitted to the commandant of the naval district in which burial is made. When available services of the government are proffered and refused and the relatives take charge of the remains, they may be reimbursed for expenses of preparation and casketing as follows: (1) where an Armed Forces contract or mortuary was available but not utilized, in an amount not to exceed what procurement would have cost the Navy, or (2) where an Armed Forces contract or mortuary was not available, in an amount not to exceed $400. In addition, they may be reimbursed for transportation costs in an amount not to exceed what transportation would have cost the government.

An escort, not to exceed one person, may be provided to accompany the body to the place of burial if so requested. The escort may be a relative or friend (civilian or military) of the deceased.

Retired or Inactive Personnel. The Veterans' Administration allows an amount not to exceed $250 for burial, funeral and transportation expenses of a discharged or retired veteran of any war, and of a veteran of other than wartime service who was discharged or retired for disability incurred in line of duty or in receipt of pension for a service-connected disability. A prerequisite to entitlement is that discharge or release from active service must have been under conditions other than dishonorable.

Claim must be filed within two years subsequent to the date of permanent burial or cremation of the veteran and completed by the submission of the necessary supporting evidence within one year after the date of the request therefor by the Veterans' Administration or no allowance may be paid. This benefit is payable to the undertaker if he is unpaid or, if paid, to the person whose personal funds were used in payment of that expense.

Where death occurs in a Veterans' Administration Hospital, or as a Veterans' Administration patient in a naval or military hospital within the continental limits of the United States, the VA will pay the actual cost of burial and funeral (not to exceed $250) and the body will be transported to the place of burial within the continental limits of the United States.

See Section 1815 for allowances for funeral expenses in addition to the above for contributing participants in the social security program.

1714. OTHER BENEFITS. *Funeral Flag.* If the remains are to be sent home or to another designated place for private burial, a United States flag to drape the casket will accompany the remains and may be retained by the family after funeral services. When death occurs at a place where a national flag cannot be obtained from a naval activity, the nearest county seat postmaster may be requested to furnish a flag, which will be replaced by the Navy Department through the Veterans' Administration.

Honors. When burial is made in a cemetery in the immediate vicinity of a naval station, military honors will be provided at the funeral, if practicable and if requested by the next of kin. However, it is not possible for the Navy Department to provide military honors at cemeteries that are not located within a 50 mile radius of naval stations, and in such cases, it will be necessary for the relatives to arrange for the funeral services. More information is contained in BuPers Manual, article C-9813.

Certificate of Death. The widow should obtain from the Bureau of Medicine and Surgery, Navy Department, certified copies of the *official certificate of death* of her husband, if he died on active duty (from the Naval Hospital or civilian coroner, if retired). A copy of this certificate must accompany claims, including settlement of commercial insurance policies. She should also ask two officers or other friends, who knew her husband intimately, to identify his remains before the coffin is closed. They will then be prepared to furnish the affidavit sometimes required by commercial insurance companies to be filed with claim for insurance due. Five or six copies are desirable. In the case of active duty personnel, Report of Casualty (DD Form 1300), suffices for proof of death for purposes of commercial insurance.

Survivors' Benefits

1715. SURVIVOR BENEFITS. *Unpaid Pay and Allowances (Arrears in Pay).* Settlement of unpaid pay and allowances may include any of the following due to the decedent from the Department of the Navy: per diem travel, transportation of dependents, transportation of household goods, mustering-out payment, savings deposits, etc. Settlement of any monies found due and unpaid will be made to the beneficiary(ies) named to receive any such amount. If there be no designated beneficiary, then payment may be made to the surviving spouse, child or children, parents, the duly appointed legal representative of the estate or if there be none, to the person(s) determined to be entitled thereto under the laws of the domicile of the deceased member. In the case of death occurring on active or training duty the appropriate form is forwarded to the person entitled to payment by BUPERS. Upon completion and return, BUPERS certifies entitlement and forwards the claim for payment to the Navy Finance Center, Cleveland, Ohio, 44114. In the case of Fleet Naval Reserve or Retired members the appropriate form is forwarded to the person(s) entitled to payment by the Navy Finance Center.

Death Gratuity. The death gratuity is a gratuitous payment made immediately following death occurring on active or training duty or enroute to or from, or within 120 days of discharge or release, from service-connected cause as determined by the Veterans' Administration. The payment may not be less than $800.00 nor more than $3,000.00. It is payable first to a widow, then to a child or children, designated parents or brothers or sisters, undesignated parents in equal shares, undesignated brothers or sisters, in equal shares, etc. Adoptive and *in loco parentis* parents and illegitimate children who have been acknowledged may receive the payment. Normally, payment to a widow is made within 24 hours if she resides at or near the activity to which her husband was assigned, except for the 120-day case when determination of service-connection is required by the Veterans' Administration. When payment has not been made in the field to a widow or when parents are entitled to the death gratuity, BUPERS certifies entitlement to the Finance Center after an application has been filed, except that when payment is needed urgently BUPERS will certify entitlement by message or teletype to the Finance Center. The appropriate form on which to make application is DD Form 397.

1716. DEATH PENSIONS. If veteran's death occurred while on active duty or as a result of disease or injury received in service, the award granted is referred to as "compensation" and is described in Section 1717. If an award is based only on the fact of service in a war, it is referred to as "pension."

The following is the condition under which dependents of veterans presently may qualify for pension and the rates applicable. A widow

COLUMN I			COLUMN II	COLUMN III
ANNUAL INCOME			WIDOW ALONE[1]	WIDOW PLUS ONE ELIGIBLE CHILD[2]
MORE THAN—	BUT	EQUAL TO OR LESS THAN—		
		$300	$74	$90
$300		400	73	90
400		500	72	90
500		600	70	90
600		700	67	89
700		800	64	88
800		900	61	87
900		1,000	58	86
1,000		1,100	55	85
1,100		1,200	51	83
1,200		1,300	48	81
1,300		1,400	45	79
1,400		1,500	41	77
1,500		1,600	37	75
1,600		1,700	33	73
1,700		1,800	29	71
1,800		1,900	23	69
1,900		2,000	17	67
2,000		2,100		65
2,100		2,200		63
2,200		2,300		61
2,300		2,400		59
2,400		2,500		57
2,500		2,600		55
2,600		2,700		53
2,700		2,800		51
2,800		2,900		48
2,900		3,000		45
3,000		3,100		43
3,100		3,200		41

Public Law 90-275, Act of March 28, 1968, was effective on 1 January 1969.

[1] There is no pension payment if the annual income of the widow is over $2,000.

[2] There is no pension payment to the widow and the one dependent child if the annual income is over $3,200. The monthly pension is increased by $16.00 for each additional child.

FIGURE 1702. Monthly Pension Table.

should apply immediately after husband's death to determine her eligibility for a pension:

Ninety days service in World War I or II, or Korean conflict, will justify a pension as indicated: Effective war periods—World War I, April 6, 1917 to November 11, 1918; World War II, December 7, 1941 to December 31, 1946; Korean conflict—June 27, 1950 to January 31, 1955; Vietnam conflict—August 5, 1964 to present.

Monthly pensions vary widely depending on widow's and child's income and the monthly Social Security benefits received. Rates of pensions are subject to change from time to time by acts of Congress. Consult the local office of the Veterans Administration for this and other information.

Marriage Date Requirement of Widow. (1) Vietnam conflict—married to veteran for one year or more or for any length of time if a child was born of the marriage. A termination date will be determined by the President or the Congress. (2) Korean conflict—married to veteran prior to 1 February 1965. (3) World War II—married to veteran prior to 1 January 1957. (4) World War I—prior to 14 December 1944. (5) Spanish-American War—not applicable to this guide.

In all other cases a widow must have been married to the veteran five or more years or for any length of time if a child was born of the marriage.

Income Defined for Pension Purposes. All income, regardless of source, counts except:

a. Payments of the six months' death gratuity;

b. Donations from public or private relief or welfare organizations;

c. Payments by the Veterans' Administration of pension, compensation, and dependency and indemnity compensation;

d. Payments under policies of U. S. Government Life Insurance (USGLI) or National Service Life Insurance (NSLI), and payments of servicemen's indemnity;

e. Lump sum social security death payments;

f. Payments to an individual under public or private retirement, annuity, endowment, or similar plans or programs equal to his contributions thereto;

g. Amounts equal to amounts paid by a widow or child of a deceased veteran for:

1. His just debts;

2. The expense of his last illness, and

3. The expense of his burial to the extent such expenses are not reimbursed by the Veterans' Administration;

h. Proceeds of fire insurance policies.

Payment of pension commences the day following the date of death of the veteran if claim is filed within one year following the date of death; otherwise, from the date of receipt of the application. This provision adds strength to the advice to officers to obtain and place on file the required legal documents, including birth and marriage certificates. If a proper claim exists, it should be filed promptly with the nearest Regional Office of the Veterans Administration or the Veterans Benefits Office, Washington, D.C. 20421. Considerable research is necessary before a pension claim can be approved.

The Claim should be filed on VA Form 21-534 by the widow, guardian or custodian of child or children. VA Form 21-535 should be used by a father or mother. It should be accompanied by the following papers:

1. Proof of death of veteran. Death of a veteran in active service or on the retired list of the Army, Navy, Marine Corps, or Coast Guard or in a government institution does not need to be proved by a claimant.
2. Proof of marriage of claimant to veteran; if claimant or veteran has been married before, a certificate of custodian of public records or other acceptable proof of death of former spouse or certified copy of decree of divorce from the former spouse.
3. Proof of date of birth of children. Child must be under 18 years or under 23 years if in an approved school. A child so disabled before age 18 as to be helpless continues eligible.
4. If claim is submitted by a dependent parent, proof of birth of veteran showing relationship of parent.

Although one may qualify for more than one rate, only the maximum rate will be awarded.

1717. DEPENDENCY AND INDEMNITY COMPENSATION. The Survivors' Benefits Act (Public Law 881, 84th Congress) administered by the Veterans' Administration provides *compensation* for the eligible survivors of officers or enlisted men who *die on active duty* or as the result of a *service-connected disease or injury* after retirement or separation from the service. This compensation is tax free. If you once held U. S. Government Life Insurance or National Service Life Insurance and if you executed a waiver to obtain free protection under the indemnity plan, *you must discontinue the waiver before your death* to qualify your survivors for compensation under this act. Since the great majority of naval officers die after retirement from *nonservice-connected* disease or injury, compensation under this act cannot be counted upon (see Sections 1703 and 1814 for Retired Serviceman's Family Protection Plan to protect your dependents after retirement).

An officer or man who dies on active duty from any cause is generally considered to have died from a *service-connected* cause. For his dependents to be eligible for indemnity compensation, his death must be held to be service connected. The dependents of a retired officer, or other officer or man not on active duty, must demonstrate by the records of his active service that service-connected disability was in fact the *principal or contributory* cause of death. A widow can often be helpful by recalling dates and locations, when her husband suffered from ailments similar to the cause of his death (see Section 1816 for advice on facilitating this determination by the Veterans' Administration after your retirement or separation from the service).

Regulations state that service-connected disability will be determined by exercise of sound judgment, without recourse to speculation, after a careful analysis has been made of all the facts and circumstances surrounding the death, including autopsy reports. This would encourage the performance of an autopsy in those instances where it is believed that the service-connected disability of a veteran may have materially contributed to his death.

Minor service-connected disabilities which do not materially affect a vital organ would not usually be held to have contributed to death in a case in which the primary cause of death was unrelated to the service-connected disability. In those instances where service-connected diseases or injuries which affect vital organs have resulted in debilitating effects and general impairment of health to an extent that it would render a person materially less capable of resisting the effects of a disease or injury which causes death, then it may be held that the service-connected disability materially contributed to the death. Basic entitlement for Dependency and Indemnity Compensation to dependents of veterans might be decided on such a basis.

In any case which presents a question in which a death may be a result of contributory causes, full information is important, such as:

1. Statements from physicians who have been aware of the nature and degree of the veteran's service-connected disabilities, and

2. Statements from other persons who possess knowledge of this nature.

VA Regulations state further that "When, after careful consideration of all procurable and assembled data, a reasonable doubt arises as to whether a service-connected disability was the principal or contributory cause of death, such doubt should be resolved in favor of the claimant."

All deaths, whether in war or peace, are placed on the same basis. The formula for determining this monthly compensation is $120 plus 12 percent of her husband's monthly basic active duty pay. For officers already retired or for other veterans, this formula is applied to the pay they would be receiving if on active duty. For full details, consult the disbursing officer or local Veterans Administration Office.

A widow with children under the age of 18 receives benefits for the support of these children from Social Security (see Section 1815).

Orphaned children (where their mother died or was divorced from the serviceman before his death or if she dies or remarries after his death) will receive compensation from the Veterans' Administration. This payment would be in addition to benefits which the children may receive from Social Security. Compensation normally ceases when a child becomes 18, but may continue to age 23 if the child is still in school or for as long as the child is helpless.

A *special school benefit* is paid by the Veterans' Administration to children between the ages of 18 and 23 who are attending a school or college approved by the VA. This benefit, intended to assist children not covered by social security payments after age 18, will be paid concurrently with dependency and indemnity compensation but will not be paid in addition to payments under the War Orphans Educational Assistance Act (see following paragraph).

All of these compensations are payable without regard to the other income of the dependents.

Compensation for dependent parents is paid by the Veterans' Administration on a sliding scale according to their other income.

Under the provisions of the War Orphans Educational Assistance Act (Public Law 634, 84th Congress), any child between the ages of 18 and 26, whose parent or parents *died of injuries or disease resulting from service in the Spanish-American War, World War I, World War II, the Korean conflict or the Vietnam era,* is entitled to a maximum of 36 months of schooling at a rate of $130 per month for a full-time student.

Dependents' claims for these compensations or pensions, government insurance, and burial allowance, as applicable, must be submitted to the Veterans' Administration. Claims for arrears of pay and death gratuity are paid by the Navy Department. Dependents are cautioned that it is unnecessary to obtain the assistance of attorneys or any other agent to prosecute these claims. The Navy Mutual Aid renders excellent assistance to survivors of its members. Other survivors may apply to Navy chaplains, legal assistance officers, the Navy Relief Society, the American Red Cross, the Bureau of Naval Personnel Casualty Branch, and any veterans' organization of which their serviceman was a member (see Sections 1720-21). The Casualty Assistance Calls Officer of any nearby Naval Base or Station will assist in completing survivor benefits forms in the case of active duty deaths.

1718. ACTION REQUIRED BY NEXT OF KIN. If death of an active or retired officer occurs in a naval or military hospital, the commanding officer will notify the Secretary of the Navy and give the survivor's wishes as to burial arrangements. If death occurs at home or anywhere else than a naval or military hospital, the next of kin should immediately notify his commanding officer, or the commandant of the naval district in which the service member resided, giving all pertinent information. Obtain a death certificate from appropriate authority.

Return retired pay checks and any other U. S. Government checks to the agencies from which they were received with a request for further instructions. The designated beneficiary of the deceased officer will be furnished a claim form on which to apply for unpaid pay and allowances and death gratuity, to which entitled.

Seek assistance from the most appropriate agencies listed in Sections 1720 and 1721. With their help, apply to the Veterans' Administration for VA compensation or pension. Submit claims for government insurance to the Veterans' Administration and for commercial life insurance to the appropriate companies at their home office. Submit claims for social security benefits to the nearest local social security office, the address of which can be obtained from the Post Office. Claim under Retired Servicemen's Family Protection Plan (see Section 1814) should be submitted to the Navy Finance Center, Cleveland, Ohio. Do not forget, if your husband was on active duty when he died, that you are entitled to travel and transportation of household effects allowances.

1719. OTHER SURVIVOR BENEFITS. *Identification Cards.* Upon death of the retired member, the Uniformed Services Identification and Privilege Card (DD Form 1173) becomes void and should be surrendered at the nearest naval facility.

Medical Care. Unremarried widows and minor children are eligible for medical care at Armed Forces medical activities having dependents' facilities for hospital and medical care. A new Uniformed Services Identification and Privilege Card (DD Form 1173) should be automatically supplied to a widow after her husband's death. Should she not promptly receive one, she should surrender her previous DD Form 1173 at the nearest naval facility and apply for a new one as a widow. This card will be renewed upon application to unremarried widows and minor children (unmarried) under 21 years of age. Application for renewal should be made to the Chief of Naval Personnel, Washington, D.C. 20370 (see Section 1606 for details of medical care available).

Armed Services Exchange and Commissary Privileges. Unremarried widows of deceased active duty, Reserves on active duty for training personnel and those who were on the Regular Navy Retired List or the

Naval Reserve Retired List, are eligible for armed services exchange and commissary store privileges. Application may be made to the Chief of Naval Personnel.

Officers' Messes. If facilities permit, the commanding officers are authorized to extend the privileges of commissioned officers' messes, open, to unremarried widows and dependents of commissioned officers.

Social Security. If the service member is covered by the Social Security Act, the widow and/or service member's minor children under 18 years of age may be entitled to monthly benefits. The widow should check with the local social security field office for full information (see Section 1815).

Retired Serviceman's Family Protection Plan. If the service member elected to receive a reduced amount of retired pay to provide an annuity for his wife or family under the Retired Serviceman's Family Protection Plan, the widow should notify the Commanding Officer, U. S. Navy Finance Center, Cleveland, Ohio.

Household Effects. If an officer dies on on active duty the Navy will ship his household effects under the following limitations: 1) Shipment must be from the last permanent duty station or place of storage, and 2) shipment must be made within one year from date of death or one year from date of official report that the officer is dead, injured or missing for a period of 30 days or more. One privately owned automobile may also be shipped to the same destination as the household effects. When necessary, in connection with a shipment, the Navy will also pay for as much as six months' storage of your household goods to be shipped.

Application for shipment or temporary storage should be made to the designated shipping activity which is nearest to the household goods to be shipped.

Dependents' Transportation. When an officer dies while on active duty, his dependents will be authorized transportation from the place at which the notice of death was received to: 1) The official residence of record as listed in the personnel record of the deceased, or 2) to any other place designated by the surviving dependent. The survivor should apply to the disbursing office in the nearest naval activity or to the station to which the officer was attached. Escort will be provided for dependents if considered necessary.

If a widow (or other survivor) performs the travel at her own expense, she may submit a claim for reimbursement to the Chief of Naval Personnel, Washington, D.C. 20370.

Homestead Privileges. Homestead rights (preference in staking claims to government land for purposes of establishing a home) may be available to surviving widows of eligible veterans, or widows of men who died on active duty. To take advantage of this, you may request information from Bureau of Land Management, Department of the Interior, Washington, D.C.

Federal Employment Preference. Certain Civil Service preference benefits are granted to widows of service personnel in connection with examinations, rating, appointments, and reinstatements—if they have not remarried. Unremarried widows of Navy men who have served in time of war are given 10 points in addition to their earned ratings in Civil Service examinations.

Under certain circumstances, a mother of a navyman who dies in service may also be entitled to preference.

Specific details concerning preference eligibility may be obtained from any U. S. Civil Service office or from your local U. S. Post Office. A dependent who is interested in getting employment should visit the nearest United States Employment Service Office for information about job opportunities.

Personal Effects. When an officer dies on active duty, his personal effects will be delivered to the next of kin:

If the death occurs within the continental limits of the U. S. and there is no doubt as to next of kin, personal effects may be shipped direct, shipped with the remains, or delivered by the escort accompanying the remains.

If death occurs outside the U.S. and the next of kin is unknown, the navyman's effects are shipped to either the Material Department, Naval Supply Center, Oakland, California or Cheatham Annex, Naval Supply Center, Norfolk, Williamsburg, Virginia. They are held until the Bureau determines who is entitled to them or turns them over to the legal administrator of his estate. That office also instigates search to locate missing effects.

If personal effects are damaged or lost in connection with naval service, a claim for reimbursement may be substituted.

Information on submitting claims and claim forms may be obtained by writing to the Chief of Naval Personnel (Pers E-3), Washington, D.C.

Scholarship. Scholarship assistance for children of retired and deceased officers is provided at many schools, colleges, and from special scholarship funds. For additional information, write the Chief of Naval Personnel, setting forth the particular area or schools in which you are interested.

The Retired Officers' Association has a scholarship program to assist worthy sons and daughters of military personnel to further their education.

1720. ASSISTANCE BY THE NAVY. *Bureau of Naval Personnel,* upon notification of death, sends a letter to the next of kin, offering to help establish rights to any benefits for which the next of kin may be eligible by reason of the service of the deceased. A Uniformed Services Identification and Privilege Card (DD Form 1173) is forwarded to the widow. The casualty branch of the Bureau forwards to any commercial insurance companies listed on the Record of Emergency Data (see Section 1706), a certification of casualty which is acceptable for the purposes of expeditious settlement of most insurance claims. If the retired member had previously submitted an election of options under the Retired Serviceman's Family Protection Plan (see Sections 1703 and 1814), an application for annuity is mailed to the designated beneficiary.

Casualty Assistance Calls Program. For an officer who dies on active duty, the Navy appoints an officer to extend aid to the deceased's family. This officer will call within 24 hours of notification of death to extend the Navy's condolences and counsel the survivors on funeral arrangements, financial assistance, rights, benefits and privileges. He will assist the family with problems on death gratuity, arrears in pay and allowances, social security, dependency compensation or pensions, personal effects, insurance, and all the other rights and benefits previously mentioned.

The Navy Chaplain of your husband's ship or station or the nearest naval station will provide condolence, advice, and counsel to survivors of either active or retired officers. Widows or other members of the family of a deceased officer should in all cases not fail to consult a naval chaplain. They have extensive experience in assisting the families of deceased personnel. Their fine understanding of the problems of the dependents of service persons makes them especially well equipped to aid and comfort widows and children at this difficult time. In addition to spiritual ministration and help with claims, chaplains are also available for making arrangements for interment and for conducting funeral services.

The Legal Assistance Officer of the nearest naval command is available to help the families of deceased officers with claims and legal problems incident to the death of the head of their family.

1721. AID FROM ORGANIZATIONS. Government agencies are helpful and considerate in the method of handling claims of dependents of deceased officers and enlisted men. Additional advice and assistance may be obtained from several private organizations.

The American Red Cross. While an officer is on active service or under treatment in military hospitals, aid for his family or dependents may be obtained from the American Red Cross. The organization assists widows, orphans, parents, or other dependents in adjustments of all types of governmental claims. Personal and relief problems are solved. Proof of dependency is necessary. The applicant should consult the Field Director at the post or station or the Red Cross chapter in the city where the dependents reside.

Navy Relief Society gives aid to dependents, widow and minor children of deceased officers and enlisted men. A proof of dependency and need is required. Applications may be submitted, in person, if possible, to any auxiliary of the society which are located at the headquarters of the naval districts and at larger naval stations. If residing in the Ninth Naval District, requests should be submitted to the Great Lakes Auxiliary, Navy Relief Society. Applications may also be made directly to the Headquarters, Navy Relief Society, Room 1030, Munitions Building, Navy Department, Washington, D.C. 20360.

Veterans' Groups, including the American Legion, Veterans of Foreign Wars, Disabled American Veterans, Military Order of the World Wars, the Retired Officers' Association, render aid to surviving dependents of members and other military personnel.

The Navy Mutual Aid Association. Survivors of members of this Association should avail themselves of the assistance of the Association in settling insurance and pay claims, applications for pension and compensation, and appeals of adverse decisions by the Veterans' Administration. Of the $7,500 face value of the policy, $1,000 is wired or cabled to the beneficiary of record immediately upon receipt of official report of death from the Navy Department. The terminal dividend provides an additional $4,500 to the beneficiary. At the Association's central repository, a member may deposit the documents which a widow or other survivor will require in case of death of the member. The Association is happy to send to any naval officer, active or retired, its pamphlets on the advantages of joining the Association, estate planning, a life insurance program, and its excellent personal log for recording the data recommended in Section 1723. In its annual report, the Association publishes recent information on pay changes, compensation, members rights, a brochure on what to do immediately in case of death, etc. A membership in the Association is a valuable asset to an officer during his lifetime, and especially to his dependents upon his death.

For Benefit of Your Dependents

1722. FOR URGENT ACTION. Secure at once a certified copy of the following:

Your birth certificate and one for each member of your family.
Naturalization papers if not born in the United States.
Marriage certificates including former marriages of you or your wife.
Court decrees of divorce or annulment if either you or your wife were previously married.
Court orders pertaining to support and custody of your legal dependents.
Death certificates of children, former wife, or former husband of your wife.
Deeds and mortgage documents.
Insurance policies.
Bank accounts, Saving Bonds, securities.
Wills.
Power of attorney.
Proof of service.
Retirement orders.
Record of Emergency Data (NavPers 601-2).

Place these papers in a secure envelope with your other valuable records and papers. Discuss all these affairs with those who will have to act upon them. Leave them in a readily accessible place, such as a safe-deposit box in a convenient bank, and obtain the peace of mind of a task well done.

Make a list of the insurance policies you carry, giving the names of the companies, numbers of the policies, names of beneficiaries, and where policies are located. Include this list also in your Personal Affairs Record (see Section 1723).

If a member, you may file the previously listed items in your jacket in the Navy Mutual Aid Association, keeping a duplicate copy of each.

File with your will and other valuable papers a copy of your latest income-tax return.

Consider carefully the terms of ownership of all real and personal property. Consult an attorney if the nature or amount of the property justifies the action. It may be possible that joint ownership or transfer by deed offers material advantages.

Arrange a detailed plan with your family as to where they will reside in the event you are ordered suddenly to sea duty or a foreign station.

Death is not pleasant to contemplate, even as an incident of the hazards of battle in the service of the nation. If you neglect to protect your loved ones through failure to explain their rights and privileges to them or, having explained such rights and privileges, fail to do everything within your power to secure the necessary evidence and supporting papers upon which a legal claim for death benefits can be made, you will be guilty of gross neglect.

All officers are subject to temporary or permanent change of station on short notice. Arrange your personal and financial affairs accordingly.

1723. A RECORD OF YOUR PERSONAL AFFAIRS. Start *now* to prepare and keep up to date a record of your personal affairs. Members of the Navy Mutual Aid Association will find its Personal Log excellent for this purpose. It will be helpful to your wife (or your child, if your wife has predeceased you) if she will help you prepare your record. At the very least, she must read it and know where you keep it, for it will be invaluable to her after your death when so many things that you have done for the family fall upon her shoulders.

Your heirs and executor will require the following information:

1. *Personal and Family Record.* Record your place and date of birth; your citizenship and naturalization (if any); your parents' full names; your marriages, giving full maiden names of your spouses and places and dates of ceremonies; full names of children and grandchildren and place and date of birth; name and address of your lawyer or close and trusted personal friend who may be consulted as to your personal or business affairs; and the location of birth certificates of yourself and of each member of your immediate family, naturalization papers, marriage certificates, and divorce decrees or certified copies thereof.

2. *Important Papers.* Your will (location, name and address of lawyer and executor, suggested fee for lawyer); power of attorney (name of persons to whom powers of attorney were granted and dates and purposes); income-tax information (location of latest returns of Federal and state income taxes and substantiating data therefor); and data on other taxes due, paid, or in a state of contest.

3. *Life Insurance.* State the full data on all your policies, whether government, commercial, or mutual, including the method of payment of benefits, how you have been paying premiums, location of premium receipts if you have not been paying by allotment; location of policies; and data on any policy loans or any other obligations against the policies. It is probably a good plan to give the names and addresses of the beneficiaries.

4. *Social Security.* All data on your number, card, state of tax payments, employment record, etc. This may be a considerable asset to your estate under the new laws and regulations (see Section 1815).

5. *Real Estate.* Full data on all property owned, giving location; improvements; condition of ownership (owned outright, partnerships, joint tenancy, etc.); encumbrances and method of payment; last taxes, whether paid, when due, and about how much; insurance on buildings, with whom, and what it covers; and the location of deeds, abstracts of title, receipts for mortgage payments, etc. Make such a record for each piece of property owned or in which you have an interest.

6. *Automobile.* Complete data as to make, model, etc.; titling data; who can use it and have insurance be effective, insurance, what company and what it covers; premiums and when next payment due; any encumbrances; where papers are located.

7. *Other Personal Property.* Cover each item as thoroughly as for real estate and your automobile.

8. *Bank Accounts.* List the banks in which you have accounts; state the nature of the accounts: savings or checking, joint or personal, etc.

9. *Safe-deposit Boxes.* Name of bank or trust company, location of keys, the type of tenancy with your wife or other person.

10. *United States Bonds.* List all bonds, tell where located, amount and person designated as co-owner or beneficiary. Give their serial numbers, as these are required to replace lost bonds.

11. *Other Securities.* List all stocks and bonds which you now own, give their location and whether they are liquid assets or pledged in any way. State the ownership, whether with a joint tenant, tenancy in entirety, etc.

12. *Notes payable and other obligations,* which must be paid by your estate, giving amount still due, interest rate, when interest and principal are due, procedure for renewal, securities or property pledged as collateral.

13. *Debts owed to you,* giving the amount, interest, name and address of person indebted to you, whether a liquid or uncertain asset, where notes and papers are located.

14. *Other Assets.* Such as investments in partnerships, businesses of others where investments are not of a formal nature, and any other properties or investments of value.

15. *Burial Wishes.* Include honors or fraternal ritual desired, notices to clubs, organizations, journals, and newspapers, uniform, disposal of class ring or other jewelry, type of service, headstone, approximate cost of funeral, and desires as to cremation or where to be buried.

16. *Miscellaneous.* Add any other notes or instructions, information, or advice which may be useful to your lawyer, executor, or dependents in the management of your estate after your death.

Date and sign this record of your personal affairs. You can make several copies and send them to those who you think should have the information and will be discreet. It is probably a better plan to show it only to your wife, inform your attorney and executor as to where it is, and put it away in a safe place.

Remember, start your personal record now, keep at it until you complete it, and keep it up to date. Your family have a right to expect such consideration on your part.

CHAPTER 18

Retirement

Then is the time when he may become a lonely man, for there are none to guide him, save that Power which directs us all.
—ADMIRAL WILLIAM V. PRATT, USN

Retirement Procedures

1801. GENERAL. Officers of the Regular Navy and the Naval Reserve establish legal rights to retirement under a variety of conditions. For Regular Navy officers, retirement is usually accompanied with retired pay. Retirement for Naval Reserve officers may be honorary or accompanied by retired pay. This difference is attributable to the contrast in purpose and length of service, for Regular Naval officers devote their life's work to the service of their country, whereas Naval Reserve officers offer their services primarily in a national emergency or war. For this patriotic action, officers of the Naval Reserve, for physical disabilities incurred in the line of duty and for service, are entitled to retirement compensation similar to that received by Regular Navy officers.

The system of retirement for officers of the Regular Navy is mutually advantageous both to the government and to the officers themselves. It preserves and promotes efficiency by enabling the government to retire from active duty those officers who are physically incapacitated, who lack proficiency, or who have exceeded maximum age limits. And to officers who have given many years of service, accepting the rigors of naval life and frequent separations from their families, there is partial compensation in retired pay based on rank and years of service. Retirement with pay, moreover, is a strong factor in inducing young men to consider the Regular Navy as a permanent career.

518

The average officer knows little about his retirement procedures and benefits. For a full discussion and description, see Officer Fact Book (NavPers 15898), Chapter 10.

1802. REGULAR NAVY—VOLUNTARY RETIREMENT. When an officer of the Regular Navy, Regular Marine Corps, Army, Air Force or Reserve components thereof has completed more than 20 years' total active service in those services, or their Reserve components, 10 years of which must be active commissioned service, he may, at his own request, in the discretion of the Secretary of the Navy, be transferred to the retired list with retired pay as shown in Figure 1801.

The words, *in the discretion of the Secretary of the Navy,* should be noted with particular interest, for 20-year retirements have been suspended from time to time.

When an officer of the Navy has completed at least 30 years of active service, he may, upon his own application, in the discretion of the Secretary of the Navy, be retired from active service and be placed upon the retired list with 75 percent of his basic pay as described in Figure 1801.

When an officer has completed at least 40 years of active service to the United States, he shall, upon his own application, be retired from active service by the Secretary of the Navy. Retired pay is 75 percent of his basic pay.

A request for retirement is submitted via chain of command and the Chief of Naval Personnel to the Secretary of the Navy. The request may read as follows: "Having completed 30 (40) (20) years' service, it is requested that I be transferred to the retired list of officers of the Navy, effective June 1, 19—." It is not necessary to state the reason for the request, nor is it necessary to refer to pertinent law. Orders for release from active duty in response to such a request will normally provide for detachment "when directed" during the month immediately preceding the effective date of transfer to the retired list.

Non-disability retirements must be effected on the first day of a month. Disability retirements may be effected on or after the date the Secretary of the Navy approves such retirement, but not later than the first day of the month following such approval. When a request for retirement is received in the Bureau of Naval Personnel, detachment will depend upon whether a relief is required and when relief is available.

No person may accrue more than 60 days' leave. Unused accrued leave up to 60 days creditable at date of retirement is compensated by a lump-sum cash payment based on active-duty pay and allowances in effect on the day prior to date of retirement. Any leave which may be

VOLUNTARY RETIREMENT PROGRAM
FOR COMMISSIONED AND WARRANT OFFICERS, USN

LAW— TITLE 10	TYPE OF RETIREMENT	APPLICABLE TO	CREDITABLE SERVICE	PAY	RANK ON RETIRED LIST
Sec. 6321	40 years' service	Permanent officers	Active duty, including active duty for training in Regular or Reserve components of Armed Forces	¾ of applicable basic pay of rank in which retired	Rank held at time of retirement (unless entitled to higher rank under other law)
Sec. 6322	30 years' service	Permanent officers	Same as above	Same as above	Same as above
Sec. 6326	30 years' service	Temporary officers and warrant officers with permanent enlisted status	Active duty in Regular or Reserve components, including any active duty for training performed subsequent to 9 August 1958	Same as above	Rank held at time of retirement (unless entitled to higher rank under other law)
Sec. 6323	20 years' service	Permanent officers and officers whose permanent status is enlisted	Active duty in Navy, Army, Marine Corps, Air Force Coast Guard or Reserve components thereof, including active duty for training, at least 10 years of which shall have been commissioned	2½% × applicable basic pay of rank in which retired multiplied by the sum of the following: (a) total years of service creditable for basic pay purposes as of 31 May 1958; (b) total years of active service, including active duty for training, performed subsequent to 31 May 1958; (c) if not included in (a) above, total years of constructive service credited for basic pay purposes by the Act of 30 April 1956 (applicable only to MC and DC officers); and one day's credit (with maximum of 60 days credit for any one year) for each retirement point earned as a member of a Reserve component subsequent to 31 May 1958 through attendance at drills, periods of equivalent instruction or appropriate duty performed as authorized by competent authority, completion of correspondence courses, plus 15 points per year gratuitous credit for Reserve membership	Rank held at time of retirement (unless entitled to higher rank under other law)
Sec. 1293	20 years' service	Warrant officers	Same as for Section 6321		Warrant officer grade in which serving at time of retirement, unless entitled to higher rank or pay under other law, at member's election

FIGURE 1801. Voluntary retirement program, Reserve officers.

permitted to accrue over 60 days should be taken before retirement as leave cannot be granted to an officer on inactive duty.

After a request for retirement is received in the Bureau of Naval Personnel, the Bureau issues orders which will include detachment date, retirement date, and request report of physical examination, if applicable. If you are on sea duty or stationed ashore beyond the continental limits of the United States, you may first be ordered to the nearest naval separation activity (except that captains and officers of flag rank are ordered to report to the Commandant of the nearest naval district) in the continental United States, where you will receive further orders releasing you from active duty. Unless the Bureau of Naval Personnel is advised sufficiently early that you are not physically qualified for transfer to the retired list and release to an inactive status, your request is forwarded for approval via the Judge Advocate General approximately one month before the effective date of retirement.

If you are contemplating voluntary retirement or are subject to involuntary or statutory retirement and you are in any doubt as to your physical qualification for release from active duty, it is mandatory that you obtain a preliminary physical examination. Any defects existing may be corrected before retirement and not complicate and delay actual processing for release. If a disability is disclosed on this preliminary examination, you may, of course, be subject to physical retirement, but adequate information must be received in the Promotions and Retirements Division of the Bureau of Naval Personnel in time to stop final action on the retirement papers then being processed.

After a request for retirement has been approved and the retirement has become effective, there is no process of law whereby the retired status may be changed except by reason of physical disability incurred subsequently while serving as a retired officer on active duty.

If you are found not physically qualified for release, it does not necessarily follow that you will be ordered to appear before a physical-evaluation board. An operation or treatment may correct the defect and, after hospitalization, retirement may be effected. When the Bureau is cognizant that hospitalization is required (release orders provide for this contingency), orders are modified, except in those cases of involuntary retirement where a mandatory date is fixed by law and physical retirement proceedings cannot be processed to conclusion prior to that date.

1803. Regular navy.—involuntary separations and retirements. In the discussion of retirement and separation from the service in this section, two definitions of pay are of importance for an understanding of the subject.

Retired Pay.—Amount of pay to be received by an officer when he goes on the retired list (see Figure 1801 for details). After retirement, various percentages for cost of living increase will be added from time to time in accordance with law.

Severance Pay.—Lump-sum payment made to an officer discharged from the naval service, based upon 2 months' active-duty pay for each year of commissioned service, the total not to exceed 2 years' pay.

Revocable Commissions.—Commissions of all officers are revocable for 3 years after initial appointment.

Lieutenants and Lieutenants (jg).—Navy nurses are retired upon attaining age 50 or upon completion of 20 years of service, whichever is later.

Women officers who have completed 13 or 7 years, respectively, without being on the promotion list to the next grade are honorably discharged on June 30 of the fiscal year in which they complete such service, with severance pay.

Other officers failing twice of selection to the next higher grade are honorably discharged, with severance pay.

Lieutenant Commanders.—Navy nurses retire upon attaining age 55 or completion of 30 years of service, whichever is earlier.

Women officers retire at the age of fifty on June 30 of the fiscal year in which they complete 20 years of commissioned service, if they are not on the promotion list to the next grade.

Other officers, who have failed twice of selection and have completed 20 years of commissioned service, are retired.

Commanders.—Navy nurses and women officers are retired upon attaining age 55 or upon completion of 30 years of service, whichever is earlier.

Officers of the Medical Service Corps are not retired until they complete 30 years of commissioned service.

Other officers, who have failed twice of selection and have completed 26 years of commissioned service, are retired.

Captains.—Officers not restricted in the performance of duty, who complete 30 years of service and have failed twice or more of selection, and all other captains not on the promotion list upon completion of 31 years of commissioned service, will be retired.

Captains of restricted line and of the staff corps, if not on promotion list and if not selected for continuation on the active list, shall be retired on July 1 after completion of 31 years total commissioned service.

Limited-duty Officers.—Officers who fail twice of selection have the option of being discharged with severance pay or retired as provided above or of reverting to warrant officer status to complete 30 years of service. All limited-duty officers will be retired on completion of 30 years' service (exclusive of active duty for training).

Unsatisfactory Officers.—If a selection board reports that the records and reports of an eligible officer with less than 20 years' service indicate unsatisfactory performance of duty in his present grade and that he would not satisfactorily perform the duties of the next higher grade, such officer will be discharged from the Navy on June 30 of the fiscal year in which so reported, with severance pay.

Creation of Vacancies in the Grade of Rear Admiral by Selection for Retention.—Line rear admirals not designated for engineering, aeronautical engineering, or special duty must undergo selection in the fiscal year in which they complete 5 years of service in that grade or 35 years of total commissioned service, whichever may be later, to determine whether or not they are to continue on the active list. If they fail of such selection, they will be retired. At least 50 percent and not more than 75 percent of those eligible for such selection must be continued on active duty (Public Law 570, 81st Congress).

Selection of rear admirals for retention on the active list is also provided for ED, AED, and SD categories and for the staff corps. In these cases, rear admirals become eligible for consideration in the fiscal year in which they complete 7 years of service in that grade or 35 years of total commissioned service, whichever is later, and in each fiscal year thereafter as long as they remain on the active list. They will be retired on June 30 of any fiscal year in which they are not selected for retention or in which no board is convened to consider officers of their category for retention. See Sec. 712 for early involuntary retirement of captains and commanders.

1804. REGULAR NAVY—PHYSICAL RETIREMENT. The physical-retirement provisions of the Career Compensation Act (now codified in Chap. 61, Title 10, U. S. Code) are too long and involved to explain in detail here. Among them are the following:

Members of the uniformed services unfit to perform duties of their office because of physical disability may be retired *or separated* from the service. If the percentage of disability is less than 30 percent and the member has completed less than 20 years of active service, the individual may be discharged with severance pay.

A temporary-disability retired list was established to which individuals whose physical disability may be permanent will be transferred, unless permanently retired because their disability was of a permanent nature. Retired pay on this list may be either at a percentage of basic pay equal to 2½ percent times the number of years of active service or the percentage of disability with which an individual was placed on the list, but the retired pay in no case will be less than 50 percent or more than 75 percent. Individuals placed on this list are given periodic physical examinations at intervals of net less than 18 months. After 5 years, or earlier if such examination shows that the individual is permanently disabled, he may be permanently retired. If his disability is less than 30 percent on any examination and he has completed less than 20 years of active duty, he may be separated from the service with severance pay. If he is found physically fit to perform all the duties of his rank, he shall, subject to his consent, be recalled to active duty and reappointed to the active list.

There are a multiplicity of other provisions in the act, and there are many administrative regulations and decisions to implement it. If you contemplate physical retirement, consult the Career Compensation Act and Disability Separation Manual.

The purpose of physical retirement is to separate from active service those individuals who are physically unfit to perform their duties and at the same time to safeguard the interests of the individual and provide for his welfare, insofar as his naval service is responsible for his physical incapacity.

Retirement proceedings are initiated as a result of a report by a medical board of a naval hospital. When an officer has been hospitalized for 3 months, depending upon circumstances and the nature of his disease or injury, a medical board will usually recommend:

1. Appearance before a physical-evaluation board.
2. Return to duty.
3. Further treatment.
4. Limited duty and subsequent examination.

If appearance before a physical-evaluation board is indicated, the convening authority will issue appropriate orders. An officer may waive his right to appear before the board in person, but this procedure is not recommended, except when the medical evidence is clear-cut and not subject to question.

In most cases, an appearance before a physical-evaluation board requires only a part of one day. After discharge from further attendance by the board, an officer then awaits final action on the proceedings and findings of the board by the Secretary. If the board has found him incapacitated and his physical condition does not require return to the hospital, the officer may take leave or be sent to temporary duty.

When retired, in order to be reimbursed, travel home must be completed within:

1. One year from date of retirement.

2. One year from date of discharge from hospital, if hospitalization continues upon retirement.

Whichever date is later is the one that is effective. An officer of the Regular Navy may choose any residence he desires without regard to his official address of record in the Bureau.

After the proceedings and findings of a physical-evaluation board have been recorded in writing and signed by the members of the board, each case is reviewed by the Physical Review Council. The Council may return the case to the board for further consideration or revision. This is the exception, occurring only when there is an error in the proceedings or the findings are not consistent with the facts in the record or with naval law. Final determination is vested in the Secretary of the Navy. If a physical-evaluation board has found an officer unfit for duty by reason of physical disability, his case meets all the requirements of the act, and the findings are approved by the Secretary, the officer is transferred to the temporary-disability retired list or permanently retired, depending upon the recommendation of the board as to permanent disability. Retirement may be effected on the date final action on disability retirement proceedings is taken by the Secretary of the Navy or on any subsequent date up to and including the first day of the following month.

If the officer's disability was not the proximate result of active duty and he has less than 8 years of active service or his disability is less than 30 percent, he may be separated from the service with severance pay as previously indicated.

1805. REGULAR NAVY—STATUTORY RETIREMENT. The statutory retirement age for Regular officers is sixty-two years. An officer is transferred to the retired list on the first day of the month following that in which he attains this statutory age. An officer, whose statutory age is approaching, should obtain a complete physical examination 3 or 4 months prior to his prospective date of retirement in order that there will be time to evaluate his physical condition for physical retirement proceedings, if such be warranted.

1806. PROMOTION UPON RETIREMENT. Prior to 1 November 1959 any officer of the Navy or Marine Corps, regular or reserve, who had been specially commended for performance of duty in combat was advanced to the next higher grade upon retirement. This promotion, of itself, did not carry with it any increased pay on the retired list. Officers advanced on the retired list to a rank above that of captain in the Navy or colonel in the Marine Corps solely because of this provision of law, if recalled to active duty, may be recalled in either the rank to which advanced on the retired list or that in which he otherwise would have been entitled to retire, in the discretion of the Secretary of the Navy.

1807. RANK AND PAY ON THE RETIRED LIST. As a general rule, an officer is retired in the rank in which serving at the time of retirement, unless some other provision of law permits him upon retirement to be advanced on the retired list to a higher grade and become entitled to the retired pay based on that rank effective on the date of retirement. However, the amendment of the basic Career Compensation Act of 1949 by the Pay Act of 1958 (PL 85-422) and Military Pay Act of 1963 have so complicated the situation as to produce five different retired pay scales for the same rank and length of service, that it is impossible to describe them all here. Some of the basic rules are given below and in Figure 1801:

1. An officer who is voluntarily retired under law requiring 30 or more years of active service for retirement, is entitled to retired pay at the rate of 75% of the basic pay to which he was entitled when serving on active duty in the grade in which retired, or to which advanced on the retired list under Title 10, U. S. Code, Section 6151, as amended.

2. For an officer who is voluntarily retired under law requiring more than 20 years but less than 30 years of active service for retirement, or is involuntarily retired for age and/or statutory service, see Figure 1801.

3. In the future, retired pay of members will be based solely on the active duty basic pay a member was earning on the day that he retired. Increase in retired pay will be by percentages based on periodic increases in the cost of living index. Retired members recalled to active duty may, upon release from that active duty, have his retired pay recomputed on the then current basic pay rates *only* if he has served on active duty for a continuous period of at least *two* years while those pay rates were in effect. (10 U.S.C. 1402 notes)

1808. CHANGE IN RETIRED STATUS. Except as explained under Physical Retirement in Sec. 1804 and for an officer who is re-retired by reason of physical disability incurred while serving on active duty in his retired status during a period of national emergency, there is no provision of law that permits a change in the retired status of an officer once he is retired. If called back to active duty, an officer can be re-retired for physical disability incurred during that active duty, but if he was originally retired for other than physical disability, disability must be at least 30 percent disabling to permit re-retirement under the disability.

1809. NAVAL RESERVE. *The Retired Reserve* is composed of members of the Naval Reserve who have been transferred thereto without pay. *The Naval Reserve Retired List* is composed of members of the Naval Reserve transferred thereto with pay (10 U.S.C. 6017). Officers transferred to the Retired Reserve may subsequently qualify for the Naval Reserve Retired List.

Voluntary Retirement to Retired Reserve.

1. An officer will, on his own application, be transferred to the Retired Reserve provided he meets one of the following requirements:

a. Has completed a total of 20 years of honorable service in any component of the Armed Forces; or

b. Has been found physically disqualified for active duty as a result of a service-connected disability regardless of total years of service completed.

2. An officer of the Naval Reserve may, upon his own application, and in the discretion of the Secretary of the Navy, be transferred to the Retired Reserve provided he meets at least one of the following requirements:

a. Has completed 10 or more years of active service.

b. Has been found physically disqualified for active duty, not as a result of his own misconduct, regardless of total years of service completed.

c. Has attained the age of 37 years and

1. has completed 8 years of qualifying service (8 years in which he has earned a minimum of 50 retirement points per year) subsequent to 1 July 1949, or

2. has completed a minimum of 8 years of service provided that he has served honorably on active duty in time of war or national emergency for at least 6 months, or

3. has consistently supported the Armed Forces in an outstanding manner, as determined by the Secretary of the Navy.

Involuntary Retirement to Retired Reserve. Except under special circumstances, under the authority of 10 U.S.C. 6391, an officer in an active status or the inactive status list in the Naval Reserve in a grade of or above ensign will be transferred to the Retired Reserve without pay on the first day of the month following the month in which he becomes 62 years of age. For exceptions see BuPers Manual, H-31301.

United States Naval Reserve Retired List. Any warrant or commissioned officer of the Naval Reserve (10 U.S.C. 6323) who has completed more than 20 years of active service, of which at least 10 years was commissioned service, may, upon application therefor and at the discretion of the Secretary of the Navy, be transferred to the Naval Reserve Retired List. Only active duty as a commissioned officer, warrant officer, enlisted man, aviation midshipman, appointed aviation cadet or enlisted aviation cadet, in the Navy, Marine Corps, Army, Air Force, or Coast Guard, or in the reserve components thereof, is creditable in determining eligibility for retirement. Each officer retired under this section will be retired in the highest grade, permanent or temporary, in which he served satisfactorily on active duty. If the Secretary of the Navy determines that he did not serve satisfactorily in his highest temporary grade, he will be retired in the next lower grade but not lower than his permanent grade. Retired pay will be computed as shown in Figure 1802.

VOLUNTARY RETIREMENT PROGRAM
FOR COMMISSIONED AND WARRANT OFFICERS—USNR

LAW— TITLE 10	APPLICABLE TO	CREDITABLE SERVICE	PAY	RANK ON RETIRED LIST
Sec. 6323 as amended	Commissioned officers 20 years service	Active duty in the Navy, Army, Marine Corps, Air Force, Coast Guard or Reserve components thereof, including active duty for training, *at least 10 years of which shall have been commissioned*	See table, Figure 1801	Rank held at time of retirement, unless entitled to higher rank under other law
Sec. 6327	Commissioned officers and Warrant officers 20 years service	Fulltime active service in the Navy, Army, Marine Corps, Air Force, Coast Guard or, Reserve components thereof. (Member must have been in Reserves on 1 January 1953)	50% X applicable basic pay of rank in which retired	Highest rank in which service was satisfactory
Sec. 1293	Warrant officers 20 years service	Active duty including active duty for training in Regular or Reserve components of Armed Forces	See table, Figure 1801	Warrant officer grade in which serving at time of retirement, unless entitled to higher rank or pay under other law, at member's election
Sec. 1331	Commissioned officers and Warrant officers 20 years satisfactory Federal service *and* age 60	All service in the Armed Forces prior to 1 July 1949; subsequent to 1 July 1949 any year in which a minimum of 50 retirement points is earned	Total number of retirement points divided by 360 and multiplied by 2½% of basic pay of rank in which retired	Highest rank satisfactorily held during entire period of service

FIGURE 1802. Voluntary retirement program, Reserve officers.

Retired pay may not be more than 75 percent of the basic pay upon which the computation of retired pay is based plus periodic increases based on the cost of living.

Other requirements may meet standards for retirement, such as 20 years of active service or 30 years of active service. The provisions are too long and complicated to include here. Consult your paymaster or BuPers Manual, Part H, Section 13, *Retirement*.

1810. REVIEW BOARDS. In order to protect fully the interests of all officers when physical-retirement proceedings are involved, the Physical Disability Review Board and the Physical Review Council have been established in the Navy Department. Similar boards have been set up for the Marine Corps. These review bodies review the actions of a medical board of a naval hospital and a physical-evaluation board when the officer has been separated from active service *without pay as a result of action of the board under review, providing the officer concerned formally applies for such review within 15 years from the date of separation.*

1811. RETIRED PAY ACCOUNTS, INCOME TAX, ALLOTMENTS, AND SERVICE FOR PAY PURPOSES. The pay accounts of all retired officers are carried in the U. S. Navy Finance Center, Cleveland, Ohio. Pay accounts are not transferred to the Center until the disbursing officer carrying an officer's pay account is officially notified by certified copies of the final retirement letter, which is signed by the Secretary of the Navy.

Income tax is withheld by the Navy Finance Center except for those officers who are completely exempted from payment of income tax.

All allotments for insurance, whether government or private, are automatically continued when an officer is transferred to the retired list. All other allotments are stopped. Under present law, 6 months' service counts for a year only in computing the rate of pay which is determined by multiplying the number of years of service by $2\frac{1}{2}$ percent. Six months does not count as a year toward a "fogey." Thus, an officer with over $29\frac{1}{2}$ years but less than 30 years of service would receive 75 percent of active-duty pay prescribed for an officer of his rank with over 26 years of service.

An officer on active duty may estimate his retired pay at any stage of his career by this method, using his basic pay for years of service. If you have any questions as to the amount of your retired pay, write to the U. S. Navy Finance Center, Retired Pay Department, Cleveland, Ohio 44114, giving your name, rank, file number, date of your retirement and years of service.

Retired Officer Rights, Benefits, and Restrictions

1812. PUBLICATIONS OF INTEREST TO RETIRED OFFICERS. The Retired Officers' Association publishes a bi-monthly magazine giving information of vital interest to the retired officers of all services. Every officer should join this association, which is in the forefront of the fight for preservation of the rights and privileges of all retired officers.

The Bureau of Naval Personnel publishes two excellent booklets of information, Navy Guide for Retired Personnel and their Families (NavPers 15891B) and Your New Career—Planning For Retirement (NavPers 15895C). The latter booklet will be of especial benefit to the newly retired officer, as it provides advice and counsel for the difficult transition from a very active life in the naval service to retired status. The first discusses in much more detail than is possible here, the rights, obligations, privileges and benefits which accrue to an officer on retirement. In addition, the Retired Naval Personnel Newsletter (NavPers 15886), published by the Bureau of Naval Personnel, is distributed every other month to members retired in pay status. This Newsletter publicizes changes to the Guide as they occur and keeps retired members informed of new legislation and policy, and new developments in the Navy.

1813. EMPLOYMENT ACTIVITIES AFTER RETIREMENT. By all means, if physically able, find yourself interesting and agreeable employment. It is advisable to obtain a position covered by Social Security. Certain laws limit the freedom of a retired officer to accept employment and to received retired pay. Some of the laws and regulations governing employment of military personnel described in this section, are under review and may be changed by the time you seek civilian employment. It is *your responsibility* to keep informed of such changes and *not to violate the law*.

Dual Compensation Act of 1964.—All retired members are now eligible for employment in a civil position with the Federal Government, provided that no retired officer or enlisted man, Regular or Reserve, of any category may accept any position in or under the Department of Defense within 180 days of retirement or transfer to the Fleet Reserve, unless the salary of the position has been raised under 5 U.S.C. 1173 to make it competitive with the salary of comparable private employment, or under certain critical employment situations if the Secretary of the department concerned and, if necessary, the Civil Service Commission grant approval to an earlier appointment. (See appropriate DOD directive for further details.)

Compensation Under the Act.—Regular officers, retired for years of service or for noncombat physical disability, including both commissioned and warrant officers of all grades, may receive the full salary of the civilian office, plus military retired pay at an annual rate equal to the first $2,241 of such pay plus one-half of the remainder thereof, if any. Such reduction does not apply where employment is on a temporary (full or part-time) basis, any other part-time basis, or any intermittent basis, for the first 30-day period for which salary is received under any one appointment.

Regular officers retired for disability incurred in combat or caused by an instrumentality of war during a period of war, retired reserve officers and retired enlisted members so employed, are not subject to any restrictions upon total income.

Civilian office, as employed in the Dual Compensation Act of 1964, means a civilian office or position (including a temporary, part-time or intermittent position), appointive or elective, in the legislative, executive or judicial branch of the Government (including any corporation owned or controlled by the United States and including nonappropriated fund instrumentalities under the jurisdiction of the armed forces) or in the Government of the District of Columbia.

Conflict of Interest.—Certain classes of employment by private interests after retirement constitute conflict of interest with a naval officer's retired status, which may operate to deprive him of his retired pay and in some cases produce criminal liabilities. In general this involves acting, within three years after his retirement from the service while drawing retired pay, as an agent to sell, contract to sell, negotiate to sell, any supplies or war materials (any tangible item, whether jacknives or weapons systems) to any agency of the Department of Defense, Army, Navy, Air Force, Coast Guard, Coast and Geodetic Survey or the Public Health Service.

A section of the criminal code (18 U.S.C. 281) has been interpreted as prohibiting a retired Regular officer, for his lifetime, from selling *anything* to the department in which he holds a retired status. In the case of a retired officer of the Regular Navy, this interpretation would prohibit selling to the Department of the Navy.

Neither of these statutes applies to retired Reserve officers or to retired enlisted members, including those retired enlisted personnel advanced to temporary officer status.

There are many restrictions, also, against representing anyone other than the United States, prosecuting claims against the United States or negotiating contracts with its agencies.

"Reference Guide to Employment Activities of Retired Naval Personnel" is a pamphlet prepared by the Judge Advocate General of the Navy, which the pamphlet states "is merely intended as a general guide to retired naval personnel" and which advises that "in situations deemed unusual . . . the Judge Advocate General will attempt to assist naval personnel in determining the propriety of any activities in which they propose to engage upon retirement." All officers should obtain a copy of this valuable pamphlet before retirement or accepting government or private employment after retirement. Opinions rendered must be regarded as advisory only.

1814. RETIRED SERVICEMAN'S FAMILY PROTECTION PLAN. Dependency and indemnity compensation for the survivors of officers who die while on active duty or whose deaths are service-connected has been discussed in Section 1717. The protection of the survivors of an officer who dies after retirement is very much his responsibility and can be ensured by his participation in the annuity plan.

The Retired Serviceman's Family Protection Plan (RSFPP) provides that members of the uniformed services can elect to receive reduced retired pay in order to establish an annuity for their survivors. While on active duty, officers are required to make an election and to choose from three basic options: annuity for the widow, annuity for a child or children, or annuity for widow and children.

A discussion of this plan is included in Section 1703. You should read it carefully and be certain you understand it completely, as entry into or withdrawal from the plan is strictly controlled.

1815. SOCIAL SECURITY. Social Security is a government-sponsored old-age and survivors' insurance program which provides protection to nine out of every 10 employed citizens of this country—and their families—as well as giving you, as a career officer, added old-age, health, and survivor benefits. Military officers were not covered by Social Security when the program was initiated, as retirement provisions then in effect were considered adequate. As an example of the increasing impact of Social Security (and computer usage) the traditional serial and service numbers are being abolished in favor of Social Security numbers.

Social Security provides you with monthly income, in addition to your military retirement pay and disability compensation by the Veterans' Administration, as follows:

If you are totally disabled.

Upon reaching age 65 (age 62 optional at reduced amount).

For wife or widow in the event you die and are survived by children under 18 years of age or disabled children over 18, if they become disabled before age 18.

For wife or widow upon reaching age 62, with increased monthly income, if retired at age 63-65.

For orphaned children if they are under 18 years of age, or over 18, if disabled as previously described, or under 22 for full-time students.

For dependent parents.

All Officers on active duty are contributing participants in the Social Security and Medicare programs and entitled to all the rights, benefits and privileges of the Social Security Act. For those officers whose base pay is less than the current wage base (1968: $7,800), the tax rate (1968-1987: 4.4% to 5.9%) is a percentage of base pay. For those officers whose base pay is more than the current wage base, the tax rate is a percentage of the current wage base; this amount is called the maximum tax. The tax rate includes contributions for Social Security and Medicare. The U.S. Navy like the civilian employer matches the officer's and civilian employee's Social Security and Medicare contribution. Self-employed persons also pay a tax rate which runs from 6.4% in 1968 to 7.9% in 1987. Since Congress frequently improves Social Security and Medicare benefits and raises their tax rates, your disbursing officer will be able to provide the current tax rates and wage base.

The Survivors' Benefits Act gives an officer six years of free coverage as of 1 January 1957, based on a wage scale of $160 per month, if he has active service after that date. You are entitled to "drop out" five years of lowest earnings or years in which you had no earnings. The amount to be used in figuring your benefits, assuming you continue serving on active duty or retire and start working in private industry until retirement age, will be an average of all of the amounts of salary on which you paid Social Security tax, with the five lowest years dropped out. When you approach retirement from the service, consult your local Social Security office or write for a booklet which will give you information then effective.

Social Security deductions are not taken from your retired pay. If you accept seasonal employment, you may draw a social security check for any month in which you earn $140 or less, after you reach the age of 65 (62 optional). For earnings over $1,680 per year, deductions will be made from your Social Security payments according to a formula; but note, if you are not employed on a regular basis, but earn more than $140 in a certain month, even though it be more than $1,680, you will lose your Social Security only for the month in which you earn this large sum. Also note, that this maximum earned income permitted has been, and probably will be changed by Congress. If you reach 72 and are still employed, you may collect your full Social Security payments without regard to earnings.

In the event of your death leaving dependents, they would receive varying benefits depending on your average monthly wage.

Health Benefits.—All persons in the United States, after reaching age 65, are protected against all hazards by Plan 1: extended hospitalization and convalescent care, and Plan 2: major doctor bills. Plan 1 is financed by the employer and employee payroll taxes; Plan 2 is financed by voluntary payment of the insured of $4.00 per month, in 1968 which the U. S. Government matches. This payment may be deducted from your monthly benefit check.

Health benefits are a right, not charity.

1. You become eligible on attaining age 65, whether working or retired, drawing Social Security benefits or having a large private income or many assets.
2. If you choose early Social Security retirement, you will not be eligible until you are 65.
3. These plans do not give you *complete protection*. You will pay some of the costs before either plan takes effect and a percentage of the rest. Some benefits are limited in duration.

Private insurance carriers and health plans offer benefit programs to fill the gap in total protection. It will pay you to investigate before you become 65, as Navy civilian medicare ceases on that date.

You have *free choice* of doctors or hospitals, but hospitals must be qualified to participate under the program. Licensed physicians, including osteopaths, are qualified, but some doctors may elect not to participate. Check with the hospital or physician before undergoing treatment.

Plan 1: The Hospital Insurance Program provides payment for the following services:

Hospitalization for 90 days in one spell of sickness with the program paying for all but the first $44 for 60 days, and but $11 daily for the next 30 days, plus a lifetime allowance of 60 additional days at all but $22 per day.

Up to 100 days of *post-hospital* care in an extended care facility with the program paying for the first 20 days and all but $5.50 daily for the next 80 days.

Post-hospital home health care services in the 365 days following your discharge from a hospital or extended care facility, with the program paying for up to 100 visits to your home by visiting nurses, physical therapists and other health workers.

Plan 2: The Medical Insurance Program is voluntary. It will pay 80 percent of the reasonable costs or charges, except for the first $50 each calendar year, for the following services:

Physician's and surgeon's services, whether performed in a hospital or clinic, in a doctor's office or at home.

Outpatient hospital diagnostic services with the program paying 80 percent of the cost during a 20-day period except for the first $20 for each 20-day period.

Medical and health services, including diagnostic tests, X-rays or radium treatments; rental of medical equipment, and many other medical items and services.

Home health care services, with no requirement for prior hospitalization, which provides for up to 100 visits yearly by visiting nurses, physical therapists and other health workers.

Other Social Security Benefits.—For permanent disability, you may be eligible for the same benefits you would otherwise receive at age 65.

When you die, your widow (or the person who pays your burial expenses) will be entitled to a lump sum payment in addition to her monthly annuity equal to three times the amount of the monthly old-age benefit, which you would be entitled to receive at age 65, but not more than $255. Your widow's monthly benefit at age 62 will be 82½ percent of your benefit at age 65.

Important.—The social security benefits are not paid automatically—you must file an application upon reaching retirement age, or when you become disabled. You must also notify the Social Security office when you reach age 72 in order to receive benefits regardless of the amount of your earnings. Your widow or other survivor should apply promptly to the nearest local Social Security office for benefits, as these benefits do not commence until the date that the application has been received by the Social Security Administration.

Periodically, request from the Accounting Department of the Social Security Administration in Baltimore, Maryland, information as to the status of your account, and request the Administration to correct your record if it is in error. File the answers to these requests with your important papers.

For further information on Social Security, consult your local Social Security Office.

1816. ADDITIONAL RIGHTS AND BENEFITS. *Orders to Active Duty.*— Retired officers may not be ordered to active duty in peacetime without their consent, although they may be ordered to active service in time of war or national emergency.

Military Law.—Persons entitled to retired pay continue to be subject to the Uniform Code of Military Justice, even though retired pay is waived.

Uniform.—On appropriate occasions, retired personnel are entitled to wear the prescribed uniform of the rank or rate held on the retired list. They are prohibited from wearing the uniform in connection with non-military, personal or civilian enterprises, or activities of a business nature. Retired personnel in a foreign country may not wear the uniform except when attending, by formal invitation, ceremonies or social functions at which the wearing of the uniform is required by the terms of the invitation, or by the regulations or customs of the country.

Use of Titles.—Retired persons are permitted to use their military titles in connection with commercial enterprises, but must not use them so as to discredit the naval service.

Commissary, Ships' Stores and Officers' Messes.—Officers *retired with pay* may be accorded the privileges of Armed Forces commissary stores and exchanges, as well as Navy clothing and small stores and ships' stores. Privileges of Commissioned Officers' Messes, Open, are available to officers retired with pay, subject to the limitation of facilities.

Hospitalization.—A member or former member of the Navy or Naval Reserve, as well as his dependents, who is entitled to retired pay, including a member or former member who is entitled to retired pay under Chap. 67, Title 10, U.S. Code, may be hospitalized on a space available basis in naval and other uniformed services' medical facilities for the treatment of most ailments.

Retired members entitled to hospital care are also eligible for dental care, subject to the availability of dental facilities. They, and their dependents, are also entitled to out-patient treatment. See Section 1606 for a description of uniformed services' and civilian medicare available after retirement with retired pay.

Veterans' Benefits.—Many navymen (both active duty and retired) frequently overlook the fact that they may have acquired a veterans' status and therefore are entitled to the many benefits available to veterans. Some assume that the receipt of retired pay (or active duty pay) is in itself a bar to most veterans' benefits, or at least to the financial compensations which accompany veterans' benefits. Some VA benefits accrue to survivors of veterans, and in most cases survivors of active duty and retired officers may be eligible. The VA gives hospital or out-patient care when needed for all service-connected medical or compensable dental conditions. The treatment will be given at one of the many VA hospitals or clinics, or the VA may pay for outpatient care by a hometown doctor or dentist.

The Veterans' Readjustment Benefits Act (Public Law 89-358), extends to veterans whose sole service was after January 31, 1955, hospital care from the VA on a bed-available basis for treatment of their non-service-connected conditions, provided such veterans state under oath their inability to defray the costs of such care. This law does not extend hospital care to the person whose entire period of service was in an active duty status, unless he was disabled from a disease or injury incurred or aggravated in line of duty.

Employment.—You are entitled to use the specialized counseling and placement services provided for all veterans by federal and state law. When you retire, you may register with the appropriate state or local employment office, or you may contact the veterans' employment representative assigned to your locality.

Non-disabled war veterans are entitled to a five-point preference in addition to their earned ratings in Civil Service examinations. Disabled veterans are entitled to 10 points. Certain widows and certain mothers also may be granted veteran's preference.

Home and Farm Loans.—World War II and Korean conflict veterans are still eligible for the G.I. loan program until July 25, 1970. Under The Veterans' Readjustment Benefits Act of 1966 and The Veterans' Pension and Readjustment Assistance Act of 1967, veterans of at least 181 days continuous duty, or discharged for disability, any part which occurred after January 31, 1955 and persons on active duty at least two years, even though not discharged, are eligible to obtain G.I. loans made by private lenders for homes and farms or for farming purposes. In certain designated areas, direct loans can be made by VA for homes and farmhouses. Persons whose military service consisted of "active duty for training," are *not* eligible.

Each eligible veteran has a minimum of 10 years from the date of his separation from active duty. He will be eligible for an additional year for each three months (90 days) of active duty up to a maximum of 20 years. A veteran released because of service-connected disabilities will be eligible for the full 20 years from the date of discharge or release. However, no veteran's eligibility will expire before March 3, 1976.

For a veteran or serviceman, VA may guarantee a home loan made by a private lender up to $7,500 or 60 percent of the loan, whichever is less. For a farm real estate loan other than for the acquisition of a home, the guaranty may not exceed $4,000 or 50 percent of the loan; and for non-real estate farm loans, the guaranty may not exceed $2,000 or 50 percent of the loan. This means you have a better chance to borrow at a favorable interest rate, with little or no down payment and a long-term repayment possibility. Use of entitlement by a veteran or serviceman cancels unused entitlement derived from World War II or the Korean War. Entitlement may be reduced by used World War II or Korean War entitlement. However, under certain circumstances, entitlement previously used can be restored.

Loans may be for the purchase of homes; to make alterations, repairs or improvements in homes already owned and occupied; to purchase farms or farm supplies or equipment; to obtain farm working capital; or to refinance delinquent indebtedness on property to be used or occupied by the veteran as a home or for farming purposes. Direct loans may be made by VA, however, only for the purchase of homes and farmhouses. Business loans are not authorized under the new law. There is no maximum on the amount of a guaranteed loan. Direct loans made by VA may not exceed $17,500 as a general rule.

Home loans can be made for a maximum of 30 years, farm real estate loans for a maximum of 40 years, non-real estate loans for a maximum of 10 years.

A fee of $\frac{1}{2}$ of 1 percent of the loan amount must be paid to VA in the case of loans for veterans and servicemen. The fee will not be required, if, when a loan is closed, the veteran or serviceman was also eligible for a loan based on World War II or Korean conflict service. The loan fee may be added to the loan amount if the loan as so increased does not exceed the maximum loan amount. This fee is in addition to the allowable closing costs.

Loan benefits are not a gift. If the VA loses money because the loan is not paid as agreed, such loss will be a debt the veteran or serviceman owes the Government.

Accurate determinations of eligibility can be made *only* by the Veterans Administration and no person should obligate himself for the purchase of a home or farm solely on the basis of this summary. Before undertaking any such obligation, he should ask VA to determine his eligibility. A Request for Determination of Eligibility and Available Loan Guaranty Entitlement, with required supporting documents, should be sent to VA to secure a Certificate of Eligibility.

Education and Training.—Under the Veterans' Readjustment Benefits Act of 1966 (Cold War G.I. Bill) and The Veterans' Pension and Readjustment Assistance Act of 1967, an eligible person may select a program of education, an apprenticeship, on-the-job, farm or flight training at any approved educational institution or training establishment which will accept and retain him as a student, apprentice or trainee in any field or branch of knowledge or vocation which he is qualified to undertake. Eligibility ceases at the end of eight years from the date of retirement or release from active duty after January 31, 1955, except veterans released from active duty before March 3, 1966, have eligibility until May 31, 1974. An additional entitlement has been set for veterans who are pursuing farm cooperative, apprentice, on-the-job or flight training. Completion of the program must be within eight years after release from active duty or retirement, or within eight years after August 31, 1967, if released prior thereto. Educational and vocational counseling will be provided by the Veterans Administration upon request.

Vocational Rehabilitation.—The same regulations apply to vocational rehabilitation. A member entitled to both must choose which program he will pursue. Counseling may be obtained at any office of the VA.

Disability Compensation.—Regardless of the receipt of retired pay from one of the uniformed services, important benefits may be available to retired officers who establish the existence of service-connected disability to the satisfaction of the Veterans' Administration. Immediately after your retirement, investigate your eligibility for a disability compensation under the Veterans' Readjustment Benefits Act of 1966 and The Veterans' Pension and Readjustment Assistance Act of 1967. It has the following advantages:

Tax Exemption may effect a considerable Federal income tax saving. In order to accept a disability compensation award, you may waive all or part of your retired pay and receive a like amount as tax-exempt compensation from the VA.

Hospitalization on a priority basis in Veterans' Administration hospitals.

Medical Treatment as an out-patient may be received at VA out-patient facilities for conditions determined to be service-connected.

Death Benefits claims for compensation by your survivors will be considerably advanced if you have already established a service-connected disability for compensation while still alive and if you have obtained a VA claim number.

Other Benefits may include residence in Veterans' Administration homes, prosthetic appliances, vocational rehabilitation, cars for disabled veterans, and wheel chair homes.

Application for disability compensation may be filed any time after retirement or separation from the service at the regional office of the Veterans' Administration nearest your home.

Homestead Preference.—Veterans must have an honorable discharge and at least 90 days' war service. Information concerning public lands available may be obtained from any Federal Land Regional Office or the Bureau of Land Management, Department of the Interior, Washington, D.C. 20240.

U. S. Naval Home.—The U. S. Naval Home, located in Philadelphia, Pa., provides an honorable and comfortable home for old and infirm or disabled, but not bedridden officers and men of the Navy and Marine Corps. Relinquishment of retired pay or being on a retired list, are not prerequisites for admission.

FIGURE 1803. The Naval Home—Snug harbor for the retired.

CHAPTER 19

Maxims of Naval Leadership[1]

Now there may be "too much Nelson" for the
Times have changed since then,
But as long as man is human, we shall
Have to count on men;
Though machines be ne'er so perfect, there
May come a day perhaps—
When you find out just how helpless is
A heap of metal scraps.

—CAPTAIN R. A. HOPWOOD, R.N

NO MATTER how important a man at sea may consider himself, unless he is fundamentally worthy, the sea will some day find him out. If a wrong move is made at sea, in a critical moment, death may be the penalty for the most simple failure—not only death to one but to many. Incompetence may prevail upon the shore but at sea it sooner or later is ruthlessly uncovered and utter disaster often follows in its wake.

* * * * *

Act as if it were impossible to fail.

* * * * *

Don't worry about how well your uniform fits you. Concentrate instead on how well you fit the uniform.

* * * * *

It is the man you are capable of making, not the man that you have become, that is most important to you.

* * * * *

Bear in mind that you have entered a profession which requires you to place service above self during your entire career.

[1] Original compilation (Courtesy of Capt. C. F. Martin, USN) plus additional maxims in each edition.

Since the unaided achievement of the individual is meager, the most useful accomplishment you can early acquire is to learn to work harmoniously with other people.

* * * * *

Decide, knowingly, if you can, ignorantly if you must, but in any case, decide and have no fear.

* * * * *

Have a course; choose your course; be decisive; be faithful to it.

* * * * *

Personal anger has no place in official relations, and it is cowardly to humiliate one powerless to resent it.

* * * * *

Remember that the mistakes, failures, and humiliations of yesterday are gone; they are water under the bow. Get up each day remembering that it is a new day and with the determination that it shall be a day of accomplishment.

* * * * *

It is by no means enough that an officer of the Navy should be a capable mariner. He must be that of course, but also a great deal more. He should be as well a gentleman of liberal education, refined manners, punctilious courtesy, and the nicest sense of personal honor.—JOHN PAUL JONES.

* * * * *

Coming now to view the naval officer aboard ship and in relation to those under his command, he should be the soul of tact, patience, justice, firmness, and charity. No meritorious act of a subordinate should escape his attention or be left to pass without its reward, if even the reward be only one word of approval. Conversely, he should not be blind to a single fault in any subordinate, though at the same time he should be quick and unfailing to distinguish error from malice, thoughtlessness from incompetency, and well-meant shortcoming from heedless or stupid blunder. As he should be universal and impartial in his rewards and approval of merit, so should he be judicial and unbending in his punishment or reproof of misconduct.

* * * * *

Truthfulness is the warp and woof of our naval fabric.

* * * * *

Praise, following censure, is like sunshine following a storm.

Remember, commend *publicly*—reprove *privately*. And *don't lose your temper*.

* * * * *

Make no promise that you cannot keep.

* * * * *

Whenever you receive an order requiring its transmittal to subordinates for action, it is up to *you* to see that order *promptly* and *smartly executed*. Your responsibility in the matter does not end until the order has been *properly executed*.

* * * * *

A test of your leadership is to get men to do willingly things which they would not choose to do voluntarily, and in the performance of such tasks to give their best.

* * * * *

It should be remembered that, whether on the bridge at sea, or on the quarterdeck in port, the best officers are those who possess powers of observation, and having those powers *know how to use them*. And bear in mind that it is the smart, quick, and, if possible, *cheery* voice that gets the work done and the men to hop.

* * * * *

The value of any officer to the government depends upon how much attention he gives to his duty.

* * * * *

Sound leadership never takes another man's task from him, but encourages him and stimulates others to give their best efforts.

* * * * *

Don't nag your men; don't neglect them; don't coddle them; don't play the clown.

* * * * *

Every machine and every instrument is capable of vast improvement. So is every man.

* * * * *

Careful preparation is the best safeguard against failure.

* * * * *

The great universal cause of inefficiency is not ignorance, but the failure to use knowledge possessed.

The greatness of a man may well be measured by the distance he looks ahead.

* * * * *

Often an explanation of the result of faults is the most effective means of correcting them.

* * * * *

Remember that the purpose of all forms of punishment is correction.

* * * * *

Every person in the fleet, who through cowardice, negligence, or disaffection, shall in time of action . . . not do his utmost to take or destroy every ship which it shall be his duty to engage; and to assist all and every of His Majesty's ships, or those of His allies, which it shall be his duty to assist and relieve . . . being convicted thereof by sentence of a court-martial, shall suffer death.

* * * * *

Be an *optimist*. Cultivate the habit. There are some men who always see their troubles with great clearness. They always are afraid that things will not turn out just right. The man who is an optimist is like a breath of fresh air. He cheers all with whom he comes in contact. One of the great sayings of the greatest of all naval officers, Lord Nelson, was: "I am not come forth to find difficulties, but to remove them."

* * * * *

The officer who possesses self-control is the kind who is always calm and collected in an emergency, who never lacks self-possession, presence of mind, who never loses his head; the kind who is not affected by the contagion of wild excitement among those about him.

* * * * *

Faith is a strong factor in an officer's ability to handle delinquents. If you tell a man forcibly enough that he is too good a man to be misbehaving, that he has it in him to reform, to snap out of it, to come back, and show up some of the others who haven't the "guts" to take a chance of getting on the report, he presently will think so too, and the results will be amazing. You will have aroused faith in him because of your own convincing belief in him.

* * * * *

Truthfulness is the essence of nobility. *It is utterly impossible for a liar to be a gentleman.* Shading or distorting the truth is adding a base alloy to the true metal of a man's character. Truth—of thought and action—is the highest of moral attributes.

No man of small character can aspire to the greatest heights of leadership.

*   *   *   *   *

Good example on the part of officers is one of the prime requisites to a maintenance of good discipline. In fact, it is no exaggeration to say that the true, desirable brand of discipline can neither be instilled nor maintained unless the officers *practice what they preach.* Our men are too intelligent and too high-spirited to extend respect and loyalty to men of hypocrisy, insincerity, and sham.

*   *   *   *   *

Think more of the success of your work for the sake of your work than you do for the effect of success or failure on your record and reputation.

*   *   *   *   *

Opportunity has a strange, almost uncanny way of abiding where it knows it will find a fitting home.

*   *   *   *   *

The outward manifestations of good discipline are many and unmistakable. Cleanliness of person and attire; neatness and correctness of uniform; erectness of carriage; smart and energetic bearing; alert expression; general atmosphere of health in mind and body; and last, but by no means the least in importance, the correct, smart, and cheerful rendering of the salute.

*   *   *   *   *

By your character and skill, give positive leadership to your command, and maintain its discipline, welfare, and contentment.

*   *   *   *   *

Praise will usually better promote interest and efficiency than censure or punishment. Be strict, but considerate of the limitations of others. Remember that you are dealing with individuals as sensitive and jealous of their rights as yourself. Fairness and impartiality in dealing with men are essentials. Little good and great evil is often accomplished by unnecessary shouting. Nothing is *more* discouraging to a man than the finding of fault with him when he is using his best endeavors.

*   *   *   *   *

You may depend on it, that it is more in your own power than in anyone else's to promote both your comfort and advancement. A strict and unwearied attention to your duty, and a complaisant and respectful behavior, not only to your superiors but to everybody, will ensure you their regard; and the reward will surely come, and I hope soon, in the shape of preferment; but if it should not, I am sure you have too much good sense to let disappointment sour you. Guard carefully against letting discontent appear in you; it is sorrow to your friends, a triumph to your competitors, and cannot be productive of any good. Conduct yourself so as to deserve the best that can come to you; and the consciousness of your own proper behavior will keep you in spirits if it should not come. Let it be your ambition to be foremost on all duty.

* * * * *

Let your companions be such as yourself, or superior; for the worth of a man will always be ruled by that of his company.

* * * * *

If there is any occasion when an officer should be ruthless in his requirements of instant obedience and attention to duty, it is as officer of the deck.

* * * * *

The presence of liquor among the men should be a matter of the most vital concern to the officers. It well may result in accident, disaster, loss of life, and even the destruction of the ship.

* * * * *

On coming off in the one o'clock A.M. boat from the landing, no one meets you at the gangway and you go below without seeing the petty officer of the watch. You are annoyed, but dismiss the matter from your mind and turn in. A day or two later you mention the incident quite casually in the wardroom and are very promptly and properly taken to task by the executive officer for not investigating the whereabouts of the petty officer of the watch at the time, and for not reporting the case. Your only comeback is that you were not on duty and that under the circumstances you felt no obligation to take action!

You were wrong. You *were* on duty. When it comes to irregularities of this nature and breaches of discipline in general, and especially when it comes to matters which may affect the safety of your own or some other ship, an officer of the Navy is *always on duty.*

* * * * *

A young officer cannot learn too soon that every officer has two personalities, the official and the unofficial. A young officer also should remember that when a senior—such as the captain or executive—finds it necessary to reprimand him for an official mistake, the senior is acting in his official capacity and discharging his duties. The opinion that the senior entertains for the junior probably has not been altered, and there need be no change whatever in their personal and unofficial relations.

* * * * *

Whatever else you are, be a seaman. Know the ways of the sea and of the men who go down to the sea in ships.

* * * * *

A ship is only as smart as the officers in her.

* * * * *

Know your stuff—and be a man. Look after your men.

* * * * *

Aim at success, but never think you have achieved it.

* * * * *

THE POWER OF EXAMPLE

The rules a Leader keeps are written here—
Of Loyalty, Simplicity, and Tact,
Of Honor, Self-control, and Duty clear.
Among them all we find one grievous lack:
"Do not do as I *do,* but as I *say.*"
In vain is all we know and all we teach,
However we may strive to find the way,
Until we learn to practice what we preach.

Whatever we would like our men to be.
Clean and alert and wholly unafraid—
Then must we go before and let them see
That we will *do* the things that we have *said.*
So will they know that we are men to lead,
And we will have the grasp for which we reach
When we can show, by every word and deed,
That we have learned to practice what we preach.

'Tis well that we should know the Rules of Road
And how to stand a watch and thread a pipe,
And teach our crews to point and fire and load,
And hold our tongue when we would like to gripe.
Above all these, we know one vital need—
And this, our prayer, O Lord, we now beseech—
As we would have men follow where we lead,
Give us the strength to practice what we preach.

Professional Reading

Books to Have with You Always

BRITTIN AND WATSON, *International Law for Seagoing Officers*, U. S. Naval Institute.
BRODIE. *Guide to Naval Strategy*. Princeton University Press.
DUNLAP AND SHUFELDT. *Dutton's Navigation and Piloting*. U. S. Naval Institute.
HARRAL AND SWARTZ. *Service Etiquette*. U. S. Naval Institute.
KNIGHT. *Modern Seamanship*. D. Van Nostrand Company, Inc.
KNOX. *A History of the United States Navy*. G. P. Putnam's Sons.
LOVETTE. *Naval Customs, Traditions, and Usage*. U. S. Naval Institute.
NOEL. *Division Officer's Guide*. U. S. Naval Institute.
——— *Naval Terms Dictionary*. U. S. Naval Institute.
POTTER (ed.). *The United States and World Sea Power*. Prentice-Hall, Inc.
PRUNSKI (ed.). *Farwell's Rules of the Nautical Road*. U. S. Naval Institute.
WOLFE, MULHOLLAND, LAUDENSLAGER, CONNERY, McCANDLESS AND MANN. *Naval Leadership*. U. S. Naval Institute.
The Ships and Aircraft of the U. S. Fleet. U. S. Naval Institute.
Watch Officer's Guide. U. S. Naval Institute.

Essential Reading List

The Bluejackets' Manual. U. S. Naval Institute.
BREYER. *Guide to the Soviet Navy*. Henley (tr.). U. S. Naval Institute.
DANIELS. *The Nature of Communism*. Random House.
DYER. *Naval Logistics*. U. S. Naval Institute.
ECCLES. *Military Concepts and Philosophy*. Rutgers University Press.
FAIRGRIEVE. *Geography and World Power*. University of London Press.
FIELD. *History of U. S. Naval Operations: Korea*. U. S. Government Printing Office.
GARTHOFF. *Soviet Strategy in the Nuclear Age*. Praeger.
HITCH. *Decision Making for Defense*. University of California Press.
HOOVER. *A Study of Communism*. Holt, Rinehart and Winston.
HUNTINGTON. The Common Defense: *Strategic Programs in National Strategy*. Columbia University Press.
HUNTINGTON. *The Soldier and the State: The Theory and Politics of Civil-Military Relation*. Harvard University Press.
JEFFRIES (ed.). *Geography and National Power*. U. S. Naval Institute.
JONES. *Destroyer Squadron 23*—The Combat Exploits of Arleigh Burke's Gallant Force. Chilton Company.

KAUFMAN. *The McNamara Strategy*. Harper and Row.
LEVINE. *The Arms Debate*. Harvard University Press.
MORISON. *John Paul Jones*. Little, Brown and Company.
POTTER AND NIMITZ. *Seapower: A Navy History*. Prentice-Hall, Inc.
SAUNDERS. *The Soviet Navy*. London: Weidenfeld and Nicolson.
Social Usage in the Foreign Service. Foreign Service Institute.
TARRANT. *Social Usage and Protocol*. Office of Naval Intelligence.
WOLFE AND MULHOLLAND (ed.). *Selected Readings in Leadership*. U. S. Naval Institute.

Reference Works

AGETON AND HEINL. *The Marine Officer's Guide*. U. S. Naval Institute.
Annual Report. Navy Mutual Aid Association.
BREDT (comp.). *Weyer's Warships of the World, 1969*. U. S. Naval Institute.
BRODIE. *Seapower in the Machine Age*. Princeton University Press.
BUELL. *Paul Jones, The Founder of the American Navy*. Charles Scribner's Sons.
BYRNE. *Military Law: A Handbook for the Navy and Marine Corps*. U. S. Naval Institute.
DE KOVEN. *Life and Letters of John Paul Jones*. Charles Scribner's Sons.
FURER. *The History of Naval Administration in World War II*. U. S. Navy Department, Government Printing Office.
ISMAY. *NATO, 1949-1954*. Acme.
JOHNSON. *Welcome Aboard*. U. S. Naval Institute.
LEWIS. *The Navy of Britain*. George Allen and Unwin, Ltd.
MARDER. *The Anatomy of British Sea Power*. Alfred A. Knopf, Inc.
MORISON, *The History of Naval Operations in World War II*. Little, Brown and Company.
SPROUTS. *Toward a New Order of Sea Power*. Princeton University Press.
Suggested Life Insurance Program. Navy Mutual Aid Association.

Official Publications

Bureau of Medicine and Surgery Manual.
Bureau of Naval Personnel Manual.
Ship Systems Command Manual.
Supply Systems Command Manual.
Catalog of Naval Shore Activities (OpNav P213-105).
The Communication Officer (NavPers 16101).
Communications Instructions, U. S. Navy.
Comparative Rules of the Road and How to Obey Them (USCG #143).
Court-Martial Reports, Department of the Navy.
Courts-Martial, Special, A Guide for Presidents and Members, The Office of the Judge Advocate of the Navy.
Department of the Navy Security Manual for Classified Information.
Digests of Opinions.
Elements of Naval Tactics and Operations (NavPers 16043-A).
General Orders, U. S. Navy.

Handbook of Survival in Water (NavPers 16046).
Joint Travel Regulations.
Landing Party Manual.
Manual for Courts-Martial, United States, 1951 with the Naval Supplement to Manual for Courts-Martial.
Manual for Mail Clerks.
Manual for Navy Instructors (NavPers 16103-B).
Manual of Qualifications for Advancement in Rating (NavPers 18068).
Manual of Qualifications for United States Navy Line Officers.
Military Justice Handbook, The Trial Counsel, and the Defense Counsel, 1954, Departments of the Army and Air Force.
Moral Leadership (NavPers 15890).
Naval Orientation (NavPers 16138-C).
Naval Warfare (NWP-50).
Navy and Marine Corps Awards Manual (NavPers 15790).
Navy Correspondence Manual.
Navy-Marine Corps Standard Subject Classification System.
Navy Guide for Retired and Fleet Reserve Personnel (NavPers 15891B).
The Navy Staff (NWP-12).
Navy Travel Instructions.
Officer Fact Book (NavPers 15898).
Reference Guide to Employment Activities of Retired Personnel. The Office of the Judge Advocate of the Navy.
Registered Publication Manual.
Reports, United States Court of Military Appeals.
The Rights and Benefits of Navy Men and Their Dependents (NavPers 15885-A).
Shipboard Communications (NavPers 10806).
Shipboard Procedures (NWP-50A).
Shipboard Training Manual (NavPers 90110, 90110-1).
The Ships Organization and Regulations Manual.
Shore Patrol Manual (NavPers 15106).
U. S. Navy Uniform Regulations.
The United States Government Organization Manual.
U. S. Navy Regulations, 1948.
Your America (NavPers).
Your Navy (NavPers 10600).
Your New Career (NavPers 15895-A).

Periodicals

Air Force, The Air Force Association.
All Hands, The Bureau of Naval Personnel Bulletin.
Armed Forces Journal, Army and Navy Journal, Inc.
Armor, U. S. Armor Association.
The Army, Association of the United States Army.
The JAG Journal, Office of the Judge Advocate General of the Navy.
The Marine Corps Gazette, The Marine Corps Association.
Military Engineer, Society of American Military Engineers.

Military Review, The U. S. Army Command and General Staff College.
Naval Aviation News, Air Systems Command.
The Naval Aviation Training Bulletin, BuPers.
The Naval Reservist, BuPers.
The Navy Department *Bulletin,* EXOS.
The Navy Times, Army Times Publishing Co.
Our Navy (written for the enlisted man)
Proceedings, United States Naval Institute.
Shipmate, The Naval Academy Alumni Association.
The U. S. Naval Training Bulletins, BuPers.

The Responsibilities of Leadership[1]

By Fleet Admiral Ernest J. King, USN[2]

IT IS always an honor to address the graduating class at the Naval Academy. It is doubly an honor today in these times when we are engaged in the greatest war in history—a war which we can be fully confident of winning, but only at the cost of unremitting labor and a multitude of heartaches and sacrifices such as this country has never before known. But victory will bring not only the preservation of our own freedom and the restoration of the lost liberties of uncounted millions but also the firm confidence that, when we have won this war, we Americans, under the leadership of the President, will take steps to see to it that the ability of any person or of any people to enslave others, physically or mentally or spiritually, shall be forever destroyed.

This is both a proud day and a serious day for you and for your families. It is a fitting occasion to present to you some matters that should engage your interest and attention as you go forth, in paraphrase of the "Marine Corps Hymn," to fight your country's battles on the land and on the sea—and in the air.

We hear very much indeed, in this day and age, of machines and of

---

[1] Address delivered to the Class of 1942, at Annapolis, Md., June 19, 1942, on the occasion of their graduation from the United States Naval Academy.

[2] A graduate of the United States Naval Academy, Class of 1901, he served through all ranks, and was appointed rear admiral in 1933. From 1938 to 1939, he served as Commander Aircraft, Battle Force, United States Fleet, with the rank of vice-admiral. In 1941, when he assumed command of the United States Atlantic Fleet, he was promoted to admiral. Shortly after the outbreak of World War II, he was called by the President to the supreme naval command, as Commander-in-Chief, United States Fleet and so served all through World War II. His decorations include the following: Navy Cross; Distinguished Service Medal (and Gold Stars for its further award); Sampson Medal; Spanish Campaign Medal; Mexican Service Medal; Victory Medal, Atlantic Fleet Clasp; Defense Medal; Order of Vasco Núñez de Balboa, grade of commander, government of Panama.

war waged with machines. We hear so much that we do not, all of us, stop to think that war is not different, in principle, from what it has been since before the dawn of recorded history. Mechanized warfare is no more than evolution from the time when men first fought each other by the aid of stones and clubs, down through the ages to this day of mechanized ships of the sea, mechanized ships on land, and mechanized ships of the air.

We must not fail to realize that machines are as nothing without the men who man them and give them life. War is force—force to the utmost—force to make the enemy yield to our own will—to yield because they see their comrades killed and wounded—to yield because their own will to fight is broken. War is men against men—mechanized war is still men against men. Machines are mere masses of inert metal without the men who man them.

We must realize that men are not effective, individually or collectively, unless they are imbued with high morale. Morale may be defined as a state of mind wherein there is confidence, courage, and zeal among men united together in a common effort. In brief, it may be considered mental teamwork. Some years ago, Captain Dudley Knox defined morale as "conviction of excellence" which means, in other words, "We're sure we can do the job in hand" and indicates a certain amount of "cockiness"—which is quite all right!

We cannot forget—we must not forget—in our haste to arm ourselves, that we must also equip our men, not with machines alone, but with the training—and the spirit—that will bring about the teamwork which enables us to be strong in battle, steadfast in danger, and indomitable should disaster threaten. Machines and the men who man them are as nothing without morale.

The means of building, and maintaining, high morale and the consequent effective teamwork can be summed up in one word—discipline— a word very much misunderstood and very much abused. True discipline is intelligent obedience of each for the consequent effectiveness of all. It is willing obedience to attain the greatest good by the greatest number. It means laying aside, for the time being, of ordinary, everyday go-as-you-please and do-what-you-like. It means one for all and all for one—teamwork. It means a machine—not a machine of inert metal, but one of living men—an integrated human machine in which each does his part and contributes his full share for the success of all.

To sum up: Machines are as nothing without men. Men are as nothing without morale.

You are about to join the great brotherhood of American fighting men—of men who are fighting for freedom of thought, of speech, of worship and of our own American way of life. In joining this great brotherhood of American fighting men, I ask of you always to bear in mind the significance of membership in that brotherhood. Take all proper pride in the prestige and power of the Navy, but do not forget that the other great armed service—the United States Army—also wears the uniform of our country, as do our fellow services of the Navy—the Marine Corps and the Coast Guard.

This is a day and age of specialization and it is duly exemplified in the armed forces—in the Navy in surface vessels, aircraft, submarines and in amphibious troops; in the Army, in the ground forces, the armored forces, the parachute troops, and the air force.

Do not allow yourselves to become prejudiced because another wears a different uniform and is skilled in the uses of different weapons. Let there be no narrow-minded jealousy, no bootless controversy, but, rather, a firm determination to gain the victory by wholehearted cooperation, and by thorough appreciation and cordial emulation of the capacities and abilities of all those who are, in fact and in deed, your brothers-in-arms.

To this end, we have only to bear in mind the association of United States armed forces in Bataan, on Corregidor, in Java, in the Coral Sea, and, more recently, in the actions off Midway and in Alaskan waters, to have it impressed upon us that we are—all of us—working *together* for victory.

You will soon find yourselves in daily contact with enlisted men. A great many of them will be experienced in the ways of the Navy and particularly capable in their several specialties. If you are smart, you will listen to what they say of their various jobs, because they know more about them than you do—or will, until you have had their experience. Other men, you will find, are inexperienced. It will be part of your duty to instruct them. In any event, remember that their respect must be earned—it cannot be gained otherwise—and that the best way to earn it is to learn everything there is to know about your own job. You cannot fool the American bluejacket, and I advise you not to try. You can, however, readily gain his loyalty and earn his respect. You will then have something that money cannot buy.

Your graduation from the Naval Academy today means a great deal more than recognition of the successful completion of your academic course. It means that, after three years of the closest scrutiny, you are being accepted as full-fledged officers of one of the proudest organizations in the world—the United States Navy.

You have undoubtedly been told by your instructors at the Naval Academy, and probably by your parents, that you must continue to learn. Even so, I shall repeat that advice. It is your duty to yourselves and to the naval service to apply yourselves to each assignment you are given until you have mastered it. You cannot possibly know all the answers now.

As you progress in the Navy, you will acquire what is generally known as a "service reputation." For years and years the Navy has worked, and is still working, on a satisfactory system of evaluating the capabilities of naval officers. For the details of what points are considered in this evaluation, made twice a year, and how these points are expressed, I suggest you consult a blank Fitness Report—and consult it often—as a guide to your evaluation of yourself. It will give you a fairly clear picture of what is expected of you and of what, after repeated reports, will finally establish your service reputation. Only you yourself are responsible for what that reputation is!

We are hearing often in these days of actions with the enemy wherein officers and men of the Navy have conducted themselves in accordance with the best traditions of the naval service. This is as it should be, because it emphasizes the real value and the true significance of traditions. But traditions, of themselves, are no more than testimonials to the successes of our predecessors. We revere them, to be sure, and we are sometimes prone to boast of them, but that is not enough. Before we may rightfully claim them as our own property, intangible though they may be, we must prove ourselves worthy of them, and view them as inspirations to go and do likewise—to make some traditions ourselves, if you will. Whether the traditions be those of the Navy, of the Marine Corps, or of the American people, they are obligations imposed upon us by those forbears whose thoughts and beliefs and deeds created them.

I take leave to commend to your individual consideration three pieces of what may be called "philosophy" which I have found helpful. The first is "Do the best you can with what you've got"—that is, don't expect perfection in men or in tools. The second is a modern version of "Don't worry about water that has already gone over the dam" but, rather, pattern your thought and deeds on "Where do we go from here?" The third is, so to speak, interlocked with the other two; it is this: " 'Difficulties' is the name given to things which it is our business to overcome."

One of the most important things you must remember is that, to date, you yourselves have been the only ones affected by your mistakes. This will no longer be the case. Under your command, in varying numbers as you gain experience, will be men who are depending on you and your decisions. You cannot, you must not, fail them.

I need not exhort you to do well in the fleet. I know that every one of you is eager to make good, eager to take his assigned place, eager to see action, and eager to contribute your full part to victory over the enemy.

Let me enjoin you, however, to give all heed to the words you will find in the commissions which you are about to receive. They are laid as a charge upon you that you shall merit "special trust and confidence" in your "patriotism, valor, fidelity, and abilities."

On behalf of the officers and men of the seagoing forces of the Navy—now in contact with the enemy throughout the seven seas—I welcome you as brother officers and shipmates.

Code of Conduct for Members of the Armed Forces of the United States

I

❡*I am an American fighting man. I serve in the forces which guard my country and our way of life. I am prepared to give my life in their defense.*

A member of the Armed Forces is always a fighting man. As such, it is his duty to oppose the enemies of the United States regardless of the circumstances in which he may find himself, whether in active participation in combat, or as a prisoner of war.

II

❡*I will never surrender of my own free will. If in command I will never surrender my men while they still have the means to resist.*

As an individual, a member of the Armed Forces may never voluntarily surrender himself. When isolated and he can no longer inflict casualties on the enemy, it is his duty to evade capture and rejoin the nearest friendly forces.

The responsibility and authority of a commander never extends to the surrender of his command to the enemy while it has power to resist or evade. When isolated, cut off, or surrounded, a unit must continue to fight until relieved, or able to rejoin friendly forces, by breaking out or evading the enemy.

III

❡*If I am captured I will continue to resist by all means available. I will make every effort to escape and aid others to escape. I will accept neither parole nor special favors from the enemy.*

The duty of a member of the Armed Forces to continue resistance by all means at his disposal is not lessened by the misfortune of capture. Article 82 of the Geneva Convention pertains and must be explained. He will escape if able to do so, and will assist others to escape. Parole agreements are promises given the captor by a prisoner of war upon his faith and honor, to fulfill stated conditions, such as not to bear arms or not to escape, in consideration of special privileges, usually release from captivity or a lessened restraint. He will never sign or enter into a parole agreement.

IV

¶*If I become a prisoner of war, I will keep faith with my fellow prisoners. I will give no information or take part in any action which might be harmful to my comrades. If I am senior, I will take command. If not I will obey the lawful orders of those appointed over me and will back them up in every way.*

Informing or any other action to the detriment of a fellow prisoner is despicable and is expressly forbidden. Prisoners of war must avoid helping the enemy identify fellow prisoners who may have knowledge of particular value to the enemy, and may therefore be made to suffer coercive interrogation.

Strong leadership is essential to discipline. Without discipline, camp organization, resistance, and even survival may be impossible. Personal hygiene, camp sanitation, and care of sick and wounded are imperative. Officers and noncommissioned officers of the United States will continue to carry out their responsibilities and exercise their authority subsequent to capture. The senior line officer or noncommissioned officer within the prisoner of war camp or group of prisoners will assume command according to rank (or precedence) without regard to Service. This responsibility and accountability may not be evaded. If the senior officer or noncommissioned officer is incapacitated or unable to act for any reason, command will be assumed by the next senior. If the foregoing organization cannot be effected, an organization of elected representatives, as provided for in Articles 79-81 Geneva Convention Relative to Treatment of Prisoners of War, or a covert organization, or both, will be formed.

V

¶*When questioned, should I become a prisoner of war, I am bound to give only name, rank, service number, and date of birth. I will evade answering further questions to the utmost of my ability. I will make no oral or written statements disloyal to my country and its allies or harmful to their cause.*

When questioned, a prisoner of war is required by the Geneva Convention and permitted by this Code to disclose his name, rank, service number, and date of birth. A prisoner of war may also communicate with the enemy regarding his individual health or welfare as a prisoner of war and, when appropriate, on routine matters of camp administration. Oral or written confessions true or false, questionnaires, personal history statements, propaganda recordings and broadcasts, appeals to other prisoners of war, signatures to peace or surrender appeals, self criticisms or any other oral or written communication on behalf of the enemy or critical or harmful to the United States, its allies, the Armed Forces or other prisoners are forbidden.

It is a violation of the Geneva Convention to place a prisoner of war under physical or mental torture or any other form of coercion to secure from him information of any kind. If, however, a prisoner is subjected to such treatment, he will endeavor to avoid by every means the disclosure of any information, or the making of any statement or the performance of any action harmful to the interests of the United States or its allies or which will provide aid or comfort to the enemy.

Under Communist Bloc reservations to the Geneva Convention, the signing of a confession or the making of a statement by a prisoner is likely to be used to convict him as a war criminal under the laws of his captors. This conviction has the effect of removing him from the prisoner of war status and according to this Communist Bloc device denying him any protection under terms of the Geneva Convention and repatriation until a prison sentence is served.

VI

¶*I will never forget that I am an American fighting man, responsible for my actions, and dedicated to the principles which made my country free. I will trust in my God and in the United States of America.*

The provisions of the Uniform Code of Military Justice, whenever appropriate, continue to apply to members of the Armed Forces while prisoners of war. Upon repatriation, the conduct of prisoners will be examined as to the circumstances of capture and through the period of detention with due regard for the rights of the individual and consideration for the conditions of captivity. A member of the Armed Forces who becomes a prisoner of war has a continuing obligation to remain loyal to his country, his service and his unit.

The life of a prisoner of war is hard. He must never give up hope. He must resist enemy indoctrination. Prisoners of war who stand firm and united against the enemy will aid one another in surviving this ordeal.

Communism, its History
and Challenge

1. THE MAINSTREAM OF HISTORY. In the modern history of mankind, a well-defined stream of history can be clearly discerned. It flows from the supremely authoritative feudalism of the "divine right of kings" to rule and from the inherited duty of the nobility to *noblesse oblige* through the liberalism of limited monarchy, release from serfdom, the Industrial Revolution, and the emancipation from slavery into the once radical theory of the inherent freedom and dignity of the individual and representative government responsive to the will of the people who elect it. It must be remembered that, when our American Revolution was new, its philosophy was considered libertarian, a radical creed of the most dangerous sort. For anyone to declare that ordinary man was endowed with any "unalienable Rights" and that among them were "life, liberty, and the pursuit of happiness" was regarded as sedition of the most outrageous nature to be ruthlessly repressed. When this philosophy extended in the subsequent French Revolution to "liberty, equality, and fraternity," kings and their ministers stood aghast.

How could there be complete liberty for every person, how could anyone believe in anything so preposterous as the equality of every individual, and, even philosophically, who could claim as a brother or sister the unspeakable dregs of the city slums? With strengthened authoritarian controls of kings and dictators, it seemed at times as though this mainstream were diked or dammed or had reversed its flow. But the stream has always burst through the floodgates or moved around mountainous obstacles, carrying forward with it steadily improving conditions for the workingman and the peasant—the "exploited"; sometimes extravagant rewards for the industrialist, landlord, and financier—the "exploiters"; and sometimes increased government regulation of capitalism and capitalists[1]; and an accompanying decreased return on their

---

[1] These terms, *capitalism* and *capitalist* are epithets introduced into the Communist dialectic by Karl Marx. Many Free World rhetoricians prefer *free enterprise* or the present American *modified free enterprise* system.

capital investments. In the flow of this mainstream of history, the power of royalty was restricted; the privileges of the nobility decreased with the rise to wealth and importance of the middle class (bourgeoisie) during the Industrial Revolution (1760-1840); serfs were freed; slaves emancipated; and even in backward Russia and China, which had not yet experienced the Industrial Revolution, governments increasingly "derived their just powers from the consent of the governed."

Where now flows the mainstream of history?

2. SOCIALISM AND COMMUNISM. Socialism is no new theory. Born in Barmen, Germany, Friedrich Engels (1820-95) was one of its principal theoreticians and exponents. A native of Trier, Germany, Karl Marx (1818-83) read Engels' tracts and books. Living much of his life in exile, Marx, by middle age, had become one of socialism's most important doctrinaires. Differing with Engels, his philosophical theories grew through controversy with contemporaries and changed radically during his lifetime. Just before he died, he said to an enthusiastic disciple, "You know, I am not a true Marxist."

At the risk of oversimplification, here is a brief of Marx's beliefs:

1. Progress is an evolutionary process flowing from feudalism inevitably toward "pure" socialism, when all men would be equal.
2. There is an irreconcilable conflict between the two classes of capitalist society—the exploiters (nobility, industrialists, financiers, and petty capitalist bourgeoisie) and the exploited (the workers). The mainstream of history was interpreted by Marx as being directed by this conflict.
3. The purpose of the state is to safeguard private ownership. Therefore, the state must be smashed, not taken over by the proletariat in their revolution.
4. Antagonism to all religion is basic to the Marxist doctrine. Marx used the phrase, "Religion is the opiate of the people."
5. Marx expounded an extremely simple ethical code. *Anything that tends to bring about the ideal socialist (communist) society is morally good. Anything that works against this end is morally bad.*
6. In his "dialectic of revolution," Marx held that the bourgeois revolution must first destroy or take over a feudal state and establish capitalism before a country would be ready for the revolution of the proletariat leading to "pure" socialism. To be successful, the social revolution must be extended until it controls every country in the world. Communism cannot live in the same world with capitalism.
7. Since the proletariat would be unready to take over and operate a state and its economy, and since most countries would be unready for socialism, there would have to be a "dictatorship of the proletariat" to take the necessary steps to organize the country for "pure" socialism.
8. Marx described a mystic utopian communistic society of the future which would be the final stage of the social revolution.

Every movement which hopes to capture the uneducated masses must have a mysticism, a neoreligious sort of faith, which seizes an unsophisticated peoples' emotions and holds their loyalty. With his extravagantly eloquent description of the utopian society of the future, Marx probably made his greatest contribution to the communist movement.

Harmony will prevail. Culture and education will advance to a new high level of excellence. Mankind will become so nearly perfect and so social-minded that men will govern themselves without a government. For the first time in history, complete equality will prevail among men. In the words of Marx, "Only then can the narrow horizon of bourgeois right be left behind and society inscribe on its banners, 'From each according to his ability, to each according to his need.' "

This is the idealistic goal of "pure" socialism which provides communists with a mystic cause for which they will fight with fanatical and religious fervor. If this seems fantastic in the light of humankind as we know it, Marx recognized that a drastic change in human nature would be required. This, in his thinking, would take place during the period of the dictatorship of the proletariat.

The theories of Marx were a product of his time. His famed *Communist Manifesto* was an outcry of rage and anguish against the terrible conditions of the workers during the Industrial Revolution. His *Das Kapital* (1867) was a compilation of his theories, as briefed above. Nowhere in his writings does one encounter a plan for the take-over and the operation of the government and industry of a country.

3. **DEVIATIONS OF LENIN.** Lenin was basically an honest thinker, who readily admitted his mistakes. Before he came to power in Russia, he subscribed enthusiastically to the Marxist doctrines; even after his Bolshevik Party took power in November 1917, he took violent issue with his followers who advocated "deviation" from the dialectics of Marx. As a practical matter, Lenin abandoned the Marxist dialectic of revolution for immediate revolution in Czarist Russia without waiting for the bourgeois government of Kerensky to establish capitalism, and he seized the existing government instead of immediately smashing it. As a pragmatist, he found that, in the strategy and tactics of staging a revolution and establishing his dictatorship of the proletariat, he had to make many compromises. He had to set up an even more authoritative regime than the Czar had maintained. He could not go directly to socialism—initially, he seized only the banks and the few large industries. He postponed egalitar-

ianism and permitted salaries to be paid on the basis of work accomplished. Antagonistic to religion, he permitted its practice so as not to antagonize the devout. He recognized that the dictatorship of the proletariat in Russia could be run only by the Party; in respect for a possible counterrevolution and the backward condition of Russia, the dictatorship must be continued much longer than Marx had contemplated. Yet, Lenin was truly international in his thinking. When he organized the Third International in Moscow in 1919, he advocated worldwide communist revolution but he preached working from within bourgeois governments and other organizations, especially trade unions, and the seizure of power within the existing governmental framework. He expected the eventual end of the dictatorships and wrote eloquently of the mystic communist utopia of the future after the establishment of "pure" socialism.

Thus, in Russia, a small group of determined revolutionists, backed by a Bolshevik party of 200,000 in a proletariat of no more than 3,000,000, took over a country of some 100 million people either hostile to the Bolsheviks or uncompromisingly neutral.

4. DEVIATIONS OF JOSEPH STALIN. Recognizing Stalin's overweening thirst for power, Lenin, in his disputed "last will," warned against him. On Lenin's death in 1924, he tried to leave his position and authority to Kamanev and Zinoviev, who made the mistake of inviting Stalin into their *troika* of power. In his struggle for succession, Stalin first came up against Leon Trotsky, War Commissar, who had tasted of power and hungered for more. Their struggle can best be summarized by competing slogans—Stalin's, "Socialism is one country" and Trotsky's, "The Permanent Revolution."

To Marx, the reason for violent revolution and a radical change in productive relations was to introduce a new order of relations based on "democratic" principles. This Lenin might have tried to do. Under Stalin, what he understood of Marxism as interpreted by Lenin was superimposed upon a Russian-European revolutionary tradition. This resulted in a return to authoritarian rule.

Not that Stalin renounced world revolution for his "Socialism in one country," as Trotsky countered, but to Stalin, firm establishment of socialism in Russia came first. Trotsky held that the communists had not "even approached the task of creating a socialist society in Russia" and that "a genuine advance of socialist economy will become possible only after the victory of the proletariat in the most advanced countries of Europe." This dispute caused a schism down the middle of Russian

Communism. Trotsky was exiled, tried *in absentia,* sentenced to death during the bloody purge trials of 1936-39, and assassinated in Mexico City in 1940 by an obscure but dedicated Party member.

With this division in the Politburo, Stalin had a weapon against Kamanev, Zinoviev, and the other three members. One or two at a time, he accused them of counterrevolutionary activities, had them expelled from the Party, and later charged them with espionage for the Nazis. Four were tried and executed; one committed suicide on the eve of arrest. The survivor, Joseph Stalin, firmly entrenched as Secretary-General of the Russian Communist Party, had complete control of the *troika* of power: the Party, the State, and the secret police.

Like Lenin, Stalin was led to give new direction to communism by force of circumstances. Never admitting mistakes, he tried to justify his actions by reference to the writings and actions of the "great" Lenin. But Stalin was a basically dishonest thinker. He knew and used all the Marxist slogans, but, in the course of his 25 years in power, he so transformed the teachings of both Marx and Lenin that neither of them would have acknowledged these transformed teachings as his own.

Before the Bourgeois Revolution in many parts of Czarist Russia a revolutionary society called a soviet was organized among the workers of a single factory or among the peasants of one rural locality. During the Bourgeois Revolution of March 1917, these soviets combined into a large Soviet of Workers' and Peasants' Delegates. The Mensheviks subsequently organized soviets in the Czarist Army and Navy. Lenin used the organization of soviets in his November 1917 Revolution. Combined into city and village soviets under Stalin, they now elect the huge Union Congress of Soviets, which theoretically holds the ultimate power in Soviet Russia.

When Stalin discussed the relationship among the Party, the dictatorship, and the soviets, he was necessarily and expertly vague. He gave lip service to the ultimate goal of "pure" socialism when the state would "wither away."

According to Stalin, Lenin wrote that the dictatorship is exercised on behalf of the proletariat for the people of Russia. This proletariat is organized into soviets led by the Party. While the Party operates the dictatorship for the proletariat, and the dictatorship *is,* in its essence, the dictatorship of the Party, this does not mean that the Party *is* the dictatorship.

The soviets lost what constitutional authority they once had. The Party ruled and in turn was ruled by its Politburo (formerly *Presid-*

ium). At the top of this pyramid of power stood Stalin. A more complete and effective centralization of political, economic, and military power into one pair of hands had never been seen in history. Thus progressively less proletarian and less democratic under Stalin, the Party operated a highly centralized bureaucracy a form of government that was anathema to Lenin.

In 1929, Stalin abandoned Lenin's agrarian policy and proceeded with forced and bloody collectivization of peasants into state farms.

In 1934, Stalin denounced "egalitarianism." In Marxism, Stalin said, equality stood not for equalization of individuals but the abolition of classes.

Under Lenin, the rewards of power were modest, for he lived in the Kremlin in spartan simplicity comparable to his poverty-stricken exile. Under Stalin, with the definition of "ability" and "need" left to the Soviet rulers, strange were the inequalities of reward in the Soviet Union, running a gamut from degrading poverty, poor housing, and insufficient food and clothing, to a standard of living at the top which a Byzantine Emperor might well have envied. And this in a "classless society."

Stalin came to embrace the Russian nationalism of the Czars so vigorously that the organizations of international communism, the Comintern and the Cominform, were hard pressed to justify other communist parties positions as communists *and* nationalists with respect to each other. Internally, this caused little difficulty for the Soviet Communist Party because the nationalist expansion of Russian territory generated the power to establish communist regimes in countries where the local communist parties were unable to accomplish it by themselves.

In 1938, Stalin settled his long, long struggle with the Trotskyists— he announced that *socialism had been achieved in one country, in Soviet Russia.* Yet the progress to pure socialism and *the victory of socialism* was not complete, nor could it be as long as Communist Russia was surrounded by capitalist states. He believed with Lenin that ". . . it is inconceivable that the Soviet Republics should continue to exist for a long period side by side with imperialist states. Ultimately one or the other must conquer. Meanwhile, a number of terrible clashes between the Soviet Republics and the bourgeois states is inevitable."

To pursue his aims, Stalin made the following moves before World War II:

In 1924, he commenced long-continuing penetration into Outer Mongolia, for centuries nominally a part of China.

In January 1925, he divided semi-independent Turkestan into Turkestan and Uzbekistan and incorporated both into the Soviet Union as socialist republics.

In September 1939, in cynical partnership with Hitler, he attacked Poland and divided the Polish territory with the Nazis.

In November 1939, he attacked Finland in the "Winter War" of 1939-40 and obtained territorial and other concessions from free Finland.

In June 1940, he occupied the free Baltic States of Estonia, Latvia, and Lithuania and incorporated them into the Soviet Union as socialist republics.

World War II brought a terrible challenge to the Soviet Union. Despite a nonaggression treaty, Hitler turned from a stunning victory in Western Europe and, in June 1941, struck in strength against the Soviet Union. He overran most of European Russia and nearly defeated the Red Army. Timely logistic and military support from its Western allies helped to save the Soviet Union from defeat, although the Communist Party line holds that the glorious Russian people rose from the ashes of their cities to throw out the invaders. Aided by withdrawal of Nazi troops to defend the West, the Red Army rolled across Eastern Europe to Berlin. On May 7, 1945, Nazi Germany surrendered unconditionally to the Supreme Headquarters of the Western allies.

Far from grateful for the western democracies' economic and military support, which had saved it, the Stalinist regime felt even more insecure and threatened because of the display of their military power, and Stalin set about establishing a *cordon sanitaire* in Eastern Europe to protect the Soviet Union's western border. Employing a technique adapted from the Bolshevik seizure of power in Russia, the communist minority in a country first obtained participation in a coalition or popular front government. By moving into the ministries which controlled the police and the armed forces, an often bloodless *coup d'état* made possible seizure of power and established a "people's republic" and a dictatorship of the proletariat. Promised and delivered was distribution of the land to the peasants and of industry to the workers. Collectivization and nationalization programs came later. The hand of Soviet Communism was concealed, but very active. Except to maneuver troops along the border or to employ garrison troops to "preserve order" during a change of government, rarely was it necessary to use Soviet troops.

As Winston Churchill expressed it in a memorable speech in Fulton, Missouri, on March 5, 1946, "From Stettin in the Baltic to Trieste in the Adriatic, an iron curtain has descended across the continent." By April 1, 1948, the communist reorganization of the buffer states along the Soviet Union's western border into the communist bloc was complete. Subsequent forays into Greece, Turkey, and Iran were rebuffed by prompt action and resistance, thanks in no small degree to President Harry Truman's will and determination. One-third of Germany was under Soviet domination. Austria was divided, with Vienna in the Red zone. Yugoslavia and Albania soon had Red regimes in control. Strongly supported by Soviet Russia from Manchuria and Siberia, the Red Chinese People's Army defeated a disorganized, poorly trained, and disheartened Nationalist Army. On October 1, 1949, Mao Tse-tung proclaimed from Peking a new Chinese People's Republic, which the Soviet Union quickly recognized.

Except for dominated Finland, free but cowed Greece, Turkey, Iran, Afghanistan, and Japan, Soviet Russia was now surrounded by satellites or "People's Republics" with governments responsible to the will of the Communist International, that is, to Joseph Stalin and his Politburo.

5. WAR IN KOREA. Urged on by Red China and promised military advisers, arms, and munitions by the Soviet Union, on June 25, 1950, the North Korean People's Army struck in force across the 38th Parallel and fell upon the ill-prepared troops of the Republic of Korea. President Truman appealed to the Council of the United Nations, which vigorously denounced the North Korean aggression and both authorized the United States and requested all others of the United Nations to send military aid to South Korea. Thus the United States embarked on its first land war in Asia. The United States forces were not well prepared for the job. Disaster followed disaster for the United Nations' Command under General MacArthur, until the amphibious landing at Inchon turned the tide. By 19 November 1950, some American units stood on the Yalu River, the border with Red Chinese Manchuria. The People's Army of North Korea had been defeated and the end of the war was in sight. On 25 November, the "volunteers" of two Red Chinese route armies struck the ROK and American 8th Army troops. As General MacArthur put it, "The United Nations Command has met conditions beyond its control and its strength . . . we face an entirely new war."

Under the pressure of some 30 divisions of Red Chinese troops, the United Nations forces withdrew deep into South Korea, only to fight their way back to the 38th Parallel and defeat of the Chinese Armies. With United Nations and United States decisions that unification of Korea would not be accomplished by military force, negotiations for an armistice began at Kaesong, North Korea on July 10, 1951, with Admiral Turner Joy heading the United Nations delegation and with both

Chinese and North Korean generals on the other side of the table. The conference later moved to Panmunjon for better access for the United Nations Delegation, and the exasperating and frustrating negotiations continued for two years, while the war went on. On 19 July, 1953, the Chinese and Korean Communists agreed to an armistice on a demarcation line somewhat to the north of the 38th Parallel with a demilitarized zone. The Communists used the conference as a front for reinforcement and resupply of their defeated forces and as a forum for propaganda, vituperation, and vilification. For this, the United States paid the price of billions of dollars in treasure, 33,629 killed, and 103,284 wounded in action, over half of these casualties during the course of the two years of negotiation.

The United States had ended it first war for limited objectives in a shaky truce, as witness the frequent acts of sabotage, the armed attempt on the life of President Park, the capture of the USS *Pueblo* on January 23, 1968, and the shooting down of a reconaissance plane on April 15, 1969.

6. **THE COLD WAR.** Upon the surrender of the Axis powers which ended World War II, the people of the Western democracies had hoped for a real peace. Instead, we lived and still live in a world of insecurity. Although the United Nations had been established, Foreign Ministers met in conference with increasing frustration. Except for the liberation of a neutralized Austria (May 15, 1955), the conferees accomplished little. Germany, Korea, and Vietnam remain divided between communist and "free" regimes, and the German peace treaty remains unsigned. War has remained with us. The heavy burden of military expenditure has greatly increased. The Soviet Union and Communist China, in their different ways, challenge free nations everywhere in order to promote insecurity and to assist "indigenous revolution" in many countries of the free world. The communist determination to master the world has troubled mankind for fifty years and will continue to do so for many years to come. To invert Clausewitz, peace has become a continuation of war by other means.

A protracted worldwide conflict has been joined between, on the one hand, Western systems of government selected and supported by the consent of the governed, and on the other, authoritarian communist systems of government by "dictatorship of the proletariat." The former are based on a philosophy of unalienable human rights, freedom and dignity of the individual, and free choice under God. The latter are committed by written word and deed to the "systemic revolution" to over- throw every neutral, uncommitted, and democratic government in the world and to the establishment of communist dictatorships, atheistic or agnostic, and antagonistic to all religion. This is the Cold War.

7. **NIKITA KRUSCHEV.** Upon Stalin's death on March 5, 1953, Ni- kita Kruschev commenced a long struggle for accession to the power which Stalin possessed. The "hero of Stalingrad" as a lieutenant gen- eral, a member of the Presidium of the Party, and brother-in-law to Malenkov who initially succeeded to Stalin's position, Kruschev was delegated control of the Party Secretariat as First Secretary. In this po- sition, he assisted Malenkov with the disgrace of Lavrenti Beria, Chief of the Secret Police, his trial, and his execution. Employing a myth of "collective leadership", with control of the Party organization, Krus- chev was more merciful to the husband of his sister; he arranged a ma- jority of the Presidium to vote Malenkov out of office and assigned him an insignificant post in Asiatic Russia. Using the same methods, Krus- chev eliminated his opponents in the Presidium until he controlled the historical *troika* of power in the Soviet Union.

Kruschev was a dictator with minor differences. He appeared to feel the necessity to pay more attention to the opinions and advice of other members of the Presidium and to the consumer demands of the people than Stalin ever did. He frequently tried to justify his policies and his actions to the Russian people and to world public opinion. During his maneuvers to supreme power, it took six months for Kruschev to have the "collective leadership" acknowledge his authority as Chairman of the Communist Party and two years to arrange the replacement of Malenkov with Marshal Bulganin as Chairman of the Council of Min- isters. Yet the leadership of the Party moved as determinedly and even more smoothly and effectively than did Stalin to consolidate the gains within Russia and among the satellite states. On March 27, 1958, he replaced Bulganin as Chairman of the Council of Ministers. With changing strategy and tactics, lessening and increasing tension with the Western World, vacillating amiability, contrived crises, and threats of nuclear war, Kruschev's Presidium had the same goal: Communist domination of the entire world.

To achieve his ends without using Soviet troops, Kruschev called for "peaceful coexistence" and employed economic and political penetra- tion, infiltration, initiation, and support of "indigenous revolution." His "collective leadership" made these moves:

In 1953-1954, he attempted to bring Yugoslavia and Albania back into the Soviet bloc by state visits of Bulganin and himself and by receiving their reciprocal visits.

From 1955 to 1958, he experienced many instances of restlessness in the Eastern European satellites.

In 1956 during the revolt in Hungary and riots in Poznan, Poland, Kruschev used Red Army troops for bloody repression and installed Wladlyslaw Gomulka and Janos Kadar as "hard-line" chairmen of the Communist Parties of Poland and Hungary.

In January 1959, Castro assumed power in Cuba. As the communist nature of the Castro regime became apparent, Kruschev offered and supplied oil, arms, and money to support the Red Cuban economy.

In September 1959, Kruschev visited the United States and conducted talks with President Eisenhower which resulted in the euphoria of the "Spirit of Camp David" and the hope that "peaceful coexistence" with the Union of Soviet Socialist Republics was possible.

In April 1960, the Soviet Union finally was able to bring down one of the United State's U-2 reconaissance planes flying across the Soviet Union.

On May Day 1960, in Paris for a summit conference with President Eisenhower, Kruschev staged a dramatic performance of rage and disappointment at a press conference for the world press and walked out on the summit conference. The "hard line" returned.

In October 1962, Kruschev overreached himself and tried to establish on Cuban territory emplacements of intermediate-range ballistic missiles, a definite threat to the security of the United States. President Kennedy directed the United States Navy to quarantine Cuba from delivery of the Soviet missiles and demanded removal of those already delivered. Unable to support his merchant ships delivering the missiles with adequate naval forces, Kruschev backed down and removed the missiles.

In 1963, enemies in the Presidium of the Soviet Communist Party attempted to oust Kruschev from his Party and government posts. Kruschev quickly assembled the Central Committee and obtained sufficient support to retain his positions.

On October 5, 1964, Kruschev's final degradation came peacefully—no exile to Siberia, no propaganda trial and prison sentence, no secret firing squad—the Presidium and then the Central Committee of the Party simply voted him out of office. With pension, a country *dacha* and an apartment in Moscow, he retired and became a nonperson in Soviet Russia.

8. THE NEW "COLLECTIVE LEADERSHIP." Kruschev's successors were Alexi N. Kosygin, who became Chairman of the Council of Ministers, and Leonid I. Brezhnev, who became Chairman of the Presidium and First Secretary of the Communist Party; both, who had come up

through the party apparatus, were younger men than Kruschev. Kosygin has been an alternate or full member of the Politburo or Presidium of the Party since 1947. Brezhnev holds the rank of lieutenant general and formerly was a military-political officer in the Ministry of Defense. Indisputably in power, the Brezhnev-Kosygin regime is less liberal than was Kruschev, depends more upon the collective support of members of the Presidium than Stalin or Kruschev did, and has severely limited the adventures of the Soviet Union in the affairs of neutral and Free World countries.

Inherited from Kruschev, their belief in peaceful coexistence is strong and has brought them into conflict with the leaders of that former member of the monolithic Communist International, Communist China. The Brezhnev-Kosygin regime believes just as firmly as Lenin, Stalin, and Kruschev that the Soviet Union cannot continue to exist surrounded by imperialist, capitalist states.

9. CHINESE COMMUNISM. Also inherited from Nikita Kruschev, who had pulled the Soviet technicians out of Red China in 1960 and had steadfastly refused to give Chinese scientists assistance in developing an atomic or nuclear capability, was a quarrel with Chairman Mao Tse-tung and the Chinese Communist leadership. A complete split between the giants of International Communism occurred in 1963, when Kruschev recalled his Ambassador to Peking and left the Soviet Embassy manned by a fourth-level Chargé d'Affaires. They key to the dispute rests in the contrast between Kruschev's slogan of "peaceful coexistence" and economic, cultural, and political penetration of "capitalist" and nonaligned countries and, Chairman Mao's insistence on support of "indigenous revolution" in any part of the world with arms, ammunition, men, and money, and his adventures with guerilla warfare in many countries bordering China. As early as the 1950s, the Red Chinese had trained guerilla cadres from Vietnam, Laos, Thailand, Malaysia, and Burma, and had sent them home with arms, ammunition, other supplies, and military advisers.

In October 1950, Communist China's People's Liberation Army (PLA) troops occupied Tibet.

In 1962, from conquered Tibet, the People's Liberation Army fought an undeclared border war with the Republic of India.

From 1960 to 1967, Mao supported Castro's attempts to spread communism throughout Latin America by guerilla warfare in defiance of the Soviet Union's aim to communize these countries by peaceful penetration.

Disgusted with the corruption that had grown up around his revolutionary government, in June 1966, Mao called out his Red Guards to purify the regime in a so-called Cultural Revolution. Lasting well into 1968, this revolution led to breakdown of agriculture, industry, communications, and public order, and it brought Communist China to the brink of chaos. When Mao called on his People's Liberation Army to stop the revolutionary activities of the Red Guards, open civil war broke out in many provinces. For a time, it appeared that China might revert to the situation prevailing in the 1930s—many independent regions dominated by "war lords." However, with the assistance of the Army, by late 1968, the Red Guard Cultural Revolution was controlled.

10. VIETNAM WAR. The "indigenous revolution" in South Vietnam prosecuted by the guerilla soldiers of the Viet Cong commenced almost as soon as the French moved out of Indochina after signing the treaty of Geneva on July 20, 1954. With Vietnam divided between a Communist People's Republic in the north and a noncommunist dictatorship with democratic trappings in the south, the communist nature of the revolution soon became apparent. Separately and for different reasons, the Soviet Union and Communist China encouraged North Vietnam to support the Viet Cong by guerilla training, infiltration of individual replacements for the guerilla forces and of organized units of the North Vietnam Army, arms, munitions, and food supplies.

United States involvement in Vietnam began in the Eisenhower Administration with the establishment of a Military Assistance Advisory Group (MAAG) in Saigon with a small number of military advisers to help organize and train the South Vietnam Army. The size of the United States commitment increased under President Kennedy and even more extensively under President Johnson. After North Vietnamese motor torpedo boats attacked units of the United States Seventh Fleet in the Gulf of Tonkin, our commitment steadily grew, with the Tonkin Gulf Resolution of August 10, 1964 as legal authority. The Johnson Administration adopted a policy of gradualism to meet increasing resistance by committing first small then larger reinforcements until 550,000 officers and men in South Vietnam and thousands more in the Seventh Fleet were fighting the second war on the Asiatic mainland for limited objectives.

Against the guerilla warfare tactics of hit and run, the United States Armed Forces faced new problems of counterinsurgency. The Marines had learned to defeat guerillas in Nicaragua, and the United States

Navy had conducted guerilla warfare against the Japanese in China during World War II; but guerilla warfare in South Vietnam was different in terrain, philosophy, and sophistication. The policy of gradualism; the severe restriction on bombing targets in North Vietnam; the acceptance of enemy, privileged sanctuaries in Cambodia, Laos, and north of the DMZ—all served to limit the options and the operations of the field and area commanders in the prosecution of the war.

With its many troubles at home, Communist China could provide little logistic support to North Vietnam; eventually had to withdraw the hundred thousand coolies sent down to repair damages to roads, railroads, and bridges; and could not even guarantee the safety of Soviet shipments of war supplies across China. Thus the supply of arms and munitions fell to the Soviet Union, which delivered by far the largest amount by sea to the port of Haiphong and smaller North Vietnamese ports. Without this support, North Vietnam could not long have continued its participation in the war. To encourage Chairman Ho to come to the conference table, President Johnson announced, on March 31, 1968, a partial cessation of bombing of North Vietnam. Even with much heavier bombing of the Ho Chi Minh Trail in Laos and above the DMZ, interdiction of supplies and reinforcements into South Vietnam became a practical impossibility.

On May 13, 1968, the "peace conference," which President Johnson so ardently sought, met for the first time in Paris and promptly adjourned. The conferees for "our side" soon experienced once again the frustration of negotiating with the communists. Despite cessation of all bombardment of North Vietnam on November 1, 1968, in the twilight days of the Johnson Administration, the only accomplishment at Paris was agreement as to the shape and arrangement of the conference tables. The long war continued with more American casualties than during the Korean War.

11. THE BREZHNEV-KOSYGIN REGIME IN THE LATE 1960s. In pursuing its tactic of "peaceful coexistence," sometimes called a "détente" —the Brezhnev-Kosygin regime has been less active than any of its predecessors in attempting military or peaceful penetration of other countries. Attempts at economic and political penetration into newly established African countries were far from successful and were soon abandoned. Economic penetration of Latin American countries met with the resistance of Chinese Communist-supported efforts of Castro to promote guerilla warfare in several countries. In moving into the Middle Eastern cauldron of suspicion and hatred, infiltration into Le-

banon, Syria, Jordan, and Iraq were fiercely resisted. Basing efforts in the United Arab Republic on the Aswan Dam venture, the Soviet Union trained the Egyptian Army and equipped it with the most modern land and air weapons systems in the Soviet arsenal. This adventure blew up in their faces with humiliating defeat of the Egyptian armed forces in the Six-Day War of June 1967. To regain face, the Soviet Union again equipped Nasser's armed forces and assigned huge cadres to retrain his army and air force. Once again feeling his strength, Nasser seemed determined to make further attempts against Israel. The Soviet Union appeared to be anxious to calm the turbulence always present in the Middle East.

While attending a session of the United Nations Assembly in June 1967, Chairman Kosygin met for two days with President Johnson at a small college in Glasboro, New Jersey. No euphoria, no Spirit of Glasboro resulted. As junior member of the Brezhnev-Kosygin Regime, Kosygin had no authority to make commitments without approval of the Presidium of the Party.

At home in the European satellites, the collective leadership became alarmed at the liberalization in Czechoslovakia and Poland and at the restlessness of the people in the satellites and inside Soviet Russia. Border incidents with Communist China continued to trouble the leadership, culminating, on 2 March, 1969, in the armed clash on the Ussuri River border with Red China. Subsequently, both countries strongly reinforced their armed forces all along the border. The split became much more serious.

Even before the inauguration of President Nixon, the Kremlin began to show interest in a Summit Meeting with the new President, in American approval of the Nonproliferation Treaty, and in negotiations for limitation of strategic weapons.

Kremlin vacillation over the liberalization in Czechoslovakia and the intransigeance of Rumania exemplifies the split that often occurs in making decisions in the Presidium of the Party between the liberals and the conservatives, among the latter being numbered several active duty four- and five-star admirals, generals, and marshals. The decision to occupy Czechoslovakia came only after a close vote in the Presidium, with Soviet Armed Forces leaders opposed to that drastic action. That the Kremlin chose to implement the occupation with troops of several satellites as well as the Red Army, and in the name of the Warsaw Pact, was significant. Even more significant was the fact that Chairman Ceausescu of Rumania declined to participate and the clear proof that the Union of Soviet Socialist Republics was not ready to relax its control over one square foot of the territory of its satellites. The abruptness of this action, after extensive negotiations with the Czech leadership and assurances that such action would not be taken, confirmed the trend of the Brezhnev-Kosygin regime back toward the rigidities of Stalinism.

Let us not forget that, despite their intermittent amiability and personal goodwill visits to many countries, the collective leadership of Brezhnev and Kosygin had the same historical goal: communist domination of the entire world. They will not be persuaded to abandon this goal by any force of argument; because of any international agreement made or to be made; or for any reason of morality, justice, or international comity.

12. **WHY DO THE COMMUNIST RUSSIANS BEHAVE AS THEY DO?** In the period of the long civil war, the resistance of the White Russians and the attack on the Bolshevik regime by the Western powers (including the United States in Siberia) convinced Lenin that Soviet Russia was surrounded by capitalist-imperialist states determined to overthrow the Bolshevik regime. The terrible ordeal of World War II convinced Stalin of this and developed in him and other Soviet leaders a feeling of insecurity and fear at home and abroad. That we may better understand the protracted conflict in which we are embroiled, it will be well to compare the philosophies, objectives, and policies of the two world powers.

13. **THE GAGE (USA) AND THE MEASURE (USSR).** Rights and Privileges:

USA	USSR
Each person is important as an individual.	The state is important; the individual is important only as to the way he can serve the state.
He is a free American; he enjoys more freedom than any other individual in the world. He can go where he pleases, work anywhere, quit his job, and move on. No person can be forced to work for another.	He has no inherent freedom and dignity. He is severely restricted in movement, local and foreign. He works where he is ordered; he cannot quit his job. He can be assigned forced labor.
He can attend the Catholic or any Protestant church, the Synagogue, Bhuddist or Moslem rites—or be an agnostic or atheist.	Communists are antagonistic to all religion, persecute the performance of any religious services, and regard religion as an "opiate for the people" and a danger to the regime.

USA	USSR
The individual has freedom of choice and opportunity in many fields.	The individual is limited in his personal choice and opportunity. Communist dogma theoretically regards each person as alike in what he contributes and what he receives.
Each individual has the right to gather in assembly in any society, association, or organization which he may choose.	Right of assembly is severely restricted. No political parties other than communist are permitted, and membership in the Communist Party is rigidly controlled.
The individual has a right to say any thing he likes, short of slander or libel against others. This right extends to publishing, radio, television, the stage, motion pictures, and elsewhere in public or private.	Freedom in this area is very limited. Speaking, writing, and performing must not be contrary to public policy. Persons have been tried and sentenced, sent to concentration camps, or assigned long prison sentences for antistate speech or writing.
The government is the servant of the people; he who is least governed is best governed. It is a right and a privilege to vote in free elections on secret ballot to select any qualified individual to represent us on local, state, and federal levels. Voting is considered a duty by most citizens.	The people are the servants of the state which is managed by the Presidium of the Communist Party. Single-slate elections, with candidates selected by the Party, are held at all levels. A strong central government directing all activities of the people is an utter necessity.
The honest, law-abiding citizen considers the policeman a friend. His right to security of person and property and the inviolability of his home are protected by law and guarded by the police. Only criminals, conspirators, and the lawbreakers need fear the police, the "knock on the door."	Most citizens regard police (especially secret police) with suspicion and fear. None of these rights are protected by law or respected in practice. Many people fear the "knock on the door."
If charged with breaking the law, the citizen knows he will be treated and tried in accordance with established legal practices. He will be provided with defense counsel if unable to provide his own. He has the guarantees of freedom on bail, trial by jury, appeal of a conviction to higher courts, and *habeas corpus.*	The citizen can be arrested and jailed without trial; if tried, he has no right to jury, he has often been so severely handled during interrogation that he admits in court to faults and crimes of which he is not guilty, he has no right to bail or *habeas corpus;* public defenders often assist a client's conviction.

USA

Every person has a right to an education to the limit he will accept. Higher education is costly, but most qualified students can go to the university.

A person may work for another person or a corporation, or start a business of his own. He can own his home and acquire other property in his name or in the name of himself and associates. Subject to agreement of partners or management, he can conduct his own affairs. If he loses his job and cannot find employment, the government accepts the responsibility to help him find another or, for his welfare through social security, to provide unemployment insurance or work relief.

From his labor and ingenuity, a person is entitled to a fair share of that which he produces.

A person must not infringe on the rights of others. He must not so exercise his rights as to endanger the common welfare.

A man shall make his own way on his own merits; he shall be judged upon his record. Along with willingness to work, a man must aspire to do a competent job and be eager to improve his performance.

Americans believe the only true security in life is what a man stores up for himself. They also believe that no man, woman, or child should be allowed to go hungry. No man who is able to work should be a burden to society.

Citizens believe that Americans should try to live by the Golden Rule and to

USSR

Education is compulsory through age 15 or 16 and in cities to 17. Higher education is reserved to the highly talented, to sons of Party members and government officials, and to individuals who will advance the interests of the state.

Most citizens work for the state or state-owned corporations. Private enterprise is anathema to the Communist Party. The state owns all industry, housing, and property. The citizen is severely limited as to how much of his own affairs he may manage. He must work where and at the trade or profession to which the state assigns him. The government accepts responsibility for him in sickness and old age and assigns him new employment when he is well.

A citizen works for the wage of the job to which assigned, often too little to provide adequately for his needs.

The rights of citizens are considered of little importance by organs and officials of the government. Restrictive laws are rigidly enforced.

A man makes his living where and as told. Preference for advancement to what has been called the "elite" class is simpler for Party members.

Citizens may save if they *can*. The usual methods of providing for personal security—buying a house, purchasing shares in industry, operating a private business are not available under communism. The state provides such social security as there is.

"The end justifies the means." Under Stalin, this was distorted into a corol-

USA

cooperate for the common good. The Soviet philosophy of moral good is repulsive morally, religiously, and politically. Americans do not believe in the practicality of communist beliefs. They would hate to live under the terrorism and regimentation of their interim garrison-police regime, which may continue for a century.

USSR

lary, "If it is morally good for the Soviet Union to enter into agreements and commitments which serve her ends, then it is morally good to break agreements whenever they no longer accommodate her purposes."

In summary, then, every American is entitled to freedom and dignity of person and equality of opportunity. America is not perfect. Inequalities, inequities, and injustices do exist—some pronounced, others outrageous. *But,* under our democratic system of government and modified free-enterprise economic system, they are less pronounced, less prevalent, and less grievous than in any other country in the world. To the workingman for his labor, these systems have enabled America to produce more goods, more widely shared and more fairly divided than under any other system.

14. National Objectives. The United States and the Union of Soviet Socialist Republics have the following national objectives:

USA

To attain peace and security without sacrifice of either the rights of the individual or the present sovereignty we cherish. We will not wage a preventive war even against an archenemy of our system. We will not seek this goal by appeasement or "peace at any price."

To protect and maintain our way of life and form of government against any challenge at any cost. We do not require any other nation to conform to a similar way of life or form of government. We have no reason to attack the Soviet Union or Communist China.

USSR

Soviet leaders continue to proclaim abhorrence of war and a goal of peaceful coexistence between the two large world political and social systems. *But* peace to a Soviet Communist means continuation of the struggle by other means. This contrasts with Chinese Communist scorn of peaceful coexistence and demands for continuing world revolution in every noncommunist country. They revile the Soviet Communist short-range goals as abandonment of the principles of Marx and Lenin.

"Ultimately, the communist or capitalist system must conquer."—Lenin-Stalin. "We will bury you. Your grandchildren in America will live under socialism. We can blast you off the earth."—Kruschev. "The fundamental make-up (of the present era) is transi-

USA	USSR
	tion from capitalism to socialism; is an era of conflict between two opposite social systems, of the downfall of capitalism, and of the liquidation of the colonial system; and is the era of transition of more and more nations to socialism, of the triumph of socialism and communism on a worldwide scale." —*Military Strategy*, Moscow, 1968.
To maintain and raise our standard of living.	"Long before Goebbels, the people truly knew the meaning of 'guns before butter' . . . the Soviet Union is able to increase military expenditures to any level desired."—"The Soviet Military Budget." *Foreign Affairs*, Moscow, April 1964.
To seek and work for an effective world organization under the United Nations. World peace is an integral part of American peace.	Under the Stalin, Kruschev, and Brezhnev-Kosygin regimes, as a permanent member of the Security Council of the United Nations, the Soviet Union has proved intransigeant, using her veto many times to hamstring United Nations peace efforts.
Ultimately to eliminate warfare as a means of settling international disputes.	The United States is the embodiment of the social system, which they call capitalism and which the Soviets have sworn to eliminate. Only the United States has the strength to stand between the Union of Soviet Socialist Republics and its goal.
If war be forced upon us, we wish to win the war in such a way that it can be followed by a stable, livable peace.	The communists strive to stir up strife, support revolution, create chaos, and expect to build the "new order of pure socialism on the ruins of the old."

The Soviet Union's national objectives obviously go far beyond protecting its national security and its national interests. The important difference between the objectives of the two countries is that the Soviets intend to dominate the world by imposing their economic and social system on every nation in the world; the United States objectives leave states independent of coercion, "free to choose their own future and their own system."

15. NATIONAL POLICIES. From national objectives derive national policies. The national objectives of countries engaged in the protracted conflict remained remarkably constant through the post–World War II years, but their national policy has been as changeable as the wind in a typhoon. In the case of the United States, this change has been from confrontation and containment to an era of negotiation, as witness the following pronouncements.

> I believe that it must be the policy of the United States to support free peoples who are resisting attempted subjugation by armed minorities or by outside pressures. I believe that we must assist free peoples to work out their own destinies in their own way. I believe our help should be primarily through economic and financial aid . . .
> The free peoples of the world look to us for support in maintaining their freedoms. If we falter in our leadership, we may endanger the peace of the world—and we shall surely endanger the welfare of our own nation.
> The Truman Doctrine, before Congress, March 12, 1947.

On June 25, 1950, President Truman ordered the United States Armed Forces to the defense of South Korea.

> We, on our part, know that we seek only a just peace for all, with aggressive design against no one . . . Keeping the peace in today's world more than ever calls for the utmost in the Nation's resolution, wisdom, steadiness, and unremitting effort.
> President Eisenhower before the Congress, January 9, 1959.

To President Truman's Doctrine, President Eisenhower added the Doctrine of Massive Retaliation of Secretary of State John Foster Dulles. He used the United States Armed Forces to confront Soviet Communism in the Middle East with the landing of troops in Lebanon. His administration laid the basic plans for the emergency invasion of Cuba, which were almost executed in the Kennedy Administration.

> Our basic goal remains the same, a peaceful world community of free and independent states—free to choose their own future and their own system, so long as it does, it does not threaten the freedom of others.
> President Kennedy before the Congress, January 11, 1962.

President Kennedy accepted the basic policy of confrontation and containment, but, for the Dulles' policy of massive retaliation, he substituted "flexible response" and began to strengthen the conventional warfare capability of the United States Armed Forces to give his administration more options in the kind of military power to deploy in possible crises. He accepted President Eisenhower's concept of an invasion of Cuba by Cuban refugee troops and the altered CIA plan for landing them at the Bay of Pigs. He committed many more military advisers to the war in South Vietnam. In the missile crisis in Cuba, he confronted Kruschev with a blockade (called a quarantine) of Cuba. Fortunately, the Kremlin backed down, and Kruschev removed the threatening missiles from Cuba.

Speaking of the problems in Asia, President Johnson stated the policy of his administration:

> Most of the noncommunist nations of Asia . . . cannot resist the growing might and the grasping ambition of Asian communism. We did not choose to be the guardian at the gate, but there is no one else . . . we must have the courage to resist . . . We do not seek the destruction of any government, nor do we covet a foot of territory. But we insist that the people of South Vietnam . . . shall not have any government imposed upon them so long as we can prevent it . . . We cannot now dishonor our word, or abandon our commitment, or leave those who believed in us and trusted us to the terror and repression that would follow.

After the attack on our ships in the Tonkin Gulf, President Johnson committed the United States Armed Forces to the limited objectives of the war in Vietnam, the longest and, in many ways, the most onerous and costly war in United States history. When a communist take-over threatened in the Dominican Republic, he committed troops and aircraft which, with the help of Dominican troops, put down the attempted coup against the legitimate government.

Troubled by the increasing price of participation in the Vietnam War, on October 31, 1967, President Johnson ordered all bombing and bombardment of North Vietnam stopped. Not until May, 1968 did emissaries to a "peace conference" meet in Paris with an enemy determined to continue fighting while it talked. The United States conferees again learned the frustration of negotiating with communists.

President Richard Nixon, both before his election and after, stated his policy in support of his goals as follows:

> The Soviet Union is a power which is still attempting to expand around the world. The United States on the other hand is a power whose goal is only peace . . . Where peace is unknown, make it welcome; where peace is fragile, make it strong; where peace is temporary, make it permanent. After a period of confrontation, we are entering an era of negotiation. Let all nations know that during this administration our lines of communication will be open . . . the peace we seek to win is not victory over any other people, but the peace that comes "with healing in its wings" . . . But to all those who would be tempted by weakness, let us leave no doubt that we will be as strong as we need to be for as long as we need to be.
>
> October 17, 1968 and Inaugural Address, January 20, 1969.

In visits of state to our NATO allies and to seven countries in his trip around the world in July and August, 1969, President Nixon renewed the United States commitment to stand by its allies under the

NATO and SEATO Pacts, but he cautioned that he expected them to strengthen their economies and their police and military power, because never again should the United States have to intervene militarily. He also stressed his administration's continuing interest in Europe and the SEATO allies and stated that, as it has for more than a century, the United States would remain a Pacific power. Furthermore, he told the United States allies and friends, "I want to end this war . . . But we want to end it permanently, so that the younger brothers of our soldiers in Vietnam will not have to fight in the future in another Vietnam in some place in the world." He made it quite clear to both NATO and SEATO nations that many of our troops deployed around the world would be coming home—and soon.

As noted above, President Nixon expressed his policy to abandon confrontation for a policy of negotiation. We have seen that the long-range objectives of communism derive from their historic and continuing basic objective—a communist world controlled and directed from the Kremlin. Soviet and Chinese Communists bitterly disagree as to the immediate goals and the methods to be used to reach them. The immediate goal of Soviet Communism *seems* to be to reach their long-range goal by peaceful competition and coexistence, meanwhile encouraging the take-over of free countries by subversion and conspiracy short of actual engagement in war. The short-range goal of Chinese Communism is the immediate take-over of "capitalist," free-world, and uncommitted countries by any and all means, including the encouragement and spread of the *systemic revolution* and the support and prosecution of guerilla warfare from all communist countries into adjoining independent countries.

Under pressure from its ideological quarrel and its border incidents with Communist China, the Soviet Union has opted for the soft-line with the United States, and has confirmed its desire for peaceful coexistence. Even before President Nixon was inaugurated, the Soviet press put out feelers for summit and other negotiations with the new administration. In his report to the USSR Supreme Soviet on July 10, 1969, Foreign Minister Gromyko expressed Soviet readiness for negotiations with the United States on limitation of strategic arms to ban totally all nuclear arms tests, including underground tests, to ban use of the bottom of the seas for military purposes, and to ban effectively the use of chemical and biological means of warfare. He again expressed the Soviet desire for peaceful coexistence with the United States:

> The Soviet Union has always attached great importance to relations with the United States. We are for developing good relations with the United

States and would like these relations to be turned into friendly ones, since we are convinced that this would be in line with the interests of both the Soviet and American peoples. Our two countries are divided by deep class differences . . . but the Soviet Union has always . . . (believed) that in questions of maintaining peace, the Union of Soviet Socialist Republics and the United States can find common language.

For his part, President Nixon indicated a willingness to negotiate on these problems and on limitation or elimination of antiballistic missile systems, as well as on such political problems as regularizing the situation of West Berlin, assistance in settling the Vietnam War, and lessening the tensions between the countries. In his Inaugural Address, Nixon said:

> Those who would be our adversaries, we invite to a peaceful competition— not in conquering territory or extending dominion but in enriching the life of man . . . I know that peace does not come through wishing for it—that there is no substitute for days and even years of patient and prolonged diplomacy.

16. NEGOTIATING WITH THE COMMUNISTS. Negotiators from the West approach international negotiations with a tentative program, an attitude of gentlemanly conduct from another era, a belief that compromise is the essence of the negotiation process and that, with the communist negotiators, they have a common desire to arrive at a mutually acceptable agreement. To the communists, compromise is a sign of weakness; their negotiators arrive at the conference with a list of demands, to which they cling with fervor and devotion, often with no intention of making an agreement acceptable to our side, and they address their polemics not to our negotiators but to our people and the world at large to make propaganda while increasing their military pressure on "our side."

At Panmunjom and Paris, American negotiators hoped to achieve a solution to the problems under discussion which would lead to a peaceful and liveable postwar world. The communists used the conferences for propaganda, vituperation, and vilification and as a continuation of the war by another means. Meanwhile the slaughter of young American men went on. Being less eager for peace or accommodation, the "other side" had a distinct advantage because it felt that it could outwait and outlast our American impatience if it could not militarily defeat us. As Admiral Arleigh Burke, who had considerable experience negotiating with the communists, expressed it:

> When negotiating with the communists, you must simply ignore their propaganda, personal abuse, vituperation, and vilification of your country and your social system and hew to the line set for you with grim determination. You

can expect no "courteous discussion among gentlemen," adherence to protocol, or even rudimentary decency.

The conference at Panmunjom continues to meet to discuss violations of the armistice arranged there 16 years ago. Its latest accomplishment was release of the crew of the *Pueblo* after humiliating but necessary admissions by the United States that the ship had invaded North Korean waters, even though she hadn't. The *truth* of these admissions was categorically denied by the United States, but the *fact* of the admissions saved "face" for North Korea and led to the release of the *Pueblo's* crew.

President Nixon decided to continue negotiations in Paris while the fighting went on in Vietnam. From May 1968, the conferees from North Vietnam and the National Liberation Front on the "other side" and the United States and South Vietnam on "our side" met, never more than once a week. In the Spring of 1969, each party laid on the conference table a program for discussion; the "other side" used the conference for the usual polemics, vituperation, and vilification; no fruitful discussion resulted from any of the four programs.

17. NUCLEAR STALEMATE. In the years immediately following World War II, the United States possessed the known atomic or nuclear capability to destroy much of the Soviet Union without receiving unacceptable damage in retaliation. Speaking at a dinner in New York in March, 1949, Winston Churchill said:

> It is certain, in my opinion, that Europe would have been communized and London would have been under bombardment some time ago, but for the deterrent of the atomic bomb in the hands of the United States.

Much more rapidly than our experts thought possible, the Soviet Union caught up with the United States in the field of atomic and nuclear weapons and the vehicles to deliver them.

We have reached a condition of nuclear stalemate. The threat of devastation has become mutual. Creation of invulnerable deterrent forces by both the Soviet Union and the United States and a balance of such forces after a nuclear attack, which would make massive retaliation inevitable, combine to make all-out war unprofitable and to convince United States and Union of Soviet Socialist Republics leaders that initiation of a nuclear exchange would be suicidal. The establishment of a partial antiballistic missile screen around Moscow and the development of atomic and nuclear capability by Communist China confuse the situation, but strategic deterrent between the United States and Union of Soviet Socialist Republics seems to be still assured. Faced with nuclear stalemate, the communists have become more aggressive in limited and guerilla warfare and in promoting economic, cultural, and political penetration and subversion in independent states.

The United States must continue to have a strategy to maintain a deterrent force-in-being capable of delivering against a possible enemy so devastating a blow that he will not initiate nuclear attack. Our nuclear weapons must be so dispersed and mobile that a sufficient retaliatory capability will remain after a possible first strike by an enemy to inflict substantial destruction on the enemy homeland. The American people know that no United States objective will require our government to initiate a nuclear attack on any other nation, but our use of atomic bombs against Japan leads potential enemies to understandable doubt. Our government must strive to convince the Soviets and Communist Chinese as to the validity and integrity of this policy.

18. THE CHALLENGE OF SOVIET MILITARY POWER. The Soviet Union possesses a well-balanced military force, equipped with modern arms and weapons systems and trained to fight any kind of war. In a general war, in the communist view, the initial nuclear exchange would be but a prelude—a terribly devastating prelude—to a long and bitterly contested conflict with the objectives of defeating the enemy's armed forces and subjugating its people. To the contestant best prepared to conduct balanced operations with its remaining military forces would go the victory.

Soviet Army—The Soviet Army has about 2.5 million officers and men, organized into some 100 infantry divisions, 75 armored divisions and supporting units, plus an enormous trained reserve. The active divisions are well trained and equipped, are highly mobile, and possess great firepower. The troops are continuously trained to use nuclear weapons or to engage in conventional warfare, as conditions dictate.

Soviet Navy—During the decade of the 1960s, the Soviet Navy built up its surface strength significantly in cruiser, destroyer, helicopter carrier, and amphibious warfare capability and equipped its new types with modern, effective weapons systems, including a very accurate surface-to-surface missile designed to counter United States Navy superiority in carrier attack aircraft. Obviously determined to challenge American control of the seas, the Soviet Government employs this increasing naval strength in fleets and task groups in several seas to support its national policies. Operation of Soviet naval task groups in the Mediterranean Sea and the Sea of Japan has challenged the former United States naval superiority in those vital areas. Soviet naval maneuvers in the Atlantic and the Mediterranean have demonstrated their naval capability to operate at great distances from home bases, as witness the Soviet task group of two missile cruisers, two destroyers, and two logistic ships which maneuvered off the Florida coast before and during the launch of the Apollo 11 moon shot in July 1969, while this task group was enroute to communist Cuba.

Although the Soviet Navy has no attack carriers, its amphibious forces can be supported by missile cruisers and destroyers. Its contest for control of the seas is no longer limited to the radius of action of land-based aircraft. During the Korean War, the Soviet Navy demonstrated an uncomfortable technical proficiency in mine warfare.

Concentration on shipbuilding in recent years has provided a growing merchant fleet as well as increased capacity for naval construction. The Soviets employ this enlarged merchant fleet for competition on the ocean trade routes, for economic penetration, and for subversive activity in unstable political situations anywhere in the world.

Soviet Air Force—The Soviet Air Force possesses some 15,000 aircraft. Recent emphasis has been on development of air defense and ground-support aircraft, whose construction indicates a determination to have balanced armed forces capable of conducting any type of warfare ranging from guerilla war to total war.

Soviet Rocket Forces—Unlike the United States, Soviet missiles are designed, produced, and operated under a separate entity called "Rocket Forces." Soviet accomplishments in space and in missile tests into the Central Pacific demonstrate an intercontinental missile capability and development of multiple reentry vehicles. Especially in recent years, the Soviet Union has also greatly increased her capability to deliver nuclear weapons. It has been reported that they have produced many more ICBMs, hardened their launch sites, developed a fractional orbital bomb, installed an ABM system, produced advanced nuclear submarines (both for attack and missile launch), and produced the SS-9 missile capable of delivering a 25-megaton warhead. Some of these weapons would be exceptionally valuable for a devastating first strike. In judging these actions and accomplishments, it seems obvious that the Soviet Union intends to change her nuclear stalemate with the United States to a position of nuclear superiority. The Soviets have the capability to hit any target in Western Europe, England, China, or North America.

19. THE CHALLENGE OF CHINESE MILITARY POWER. Despite the division between the onetime friendly giants of International Communism and the serious internal disorders during and following the Cultural Revolution, the five million men under arms and the estimated five thousand combat aircraft of the Communist Chinese Armed Forces constitute a potentially powerful addition to the military strength of the communist world. These are the troops used to support military adventures and guerilla activity in countries along the borders of Communist China. The Chinese Communist armed forces are efficient and effective, as witness the decisive entry of Chinese "volunteers" into the Korean War.

Like the marshals of the Soviet Red Army, the Chinese Communist military leaders prefer to remain one country removed from the actual combat. Examples are the use of North Korean troops for the invasion of South Korea and the support of North Vietnamese troops in their infiltration into the war in South Vietnam following the guerilla war doctrine of Chairman Mao, in which they have been all too effective. In Korea, Communist Chinese troops showed up in the order of battle *only* when American troops threatened China on the border at the Yalu River. Should the Chinese border with North Vietnam have been threatened, as in North Korea, certainly Communist China would have intervened with "volunteers" from its Peoples Liberation Army in a determined attempt to retrieve the situation.

20. A POSTURE OF MILITARY STRENGTH. The United States believes that mutually deterrent forces will prevent total war. In addition, the United States must possess adequate conventional armed forces to provide our President with options in a critical situation to apply a gentle hint, a firm warning, a strong demonstration of force, or a solid blow at the proper time and place. Since World War II, our nuclear deterrent has had but little utility in the kind of economic, political, and military crises which have developed and may have but little usefulness in serious situations likely to develop in the future.

In peace and war, the United States Navy must possess the capability to gain and maintain control of any sea area we wish to use, despite the challenge of any aggressor, whether from the air above, the surface, or the depths below.

21. A POSTURE OF ECONOMIC STRENGTH.—We must also possess the economic strength required to support our military establishment and all the other needs of our people. For the past few years, we have experienced the most fabulously prosperous era of our economic history under our modified free-enterprise system. We have had 96 percent employment of employables, the largest gross national product with each

succeeding year surpassing the previous one, the greatest volume of exports, and the highest standard of living in the world.

By compromise between the demands of our military and the needs of our civilian establishments, our industrial establishment must be able to sustain the required expenditures without damage to our economy. Our economic system depends upon our ability to buy from other nations the raw products we must have to keep our industries operating efficiently *and* upon selling to other nations more products from our abundant production in agriculture and industry than we buy from abroad. We must frequently remind ourselves that the communist credo holds that there are elements in our "capitalist" system—the alternating periods of boom and severe depression—which will ultimately destroy it—*The Communist Dream*.

The United States Navy helps to promote a favorable economic climate and freedom of access to markets, so that increased foreign trade will be feasible and continually expanding.

22. A STANCE FOR NEGOTIATION.   For Americans who must negotiate with the communists, the following lessons from the past are important:

1. We must not demonstrate more eagerness than the enemy for negotiations. Such an attitude indicates to the "other side" that our determination is weak, that they hold the position of strength, and that they can outwait our side and win the contest.
2. Expect the "other side" to go to ridiculous lengths to score a propaganda point.
3. Do not expect the enemy to have the same objective as "our side"; he will use the conference to make propaganda against "our side" to attempt to win by negotiation what he could not win in battle.
4. Never make a concession for which the "other side" does not reciprocate.
5. Do not go to a conference with an enemy who intends to fight and kill our troops while talking.
6. If the "other side" procrastinates, break off negotiations, threaten to resume use of military force, and then use it if enemy remains recalcitrant.
7. Let the enemy earn your trust only by actions, not promises. Do not assume that you can accept the word of the "other side" as a valid agreement.
8. Swallow your anger and frustration; ignore insults and personal abuse; hew to the negotiation program set for you; a firm stance is more apt to produce acceptable agreements and reduce danger of escalation into total war.

As President Eisenhower expressed it:

We can have no confidence in any treaty to which the communists are a party, except where such a treaty provides within itself for self-enforcing mechanisms. Indeed, the demonstrated disregard of the communists of their own pledges is one of the greatest obstacles to success in substituting the rule of law for the rule of force.

23. A POSTURE OF MORAL STRENGTH. Vigilance is the price of remaining a free American. Freedom cannot remain static—it must be defended in every generation. International communism fights a continuing battle in all fields, lessening pressure here, increasing it there, sometimes appearing to go along with the force which resists it. We must not be misled by the devious twists and turns of communist strategy and tactics. Its determination to destroy the free institutions in independent nations never falters. Pressure will soon be applied where resistance weakens.

The economic strength, the freedom, and the security of our country rest upon the moral and spiritual vigor of our people and upon the continuing freedom of choice for the vast numbers of other peoples of the world. We owe our position of leadership in the noncommunist world today not so much to our economic power and military might as to the unusual kind of idealism we have presented to the world. We must be vigilant to maintain the opposite to the spurious moral code which Marx and Lenin gave to the communist world. If an objective be sound, we must always strive to achieve it only by means which are morally correct.

We must return to fundamentals. Our philosophy is dedicated to the belief that the individual must have an opportunity to develop his individual capacity—morally, intellectually, and materially—but that this freedom of opportunity entails certain individual responsibilities.

We must recognize Soviet and International Communism for what it is—an international conspiracy for power and conquest. It is powerful militarily and economically, but it is weak morally, for there is no basis in the ethics of mankind for the communist philosophy of moral good. The motivating force of communism is lust for personal power and position and their perquisites.

"What is it that the Gentlemen wish?" Patrick Henry asked almost 200 years ago "Is life so dear, or peace so sweet, as to be purchased at the price of chains and misery? Forbid it, Almighty God!"

In 1858, Abraham Lincoln said, quite simply, "As I would not be a slave, so I would not be a master."

In every communist dictatorship in the world, the communist leadership says, "I will not be a slave. I will be the master."

This is a vital and fundamental difference. Our nation covets nothing that the nations of the communist world possess. The United States has no objective, no policy, no reason to attack the Soviet Union or Communist China. Should the communist dictatorships turn their attention inward to try to eliminate the many inequities of their social system and refrain from intervention in the affairs of free and independent nations, the communist world and the western world would be able to work together and to enjoy free trade among nations, true peaceful coexistence, and immensely improved conditions for all peoples on this small planet.

APPENDIX 4

Military Law[1]

1. INTRODUCTION. Every naval officer should have a general knowledge of the fundamentals of military law. At the most unexpected times in his naval career, he may be called upon to perform some function in the administration of naval justice. He may have to act as prosecuting attorney if detailed as trial counsel of a special court-martial. He may be detailed or requested to act as defense counsel for some enlisted man who is being tried by court-martial. He may have to perform the dual duties of judge and jury member if ordered as senior member of a special court-martial (although he would not perform the duties of a judge if a military judge has been detailed to the case). If ordered to conduct a formal pretrial investigation (in accordance with Article 32 of the UCMJ), which must precede a general court-martial, he may find himself performing the equivalent of the grand jury in civilian life.

Military law comprises the body of rules prescribed by competent authority for the governing and regulation of the armed forces. The basic sources of military law include the Constitution of the United States, statutory enactments of Congress (UCMJ), executive orders of the President of the United States (MCM), directives issued by the Secretary of the Navy (JAG Manual), and decisions of the military and federal appellate courts (the U.S. Court of Military Appeals and the Supreme Court of the United States) for the naval services.

Constitution of the United States. The source of all our military justice may be found in the Constitution. Article 1, Section 8 of this document delegates to the United States Congress the power "To make

[1] By Lieutenant Commander Edward M. Byrne, JAGC, USN. Mr. Byrne is the author of *Military Law: A Handbook for the Navy and Marine Corps,* published by the U.S. Naval Institute. This book is an authoritative and up-to-date reference, covering in detail the duties of the preliminary inquiry officer, court member, president of a special court-martial, convening authority, summary court officer, legal officer, line of duty/misconduct investigating officer, trial counsel, and defense counsel; the broad sweep of military law for the nonlawyer; the changes of UCMJ effective 1 August 1969; and the pertinent decisions of COMA.

591

Rules for the Government and Regulation of the land and naval forces." In another paragraph of Section 8 Congress was given similar authority as regards the militia (U. S. Army).

Uniform Code of Military Justice (UCMJ). Pursuant to its Constitutional authority, Congress enacted the Articles for the Government of the Navy and the Articles of War (for the Army). These systems of military law remained separate until 1950. On 5 May 1950, Congress passed the Uniform Code of Military Justice. Its provisions are applicable to all the uniformed services.

Manual for Courts-Martial (MCM). In enacting the UCMJ, Congress specifically delegated to the President the responsibility for prescribing the procedure and rules of evidence for this uniform code utilizing the federal rules as his guideline. Pursuant to this authority the President of the United States, by executive order, promulgated the Manual for Courts-Martial. It was prepared by a joint committee of the armed services.

Manual of the Judge Advocate General of the Navy (JAG Manual). In drafting the UCMJ, it was recognized that certain matters could best be regulated within the individual services. The Secretary of the Navy was granted authority to promulgate these rules. These rules are contained in the JAG Manual and are applicable to the Navy and Marine Corps.

U. S. Court of Military Appeals (COMA). The court, established by Congress, is the highest military court in the military judicial system. It consists of three civilian judges who are appointed by the President of the United States, by and with the advice and consent of the Senate, for a term of fifteen years. Article 67 of the UCMJ discusses the Court.

The Court of Military Appeals basically determines questions of law. For example, in determining what the law is, the Court interprets and, if necessary, modifies the UCMJ, the MCM, the JAG Manual, and other regulatory publications of legal efficacy. It applies Supreme Court decisions of constitutional import to the military judicial system unless they are excluded directly or by necessary implication by the provisions of the Constitution itself.

The *Court of Military Review* is a lower court established within the office of each Judge Advocate General. These lower courts review questions of both law and fact. Sentences, as approved, that extend to dishonorable or bad conduct discharge, to dismissal of an officer, cadet, or midshipman, or to confinement for one year or more; or that affect a general or flag officer, must be reviewed by a Court of Military Review.

2. THE PRELIMINARY INQUIRY AND PREMAST SCREENING. When a service man is reported for an offense, the report slip (entitled the "Report and Disposition of Offenses"—NavPers 2696) is routed to an officer of the command for a preliminary inquiry (i.e., an investigation). The investigation of the preliminary inquiry officer should determine if the reported misconduct was actually committed by the person on report and if the reported misconduct is an offense under the UCMJ.

All information and recommendations concerning the reported misconduct is assembled and presented to the Executive Officer. This would include a completed Charge Sheet (DD Form 458) if the preliminary inquiry officer recommends that the case be resolved by a court-martial.

The Executive Officer is generally empowered by the Commanding Officer to dismiss any case if the charge is minor or if the charge is unwarranted by the evidence. If the facts and circumstances warrant, the Executive Officer presents the case to the Commanding Officer. The Commanding Officer has several alternatives. He may:

(1) Dismiss the charges;
(2) Return the record for further investigation;
(3) Hear the case at Captain's Mast;
(4) Refer the case to a court-martial;
(5) Refer the case to a pretrial investigation;
(6) If he considers the case may warrant a general court-martial, he may refer the case to a pretrial investigation required by Article 32 of the UCMJ. Members of the armed forces, except those attached to or embarked on ships, have the right to refuse punishment by Captain's Mast and demand trial by court-martial in lieu thereof.

3. CONDUCT OF CAPTAIN'S MAST. Captain's Mast should be conducted with dignity in a suitable location. Mast is no longer held before the mainmast as it was in the days of sail. The Executive Officer now designates an area of the ship spacious enough to accommodate the necessary number of accused persons, witnesses, and other persons involved. The area should be reasonably private and should be capable of being transformed into a place of appropriate dignity. A portable desk or lectern is provided for the Commanding Officer's use.

The Chief Master-At-Arms or other senior petty officer is detailed to maintain order and ensure that proper military etiquette is observed. If feasible, the following personnel should be present: the Legal Officer,

Division Officer of each accused, the accused, witnesses for and against the accused (including the preliminary inquiry officer), a yeoman, and the Chief Master-At-Arms.

The Division Officer of each accused is informed of the nature of the offense in order that he may be able to speak properly for the accused. The Division Officer should review the man's service record and talk with the leading petty officer of the division to obtain his opinion of the accused's reputation. It is important that the accused present an excellent personal appearance and understand the essential features of the mast procedure.

The principals are assembled about 15 minutes prior to the scheduled time of mast. The Chief Master-At-Arms inspects each man for correctness of uniform and appearance and instructs him in the procedures at mast. The accused and all witnesses who will appear at mast are advised of their rights under Article 31, UCMJ. In some commands, the Commanding Officer himself prefers to give this warning or repeats it during the mast proceedings. The accused men usually face the lectern in one rank about three paces in front of it. Witnesses fall in on the left side of the lectern, and Division Officers and officer witnesses fall in on the right side of the lectern. The Chief Master-At-Arms informs the Executive Officer that mast is ready. The Executive Officer advises the Commanding Officer of that fact.

As the Commanding Officer reaches the mast area, the Chief Master-At-Arms calls "Attention on deck," and after the Commanding Officer has assumed his position behind the lectern states: "Hand salute. Two." After the Commanding Officer returns the salute, the cases are called. The Chief Master-At-Arms calls each man forward by name and the man takes position one pace in front of the lectern and uncovers. The Commanding Officer either warns the accused in accordance with Article 31 or advises the man that the warning previously given is still effective. Most Commanding Officers then consider the report of preliminary investigation and ask witnesses appropriate questions to establish as clearly as possible the nature of the offense. After all witnesses against the accused have been heard, the Commanding Officer asks the accused if he desires to make any statement or to present matters in defense, mitigation, or extenuation. The accused is privileged to question witnesses against him. The Commanding Officer, at this state of the proceedings, acts to assist the accused to protect his rights and to see that his case is fairly heard. After hearing all of the evidence, the Commanding Officer asks the man's Division Officer questions concerning the man's record, reputation, and performance of duty.

After completion of this procedure, the Commanding Officer announces his decision. He may:

(1) Dismiss the charges;

(2) Excuse the offense with or without a warning;

(3) Determine guilt and impose nonjudicial punishment as authorized under Article 15, UCMJ;

(4) Refer the case to a summary or special court-martial or recommend such trial to a superior;

(5) Order a formal (Article 32, UCMJ) pretrial investigation if offenses appear serious enough to warrant possible recommendation to trial by general court-martial; or

(6) Postpone action pending further investigation or for other reasons.

If the Commanding Officer has imposed nonjudicial punishment, those men who have been punished are advised of their rights to appeal. Appeals from nonjudicial punishment in accordance with paragraph 135, MCM, must be made in writing via the Commanding Officer to his immediate superior within a reasonable time, usually considered to be 15 days after imposition of punishment.

The Commanding Officer writes the disposition of each case on the NavPers 2696 (Report and Disposition of Offenses) as he awards punishment at mast or has someone else make such entry. Upon completion of the last case, the Chief Master-At-Arms orders "Hand salute. Two." The Commanding Officer returns the salute and retires.

After the imposition of nonjudicial punishment, the Executive Officer, or someone under his direction, ensures that all necessary steps are taken immediately to execute punishments not suspended by the Commanding Officer. Other officers ensure that appropriate entries are made in the Unit Punishment Book, that punishments are recorded in the Log or Station Journal, and that proper service record entries are made.

The Navy Department advocates the use of nonjudicial punishment in every possible case where the ends of justice and naval discipline may be attained by its use. Mast proceedings are brief and direct, and, most important, the punishment is prompt. This is far more conducive to good discipline than punishment deferred long after the commission of an offense.

4. SUMMARY COURTS-MARTIAL. The function of the summary court-martial is to exercise justice promptly for relatively minor offenses under a simple form of procedure. Any person subject to the UCMJ, except officers, warrant officers, cadets, aviation cadets, and midshipmen, may be tried by summary court-martial. A summary court-martial by law is composed of one commissioned officer. Whenever practicable, the summary court should be a lieutenant in the Navy or captain in the Marine Corps, or higher. A summary court-martial may be convened by any officer having authority to convene a general or special court-martial or the commanding officer or officer-in-charge of any command when empowered by Article 24 of the UCMJ or the JAG Manual.

In cases where only one officer is attached to a vessel or station, the Commanding Officer shall be the summary court-martial of that command (or detachment) and shall hear and determine all summary court-martial cases brought before him. When more than one officer is present in a command, a subordinate officer shall be appointed summary court-martial. The summary court-martial officer is not sworn as such. He performs his duty under the sanction of his oath of office.

A reporter is not ordinarily appointed for summary courts-martial, but the convening authority may, if he wishes, order any person under his command to perform such duty. If appointed, the reporter is to keep a true record of the case. The appointment of a reporter need not be in writing.

The examination of witnesses, who testify under oath, is conducted by the summary court-martial. If the convening authority of a summary court-martial, or the summary court-martial, is the accuser of the person or persons to be tried, it is discretionary with the convening authority whether to forward the charges and specifications to superior authority with a recommendation that the summary court-martial be convened by the senior. Although the fact that the convening authority or the summary court-martial is the accuser in a particular case does not invalidate the trial, such a practice is inadvisable in the interest of military justice.

An enlisted person who is brought before a summary court-martial for trial must signify his willingness to be tried by such a court by signing a statement to that effect in the record. If he objects, he may be ordered to be tried by a general or special court-martial, as may be appropriate. Enlisted men usually do not object to trial by a summary court-martial because its limits of punishment are more restricted than those of other courts-martial.

It is the duty of the summary court-martial to advise the accused as to his rights on a variety of matters including: the general nature of the charges, who appointed the court, the name of the accuser, the maximum sentence which the court can adjudge, the names of witnesses and the right of the accused to cross-examine them, the right to call his own witnesses and produce evidence in his own behalf, the right to testify or remain silent, and the right to produce evidence in his own behalf in the event he is convicted. (MCM 79d).

For punishments authorized, see UCMJ, Article 20; MCM, Chapter XXV; and MCM, paragraph 16b.

In case of acquittal, the accused is so informed by the summary court-martial. In case of conviction, the findings and sentence are announced to the accused during the trial. The results of the trial are entered in the ship's log, an entry is made in the man's service record in the event of conviction, and an entry is made in the record of trial consisting of page four of the Charge Sheet (DD Form 458). If the commanding officer or higher reviewing authority so directs, the summary court must summarize the evidence and attach it to the record for review. However, even this summarization is not required if the court-martial has resulted in a finding of not guilty as to all charges and specifications.

5. SPECIAL COURTS-MARTIAL. Some of the special court-martial convening authorities include commanding officers of ships, shipyards, bases, or stations; commanding officers of all battalions, squadrons, units, and activities of the Navy; the commanding officer or officer in charge of a separate or detached command if designated by a flag or general officer in command; and any commanding officer whose subordinates in the tactical or administrative chain of command have authority to convene special courts-martial. Any person who can convene a general court-martial can convene a special or summary court. Officers and enlisted men may be tried by special court-martial for any offense (with the exception of capital offenses) that the convening authority does not deem serious enough to warrant trial by general court-martial.

A special court-martial is composed of any number of members, but not less than three. The accused is entitled to be represented by one or more defense counsels. The government is represented by one or more trial counsels. A bad conduct discharge (a BCD) may not be adjudged unless a certified lawyer counsel (see Article 27b of the UCMJ) is detailed to represent him and a military judge is detailed to the trial, except in any case in which a military judge could not be detailed because of physical conditions or military exigencies. This means that only under rare circumstances, and for compelling reasons, may such a trial commence without a military judge detailed. "Mere inconvenience" is not sufficient. A verbatim record of the proceedings is required.

In every non-BCD case the accused must be afforded the opportunity to be represented by a certified lawyer counsel. If the accused so requests, such a counsel must be obtained unless physical conditions or military exigencies prevent such detailing.

The trial counsel in a special court-martial is not required to be a certified lawyer, but it is strongly recommended that if the accused is represented by such counsel, the government be so represented.

Officers or enlisted men may be temporarily attached to the command of the convening authority for court-martial duty as a member of the court or as trial or defense counsel.

The officer of highest rank on the court is the president, and the others are members. A president may have to act as both judge and member, if a military judge is *not* detailed to the court. If a military judge is detailed, he presides in court, regardless of his relative seniority in comparison with the president. In such a case, the president would be considered the equivalent of the foreman of a jury, and would speak on behalf of the other members and preside when the court is closed for deliberations.

If a military judge is not detailed to the court, the president presides. He would then be both the judge and a member of the court. The president sitting without a military judge would then rule upon such matters as the admissibility of evidence, competency of witnesses, continuances, adjournments, recesses, motions, order of the introduction of witnesses, and the propriety of counsel's arguments. (See paragraph 57 of the MCM.) As a member he weighs the evidence presented to the court and decides on the guilt or innocence of the accused and participates with the other members in the awarding of an appropriate sentence. The trial counsel acts as prosecuting attorney and conducts the case for the government; the defense counsel acts as defense attorney for the accused.

If an enlisted person requests enlisted members in writing, he may not be tried by a special court-martial unless at least one-third of the court is comprised of enlisted persons (unless eligible enlisted persons cannot be obtained because of physical conditions or military exigencies). Enlisted members shall not be members of the same company, air squadron, ship's company, or corresponding unit. When enlisted members cannot be obtained, the court may be convened and the trial held without them, but the convening authority must explain his reasons in detail in a written statement appended to the record. Whenever possible, the senior member should be an officer of a rank not below that equivalent to lieutenant in the Navy, and no member of a court-martial should be junior to the accused in rank or grade (MCM 4 and 5b). For punishments authorized, see UCMJ, Article 19, and MCM 15b and 125-127.

6. GENERAL COURTS-MARTIAL. A general court-martial is the highest tribunal in military law. It is convened for the trial of persons subject to the UCMJ. General courts-martial may adjudge the sentences of death, dismissal, dishonorable discharge, confinement at hard labor, and any punishment authorized to be inflicted by any other court. General courts-martial may be convened by the President, the Secretary of the Navy, the commander-in-chief of a fleet, the commanding officer of a naval station or larger shore activity beyond the continental limits of the United States, and such other commanding officers as may be authorized by Article 22 of the UCMJ and the JAG Manual.

A general court-martial is composed of not less than five commissioned or warrant officers, enlisted persons if an enlisted accused has so requested in writing, and a military judge. The MCM requires that the president shall have rank at least equivalent to that of a lieutenant in the Navy, but the Navy Department has long maintained a policy that he should be a senior officer. For trial of an officer, all members, except the military judge, should be senior to the accused.

As with special courts-martial, an accused enlisted person has a right to trial by a general court-martial composed of at least one-third enlisted members.

The military judge of a general court-martial is appointed by the convening authority. He must be a commissioned officer who is a member of the bar of a Federal court or of the highest court of a State of the United States and be certified to be qualified for duty as a military judge by the Judge Advocate General of the armed service of which he is a member. The military judge may consult with members of the court only in the presence of the accused, trial counsel, defense counsel, and reporter. A military judge, whether detailed to a special or general court-martial, performs substantially the same functions during trial as a civilian judge in a federal court. He does not vote with the members of the court.

7. INVESTIGATION OF CHARGES. The MCM requires the convening authority to make or cause to be made a preliminary inquiry into the charges sufficient to enable him to make an intelligent disposition of them. If the incident is not of a serious enough nature to warrant referral to the Naval Investigative Service (see SecNavInst 5430.13), the Commanding Officer will normally refer the responsibility for conducting the preliminary inquiry (i.e., the investigation of the case) to a junior officer attached to his command. He is the *Preliminary Inquiry Officer*.

This inquiry is usually informal. It may consist only of an examination of the charges and the summary of the evidence which accompanies them when unnecessary to investigate further. In other cases it involves a more extensive investigation and the collection of evidence. As a very minimum, the preliminary inquiry officer should attempt to resolve such questions as:

1. Whether the reported misconduct actually occurred;
2. Whether the misconduct constituted an offense under the UCMJ; and
3. The amount of evidence present to link the accused with the offense.

Paragraph 32b of the MCM states that it "is not the function of the person making the inquiry merely to prepare a case against the accused. He should collect and examine all evidence that is essential to a determination of the guilt or innocence of the accused, as well as evidence in mitigation or extenuation."

Article 32, UCMJ, provides that no charge shall be referred to a general court-martial for trial until a thorough and impartial investigation has been made. This is called a pretrial investigation and is separate and distinct from the preliminary inquiry. Under certain limited circumstances, a court of inquiry or formal investigation will suffice as a pretrial investigation as required by Article 32, UCMJ. (See 0908, JAG Manual.)

8. PRETRIAL RESTRAINT. Prior to disposition of an accused's case, military authorities may consider some type of pretrial restraint may be necessary. The type of restraint required depends upon the particular reason for the restraint. There are three types of pretrial restraints: confinement, arrest, and restriction in lieu of arrest.

a. *Confinement.* This is the physical restraint of a person, generally in a brig or guardhouse. It may only be imposed if deemed necessary to ensure the presence of the accused at the trial or because of the seriousness of the offense involved. For example, a person charged with an offense normally tried by summary court-martial ordinarily should not be confined prior to trial.

b. *Arrest.* Arrest is moral restraint imposed upon either officers or enlisted men by oral or written orders of competent authority limiting the person's personal liberty pending disposition of the charges. For example, an order for a person to remain within his quarters or barracks would constitute an arrest. The restraint is not enforced by physical force but by virtue of the accused's moral and legal obligation to obey the order. A person in arrest cannot be required to perform his full military duties. He can, however, be required to do ordinary cleaning or policing of his personal area and to take part in routine training or duties not involving the exercise of command or the bearing of arms.

c. *Restriction In Lieu of Arrest.* Restriction is a restraint on the liberty of the individual imposed by an order directing him to remain within certain specified limits. Although very similar to the status of arrest, it is a lesser restraint because it involves broader limits and permits the restricted person to perform his military duties. For example, restriction in lieu of arrest would encompass the limits of a naval or marine base less certain areas. Restriction in lieu of arrest is generally imposed either because the accused's presence during an investigation of his conduct may be necessary or because restriction prevents further exposure to the temptation of misconduct similar to that for which he is already under charges.

No punishment associated with the pretrial restraint (other than minor punishments for infractions of discipline while confined) may be imposed either prior to trial or until the sentence has been ordered executed after trial. If an accused is compelled to work with sentenced prisoners, performing hard labor under the same conditions and directives and if he receives the same treatment accorded such other prisoners, he is being "punished."

Any officer placed under arrest or restriction must confine himself to the limits assigned him under pain of disciplinary action. He cannot visit his commanding officer or other superior officer officially unless he is sent for or, in case of business requiring attention, until he has made a written request to do so.

An officer placed under arrest or restriction aboard ship should not be confined to his room or deprived of the proper use of any part of the ship to which he had a right before his arrest. If also suspended from duty, he may not visit the bridge or quarterdeck, unless the safety of the ship so dictates. Similarly, confinement or restraint on a naval shore station shall not be unduly rigorous.

9. TYPES OF ADMINISTRATIVE FACT-FINDING BODIES. A fact-finding body may be either a court of inquiry or an investigation. Investiga-

tions are of two types: formal and informal. Therefore, there are really three types of fact-finding bodies: courts of inquiry, formal investigations, and informal investigations.

The proceedings of inquiries and investigations are in no sense a trial of an issue or of an accused person. Detailed instructions concerning courts of inquiry and investigations are contained in the JAG Manual.

Court of Inquiry. Article 135, UCMJ, provides as follows:

> a. Courts of inquiry to investigate any matter may be convened by any person authorized to convene a general court-martial or by any other person designated by a Secretary of a Department for that purpose whether or not the persons involved have requested such an inquiry.
>
> b. A court of inquiry shall consist of three or more officers. For each court of inquiry the convening authority shall also appoint counsel for the court.
>
> c. Any person subject to this Code whose conduct is subject to inquiry shall be designated as a party. Any person subject to this Code or employed by the Department of Defense who has a direct interest in the subject of inquiry shall have the right to be designated as a party upon request to the court. Any person designated as a party shall be given due notice and shall have the right to be present, to be represented by counsel, to cross-examine witnesses, and to introduce evidence.
>
> d. Members of a court of inquiry may be challenged by a party, but only for cause stated to the court.
>
> e. The members, counsel, the reporter, and interpreters of courts of inquiry shall take an oath or affirmation to perform faithfully their duties.
>
> f. Witnesses may be summoned to appear and testify and be examined before courts of inquiry as provided for courts-martial.
>
> g. Courts of inquiry shall make findings of fact, but shall not express opinions or make recommendations unless required to do so by the convening authority.
>
> Each court of inquiry shall keep a record of its proceedings, which shall be authenticated by the signatures of the president and counsel for the court and forwarded to the convening authority. In case the record cannot be authenticated by the president, it shall be signed by a member in lieu of the president; in case the record cannot be authenticated by the counsel for the court, it shall be signed by a member in lieu of the counsel.

Investigations. *Formal investigations* may consist of one or more commissioned officers. They are convened by a written appointing order and utilize a formal-hearing procedure. The appointing order *may* direct that the body take all testimony under oath and record the proceeding verbatim. Persons who may be parties may *not* be designated such unless such designation is expressly authorized in the appointing order.

A formal investigation does not have the power to subpoena witnesses.

Informal investigations need *not* be conducted by officers. Senior enlisted persons or civilian employees of the Department of the Navy may serve as members. They may be convened orally and are ordinarily not directed to take testimony under oath or to record testimony verbatim. These investigations utilize informal procedures in collecting evidence. They may *not* designate any persons or parties ᵗo the investigations, nor do they possess the power to subpoena civilian witnesses. For further information on fact-finding bodies, the JAG Manual should be consulted.

10. OTHER INFORMATION SOURCES. The Judge Advocate General of the Navy prepares, and the Bureau of Naval Personnel distributes, special and summary court-martial trial guides and other instructional material for use in courts-martial. They are "NavPers" publications and may be ordered through stock points for such materials. The *JAG Journal* publishes timely and informative articles relating to military law. It is available in most ships and stations.

Roads to a Naval Commission

1. **COMMISSION OPPORTUNITIES.** There are some 20 roads to a naval commission in the Regular or Reserve navy, on active or inactive duty, as line or staff officers. Line officers are specifically trained for command afloat and in the air; staff officers reflect specialized duties in such areas as supply, civil engineering, medicine, religion, and law and exert command over activities within their specialty. Officers' occupations fall into two major categories: operations and management *and* scientific and technical. The Regular Officer Programs include the U. S. Naval Academy, Naval Reserve Officer Training Corps (NROTC Midshipmen), Navy Enlisted Scientific Education Program (NESEP), Augmentation, Limited Duty Officer (LDO) Program, and Warrant Officer (WO) Program. The Reserve Officer Programs include Naval Reserve Officer Training Corps (NROTC College Students), Reserve Officer Candidate (ROC), Aviation Officer Candidate (AOC), Naval Aviation Officer Candidate (NAOC), Air Intelligence Officer (NAOC-AI), Aviation Reserve Office Candidate (AVROC), and Officer Candidate School (OCS) programs. The Direct Appointment Program offers commissions in the professional and certain specialty fields for active and inactive duty. The Staff Corps Programs provide officers for the Medical, Dental, Medical Service, Nurse, Chaplain, Judge Advocate General's, and Civil Engineer Corps. Women Officer Procurement certainly provides quality officers for the Staff Corps and the Line. Graduates of the U. S. Merchant Marine Academy, state Maritime Academies, and the U. S. Coast Guard Academy are to be found as officers abroad merchant, Coast Guard, and Navy ships. These programs are briefly described in this appendix. Complete information on programs for a naval commission may be obtained in the *Naval Officer Programs Counseling Guide* and the *Recruiting Manual* by writing the nearest Office of Naval Officer Procurement or main Naval Recruiting Office or Recruiting Division (Pers-B6), Bureau of Naval Personnel, Washington, D.C.

The U. S. Naval Academy

2. BACKGROUND AND FACILITIES. Founded in October, 1845, at Annapolis, Maryland, the U. S. Naval Academy occupies the unique position of being the only institution in this country established and maintained for the sole purpose of providing career officers for the naval service.

From small beginnings in old Fort Severn at the mouth of the Severn River, the Academy has expanded to a brigade of about 4,100 midshipmen. Graduates who complete the strict educational curriculum and are physically qualified are commissioned as ensigns in the Navy or as second lieutenants in the Marine Corps.

Naval Academy life centers about Bancroft Hall, which houses all members of the brigade and contains such facilities as the galleys and mess hall, a store, soda fountain, recreation rooms, post office, sick quarters, and barbershops. Situated within close walking distance of Bancroft Hall, the buildings of the Academic group are named after naval heroes and contain modern laboratories for chemistry, physics, electronics, fluid mechanics, thermodynamics, electrical engineering, and many other subjects. The Yard and the Naval Station contain fine playing fields, tennis courts, an 18-hole golf course, a field house, a gymnasium, swimming pools, and a rifle range.

3. MISSION. The Mission of the U. S. Naval Academy has been officially stated as follows:

> To develop midshipmen morally, mentally, and physically and to imbue them with the highest ideals of duty, honor and loyalty in order to provide graduates who are dedicated to a career of naval service and have potential for future development in mind and character to assume the highest responsibilities of command, citizenship, and government.

4. THE REGIMEN. The Naval Academy is administered by its Superintendent, who is a flag officer of the line of the Navy, under the direction of the Chief of Naval Personnel. A system of rotation of midshipmen officers affords maximum opportunity for first class midshipmen to exercise tactical and administrative leadership.

From early Monday morning until after noon meal formation on Saturday, life for a midshipman is very rigorous. From reveille to taps, he follows a closely scheduled routine. The academic day is divided among individual study and group-recitation periods, laboratory work, and practical drills.

Life at the Academy is by no means "all work and no play." On Saturday afternoons, the midshipman may attend an interesting athletic event. Frequently, Saturday evening features a dance ("hop"), which the three upper classes may attend.

5. THE CURRICULUM. Primary emphasis is placed on basic education rather than training in order that a firm foundation in education may be laid for future development of the graduates.

In order to qualify for graduation and a degree, each midshipman must complete a minimum of 140 semester hours of work, complete required professional courses, specified distribution requirements, and the course requirements in one of the 24 majors offered. They are: Analytical Management, Applied Science, Chemistry, Economics, European Studies—French, German, or Italian, Far Eastern Studies—Chinese, Foreign Affairs, General Management, History, Latin American Studies, Spanish or Portuguese, Literature, Mathematics, Oceanography, Operations Analysis, Physics, Political Science, Soviet Studies—Russian, Aerospace Engineering, Electrical Engineering, Marine Engineering, Mechanical Engineering, Naval Architecture, Ocean Engineering, and Systems Engineering.

Training is included in the naval science portion of the curriculum to develop skills in some of the operating techniques which the graduates will have to use when they join the fleet as junior officers. Cruises during the summer months in combatant ships of the Navy to domestic and foreign ports, during which the midshipmen fill regular billets in the officer and enlisted complements of the ships, give them firsthand experience in the duties of petty officers and nonrated men as well as those of junior officers. For part of one summer, each midshipman makes an "air cruise" in transport aircraft to visit and become acquainted with the far-flung activities of naval aviation. Each class participates in an amphibious exercise during one of the summer programs. Thus, through performance of duties in engineering, weapons, navigation, communications, aviation, and tactics on these cruises, the midshipmen confirm the basic education they have received in the classroom.

6. EXTRACURRICULAR ACTIVITIES. Varsity teams, junior varsity teams, and class teams are fielded in virtually every intercollegiate sport.

The Academy also gives the midshipman opportunity for self-expression in a wide variety of activities—as racing yachtsman, actor, musician, chorister, artist, writer, journalist, orator, and photographer.

7. APPOINTMENT AS A MIDSHIPMAN. All candidates for admission to the United States Naval Academy must have certain general qualifications. They must be citizens of the United States, except that the law provides that a limited number of citizens of other American Republics and the Philippine Republic may be appointed.

Candidates must be between the ages of 17 and 22, must be of good moral character, and must be unmarried. Any midshipman who is found to be or to have been married will be discharged.

If a young man meets these qualifications and wants to become a midshipman, he must accomplish three basic steps before he can receive an appointment.

(1). *Acquire the Necessary Scholastic Background.* This is put first because, unless it is considered at an early age, a boy may find himself on graduation from high school with a burning ambition to become a midshipman yet seriously lacking in the basic scholastic requirements for admission. Sometimes, if the lad is young enough, this situation can be remedied by special preparatory school work after graduation from high school, but the wisest course is a well-planned high school program. Parents who think their sons might be interested in the Naval Academy should, before they register for Freshman year in high school, obtain from the Naval Academy a copy of the USNA catalogue. Adequate preparation is evidenced by high-school and college records, performance on College Entrance Examination Board tests, athletic and other extracurricular activities, and instructors' recommendations. Qualification for admission is based on all of the above factors.

(2). *Obtain an Appointment.* The above-mentioned catalogue gives the details of obtaining a nomination for such appointment. Briefly, the following appointments are available:

By the President	100 midshipmen per year, selected from among the sons of officers and enlisted personnel, Regular or Reserve, of the Army, Navy, Marine Corps, Air Force, and Coast Guard, who are on active duty or are retired.
By the Vice-President and Members of Congress	Five midshipmen in the Naval Academy at any one time. Vice-Presidential appointments from the United States at large. Senators' appointments from residents of their own states. Congressmen's appointments from residents of their congressional districts or territories.

From the Regular Navy and Marine Corps	85 enlisted men each year.
From the Naval and Marine Corps Reserves	85 enlisted men each year.
Sons of deceased or disabled officers, soldiers, and Marines of the two World Wars and the Korean or Vietnamese conflicts	Includes any son of male and female members of the Army, Navy, Marine Corps, and Coast Guard, who were killed in action or have died, or may hereafter die, of wounds or injuries received, or disease contracted or aggravated, in active service during World War I or World War II or during the period beginning 27 June 1950 and ending 31 January 1955. Maximum of 40 such appointees to be in the Naval Academy at any one time.
Sons of Medal of Honor recipients	The son of anyone who has received, or may hereafter receive, the Medal of Honor.
Honor graduates of the military and naval schools designated as honor schools by the Department of the Army, Navy, and Air Force.	10 each year.
NROTC units	10 each year from among members of the NROTC units (limited to NROTC midshipmen)
Panama Canal Zone and Republic of Panama	One midshipman in the Academy at any one time from sons of civilians residing in the Canal Zone and sons of civilian employees of the United States Government and the Panama Railroad Company residing in the Republic of Panama
District of Columbia	Five midshipmen in the Naval Academy at any one time
Governor of Puerto Rico	One midshipman in the Naval Academy at any one time, a native Puerto Rican
Resident Commissioner of Puerto Rico	Five midshipmen in the Naval Academy at any one time, appointed from residents of Puerto Rico
Qualified Congressional Alternates	150 qualified congressional alternates appointed by the Secretary of the Navy

The Secretary of the Navy is authorized to appoint 150 qualified congressional alternates. These appointments are awarded to the best-qualified alternates as recommended by the Academic Board of the Academy. Additional appointments from qualified alternates and competitors may be made by the Secretary to bring the Brigade to authorized strength. At least 75 percent of these must be congressional alternates.

For non-United States citizens, the following sources of appointments are authorized:

a. A maximum of 20 young men at a time from American Republics and Canada, but not more than three from any one of such countries may be in the Academy at any one time. Midshipmen from these other countries receive the same pay, allowances, and emoluments as midshipmen from the United States; they are subject to the same rules and regulations; but on graduation are not appointed to any position in the U. S. Navy.

b. A total of four Filipinos, to be designated by the President of the United States, may be admitted as midshipmen under much the same conditions.

(3). *Pass the Required Physical Examination.* Formal physical examinations for entrance to the Academy are conducted at many different military installations in continental United States and abroad. The physical requirements are exacting. The best interests of the government, the Navy, and the individual demand that they be so. The Naval Academy catalogue gives detailed information.

A careful preliminary physical examination should be taken by all prospective candidates before they seriously pursue the ambition to become a midshipman. The Departments of the Army, Navy, and Air Force have made available to all prospective candidates places, such as recruiting offices and military establishments, where service medical officers will examine a candidate without expense other than the cost of travel. The Congressman of his district or his Senator will give him a letter requesting such examination.

8. THE PRODUCT. The graduates of the Naval Academy have served their country and the Navy with honor and distinction in all its wars since its establishment in 1845. Many alumni have risen to high places in the councils of our government. Many a Naval Academy graduate has served in positions of high command and great trust where military experience and knowledge had to be combined with diplomacy, wisdom, and tact. They have met their responsibilities fully. They have served their country well.

The Naval Reserve Officers' Training Corps

9. HISTORY. In 1926, units of the Naval Reserve Officers' Training Corps were established at various universities to offer the opportunity to young men to qualify for a reserve appointment while attending college. It was the intention of the Navy Department at the time to work these young men into the Organized Reserve at the bottom and gradually to retire the older Reserve officers from the top.

In 1946, to meet the increasing demands for greater numbers of career officers, Congress authorized the award of regular commissions to graduates of a subsidized NROTC program rather than create a second Naval Academy. The Holloway Plan of 1947 provides students with appointments as midshipmen in the naval reserve, full tuition at the nation's leading universities, retainer pay, uniforms, and books. The naval service on the other hand continues to receive a career officer of liberal education and civilian orientation to add breadth of experience to wardrooms throughout the world.

The two training programs for Regular and Reserve officers now go hand in hand. Students are known as NROTC midshipmen and NROTC college students, respectively. Both take the same naval science courses and drills and are subject to the same privileges and discipline. Methods of selection, benefits received, obligations entailed, and cruises required vary widely.

Students enrolled in the NROTC programs lead approximately the same life as their civilian contemporaries. They wear the uniform when attending drills and other ceremonies and while engaged in summer training cruises.

Under the provisions of the 1951 Amendments to the Universal Military Training and Service Act, all NROTC students who are subject to induction under the provisions of that act are required to agree in writing to accept a commission upon completion of their training and to serve, subject to call by the Secretary of the Navy, not less than three years on active duty after receipt of their commission. Having signed this agreement, they will then be deferred from induction until the completion or termination of the course of instruction, but shall not be exempt from registration. In the case of students, who are commissioned in the Reserve, this does not necessarily mean that they will be permitted or required to serve for three years on active duty. To be deferred from induction, however, they must agree to accept a commission and to serve on active duty if called to do so.

10. NROTC MIDSHIPMEN. For those applicants from civilian life and from among enlisted personnel on active duty in the Navy and Marine Corps, who desire financial assistance from the Navy, with the prospect of a career in the Regular Navy or Marine Corps, the Navy now offers a status as a Regular student in the NROTC, which provides not more than four years of Navy-subsidized education. Students, upon enrollment, are appointed Midshipmen, USNR. The government pays tuition, the cost of textbooks, and laboratory and other fees of an instructional or administrative nature and furnishes the necessary uniforms. Midshipmen also receive monthly retainer pay to assist in defraying other expenses. Students will normally attend college for four years, taking a course leading to a baccalaureate or higher degree.

In return for benefits received under this program, the NROTC midshipman is subject to the following requirements and obligations:

To remain unmarried until commissioned.

To complete such naval science courses and drills as may be prescribed.

To make three summer cruises (one to be aviation indoctrination), each of approximately six to eight weeks' duration.

To accept a commission in the Regular Navy or Marine Corps, if offered, to serve on active duty for four years, and to retain commissioned status for a total of six years.

He is liable to release from his contract and separation from the NROTC program at any time that, in the opinion of the Secretary of the Navy, the best interest of the naval service requires such action.

11. NROTC COLLEGE STUDENTS. For those college students who desire neither financial assistance from the Navy nor a naval career but who do wish to be available to serve their country in time of emergency as a Reserve officer of the Navy or Marine Corps, the Navy offers the NROTC college program. NROTC college students are civilians who enter into a mutual contract with the Department of the Navy, in which they obligate themselves to take certain naval science courses and drills and one summer training cruise. In return the Navy provides the required uniforms, gives them monthly retainer pay during their Junior and Senior years, and offers a Reserve commission on graduation, if qualified. NROTC college students must meet the same standards for enrollment as NROTC midshipmen, except that the lower age limit may be reduced to 16 years in some instances. In addition, visual acuity standards are somewhat less restrictive.

12.   ELIGIBILITY.   To be eligible for either NROTC midshipmen or NROTC student status, a candidate must:

Be a male citizen of the United States.

Have reached his seventeenth birthday, and not have passed his twenty-first birthday on July 1 of the year he enters, unless contemplating undertaking a college course which takes 5 years to complete, in which case he shall not have passed his twentieth birthday on July 1 of that year.

NROTC students may marry.

Be physically qualified in accordance with the standards for midshipmen.

Be prepared to enter into an appropriate contract with the Secretary of the Navy providing for the obligations set forth in the preceding paragraphs. Minors must obtain an agreement to the contract signed by their parent or guardian.

Be a high-school graduate or possess an equivalent certificate: high-school students who will graduate by the end of the current academic year may apply.

Have no moral obligations or personal convictions which will prevent him from conscientiously supporting and defending the Constitution of the United States against all enemies, foreign or domestic.

13.   SELECTION OF CANDIDATES, REGULAR STATUS.   The procedures for selection of naval enlisted personnel on active duty are promulgated in instructions issued annually by the Bureau of Naval Personnel to all ships and naval stations. Naval Reserve personnel on inactive duty are selected by the same competitive system as other civilian candidates.

An NROTC Bulletin of Information, published each year by the Bureau of Naval Personnel gives full details as to eligibility, procedure for application, physical examination and interview of candidates, admission to college, appointment as a Midshipman, USNR, a list of universities and colleges where NROTC units are established, full details on physical requirements, and a wealth of other information. For a copy, apply to the Bureau of Naval Personnel, Pers B641, Navy Department, Washington, D.C.

14.   CURRICULUM.   Since the mission of the NROTC is to provide, by a permanent system of training and instruction in essential naval subjects at civilian educational institutions, a source from which qualified officers may be obtained for commissioning in the lowest grades of the Regular and Reserve components of the Navy and the Marine Corps, the objectives of the Naval Science Department of a university are as follows:

1. To assist in the education of the midshipman in a major field of study of interest to the Navy or Marine Corps leading to a baccalaureate degree.
2. To provide the midshipman with the fundamental concepts and principles of Naval Science and with the professional Naval knowledge necessary to establish a sound basis for his future growth as a Naval or Marine Corps officer.
3. To prepare the midshipman for service with the highest sense of honor and integrity as a commissioned officer; to cultivate the essential elements of military leadership; and to foster the growth of a strong sense of loyalty and dedication to his Service and to the Nation.
4. To prepare the midshipman to undertake successfully in later periods of his career, advanced and continuing education in a field of application and interest to the Naval Service.
5. To inject the values of civilian higher education into the Naval Service by utilizing the expertise of civilian faculty instruction where applicable.

15. The course of instruction. Instructors in the various units are Regular Navy and Marine officers on shore duty. As far as possible, the technical naval subjects are presented in about the same scope as at the Naval Academy. Adherence to the conventional lecture system is expected in many universities, but the Navy also expects the students to study, be told, be shown how, and learn by doing.

Cruises.—The NROTC midshipman obligates himself to make three summer cruises, one of which is for aviation indoctrination. The NROTC student obligates himself to make one summer cruise.

These summer cruises are very similar in purpose and schedule to, and are often combined with, those taken by midshipmen from Annapolis.

16. Extracurricular. While NROTC students may join fraternities and engage in all the usual outside activities of the college, including athletics, dramatics, art, journalism, etc., they find themselves particularly drawn to the naval group with which they work. The unit has its dances, luncheons, picnics, and "smokers." Many units form local

naval societies on the campus, with such seagoing names as The Conning Tower, The Sextant, and The Quarterdeck, whose members run these affairs for their own amusement and sociability.

17. PROSPECTS UPON GRADUATION. A NROTC midshipman who successfully completes his college course and his course in naval science may apply for a commission as an ensign in the Line, Supply Corps, or Civil Engineering Corps or as a second lieutenant in the Marine Corps. Within quotas allotted, their requests will be approved. At the end of four years' active service, the officer may resign from the Regular Navy or Marine Corps, and accept a commission in the Reserve. During his time on active duty, he competes on equal terms with all other Regular officers of whatever source. He is a professional naval or Marine officer with all the rights, privileges, and obligations which that career entails in our world of today.

The Navy Enlisted Scientific Education Program

18. THE PROGRAM. The Navy Enlisted Scientific Education Program provides an uninterrupted four-year college education in one of more than 20 colleges or universities for qualified enlisted men and women. A baccalaureate degree in science or engineering may be earned. NESEP's attend OCS during the summer between junior and senior years.

Applicants are given a special examination administered annually in November. Those selectees are ordered to the Naval Preparatory School at Bainbridge, Maryland, or to the Naval Training Center at San Diego, California, for nine weeks' instruction pending admittance to colleges or universities.

19. ELIGIBILITY. Eligibility requirements and procedures for applying are contained in BuPers Instruction 1510.69 series. In addition to the general qualifications required of all officer candidates, they must not have reached their 24th birthday by 1 July of entry into the program. Service obligation is six years obligated enlisted naval service on acceptance into the program and a two year extension at the completion of the second year of college. Minimum active duty as an officer is four years.

Augmentation Program

20. THE PROGRAM AND ELIGIBILITY. The Augmentation Program provides for the transfer of officers from the Reserve Navy to the Regular Navy. A Reserve officer must have served for a period of active duty in commissioned status and be in a grade and have seniority in that grade for which a need exists in the regular component. For eligibility and transfer a reserve officer does not have to be on active duty at the time of application.

The Limited Duty Officer Program

21. THE PROGRAM. The Limited Duty Officer Program also gives the Navy's outstanding young men an excellent chance for advancement. While the number of commissions awarded each year is not large in proportion to the number of applicants, there is a definite opportunity for top-notch candidates.

22. REQUIREMENTS. The program is for Regular Navy Personnel who:

Hold the permanent or temporary rank of chief warrant officer (W-2 or W-3).

Applicants must be able to meet the physical standards prescribed for original appointment in the Navy, for the corps to which appointed. Eligibility requirements are contained in BuPers Inst. 1120.18 series. NavPers 18564, *Manual of Qualifications for LDO* also provides information regarding selection process, general and professional qualifications, and career planning.

The Warrant Officer Program

23. THE PROGRAM. The Warrant Officer has long been a mainstay of the officer corps, providing a source of technical skill and supervisory abilities. In 1959, phase out of the Warrant Officer Program was commenced. In 1964 Secretary of the Navy approved a revised Warrant Officer Program, providing a path of advancement for outstanding Chief and First Class Petty Officers (pay grades E-6 through E-9).

All appointments will be made to Warrant Officer (W-1). There are four Warrant Officer grades, W-1 through W-4.

24. REQUIREMENTS. Applications are called for annually to be submitted by December. A selection board usually convenes in February. Eligibility requirements are contained in the BuPers Instruction 1120.18 series. NavPers 18455, *Manual of Qualification for Warrant Officers,* also provides information regarding selection process, general and professional qualifications, and career planning.

The Naval Reserve Officer Candidate (ROC) Program

25. THE PROGRAM. On September 9, 1948, the Secretary of the Navy approved the establishment of the Naval Reserve Officer Candidate Program designed to maintain a continuing flow of newly commissioned officers into the Naval Reserve in sufficient numbers to offset attrition and keep the Naval Reserve at authorized officer strength.

Each year the Navy selects several hundred college juniors for officer training. Candidates selected will attend two summer courses, beginning about the middle of June and lasting about eight weeks each, at the Navy's Reserve Officer Candidate School located at Newport, Rhode Island. They study naval customs and history, seamanship, weapons, navigation, communications, and other seagoing skills. During both summer courses, they receive pay of pay grade E-5 or the rate held in the Naval Reserve, whichever is higher. Members in pay grade E-4 or lower are administratively advanced to E-5 for the duration of training, and pay starts when they leave home. Transportation to the training activity and back again is paid by the Navy. During this school period, quarters and food and necessary textbooks and supplies are provided.

Candidates successfully completing two summer training sessions not later than the summer immediately following graduation will receive commissions as ensigns in the Naval Reserve in the Line, Supply Corps, or Civil Engineering Corps, and may look forward to three years of active duty. Candidates may apply for appointment in the Regular Navy.

26. REQUIREMENTS. To be eligible, a candidate must be:
A citizen of the United States.
At least 19, not have reached 27½ upon commissioning.
Physically qualified.
Mentally and morally qualified and show capacity for leadership.

A student in good standing in his junior class at an accredited college or university.

A member of the Naval Reserve program or agree to serve in an enlisted status in the Naval Reserve until commissioned.

27. APPLICATION. Members of the Ready Reserve, apply to their commanding officer; others to the Commandant of the naval district within which they reside.

Aviation Officer Candidate (AOC) Program, Naval Aviation Officer Candidate (NAOC) Program, Air Intelligence Officer (NAOC-AI) Program, and Aviation Reserve Officer Candidate (AVROC) Program

28. THE PROGRAMS. Another program leading to a commission and Navy wings is Aviation Officer Candidate training, which is open to eligible college graduates serving on active duty as enlisted men in the Regular Navy or Naval Reserve. It is also open to qualified college graduates who are civilians.

Under this program selected applicants are ordered to the Aviation Officer Candidate School, Naval Air Station, Pensacola, Florida, and upon successful completion of the first 16 weeks of officer indoctrination and preflight training, are appointed ensigns in the Naval Reserve. After appointment they undergo approximately 14 months of flight training, after which they are designated as Naval Aviators (1315). They are required to serve on active duty for a period of 4½ years, following designation as naval aviators, and to retain their Naval Reserve commissions for a total of six years.

Applicants must be citizens of the United States; they may be married; must be at least 19 but under 26 years of age at the time of submission of application; must have a baccalaureate degree from an accredited college or university, except that they may apply 12 months prior to graduation; and must pass certain mental and physical tests.

The Naval Aviation Officer Candidate (NAOC) Program provides training for designation as Naval Flight Officer (1325). Candidates are commissioned Ensign, U.S. Naval Reserve, upon successfully completing 16 weeks NAOC indoctrination at Pensacola, Florida. In advanced training, NFO's concentrate on the weapon system of the type of aircraft

to which they will be assigned. The six specialties are: Early Warning Systems Operations, Airborne Electronic Counter-Measure Operator, Airborne Tactical Data System Operator, Antisubmarine Tactical Co-ordinator, Bombardier-Navigator, and Radar Intercept Officer. Appointees serve three and one-half years on active duty upon completion of all training.

The Air Intelligence Program is designed to train those who desire a nonflying assignment as an Air Intelligence Officer. Basic requirements and training are the same as the NAOC Program except advanced training which consists of a 28-week Air Intelligence Course at Lowry Air Force Base, Denver, Colorado. Appointees serve on active duty four years from the date of commission.

The Navy's Aviation Reserve Officer Candidate Program takes applicants in their second or third year of college. During two separate summers candidates attend an eight-week Naval Aviation training course. After graduation they are commissioned as ensigns, U.S. Naval Reserve and are ordered to pilot or NFO training. Pilots are required to serve four and one-half years after completion of training, and NFO's three and one-half years. Pilot training applicants must be between 17 and 26½ years of age when commissioned; NFO training applicants, between 17 and 27½.

29. METHOD OF APPLICATION. Application for appointment to these programs may be made at any Office of Naval Officer Procurement or Naval Air Station. Information is available at the nearest Navy Recruiting Station. The following documents are required: birth certificate, complete college transcript, and evidence of citizenship if not born in the United States.

Officer Candidate School

30. THE PROGRAM. The purpose of the Officer Candidate School Program is to provide a ready and adequate reserve of qualified junior officers. It is an active duty program under which candidates are trained at the U. S. Naval Officers Candidate School, Newport, Rhode Island. Those young men selected for the Officer Candidate Program are trained in naval subjects at the school for 18 weeks. Upon successful completion of this training, candidates are appointed in the U. S. Naval Reserve in which they are required to serve on active duty for three years from date of acceptance of appointment and to retain their commissioned status in the Naval Reserve for a period of six years (including periods of active duty). Further specialized training of certain designated officers is conducted under the cognizance of the appropriate Bureau or office. This training would be applicable to those officers assigned to the Nuclear Propulsion program, Supply Corps, Civil Engineer Corps, Intelligence, and Hydrography.

31. ELIGIBLE APPLICANTS. An applicant must be a graduate of a regionally accredited college or university with a baccalaureate or higher degree. He must be 19 but not more than 27½ years of age at time of commissioning. Applicants may apply upon completion of their junior year; however, they must provide evidence of graduation before they commence training at the Officer Candidate School. Individuals who desire to apply for the Officer Candidate School Program must be citizens of the United States. However, applicants for certain designators must be citizens by birth. An applicant must meet the physical qualifications established for the Officer Candidate School Program in accordance with current Navy directives.

Enlisted men on active duty in either the Regular Navy or the Naval Reserve are eligible.

32. APPLICATION. An enlisted man of the Regular Navy or Naval Reserve on active duty should apply for the program through his commanding officer.

An enlisted man of the Naval Reserve on inactive duty or a civilian should apply to the nearest Navy Recruiting Main Station. There, each person must submit a formal application, must take the Officers Qualification test and a physical examination, and be interviewed by two or three officers. The completion of the processing of papers takes approximately two months (in some cases longer). The application is then forwarded to the Bureau of Naval Personnel, which forwards the physical examination to the Bureau of Medicine and Surgery for recommendation concerning physical fitness for the program. The cases are then referred to the OCS Review Board in the Bureau of Naval Personnel for final consideration. The time required to complete the final action is dependent on many variables and cannot be determined; however, it may be as long as three months. An applicant will be notified of one of three possibilities after the final action has been taken on his case: (1) that he has been selected; (2) that he has not been selected (because of quota limitations); (3) that his application is disapproved because of either physical or other reasons.

If an applicant is selected as an Officer Candidate, he will be notified by the Navy Recruiting Main Station which processed his application, to the effect that he has been selected and that he must appear at that office for enlistment as an Officer Candidate. After enlistment he will be placed on inactive duty with orders to report to the Officer Candidate School in time for the convening date of the class of which he will be a member.

33. OFFICERS CANDIDATE SCHOOL.   This school is located at the U. S. Naval Schools Command, Newport, Rhode Island. At the school, the Officer Candidate will be furnished uniforms, food, living quarters and medical and dental treatment, as needed. His course of instruction will include courses in seamanship, weapons, engineering, communications, navigation, operations, military justice, and leadership. The plan of the day, during Officer Candidate training, is very similar to Recruit Training with the exception that much more time is devoted to classroom work and required study hours. Housing is scarce and expensive in the Newport area, and shore liberty for officer candidates is granted only from 1200 Saturday to 1900 Sunday. In view of this fact, it is not advisable for the individuals selected for Officer Candidate training to bring their families. Assignment after completion of the officer course is under the cognizance of the Officer Detail Section of the Bureau of Naval Personnel. Every attempt, however, is made to place an individual in the billet where his service can be utilized to the best advantage of the individual and the naval service.

Direct Appointment

34. THE PROGRAM.   The direct appointment program provides a means of procuring naval officers with specific talents in certain areas. The active-duty direct appointment programs are Judge Advocate General's, Chaplain's, and Civil Engineer Corps. The inactive-duty direct appointment programs are the three Corps of active duty programs and engineering (1405), aeronautical engineering (1515), cryptology (1615), air and surface intelligence (1635), public affairs (1655), and meteorology (1815) in the Naval Reserve. Officers are appointed as ensigns, lieutenants (junior grade), or lieutenants in the Naval Reserve based on age, qualifications, and civilian or military experience and the needs of the naval service.

35. APPLICATION. Candidates for direct appointment should apply to the nearest Navy Recruiting Station. Additional information on exact eligibility requirements may be procured from this source.

Staff Corps

36. MEDICAL CORPS PROGRAMS. These programs are for men and women who are medical students (1915) on inactive duty, senior medical students (1915) on active duty, medical interns (2100/2105) on active duty as Regular or Reserve, and doctors after internship (2100/2105) in the Medical Corps. The medical student program is a nonsubsidized program which provides deferment from military service while the student is completing medical school. The medical student is appointed ensign, Medical Corps, in the Naval Reserve; upon graduation, lieutenant in the Naval Reserve on active duty. During summer vacation the medical student is eligible for 60 days of active duty with full pay and allowances. The subsidized and nonsubsidized senior medical student programs require a minimum of three years of active duty upon graduation and immediately following completion of a civilian or naval internship as a lieutenant in the Regular Navy. The age-limit for the medical student and senior medical student in these programs is 33 upon graduation with an adjustment of three years for previous active duty. The medical intern is a graduate of a medical school approved by the Council of Medical Education, American Medical Association (AMA) or the American Osteopathic Association (AOA), who as a lieutenant is assigned for a minimum of two years' active duty to one of the ten Naval hospitals providing intern training. The upper age-limit is 41 and 42; an additional requirement for foreign medical graduates to qualify in the intern training is successful completion of the American Medical Qualifications Examination (AMQE). Medical Doctors and Doctors of Osteopathy who have completed internship may be commissioned in the medical corps as lieutenant (2105) in the Naval Reserve or as lieutenant or lieutenant commander (2100) in the Regular Navy depending on qualifications; there is a service requirement of two years' active duty.

37. DENTAL CORPS PROGRAMS. These programs are for dental students (1925), dental interns (2200/2205), and dentists (2200/2205) in the Dental Corps. The dental corps programs are comparable to the medical corps programs. The dental student in a dental school ap-

proved by the ADA may be selected for 28 days of active duty with full pay and allowances between scholastic years. The dental intern who is a graduate of a dental school approved by ADA is assigned to one of the eight Naval Hospitals providing a one-year rotating internship approved by ADA. Dentists must have graduated from dental school within ten years of application for the dental corps. The service requirements, rank, etc. for the dental corps is the same as for the medical corps.

38. MEDICAL SERVICE CORPS PROGRAMS. The Medical Service Corps offers programs for students and interns and medical specialists in physical therapy, occupational therapy, dietetics, administration and supply, allied sciences, and optometry and pharmacy in the Naval Reserve.

For the dietetics program the applicant must have a baccalaureate degree with a major in foods and nutrition or institution management and have completed a hospital dietetic internship approved by the American Dietetic Association; or have a baccalaureate degree in medical dietetics; or have a Master of Public Health degree with emphasis on hospital dietetics and public health nutrition. The Navy Enlisted Dietetic Education Program (NEDEP) is a one- to three-year college program (depending upon prior college work) which leads to a baccalaureate degree in Medical Dietetics and to appointment to ensign, Medical Corps, (2305) after OCS training. See BuPers Inst. 1120.38 series for eligibility requirements.

For the occupational therapy or physical therapy program the applicant must have a baccalaureate degree and certification of completion of a course in occupational therapy or physical therapy approved by the Council on Medical Education and Hospitals of the American Medical Association.

For the supply and administration program in the Medical Services Corps the applicant must have a baccalaureate degree in sanitary science or environmental health, a Master of Public Health degree in sanitary science or environmental health, or a Master's degree in hospital or health care administration. For the allied sciences' program the applicant must have completed requirements for a Masters Degree or the first two years of a doctorate program, in or relating to one of the specialties, except those applying for the specialties of medical technology, aviation physiology, and radiation health. Applicants for appointment as medical technologists must have a baccalaureate degree and be registered as a medical technologist by the American Society of Clinical

Pathologists. Applicants for appointment in the specialties of aviation physiology and radiation health must have a baccalaureate degree with a major in physics, chemistry, or one of the biological sciences. For the optometry and pharmacy program the applicant must have a degree in optometry or pharmacy and evidence of state or District of Columbia licensure, or registration must be furnished prior to appointment. Optometrists may present evidence of having passed Parts I and II of the National Board of Optometry Examination in lieu of evidence of state licensure.

The Medical Service Corps Inservice Procurement Program is a continuing program on an annual basis which provides a path of advancement to commissioned officer status for senior HM and DT personnel who possess the necessary potential, outstanding qualifications, and motivation. This program also provides an opportunity for other eligible personnel, as specified herein, to obtain appointment in the Medical Service Corps, Regular Navy. These personnel are given a four-week orientation course at the School of Hospital Administration, Bethesda, Maryland.

For the entire Medical Corps Service programs men are trained for four weeks at the School of Hospital Administration, Bethesda, Maryland; and women for four weeks at Women Officers School, Newport, Rhode Island. Depending upon the individual's qualifications, the ranks at commissioning may be ensign, lieutenant (junior grade), or lieutenant, Medical Service Corps, in the Naval Reserve.

39. NURSE CORPS PROGRAMS. For the Navy Nurse Corps Candidate (NNCC) Program the applicant may be a student nurse or a registered professional nurse through a hospital nursing program or a baccalaureate degree nursing program accredited by the National League for Nursing (NLN). While in nursing school, the applicant holds the rate of OCHN; when within six months of completion of degree requirements, the applicant holds the rank of ensign (1905) in the Naval Reserve; upon completion of the four weeks' Nurse Corps Indoctrination course at Women Officers School, Newport, Rhode Island, the applicant is then appointed ensign, lieutenant (junior grade), or lieutenant (2905) in the Naval Reserve depending on qualifications and length of professional nursing experience.

For the Navy Nurse Corps Candidate Program (Hospital) the applicant must be matriculated in a nursing program of at least three academic years duration which leads to a diploma in nursing. Applicants are enlisted as OCHN during the third year of schooling. Upon graduation they are commissioned as ensign, Nurse Corps, (2905).

The Navy Enlisted Nursing Education Program (NENEP) is a three- or four-year college program for outstanding petty officers of the Hospital Corps. This program leads to a baccalaureate degree in nursing, licensing as a registered nurse, training in officer candidate school, and a commission as an ensign, Nurse Corps, (2905) in the Naval Reserve. See BuPers Inst. 1120.37 series for eligibility requirements.

The Navy Nurse Corps Candidate Program and Nurse Corps are open to graduates of nursing schools providing a minimum of a three-year diploma program, NLN or state approved. A graduate registered nurse must be engaged in the ethical practice of nursing for appointment as lieutenant (junior grade), or lieutenant, Nurse Corps.

40. CHAPLAIN CORPS PROGRAMS. The theological student (1945) program accepts students enrolled at approved theological schools for the rank of ensign in the Naval Reserve on inactive duty. The student is ordered to active duty for eight weeks' Chaplain School, Newport, Rhode Island during the summer prior to graduation from the seminary. Upon completion of the course the officer is considered qualified for the superseding appointment as lieutenant in the Naval Reserve. The Chaplain Corps (4105) program accepts applicants with 90 semester hours of graduate theological school work and 120 semester hours of undergraduate work at properly accredited institutions. The applicant must be an ordained minister, have ecclesiastical approval, and be recommended by the District Chaplain. The service requirements are three years' active duty; the commission must be retained for six years. The priest, minister, or rabbi is commissioned a lieutenant, Chaplain Corps, in the Naval Reserve and ordered to eight weeks of indoctrination training at Chaplain's School.

41. JUDGE ADVOCATE GENERAL'S CORPS PROGRAM. The Judge Advocate General's Corps (1955) student program accepts college seniors who anticipate enrollment at a Law school approved by the American Bar Association. The student with the rank of ensign in the Naval Reserve is ordered to active duty for training for eight weeks of Officers Indoctrination School during the summer preceding graduation from Law School. Upon completion of the course, awarding of Law Degree, and admittance to the Bar of a federal court or highest court of state or territory of the United States or District of Columbia, the ensign is considered qualified for the superseding appointment as lieutenant (2505) in the Naval Reserve. The service requirement for this appointment is four years of active duty. The JAG Corps (2505) program accepts law-degree graduates from law schools accredited by the American Bar Association; the graduate must be a member of the Bar of a Federal Court or highest court of state or territory of the United States or District of Columbia. The applicant attends nine weeks of officer indoctrination and seven weeks of Justice School, both at Newport, Rhode Island. The lawyer is commissioned a lieutenant, Judge Advocate General Corps, in the Naval Reserve with a service requirement of four years' active duty and with a commission commitment of six years.

42. CIVIL ENGINEER CORPS PROGRAM. The Civil Engineer Corps accepts applications from graduates with baccalaureate degrees from a regionally accredited college or university in civil, mechanical, electrical, mining, petroleum, or architectural engineering; or architecture. In addition to the degree, four years of appropriate experience is required for a commission as a lieutenant; nine years' experience is required for a lieutenant commander. The appointments available are lieutenant or lieutenant commander (5105) in the Naval Reserve with an active duty requirement of two years and with a commission commitment of six years.

Women Officer Procurement

43. HISTORY. When the President on July 30, 1942, signed a bill which created the Women's Reserve of the U. S. Naval Reserve, the Navy immediately set up, at Smith College, a Naval Reserve Midshipmen's School (WR) for training women Naval Reserve midshipmen. Originally, the young women applicants were required to have a baccalaureate degree from an accredited college or to have completed 2 years of college and have had at least 2 years of business or professional experience. Women accepted initially had to be between the ages of twenty and fifty years.

Considering the different physical capacities and emotional attitudes of women, the regulations of the school said:

> In organizing the Women's Reserve, the questions arising from mental and character traits of women, insofar as they differ from men, are the same as those which have been successfully answered in the business and industrial world. The real and only problem is to produce "properly trained women" who will be able to perform assigned naval duties as well as the men whom they will relieve. The women who have preceded you have shown that this problem can be solved. They have set extremely high standards. For the continued success of the Women's Reserve you must meet them.

44. WOMEN IN THE POSTWAR REGULAR NAVY. When, along with the women's corps of the other services, the WAVES were incorporated into the regular establishment, a different system of training new women officers was considered more economical and better adapted for peacetime. Accordingly, an Officer Indoctrination School (W) was established as a component of the U. S. Naval Schools Command, Newport, Rhode Island.

45. CURRICULUM. The first phase, or basic course, consists of eight weeks of indoctrination stressing orientation and administrative techniques and, for successful candidates, results in an ensign's commission in the Naval Reserve. The new officers then remain for an additional eight weeks for the advanced course in officer indoctrination, during which leadership and skill areas are emphasized. Military drill, counseling, hygiene and physical education continue throughout the course.

The curriculum is prescribed by the Bureau of Naval Personnel and includes:

Introduction to the Navy.—This course is a general orientation to the Navy and Navy life. It is intended to familiarize the student with naval terminology; military customs, traditions, ceremonies and courtesies; officer and enlisted uniforms and uniform attachments; concepts of precedence, authority and chain of command; Navy Regulations; and the history of contributions of women in the armed forces.

The Operating Forces.—A general introduction is provided to the naval units and their components which comprise the Operating Forces of the Navy. Students are acquainted with the construction, characteristics, and equipment of naval ships and aircraft, and with shipboard organization and the methods of employing this naval power.

The Navy's Role in Support of National Policy.—In this condensed review of U. S. Naval history, the student is made aware of the principles of seapower, as defined by Admiral Mahan, and of the highlights of naval activity and warfare from 1775 to the present history. Additionally, the course is concerned with collective security, the Communist threat in the post–World War II period, counterinsurgency, and with a treatment of the Navy's role and mission in today's world.

Organization for National Security.—This course is directed toward acquainting the student with those national organizations which mobilize our political, military, economic, and psychological resources to meet the requirements of national security. Special emphasis is placed on organization principles which are then related to a detailed study of the Department of the Navy and its relationship to the executive and legislative branches of the government including the Department of Defense.

Personnel Administration.—General information pertaining to the Navy's program of personnel management is imparted in this course. Specifically, the administration and distribution of officer and enlisted personnel including recruiting, classification, promotion and advancement, assignment, training and personnel accounting procedures are discussed.

Naval Correspondence.—Instruction is provided in the preparation and maintenance of official correspondence and the student is introduced to the publications and documents which are basic references in performing naval duties.

Military Justice.—The student is acquainted with the fundamentals of naval justice and discipline predicated on military law.

Leadership.—The course deals with concepts and methods of leadership, particularly military leadership. It examines the written sources which commit the naval officer to the exercise of leadership, the basic concepts of psychology which the military leader should apply in handling individuals and groups, methods of achieving discipline and morale, and means of effecting sound relations with seniors, peers, and subordinates. It also offers opportunity for practical application of information discussed.

Communciations.—Basic instruction is provided regarding the organization, administration, employment, and operation of communication systems.

Training Responsibilities.—An overview of the naval officer's significant responsibility for training subordinates is followed by brief examination of the methods and techniques of instructing.

Responsibilities, Rights and Benefits.—This course details the responsibilities, rights, and benefits of naval officers and enlisted personnel. Specifically, personal, civic, and financial responsibilities; insurance programs; pay; leave; educational and other benefits are described.

Professional Appearance.—This course provides instruction in facets of good grooming with particular stress upon correct appearance in uniform.

Hygiene and First Aid.—Provides instruction on good health habits and their importance to daily efficiency; basic information on first aid measures.

Military Drill and Physical Education.—Encompasses an active program of drill, swimming, and sports activities designed to promote good military bearing and appearance, provide for survival in the water, and improve general health, posture, and weight control. Military drill includes standard techniques for orderly maneuverability of personnel, and for dress parades. Its indoctrinational value is the development of leadership qualities and immediate obedience to commands.

With the coming of the last term, discipline is relaxed for the successful candidates. Liberty is granted on the same basis as for male officer students at the school. All recreational facilities of the station are available to WAVES. The Officers' Club is open to them. The station hobby shop provides amusement for those interested in leathercraft, wood carving, drawing, or painting. Frequent station dances and other entertainments help to occupy the limited leisure time.

46. ACTIVE DUTY. Women candidates who successfully complete the course serve on active duty for a period of 24 months following the date of their appointment in the grade of ensign, Naval Reserve, if required by the needs of the Service. They are ordered to various shore activities for duty in connection with personnel, public relations, training, publications, intelligence, communications, logistics, operations or similar types of duty.

Women officers of the Naval Reserve while in the grade of ensign and lieutenant (junior grade) may apply for transfer to the Regular Navy provided they meet all the requirements of the Navy Augmentation Program and are recommended by their commanding officers.

Women officers perform outstandingly in the Medical, Dental, Medical Service, and Nurse Corps, and unrestricted line, both in the Regular and Reserve Navy; in special duty officers assignments and in restricted line billets in the Naval Reserve.

The U. S. Coast Guard Academy

47. BACKGROUND. Founded in 1910 in old Fort Trumbull, New London, Connecticut, the U. S. Coast Guard Academy is one of the finest institutions of learning in the United States. Its present plant with its Georgian colonial-type buildings dates from 1932. A four-year course of academic studies and military training leads to a degree of bachelor of science in engineering and a commission as ensign in the Regular Coast Guard.

48. THE REGIMEN. The purpose of the Coast Guard Academy is to

provide officers for a military organization. As at the Naval Academy, life is run on military lines. The principal source of military training is in the Cadet Battalion, a corps officered by the cadets.

The curriculum is similar to that at the Naval Academy. The Coast Guard Academy ranks with the top engineering schools of the country. Although the cadet receives a free education and his degree is in engineering, the course includes nearly three-fourths of the cultural subjects required for a bachelor of arts degree in a liberal arts college.

Summer cruises give the cadets an opportunity to prove their Academy motto *Scientiae Cedit Mare*—the sea yields to knowledge. The Academy has retained the feature of sea training in square-riggers. Cadets also make cruises in the big, modern cutters of the Coast Guard.

49. APPOINTMENT AS A CADET. While the requirements for eligibility are essentially the same as for midshipmen in most details, appointments are made strictly on a competitive basis. Any young man who believes he can meet the mental, physical and aptitude requirements is encouraged to make application. There is no requirement for appointment by any Senator or Congressman or any other official of the government. Competitive mental examinations are held once a year in several cities in the country. Character, officer-like qualities, and physical-aptitude tests as well as a physical examination are considered in the selection of successful candidates.

Pay and Allowances

1. **AUTHORITY FOR PAY OF OFFICERS.** The annual pay and allowances of officers are specified and fixed by Title 37 of the United States Code. The Code also includes the following:
   1. It defines the word "dependents."
   2. It provides for a subsistence allowance for officers.
   3. It provides for a rental allowance for officers.
   4. It saves to officers their old base pay, plus longevity, in the event that it is greater than the pay provided by the act.

2. **BASIC PAY OF OFFICERS.** An officer appointed to the Navy is entitled to pay from the date of acceptance of appointment only, except that a person commissioned as a naval officer by reason of graduation from the United States Naval Academy becomes entitled, upon acceptance of his commission, to pay from the day of graduation. However, if a midshipman is not commissioned within six months after date of graduation, then his officer pay commences from the date of execution of the acceptance and oath of office.

Under the present conditions, the President continues the practice of temporary appointments, established during World War II, which are promulgated by various ALNAVS and by individual letters. The date of rank and the effective date of pay and allowances for appointees are included in the notification.

Under such appointments, if an appointee included in the ALNAV cited holds a letter appointment to increased rank dated earlier than the appointment of the ALNAV, the date of the appointment on the letter (as distinguished from date of rank) is the effective date for pay purposes. Officers temporarily appointed under Sections 5596, 5784 and 5787a of 10 U.S. Code, are entitled to pay and allowances of the higher grade from and including date of acceptance of appointment.

The sums received by the officer as "pay" in the civilian sense include the following:
   1. Basic pay.
   2. Basic allowance for subsistence.

3. Basic allowance for quarters under prescribed conditions.

In addition to the above, those officers whose duties, status, or assignment qualify them under law become entitled to incentive and special pay (see Secs. 5 to 8 following).

All pay following retirement, except on being recalled from retirement to active duty, is computed on the basis of basic pay only.

3. BASIC PAY.[1] The basic pay of an officer is computed on the basis of the pay grade in which he is placed. The pay grade of an officer is determined by his grade or rank, and his pay also depends on his length of service.

There are ten grades. An officer is placed in a pay grade according to the following:

Rank. If an ensign, he is placed in 0-1; if a lieutenant, in 0-3; etc. to 0-10 for Admiral. But note that officers in pay grades 0-1E through 0-3E, who have been credited with over four years' active service as enlisted members, are authorized increased basic pay for additional years of service.

4. SERVICE CREDITABLE IN COMPUTATION OF BASIC PAY. In computing the cumulative years of service to be counted by members of the uniformed services for determining the amount of basic pay they are entitled to receive upon completion of such years of service, service personnel shall be credited with:

1. Full time for all periods of active service as a commissioned officer, commissioned warrant officer, warrant officer, Army field clerk, flight officer, and enlisted person in any Regular or Reserve component of any of the uniformed services.

2. Full time for all periods during which they were enlisted or held appointments as commissioned officers, commissioned warrant officers, warrant officers, Army field clerks, or flight officers, in any of the Regular components of the uniformed services, or in the Regular Army Reserve, or in the Organized Militia prior to July 1, 1916, or in the National Guard of the United States, or in the Organized Reserve Corps, or in the Officers' Reserve Corps, or in the Enlisted Reserve Corps, or in the Medical Reserve Corps, or in the Medical Reserve Corps of the Navy, or in the Dental Reserve Corps of the Navy, or in the Naval Militia, or in the National Naval Volunteers, or in the Naval Reserve

[1] Since basic pay, allowances, special pay for various purposes are frequently changed by amendments to Public Law 351, the tables and figures included in previous editions of this *Guide* have been deleted. See your Disbursing Officer for pay tables and detailed figures on money allowances.

Force, or in the Naval Reserve, or in the Air National Guard, or in the Air National Guard of the United States, or in the Air Force Reserve, or in the officers' section of the Air Force Reserve, or in the Air Corps Reserve, or in the Army of the United States without specification of any component thereof, or in the Air Force of the United States without specification of any component thereof, or in the Marine Corps Reserve Force, or in the Marine Corps Reserve, or in the Coast Guard Reserve, or in the Reserve Corps of the Public Health Service, or in the Philippine Scouts, or in the Philippine Constabulary.

3. For commissioned officers in service on June 30, 1922, all service which was then counted in computing longevity pay and service as a contract surgeon serving full time.

4. Full time for all periods during which they held appointments as nurses, Reserve nurses, or commissioned officers in the Army Nurse Corps, the Navy Nurse Corps, the Nurse Corps of the Public Health Service, or the Reserve components thereof.

5. Full time for all periods during which they were deck officers or junior engineers in the Coast and Geodetic Survey.

6. All service which, under any provision of law in effect on January 10, 1962, is authorized to be credited for the purpose of computing longevity pay.

Such service under previous provisions of law included:

Full time for all service (active and inactive) as commissioned officer, chief warrant and warrant officer, Army field clerk, enlisted man in the Army, Navy, Marine Corps, Coast Guard, Coast and Geodetic Survey, Public Health Service, Regular Army Reserve, Organized Militia prior to July 1, 1916, National Guard, National Guard Reserve, National Guard United States, Officers' Reserve Corps, Enlisted Reserve Corps, Naval Militia, National Naval Volunteers, Naval and Marine Corps Reserve Forces, Naval and Marine Corps Reserves, Coast Guard Reserve, Reserve Corps Public Health Service, Philippine Scouts, and Philippine Constabulary. Officers in service on June 30, 1922, are entitled to count, in addition to the foregoing, all service then counted and service as a contract surgeon serving full time with one of the services. Inactive service on the retired list is included.

Members of the uniformed services shall accrue additional service credit for basic-pay purposes, for periods while on a temporary-disability retired list, honorary retired list, or a retired list of any of the uniformed services, or while authorized to receive retired pay, retirement pay, or retainer pay as a member of the Fleet Reserve or Fleet

Marine Corps Reserve, from any of the uniformed services or from the Veterans' Administration, or while a member of the Honorary Reserve of the Officers' Reserve Corps or Organized Reserve Corps: *Provided,* That, except for active service as prescribed under (1), the service credit authorized in this section cannot be included to increase retired pay, disability retirement pay, retirement pay, or retainer pay while on a retired list, on a temporary disability retired list, in a retired status, or in the Fleet Reserve or Fleet Marine Corps Reserve, except as provided in Title IV of the act.

The periods of time authorized to be counted in the computation of basic pay include all service performed by service personnel while under the age of eighteen years.

The period which any individual may count in the computation of his basic pay is the total of all periods authorized to be counted in any of the uniformed services, but the same period of time cannot be counted more than once.

5. SPECIAL PAY, PHYSICIANS AND DENTISTS. In accordance with Sec. 203 of the Career Compensation Act of 1949, as amended, physicians and dentists of the armed services and the Public Health Service are entitled to special pay. This special pay is hedged about with provisions as to *voluntary* service, service as an intern, and the list of those qualified to receive the pay is so long and complicated that it is best to consult the basic law and your disbursing officer as to your entitlement under this section of the act.

6. SPECIAL PAY: DUTY SUBJECT TO HOSTILE FIRE. Except in time of war, declared by Congress, special pay for duty subject to hostile fire, may be paid to members of the uniformed services under any of the following conditions:

(1) When a member is on duty in an area designated to be a hostile fire area.

(2) When a member is subject to hostile fire or explosion of hostile mines.

(3) When a member is killed, injured or wounded by hostile fire, explosion of a hostile mine, or any other hostile action.

7. INCENTIVE PAY FOR PERFORMANCE OF HAZARDOUS DUTY. For the performance of hazardous duty directed by competent orders, extra pay is provided to members of the uniformed services; in time of war however, the President may suspend payment of incentive pay. The

various types of incentive pay for performance of hazardous duty are:

a. *Aviation pay*—may be payable when performing duty as a crew or non-crew member, involving frequent and regular participation in aerial flight. Aviation pay may be payable also to qualified members holding certain aviation designations for 15 or more years, without having to fly.

b. *Flight deck pay*—may be payable to a member assigned to duty requiring frequent and regular participation in flight operations of an attack (CVA) or antisubmarine aircraft carrier (CVS).

c. *Submarine duty pay*—Qualified members may be entitled to this pay when assigned to duty on a submarine or on an operational, self-propelled submersible, including undersea exploration and research vehicles. Under certain conditions submarine duty pay may be paid for periods of training, rehabilitation, and to a prospective crew member of a submarine under construction.

d. *Parachute duty pay*—may be payable to a member designated as a parachutist or student parachutist, and who is required to engage in parachute jumping from an aircraft.

e. *Demolition duty pay*—may be payable when a member's primary duty involves the demolition of explosives; this may also include periods of training.

f. *Leprosarium duty pay*—may be payable for duty involving close contact with persons having leprosy or with articles used by such persons.

g. *Experimental stress duty pay*—may be payable for duty performed in experiments which competent medical authority has determined involve the risk of exposure hazards such as severe strain, injury, or collapse.

No member is entitled to receive incentive pay for more than two purposes at the same time.

8. SPECIAL PAY FOR DIVING DUTY. Officers and enlisted members who are designated divers and occupy diving billets within an authorized allowance established by the Chief of Naval Personnel are entitled to diving pay. Members are not entitled to receive both diving duty pay and incentive pay for performance of hazardous duty for the same period.

9. ALLOWANCE FOR SUBSISTENCE. All officers on the active list or on active duty are entitled to receive a basic allowance for subsistence, without regard to rank, grade or dependency status.

10. Basic allowance for quarters. All officers are entitled to a basic allowance for quarters, except as provided here:

1. When assigned to government quarters, appropriate to their rank or grade and adequate for themselves and their dependents, if they have dependents. Officers without dependents in rank of lieutenant commander or above may receive allowances if they elect not to occupy available government quarters.

2. While on field or sea duty, unless the commanding officer certifies that they were necessarily required to procure quarters at their own expense. Field or sea duty for temporary periods of less than 3 months is not considered applicable under this provision.

3. When, by reason of orders of competent authority, his dependents are prevented from occupying quarters assigned to him.

11. Rights to basic allowance for quarters while in a leave or travel status. An officer with dependents is entitled to basic allowance for quarters as follows:

1. When on sea (or field) duty, including time absent therefrom on authorized leave (not in excess of statutory leave limit), on sick leave, in hospital, under arrest, or on temporary duty away from such sea (or field) duty.

2. For the interim following detachment from permanent station and preceding reporting at a new permanent station, including time on authorized leave, inclusive of the 4 days or lesser period of authorized delay in proceeding.

3. For the interim between date of oath of office and reporting for first duty, unless occupying government quarters.

4. If while on leave of absence he is relieved from duty at a permanent station where quarters are assigned him, and such assignment is terminated, basic allowance for quarters accrues thereafter, unless his dependents occupy quarters.

An officer without dependents is entitled to basic allowance for quarters as follows:

1. When stationed on permanent shore duty (either within or without the continental limits of the United States), except when assigned quarters thereat. This allowance continues for time absent from station on authorized leave, on sick leave, in hospital, under arrest, or on temporary duty away from such permanent station, including temporary sea duty not exceeding 3 months. See Section 10.

12. Family separation allowance.

a. *General.* A member with dependents may qualify for an additional allowance, referred to as family separation allowance, under any of the following conditions:

(1) A member whose dependents are not authorized to travel at Government expense to his permanent duty station in Alaska or outside the United States or to a place nearby, and whose dependents do not reside at or near that station, or

(2) A member who is on duty on board a ship away from the home port of the ship for a continuous period of more than 30 days, or

(3) A member who is on temporary duty away from his permanent station for a continuous period of more than 30 days and his dependents do not reside at or near his temporary duty station.

There are two types of family separation allowance and a member may qualify for both concurrently; family separation allowance is in addition to any other allowance or per diem to which the member may otherwise be entitled.

b. *Family separation allowance, type I.* The purpose is to pay an additional quarters allowance when, because of circumstances cited in subparagraph a(1) above and which of nonavailability of Government quarters or housing facilities for the member at his permanent station, he must maintain a home for himself and one for his dependents. The rate of family separation allowance payable is equal to basic allowance for quarters payable to a member without dependents in the same pay grade. This allowance is not payable to a member who is on permanent duty in Hawaii.

c. *Family separation allowance, type II.* The purpose is to compensate a member for added expenses incurred, because of enforced separation from his dependents due to circumstances cited in subparagraphs a(1), a(2), or a(3) above. This allowance is not authorized in time of war or national emergency declared by Congress. Only members serving in pay grade E-4 (over 4 years service) or above and who are entitled to a basic allowance for quarters with dependents may qualify for this type of family separation allowance.

13. DEFINITION OF "DEPENDENT." The term "dependent," as used in connection with pay and allowances, means a member's:

a. Lawful spouse.

b. Unmarried legitimate child (or children) (including a stepchild, or an adopted child, who is in fact dependent on the member for support), who either is under 21 years of age, or is incapable of self-support because of mental or physical incapacity and is dependent on the member for over one-half of his or her support.

c. Parent(s) (including a stepparent or parent by adoption, and any person, including a former stepparent, who has stood *in loco parentis* to the member at any time for a continuous period of at least five years before he became 21 years of age). The parent(s) must be dependent on the member for over one-half of his support and actually residing in the member's household.

In the case of a female member a person is not her dependent unless he or she is dependent on the female member for over one-half of his or her support.

14. STATION ALLOWANCES OUTSIDE THE UNITED STATES. Because of the continuing change in allowances outside the United States, it is recommended that you contact your disbursing officer for up-to-date allowance tables.

15. PERSONAL MONEY ALLOWANCES. Flag and general officers, while serving in ranks and positions of great authority with ranks higher than major general and rear admiral, are granted certain personal money allowances. These are as follows: for lieutenant general or vice-admiral, $500 per annum; for general or admiral, $2,200 per annum; for the Chairman of the Joint Chiefs of Staff, Chief of Staff of the Army or the Air Force, Chief of Naval Operations, Commandant of the Marine Corps, Commandant of the Coast Guard, in lieu of any other personal money allowance, $4,000 per annum, for fleet admiral and general of the army, in lieu of any other personal money allowance, $5,000 per annum; for the senior member of the Military Staff Committee of the United Nations, who is entitled to the grade, pay and allowances of a lieutenant general or vice admiral, $2,700 per annum ($2,200 plus $500 authorized for the rank involved).

16. UNIFORM AND REQUIREMENT ALLOWANCES FOR OFFICERS. The following officers may be entitled to an initial uniform allowance upon call to active duty (other than for training) for a period of more than 90 days, or upon completion of 14 days active duty or active duty for training:

(1) Officers of the Naval Reserve.

(2) NROTC graduates appointed in the regular Navy on and after October 13, 1964. (Those appointed prior to that date are not entitled to uniform allowances.)

(3) Officers previously separated from the regular Navy who perform active duty, provided such duty is two years subsequent to the

separation; it is noted that the period of active duty may begin within the two-year period without jeopardizing entitlement to the uniform allowance.

(4) Former enlisted personnel of the regular Navy or Naval Reserve on active duty upon appointment as temporary officer.

The initial uniform allowance is payable only once to an officer and amounts payable vary, depending on the source from which an officer is appointed and the uniform items furnished to him in kind.

In addition to the initial uniform allowance officers may also qualify for an additional active duty uniform allowance for additional uniforms required while they are on active duty or active duty for training. This allowance may be payable each time on entry or reentry on active duty, or active duty for training for more than 90 days; however, it is not payable if the officer has received an initial uniform allowance during his current tour of active duty, or within a period of two years prior to entering on that tour.

A uniform maintenance allowance may be paid to an officer of the Naval Reserve who has not become entitled to a uniform allowance during the preceding four years. This is payable upon completion of each four-year period of satisfactory service in an active status in one or more reserve components, including at least 28 days of active duty or active duty for training.

17. PAY OF AVIATION CADETS. The grade of aviation cadet is a special enlisted grade although the pay and allowances are a mixture of officer and enlisted. Pay and allowances are as follows:

a. *Basic pay*—is 50% of the basic pay of an ensign (pay grade 0-1) with 2 or less years of service.

b. *Basic allowance for subsistence*—entitlement is the same as that provided for an officer.

c. *Basic allowance for quarters*—entitlement is the same as that provided for an enlisted member in pay grade E-4 (over 4 years service).

d. *Incentive pay* for performance of hazardous duty—an aviation cadet may be entitled to aviation pay when designated as a crew member.

e. *Cash clothing allowances*—an aviation cadet is authorized a special initial clothing allowance in an amount specifically authorized for aviation cadets; clothing maintenance allowances are also authorized.

18. PAY OF MIDSHIPMEN AT THE UNITED STATES NAVAL

ACADEMY. Midshipmen are entitled to pay at the rate of one-half that of ensign (0-1), under two years of service. They are further entitled to an allowance of 6 cents per mile from the place of their appointment (usually their home) to the Naval Academy at Annapolis, Md., on first being appointed as midshipmen. They are also entitled to a subsistence allowance per day fixed by law periodically. Cadets at the Military Academy and Air Force Academy receive the same pay and allowances.

19. PAY AND ALLOWANCES OF ENLISTED MEMBERS.

a. *General.* As in the case of officers enlisted members' rates of pay and allowances and conditions of entitlement are fixed by public law. Enlisted members are equally eligible for the majority of pay and allowances available to officers and in some cases may be entitled to items for which officers are not. A brief summarization of enlisted members' pay and allowances is contained in subsequent subparagraphs; for more detailed information see your disbursing officer.

b. *Basic pay*—Rates of pay are based on the member's pay grade (pay grades E-1 through E-9) and years of creditable service. Service creditable in computation of basic pay is similar to that for officers except for a few minor differences. Entitlement to pay commences on date of enlistment for regular Navy personnel, and on date of departure from home for the first duty station in the case of a Naval Reserve member on active duty.

c. *Foreign duty pay*—is in addition to basic pay and is payable only to enlisted members who are assigned to duty at certain designated places located outside CONUS; Alaska and Hawaii are considered foreign duty stations for pay purposes.

d. *Sea duty pay*—is in addition to basic pay and is payable only to enlisted members who are assigned to a vessel; a ship-based staff; a fleet, force, flotilla, squadron, or division commander afloat; a ship-based aviation unit; a commissioned landing craft or motor torpedo-boat squadron which is a tactical component of an operating fleet in active status; or on an artificial island on the outer Continental Shelf outside the territorial waters of the United States.

e. *Proficiency pay*—is intended as an incentive to enlisted personnel in certain designated highly skilled military occupations to remain in service. There are two types of proficiency pay: (1) proficiency pay (specialty) for qualified personnel with highly skilled military specialties requiring relatively long and costly training, and, (2) proficiency pay (superior performance) for personnel demonstrating superior performance while serving in a billet designated as eligible for that type of pay. Proficiency pay is in addition to basic pay but only one type of proficiency pay can be earned at any time. Due to continuing changes in personnel retention problems, military skill needs, and availability of funds the eligibility requirements and rates of payment for proficiency pay periodically change.

f. *Reenlistment bonus*—is payable to enlisted members upon reenlistment in the regular Navy provided the reenlistment occurs within three months from date of last discharge or release from active duty. Extension(s) of enlistments may be considered as "reenlistment" for the purpose of entitlement to reenlistment bonus. There are two types of reenlistment bonus: (1) regular reenlistment bonus, for which all reenlistees may be eligible, and, (2) variable reenlistment bonus, intended as an additional reenlistment incentive to those enlisted members possessing certain designated critical military skills. The regular reenlistment bonus may be payable on the first and subsequent reenlistments but the cumulative total of regular reenlistment bonuses can not exceed $2,000; the amount payable upon each reenlistment is computed by multiplying a prescribed percentage of the basic pay by the number of years for which the member is reenlisting and is payable at the time of reenlistment. The variable reenlistment bonus is payable to qualified personnel on their first reenlistment only and is in addition to the regular reenlistment bonus; the amount payable is computed by multiplying the amount of the regular reenlistment bonus by the multiplier (1, 2, 3, or 4) prescribed for the particular critical skill held by the member. The variable reenlistment bonus is paid in equal annual installments but may be paid in fewer installments in meritorious cases and when so authorized. A pro rata portion of the regular reenlistment bonus and the variable reenlistment bonus must be refunded when a member, either voluntarily or as a result of his own misconduct, does not complete the reenlistment.

g. *Hostile fire pay*—This is payable both to officers and enlisted members.

h. *Diving duty pay*—see section 8 of this appendix for details. This is payable both to officers and enlisted members.

i. *Incentive pay for performance of hazardous duty*—see section 7 of this appendix for details. This is payable both to officers and enlisted members.

j. *Subsistence allowance*—Enlisted members are entitled to a basic allowance for subsistence only when rations in kind are not available to them or, although rations may be available, when authorized to mess separately. Rates payable vary according to the circumstances involved, and entitlement to subsistence allowances may be affected during periods of temporary duty and when receiving a per diem allowance while in travel status.

k. *Quarters allowance*—Enlisted members without dependents are entitled to a basic allowance for quarters only when Government quarters are not available to him at his permanent duty station, and generally may continue to be eligible for it during temporary periods of absence (e.g., leave, temporary additional duty, hospitalization, etc.). Basic allowance for quarters for enlisted members with dependents may be payable when adequate Government quarters are not available for him and his dependents. See section 13 of this appendix for the definition of the term "dependents". When Government quarters are available only to the member but not to his dependents his entitlement to the quarters allowance continues. When dependents of a member are in military service entitlement to basic allowance for quarters can be affected. Rates of basic allowance for quarters vary, depending on the pay grade and number of dependents. Members in pay grades E-1 through E-4 (with 4 or less years service) are required to allot prescribed amounts of their pay to their dependents in order to be eligible for basic allowance for quarters for dependents.

l. *Family separation allowance*—See section 12 of this appendix for entitlement; both enlisted and officer members may be eligible for this allowance.

m. *Station allowances outside the United States*—See section 14 of this appendix for entitlement; both enlisted and officer members may be eligible for these allowances.

n. *Clothing allowances*—Upon first enlistment or reporting to active duty enlisted members are authorized an initial clothing allowance for procurement of uniform items; in addition a monthly maintenance allowance is provided. A civilian clothing allowance and monthly maintenance allowance may also be authorized when an enlisted member is assigned to duty requiring the wearing of civilian clothing. There are also provisions for a special clothing allowance when a member is promoted to pay grade E-7. Rates vary according to type of allowance and costs of uniform items.

20. Travel expense and mileage. *General.*—Title 37 United States Code provides for travel expenses of naval personnel, on mileage or per diem expense basis, by rail, privately owned conveyance, and aircraft. The act authorizes the Secretaries of the uniformed services to prescribe the conditions under which travel and transportation allowances are authorized, including advance payments, and the allowances for types of travel not to exceed:

1. Transportation in kind, reimbursement therefor, or a monetary allowance in lieu of cost of transportation at a rate not more than seven cents a mile based on distance in mileage tables prepared by the Chief of Finance, Department of the Army.

2. The allowance in (1) plus a per diem in lieu of subsistence not to exceed $25.

3. A mileage allowance of not more than seven cents a mile according to current mileage tables. Although the law authorizes the maximum amounts payable, these amounts are further limited by the provisions of the Joint Travel Regulations.

Under current regulations, allowances have been authorized as described in the following paragraphs.

Types of Orders.—There are four types of orders which give authorization to perform travel:

Permanent change of station, unless otherwise qualified, means the transfer or assignment of a person from one permanent station to another. This includes the change from home, or from the place from which ordered to active duty, to first station upon appointment; call to active duty; enlistment or induction; and from last duty station to home or to the place from which ordered to active duty upon separation from the service, placement upon the temporary disability retired list, release from active duty, or retirement. It also includes a duly authorized change in home yard or home port of a vessel.

When permanent change-of-station orders do not involve temporary duty en route, the effective date of orders for all purposes is the date of detachment from the last permanent station except that leave, delay, or additional travel time, when authorized, will be added to the date of detachment to determine the effective date.

Temporary duty means duty at a location other than at your permanent station under orders which provide for further assignment to a new permanent station.

Temporary additional duty involves one journey away from the individual's duty station, in the performance of prescribed duties at one or more places, and direct return to the starting point upon completion of such duties. Personnel on temporary additional duty remain permanently assigned to the station from which they proceeded on temporary additional duty.

Blanket travel orders are defined as orders issued to members who regularly and frequently make trips away from their permanent duty station within certain geographical limits in performance of regular assigned duties.

Repeated travel orders allow any necessary number of separate round-trip journeys from the permanent duty station to and from or between specified locations.

Travel must not be solely between place of duty and place of lodging. These orders continue in effect until expiration by time limit or by automatic cancellation upon detachment from permanent duty station to which such orders pertain or upon revocation.

Per diem allowance is an allowance designed to cover the cost of quarters, subsistence, and other necessary incidental expenses related thereto (exclusive of reimbursable expenses).

Reimbursable expenses are expenses in addition to per diem such as tips, streetcar or taxi fares and other similar expenses which are directly attributable to the ordered travel and temporary duty.

Transportation expenses are travel expenses in addition to per diem and reimbursable expenses to cover the cost of bus, air, railroad and steamship tickets (including sleeping accommodations or parlor-car seats).

Types of Travel.—The mileage form of allowances for *permanent* change of station travel at the rate of 6 cents per mile is effective when travel is performed by privately owned conveyance; by rail and available transportation when Government Transportation Requests were not utilized; upon relief from active duty other than active duty for training; upon separation from the service under honorable conditions; upon transfer to the temporary disability retired list; upon retirement; and upon transfer to the Fleet Reserve or Fleet Marine Corps Reserve.

Except for group travel and travel directed by a particular mode of travel, naval personnel may otherwise elect any one of the following travel allowances on permanent change of station for travel within the United States:

1. mileage at the rate of 6 cents per mile
2. transportation in kind or transportation request(s), plus a per diem allowance
3. transportation in kind or transportation request(s), plus meal tickets
4. reimbursement for the actual cost to the traveler for the mode of transportation authorized and used plus per diem if TR's are not available or if TR's are available and the traveler procures transportation at own expense on common carrier in amounts of $15 (plus tax) or less.

When a person travels under the circumstances contemplated in (4) he may elect between that type of allowance or mileage as described in (1); but he must indicate his choice prior to payment of an advance or upon termination of the travel. Such choice once indicated is final.

Applicable mileage is computed by the *shortest usually traveled route* as given in the official tables of distances established by the Chief of Finance, Department of the Army. The basis of this computation is applicable to travel by rail or privately owned conveyance when no Government Transportation Request (government ticket) has been furnished and no government-owned carrier has been used for such transportation.

For temporary additional duty orders, temporary duty orders between permanent stations which specify per diem reimbursement, and *permanent change of station orders,* where a per diem was elected, transportation is furnished in kind or by Government Transportation Request, and reimbursement is at a per diem of $25 per day. If you elect to pay for your own travel expenses, you will be reimbursed a monetary allowance in lieu of transportation at the rate of 5 cents per mile for the official distance as described above.

In the event the use of a privately owned automobile is authorized as more advantageous to the government and such means of transportation is actually used, reimbursement is made at the rate of 7 cents per mile computed by the same method. But note, travel time by automobile when on a per diem basis is not necessarily at the rate of 300 miles per day. If such travel is authorized as more advantageous to the government, actual time necessary to perform the directed travel is allowed. If such travel is not considered more advantageous, the allowed travel time is limited to the usual time by common carrier.

Per diem allowances are applicable for all periods of necessary temporary duty and travel in connection therewith, including periods of necessary delay awaiting further transportation, periods of delay at ports of embarkation and debarkation in connection with a permanent change of station, and periods of temporary duty directed in a permanent change of station order. For special cases under which temporary duty per diem allowances are not payable, see Joint Travel Regulations.

Per diem allowances in the United States are also given in that publication, Par. 4205, and are rather lengthy and complicated. Where government quarters and mess are available, the per diem allowances are generally reduced. See the references and Navy Travel Instructions for full details.

Per diem allowances outside the United States vary widely from country to country and are frequently changed, both for station allowances and for travel. They are discussed in Joint Travel Regulations, Chap. 4, Parts F, G, and H, and the rates are given in an appendix to that publication, which is changed from time to time or reissued as living conditions in foreign countries change.

Expenses Reimbursable in Connection with Travel and Temporary Duty.—Certain items of expense incurred in connection with travel and temporary duty are reimbursable in addition to cost of travel and authorized per diem payments. See JTR in regards to the following items not reimbursable when traveling on a mileage or mileage in lieu of transportation basis. Some of these are:

Taxi fares, or fares for streetcar, bus, or other means of local transportation, between places of abode and common carrier terminals and between terminals, when free transfer is not included in price of ticket.

Pullman tips, tips to baggage porters at terminals, fees for checking of baggage, for excess baggage when properly authorized, and toll fares for ferries, roads, bridges and tunnels when traveling by *government vehicle.* For travel by commercial vessel, a per diem is allowed in lieu of tips in accordance with the Joint Travel Regulations.

In *government aircraft,* costs of gasoline, oil, repairs, nonpersonal services, guards, and storage at other than a government field. In a *government automobile,* cost of storage of the automobile.

Cost of *telephone, telegraph, cable,* etc., when incident to the duty enjoined or in connection with items of transportation.

Registration fees incident to attendance at meetings of technical, professional, scientific, or other non-Federal organizations when attendance thereat is authorized or approved.

Returns required to collect for the above items vary considerably and are somewhat complicated. Consult Joint Travel Regulations, Navy Travel Instructions, and your disbursing officer, before leaving on temporary duty.

Determination of Type of Carriers from Orders.—Except where travel by a particular type of transportation is necessary because of requirements of the service concerned, orders for travel on a per diem basis will normally be silent as to the mode of transportation authorized. Transportation in kind may be furnished. If orders do not direct any particular mode of transportation, you may choose any type of carrier at your own expense subject to reimbursement.

Government Transportation Request.—Officers ordered to duty involving travel may obtain from the designated T/R Officer completed Government Transportation Requests. These forms are presented to the agent of the carrier and exchanged for tickets.

Travel Advice.—*Travel time* on permanent change of station in a privately owned vehicle is allowed on the basis of 300 miles per day, with increments over 150 miles counting as another day. Prior to departure, officers should be particularly careful to determine the time allowed to report to the next duty station. In many cases, officers report one or two days late because they have not taken care to interpret their orders correctly as to date of reporting, when proceed time or delay time is allowed.

Travel by commercial air is fast and convenient. Officers should consider the financial advantage to be gained by traveling with their families in slack times when air lines allow half fare for spouses and give special rates for various reasons. Coach travel on *established air lines* is less expensive and no great hardship. The convenience of getting travel completed quickly when small children are involved causes air travel to appeal to many families.

Travel by privately owned automobile, with delay time en route, often provides a family vacation; permits varying route to visit scenic and historic spots, members of the family, and vacation resorts; and can be made at a considerable saving over other methods of travel, particularly when the cost of transporting the automobile by other means is considered.

The best advice is to balance up all the considerations of pleasure, convenience, accommodation, and expense and see which suits your plans and wishes the best.

Travel in Naval Aircraft.—Officers under orders to travel by naval aircraft (or other government conveyance) other than for training flights are paid on a per diem basis. This allowance is given for meals and room accommodations.

Ferrying Aircraft.—When naval aircraft are ferried from one station to another, officers are paid on a per diem basis. If the aircraft is delivered to a station other than the home station of the crew, they usually return to their home station by naval aircraft.

For payment of per diem allowances and mileage allowances for ferrying aircraft, orders from competent authority must be issued, except that naval personnel on duty with or under training for the command, Naval Aircraft Ferrying Squadrons, Fleet Tactical Support Squadrons or Marine Corps Transport Squadrons, while away from their permanent station, are authorized per diem allowances without the issuance of orders for specific travel. Travel as a crew member in these units, unless engaged in tactical exercises, maneuvers, field exercises, etc., is not considered as travel with troops. Claims are certified by the appropriate unit commander.

Transportation of Dependents on Change of Station.—Transportation of dependents (lawful wives, dependent parents, and dependent children) is authorized at government expense upon permanent change of station.

A member may procure transportation requests for the travel of his dependents or he may transport them at his own expense by any means including private vehicle and claim reimbursement therefor after travel has been completed. Reimbursement will be in accordance with Joint Travel Regulations and Navy Travel Instructions.

21. SHIPMENT OF HOUSEHOLD GOODS. Military personnel are entitled to shipment and/or storage of their household goods at government expense upon issuance of change of station orders. Shipment includes packing, unpacking, crating, uncrating, drayage, transportation, storage and servicing of applicances.

Shipments are authorized under the following conditions:

1. Orders to change from duty at one station ashore to duty at another station ashore, either within or without the United States, and orders to active duty of more than six months.

2. Orders to change from duty on one vessel to duty on another vessel, having a different home yard and/or home port.

3. Orders to change of duty from a shore station to duty on board a vessel.

4. Orders to change from duty on board a vessel to duty ashore.

5. Receipt of letter from Chief of Naval Operations changing a home yard and/or home port of vessel, or specifying that the vessel will operate in an overseas area for a contemplated continuous period of 1 year or more.

6. Receipt of retirement orders, orders to transfer to the fleet reserve, or release from active duty.

7. Emergencies in which approval may be obtained from the Naval Supply Systems Command for shipment prior to issuance of permanent change of station orders.

Shipment on Temporary or Permanent Change of Station. On change of station military personnel should arrange through the nearest Navy or Marine Corps Household Goods Transportation Office for shipment of household goods at government expense.

Professional books, papers, and equipment owned by Navy personnel, certified to be necessary in performance of official duties, may be shipped in the same manner as household goods but without charge against the weight allowance. The weight of such professional books, papers, and equipment must be shown separately on the following documents:

(a) Application for Shipment of Household Goods, DD Form 1299, which will be filled out when arranging the shipment at the Household Goods Transportation Office.

(b) Statement of Accessorial Services Performed, DD Form 619, which the mover will ask you to sign on pickup of your household goods.

(c) U. S. Government Bill of Lading, Standard Form No. 1103, which the mover will ask you to sign on delivery.

It is important to note that if storage-in-transit at destination is involved in the shipment you will not be requested to complete the bill of lading. So it is important that the DD 619 accomplished at origin show the weight of professional items in all cases.

CAUTION: Unless the weight of the professional books, papers, and equipment is shown as above, special credit for these professional items cannot be allowed in the determination if excess weight is involved.

Expedited Mode Shipments.   Military personnel may arrange with the household goods transporatation officer for the shipment at government expense of unaccompanied baggage, including air shipment, when such mode is necessary in order to carry out assigned duties or to prevent undue hardship to member and/or dependents. When the expedited mode selected is commercial air, not to exceed 350 pounds net weight may be shipped by such mode unless the transporation of such baggage in excess of 350 pounds net weight is approved by the Naval Supply Systems Command.

Easily pilferable articles of substantial value may also be shipped by an expedited mode of transportation which will provide for transportation at a higher released valuation (provided in the tariff), than would be available by freight or van modes. If the member desires protection in excess of the tariff released valuation he may also specify upon agreement to pay the cost of the excess valuation.

Subsequent claims for loss and damage of easily pilferable articles of substantial value will be disallowed unless they were transported by an expedited mode of transportation.

Excess Costs.   Household goods in excess of the weights allowed may be shipped, but the prorated costs of the excess portion will be paid by the owner. The current weight allowances are prescribed in paragraph M 8003 of the Joint Travel Regulations, Volume 1. Similarly, costs for shipment in excess of the distance between authorized points; for shipment in excess of the distance between authorized points; for unauthorized articles; for storage-in-transit over 90 days without authorization, or 180 days in any case; for the excess cost of a second shipment by the same mode when one combined shipment could have been made; and for the excess cost of a higher cost mode of shipment, specific routing or other special service will be paid by the owner. The Navy Finance Center, Washington, D.C. is responsible for determining and collecting excess costs.

Loss and Damage. Generally, the carrier is responsible for loss and damage to your property which occurs while under his care, but only to the extent of the lowest released valuation and conditions on the government bill of lading. The carrier's liability under the terms of the Government Bill of Lading is limited to the following:

Motor van shipments	60 cents per pound per article
Freight forwarder	30 cents per pound per article
Rail or motor freight	10 cents per pound per article
Air or Railway Express (over 100 pounds)	50 cents per pound actual weight
Air or Railway Express (100 pounds or less)	$50.00 for total shipment

For van shipments you may declare a lump sum value for the entire shipment up to a maximum of $1.25 times the total net weight (in pounds) of the shipment. When this is done the additional valuation charges in excess of 60 cents per pound per article will be paid by the member direct to the carrier.

In determining the desirability of declaring a lump sum value up to $1.25 times the net weight of the shipment at your expense for the excess valuation, or of taking out commercial insurance, consider your shipment of household goods by ordinary mode separately from your expedited shipment.

In the regular shipment of your household goods you may want to purchase sufficient additional valuation or commercial insurance to cover:

(a) the value of your total effects in excess of $10,000, the maximum protection provided by the Government; or

(b) items of very high value which cannot be shipped by expedited mode because of size of volume, such as bulky antiques. These items are subject to an allowance by the Government based on the fair and reasonable purchase price of substitute articles of a similar nature appropriate for the claimant under the particular circumstances of his service; or

(c) unusually large numbers of particular categories of items individually not expensive but collectively of high value such as hobby items, books, or individual wardrobes. Items of this nature are subjected to maximum allowances by the Government.

Items of extraordinary value and easily pilferable items will not be honored in your claim against the Government unless they were shipped by expedited mode. Most items of extraordinary value are subjected to maximum allowances by the Government; consequently, you should consider acquiring insurance coverage for the full value of these items. When this has been done and you suffer damage or loss, you are protected by the coverage you have purchased; or, if for any reason the carrier or insurer denies liability in whole or in part, the Government will make settlement without regard to maximum allowance tables up to the $10,000 maximum.

Be sure to place a true valuation on your property. Remember the Government and, usually the insurance company or carrier will not pay more for an item than its depreciated value at time of loss or damage; and, your combined recovery cannot exceed this value. Under normal circumstances, neither the Government nor an insurance company will pay full replacement value.

For your guidance, typical items subjected to maximum allowances* are as follows:

Jewelry	$750 per claim, $250 per item
Sterling Silverware	$1000 per claim
Painting and Pictures	$1000 per claim, $250 per item
Furs	$750 per claim, $500 per item
Fine china, crystal	$1000 per item
Rugs	$1000 per item
Books	$1000 per item
Appliances	$750 per item
Musical instruments	$1000 per claim, exclusive of pianos and organs
Hobby items	$1000 per claim, $500 per family member.

At the time of delivery should you discover losses and damages you should record them on the inventory and shipping documents that you will be requested to sign. Notation of losses and damages should be made on the reverse side of the bill of lading. If circumstances do not

* Maximum allowances are subject to change by Armed Services Joint Committee on Claims.

permit you to complete your inspection, such as insufficient time to unpack all items, have the person in charge of the delivery for the delivery carrier countersign your statement to this effect. After these notations have been made it is proper that you sign the face of the bill of lading for the weight of the household goods actually received. The complete inspection of the shipment should be made as soon as possible and any losses and damages reported promptly in writing to both the delivery carrier and the destination household goods transportation officer. Damaged items must be retained for inspection by the carrier and the household goods transportation office inspector. The destination household goods transportation officer will assist you in the procedures for submitting your claim against the carrier, the insurance company, if you had insurance, and the Government.

General. Regulatory provisions concerning the shipment of household goods, baggage, house trailers and privately owned vehicles are contained in Joint Travel Regulations, Volume I, Chapters 8, 10, and 11, and in the Naval Supply Systems Command Manual, Volume V, Chapter 8. General information designed to assit you in arranging for shipment of your household goods, baggage, house trailer and privately owned vehicle is contained in NavSup Publication 380, entitled *It's Your Move!* A copy may be obtained from the nearest designated household goods shipping activity. A list of designated shipping activities is contained in NavSup Manual, Volume V, Chapter 8, paragraph 58027-2a. *Caution:* It is important that you contact the household goods shipping activity for assistance in arranging for shipment/storage of your property.

22. ALLOTMENTS. As a matter of convenience and to ensure regular monthly payments, naval personnel are privileged to make allotments of their pay for certain purposes. Allotments may be registered to dependents, to banks for the use of dependents or for savings, to pay insurance premiums, to purchase United States Savings Bonds, to repay loans made by the American Red Cross or Navy Relief Society, or for other miscellaneous purposes as authorized from time to time. The amounts allotted are deducted from the pay of the person concerned and are mailed to the designated payees on the last day of each month by the Navy Finance Center, Cleveland, Ohio. Personnel should register allotments as soon as they report for duty, even though they are stationed ashore and have their families with them. Thus, in the event of a sudden move, their dependents are ensured of continued and periodic payment of funds regardless of the location of the officer, and insurance policies will not lapse. It is especially important that officers engaged in operations against the enemy avail themselves of this right. In case of capture by an enemy, the Secretary of the Navy is authorized to continue the payment of allotments while the alloter is in the status of prisoner of war or missing. Disbursing officers should be consulted on all questions of allotments.

23. SOCIAL SECURITY. All service personnel on active duty are contributing participants. See Section 1815, your Disbursing Officer and Social Security publications for details.

Index

Naval Service
Customs, 402. *See also* Traditions and Customs of the Naval Service
Customs, origin of, 407

Dead Horse, term, origin, 407
Death and Burials. *See also* Survivors' Benefits
  action required by next of kin, 1718
  aid
    American Red Cross, 1605, 1609, 1717, 1720
    Navy Mutual Aid Association, 1609, 1703, 1704, 1721, 1722
    Navy Relief Society, 1605, 1609, 1717, 1721
    Veterans' groups, 1721
  arrangements, 1709
  assistance by chaplains, legal officers, and Navy, 1720
  burial allowance, 1713
  burial honors, 1714
  certificates of death, 1714
  claims, insurance, 1704
  death gratuity, 1715
  funeral flag, 1714
  headstones, 1710
  instructions, procedures, for survivors, 1711
  interment in
    Arlington National Cemetery, 1711, 1712
    national cemeteries, 1710
    Navy funeral service, 1712
    space reservation, 1710
  Survivors' Benefit Act, 1703
  survivors' death benefits, 1715, 1719, 1816
  veterans' benefits, 1716, 1816
Deck Watch
  in-port, 307
  underway, 306
Defense Department. *See also* Armed Forces, U.S.; Department of Defense
  Armed Forces Policy Board, 906
  boards, committees, offices, 908
  Deputy Secretary, 906
  joint secretaries, 906
  mission, 906
  National Security Act of 1947, 908, 909
  Office of the Secretary, Staff, 907
  Reorganization Act of 1958, 910
  Secretary, 906
Defense Intelligence School, 1408
Dental Corps, Navy, 1030
Dental Officers, Navy, 1210

Department of Defense, 906
Department of the Air Force. *See also* Air Force, U.S.
  composition, 934
  function, 929
  Headquarters, 932
  mission, 928
  organization, 930
  Secretary and assistants, 931, 932
  Staff functions, 932
Department of the Army. *See also* Armed Forces, U.S.; Army, U.S.
  area organization, 924
  Chief of Staff and Staff duties, 919
  Combat Developments Command, 922
  Continental Army Command, 923
  functions, 916
  General Staff function, 920
  major commands, 922
  Material Command, 922
  mission, 915
  National Guard, 923, 925, 927
  officer candidate training, 927
  organization, 917
  Reserves, 925
  Reserve Officer Training Corps (ROTC), 923, 925, 927
  responsibilities, duties, 925
  saluting uncovered, 503
  Secretary and assistants, 918
  Special Staff, function, 921
  U.S. Military Academy, 927
  women in the Army (WACS), 926, 927
  Zone of Interior, 924, 925
Department of the Navy. *See also* Naval Establishment; Navy Department
  Air Systems Command, 1021
  Assistant Secretaries, provision for, 1003
  Assistant Secretary for:
    Air, 1003
    Material, 1003
    Personnel, 1003
    Research and Development, 1003
    Reserve Forces, 1003
  Board of Naval Commissioners of 1815, 1003
  Bureau of:
    Aeronautics (BuAer) merged in BuWeps, 1003
    Medicine and Surgery (BuMed), 1021
    Naval Personnel (BuPers), 1021
    Naval Weapons (BuWeps) combined BuAer and BuOrd, 1003
    Ordnance (BuOrd) merged in BuWeps, 1003
  Bureau reorganization, 1021

Composed, printed, and bound by George Banta Company, Inc., Menasha, Wisconsin.

Composed in eleven point Linotype Old Style No. 7 with one point leading.

Printed letterpress on fifty-pound White Printone.

Bound in Fictionette FNV 3750.